KINGDOM
in the
WEST

The Mormons and the American Frontier

VOLUME I

THOMAS BULLOCK, CLERK OF THE CAMP OF ISRAEL, ABOUT 1860.
Courtesy, LDS Archives.

THE PIONEER CAMP OF THE SAINTS

The 1846 and 1847
Mormon Trail Journals of
Thomas Bullock

Edited by
Will Bagley

UNIVERSITY OF OKLAHOMA PRESS
NORMAN

Library of Congress Catalog Card Number 2006027640

Library of Congress Cataloging-in-Publication Data

Bullock, Thomas, 1816-1885.

The pioneer camp of the saints : the 1846 and 1847 Mormon trail journals of Thomas Bullock / edited by Will Bagley.

p. 396 cm.—(Kingdom in the West; v. I)

Includes bibliographical references and index.

ISBN 978-0-8061-9026-6 (paper)

I. Bullock, Thomas, 1816—1885—Diaries. 2. Mormon converts--United States—Diaries. 3. Mormons—United States—Diaries. 4. Mormon Pioneer National Historic Trail—Description and travel. 5. Mormon Pioneer National Historic Trail—History—19th century. I. Bagley, Will, 1950- II. Title. III. Series.

BX8695.B84A3 1997

289.3'73'09034—dc21

96-51745
CIP

The paper in this book meets the guidelines for permanence and durability of the Committee on Production Guidelines for Book Longevity of the Council on Library Resources, Inc. ∞

Copyright © 1997 by Will Bagley
Published by the University of Oklahoma Press, Norman,
Publishing Division of the University.
Paperback edition published 2022.
Manufactured in the U.S.A.

All rights reserved. No part of this publication may be reproduced, stored in a retrieval system, or transmitted, in any form or by any means, electronic, mechanical, photocopying, recording, or otherwise—except as permitted under Section 107 or 108 of the United States Copyright Act—without the prior written permission of the University of Oklahoma Press. To request permission to reproduce selections from this book, write to Permissions, University of Oklahoma Press, 2800 Venture Drive, Norman OK 73069, or email rights.oupress@ou.edu.

For Laura

Contents

Acknowledgments	11
Editorial Procedures	13
Introduction	15
Thomas Bullock: A Life Sketch	25
1. The Great Western Measure: The Mormons and the West, 1845–1847.	39
2. The Poor Camp Journal: Nauvoo, Illinois, to Winter Quarters, Indian Country, 1846	63
3. "The Celebrated Platte—The Highway of Our Future Journey": The Camp of the Pioneers to the Oregon Trail, April 1847	111
4. "The Tracks of Buffalo": Kearney, Nebraska, to Fort Laramie, May 1847	139
5. "To the Tops of the Mountains": Fort Laramie to South Pass, June 1847	173
6. "The Council in the Grove on Little Sandy River with Mr. Bridger": South Pass to Green River, June 1847	205
7. "Hurra, Hurra, Hurra, There's My Home At Last": Green River to the Salt Lake Valley, July 1847	215
8. "The Great Salt Lake City of the Great Basin": Salt Lake Valley, July–August 1847	235
9. "The Best & Nighest Road": The Returning Pioneers, Great Salt Lake City to Winter Quarters	267
Afterword: The Triumph of Brigham Young	319
A Galaxy of Mormon Pioneers: Biographical Sketches	325
Appendix A: Thomas Bullock Papers and Journals	351
Appendix B: Bullock's Notes at the End of Journal No. 1, 1847	356
Appendix C: Notes from the Returning Pioneer Journals	360
Bibliography	365
Index	377

TABLES

Persons who Volunteer to go	75
[The Iowa Trail, Camps and Mileages]	100
[The Night Guard]	122
[The 1847 Brigham Young Pioneer Company]	130
[The Advance Guard of the Mississippi Saints]	181
[The Battalion Advance Party]	219
[Orson Pratt's Advance Company, 13 July 1847]	226
[Distances from Winter Quarters to Salt Lake Valley]	233
[The Ox Company of Returning Pioneers]	258
[The Returning Pioneers]	276
[Hosea Stout's Relief Party from Winter Quarters]	315
[Ferry Accounts on the North Platte]	356
[Camps and Mileages, 1847]	358
[Miles] from Great Salt Lake City	360
Military Organization	362
Teamster Company	363
[Returning Pioneers] Traveling Organization	363

Illustrations

Thomas Bullock, about 1860 . . . . *frontispiece*
Thomas Bullock, about 1847 26
Henrietta Rushton Bullock, first wife of Thomas 27
Lucy Caroline Clayton Bullock 31
Brigham Young, in 1851 33
Betsy Prudence Howard Bullock 35
Henrietta Bullock, 1897 38
Bullock's drawing of the medal carried by Lakota chief . . 167
Bullock's drawing of Fort Laramie 177
Map of Great Salt Lake region 251

Acknowledgments

I owe a tremendous debt of gratitude to the staff of the Historical Department and Library of the Church of Jesus Christ of Latter-day Saints (LDS), without whose assistance this work would have been impossible. I am especially indebted to them for providing copies of the Edyth Jenkins Romney typescripts of Bullock's journals. I must salute the late Mrs. Romney, who over her long career created hundreds of typescripts of important LDS documents; her contribution to this work is immense. W. Randall Dixon tracked down many obscure and difficult requests for documents with extraordinary patience. I also recognize the assistance and professionalism of Steven Sorenson, Ronald O. Barney, Larry W. Draper, Pauline Musig, Chad Orton, William W. Slaughter, Ronald G. Watt, Linda Haslam, Nancy Hurtado, Scott Christensen, Melvin L. Bashore, JoAnn Bitton, Kim Farr, April Williamson, and James L. Kimball, Jr., who have shown tireless courtesy and patience. Michael N. Landon has shared the adventures of trail research with me.

The Thomas Bullock journals and other documents from the LDS Archives are published with the permission of the Historical Department of the Church of Jesus Christ of Latter-day Saints.

Researcher Robert Hoshide initially collaborated on the project, correcting the first electronic transcript of the 1847 journal against the original text. We came to a "parting of the ways" on the collaboration, but I must acknowledge the many corrections, Latin translations, and insightful suggestions he contributed to the work.

Gregory Thompson and the entire staff of Special Collections at the University of Utah's Marriott Library have been exceptionally helpful. Walter Jones in particular has solved mysteries that would otherwise be unfathomable.

Curator Edith W. Menna of the Daughters of Utah Pioneers' Pioneer Memorial Museum located several Bullock family biographies in the museum's collection. Photo Archivist Elma Olmstead helped find and copy portraits of Thomas Bullock and his family.

I wish to acknowledge the Utah Pioneer Trails Sesquicentennial Celebration Commission for its generous grant to support publication of the Bullock journals.

I want to recognize the invaluable assistance of three dedicated public employees: National Park Service Long Distance Trails Superintendent Jere Krakow, whose duties include administering the Mormon Pioneer Trail; and Interpretive Planner Kay Threlkeld and former Trails Coordinator Mike Duwe of the National Park Service, who devoted much time and hard work to creating the map that accompanies this volume.

Historians Jay Aldous, Donald E. Buck, Lyndia Carter, Robert Carter, Peter DeLafosse, William G. Hartley, F. Garn Hatch, Kristin Johnson, Merrill Mattes, Floyd O'Neil, Roy Tea, and Harold Schindler have helped me hammer out ideas and resolve perplexing puzzles. Levida Hileman of Casper, Wyoming, searched her collection of names from Independence Rock for members of the pioneer company. Randy Brown of Douglas, Wyoming, contributed his detailed knowledge of the trail through that wonderful state, making a number of corrections that will make me appear a far better trail hand than I am. Gary Clayton, a descendent of William Clayton, provided many insights into Mormon doctrine. Gail G. Holmes, an expert on the Mormon Trail in Iowa, caught many errors and prevented me from repeating old mistakes long embedded in the literature.

The mistakes that remain are solely my own.

I owe much to the great trail scholars who reviewed the entire manuscript. Stanley B. Kimball, the acknowledged godfather of Mormon Trail scholars, provided dozens of corrections, insightful suggestions, and appreciated encouragement. Violet Kimball made many stylistic and critical comments that I greatly appreciate. David L. Bigler, former president of the Oregon-California Trails Association, drove the trail with me from Salt Lake to Grand Island in August 1995, sharing his encyclopedic knowledge of the land and its history. Many of the original observations and interpretations in this work must be credited to him, and he has continued to inspire and enlighten my education in the story of the overland epic.

Finally, I must affectionately salute the author of this adventure, Thomas Bullock, whose devotion and hard work created this magnificent record of his and his people's part in the history of the American West.

WILL BAGLEY
Salt Lake City
October 1996

Editorial Procedures

The primary goal of this compilation of Thomas Bullock's 1846 and 1847 trail journals is the faithful representation of the original records in a readable format. In the interest of clarity, I have made a number of editorial changes.

Bullock provided full dates for his entries, typically on two lines, the first containing the month and year and the second listing the date and day of the week. I have put all the information on a single line using date/month/year format, supplying em dashes to set off dates from text.

Especially in the 1847 diaries, Bullock inconsistently used a complicated system to render times, showing 10:05 as 10h.5min. I have replaced these "h" and "m" references with standard notation. Bullock might also within a few lines randomly refer to time as "½ past 6," "20 min to 10," or "20 minutes to 4"; such references are preserved, but where he uses "6½ P.M.," it is rendered as 6:30 P.M.

Bullock did not always spell names consistently, and I transcribe names using the variant spellings in the manuscripts. As much as possible, the biographical sketches and index use the correct spellings. I spell out and capitalize abbreviated names and all personal, religious, and military titles, such as Brother, Sister, Elder, Captain, Colonel, and President. In particular, Bullock often referred to his adopted father, Apostle Willard Richards, as "Dr." or "Dr. Richards." References to "Dr. Richards" are preserved, but references to "Dr." are changed to "Doctor."

I italicize Bullock's occasional Latin phrases and spell out abbreviations for the primary compass directions, while other compass points are rendered using initials only, as in NE for northeast. Bullock occasionally used "c" to indicate "and," and "r" for "are," and they are so rendered.

Grammar and diction are presented as in the original. The dashes that provided punctuation in the manuscript diaries are eliminated or replaced with commas, periods, or em dashes, depending on context. Capitalization is generally Bullock's, except that the first letters of sentences and of personal names are capitalized; where the case used in the manuscript is ambiguous, I use standard capitalization. I standardize punctuation (or its absence) and add periods to the ends of sentences. In general, I have simplified punctuation for readability.

Where missing, I add apostrophes to possessive nouns, contractions, and to "o'clock." I generally use Bullock's original spelling, except when the correction of a simple misspelling, such as that of an article, improves the readability of the passage. Brackets enclose added letters, missing words, and conjectural readings. [Blank] indicates a blank space. I have dropped superscripts and place interlined information in its proper location in the text. Crossed-out text is rendered as ~~strikethrough~~.

As a personal preference, I use the contemporary term mountaineers to refer to the fur trappers and traders who are today usually called mountain men.

To simplify the annotations, quotations from published pioneer journals are identified by their writer and can be found under the date referenced. I cite published sources by author and title; I italicize book titles and put newspaper and magazine articles and thesis titles in quotation marks. Manuscripts are listed in plain text. The bibliography contains complete listings of all the books, articles, newspapers, journals, and manuscripts used to annotate Bullock's journal. Footnotes contain editorial comments, including definitions and the location of place names. The biographical sketches in "A Galaxy of Mormon Pioneers" provide personal information on many, though not all, of the Latter-day Saint mentioned in the journals. Biographical information on non-Mormons, such as fur traders, fellow overlanders, and Catholic and Protestant missionaries (in Mormon parlance, the "Gentiles"), and Indians is placed in the footnotes.

INTRODUCTION

No other group in America is as obsessed with history as the Latter-day Saints. The Mormon people are justly proud of their colorful heritage and are renowned for the completeness of their records and their devotion to the past. Perhaps no single person is more responsible for the vast scope of the rich documentary record of this singular American religion than the "Clerk of the Camp of Israel," Thomas Bullock. An English scribe who served as clerk and personal secretary to two Mormon prophets, Joseph Smith and Brigham Young, Bullock spent the last forty-five years of his life in the service of his adopted religion, in addition to holding innumerable city, county, and territorial offices in Utah. His twenty-one years in the Church Historian's Office produced most of the volumes in the classic (if not infallible) documentary history credited to Joseph Smith, but ultimately edited and published by B. H. Roberts as *History of the Church*. His life's work assured the collection and preservation of a host of maps, letters, and documents of invaluable worth not only to the study of LDS history, but also to the interpretation and understanding of the American West.

Ironically, though Bullock wrote thousands of pages that would ultimately be released under other men's names, only a single recently published volume bears his name, Greg R. Knight's 1994 edition of *Thomas Bullock Nauvoo Journal*. And while the 1847 trek of Brigham Young's pioneer company is arguably the most documented event in Western American history—excepting, of course, the Battle of the Little Bighorn—no one has ever published the official chronicle of the journey, Thomas Bullock's "Journal of the Travels of the Pioneer Camp of the Saints, from Winter Quarters, in search of a location for a Stake of Zion."

This volume corrects that oversight. The trail journals Bullock kept between September 1846 and October 1847 describe the entire trip from Nauvoo to Salt Lake and back to the Missouri River.[1] These doc-

---

[1] See Appendix A for information about Thomas Bullock's papers and physical descriptions of the journals published here.

uments paint a colorful and personal picture of the Mormon Trail from the Mississippi to the Great Basin. They capture the suffering of the poverty-stricken Saints (as they called themselves) during their struggle across Iowa in 1846. They tell the legendary tale of Brigham Young's pioneer company, describing the beginnings of a great exodus that moved a people from the American frontier into the heart of a land they considered a wilderness. While our modern perspective makes the success of the Mormons' western venture seem foreordained, Bullock's journals show that this massive movement of thousands of families into "the wilderness" was much more complicated—and riskier—than is generally assumed.

These wonderfully detailed documents paint a vivid picture of the Mormon exodus. Bullock's 1846 diary tells the story of the Poor Camp, created when the last of the Mormon refugees were driven from Nauvoo, their fallen capital on the Mississippi River, and the renowned "miracle of the quail." The Poor Camp was among the last of the 1846 Mormon wagon trains to cross Iowa to the LDS church's settlements on the Missouri River. While their trip was difficult, it did not match the suffering of the leading companies that made the crossing during the late winter and early spring of 1846. Still, this journal tells a compelling story. Finally, the diary includes details of life at Winter Quarters, the Mormon camp built on Indian lands west of the Missouri River.

Bullock's 1847 diary of "the Pioneer Camp of the Saints," the first trail-blazing party of overland Saints, tells the intriguing story of Brigham Young's rise to power. With the anti-polygamy faction of the church determined to oppose him, Young had been engaged in a rough-and-tumble struggle to succeed Joseph Smith that had begun as soon as a mob had murdered the prophet in 1844. Although he was confirmed president of the LDS church as early as 1845, opposition from fellow apostles prevented Young from forming a First Presidency and establishing his power as equal to that of the Quorum of the Twelve Apostles. It was Young's brilliant management of the 1847 trek that firmly established his claim to lead the Saints; in the face of his *tour de force*, opposition to him within the church's hierarchy collapsed. The 1847 journals conclude with an account of the returning pioneers, the band of men who returned from the Great Salt Lake Valley to the Missouri

River in the fall to bring their families to the Rocky Mountains in the next spring.

Few historians have recognized how close the initial Mormon emigration came to disaster. In 1848 Bullock commented, "It appears as if we are to get to our journey's end by a miracle, or very narrowly indeed." Bullock's journal gives an intimate view of the tremendous gamble Brigham Young took when he led his people 1,000 miles from the Missouri River with few livestock or supplies. In the spring of 1847, the Church of Jesus Christ of Latter-day Saints was broke—flat broke. More than 10 percent of the Saints in the Mormon camps on the Missouri perished during the preceding winter, and many of those who survived were demoralized and desperately sick.[2] In January 1847, Brigham Young organized the emigration along military lines with his only canonized revelation, "The Word and Will of the Lord," which outlined the "Plan of organization for migration to the West." It defined companies "with captains of hundreds, captains of fifties, and captains of tens, with a president and two counselors at their head, under the direction of the Twelve Apostles" that would define the structure of hundreds of Mormon overland parties.[3]

Young grasped for money to carry the Saints through the winter whenever the opportunity offered, but opportunities were scarce. At the start of the 1847 emigration, a last-minute infusion of English sovereigns from the enormously successful LDS missionary efforts in Great Britain eased the Saints' desperate financial plight, but the Mormons remained spectacularly poor. Ten years after reaching the Salt Lake Valley, Brigham Young recalled, "I came here in debt, owing for my outfit."[4] Young relied on the draft animals and wagons his followers had assembled before evacuating Illinois for transport, and the Mormons depended heavily on game for food. Young planned for the pioneer com-

---

[2] Gail Holmes notes that the sexton's records for Winter Quarters from 23 December 1846 to 21 March 1847 listed only seventy burials, many fewer than the traditional figure of 600 deaths out of 6,000 inhabitants. Richard Bennett, however, estimated there were 723 deaths in the Mormon settlements from June 1846 to May 1847 and that the total population of the Mormon camps on the Missouri at the end of 1846 totaled 6,950. See Bennett, *Mormons at the Missouri*, 90, 136–37.

[3] *Doctrine and Covenants*, Section 136. This revelation eventually governed the organization of all Mormon overland parties.

[4] Brigham Young, A Discourse, 16 August 1857, in Edyth Romney Typescript Collection, MS 2737, box 79, folder 4, LDS Archives.

pany to blaze the trail to the Saints' new Zion. They would travel quickly to the Great Basin in carriages and light wagons, leaving six weeks before there was even sufficient grass on the plains for the impoverished stock, breaking trail where necessary and hurrying to arrive in the mountains in time to plant crops. The bulk of the 1847 emigration—1,553 people—followed in the "second division," which was even more poorly equipped and supplied than the pioneers.

The ratio of animals to wagons in the pioneer company, 3 to 1, is one measure of the desperation of the Saints—and this for the spearhead of the movement, an elite group that included eight of the Twelve Apostles who led the church. By comparison, the ratio of animals to wagons in the Donner party of the previous year was closer to 10 to 1, and military and freighting companies of the next decade preferred a ratio of 12 to 1. The Mormon "down-and-back" trains of 1861 used ratio of 8 oxen to 1 wagon—but these were animals born and bred in the Rocky Mountains that were acclimatized to the challenges of overland travel.[5]

Bullock's 1847 journal paints an especially compelling portrait of Brigham Young in his glory: this is a dynamic, hands-on leader who personally scouts out the route and selects camping sites, negotiates with traders and mountaineers, interrogating them closely about the lay of the land, wades rivers, hauls rafts, and jumps into the mire to pull on a rope when necessary. This is the man whom Patty Sessions watched in 1846: "Brigham Young came up with his company driving his team in mud to his knees, as happy as a king."[6] We watch as "Prest. Young stript himself" on the banks of the North Platte and "went to work with all his strength" to build "a first rate White Pine and White Cotton Wood Raft." In this adventure Young is a rough-and-ready leader who knows exactly what he wants—an independent empire isolated in the Rocky Mountains—and he uses all the force of his personality to cajole, exhort, and inspire his people to achieve that dream. Young blazes trail, hunts antelope, stands guard, stares down Indians, and clambers up the canyon wall at Deer Creek to escape a mother grizzly bear. Here the American Moses is, at bottom, a frontiersman.

Besides its sweeping view of the historical landscape, this collection

---

[5] Lass, *From the Missouri to the Great Salt Lake*, 7; and Hartley, "Down-and-Back Wagon Trains," 24.
[6] Kimball and Kimball, *Mormon Trail*, 13.

tells a very personal story of the metamorphosis of an English excise clerk into a rough approximation of an American frontiersman. On these journeys we see a timid Thomas Bullock overcome his fear of horses, drive oxen, herd cattle, read Indian sign, hunt buffalo, and kill rattlesnakes. While Bullock seldom enjoyed the process, it is a remarkable transformation. The modest clerk seldom made much of his exploits as a plainsman—and he sometimes even mocked his failings as a hunter or cowboy: "Elder Woodruff returned from shooting as the Sun set. I killed a Mosquito"; and "After a long day's hunt, T. B. trailed two lame [pronghorns] & in a gully or ravine came up to one, which after Six or seven shots lay down & gave the Ghost." After riding through the tall grass at the mouth of Emigration Canyon he credited the Lord for this remarkable change: "I am not afraid now but that by a little practice I could make a good Equestrian & thank the Lord for my improvement." These experiences graphically show the effect of the frontier on a quiet English clerk and describe a profound and unlikely transformation of the man's character.

Bullock's 1847 journal tells the story of the pioneer band in both its grandeur and tedium, but despite its status as the "official" journal, it remains an intensely personal document. Perhaps this is most evident in Bullock's many complaints about the difficulties of keeping the record:

> it is utterly impossible for me to do justice in writing a Journal. Having besides team to drive, to run after the cow, fetch Water, hunt up and carry Wood, look after the oxen, stand guard over the cattle, load and unload my Wagon of its contents, and run to do every job that is wanted, & when I pick up items not allowed time to fill them out. Almost every man in Camp has more or less time to spare, but I have not now spare time allowed to fill up the Journal, to fulfil the very office I was brought out to fill—namely, keep the Camp Journal.

Bullock complained that he was at everyone's beck and call—"I have so many commanders; it is hard for me to do every thing"—and keeping a detailed journal was no one's priority but his own: "I was sent to gather Dandelions, then pick them—this instead of writing a Journal." The indignities he suffered were many and varied: "I have Eight sections of maps to copy, besides bringing up the arrears of notes in this Journal—and yet I was sent out on Guard. In running after the Animals, sweating, & then sitting down to map brought on sickness again. I write this to show the difficulties I have to encounter even in doing this fragment of a Journal." He was even "kicked three times by cow, while milking."

Bullock apologized for the brevity of his 1847 journal, explaining that having to "attend to cattle, & drive a team is the cause that I have so little down in my Journal. I could wish to have had the best, & fullest Journal of this Mission, but am sorry I cannot do more; may the Lord accept what I have written & done in this Journey." Still, while William Clayton's journal shows more literary talent, Orson Pratt's diary is much more precise and scientific, and the Norton Jacob and Howard Egan accounts provide a more entertaining telling of the story, Thomas Bullock's 1847 chronicle gives a comprehensive picture of this intriguing American adventure. In rating Bullock's 1847 journal, the dean of trail historians, Merrill Mattes, gave it only three stars out of five, but he recognized that "this record is of vital importance to establish a complete record of the Mormon Pioneer trek."[7]

The journals display a remarkable awareness of and sympathy for animals and nature, and these greenhorn frontiersmen are full of surprises. The pioneers occasionally remembered "the Prophet Joseph's instructions, not to kill any of the animals or birds, or any thing created by Almighty God that had life, for the sake of destroying it." Bullock noted that "a large Wolf came out of the Wood on our right hand & walked very leisurely within about 50 rods past our camp; as much as to say the Devil & I are determined to prove whether you will practice what is now taught." Bullock's record provides a surprising insight into the humanity of these pioneers, as when Bullock restores a desecrated Indian grave, or when "A young Fawn ran thro' the Camp, the dogs run it down & Andrew Cahoon rescued it alive & carried it to his Wagon [and] in the evening turned it loose again." On a kindly impulse, Brigham Young orders several men who are prodding at an exhausted buffalo cow "to come away & leave her alone."

Bullock's journal may be the only pioneer company account to remark on butterflies and bats. Beyond the bear and the buffalo, the wolves,

---

[7] Mattes, *Platte River Road Narratives*, 90, 113. The low rating may simply express Mattes' frustration at his inability to get copies of manuscript journals from the LDS Archives.

foxes, and coyotes, the deer, elk, and pronghorn that caught the attention of all overlanders, Bullock's account teems with small animals, from "a Mud Turtle [I caught] with my hands" to "a small Chamelion, a pretty little harmless reptile." Bullock remarks on a "Prairie Dog Town," "Snipes & Geese," skunks, badgers, and birds large and small—swallows, magpies, sand hill cranes, hawks, geese, ducks, and prairie hens—while on occasion we hear "the Whip poor will & Red breasts enliven the Grove." Bullock sees "two perfect rainbows in the heavens and an Eagle flying in the Air" and hears "after Sunset a full Frog Symphony, full of music & variety."

Bullock shows a continuing fascination with all aspects of this "most beautiful country," evoking its flora—"dandelions, White flowers called Pickpockets, Onions, Gooseberries, a Strawberry Vine...Daisies, Pinks, Artimesia," "the Prickly Pear," "Sunflowers & Hollyhocks,"—and its trees: "Oak brush, many Sugar Maple, & Balm of Gilead Trees," "Service Bushs, Scrub Oak, Choke Cherries," and "Spruce Pines," noting that "Cedars are beginning to flourish; Pines are seen on the Mountains, Cotton Wood Trees on the River banks...& the Artimesia." He remarks on the land's geology from its massive trail landmarks down to its "many Curious & Clear Stones." And he evokes the wonder of the western scenery to a man born in green Great Britain: "bold ragged bluffs, speckled with Cedar and Pine Trees."

Bullock tried to plant a hill of corn at each camp—as a sign of hope for those who followed the pioneer company. This act is symbolic of the revolutionary nature of the Latter-day Saint's contribution to America's overland heritage: the Mormons were consciously and conscientiously building a road, not merely following a trail. Until 1847, overland emigrants showed little if any concern for those who would follow them, but the Saints were engaged in a vast communal endeavor: they were moving the Children of Israel to a new Zion. "It should be understood," Wilford Woodruff wrote after breaking trail with Heber Kimball on 27 May 1847, "that we are piloting A road for the House of Israel to travel in for many years to come. Therefore it requires the greater care." They were also laying out a separate and distinct route from the wagon road that by 1846 was already famous as the Oregon Trail. Although it remained for their descendants to name the route the Mormon Trail, as Woodruff noted early in May, "we thought it best to keep on the north side of the [Platte] river & brave the difficulties of Burning Prairies & make A road that should stand as a permanant [sic] rout for the saints independant [sic] of the old emigration rout." There was no name attached to the North Platte road when the Mormons set out across it in 1847, and those who judge the name "Mormon Trail" to be inappropriate should consider the judgment of Wallace Stegner: "By the improvements they made in it, they earned the right to put their name on the trail they used."[8]

Merrill Mattes correctly observed that the name Mormon Trail has obscured the fact "that the great majority of travelers along the north side [of the Platte River] were not Mormons but others with a different history." The returning Astorians came down the river on their return from Oregon in 1812–13, and overland travel on the north side of the Platte began as early as 1820 when Lieutenant Stephen H. Long's exploring party left Cantonment Missouri. Fur traders and missionaries used the trading post at Bellevue as a jumping off point to the West through the next two decades. Even the Stephens-Murphy-Townsend party of 1844, the first emigrants to get wagons into California, used the northern route, but the fact remains that these passages left mere scratches on the prairie. Brigham Young's pioneer company of 1847 explored, blazed, marked, and improved "a new road on the North side," a road that carried one of the "two great streams" of the massive gold rush migration to California and ultimately served as the road west for some 70,000 Mormons and as many as 150,000 other emigrants.[9] Trail historians who have long joked that the only part of the Mormon Trail actually opened by the Mormons was the last 300 yards at the mouth of Emigration Canyon should consider Bullock's account before again burnishing this chestnut.

Readers who are familiar only with modern LDS practices may be surprised to find that the 1847 pioneer company started the day with coffee or learn that Brigham Young distributed "a Canteen of Spirits

---

[8] Stegner, *The Gathering of Zion*, 12.

[9] The "new road" quote is from Bullock, while the others are from Mattes, "The Northern Route of the Non-Mormons," 2-14. The figures are my own, using some of the most liberal estimates. Mattes, "The Northern Route," 4, estimated that 35,000 Mormons and 150,000 non-Mormons used the route between 1841 and 1866.

among the brethren" as the weary Saints returned to Winter Quarters in 1847. The 1833 revelation in *Doctrine and Covenants*, Section 89, called the Word of Wisdom, which proscribes hot drinks, tobacco, and alcohol, "was given as counsel or advice rather than as a binding commandment," and until the early twentieth century observance of this scripture was "sporadic" among Latter-day Saints.[10] Especially among pioneers and Brigham Young's clerks, the sage advice of the Word of Wisdom was more honored in the breach than in the observance.

Bullock relentlessly recorded the words of the Mormon leader, reporting his sermons, rebukes, orders, and especially the personal compliments that Young bestowed on his faithful scribe. The extreme nature of much of Young's speech is still provocative; while some historians dismiss his harsh talk as rhetoric and bombast, I believe the Mormon leader usually meant exactly what he said.

Observant readers will note Bullock's repeated references to minutes and letters "on file." Most of these documents are located in various collections in the Archives of the Historical Department of the Church of Jesus Christ of Latter-day Saints (referred to in annotations and in the bibliography as LDS Archives), with most of the relevant documents probably located in the Brigham Young Papers. This collection is restricted, and though the professional staff at the archives has shown me every assistance and has given me access to nearly every document I requested, I have not been able to track down and evaluate every item referenced in Bullock's journals. This failing, however, is due more to time constraints than to archival restrictions. Some of these documents can be found in the Journal History, a daily scrapbook of Mormon history consisting of journals, letters, and articles extracted from church records by Andrew Jenson. Whenever possible, for documents Bullock references I have identified published sources or their location in the Journal History. I have reviewed most of the documents that seemed interesting and important, but there is certainly much remarkable material that I have been unable to access or have merely overlooked.

Bullock's diary of the great exodus of 1848 and his short 1858 missionary journal from Florence, Nebraska, to Great Salt Lake City complete the set of Bullock's overland trail accounts. In a perfect world, this

---
[10] Lyon, "Word of Wisdom," in *Encyclopedia of Mormonism*, 4:1584.

book would consult and reproduce these journals and every document connected with Thomas Bullock's trail adventures, including the minutes of meetings, transcriptions of sermons and harangues, Bullock's personal letters published in the *Millennial Star* (the LDS missionary newspaper in England), the official letters dictated by Brigham Young and Willard Richards, notes to Bullock's wife, Henrietta, the clerk's hand-drawn maps, and the many waybills and mileage charts included in the Thomas Bullock Papers at the LDS Archives. Perhaps by the bicentennial of the Mormon Trail in 2047, the LDS church will see fit to produce comprehensive documentary editions of some of the remarkable trail documents in its possession; until then, this less-than-definitive sesquicentennial edition will make Bullock's key Mormon Trail journals accessible to scholars and buffs alike.

Bullock's lively record of the "Pioneer Camp of the Saints" presents in detail the daily reality of a journey that has become an American legend. Within my limitations, I have tried to edit Bullock's trail journals as more than simply Mormon history, to place them in the context of their times as important documents in the history of the American West. This remarkable record paints an intimate and colorful picture of life on the trail in the late 1840s and encompasses a cast of characters that is as diverse as it is colorful. Within these pages, we learn that the Latter-day Saint odyssey to the West was both a hegira and an adventure.

THOMAS BULLOCK:
A LIFE SKETCH

Thomas Bullock, the eleventh of twelve children of Thomas and Mary Hall Bullock, was born in Leek, Staffordshire, England, on 23 December 1816.[1] His father was a grocer and his grandfather, Ralph, was a yeoman; by tradition, the family was deeply religious. At age thirteen the boy ended his formal education (he was "second-best scholar in his class") to work as a clerk in the law office of John Cruso.[2] Bullock worked in the law office for eight years and in 1838 became "One of Her Majesty, Queen Victoria's Officers of Excise," whose duties were to inspect and rate taxable items.[3] His "first sweetheart" was Lettice Marsh, but after a courtship of several (some say seven) years, Bullock married Henrietta Rushton, daughter of Richard Rushton, a silk manufacturer, on 23 June 1838, and they quickly had two sons, Thomas Henry (1839–1906) and Charles Richard (1840–1923), and a daughter, Pamela (1842-1921).[4] Ultimately, the couple would have nine children.

Bullock was not physically imposing—on 1 July 1846 he recorded his weight as being a mere 116 pounds.[5] The coat he wore across the plains in 1847, now preserved at the Pioneer Memorial Museum of the Daughters of Utah Pioneers in Salt Lake City, indicates that he was a slight man, perhaps 5'2" to 5'6" tall.[6] He had pleasant features set in an open face and deep-set eyes. As a young man, he wore a beard without a mustache or chin whiskers.

Bullock was proud of his service in the excise department, where he

---

[1] Family Record Book of Thomas Bullock, courtesy of Elaine Speakman; and Jenson, ed., *LDS Biographical Encyclopedia*, 2:599–600, 4:695. Bullock shared a birthday with Joseph Smith, a circumstance that probably helped Bullock's career in the LDS church.

[2] Bullock to "Cousin Thomas," 21 September 1850, in Carter, ed., "Thomas Bullock, Pioneer," 8:265.

[3] Simon, "Thomas Bullock as an Early Mormon Historian," 71, 86; and Knight, "Introduction to the 1845–1846 Journal of Thomas Bullock," 5.

[4] Family Record Book of Thomas Bullock; and Carter, ed., "Thomas Bullock, Pioneer," 8:229-30, 284.

[5] Knight, "Journal of Thomas Bullock," 74.

[6] Simon, "Thomas Bullock as an Early Mormon Historian," 86.

Thomas Bullock as he appeared about the time of the 1847 Mormon pioneer trek.
Courtesy, Daughters of Utah Pioneers.

"advanced to every grade, and in every place, with satisfaction to my superior officers and all with whom I was connected." In 1839 Bullock was promoted and sent to Ireland, where he worked for two years at the Carrickmacross distillery in Moneghan County, perhaps acquiring the taste for spirits that is reflected in many entries in his later journals. Promoted "to a ride in the island of Angleses," he petitioned to be sent "to some place where I could speak the same language." He was assigned to "a new ride in Shurbridge, where I had as pleasant a berth as a man could desire."[7]

In 1840, Bullock's in-laws were baptized into the Church of Jesus Christ of Latter-day Saints, popularly known as the Mormons, and on 20 November 1841 Thomas Bullock joined the Saints, walking "into the waters of baptism on a cold November night when ice was on the canal, and the keen frosty air was blowing in all its severity." Bullock was quickly ordained an elder and helped organize a branch in Brierly Hill. He endured the persecutions of his countrymen, being "pelted with

---

[7] Bullock to "Cousin Thomas," 21 September 1850, in Carter, ed., "Thomas Bullock, Pioneer," 8:265.

Henrietta Rushton Bullock, first wife of Thomas Bullock, as she appeared in her later years. *Courtesy, Daughters of Utah Pioneers.*

stones (in Dudley Park and Tipton)...[and] threatened to be thrown down an old coal pit (named Brierly Hill)."[8] By early the next year Bullock determined to join "the Gathering" and move his family to America, and on 8 March 1843 they departed Liverpool aboard the *Yorkshire*. Bullock paid for the passage of several families and was secretary of the ship's eighty-three Mormons, led by his brother-in-law, Richard Rushton.[9]

Life on emigrant packets in the nineteenth century was no pleasure cruise, and the *Yorkshire* had an eventful voyage during which Bullock "beheld the glory and power of God in the great deep."[10] While off Cuba early on the morning of 3 May, a sudden "whitesquall caught the foretop royal sail, which careened the vessel, when the foremast, mainmast and mizzenmast snapped asunder with an awful crash." Totally dismasted, at daybreak "all on deck was in confusion and a complete wreck," but the crew managed to jury-rig a sail to the stump of the main-

---

[8] Bullock to Angus, *Millennial Star* (3 July 1852), 299.
[9] Carter, ed., "Thomas Bullock, Pioneer," 8:230, 284-85. For an account of the voyage, see Hartley, "Broken Sails off Cuba," 9-11.
[10] Bullock to Angus, *Millennial Star* (3 July 1852), 299.

mast and sail the ship to New Orleans. The emigrants took passage on the *Dove* to St. Louis, and by the end of the month, Bullock arrived on the steamboat *Amaranth* at the Mormon capital on the upper Mississippi River, Nauvoo.[11]

On landing, Bullock met and talked with Joseph Smith, Jr., the visionary founder of the Latter-day Saints, and his brother, Hyrum. Self-taught and painfully conscious of his lack of formal education, Smith quickly recognized the abilities of the English convert, and by October Bullock had a job as clerk in the office of the Mormon prophet. Bullock bought land in Nauvoo the day after his arrival and immediately began building a two-story brick house on the lot he purchased on Block 31 of Lumber Street for $60.[12] Joseph Smith recalled that Bullock and his blind mother-in-law came caroling at one o'clock on Christmas Morning, 1843, "which caused a thrill of pleasure to run through my soul."[13]

Bullock was at the center of the business and religious life of Nauvoo, serving as secretary of the municipal council and court, clerk of the steamboat *Maid of Iowa*, and clerk of the Nauvoo Masonic lodge. Along with George D. Watt, William Clayton, and others, he took the minutes of Smith's sermons and was clerk of the April 1844 general conference. He served as deputy city recorder and clerk to church historian Willard Richards, an apostle and cousin of Brigham Young, who became Bullock's mentor and patron. Under the "Law of Adoption," a practice the LDS church has since abandoned, Bullock and his family were "sealed" to Willard Richards by Mormon temple rites, making the apostle Bullock's adopted father and further strengthening the bonds that joined the clerk to the inner circles of Mormon power.[14]

Bullock's dramatic and often poignant journals have another side that provides many insights into human reactions to the Saints' attempts to

---

[11] Smith, *History of the Church*, 5:380, 5:415; and Hartley, "Broken Sails off Cuba," 10-11.

[12] Knight, "Introduction to the 1845–1846 Journal of Thomas Bullock," 6; and Dorothy B. Blanpied, Thomas Bullock's Home in Nauvoo, Bullock Collection, Daughters of Utah Pioneers.

[13] Smith, *History of the Church*, 6:134. Since the *History of the Church* was composed after Smith's death, Bullock probably wrote this passage himself.

[14] Simon, "Thomas Bullock as an Early Mormon Historian," 87. With this ordinance, Joseph Smith adopted chosen subordinates, such as Richards, as his sons, and they in turn adopted others, like Bullock, who adopted others, and so it would go until all Israel was joined in a great family with Smith at its head. See Irving, "The Law of Adoption," 291–314.

live communally. As one of the first LDS church bureaucrats, Bullock depended on the contributions to the church for his livelihood and was paid in kind, which meant that his family's well-being depended on his fellow believers supporting the church and keeping their commitment to pool their wealth. The natural desire of people to keep what is theirs was a constant irritant to Bullock and was often the source of his many of his complaints—and his constant complaining is probably the greatest flaw in his journals.

Bullock was deeply involved in the closely guarded activities of Joseph Smith during the last dramatic year of the prophet's life. Bullock was part of the intimate circle that learned of the celestial order of marriage—polygamy—directly from the prophet. Among his many duties, Bullock was clerk of the Council of Fifty, the body that crowned Smith king of the world in April 1844.[15] This elite group, sometimes called "The Living Constitution" or, more commonly, the "Kingdom of God," was created to oversee the political organization that would rule the earth after the second coming of Jesus Christ.[16]

The clannish ways, the monolithic loyalty of the Saints to their religion, and the members' single-minded devotion to their leader angered their neighbors. The church hierarchy's adoption of polygamy and the public denial of the practice led to wild rumors inside and outside of Nauvoo. In his last months Smith lived at a frenetic pace: in April he preached the King Follett funeral oration that represented the final synthesis of his theology; in May he launched a campaign for the presidency of the United States; and in June he smashed the printing press of his opponents. All that spring Smith plunged headlong into expanding the practice of polygamy among his closest followers. "I intend to lay a foundation," he said on 12 May, "that will revolutionize the whole world."[17]

Bullock was more than a witness to this intense burst of energy—he was an active participant. In April he became a Mason and was first introduced to the Mormon temple rituals. Bullock was copyist for Smith's presidential campaign pamphlets *Views on the Powers and Policy of the*

---

[15] Hanson, *Quest for Empire*, 66, 155.
[16] Smith, *History of the Church*, 7:213.
[17] Ibid., 6:365.

Government of the United States, The Voice of Innocence from Nauvoo, and *Pacific Innuendo*. He drafted Smith's letters to Illinois Governor Thomas Ford and to Secretary of State John Calhoun. After the Law brothers published articles in the *Nauvoo Expositor* revealing Smith's doctrine of plural marriage, Bullock acted as secretary of the Nauvoo Legion's court martial of Wilson Law.[18] As clerk of the city council, he watched Mayor Joseph Smith order the destruction of the press of the *Expositor*, and he witnessed the subsequent arrest of the prophet.

The defining moment of Mormonism came on 27 June 1844 with the murder of Joseph and Hyrum Smith in Carthage Jail at the hands of a mob. Bullock experienced the martyrdom's devastating and galvanizing effect on his fellow believers. Smith's death profoundly moved his English disciple: "They were two good men and they died good men; they died martyrs for the truth and they sealed their testimonies with their blood." With just as much certainty, Bullock believed "The mantle of Joseph fell on Brigham Young."[19] The death of their prophet left the Mormons momentarily confused and leaderless, but a power struggle was partially resolved in August when the Twelve Apostles and their president, Brigham Young, asserted their authority and took control of the church.[20]

The Saints and their leaders tried to consolidate their position in Illinois, but relations between the Mormons and their neighbors quickly deteriorated to the point of civil war. By January 1845, the apostles were considering California as a possible haven for their people. Bullock recorded conversing with Willard Richards about California on 21 August, and a week later the church leaders determined to send 3,000 men and their families to California in 1846.[21] In September, Brigham Young promised that the Mormons would leave Illinois as soon as grass grew, and on 3 October, Bullock told Stephen Nixon "I was bound for California." Two days later he proudly recorded he was assigned to the "No. I Co." being "No. II on list."[22]

Bullock's 1845 journal contains more than fourteen allusions between 21 September and the end of the year to Mormon emigration

---

[18] Simon, "Thomas Bullock as an Early Mormon Historian," 80.

[19] Bullock to Angus, *Millennial Star* (3 July 1852), 299.

[20] For an account of Brigham Young's successful power struggle in Nauvoo in August 1844, see Quinn, *The Mormon Hierarchy*, 173-82.

[21] Journal History, 28 August 1845.

[22] Knight, "Journal of Thomas Bullock," 23.

plans and shows an interesting evolution. The first four entries refer specifically to "California"—then a general term for all Mexican territory west of the continental divide—but the 6 October entry shows a subtle geographical shift: "P. P. Pratt preached on the subject of leaving this place and going beyond the Rocky Mountains."[23] This and other evidence indicates that the church leaders, who closely interrogated every western traveler who passed through Nauvoo and carefully studied the writings of John C. Frémont and Lansford W. Hastings, had by this time selected the Great Basin as their likely destination.

To the puzzlement and distrust of their wary neighbors, the Saints expended tremendous energy and expense to complete the temple they were building on a bluff overlooking the Mississippi River. Their enemies could not believe that they would pour so much time and treasure into a building they planned to abandon immediately, but the temple was needed to perform the endowments and family sealings that were central to Mormon belief. Bullock received his Second Anointing in the Nauvoo Temple and was sealed to Lucy Caroline Clayton (1820–79) in the "Celestial Order of Marriage," popularly known as polygamy, on 23 January 1846.[24] She was the sister of William Clay-

---
[23] Ibid., 24.
[24] Knight, ed., *Thomas Bullock Nauvoo Journal*, 47–48; and Simon, "Thomas Bullock," 72.

Thomas Bullock's polygamous wife Lucy Caroline Clayton Bullock was the sister of William Clayton, who wrote the words to the famous LDS hymn, "Come, Come Ye Saints."
Courtesy, Daughters of Utah Pioneers.

ton, another talented English clerk whose career paralleled Bullock's in many ways. Lucy Clayton had been housekeeper of the Carthage Jail when Joseph and Hyrum Smith were killed there in 1844, "and it was her duty to clean the plaster from the floors, which was shot from the walls, and also the blood that stained the floors."[25] One biography credited her with driving a team in 1848 "the entire distance to Great Salt Lake. Thomas Bullock was more of a scholar than a handy man, and most of the heavy work fell on the women's shoulders."[26] As Henrietta Bullock was in ill health, Lucy Bullock cared for her and her children during their husband's absence with the pioneer company.

When the leadership of the church left Nauvoo in February 1846, Bullock remained in the ghost city to record its last days as the Mormon capital. He had already indexed and inventoried the church records that departed with church historian Willard Richards on 4 February 1846.[27] Throughout the spring, Bullock was afflicted with fever and Henrietta, his wife, had just given birth to a child, Willard Richards Bullock, who was in fragile health. While "the devils from nine counties laid siege to the devoted city," Bullock recorded the entry of the "Bands of armed demons" into the prostrate LDS capital.[28] This assignment spared the Bullock family the ordeals of the main Mormon companies who spent the late winter and spring of 1846 in the ice and mud of Iowa, but it exposed them to the "1500 to 2000 demoniacs, in the shape of men, who had sworn to raze our temple to the ground, to burn the city, to ravish our wives and our daughters, and drive the remainder into the river." In July, Brigham Young called on Bullock to join the Saints in Iowa, "as we frequently need more writers," but the clerk and his family were too sick to answer the call.[29] In September 1846, Bullock and all his family were afflicted with malaria when mobs descended on the Mormons who remained in Nauvoo. A "captain with a sword in his hand" offered to protect Bullock if he would renounce religion, but the sick clerk replied, "If I live, I shall follow the twelve." Seeing Bullock bid farewell to another refugee, one mobber yelled, "Look, look, there's a

---

[25] Amber R. Palmer, History of Thomas Bullock, Jr., Thomas Bullock Collection, Daughters of Utah Pioneers.

[26] Carter, "Thomas Bullock, Pioneer," 8:288.

[27] Simon, "Thomas Bullock as an Early Mormon Historian," 77.

[28] Bullock to Angus, *Millennial Star* (3 July 1852), 300.

[29] Journal History, 7 July 1846, 6; and Simon, "Thomas Bullock as an Early Mormon Historian," 81-82.

Brigham Young in a portrait taken on his fiftieth birthday in 1851. *Courtesy, LDS Archives.*

skeleton bidding Death good bye!" Bullock commented simply, "So you can imagine the poor sick condition we were in."[30] Bullock abandoned his $700 home and lot and "his tables, chairs, furniture, pigs, chickens, and all he possessed" to three men in exchange for "food amounting to two dollars seventeen and a half cents."[31]

On 9 October 1846, Bullock and 640 Mormon refugees witnessed the "Miracle of the Quail" at the Poor Camp on the banks of the Mississippi near Montrose, Iowa. Some historians explain the event as the natural result of a flock of passenger pigeons surprised to find their accustomed roost already occupied, or a covey of quail exhausted from flying across the river, but Bullock could certainly distinguish a quail from a pigeon. Whatever natural explanation there might be for the event, the desperate people who ate the quail can hardly be blamed for believing they had witnessed a miracle. The episode sheds much light on the way the Mormons saw themselves. They literally believed that they were the modern successors of the children of Israel, bound to their

---

[30] Bullock to Richards, *Millennial Star* (15 January 1848), 28.
[31] Carter, ed., "Thomas Bullock, Pioneer," 8:236.

God by a "New and Everlasting Covenant," a new chosen people enduring the ordeals of their own exodus.

Bullock's published account is the standard source for the event:

> But hark! what noise is that? See! the quails descend; they alight close by our little camp of twelve wagons, run past each wagon tongue, when they arise, fly round the camp three times, descend and again run the gauntlet past each wagon. See the sick knock them down with sticks, and the little children catch them alive in their hands!... One descends upon our tea-board, in the midst of our cups, while we were actually round the table eating our breakfast, which a little boy about eight years old catches alive in his hands; they rise again, the flocks increase in number, seldom going seven rods from our camp, continually flying round the camp, sometimes under the wagons, sometimes over, and even into the wagons, where the poor sick Saints are lying in bed; thus having a direct manifestation from the Most High that although we are driven by men, He has not forsaken us.[32]

Bullock arrived at Winter Quarters, near present Omaha, Nebraska, on 27 November 1846, "finding a city of about 700 houses, and upwards of 4,000 Saints, built in less than three months."[33] Brigham Young told Bullock "he would take me with him" on the trip to the mountains in the spring "even if he had to put me in his pocket."[34] First, Bullock and his family had to endure the winter in one of the dugouts Bullock called "gopher holes." Pneumonia, diphtheria, dysentery, and scurvy haunted the camp, intensified by the bitter weather and general malnutrition. On 17 March 1847, the clerk's infant son, Willard Richards Bullock, joined those who died in that awful season at Winter Quarters.

Bullock's 1846 and 1847 journals describe his life in detail from his departure from Nauvoo to his return to Winter Quarters. In 1848, he brought his family to the Salt Lake Valley, where he was once again a busy man. He helped plat the city and distribute lots. Late that year he drafted the scrip that served as paper money in the Mormon settlements, and in 1849 as "Secretary to the mint" he helped to stamp coins made of California gold dust. Bullock was elected recorder of Salt Lake

---

[32] Bullock to Richards, *Millennial Star* (15 January 1848), 28. Bullock's 9 October 1846 journal entry confirms this widely quoted account of the "Miracle of the Quail."

[33] *Ibid.*

[34] Carter, ed., "Thomas Bullock, Pioneer," 8:238.

Betsy Prudence Howard Bullock married Thomas Bullock in 1852 at the urging of Lucy Clayton Bullock. The couple had eight children.
Courtesy, Daughters of Utah Pioneers.

County and was appointed recorder for the Perpetual Emigration Fund that financed and managed the Mormon emigration "to remove the poor to this place." He served as secretary to the First Presidency. In December 1850, Bullock was selected clerk of the House of Representatives of the State of Deseret and later held the same office in the Utah Territorial Legislature. In 1851 Bullock conducted a census of Utah Territory that enumerated 11,354 inhabitants. From 1848 to 1856, Bullock accompanied a number of exploration parties and acted as their historian. Upon the founding of the *Deseret News* in June 1850, Bullock was named proofreader; earlier in the year, he helped set the type for the constitution of the State of Deseret. In 1852, General Daniel Wells appointed Bullock military secretary of the Nauvoo Legion, and by 1855 he was a lieutenant colonel.[35]

Somehow, Bullock found time to take another plural wife, marrying Betsy Prudence Howard on 9 December 1852. Bullock's second wife, Lucy Clayton, apparently helped arrange the marriage, which produced eight children.[36] On 30 November 1853, Queen Victoria's former excise man became a citizen of the United States.

---
[35] *Ibid.*, 8:256-266, 274, and 284 describe Bullock's Utah service in his many territorial offices and ecclesiastical callings.

[36] See *Ibid.*, 8:289–90, for a short autobiography of Betsy Bullock.

In August 1856, Bullock was called as a missionary to England. On 10 September he dedicated his family to the keeping of the Lord and set out for his homeland.[37] After an adventurous overland crossing, the missionary party reached the Missouri River in late October; and after an equally thrilling Atlantic crossing, Bullock landed in Liverpool on 11 January.

Bullock returned to America on 19 February 1858. His absence framed the "Utah War"—the drama played out when James Buchanan sent a federal army to replace Brigham Young as governor of Utah Territory—and the attendant excitement in the frontier Zion. In Chicago, Bullock met government officials recruiting mercenaries to go to Utah, offering "a bounty of beauty and booty." One of his companions "fearing being searched, destroyed my journal, which was invaluable to me and my friends," making this one of the few periods in Bullock's adult life for which there is no surviving diary.[38]

On the trail in late May, he wrote the *Millennial Star*, "I understand hell is at Fort Bridger," where Albert Sidney Johnston's troops were posted. Arriving to find Great Salt Lake City "deserted by its inhabitants" in anticipation of the arrival of Johnston's hated army, Bullock found his house boarded up "and everything carried away, which literally and remarkably fulfilled a dream I had near Grand Island when a pioneer in May, 1847." (He did not mention this dream in his journal.) Bullock met the church leaders in Utah Valley on 22 June 1858, "and then started to find our families, thus completing a hazardous and laborious journey."[39]

Upon his return to Utah, Bullock resumed many of his old offices and accumulated new ones, becoming secretary of the Deseret Agricultural and Manufacturing Society (which awarded him a diploma for the best drawn map of Utah) and, with the official establishment of the office, inspector of liquors. Bullock worked in the Church Historian's Office until 1862, when he denied Joseph A. Young, the son of the prophet, access to "a Book upon sealings." Bullock "had orders that no

---

[37] Ibid., 8:267.

[38] Ibid., 8:277. The destroyed papers included the names of 650 relatives for whom Bullock hoped to perform temple work. He later wrote, "If an angel could offer me my journal and papers in one hand, and two thousand dollars in the other, and I could have one, I would choose my journal, family records, and other papers." Ibid., 8:279.

[39] Ibid., 8:278–79.

one should see it," but his action resulted in an order from Brigham Young to "deliver up to him all of his Private records and papers that He might have in his possession."[40]

Willard Richard's death in 1854 left Bullock without his adopted father as patron in the historian's office. On 22 January 1865 Brigham Young directed George A. Smith to "dismiss Thomas Bullock from the Historian office and put Joseph /F/ Smith in his place." A petulant Young complained that he thought Richards had "used to take any paper he could lay his hands upon for waste Papers whether they was valuable or not & I believe Thomas Bullock will do the same, & I dont want him in the office any longer."[41] Whatever Brigham Young's virtues, loyalty to his old comrades and subordinates was not among them, and Bullock felt the unjustness and harshness of this rebuke for the rest of his days.

During his service in the historian's office, Bullock wrote 2,013 pages of the 2,407-page "Manuscript History" that, when edited by B. H. Roberts, emerged as the seven-volume *History of the Church*. Although attributed to Joseph Smith, the history was assembled from Smith's dictations and from newspaper articles, other people's journals, and letters. Of the published edition, Bullock wrote most of the last 300 pages of volume 3 and all of volumes 4 through 7.[42]

After his banishment from the historian's office, Bullock moved to the mountains east of Salt Lake, settling first in Wanship and later in Coalville in Summit County. He served as county recorder and clerk and was elected a regent of Deseret University, predecessor of the University of Utah. While preparing for church in February 1866, he fell through a trap door, "whereby his shoulder was dislocated, and he became a partial cripple for the remainder of his life."[43] During his last years he was

---

[40] Kenney, ed., *Wilford Woodruff's Journal*, 6:28. Woodruff's inventory of the items Bullock delivered included notebooks listing sealings and adoptions, the records of the Perpetual Emigration Fund, the "List of donations" for 1849-1853, "7 journals of kingdom of God," and "One package of minutes on file of the kingdom of God from 1849 to 52" that Woodruff thought "we may want to refer to in the Compilation of History." Bullock also surrendered forty-three promissory notes autographed by Joseph Smith, Brigham Young's journals of 1832, 1833, and 1835, and "a Box with a secret lock Containing gold dust and papers."

[41] *Ibid.*, 6:208. To his credit, Woodruff defended Bullock in his journal, stating that neither "G. A. Smith or my self have never known either Richards or Bullock [to] destroy any valuable papers But always looked upon them as faithful honest men."

[42] Simon, "Thomas Bullock as an Early Mormon Historian," 87.

[43] Thomas Bullock, Papers 1844–1881, LDS Archives.

Henrietta Bullock on the porch of her home in Salt Lake City shortly before her death in the Pioneer Jubilee year, 1897. *Courtesy, Daughters of Utah Pioneers.*

clerk, historian, and general recorder for the Summit Stake of the LDS church.

Thomas Bullock died at his home in Coalville on 10 February 1885, remembered as a "gentlemanly, unobtrusive and reliable character."[44] His second wife, Lucy Clayton Bullock, had died on her farm in South Cottonwood in 1879. Betsy Prudence Howard Bullock died in 1893, while Bullock's first wife, Henrietta Rushton Bullock, died in the Pioneer Jubilee year of 1897.

In September 1876, Bullock had composed his own obituary, "Another Old Veteran Gone":

> Elder Bullock was always Honest, and a Man of Truth; in his latter days he frequently talked with his friends, expressing his convictions that he would soon pass behind the vail for a little Season, and come up in the first Resurrection, with Joseph and Hyrum, Willard, Heber, and George A., the Apostles of the Lord Jesus and all the faithful Saints, who have embraced the doctrines of the Lord Jesus Christ. And we can add, the Old Veteran Clerk has gone home, He is not dead, but sleepeth. Blessed is he for his integrity and faithfulness.[45]

Thomas Bullock was the father of twenty-three children, thirteen of whom lived to adulthood, and he is survived today by a vast progeny.[46]

---

[44] Salt Lake *Daily Herald*, 12 February 1885, 8.
[45] Thomas Bullock, Papers 1844–1881, LDS Archives.
[46] Simon, "Thomas Bullock as an Early Mormon Historian," 73.

Chapter I

THE GREAT WESTERN MEASURE
The Mormons and the West, 1845–1847

As Wallace Stegner noted in his classic story of the Mormon Trail, *The Gathering of Zion*, the trek of the 1847 Mormon pioneer company to the Salt Lake Valley "must be the most extensively reported event in western history."[1] The journey has achieved mythic status among the Latter-day Saint people, and even the most skeptical of historians must concede the biblical dimension of the story. Like the tale of Moses and the exodus of the children of Israel, the story of Brigham Young and the Mormon pioneer company remains an enduring legacy, and their achievement is now a sacred text encrusted in legend. The large number of journals kept by members of the party shows that they recognized the significance of their trek and realized that it would be the central event in their lives. The survival of many of its veterans to great old age elevated these rowdy frontiersmen to the special sainthood of founding fathers. Their story still resonates in the empire they established in the Rocky Mountains.

The Mormons had long sought government help to support a move west, and the complicated story of how they made their way to the Great Basin must be seen against the larger history of the American West and in the context of national politics in the mid-1840s.

Although the LDS church had only existed for fifteen years in 1845, it already had a troubled history. Founded in the "burnt-over" district of upstate New York by Joseph Smith, a prophet who was not yet twenty-five years old, the Saints had already been driven from homes in Ohio and Missouri. Their capital on the Mississippi, Nauvoo, had promised to be a utopia and gathering place for followers of the young religion,

---
[1] Stegner, *The Gathering of Zion*, 111.

but the controversial political policies and religious doctrines of the visionary Smith once again turned the Mormons' neighbors against them. Smith taught his disciples to view any opposition as persecution and admitted, "I should be like a fish out of water, if I were out of persecutions...The Lord has constituted me so curiously that I glory in persecution." He used opposition to create a compelling myth that "idealized the Saints and demonized the people who actively opposed them," convincing his followers that their righteousness provoked the rage of Satan and the hatred of Babylon—one of his favored terms for the United States. The myth of "persecuted innocence" became central to Mormon belief.[2] The conviction that they were "persecuted for righteousness' sake" helped unite his people, and gave them an enduring identity as God's new "chosen people," the modern Israel of the "new and ever-lasting covenant," and let them equate their suffering with the persecution of the early Christians.

The Saints had long been fascinated with the Rocky Mountain West, and since the early 1830s their newspapers had printed reports of fur traders and explorers. As conflict with his Illinois neighbors heated up in early 1844, Joseph Smith picked "a company to explore Oregon and California, and select a site for a new city for the saints." Among others, Phinehas H. Young, Daniel Spencer, David Fullmer, Jonathan Dunham, and James Emmett either volunteered or were asked to go. On 23 February, Smith called for a "leader to drum up volunteers" and told the apostles he "wanted an exploration of all that mountain country. Perhaps it would be best to go direct to Santa Fe...Appoint a leader and let them beat up for volunteers. I want every one that goes to be a king and a priest. When he gets to the mountains he may want to talk with his God; when with the savage nations [he shall] have power to govern." He hoped the party could "secure a resting place in the mountains or some uninhabited region, where we could enjoy the liberty of conscience guaranteed to us by the Constitution."[3]

In the early months of 1844 Smith also launched a presidential cam-

---

[2] Hallwas and Launius, *Cultures in Conflict*, 91, 139, 300. The authors use contemporary accounts to analyze the Mormon persecution myth and conclude that the Latter-day Saints would have "come into conflict with Americans anywhere in the country." Ibid., 300.

[3] Smith, Jr., *Doctrines of Salvation*, 3:331–32; and Roberts, *Comprehensive History of the Church*, 2:210–11.

paign. Needing its members to support his presidential campaign, Smith delayed the departure of the scouting party until after the 1844 election. At the same time, Smith formally organized the Council of Fifty, an ultra-secret brotherhood that aimed to establish a theocratic world government that its members called the Kingdom of God. "The Fifty" remains one of the most mysterious organizations in Mormon history.[4] Since the council admitted a few Gentiles as members, it was technically not part of the LDS church, but it included all of the most favored and powerful members of the Mormon hierarchy. Joseph Smith had revealed the grand plan of the council in April 1842, but waited until March 1844 to organize the group; at a meeting of the council on 11 April, Smith was "chosen as our Prophet, Priest and King by Hosannas."[5] According to one participant, "Joseph suffered himself to be ordained a king, to reign over the house of Israel forever."[6]

In late March, with the Mormons once again becoming unwelcome to their neighbors, Smith drew up "An ordinance for the Protection of the Citizens of the United States Emigrating to the Adjoining Territories: and for the Extension of the Principles of Universal Liberty." In it, he asked Congress to authorize him to raise 100,000 armed volunteers to "open the vast regions of the unpeopled west and south to our enlightened and enterprising yeomanry." Smith proposed to police the borders from Texas to Oregon and offered his services as general. He sent apostles Orson Pratt and John E. Page to Washington "in the interest of this scheme." In April, Orson Hyde was sent to help them.[7]

Smith did not live to see anything come of these plans. After he destroyed the office of a newspaper that printed revelations about his practice of polygamy, Illinois authorities arrested the prophet. While in

---

[4] For the classic sources on the Council of Fifty, see Hanson, *Quest for Empire*; and Quinn, "The Council of Fifty and Its Members, 1844 to 1945," 163-97. The new standard is set in the chapter "The Kingdom of God in Nauvoo, Illinois," in Quinn, *The Mormon Hierarchy: Origins of Power*, 105–41. The minutes of the Council of Fifty, which would shed much light on its planning of the Mormon emigration, are in the possession of the First Presidency of the LDS church and are not available to scholars. Without access to this critical primary source, it is impossible to evaluate accurately the role of the Council of Fifty in these events or to formulate a definitive picture of the planning of the Mormon emigration.

[5] Hanson, *Quest for Empire*, 66, 155, and Smith, ed., *An Intimate Chronicle*, 129, 154.

[6] William Marks, quoted in Quinn, *The Mormon Hierarchy: Origins of Power*, 124.

[7] Roberts, *Comprehensive History of the Church*, 2:212–13.

the state's custody on 27 June 1844, a mob murdered Smith and his brother Hyrum in Carthage. The prophet had sealed his religious legacy with his blood.

The loss of its founder shook the stripling LDS church to its roots; the Saints had believed Joseph would rule over them until Christ returned, and there seemed no way to replace their leader. There was certainly no clearly defined succession policy. Smith probably would have wanted his offices to go to his son, but Joseph Smith III was barely a teenager and with the death of Samuel H. Smith later in the summer of 1845, the erratic and unpopular William Smith became the last surviving brother of Joseph Smith. He proved a poor representative to assert the Smith family's title to leadership, and Emma Smith, the prophet's widow, relied on other allies to challenge the succession claims of Brigham Young and the Quorum of Twelve Apostles. She led those who wanted to abandon the "secret things which had cost Joseph and Hyrum their lives," specifically Smith's doctrines of polygamy and eternal progression.[8] This ignited a struggle with those who saw their mission as the continuation of the dead prophet's work and who rallied behind Brigham Young and the apostles. The conflict drove a contest for power that continued for years.

The complicated hierarchy Smith had created with its numerous quorums, presidencies, and councils muddied the question of succession. The lines of authority between the First Presidency, the apostles, the bishops, and the priesthood offices were hopelessly tangled, and virtually all the LDS church's leadership was away from Nauvoo working for Smith's presidential campaign. The Council of Fifty made one of the first leadership claims when on 30 July "Bishop George Miller and Alexander Badlam wanted them to call together the Council of Fifty and organize the church." Apostles Willard Richards and George A. Smith rejected the proposition since "the Council of Fifty was not a church organization...[and] the organization of the church belonged to the priesthood alone." They directed Miller and Badlam to focus on their earlier charge from Joseph Smith "to secure a resting place in the mountains, or some uninhabited region, where we can enjoy the liberty of conscience."[9] The Council of Fifty planned the subsequent emigra-

---

[8] Quinn, *The Mormon Hierarchy: Origins of Power*, 170.   [9] Smith, *History of the Church*, 7:213, 6:261.

tion until January 1847, when Brigham Young and the twelve took over the task.

One member of the Fifty, James Emmett, considered his call to the "noble company to explore Oregon and California" a mandate from the dead prophet.[10] In September 1844 he ignored Young's orders and led a party of twenty-five families into Iowa territory on his mission "to travel among the Indians; to go on to the Rocky Mountains; to preach to the Indians along the way, and prepare them to receive the Saints in the Rocky Mountains." Emmett and his unfortunate followers wintered "150 miles west of the settlements" near today's Iowa City. The company came close to starving, but in 1845 Emmett continued to push west, wandering as far north as present South Dakota before stopping in June on the Vermillion River. LDS church leaders had kept in contact with the party and during the summer Emmett returned to Nauvoo to patch up his relations with the apostles. The apostles readmitted Emmett to the LDS church and on 7 August sent H. G. Sherwood and John S. Fullmer to "counsel and instruct" his followers. During 1845–46, the unfortunate party wintered over in the Sioux country. In April 1846, John Butler and James Cummings arrived at Camp Vermillion with orders for Emmett's followers to meet the main body of the LDS church at Fort Laramie, but instead they turned south and on 11 June came in contact with the Mormon camps in Iowa. Cummings reported "Emmett had taken seven horses, some jewelry and with a young squaw left the company."[11] A repentant Emmett eventually rejoined the Saints and his party was absorbed into the followers of another headstrong leader, Bishop George Miller.

The question of prophetic succession was further confused by the ambiguous blessings that the dead prophet had bestowed on several relatives and followers that seemed to give them rights to his offices. Based on an 18 June 1844 blessing Joseph Smith gave to James Strang, a convert of only four months, to "plant a stake of Zion in Wisconsin," Strang claimed to be the prophet's successor. Although Heber C. Kimball rejected Strang's views as "not worth the skin of a fart," Strang attracted hundreds of followers. The ambiguities of the mysterious "Second Anointing" led men

---

[10] Quinn, *The Mormon Hierarchy: Origins of Power*, 199; and Roberts, *Comprehensive History of the Church*, 2:211.
[11] Morgan, "The Reminiscences of James Holt: A Narrative of the Emmett Company," 22, 25, 29, 33.

such as Alpheus Cutler to claim that his membership in the "Quorum of Seven" conferred on him all the "rights, keys, powers, privileges, and blessings belonging to" the prophetic office. Apostle Lyman Wight viewed Smith's May 1844 call to set up a colony in Texas and stay there until "you can gather around you five hundred thousand souls" as his life's work; unaware of the scope of his calling, Wight's fellow apostles approved a mission to Texas with George Miller and Lucien Woodworth in August to carry out Smith's instructions. When Wight attempted to enlist the entire population of Nauvoo for his mission, Brigham Young tried unsuccessfully to redirect the energies of the "Wild Ram of the Mountains." Ultimately, the apostles dropped Wight from the Council of Fifty and excommunicated him in 1848.

For many Saints, however, the succession was settled when the two leading claimants, Sidney Rigdon and Brigham Young, spoke to some 5,000 members of the assembled church on 8 August 1844. As the sole surviving member of the First Presidency, that morning Rigdon offered to act as the LDS church's "guardian." After Rigdon spoke for an hour and a half, Brigham Young adjourned the meeting until 2:00. In his afternoon address, Young asserted that "the Quorum of the Twelve have the keys of the kingdom of God in all the world" and that they were "appointed by the finger of God."[12] Young presented his case so forcefully that "every saint could see that Elijah's mantle had truly fallen upon the 'Twelve.'"[13] According to the minutes of the meeting in Thomas Bullock's handwriting, the vote to sustain the Twelve Apostles "as the 1st presy of this people" was unanimous. On 1 September, Rigdon preached his last sermon in Nauvoo; and following a six-hour "inquisition" on 8 September, Brigham Young's most formidable opponent was "cut off from the church, and delivered over to the buffetings of Satan."[14]

The death of Joseph Smith delayed but did nothing to diffuse the simmering crisis between the inhabitants of Nauvoo and their neighbors. By

---

[12] Quinn, *The Mormon Hierarchy: Origins of Power*, 143–245, is the definitive study of the 1844 succession crisis. For the confrontation between Young and Rigdon, see 164–68. For James Strang's succession claims, see 210–11. For Alpheus Cutler's claim, see 204–205. For Lyman Wight's claim, see 198–203.

[13] *Times and Seasons*, 2 September 1844, 637.

[14] Van Wagoner, *Sidney Rigdon: A Portrait of Religious Excess*, 341, 354–55, 357.

late summer of 1845, it was apparent to LDS church leaders that they would be driven from Illinois if they did not leave on their own volition.

Much speculation has gone into when LDS leaders picked the Salt Lake Valley as their ultimate destination. By January 1845, the Saints had stated their determination to go to California, but in 1845 "California" included everything west of New Mexico and the Rocky Mountains and south of Oregon. Until July 1847 when he actually looked at the Salt Lake Valley, Brigham Young's statements about his destination were ambiguous and wildly contradictory, perhaps intentionally so to deceive the government and Mormon political enemies about the precise location of the new Zion. Editors and politicians variously recommended the valley of the Bear River, the San Francisco Bay, the Yellowstone Country, and the mouth of the Colorado as destinations for the troublesome Saints, and apostles John Taylor and Orson Pratt met with British government officials to investigate the possibility of settling on Vancouver Island. The Mormon leaders had determined to leave the United States and move into Mexican territory and had identified the Great Basin as their destination by the late summer of 1845, when they publicly announced their plans to abandon Nauvoo by the next spring. On 28 August 1845, the apostles voted to send an expedition to California in the spring of 1846, and on 9 September they resolved to send 1500 men to "Great Salt Lake Valley" to find a location for the saints. When the neighboring countryside rose against the Saints in September, the apostles spent much time "in seclusion" in the temple and "gave attention to the reading of books published on the subject of explorations of the west, and routes of travel therein."[15] Early that month Apostle Parley P. Pratt outlined the LDS church's emigration strategy:

> I write this letter mostly for the purpose of telling you of our council in regards to Callifornia [sic]. We have decided on sending from one to 3 thousand men to that place next spring. They will start from here with ox teams, cattle, cows, provisions, arms, tents, etc. the first of May...Our intention is to maintain and build up Nauvoo, and settle other places too. I expect we shall stop near the Rocky Mountains about 800 miles nearer than the coast, say 1,500 miles from here, and there to make a stand, until we are able to enlarge and to extend to the coast...Keep all these things Still.[16]

---

[15] Roberts, *Comprehensive History of the Church*, 2:521.

Pratt was probably already involved in a complicated plot to wrest Upper California from Mexico. In the summer of 1845, Pratt's publishing partner in New York, Samuel Brannan, one of the "young lions of Mormonism," met with promoters Lansford W. Hastings and Thomas Jefferson Farnham to outline a scheme to lure 20,000 Americans to California in 1846. Both Farnham and Hastings were lawyers, and both had been overland to the west coast and had written popular (if inaccurate) guidebooks that touted that "delightful country." Although he only spent four months in California during 1843, Hastings had made arrangements with land-baron John Sutter to promote overland emigration from the United States with an eye to establishing an independent Republic of California. Sutter's clerk, John Bidwell, recalled Hastings as "a man of great ambition" and wrote that he "desired to wrest the country from Mexico" and "was ambitious to make California a republic and to be its first president."[17] Farnham may have been as ambitious, but he was certainly even more ruthless: according to Brannan, "His doctrine is to annihilate the native Californians with the sword."[18]

These men allied themselves with two powerful New York businessmen, brothers Arthur W. and Alfred G. Benson, who in 1841 had contracted with the Navy Department "in furtherance of a national policy entered upon by the executive administration, pursuant to a cabinet decision, to establish a line of transport ships to the Oregon Territory, conveying fifty passengers by each trip without charge." In return, this confidential arrangement gave the Bensons "the benefit of transporting all government supplies to the Pacific at the rate of $3 per barrel freight," fifty cents more than the going rate.[19]

In the first weeks of the Polk administration, Secretary of the Navy George Bancroft canceled the Bensons' lucrative contract delivering supplies to the Pacific Squadron and emigrants to Oregon. Bancroft deter-

---

[16] Pratt to Rogers, 6 September 1845, LDS Archives.

[17] John Bidwell, "Life in California Before the Gold Discovery," 169, 176.

[18] Brannan to Young, 26 January 1846, Brigham Young Collection, LDS Archives. "Native Californians" referred to the province's Mexican population.

[19] See the "Report of the Committee on Naval Affairs," 3 March 1851, Senate Document 319 (31-2), 1-3. For the price of freight, details of an investigation of the firm's naval lumber contracts, and President Tyler's 26 February 1845 letter recounting the Oregon arrangement, see "Letter from the Secretary of the Navy," 3 March 1845, House Document 161, (28-2), 21-22.

mined that the contract was "unauthorized by law," since Congress had never appropriated money to subsidize emigration to Oregon. The Benson brothers hired a former postmaster general of the United States and influence peddler, Amos Kendall, to use his contacts to revive the contract.[20] To put additional pressure on the administration, Kendall and the Bensons enlisted Brannan and the Mormons, making a "conditional arrangement with the Messres Benson of New York to take fifty of our number to Oregon for nothing, and the balance at very low rates."[21]

In this complex intrigue, each element of the scheme hoped to use the other factions for its own ends. The Bensons wanted their government contract restored, while Hastings and Farnham dreamed of ruling their own nation on the Pacific. Amos Kendall acted to support James K. Polk's plan to acquire California—and to make money at it. Brannan and the Mormons had an especially ambitious agenda—they wanted to leave the United States and establish their own independent nation, the Kingdom of God.

In Nauvoo, the Council of Fifty organized and directed the Mormon western emigration. After Smith's death, the council was specifically assigned the task of moving the entire LDS church—with some 12,000 to 15,000 believers in Illinois alone—to a new home in the West. The council was also was charged with devising a plan that would bring additional converts from the British Isles to the new Zion.

William Smith, the Prophet Joseph's sole surviving brother, was a charter member of the Kingdom of God. After leaving the LDS church in 1845, Smith told the *New York Sun* "that it is [the Mormon] design to set up an independent government somewhere in the neighborhood of the Rocky Mountains, or near California."[22] This was exactly what Brigham Young hoped—and intended—to do.

Samuel Brannan had outlined his early meetings with Hastings for Brigham Young during a visit to Nauvoo in May 1845.[23] Hastings had

---

[20] For Kendall, see DeVoto, *The Year of Decision, 1846*, 240–43, 509–510; for his lobbying efforts, see Bancroft to Breese; Breese to E. D. Taylor, 18 May 1845; and Kendall to Polk, 8 June 1845, James K. Polk Papers, Library of Congress.

[21] *New York Messenger Extra*, 13 December 1845. Brannan ended the article with an appeal to his fellow Mormons to launch a letter-writing campaign to the president.

[22] *New York Sun*, cited in *Times and Seasons*, 1 December 1845.

[23] Brannan to Young, 22 July 1845, Brigham Young Collection, LDS Archives.

planned to visit the Mormon capital on his way west in July, but with the summer rapidly slipping away, the adventurer changed his itinerary to leave Independence for California in the middle of August. How much Young and the Mormon leaders knew of these plans is open to question, but it seems likely that Parley Pratt provided his fellow apostles with the details of these arrangements in late August 1845.

As they planned their departure from the United States, the Mormon leaders faced a much more practical problem than how to conquer California—they had no money. As the church looked for revenue to pay for its emigration, it turned once again to the government. Reviving and extending Joseph Smith's 1844 petition, in March 1845 Brigham Young and the apostles proposed a "Great Western Measure," a plan for the Mormons to colonize "some location, remote from the states."[24] They asked for authority to build, operate, and police a series of posts and ferries along the Oregon Trail. Through agents in Washington, Young actively sought government patronage; but as long as peace endured with Mexico and Britain, he met with no success.

If anything, the U.S. government seemed committed to blocking Mormon plans to leave the country. To the beleaguered Saints, dark forces appeared to conspire against them. In October 1845, Mormon leaders in Nauvoo received reports that "the apostates are trying to get an influence with the President of the United States to prevent the Saints emigrating westward, and that they have written to the President informing him of the resolutions of the general council to move westward, and representing the council guilty of treason."[25] On 11 December 1845, Brigham Young called the Twelve Apostles and bishops together and said that Samuel Brannan had learned in Washington that the secretary of war and other members of the cabinet:

> were laying plans and were determined to prevent the Saints from moving west, alleging that it was against the law for an armed body of men to go from the United States to any other government. They say it will not do to let the Mormons go to California nor Oregon, neither will it do to let them tarry in the states, and they must be obliterated from the face of the earth.[26]

---

[24] Hallwas and Launius, *Cultures in Conflict*, 269.
[25] Journal History, 29 October 1845.
[26] Smith, *History of the Church*, 7:544. The letter containing these charges is not in the LDS Archives.

In response to these unlikely rumors, Brigham Young accelerated his plans to complete the temple and evacuate Nauvoo. In a tremendous effort that seemed to belie the Mormon promise to evacuate Nauvoo, the Saints poured enormous resources into completing their temple. While their nervous Illinois neighbors suspected that it would serve as a fortress, the Mormons rushed to finish the building so they could conduct the rites essential to their salvation and spiritual evolution. From December to February, more than five thousand people received the ordinances.[27]

In late October 1845, the Twelve Apostles had authorized Orson Pratt and Samuel Brannan to charter a ship to take several hundred Saints from the east coast around Cape Horn to establish an advance base for the LDS church in California. In New York, A. G. Benson, a merchant "now engaged in the Pacific trade," made Brannan "the following proposition: if he can obtain the government freight consisting of naval stores, to be carried into the Pacific, he will take two hundred of us at sixteen dollars per ton for the room we occupy and fifty more for nothing."[28] Brannan chartered a ship from Benson and plunged into what Mormon historian B. H. Roberts called a "Conspiracy in Washington to bond the Saints on the Pacific Slopes." Brannan wrote Brigham Young he had "received positive information that it is the intention of the Government, to disarm you, after you have taken up your line of march in the spring."[29] Amos Kendall personally drew up a contract in which A. W. Benson pledged to "correct any misrepresentations which may be made to the President of the United States and prevent any authorized interference" with the Saints in exchange for half of all lands the Mormons might acquire in the West. The LDS clerk who filed the document called it a "Contract for Mormons to go & take California on shares."[30] Brannan claimed that James K. Polk was a "silent partner" in the plan.[31] Brannan signed the contract and forwarded it to Brigham Young along with a breathless letter assuring him, "It is no gammon,"

---

[27] Flanders, *Nauvoo: Kingdom on the Mississippi*, 335–36.
[28] *New-York Messenger Extra*, 13 December 1845.
[29] Brannan to Young, 12 January 1846, Brigham Young Collection, LDS Archives.
[30] Contract, 27 January 1846, A. G. Benson for A. Kendall, LDS Archives, Brigham Young Collection, LDS Archives.
[31] Roberts, *Comprehensive History*, 3:35

but would be done "if you say Amen."[32] What Brannan viewed as the "contract I have made for our deliverance," Brigham Young bluntly rejected as "a plan of political demagogues to rob the Latter-day Saints of millions and compel them to submit to it, by threats of federal bayonets."[33] Before the dust could settle, on 4 February 1846 Samuel Brannan sailed from New York with some 230 Saints under his command. The *Brooklyn* hoisted "a flag with Oregon on it," but it was an open secret that the ship was bound for California.[34]

On the same day that the *Brooklyn* sailed, Charles Shumway began to ferry wagons from Nauvoo across the Mississippi to the Iowa shore, signaling the beginning of the Mormon exodus. The rumors of government plans to stop and disarm the Saints led Brigham Young to begin the evacuation in the middle of winter. The precipitous removal forced the some 3,000 Saints to endure subzero temperatures and miserable conditions as they began their hegira across Iowa. This poorly organized initial movement left camps scattered from the Mississippi to the Missouri, and more than 10,000 refugees joined the emigration after spring broke.[35] The last elements of the evacuation (including Thomas Bullock and his families) did not begin their Iowa crossing until four months after Brigham Young had reached the Missouri.

As they contemplated their westward trek, the Mormons addressed the practical requirements of overland travel. They faced the same choices of draft animals and wagons as other emigrants. They chose to use mules, horses, or oxen as teams based on personal preference—and in the Mormons' case, on what they had available. For the 1846 Iowa crossing, the Saints favored ox teams. Oxen plodded along slowly, averaging only two miles an hour, but they were steady, had great strength and patience, and did not balk at crossing mud or quicksand; importantly, they could forage successfully on the native grasses of the plains. Oxen were cheaper on the frontier than horses, and emigrant guide books "almost unanimously recommended their use."[36] In contrast, grain-feed farm horses weakened if forced to rely on grazing, a lesson

---

[32] Brannan to Young, 12 January 1846, Brigham Young Collection, LDS Archives.
[33] Roberts, *Comprehensive History*, 3:35–36.
[34] Brannan to Young, 26 January 1846, Brigham Young Collection, LDS Archives.
[35] I am endebted to William G. Hartley, who has made a detailed study of the Iowa crossing, for these figures.
[36] Unruh, Jr., *The Plains Across*, 107.

the Mormons would learn by hard experience. Horses and mules required expensive harnesses and were much more prone to wander away while grazing than the oxen—and they were the favorite targets of Indian raiding parties. Still, the 1847 pioneer company with its ninety-three horses, fifty-two mules, and sixty-six oxen favored equine over bovine draft animals by a ratio of more than 2 to 1.

Despite popular legend, few emigrants in the 1840s used Conestoga-style wagons, which were heavy freight wagons built to a design developed early in the eighteenth century in Pennsylvania. Ordinary farm wagons, which were smaller and lighter, were easily available and proved to be more adaptable to trail conditions. Emigrants could sleep in or under them and at trail's end they provided a temporary shelter. The 1847 pioneer company included a surprising number of carriages, including vehicles owned by Orson Pratt, Wilford Woodruff, and Brigham Young that provided an infinitely more comfortable ride than wagons. As Bullock's references show, the 1848 emigration employed some number of "Big Wagons," but such heavy freight wagons created problems of their own, and Bullock noted unloading one big wagon and redistributing its contents.

The typical elements of a wagon included its box, top, and running gear. For a light wagon, the box was nine to ten feet long and four feet wide, with sides built of boards raised to about two feet. The box gave emigrants a home on wheels, and typically could be loaded with as much as a ton of possessions and supplies. Caulking the bed improved the wagon's ability to ford rivers, creating a vehicle that was dynamically amphibious. Bullock occasionally notes the maintenance wagons required—such as the Poor Camp orders directing "every Wagon in Camp to have their Wheels tarred." The top was generally made of canvas water-proofed with linseed oil or paint that was stretched over bent-hickory hoops. Flaps secured with a "puckering string" at the front and back created a small room of wood and canvas. The running gear was the most important of the wagon; it needed to be both light and strong—contradictory requirements that generally favored lightness, so tongues, axles, and the iron-rimmed wooden wheels often broke. The well-organized Mormon companies usually included blacksmiths, wheelwrights, and wagonwrights who came prepared to repair such accidents.[37]

---

[37] Stewart, Jr., *The California Trail*, 108–116; and Kimball, *Heber C. Kimball*, 130–131.

June 1846 found the Mormon people strewn before the wind, still hoping to cross the plains that summer. Midway through what Bernard DeVoto would call the "year of decision," the Mexican War and the poverty of the LDS church had dispersed the Saints into a dozen camps of varying sizes. One enthusiastic party outran the main body of the church by some five hundred miles. In May 1846, John Brown headed west from Independence leading a group of converts from Monroe County, Mississippi, and Illinois. Their nineteen wagons made it all the way to Fort Laramie before they learned from James Clyman that there were no Mormons on the trail ahead of them.[38] The "Mississippi Saints" turned their wagons south and wintered at present Pueblo, Colorado. John Brown formed a party that included Mormon slave owners and Oregon desperado Wales Bonney, who earlier that summer had carried a recruiting letter from Lansford Hastings to a small wagon company led by James Reed and George Donner that was now struggling across the mountains and deserts of Utah. Brown's party returned to the Missouri to determine what had happened to the promised emigration. Upon reaching their homes in Mississippi, they received a letter from the Council of the Twelve and "concluded to send some six pioneers, one of whom was to take charge of the whole, being mostly black servants."[39] John Brown led this group to Council Bluffs, which accounts for the presence of two of the three black pioneers in the 1847 Brigham Young company.

In June 1846, Young sent apostles Parley Pratt and Erastus Snow back from the Missouri to the Mormon camps in Iowa to recruit volunteers for an advance party of 150 wagons that would make a forced march to the Rocky Mountains, while 100 volunteers under Bishop George Miller established the Middle Mormon Ferry at Council Bluffs. As late as 28 June, Young "urged the importance of sending an advanced company of men as pioneers over the mountains" and called for volunteers to "make a dash for the mountains."[40]

George Miller, whose wagons had led the advance across Iowa, completed his ferry on 29 June. Nine days earlier, American Fur Company agent Peter A. Sarpy had offered the Mormons $1,000 to provide forty-five wagons to haul forty-five tons of peltries from Grand Island, and

---

[38] Clyman had left Lansford Hastings west of South Pass, waiting for Brigham Young. See Bagley, "Lansford W. Hastings: Scoundrel or Visionary?" 19, for Clyman's statement on Hastings' expectations.

[39] Brown, *Autobiography of Pioneer John Brown*, 71   [40] Roberts, *Comprehensive History*, 3:63.

Miller took the job. The apostles directed John L. Butler and the remnants of the Emmett party to join him. As the wagons were about to start, Sarpy canceled the offer, but "told the Bishop to send his wagons to the trading post" where he filled them with corn as a "forfeit." A second money-making opportunity presented itself when refugees from the Pawnee mission on Loup Fork arrived at the ferry site on 27 June. Fleeing an attack by the Sioux on their post, the Presbyterian missionaries and government agents asked the Mormons to salvage their possessions at the station. On 9 July, Miller took thirty-two wagons across the river into Indian Country and proceeded 120 miles to the station. As payment, Miller's party was permitted to harvest the mission's crops. Starting on 21 July, Young sent an additional 140 wagons west to join Miller's company and proceed to the Rocky Mountains. When Miller's wagons arrived at Winter Quarters with the missionaries' property on 27 July, however, Young had a change of heart. He directed Miller to winter over at the Pawnee village and send a small group west to Grand Island. Some thirty wagons could then press on to Fort Laramie, but no one should try to cross the mountains. Young allowed Miller to use "your own judgment with regard to wintering" and in the spring "we will overtake you & all cross the mountains together."

Quite sensibly, Bishop Miller listened to a Ponca chief who warned that his advanced party had stopped in the middle of a Pawnee, Sioux, and Ponca war zone. The Pawnees wintered their stock at Grand Island and combined with the Mormon cattle such an "immense herd would eat up all the feed before the winter was half gone."[41] On 8 August, Miller received a letter from Young that directed him to abandon the Grand Island and Fort Laramie expeditions and camp "as near together as circumstances will permit to be able to resist encroachments from Indians." Young also hinted that Miller should use his "chance to fish" for converts among the Indians. Leaving fourteen families at the Pawnee Station, Miller accepted the Ponca's invitation to winter on their lands and led 160 to 175 wagons eleven days' march to the north on the Niobrara River, some 150 miles northwest of Winter Quarters.[42]

---

[41] Morgan, "The Reminiscences of James Holt," 152–58.

[42] Hartley, *My Best for the Kingdom*, 213-15; Roberts, *Comprehensive History of the Church*, 3:157. The apostles recalled Miller's followers to Winter Quarters on 23 March 1847. On 2 April Miller came out "in open opposition" to Brigham Young and called for the LDS church to move to Texas. Miller joined Lyman Wight for a short time and then followed James Strang.

As the Saints watched their plans to cross the plains in 1846 dissolve in the Iowa mud and in face of the harsh reality of their poverty, fate turned about and smiled on them once again when Congress declared war on Mexico in May 1846. Chance brought them an important political ally in the person of Thomas Leiper Kane, son of a prominent judge and brother of a noted Arctic explorer. Kane had heard Samuel Brannan's successor as president of the Eastern States Mission, Jesse C. Little, preach in Philadelphia. Kane soon became a steadfast ally of the Mormons; he would be instrumental in helping secure authorization of the Mormon Battalion. Armed with a letter of introduction from A. G. Benson to Amos Kendall, Little was lobbying for the Saints in Washington when war was declared, and Kane introduced Little to prominent Democrats in Washington. On his own initiative, Little wrote Polk a remarkable letter, boldly stating that although the Saints "disdain to receive assistance from a foreign power," they would look for help elsewhere—Little hinted that England might be interested in the Mormons' plight—if the United States "shall turn us off in this great crisis and will not help us, but compel us to be foreigners."[43] The United States was miserably prepared to fight a war; and although his call for 50,000 volunteers was quickly oversubscribed, President Polk decided to enlist a battalion of Mormons to secure their loyalty. Polk directed Secretary of War William Marcy to recruit as many as 1,000 Mormons for the Army of the West that was assembling at Fort Leavenworth to invade New Mexico and California. (Marcy's orders to Colonel Stephen Watts Kearny directed him to make sure that the Mormons composed no more than one-third of his force.[44]) Kearny ordered Captain James Allen to go to the Mormon camps and raise four or five infantry companies. In June and July 1846, with the cooperation of Brigham Young, Allen recruited nearly 500 men, and on the Missouri formed the Mormon Battalion of Iowa Volunteers. They marched out of Council Bluffs on 21 July to the tune of "The Girl I Left Behind Me."

---

[43] *Ibid.*, 3:72.

[44] Marcy to Kearny, 3 June 1846, cited in Bigler, ed., *The Gold Discovery Journal of Azariah Smith*, 6. This book is the best general history of the Mormon Battalion. In his diary, Polk specified that the Mormons should total no more than one-quarter of Kearny's force; the military orders the secretary of war sent to Kearny on 3 June 1846 raised the limit to one-third. Except for the hundred men Kearny took from New Mexico to California and Frémont's volunteers, all of the American soldiers in California were Mormons until the 1st New York Volunteers arrived via Cape Horn in 1847.

The arrangement served the plans of the LDS church very well. Although the call deprived the emigration of a large number of able-bodied men, in return the Saints were able to equip and send these men and some of their wives, who joined the march as paid laundresses, to the West at the government's expense—and upon discharge, they would keep their arms. Allen also authorized the Mormons to settle temporarily on Indian lands along the Missouri. Finally, the enlistment brought some of the precious hard cash of the battalion's pay and clothing allowance to the LDS church's coffers. Polk, in return, effectively purchased the loyalty of the Saints and secured enough troops to ensure the conquest of California. In support of Young's decision, Heber C. Kimball's journal noted that the battalion call was "one of the greatest blessings that the Great God of heaven ever did bestow upon the people."[45] The decision was not nearly so popular among rank-and-file church members; Hosea Stout recorded, "We are all very indignant at this requisition and only looked on it as a plot laid to bring trouble on us as a people."[46]

As Bullock's journal shows, Brigham Young later put his own interpretation on the recruiting of the battalion, complaining loudly about "Polk's tyranny in drafting out 500 men to form a Battalion, in order that the women & children might perish on the Prairies." The Mormon leader suspected that Polk had made a deal with Missouri Senator Thomas Hart Benton, Secretary of War William Marcy, and other powerful anti-Mormon politicians. Although there is not a single shred of evidence to support such a charge, Young believed that if the Mormons had refused to contribute to the war with Mexico, "Missouri was ready with 3000 men to have swept the Saints out of existence on attempting to cross the Missouri River." Young carried the resentment born of his suspicions for years, and on his arrival in the Salt Lake Valley swore that "no officer of the United States should ever dictate him in this valley, or he would hang them on a gibbet as a warning to others." He hoped "never [to] have any commerce with any nation, but be Independent of all."

So it was that the Brigham Young company of 1847 was the last of the three main elements of the Saints' "Great Western Measure" to reach

---

[45] H. C. Kimball Journal, 14 July 1846, quoted in Kimball, *Heber C. Kimball*, 140.
[46] Brooks, ed., *On the Mormon Frontier*, 1:72.

the far West. By the end of 1846, both the *Brooklyn* seafarers and the Mormon Battalion were far in advance of the main body of the LDS church, which now turned its attention to surviving the winter on the shores of the Missouri River in Indian Country and Iowa.

The Mormon Battalion marched off into a series of adventures that eventually brought some 150 of its members into the Salt Lake Valley five days after the arrival of Brigham Young. Although the unit's officers were almost exclusively Latter-day Saints, this did not prevent religious discord from dividing the battalion and creating constant conflict between military and religious authority—and backbiting by everybody.[47] Captain James Brown's subordinates tried to replace him as captain of Company B the day after they left Fort Leavenworth. Private Levi Hancock, a lowly fifer in Company E, was one of the First Presidents of Seventy in the LDS Melchizedek priesthood, and as such was the only General Authority of the LDS church to serve in the battalion.[48] Hancock's religious office made him the senior ecclesiastical authority present, and he took his responsibilities seriously. When he had an ominous dream that his fellow soldiers slit their own throats, he and a fellow private, fifty-five-year-old "Father" David Pettegrew, persuaded the senior Mormon captain, Jefferson Hunt, to "call" them to help the officers manage the battalion's spiritual affairs.[49] The arrangement proved to be a disaster and the Mormon captains found themselves enmeshed in continual bickering with Hancock and Pettegrew, who won the sympathies of their fellow enlisted men.

The battalion was uniformly composed of people who had been living on the edge of survival for months. It had more than its share of aged souls and a surprising number of women and children—Jefferson Hunt, for example, brought along two wives, seven children, and four other dependents, while Lieutenant Elam Ludington took his wife and mother on the march—so it is hardly surprising that sickness and death stalked the battalion.[50] Its much-loved commander, James Allen, died at

---

[47] Aside from the battalion's three commanders, James Allen, Andrew Jackson Smith, and Philip St. George Cooke, only Lieutenant George Stoneman and surgeon George Sanderson were non-Mormons.

[48] The LDS priesthood consists of a higher, or Melchizedek, priesthood and a lower, or Aaronic, priesthood.

[49] Christiansen, "The Struggle for Power in the Mormon Battalion," 55–56.

[50] Non-combatants who departed Iowa with the battalion included about thirty-two women and forty-three children. See Larson, *Women of the Mormon Battalion*, 50.

Fort Leavenworth—and his men suspected he was poisoned. The combative Mormon Captain James Brown once had to drag himself from a sickbed to threaten to shoot one of his lieutenants. The ordinary soldiers and camp followers sought to "live by faith" and trusted in prayer and baptism to cure their afflictions, much to the aggravation of their professional medical officers. Brigham Young exacerbated the conflict when he sent the soldiers counsel on 19 August to "let the surgeon's medicine alone if you want to live." The Mormon soldiers came to hate their surgeon, George Sanderson, and called him "the mineral quack" and "Doctor Death."[51]

The death of James Allen set off a power struggle between the Mormon captains and the regular army officers. Ultimately, Lieutenant Andrew Jackson Smith took command of the battalion by virtue of his regular army commission—the irregular officers had to concede they had no idea how to fill out the paperwork necessary to keep the outfit fed and paid. On the Arkansas River, Smith had a chance encounter with John Brown and the Mississippi Saints who were returning to Missouri. Learning of the Mormon camp at the trapper's settlement at Pueblo, Smith seized the opportunity to send a few of the numerous families and friends accompanying the march to a winter camp at Pueblo. Although Brigham Young had issued strict instructions not to divide the battalion, on 16 September, Captain Nelson Higgins (who had brought along eight of his own children) and a guard of ten men led the first of the "sick detachments" away from the Mormon Battalion.

Upon learning of James Allen's death, Stephen Kearny (now a general) sent Captain Philip St. George Cooke to take command of the battalion at Santa Fé. Despite Lieutenant Smith's pruning on the Arkansas, Cooke found the outfit "enlisted too much by families; some were too old,—some feeble, and some too young; it was embarrassed by too many women; it was undisciplined; it was too much worn by travelling on foot, and marching from Nauvoo."[52] He ordered eighty-nine men, eighteen "laundresses," and all of the remaining children to go north to Pueblo under the command of the officious Captain James Brown. After marching down the Rio Grande for twenty-two days, as the battalion entered

---
[51] Tyler, *A Concise History of the Mormon Battalion*, 146, 147. See Bigler, ed., *Azariah Smith*, 20, for a defense of Sanderson.
[52] Cooke, *The Conquest of New Mexico and California*, 91.

unknown territory on short rations and with jaded stock, Cooke ordered fifty-five men to proceed to Santa Fé and Pueblo under Lieutenant William Wesley Willis. This final element of the "sick detachment" crossed the Sangre de Cristo mountains with pack animals and reached Pueblo four days before Christmas. Here, in "a wide and well-timbered bottom of the Arkansas," the Mormons built log shanties, "in which to pass the inclement winter."[53] They built a log tabernacle where they held religious services and dances with the Mississippi Saints. In the spring, seventeen people in five wagons followed mountaineer Lewis B. Myers (who seems to have taken a fancy to one of the Mormon girls) to Fort Laramie, arriving more than two weeks before the pioneer company. A small posse under Sergeant Thomas Williams set out in May on the trail of some stolen animals, and on 24 May 1847, Captain Brown led the remaining Mormons, some 150 in number, north from Pueblo to the overland trail.

After a long, hard march, the main battalion arrived in California too late to participate in the conquest or its complicated consequences, but their mere presence gave the senior military officer on the scene, Stephen Watts Kearny, the manpower he needed to corral the ambitions of John C. Frémont and Commodore Robert Stockton. After its discharge in Los Angeles in July 1847, the battalion shattered into a half dozen groups. One company of seventy-nine men re-enlisted as the Mormon Volunteers under Captain Daniel Davis; a few men stayed in San Diego or struck out on their own; most of the officers and a few of the men formed a "Fifty" to follow Jefferson Hunt up the El Camino Real, while some 200 men trusted their fortunes to Private Levi Hancock, who marched them north through the Central Valley to Sutter's Fort, where they fell in with Hunt's party. By late August 1847 the veterans were eastbound on the emigrant road where they would cross the Sierra by the pass now named for the people who had starved in its shadow the previous winter—the Donner party.

Brigham Young went to great lengths to communicate with the battalion and dictate its affairs from afar. When Lieutenant James Pace brought word of James Allen's death, Young sent Pace, Howard Egan, and John D. Lee to Santa Fé to deliver instructions and bring back the battalion's pay.

---

[53] Ruxton, *Life in the Far West*, 204. For details of the march and the winter at Pueblo, see Bagley, *Frontiersman: Abner Blackburn's Narrative*, 45–49.

In the dead of winter, two members of the sick detachment, Thomas Woolsey and John Tippets, carried word back to Winter Quarters of the battalion's progress to the Rio Grande. Young continued to devote much time and thought to directing the movements and managing the pay of the battalion. On the trail in 1847, Young sent Amasa Lyman south with orders to throw out the sick detachment's officers if need be; and when the battalion men lost a few wagons in a flash flood in Emigration Canyon just before entering the Salt Lake Valley in late July, the Mormon leader seized upon the event to justify not marching them to California for discharge. Before leaving Salt Lake Valley in 1847, Young dictated a long letter of instruction to Jefferson Hunt.

By the spring of 1847, the Saints who landed on the west coast in 1846 with Samuel Brannan felt truly abandoned. "There has been no arrival in this country this fall, from those coming by land; but we are anxiously waiting for them next season," Brannan wrote on New Year's Day. He concluded that the main body of the church "will in all probability winter on the head waters of the Platt, where they can subsist upon Buffalo meat."[54] On 26 April 1847, Brannan struck out from Sutter's Fort with three companions to find Brigham Young and guide him to the paradise he had found in California.

With the departure of the battalion in August 1846 from "the western shores of the great Missouri," Brigham Young wrote a confidential letter to the president of the United States. It outlined the reasons that the Saints chose to leave "the nation of our nativity and the Republic over which you have the honor to preside" and recommended a remedy to their predicament:

> The cause of our exile we need not repeat, it is already with you, sufficient to say that a combination of fortuitous, illegal, and unconstitutional circumstances have placed us in our present situation, on a journey which we design shall end in a location west of the Rocky Mountains and within the basin of the Great Salt Lake or Bear River Valley, as soon as circumstances shall permit, believing that to be a point where a good living will require hard labor and consequently will be coveted by no other people, while it is surrounded by so unpopular but fertile country.

---

[54] Brannan, "To the Saints in England and America," *Millennial Star*, (15 October 1847), 20.

For the Mormons, the declaration of war with Mexico and the recruiting of the battalion had done more than leave "500 of our loaded teams standing on the fringe of the Poduwidemie and Omaha Nations and nearly as many families destitute of their head and guardian": it had upset the applecart of their political plans. The LDS leaders had held fond hopes that they could march to Upper California, seize or at least settle in the Great Basin and establish an independent Kingdom of God before Mexico could comprehend the action. Having supplied a good part of the Army of the West that Polk had dispatched to conquer California, Young immediately realized he would be forced to "locate within the territory of the United States," and he asked the president for a "territorial government of our own; as one of the richest boons of earth." Young made a tactical error in not asking for statehood, but otherwise he knew exactly what he wanted: a territory "bounded on the north by the British and on the south by the Mexican dominions; & east and west by the summits of the Rocky & Cascade mountains." Young protested that he loved the Constitution, but warned he would "rather retreat to the desertes [sic], islands or mountain caves," than be ruled by a government "whose hands are drenched in the blood of innocence & virtue, who delight in injustice & oppression and whose greatest glory is to promote the misery of their fellows, for their own aggrandizement or lustful gratification."

Not knowing that the president had sent General Kearny to California with a governor's appointment in his pocket, Young told Polk "that the friends of ex-gov Boggs are endeavoring to make him governor of California." The hated Lilburn Boggs, who as governor of Missouri in 1838 had issued the notorious "extermination order" against the Saints, had left Independence for California in late April 1846. Some say that Boggs had spent the winter in Washington lobbying and went with assurances (and a wagon bottom full of law books) that "as soon as possible President Polk should appoint him" governor of California.[55] The Mormons regarded Boggs as their inveterate enemy, and Young warned Polk "that we, as a people are bound to oppose said Boggs in every point and particular that shall tend to exalt him in any country where our lot may be cast; and that *peace* and '*Mormonism*' which are always *undivided*, and

---

[55] Parmelee, *Pioneer Sonoma*, 31; and Roberts, *Comprehensive History of the Church*, 3:100.

Lilburn W. Boggs cannot dwell together; and we solicit the attention of President Polk to this important item in the justice prosperity and welfare of the newly acquired territory of our Glorious Republic."[56] Having already secured the loyalty of the Mormons by enlisting them in the U.S. Army, rather than address these issues in an atmosphere of wartime crisis, Polk let Young's questions remain unanswered.

So let us return to the banks of the Mississippi River at the end of September 1846, to watch as the last of the Saints are driven from Nauvoo to form the Poor Camp at the very head of the Mormon Trail.

---

[56] Young to Polk, 9 August 1846, Brigham Young Collection, LDS Archives; published in Roberts, *Comprehensive History of the Church*, 3:88–90. Young reported Captain Allen's promise to let the Saints "stop on any Indian lands" and asked Polk to "give us your views of Lieut. Col. Allen's permit for us to stop on Indian lands."

Chapter 2

THE POOR CAMP JOURNAL
Nauvoo, Illinois, to Winter Quarters, Indian Country, 1846

To diffuse an impending civil war in September 1845, Brigham Young promised that the Mormons would abandon Nauvoo in the spring, "as soon as grass grows and water runs." Fearing that the federal government would block the Mormon exodus, Young began the evacuation of Nauvoo on 4 February 1846, when the first wagons crossed the Mississippi and the Mormons established a camp at Sugar Creek, some seven miles from Nauvoo. On the fifteenth, Brigham Young joined the camp; on the nineteenth the bottom fell out of the thermometer and by the twenty-fourth the river had frozen over. The next day, despite below-zero temperatures, Young dispatched George Miller and sixteen wagons to lay out a road to the Des Moines River. On the first of March, the main camp began its arduous crossing of Iowa.

The road the Saints blazed across Iowa that spring headed northeast up the Des Moines River, past Farmington to cross the river at Bonaparte. Here the trail headed west to Centerville; today's Highway 2 generally follows the line of the Mormon route. As they moved west, the Mormons established way stations near Chequest Creek, at the Chariton River, and on Locust Creek, near the Missouri border. Here William Clayton composed the words to "Come, Come Ye Saints," the great hymn of the Mormon emigration. The Camp of Israel reached the limits of settlement at Wayne County, where they set out across a sea of grass, roadless save for Indian trails and game paths. As winter broke in March, the spring rains transformed the plains into a sea of mud. The camp they established at Garden Grove in late April was a mile west of the town that bears the name today, but the waystation at Mount Pisgah, on the middle fork of the Grand River, has nearly vanished, its site marked today by a nine-acre park. The trail wound northwest to today's Orient, where it then ambled west past a Pottawattamie village by present Lewis on the Nishnabotna River to meet the Missouri River. Here Henry W. Miller established a settlement, Miller's Hollow, which later became Kanesville and is today's Council Bluffs.[1]

The early crossing of Iowa was a saga of misery—it took the first Mormon companies four months in almost unremitting rain before their first wagons reached the Missouri. Their dead marked the road with graves. When the weather broke and warmed briefly in April, it brought out rattlesnakes in numbers that evoked memories of Pharaoh's plagues—and when the prairies dried out, they caught fire.

Not all the Saints suffered through the mud of the spring crossing; the majority waited for warm weather to begin the trip. The majority of the emigration—some 11,000 people—left Illinois after March and used better routes. The poorest and sickest members stayed behind in Nauvoo, and when a few of them planted crops, the worst suspicions of their Illinois neighbors seemed confirmed. Thomas Bullock and his family remained with the last few hundred of the Mormons in Nauvoo, to be struck down in August with malaria. Bullock wrote to Willard Richards, his adopted father, "I have been shaking every day for the last month and can scarce write any." He reported, "Even my little boy says 'dadda I wish I were out of this country, for when I've done shaking I can get nothing to eat.' We have all be[en] 'shake, shake, shaking' more or less for the last five weeks. A fortnight ago, I, Henrietta, & Thomas Henry were not expected to live thro the day." He added a postscript on 16 September 1846—the day before he began his "Poor Camp" journal—"I have been insensible for several days, racked with pain in my back."[2]

Fanaticism on both sides of the conflict culminated in the "Battle of Nauvoo" on 12 September, after which Illinois militia units—or, to Mormons such as Bullock, simply "the mob"—marched into the city and evicted its remaining LDS inhabitants. Bullock counted these survivors as lucky: "There have been many Saints who were preparing as fast as they could to go to the West who have gone to the grave, many literally dying for want."[3]

Thomas Kane witnessed the sufferings of these Saints on the Iowa shore of the Mississippi, who are remembered as the Poor Camp:

---

[1] For the route of the first LDS companies across Iowa, see Kimball, "The Iowa Trek of 1846," 36–45; and Kimball, "The Mormon Trail Network in Iowa, 1838–1863," 417–30.

[2] Thomas Bullock to Willard Richards, 10 September 1846, LDS Archives.

[3] Ibid.

Among the dock and rushes, sheltered only by the darkness without roof between them and the sky, I came upon a crowd of several hundred human creatures, whom my movements roused from uneasy slumber upon the ground...

Dreadful, indeed, was the suffering of these forsaken beings; bowed and cramped by cold and sunburn, alternating as each weary day and night dragged on, they were, almost all of them, the crippled victims of disease. They were there because they had no homes, nor hospital, nor poor-house, nor friends to offer them any. They could not satisfy the feeble cravings of their sick; they had not bread to quiet the fractious hunger-cries of their children. Mothers and babes, daughters and grand-parents, all of them alike, were bivouacked in tatters, wanting even covering to comfort those whom the sick shivers of fever were searching to the marrow.

These were Mormons, famishing in Lee County, Iowa, in the fourth week of the month of September, in the year of our Lord 1846...They were, all told, not more than six hundred and forty persons who were thus lying on the river flats.[4]

Brigham Young dispatched a relief train of fifteen wagons from the Missouri on 15 September, under the able command of Orval Morgan Allen. Allen is a prime example of the remarkable leadership the Mormon people could call up when faced with dire necessity. Born in Pike County, Missouri, in 1805, Allen was a "lineal descendant" of Revolutionary War hero Ethan Allen. His father disinherited him when he joined the Mormon Church in 1838. He was a member of Joseph Smith's Nauvoo bodyguard and had pushed through to the Missouri with the first of the 1846 companies.[5]

Allen's journal, which he apparently dictated to Thomas Bullock, noted on 12 September 1846, that the "Council of Twelve having decided to send some Men and Teams to Nauvoo, to bring away the poor, the sick, and a few other families, volunteers were called for that purpose." C. N. Baldwin, Newman Blauger, Clement Evans, Pliny Fisher, Evan M. Green, John Lytle, James McFate, Samuel Smith ("a very trusty man"), James M. Sprague, and Amos Tubs "were the volunteers to go with me," along with thirty-six yoke of oxen. They arrived at the Poor Camp on 7 October, and Allen's speech to the demoralized Saints was a model of simple leadership. "I was sent to bring as many as I can," he told his assembled followers, "and I will do it, and get them to Council Bluffs." He promised, "I'll get you thro' as quick as I can," and he kept his word.[6]

---

[4] Kane, *The Mormons*, in Tyler, *A Concise History of the Mormon Battalion*, 67-69.
[5] Esshom, *Pioneers and Prominent Men of Utah*, 298, 714–15.
[6] Orval M. Allen, Diary, 1846, LDS Archives.

The route of the Poor Camp improved upon the route used in the spring of 1846. It left the old road at the crossing of the Fox River, heading northwest to follow the northern border of Appanoose County to ascend the Chariton River, rather than skirt the Missouri border at Locust Creek. This "Ridge Route" followed the divide between the Chariton and Whitebreast Creek until it reunited with the old road about five miles north of Van Wert, Iowa, on the line of Interstate 35. Here the trail set out across the "big prairie," heading northwest to the waystation at Mount Pisgah. The Poor Camp then followed the established trail to the Missouri, crossing immense stretches of burnt prairies and the occasional "very beautiful rolling country."

Bullock's story begins at the very head of the Mormon Trail—at Nauvoo, Illinois, in its last days as a Mormon city.

THE POOR CAMP JOURNAL

Thursday 17 September 1846—An agreement having been made for the mob to enter this afternoon, I was aroused out of my bed to see them (at 3 P.M.) march along Mullholland Street. They went to the Temple, when the Keys were given up by Henry I. Young to the Chairman of their Committee—they marched round the Temple, & then encamped in the field adjoining the Rope Walk—on Parley Street.[7] They number about 2,000 with 500 Wagons.[8] They were led in by McCauley & Carlin & the rear brought up by the noted Captain Dunn.[9] When they had encamped, some speeches were made and the men yelled and screamed like Savages. Fine day.

Friday 18 September 1846—G. Wardle[10] packed up his goods in the

---

[7] In a letter to Franklin Richards, Bullock indicated that this ropewalk was "by Hibbards." There were at least two ropewalks—covered sheds or alleys for making rope—in Nauvoo. The first belonged to William Law, but Law left Nauvoo shortly after Joseph Smith's death, so this entry seems to refer to the ropewalk of Howard Egan and John Alley. Their operation, however, was located on Wells and Water streets, two blocks south of Parley Street. I want to thank James L. Kimball, Jr., of the library of the Historical Department of the LDS church for this information.

[8] Illinois Governor Thomas Ford estimated the size of this force at about 800 men; see Roberts, *Comprehensive History*, 3:11.

[9] Major John McAuley (or M'Auly) settled at Pontoosuc, Illinois, in 1833. He commanded the troops who occupied the Nauvoo Temple. John Carlin was appointed special constable in August 1846 to detain Mormons charged with false arrest, and helped negotiate the surrender of Nauvoo. Captain Dunn of the Illinois militia led the company of dragoons from Augusta who escorted Joseph Smith to Carthage Jail.

[10] On 16 September, brother-in-law George Wardle packed Bullock's goods "on two wagons and removed them to his house to be out of danger from the cannon balls, which were flying about too thick for anyone to feel anyway comfortable." See Bullock to Richards, *Millennial Star* (15 January 1848), 28.

Wagon. About 10 a body of men about 20 with [the] United States Flag [and] muskets, Bayonets, Swords and Belts came and surrounded my Wagons and ordered us off in 20 minutes and threatened if we were not gone when they returned, they would shoot me. Several of the men were very abusive, cursing and swearing in a awful manner. They left a guard of four men, one with a drawn sword, the others with cocked guns. I requested half an hour extra time to put in the remnant of my goods, as we were all very sick (three [of us were] shaking at the time) but was refused. We left behind all our furniture [and] a [great] many other things and started our pilgrimage. When we arrived at Mullholland St. my arms were demanded by another band of robbers. They took one pistol, promising to return it (never returned) when I got across the River. We were also stopped at four other different places between the Landing, but they did not find my arms or ammunition. When we got to the River there were a many Wagons before us, and several marauding parties searching for arms.

The mob kept up one continual stream thro' the Temple, up to the top of the Tower—ringing the bell, shouting and halloing. Some enquired "who is the keeper of the Lord's House now." Other detached bodies were roving thro the city, searching for arms, and driving the Saints from their homes—bursting open trunks, chests, tearing up floors, appropriating to themselves such things as they saw fit. A Mob preacher ascended to the top of the Tower and standing outside proclaimed with a loud voice "Peace, Peace, Peace to all the Inhabitants of the Earth, now the Mormons are driven."

Saturday 19 September 1846—On the River Bank all day, shaking as usual. [The] mob came to search my Wagons several times, but went as they came. [The] mob held Court Martial at the Temple on the principal men of the city, and ordered all to cross the River immediately.

Sunday 20 September 1846—George Wardle having ferried the flat boat over 17 times, and Edwin Markham 6 times, I had the privilege of crossing the Mississippi River at Sundown on the Trustees' Boat.[11] James Whitehead having been asked by me to give me an order to cross with

---

[11] The president is usually the trustee-in-trust for the LDS church, but after Joseph Smith's death Joseph Coolidge, Joseph Heywood, Almon Babbitt, and John Fullmer held the office until 1846; all the trustees but Coolidge signed the "treaty" that surrendered Nauvoo on 16 September 1846. The trustees disposed of the property of the Mormons in Nauvoo.

my Wagon and 3 cows, and Dr. Richards' wagon and 2 yoke of Oxen, and refused. The mob rang the bell of the Temple for preaching this evening.

Monday 21 September 1846—Went down to Bishop Higbee for some flour to eat, having been fed by my Sisters in law for some time past and having nothing to eat. Returned to my Wagon shaking. In the evening J. L. Heywood gave me an order for a barrel of flour, which I got (to be charged [to] me while all the rest was given away). [The] mob [was] continually searching Wagons—and in bodies marching men to the ferry. Fine [weather].

Tuesday 22 September 1846—There was some provisions to be delivered out on the Steam Boat and my Wife went with the rest of the Camp. J. L. Heywood let her have about a quarter of a pound [of] Tea and told the dealers out "that they have plenty of everything else" which is a bare faced fals[e]hood. At night Edwin [Rushton], his Wife and mother left us for St. Louis.

The mob took Colonel Johnson prisoner, led him to the Temple, held a Court Martial on him, passed the sentence of death on him, squabbled about the manner of his execution and finally ordered him to leave the City. Fine [day].

Wednesday 23 September 1846—About noon a most tremendous thunder storm passed over our Camp. The rain poured down in torrents, swept under the Tents, [and] it poured thro' my Wagon Cover and the Carpet was one complete pool. Altho in a raging fever I had to lad[l]e the water out with a basin, while my Wife sat up catching the Water with a Wash bowl and dishes. All the beds, bedding and clothing got thoroly drenched. There were several other storms during the evening and night which kept us miserable in our wet beds, not having one dry thread on. One poor woman took off her petticoat, and stood up, having cast it round her four children and there kept huddled together all the time. G. Wardle being in the City, endeavoring to sell his 3 Wagon works, was pursued by four men and hid himself from their grasp, in brother Robinson's Wagon, under their beds. Seven or eight poor shaking creatures and others burning with fever went to one tent and cramd themselves in, [while] others crept under Wagons, and bushes, and a more doleful day and night was seldom if ever equalled.

Thursday 24 September 1846—About 5 P.M. the mob seized upon Charles Lambert and led him to the River where amidst cursing and swearing one of them baptized him saying "By the Holy Saints I baptize you by orders of the Commanders of the Temple" (plunged him backwards) and then said "The Commandments must be fulfilled and God dam you—you must have another dip" (and then threw him on his face) and also plunged others in the River.

Friday 25 September 1846—This day a man by the name of William Jewell was seized by a band of the mob near Curtis Hodges' and was most unmercifully beaten about his head and shoulders with Clubs.[12] He was then let go, and two dogs turned loose on him. One seized him by the arm, the other by the leg and tore him bad. The monsters again beat him with their clubs on his head and body—loosed him and again started the dogs on him, which tore him again. This evening some goods were distributed to the suffering poor. G. Wardle went down, C. E. Bolton was going to let me have two woollen Singlets and G. W. begged hard for them to be given to me, but Almon W. Babbitt said I "was able to get plenty." How in the name of all that is good I ask, can I who have been writing for the Church for more than seven months, without receiving one cent for pay, am "able to get plenty"? He knows it well, Shame Shame on the Hypocrite. Fine [weather].

Saturday 26 September 1846—The mob this day baptized Daniel Davis and two others. After my Shake (which I have done every day) I got up, and Father Bosley came to me, he said he could cure me. He then cut off all my hair, or as close as he could, [and] he gave me a dose (Emetic Tartar &c I believe) which caused me to vomit and purge during the remainder of the day.

Sunday 27 September 1846—This last night there has been a keen frost, which whitened a many things—same as hoar frost does. Contrary to my expectation I had a very severe shake, but not so bad [a] fever. There was a meeting in Camp to consider where the poor brethren had best remove to out of the sickly spot where we were now encamped, when William Burton, Minor, and David DeVol were chosen a committee to look out places for their further locations.

---

[12] Despite repeated denunciations for fraud and apostasy, Curtis Hodges, Sr., had been associated with the LDS church since Kirtland. He apparently did not go west with the Saints.

Monday 28 September 1846—This morning at day break Fanny Wardle was safely delivered of a Boy, which died at ¼ past 4 in the afternoon. I missed my Shake. A meeting was held in Camp when the Committee reported three different places where they could be in a more healthy situation. Fine [weather].

Tuesday 29 September 1846—George [Wardle] buried his child on the banks of the Mississippi this P.M. and Tommy Travis (the man who made the first and last Mortar for the House of the Lord) died about 6 P.M. I feel some better this day—many Geese flying to the South. A stranger came to me and wanted me to let him have a yoke of oxen to take his Wagon four or five miles on the road to Bonapart and he said he would give me 2 bits and return them in the morning. I told him I objected to the oxen being out all night, when he turned round and said "Dam such a man as you, as will not let his cattle go all night." I replied a man who will curse and swear like you, I would not lend them to, for three dollars, and especially to a stranger like you. I afterwards found out his name was Charles Burk. He was very abusive. Fine [weather].

Wednesday 30 September 1846—To our great surprise this morning the Mob fired their canon three times at our Camp, but their shot fell short. The last struck the water in a direct line with my wagon. J. W. Brattle[13] and many others of the Mob, seized a man by the name of Silas Condiff and brought him to the River, when Brattle marched in with Condiff and plunged him in the Water saying "I baptize you in the name of Jo Smith." When Condiff arose he pulled Brattle to the bottom of the River, both went out amidst the shouts and laughter of the remainder of the crew. The mob also passed resolutions that no Mormon should be allowed to recross the River, to transact any business in the City. [It was] a very close and sickly day which was followed by a heavy thunderstorm in the evening, and continued nearly all night.

Thursday 1st October 1846—Henry I. Young called at my Wagon and gave me the following certificate which he received in Nauvoo:

"Mr. Henry Young is here on business at the Temple and has permission for today to go about the Town Sept. 30, 1846

John McAuley Commandant
By J. W. Brattle"

---

[13] J. W. Brattle shared command of the militia guards at the Nauvoo Temple with John McAuley.

He also told me that no Mormon would be allowed to go across the River to sell his property, and that it was intimated that those brethren on this side of the River who were assisted with teams to the Camp would never get a cent for the property they left behind, the Trustees being too poor to part with it. [This news] caused a great deal of murmuring &c. He also told me that when the Mob went to drive "Peepstone" Parker, he told them he was "not a long eared Jack" [and] that he was "not a friend to the Mormons, nor never was."[14] They afterwards went after him for some stolen property belonging to Patrick Dawson when he took them to a place where he had hidden the money and gave it up. He also sold three Cows belonging to Rodman Clark for [$]24.00 and forged a letter to the man who had them in [his] care. With the money [Parker] bought goods and ferried them across to Montrose.[15] The Mob troops followed on [his] trail and found not only these goods, but also a quantity of goods stolen from Dawson in the care of Parker's Wife and Daughter who were ready to start by the first Steam Boat for Chicago. Such is the man that was so very anxious to be restored to full fellowship. I was in bed till noon and had a narrow escape from shaking—[The weather was] very cold.

Friday 2 October 1846—The brethren kept moving away from the River side to different places as fast as they can and if Captain Smith buys my place today according to his promise I'll soon be on the way to "Cutler's Park."[16] A [great] many Cranes [are] flying South. I continue to improve in health but all my family continue very sick. Fanny [Wardle] has chills every day since her confinement. Fine [weather].

Saturday 3 October 1846—A cold drizzling rain [continued] till about 10 which caused nearly every person in Camp to chill. [It] then cleared up for a fine day. Nothing of any occurrence this day.

Sunday 4 October 1846—Brother Benjamin Baker called to tell me that my two Cows were at brother Perkins, an Englishman, about six miles down the River. I wrote a note to Robert Burton to fetch them for me. He also said that the Mob had taken away the Angel and Ball from

---

[14] Parker referred to the newly coined term "Jack Mormon," which in Illinois meant a person sympathetic to the Saints. Today the term identifies "backsliding" Mormons.

[15] Montrose, Iowa, was the landing point for the ferries from Nauvoo. Today it has a population of almost 1,000.

[16] After Cold Springs Camp near present Ralston, Nebraska, Cutler's Park was the first Mormon settlement west of the Missouri. It was located about three miles west of its successor, Winter Quarters.

the top of the Temple last Friday.¹⁷ At night I took a walk thro the Camp for the first time and counted 17 tents and 8 Wagons remaining, and most of those are the poorest of the Saints. [There is] not a tent or Wagon but [has] sickness in it, and nearly all don't know which way they shall get to the main camp, and yet persons who have come out of Illinois to hire men and women cannot prevail on one to go there.

Monday 5 October 1846—A very fine day, the woods all alive with the sweet music of birds which makes me feel delightful even in my exiled state. Brother Burton drove up "Whiteface" and "Star"¹⁸ from brother Perkins' field where they had been kept up after they went there. I feel thankful to the Lord for the restoration of my Cows and also thankful to the brethren for their trouble about them, may the Lord reward them. Mrs. [Henrietta Bullock] is very sick, [so I] gave her some thorowort which vomited and purged her very much. [The] fore part of morn [was] foggy, [the] rest fine.

Tuesday 6 October 1846—Mrs. continues very sick. The Birds again singing delightfully—a very windy day. The waves ran high and covered with foam. G. Wardle went to Keokuk to take brother Green's goods. In the evening I went to search for Cherry.¹⁹ [We] travelled a long distance without success.

Wednesday 7 October 1846—I was aroused out of my bed by O. M. Allen (and John Bair) who was come from Camp to fetch me, and had brought a Number of Teams for others. I was very glad to see him and hear his news, and it was agreed to call the whole Camp together at 9 o'clock and proclaim his mission. At the time appointed the brethren met close to my Wagon, and O. M. Allen called upon Tarlton Lewis to pray. After prayer brother Allen rose and spoke, he said the circ[umstanc]es of the brethren are different to what he expected. He had heard many reports about the Camp which he believed to be false. He never heard them there. Agreeable to the organization of the Church there is a Spirit of gathering and not of scattering. A [great] many have

---

[17] To the side, Bullock wrote, "I saw the Angel on [the] 8th all safe."

[18] These are Bullock's cattle. Star was a "small red cow," while Whiteface was a "light brown cow with[a] white face" and "Nose speckled with black." See Knight, "Journal of Thomas Bullock," 64. Neither animal made the trek to Salt Lake.

[19] Cherry was "A small red cow. Streak of white under her belly. Blackish hoofs. Left ear slit. Tail cut short. Seven rings on her horns." See *Ibid.*, 64. Cherry would help carry the Bullock family to Utah in 1848.

reached the West bank of the Missouri River and are pretty comfortable. The 1st camp sometimes lived on boiled corn and [for] 10 days they lived on parched Meal. There is plenty of means to sustain them where they are all Winter. Every man is known, whether he works or no. The idler shall not eat the bread of the industrious. I am sent with a p[ar]cel of teams to remove the poor, and shall organize and start from here. In regard to scattering in Missouri, Galena, Iowa &c., the President said he would start horse teams and then ox teams until they had got every man West of the U.S. The Council is to work West. Wagons will be coming and going continually. How many made the Covenant to spend the last cent?[20] I would rather fare as the brethren than be among the Gentiles, and I won't be content till I get on the big prairie again. I have no Council to give. I was sent to bring as many as I can and I will do it, and get them to Council Bluffs—you uphold me and I'll uphold you. I'll take some to Bonapart where they may get work. I know some men have left that Camp and brought back evil reports, fearing to starve!—at the same time having their Wagons so heavy laden with flour that they could scarce roll them. Has not the prophet Joseph prophesied of these things? They are now fulfilling! I have heard him say that within 5 years the Mormons would be glad to go West with a bundle under their arms. I want peace, union and friendship on the Road, and for all to spend and be spent to remove the poor. I'll get you thro' as quick as I can.

The names were called over.

I want to see all the brethren united. Yoke up your Cows and make every exertion to get away from these ponds. Those that have teams organize with us—if all were as liberal as Sister Smith and Sister Thompson we should do.[21] They gave me [$]18.00 for this Company. When we get to Mt. Pisgah I can get more means—I have made hay until I came to the Settlement. I am not going to suffer a man to run away with a load of provisions. If we have to work we go ahead. I was 9 weeks getting

---

[20] On 6 October 1845, at the only LDS church conference held in the Nauvoo Temple, Brigham Young proposed, "That we take all the saints with us, to the extent of our ability, that is, our influence and property." See Roberts, *Comprehensive History*, 2:538. At this time many Saints swore to share their "last cent" with the poor until the entire LDS church reached Zion.

[21] These are sisters Mary Fielding Smith Kimball and Mercy Rachel Fielding Thompson Smith, widows of Hyrum Smith. Mary was the mother of Joseph F. Smith; she had married Heber C. Kimball in September 1844. Thompson was also the widow of Robert B. Thompson, one of Joseph Smith's personal secretaries, who died in 1841. The sisters accompanied their brother, Joseph Fielding, to Winter Quarters.

means and sending them to the Main Camp. We can go ahead with as little as the 1st Camp did.²²

John Bair spoke and recommended the brethren to get away. The reason they did not get away was because they did not organize. Said he, I would rather die chawing a root than lie bleaching on the Banks of this River.

O. M. Allen said we can see how many need help. When the Company goes out the Clerk can leave a bill of what will be wanted with the Bishop. The people we go among don't like to see us lazy. If we have means to take us thro' we'll go the direct course and if not enough we can take jobs.

Wednesday 7 October 1846—Mrs. continues very sick indeed. I got brothers Allen and Bair to administer to her and then gave Spear mint tea which stopt her vomiting and she was some better. The day was warm, afternoon cloudy. Captain Allen was refused a passage to Nauvoo and he could not go without being arrested by the Mob. A man was in pursuit of him who threatened to kill him.

Thursday 8 October 1846—At day light an immense flight of black birds passed over our Camp, which darkened the air. The Sky [was] beautifully clear for our start. Captain Allen sent over for J. S. Fulmer who came with J. L. Heywood. He asked for the books, which they refused to send, and they told him to take brother Whitehead (a cripple) who was wounded at Nauvoo, and brother Campbell (another cripple) in the Wagon. At 10 minutes to 11 I moved out my Wagon on to the prairie, in order to organize into Companies, and Captain Allen called on the rest to go to the same point. He assisted the cripples in loading up, and visiting the whole of the Camp from begining to end and offering all assistance. Some were not prepared to go, some would not carry a Widow with only 250 pounds luggage altho' they were offered a yoke of Oxen to carry them, they being without. Some made one excuse and some another. I went down to Montrose and was overtaken in a thunder storm—took shelter in John Rushton's Wagon where I dined. At night Captain Allen and G. W[ardle] had a long talk until late at night. Tarlton Lewis went over to Nauvoo this day and received the following Certificate:

---

²² This is the end of Allen's sermon. The abbreviations in the text suggest Bullock took notes as Allen spoke.

Persons who Volunteer to Go

[Name]	[Wagons]	[Animals]	
Henry Parker	1 Wagon	1 yoke of Steers	1 Cow
Scoles and Gabbut	1 "	1 — " —	
James Bennett	1 "	1 — " —	2 Cows 1 horse
William Williams		1 — " —	"
Jonathan Crosby	1 "		
Tarleton Lewis	1 "	1 — " — —	5 [Cows]
John Worsley	1 "		2 [Cows]
Robert Burton	2 "	1 ox	3 [Cows]
Henry Eccles	1 "		
John L. Robinson	1 "	2 yoke	
Moses Whittaker	1 "		1 [Cow]
William Milam	1 "		1 [Cow]
William Dorland	1 "		1 [Cow]
Joseph Knight	1 "		2 [Cows]
William H. Pressley	1 "		2 [Cows] 1 [horse]
Millgate	1 "		1 [Cow]
Reuben Houghton	1 "		5 [Cows] 2 [horses]
Peter Spurr	1 "		
Asher Baldwin	1 "	1 [yoke]	5-sheep —1 [Cow]
James Hawkins			1 [Cow]
William D. Moreton			2 [Cows]
Alfred R. Draper			1 [Cow]
John P. Herr			2 [Cow]
Joseph V. Hawks			1 [Cow]
A. L. Lamoreaux			1 [Cow] 2 [horses]
Job E. Green			1 [Cow]
John J. Millron			1 [Cow]
Nancy Davison Widow			1 [Cow]
Hannah Carl Widow			1 [Cow]
Mary Davis Widow			1 [Cow]
Robert Campbell			1 [Cow]
Jonathan Wilson			
Alonzo Perce			
Wa. Wilsey			
Cyprian Marsh			
Ann Zemmer			
Charles Bassett and Father			
Ezekiel Peck and Son			
Josiah L. Deforest			
Ephraim M. Sherman			
Joseph Grover			
William Gray wants a driver			

"Mr. Lewis came across the River with me this morning to gett a yoke of cattle to start his journey to the West. I request that he should be permitted to pass unmolested" Octr. 8. 1846. D. M. Gerger (New Citizen Doctor)

Friday 9 October 1846—At Cock Crow the Captain called out all the men who were well, in order to make fires and prepare breakfast. I arose with a severe headache and wrote a note to the Trustees, as follows:

Messrs. Heywood and Fulmer—Trustees. Gentlemen,
I have to inform you, that my Camp is now ready to start, and shall be happy to see you with that portion of goods that you will distribute to assist the Camp on their journey, that we may take our departure, and oblige O. M. Allen, Captain of the Camp—[at] Sunrise—By Thomas Bullock clerk.

which was sent down to them by E. Bosley.

This morning we had direct manifestation of the mercy & goodness of God, in a miracle being performed in the Camp. A large, or rather several large flocks of Quails, flew into Camp. Some fell on the Wagons—some under—some on the Breakfast tables. The boys & brethren ran about after them & caught them alive with their hands. Men who were not in the Church marvelled at the sight. The brethren & sisters praised God & glorified his name, that what was showered down upon the Children of Israel in the wilderness is manifested unto us in our persecution. The boys caught about 20 alive & as to the number that were killed—every man woman & child had quails to eat for their dinner. After dinner the flocks increased in size. Captain Allen ord[er]ed the brethren not to kill when they had eaten & were satisfied. A Steam Boat passed down within 5 or 6 rods[23] of our Wagons at the time we were catching the Quails with our hands. Not a gun was afterwards fired & the Quails flew toward the camp. Many alighted in it, then all the flock would arise, fly around our Camp, again a few rods off & then would alight again, in & close to the Camp. This was repeated more than half a dozen times during the afternoon.

About 3 P. M. the Trustees arrived and delivered out Shoes, Clothing, Molasses, Salt and Salt Pork, and at ½ past 4 Captain Allen called out my Wagon to take up the line of March for the West, when I left the banks of the Mississippi, my property, Nauvoo and the Mob for ever, and started merrily over a level prairie, amid the songs of Quails and

---

[23] A rod is 16.5 feet or 5.03 meters.

Black Birds, the Sun shining smilingly upon us, the cattle lowing, pleased at getting their liberty. The Scene was delightful, the prairie surrounded on all sides by timber. All things conspired for us to praise the Lord. After travelling about a mile we came to a short but very stiff little sandy hill. With much difficulty we got up and then had a very sandy road of about another mile, when it improved and we succeeded in getting to the foot of the bluff ½ an hour after dusk, when we encamped, in order. We had scarce stopt when a very stiff wind arose and continued very cold all night. Father Bosley volunteered to superintend the herds boys the whole journey. 3 miles.

Saturday 10 October 1846—Arose with daylight, and after attending to the morning business about 10 we started, on a cold, dull morning, up a very steep hill, thro' a Wood, which proved a regular teazer to a many teams. The trees begins to cast their leaves and begins to show like autumn. On the road I picked up a nice dish of mushrooms which was sufficient for our dinner. We arrived at Charleston about noon.[24] When the sky cleared up, it became very hot and dusty. Directly after leaving Charleston, a large flock of Prairie chickens crossed the front of my Wagon within 4 yards. We crossed several prairies and thro' several deep ravines in the Woods. In the P.M. we came to some muddy water in a creek on the Prairie in a very deep place. The Oxen were taken out of the Wagons and taken to it—and what with the lowing of the cattle and the shouting of the drivers made a very exciting time of it. Many of the cattle were very contrary and obstinate to the Will of the drivers. After refreshment we again started on our journey and came to an encampment on [the] East side of Sugar Creek, after travelling about 13 miles, at ½ past 6. At 3 minutes to 9 a loud crash was heard, occasioned by the falling of a tree in the Camp. I said to the Captain I feel that no one is hurt, which on enquiry turned out so. We were detained several times on our journey by the cattle of John Rushton being restive and obstinate. 13 miles.

Sunday 11 October 1846—In the night a man passed thro' our Camp, bawling out with all the power of his voice "What new City is this, get up, get up, you['l]l be frozen with the daylight." &c &c. No man answered him, when at last an old Ox gave him three bleats for an

---

[24] Charleston is today located on Highway 218, about ten miles northwest of Nauvoo.

answer. [We] rose by day break and started at 8 across Sugar Creek bridge. Travelled over 3 Prairies and 4 hollows in the Woods, when we came to a Prairie [at] ¼ to 12 where we halted to feed our cattle, about 8 miles from last night's encampment. At 20 minutes past 1 we started again having a beautiful Sky over our head [and] a delightful breeze from the West in our teeth, over a very level prairie. After three miles further of pleasant travelling we came to a long wood with a winding road, very long, and full of Stumps. At the bottom was a mud hole with a tree on either side, and crack went my Wagon against the tree on the right. In a few minutes we were on the road again and soon arrived on the banks of the Des Moine River. At the same ugly place brother Parker and Sister Jones broke each of their Wagon tongues, which caused us considerable delay. About 6:30 I crossed the River, while raining very heavy, and the last of the Wagons crossed at 7:20. The rain poured down and it was totally impossible to kindle a fire. 14 miles.

Monday 12 October 1846—Encamped all day on the banks of the Des Moine, opposite Bonapart.[25] The River is a very pretty one and where we crossed, below the Mill, it was very shallow, being about 20 inches deep and from 50 to 60 rods across. The town appears to have some 40 or 50 houses in it, besides one of the best flouring Mills in the Country. On the opposite side is a Saw Mill, which is not at work—altogether it appears a snug place. When we arose, the captain called all the brethren together and gave them their orders for the day. The Sisters had a regular washing day, and the men were ordered to fetch water for them. He [Captain Allen] then crossd the River to buy Tar &c & get Wheat ground, and buy Corn meal for the remainder of the journey. When he went, away went the rest, some visiting, and some one thing and another. Brother Berhelow who was to carry water for me, fetch'd 2 Buckets and was not seen again until after the finish, and I had to carry Water sick as I am, whereby I got wet feet, and nursed every minute of this day. [I] collected money from the brethren and continued to organize those who joined the Camp. Very windy from NW [but it] cleared up for a fine day. My Cows went out with the drove, but as the boys and their Overlooker left them, they did not come home again.

Tuesday 13 October 1846—Heavy fog [rose] from the River in the

---

[25] Modern highways have bypassed Bonaparte, Iowa, and it is today a small farming village.

night, which cleared off about 8. Wind being South, veered round to NW. Several of the Wagons had their Wheels laid and greased. Captain fixes Sister Wheeler's Wagon Bows and Cover. In the P.M. the captain called me to go with him across to Bonapart. Altho' the River is wide and shallow the Water is the most beautiful that I have seen, for the size of the River. The bottom is solid Rock, with loose Stones on it. We bought meal, Beans &c and then return'd. The Cows have not yet returned, only 2 or 3 turned out to hunt, altho' ordered by the Captain, every one resting perfectly satisfied when they have got their own Cows and Oxen safe, altho' it may delay the whole camp several days.

Wednesday 14 October 1846—Arose before daylight and made fire. After breakfast the Captain ordered men to hunt the Stray Oxen and Cows, in order that we may go to a Prairie about 6 miles off, where we can get grass for our cattle. When they returned they had not found my Cows and immediately after dinner we started on the side of a hill, sideways, and slipping almost every yard, thro' a wood among stumps and logs. It had commenced raining during dinner and continued all the journey, which, with the dreadful road itself, made it most decidedly the worst travelling we have yet had, and may the Lord preserve us from worse; after much difficulty we got to the top of the hill where we halted, until every one of the teams got up without accident, when we started again thro' the same Wood, until we arrived at a prairie where we found a Well, about 5 o'clock, and encamped forming two sides of a square. (G. Wardle made himself very officious in dealing out Whiskey out of my Bottle, and because I objected to a man by the name of Baldwin, slobbering out of the bottle, when I had offered him a tin cup to drink out of, like the rest. Wardle was so affronted that he went and told the Captain. He is getting too big already. If it had not been for my bringing him, he would not have been in camp.) This is the first night that we have been free from pigs, and that we had a little peace, not being troubled with the brutes.[26] 6 miles.

Thursday 15 October 1846—I laid on the prairie all day, in consequence of Father Fisher not yet come up to the Camp, and to send men back to Bonapart to hunt for the strayed Oxen and Cows. They returned in the evening bringing in 3 teams, some Oxen and among others, my

---

[26] Bullock referred to feral pigs.

three Cows. In the morning I took a vomit and brought up a deal of bile and rubbish. [In the] afternoon I was better. The Captain went to Bonapart with the men. There was a brisk wind from the South all day, very cold and raw. We have travelled 36 miles the past week.

Friday 16 October 1846—Between 2 and 3 this morning Sister Joan Campbell was delivered of a child which was dead. Immediately after delivery she was seized with a chill and in less than an hour she was a corpse. When she was driven from Nauvoo she was in perfect health, but living on the Slough opposite and exposure brought on Chills, and then Shakes, which has thus cut her thread of life—this is the effects of persecution by the Illinois Mob. Got up at daylight [and] the Captain sent to Bonapart for Wood to make Sister Campbell's Coffin. G. W[ardle] & Henrietta [Bullock] had a quarrel, G. W. not being satisfied with having equal shares of Milk from my three Cows, but must grumble, altho' having more than we have in proportion. I wish I was at Cutler's Park. A very Cold NW wind blowing. William Wheeler's boy told me he had seen my three Cows, every day, while at Bonapart (my Cows went dry for want of being driven up for me). About noon, one Dr. Avery, and the Constable of Vernon Township, Van Buren Co., came [and] attached a yoke of Oxen for a debt said to have been contracted by a brother E. M. Green, amounting to [$]8.00. This causes a delay to the Camp, and as every moment is now precious to us, the Captain charges for this delay [$]500.00 as damages against Van Buren County, Iowa. A coffin was made and Sister Campbell was placed in it, with her child on her right arm. A grave was dug about 50 rods NNE of Samuel Davis' Well, in a Hazel Brush. There was a slight snow at noon, thundered at 3—a terrible black cloud, and a Snow about 8 P.M. but did not lie on the ground. Very cold, frosty night. G. W. succeeded in completing his Quarrel with me.

Saturday 17 October 1846—Still detained by the Oxen being attached by Dr. Avery, the Captain went 10 miles on foot to see the Doctor, found him very obstinate, because the property was not actually the Captain's, and if the Captain had replevined,[27] he would have had to bring the actual owner from Camp; which would have caused both expence and delay, and so thought it best to pay the debt with such

---

[27] From replevin, an action taken to recover property unlawfully taken.

goods as we had in Camp. The Doctor came to Camp and had goods of the value of [$]16.00 to pay debt and costs, thus doubling his amount. The Captain got a receipt "in full of all demands." The Captain has good reasons to believe that a noted Mobocrat named Rob was the cause of the Doctor levying. A. W. Babbit passed the Camp, and brought me a letter from Dr. Richards, which caused my Soul to rejoice, and desire more and more to be with him, that I might unpack the Records and enjoy the "good days together" as he speaks of.[28] About 3 Sister Campbell was laid in the grave. I read a portion of the 216 Hymns and Father Bosley prayed. Thus have I seen the Saints laid low in the Wilderness, followed by one single mourner, having been banished from the land of their adoption by a brutal mob (sanctioned by Governor Ford the Governor of Illinois) on account of her religion. About 5 Father Fisher arrived, with Sister Mary Smith. By these arrivals, we can now pursue our journey. At dark the Captain called the brethren and Sisters together and exhorted them to prayer, unity, diligence, obedience to the authority over them, to assist each other, [and] be kind to the sick—when he gives orders to hunt cattle, for all who are well to start, and do their duty, &c. When he had finished he called on Father Fisher to make prayer, after which all sung "How firm a foundation." They had scarce finished when there was a cry of "Wagon on fire," from Sister Mary Smith's Wagon, which was soon put out by the brethren, with much damage being done. A cold wind from NNW all day.

Sunday 18 October 1846—A very severe frost in the night which caused the ground to be white over and a thickish Ice on the Water. After breakfast Captain sends off [men] to hunt the cattle and all go. At 4 past 12 [they] found Sister Wheeler's Cow, when the camp began to hitch up and at 10 minutes to 3 we started with a beautiful blue sky over a prairie. Met brother Pitt who hitched his horse to the hind end of my Wagon without my leave, and when crossing an ugly pitch, it pulled the board completely off, rolling my Wash kettle, can, Saucepans, Bucket &c into the mud. Then we came to a scrubby Wood, Oak openings, over

---

[28] On 8 October 1846 Richards wrote from Winter Quarters, "Come, my son, & cheer up your heart—& take courage & come on and we will see many good days together yet...We are doing the best we can here & expect to start a pioneer company over the mountains early in the spring." He promised his adopted son, "Don't stop to die yet, tis no time, there is a great work before you and after much tribulation, you will inherit the blessings with a thousand times more than all their cost to you." Willard Richards to Thomas Bullock, 8 October 1846, LDS Archives.

Indian Creek bridge which is the worst we have past over, and encamped on the creek at 10 minutes to 5.[29] The day was bright, T.B. troubled with a violent pain in my head and bowels and was very bad. 4 miles.

Monday 19 October 1846—The Captain arose before daylight for an early start, but his Oxen not being fastened up last night, they had strayed away. Orders were given to hunt them. The Captain and a few of the men went in pursuit. There were 9 [men left] in Camp left sitting round the fires at one time roasting themselves. The Captain returned, and finding his orders disobeyed, ordered all to unhitch their Oxen and cows and take them to feed on the prairie 1½ miles off, and proclaimed that those who were diligent, their names should be recorded. They then all started in search and some of the brethren returned about 3 o'clock having found them. As we could not travel far this evening, we had to stay here another night, thus losing 1½ days out of 2 days thro' cattle not being fastened up. At the same time Luther Berkeley[30] (my driver) returned having shot a Buck, which was cut up and distributed by Bishop Knight among all the brethren in Camp. A very fine day.

Tuesday 20 October 1846—Captain wanting the Oxen to make an early start cried fire, fires, which caused all of them to be up before daylight and prepared so that we made a start by 8 o'clock (all went off well, except brother Gray's oxen which were very restive) thro' a continuation of Woods and Oak openings. It was a very cold morning and Big Round clouds floating in the air. We went thro' Mechanicsburg[31] at 11 and saw a Grave yard, the only one we have seen in our journey. After a mile or two journey, an extraordinary sight came in view—a whirlwind was passing over an immense field of corn. It was curious, yet wonderful to see the blossoms, leaves and pieces of Corn Stalks shoot up in the air some thirty feet, as if shot from some gun, and then whirl away round and round to about 200 and 300 feet high, keeping aloft like so many Sky larks and then again descend with a whirling motion to within 20 or 30 feet of the ground, when they would again reascend, and repeat the same whirling journey. This shews to us the God that Sits on the Whirlwind, as well as the God that fed the ancient Israelites in the

---

[29] The camp on Indian Creek was probably located near today's Lake Sugema.

[30] Luther Van Burklow may be the man variously identified in Bullock's journal as Berkeley, Berkelow, and Voerheley, but he otherwise elludes identification.

[31] Mechanicsburg no longer exists.

Wilderness [and] the Saints with Quails on the Mississippi. When we had passed this strange sight, we met Charles Decker who was going to Bonapart for a Load of provisions. About 3 we arrived at Richardson's point where we fed the cattle with Fodder. At 10 minutes to 4 we started again and arrived on the Banks of Fox River at Sunset.[32] We encamped on a prairie where the cattle were turned out to graze. After Supper I had to bake (altho almost kill'd with pain in my bowels and head and scarce able to stand) to a late hour. 16 miles.

Wednesday 21 October 1846—Captain called up the Camp by dawn of day and ordered all the Cows and Oxen turned loose to graze. Henry L. Cook, Edward M. Green, Pliney Fisher, James McFate, Daniel Corbett, and Stephen Perry, Samuel Savary, George B. Gardiner and Sally Hill joined the Camp and were organized at this place. The Captain then ordered every Wagon in Camp to have their Wheels tarred, which was done. Started at 9 along a level road with a clear blue sky in the Zenith and the Smoky horizon, which indicates the commencement of the Indian Summer. Buck Flies began to be pretty thick thro' out our journey. We again encamped on the West Fork of Fox River, having to turn out of the Road about a Mile, and travelled 14 miles.

Thursday 22 October 1846—Captain called the Camp up by dawn of day, and when the cattle were gathered together for a start, it was found that the Captain and John Robinson's Oxen and W. H. Pressley's Horse were missing. In a short time the Oxen were found and at a little after 9 we re-tracked our steps to the Road, where we took in William Meeks' family, and started from his Tent at 11 o'clock. Having a beautiful clear morning and a prairie to travel over, we met 5 teams on their way from Garden Grove[33] to the Mississippi River to fetch some of the persecuted Saints at ¼ to 1, and at 4 P.M. we encamped on Allen's Hill (named by E. T. Wheeler) at the head of Fox River, having had many hollows to pass over, which caused delays and travelled 8 miles. Our Camp now numbers 28 Wagons, with 47 yoke of Oxen, 31 Cows and 157 Souls. After we had encamped, [we] saw a new moon. Directly

---

[32] Near present Bloomfield, Iowa, the Poor Camp reached the Fox River, which empties into the Mississippi River just south of the Iowa line at Alexandria, Missouri.

[33] At the approximate mid-way point between Nauvoo and Council Bluffs, Henry G. Sherwood and Brigham Young selected the site of the waystation at Garden Grove on 24 April 1846. It survives as a Decatur County hamlet of some 229 people.

afterwards we were joined by brother Jesse P. Harmon and brother [Elijah E.] Holden. We have now left the Mississippi a *fortnight, and travelled 78 miles.*

Friday 23 October 1846—I had to carry water more than half a mile (altho' sick) receiving no assistance from either of my two drivers, altho' they are well, yet they are always ready to use it when fetched. Neither do they render me any assistance about my Cows, altho' they know and see that I have not strength to tie or untie one of them (White face) and have to seek for assistance from others. We started at 9 o'clock with a cold frosty wind in our face and soon came to an ugly hollow where my Wagon had a very narrow escape of turning over. Continued our course up the Divide, until we came to a little piece of the most dammable road I ever travelled, then over a prairie. Passed thro' an Oak Forest and then descended a very steep hill, crossed over Soap Creek[34] and encamped on the West Bank at ¼ to 4, having travelled 12 miles.

Saturday 24 October 1846—Arose at Cock Crow. After breakfast the Captain called the brethren together and spoke to them about half an hour, shewing the necessity of them going to work and repairing Chains and or Iron fixings, and making Cow yokes and bows in order to yoke up Cows and strengthen the teams, and as some of the brethren had deceived him in regard to their means, it now became necessary to trade away our property to buy corn for our cattle, and to attend to council better than they had done. When brother Whitehead and John Lytle, were named Blacksmiths; Knight and Meeks, Traders; Berkelow and Meeks, Hunters; Green, McFate, Bennett, Wardle and Corbett to make Cow Yokes and Bows; and Cook to take charge of all the rest and hunt cattle. The following persons agreed to yoke Cows: Bullock 2; Cook 2; Bennett 2; Fisher 1; Pressley 2; Green 1; McFate 1; Davison 1; Parker 1; Campbell 1; Whitehead 1; Knight 1; Meeks 1. At 10 minutes past 1 the Captain returned and reported that both blacksmiths were at work, Knight was trading, Berthelow Hunting, McFate, Meeks, Corbett and Hopkins making yokes, and Cook returned having had no assistant. At Sunset the Captain reported McFate, Meeks, Corbett and Green making yokes—Wardle 2 hours ditto. Blacksmiths both at work, Knight selling goods, Berkeley hunting, Cook and his Son and boys Hopkins

---

[34] The Soap Creek crossing was near today's Unionville, Iowa.

and Father hunting cattle, Jim carrying Wood, all the rest idle—Bennett reported sick. Fine day.

Sunday 25 October 1846—Still encamped on the West side of Soap Creek. Joseph Knight, George Wardle, and John Rushton were to unload the Captain's Wagon in order to fetch corn. Knight had to call on the Camp to assist him to empty it. McFate, Green, Meeks, and Corbett making cow yokes all day, Wardle and Bennett making bows in [the] afternoon, 5 yokes were completed. Whitehead and Lytle blacksmith all day. Berkelow hunting. A warm day, large clouds floating in the air. I was baking, carrying water, nursing, organizing Harmon and Wilson, hunting cows &c &c. My Wife washing, altho' so very sick that she had to leave the wash tub to vomit, and when spreading her clothes on the ground to dry, had to lie full length on the prairie, and had to go and wash again, receiving no assistance from any one, altho' single women and women with only one child were on each side of our Wagon. About four o'clock in the evening a man was purchasing goods from the brethren. Sister Savary let the Bishop have six plates, which he sold to the man for forty eight cents. Brother Samuel Savary returned to the Camp from hunting his cattle and commenced abusing his Wife with his tongue. She then told him, to "get them again then." He went to the Bishop to get them and was very near being the means of causing the man, not trading [to quit trading], nor of our getting corn for our cattle. The Captain returned with the Bishop to Savary's Wagon. After some words, Savary said he would not take six bits for his plates, [as] he thought more of his plates than his Wife and such like expressions. When the Captain said he would give Savary a dollar for his Wife, Savary agreed. The Captain offered it to him, [and] Savary said "give it to my Woman." He did so, [and] she accepted it. The Captain then went for the Clerk to make out the writings. When they got to Savary's Wagon, Savary said he would "not sign any paper [as] he considered he was an honorable man, his word was his bond, he did not repent of his bargain" and many similar expressions. The Captain then went to the Wagon, began conversing with Sister Savary, when brother Savary went up to him and said "you have no business talking with my woman." Captain Allen replied "You have no Woman, you have sold her, I have bought her and shall claim her in time and thro' all Eternity." Savary then ordered Captain Allen away several times, became very abusive in his language to the Captain. For proof of this, call George B. Gardiner, Solomon Wixom, Thomas Bullock, Stephen Perry, and Jesse P. Harmon. Another bell was lost of mine, off the necks of Tom & Jerry.[35] This makes [$]2.25 loss on Ox Bells. At 10 o'clock at night there came a loud cry of "fire fire" and cries for assistance, the prairie being on fire and fast threatening to destroy the fence and corn field of a man (a Gentile). Immediately Henry Parker, Gabbut, Scholes, Wixom, and Cook's Son started to the rescue. A gentle rain came on and damped the ground, which prevented any further danger & the man gave each of the brethren a pumpkin as a reward for their assistance, and said "I am mighty glad you came," thus shewing a great difference of treatment to the Gentile mob burning out the brethren and driving them from their city and their homes. Thundered several times in [the] evening.

Monday 26 October 1846—I arose by Cock Crow, the Camp still encamped on the West bank of Soap Creek. While Meeks and Knight were trading, McFate all day and Bennett and Wardle till at 10 A.M. were at the Ox Yokes and Bows, Whitehead and Lytle were blacksmithing and Voerheley Hunting. I and my Wife were sick all day, had nothing to eat and drink, not even a cup of cold water could we get for ourselves and no one rendered us any assistance. My cows at night were tied up, but in the morning they were loose, and I discovered they had been milked for use, but I did not see the milk for my family. A Load of Pumpkins were distributed among the Camp by the commissary, but as I was sick in bed, I had none. My share was distributed among those who were well, and they were also saved the trouble of carrying them, or any thing else, to my Wagon. Cold windy day.

Tuesday 27 October 1846—Last night [we had] a severe frost. Got up at Cock Crow, and fell off my Wagon tongue, flat, I was so very weak, and had a severe pain in my bowels. I allowed my cows to be yoked up, being determined to do my duty as far as I can. [We] left Soap Creek about 10, and ascended a very steep hill. Went thro' a fine Oak Forest with its rich yellow verdure, and then over a Prairie, the right side of which was burnt up and a smoking Prairie ahead. Travelled until half an

---

[35] Tom was a nine-year-old black ox with a "white head and black ears and nose and hoofs." Jerry was also about nine years old and was a "red ox with a small white star on the left side of his belly." See Knight, "Journal of Thomas Bullock," 64. Neither animal made the trek to Salt Lake.

hour before Sundown. At the Big Spring we encamped. When I went down I saw a fish swimming very lively in the hole, and plenty of clear water. 15 miles.

Wednesday 28 October 1846—Arose at 4 and found a very frosty morning. Got cooking finished by day light, hitched up [at] 7:30 and made a start at 8:15 over a prairie, and some bad hollows. Met Mr. Picket, who told me "Dr. Richards is anxiously enquiring for you." They had heard of my long sickness at the Camp. [We] also [met] three other Wagons from Mount Pisgah [going] to the Mississippi. We travelled over an immense prairie which had been burned, having a keen wind, and encamped by moonlight in a wood, having to hunt for water. In about an hour brother Robinson discovered water but it was full of Wiglers[36] and had to be strained before it was fit for drinking. 18 miles.

Thursday 29 October 1846—Arose at daylight, but on account of Stephen Perry's 2 yoke of cattle being missing, the Camp did not make a start till 10 o'clock. The Country being all knolly and undulating, the prairie was burnt for scores of miles and appears only one blackened mass. In many places the burnt prairie is covered with the webs of Spiders which has a pretty gauze like appearance. All the Camp had to stop to allow a man to pass, who was going to Garden Grove. We arrived at Wild Cat Grove about Sunset. We had to go more than a quarter of a mile for water and then it was quite black and not fit to drink, [but] after wards found some holes where we procured a sufficiency. This evening a Beef was cut up and distributed among the Camp. Here are 5 Log houses recently built, occupied by the Saints. The Captain called the entire Camp together and instructed them in their several duties. 12 miles.

Friday 30 October 1846—A very cold, brisk wind in the night. Arose by daylight. The Captain ordered the Wagons to be tarred, which was done and [we] started about 11. On the banks of the Charidon River, G. Wardle asked me if that was not some animal (pointing to an object in the distance). I told him I thought it was a cow, and to tell the Captain. They then started in pursuit, and turned up a young three year old Bull, which was driven into the drove. Here the cattle were all watered in the River. This is the most delightful country we have trav-

---

[36] "Wiglers," a common feature of emigrant water holes, were mosquito larvae.

elled thro'. [We] then ascended a very steep hill. As soon as brother Gabbut's Wagon had ascended the hill, his Wife Sarah Gabbutt [while] attempting to get into the Wagon, laid hold of a churn dasher which being cracked, gave way, and she fell against the Oxen, which so startled them, that they started off at a full run. She fell to the ground and the wheels of the Wagon passed over her loins or kidneys (about 12 o'clock). She exclaimed "oh dear, I am dying." She lingered until 5 minutes to 1 and breathed her last. This determined the Captain to come to an early camping ground. We continued over hill and dale until we came to one of the tributaries of "White Breast," which runs into the "Des Moine" at ½ past 3.[37] The hill opposite us was on fire. Here we found plenty of wood and a clear running stream, and was altogether the best Camping Ground since we left Bonapart. Laid Sister Gabbut out in her [temple] robes and part [of the company] prepared a grave. 7 miles.

Saturday 31 October 1846—Was a dull cloudy and cold morning. The grave being finished, Sister Gabbut was carried and laid low in her resting place between 8 and 10 o'clock and at 11 we started up the steepest hill yet travelled, and continued over a rolling prairie until we got to the White Oak Springs. 10 miles. The road we travelled this day was Serpentine, and at one time had a fine view of the flames rolling over and over again and leaping high in the air as if conscious of its power, and sweeping the dry grass into oblivion, leaving nothing but its black track for a remembrance. The wind was very cold, the clouds dull and heavy and [gave] every appearance of an approaching Snow Storm.

Sunday 1 November 1846—November dawned upon us as a heavy dull day, the clouds hanging very heavy. The Camp was up by day light, but in consequence of cattle being missing we could not make the early start, as intended. At 35 minutes past noon the Captain ordered all the cattle to be unhitched and turned to graze on account of brother Savary's Oxen not being found. All the men turned out to hunt, when they were found, and we finally made a start by ½ after 1. We had a very bright and pleasant day (½ day lost) and travelled to the head waters of the Welden Fork of Grand River at 5:08. [We] travelled 8 miles. Here was very little water, that in a hole and a scum on it.[38]

---

[37] Whitebreast Creek enters the Des Moines north of present Knoxville, Iowa.

[38] Water sources such as this would contribute to the cholera epidemic that killed thousands of overland emigrants when the gold rush began in 1849.

Monday 2 November 1846—Was also a dull morning and we had a delay as usual, Bennett and Corbett's horses were missing. After we had gone a short distance, we descended a very steep hill to a bridge which was in a shocking state. The brethren turned out with Axes and Spades and renewed it, over which my Wagon was the first to try its strength. Continued our course to the Raccoon Fork,[39] where we encamped at ¼ past 5 and found plenty of wood and water, and a good place to encamp. Bishops Tarleton Lewis, Hezekiah Peck and Isaac Higbee, went by the Ridge Road a distance of five miles further to them, and encamped on the opposite side of the wood to us, in order to miss going with us, and to avoid assisting our poor and sick camp, similar to the Levite of old.[40] Let it be remembered Peck [and] Lewis volunteered to go with us, while on the Mississippi, and Lewis told the Captain "I have [$]15.00 of Uncle Tommy's, which will go to assist this poor and sick camp. I shall overtake you and will assist all I can."

Tuesday 3 November 1846—Arose by day break [and] the brethren hunted the cattle by Sunrise. Bishop Knight reported that he saw the three Bishops last night, who would not go along with us, as they wanted to get thro' to the Bluffs. Isaac Higbee gave the Bishop [$]40; the others did not give any thing. Knight then said, "if you cannot assist us with your means, or labor, give us your prayers then." One of them replied "we don't pray for ourselves." Knight then said "if you was in our Camp and did not pray, the Captain would talk to you." Lewis replied "We are a disorderly set any how" two or three times over. The time proposed for starting being come, Harmon's heifers were missing. There were only six Wagons ready to start and the Captain started off with them, and I gathered the drove of cows together and went off on the road with them. The more the Captain orders the brethren to look after their cattle and be ready, the more determined they are not to do it. If he wants to start early, they are determined to start late, which drives us late in the evening to encamp. After we had left our encampment it was discovered that some one had set the prairie on fire. The crescent of fire was beautiful, as the smoke ascended on high and left naught but blackness behind it. We travelled over a rolling prairie, until we arrived at a branch

---

[39] Bullock's Raccoon Fork, apparently a tributary of the Grand River, should not be confused with the Raccoon River, which flows into the Des Moines River at the state capital.

[40] In Jesus' parable of the Good Samaritan, the "Levite of old" passed by the robbed and wounded traveler.

of the Thomson fork of Grand River, half an hour before sunset, which was a beautiful camping ground, having plenty of wood, and a stream of excellent water. 15 miles. The Captain called the brethren together and gave them a strong lesson and warning them against setting Prairies on fire.

Wednesday 4 November 1846—We all arose about 5 and a very frosty morning. Ice was on the stream and the Captain marched on to Mount Pisgah[41] in order to purchase Ox Corn and save a delay on the Road. We started on our journey with a bright sky and a Cool South wind. We had not travelled a mile before I was told that the Prairie was again on fire. I looked and saw the hill on a blaze, and the flames running fast over the prairie. This must have been wilfully done, as Captain Meeks was the last man that left the camping ground and there was no appearance of fire when he was ascending the hill. It appears as if some one was determined to try what the Captain and Company will bear. We travelled on and ascended Mount Pisgah—passed thro' and descended to the opposite side of the Town, crossed the River and encamped on its West bank. It appears admirably situated for a place of defence. 5 miles.

Thursday 5 November 1846—The Captain called all up before daylight for an early start, but in consequence of the dilatory habits of the brethren could not affect it. At ¼ to 11 the Oxen belonging to Bishop Knight were not found, and all the preaching and talking of the Captain profiteth nothing. The brethren will not go, but had rather stand with their hands in their pockets and let all the Oxen stand idle waiting to be hitched up. The delightful weather is allowed to pass unused and let slip without making the most of it. Wm. O. H. Horn and Knight joined the Camp. *Nauvoo to Mount Pisgah 193 Miles.* Destroyed my deeds to Bolander and Smith.

Thursday 5 contd. We started about 12 from Mount Pisgah and travelled over a rolling prairie with some bad hollows and encamped on the East side of the Mormon Grove at 10 minutes to 4, which is a beautiful place for encampment, having plenty of good water, wood, and grazing for the cattle. 6 miles.

Friday 6 November 1846—I arose between 4 and 5 and commenced

---

[41] Parley P. Pratt named the waystation he located on 16 May after the heights mentioned in Deuteronomy 34:1 from which Moses viewed the Promised Land. Mount Pisgah was located about three miles northwest of today's Thayer, Iowa. See Gentry, "The Mormon Way Stations: Garden Grove and Mt. Pisgah," 445–62.

cooking bread for the big prairie. A beef was killed and I was called to pick me a piece, after every one else had theirs. At ¼ to 9 [we] began to hitch up, cross the bridge and ascend a very steep hill. Many had to have assistance up it. Our journey was over a prairie, having two very bad hollows to cross over and encamped on the last branch of the Grand River, on the border of the big prairie, at ¼ past 3 having travelled only 6 miles and encamping on the spot where we intended for last Wednesday night, thus losing two entire days out of three. As we get nearer the big Camp, the brethren appear by their dilatory movements to be afraid of going there. James Sprague left Camp very early this morning, and he is strongly suspected of taking away James Bennet's Mare, which disappeared at the same time. It is also believed that he is the person who set the Prairie on fire.

Saturday 7 November 1846—Rose at daylight and found there had been a severe frost. It turned out a beautiful morning. We started at 20 minutes past 9 (brother Corbett's Oxen were lost which detained us) up a very steep hill, on the big prairie. After travelling about 12 miles, met L. O. Littlefield, who delivered a Letter from the Council of Twelve to the Camp, "to locate the poor Saints at Mt. Pisgah and Garden Grove" and bring myself and a few others on to the main Camp. He said that he was the cause of the Council being called together, and this letter being written. He told the Council we were 12 or 15 teams, all poor and sick, and expected to meet us between Garden Grove and Mt. Pisgah. The brethren assembled and after consulting together, it was determined that we should all go on as far as the Ishna Botna[42] [with] the Captain to go on, with those who were sent for, and the remainder to stay at the Ishna Botna, until the Captain could return with instructions from the Twelve. Brother Littlefield advised with us; we gave him a description of Sprague and the mare. At 10 minutes to 4 we started again, crossed a Creek, when the Sun set, then travelled over two ugly vallies and came to an encampment close to a Creek but not a stick of wood, at 25 minutes to 9. 18 miles.

Sunday 8 November 1846—Captain called all up by day break, when we made a start by 4 past 7. A very severe frost in the night. At 20 minutes to 11 we crossed a deep river, where brother Gray's Wagon Reach

---

[42] That is, the Nishnabotna, which rises in central Iowa's Carrol County and reaches the "Big Muddy" in the northwest corner of Missouri.

got broke, then ascended several steep hills. Altogether a rolling country, and encamped at ¼ to 3 on the West bank of a beautiful River called "No. 102."[43] The Captain spoke to the brethren this evening (see my minutes).

Monday 9 November 1846—The Camp staid on the Banks of the River all day. Immediately after breakfast it commenced to rain, lightning and thunder which continued at intervals thro' the day. The ground was very muddy. In consequence of the letter that came by L. O. Littlefield, the Captain requested me to make out a correct statement of the Camp as it is this day, which I did, and copied same. O. P. Rockwell & Company passed our Camp this morning but would not stay for our report.

Tuesday 10 November 1846—Very strong cold wind in the night. Bishop Knight and 2 or 3 others having washed in their tents yesterday and the ground being still muddy, the Camp staid all day on the Banks of the River, losing another day. This is the effects of not travelling when the weather was fine. Bishop Evans came to our Camp about one o'clock and told the Captain that he had seen the letter from the Council to him, brought by L. O. Littlefield, and that the Seal of the letter was broken before Littlefield came to Evans. At dusk a meeting was held in the Camp, and [we] were addressed by the Captain, Bishop Evans and Horne &c chiefly respecting this location and the Council from the Camp (see my minutes). Foggy night.

Wednesday 11 November 1846—A thick fog this morning. Brothers William H. Pressley & Benjamin Whitehead concluded to stay at this Settlement with their families. The rest of the Camp prepared to resume their journey and at 10 the first teams started on their journey up a long steep hill, but in consequence of Harmon's cows and Cook's Oxen being missing, the Camp was detained until one o'clock. We crossed several bad hollows, walked in the Indian trail and we encamped about 7:00 on the Prairie. The sky was clouded, roads slipp[er]y, [but it] cleared up at dusk. 11 miles.

Thursday 12 November 1846—It has blowed a perfect gale thro' the night, fine morning. About 10 "Shabne a Pottawatamie Chief and another Indian, from Council Bluffs to Chicago" called and had refresh-

---

[43] Bullock probably crossed the Nodaway River, not one of the forks of the One Hundred and Two River, near today's Mormon Trail Park west of Greenfield, Iowa.

ments. At 10 minutes to 11 the camp started, sun shining (but drawing rain) roads much dryer, good travelling. We only crossed a little prairie and encamped at 15 minutes to 1 at the "Sand stone Springs" having only gone 3 miles. This is a clear river, plenty of wood [and] excellent grazing for cattle. Another fine day lost. About 7:00 [it] commenced raining and continued all night, with a high wind. Wife sick in bed. Father Tubbs, Charles Lambert and Sharp encamped with 4 Wagons close to us.

Friday 13 November 1846—Staid at the Sand Springs all day. Hiram Gates & Company encamped with 5 Wagons near us, in the afternoon, also Haws & Hall with 4 Wagons. The brethren were drying their clothes that were wet by last night's rain. In the evening the Captain called the Camp together and again exhorted them to cleanliness, look to their teams, attend to the sick, to be in union, and be more saving in their provisions, as his were all delivered out, &c. Wife sick in bed. [At the] Meeting at night H. L. Cook confessed he was the cause of the delay on 11th which lost all [of] two days.

Saturday 14 November 1846—Arose before dawn, severe frost in the night, beautiful morning. I was sent to Father Tubbs to organize him into our Company, but he refused. He said, "I am not going to be organized into this Company—the Captain would not wait for me, and I am now going straight ahead & shall make my returns to Brigham." I asked him if he thought it reasonable that a Camp of Thirty Wagons should wait between a fortnight & three weeks for one man. He repeated his determination of going ahead &c, & immediately after his Wagons left our Camp, followed by Gates's Camp, again proving that when men have plenty of provisions and means, they pass by a poor and sick Camp, like the Levite of old. At 8 o'clock all the cattle were up, except Hopkin's oxen. At 9 we met a man from Musquito Creek [going] to Paw Paw Grove who told me he met Lewis, Peck & Higbee yester afternoon and O. P. Rockwell in the evening. We crossed a very bad and muddy bridge by 10.

Saturday 14 November 1846—Pursued our journey over a prairie and came to an encampment on the West side of Ottawa River at 2 P.M. where a young heifer was killed and distributed. A beautiful day. Wife continues sick in bed. 9 miles.

Sunday 15 November 1846—Father Fisher called us up before dawn of day, and we heard Allen Taylor's Camp, who was near us. We have been 37 days [on the road] and they 17, in coming to this place from the Mississippi, being more than half as quick again. It is a delightful frosty morning. When the Sun arose there was a curious cloud, pointing from East to West, which turned to the appearance of a broom, increasing in size. Captain requested me to write a letter to the President & the Twelve, telling them our situation, which I did, & we gave it to Captain Taylor to take on with him. At 25 minutes to 10 we started again over the Prairies. Came to a bad hole in sight of the Indian Town.[44] Met a many Indians & horses returning from Council Bluffs. At a quarter to 2 [we] crossed the East Fork of the Ishna Botna [and] rolled on by the Ridge Road. At ½ past 6 we encamped on the 3rd Fork of the Ishna Botna where we found Gates's Camp.[45] Most of the prairies were burnt up and we saw them burning in three different directions. Day cloudy & threatning rain. 14 miles. Gray's team not keeping up, the Captain sent a yoke of Steers to help him on. Brother Tubbs took the liberty of using one third of our hay, without consent. When a man has corn and money, it is too bad to rob the poor Saints of their only means to provide food for cattle.

Monday 16 November 1846—Raining at intervals all day, made the ground very muddy. I was wet thro' before breakfast. We encamped all day on the banks of the River. At night the rain was accompanied by lightning and thunder.

Tuesday 17 November 1846—A muddy morning, mizzling rain. Daniel Corbett left us this morning contrary to Counsel and to save his flour and money—7 Sovereigns & small money—from the Poor Camp. Brother Harmon's cattle had been driven up for a start, but thro' the negligence of the driver [they] were allowed to stray away again which delayed us till 12 o'clock, when we had to go 3 miles round the ridge road (on account of the bridge on the shorter road being burnt up, supposed by Allen Taylor's Company, who said they should encamp there and burn it). Had a keen North wind blowing all journey. We camped at dusk near a Grove. Went near a mile to fetch water, thro' grass from

---

[44] This Pottawattamie settlement was on the Nishnabotna River near today's Lewis, Iowa.

[45] The trail cut across southeastern Pottawattamie County, and this camp was probably on Walnut Creek or Indian Creek.

five to seven feet high. I had wet feet, made me very uncomfortable. Came to a pool about 8 feet deep, the most beautiful water I have seen on the journey.

Wednesday 18 November 1846—There was a slight snow before breakfast, which caused us to remain in Camp all day. Sent back oxen to draw in Wm. Gray, Knowles, John Robinson & other teams, and also some Steers which had given out. They returned about 3 P.M. with the teams. In the evening the Camp assembled for meeting. Captain Allen spoke on the duties of the Saints, followed by Thomas Bullock & others on the same and other subjects. I set before them some principles which they will remember in Eternity. It was agreed that every Wagon should be searched to see if there was anything not worth carriage, and that to be destroyed, also to get goods to go to Missouri to trade with, in order to get provisions, when Captain Allen, myself, Wm. Meeks, Joseph Knight, and James McFate were appointed a Committee for that purpose.

Thursday 19 November 1846—The Committee took a list of property that each had to give in, then [we started] hunting for cattle. Found all except my White face Cow which was left behind. There was no turn out to hunt her, but every other creature that has been lost, all have had to turn out. We left our encampment at ½ past 1. Saw a Wolf on the top of the Ridge. Travelled over 2 hills and dales. The grass being all burnt I drove my team about three miles of[f] the Road, thro' a Wood to the camping place on the East side of the Sideling Bridge over the Isna Botna. My leading oxen being sent back to draw up Gray's team, which had given out again, they returned about two hours after us. Very tired. 5 miles.

Friday 20 November 1846—A man passed us who stated that Savary's ox was dead. A meeting was called about 11, and statements made to shew that this was the best place for those brethren who had not provisions to last them all winter, to stay, and it was agreed to on all sides, and the property that was to be left for trading was locked up and left with Wm. Meeks, the foreman of the Company. I turned out a set of double trees, valued at [$]6.00 and 2 pairs of pants, which left me only one pair for Winter. About noon Orval M. Allen and James McFate baptized Lucy J. McFate for her health (in a Chair) and O. M. Allen afterwards baptized Luther Van Burklow for the remission of sins, who was confirmed about 7 in the evening a Member of the Church by O. M. Allen, Thomas Bullock and Pliny Fisher, at the same time ordaining him to the office of an Elder. All the teams were passed over the Sideling Bridge except Sister Wheeler and Jesse P. Harmon, who refused to cross to day. Harrison Burgess passed thro' our Camp and began counselling those brethren who were to stay, which brought in a Spirit of murmuring among them. A beautiful day.

Saturday 21 November 1846—The brethren being very discontented at having to stay here, Captain and I went to meet and Counsel them for their best advantage, and afterwards collected the goods that were left by the brethren who were going on, which was put into the possession of Wm. Meeks, the Foreman of the Company, also provisions to maintain them. After attending to business, we found the Captain's oxen were missing, when I and Captain started to hunt them, also one of brother Green's Horses which we found and at 20 minutes to 10 we started, leaving Wm. Meeks, Wm. Gray, Henry Parker, George Scholes, Wm. Gabbut, John Robinson and brother Bennett to make a Settlement here, and one of Savary's Steers that was missing. I drove a team up the hill, over a burnt prairie, but [it is] a very beautiful rolling country & a delightful day.

Sat. 21 continued. Saw a new moon. Encamped on the West Fork of the Ishna Botna. About six o'clock I drove my own team for about 3½ miles, my driver being sent to get Father Fisher out of the mud hole. 10 miles.

Sunday 22 November 1846—My eyes were gladdened at finding myself once more in a Settlement, there being about 20 houses here.[46] Samuel Smith came into our Camp about 10 o'clock and I organized them. John Rushton and George Wardle were sent to mend Father Fisher's Wagon and bring him into camp. They returned about 2:00 [and] we lose another day by his delay. Beautiful day. A Mr. Stringham came up with a team to assist Jesse P. Harmon and they left Camp about 10 A.M. After they were gone, the Captain was informed that Stringham had been feeding his cattle upon the Captain's hay, and refused to pay brother Edmonds any thing for it, altho' he had plenty of money, and

---

[46] This small settlement, perhaps named after coffin-maker Nelson Whipple, was south of today's Macedonia, Iowa.

that it was Allen's hay and he was come for part of Allen's Company. It is true that Harmon joined our Company, but it was because he was sick and was wanting a driver and other assistance. He did not even pay his share of the expences of the Camp, and now to leave the poor, sick camp, for fear of dealing out his flour, having upwards of 700 pounds, in this way, is a little too mean and shabby—this is also breaking the Captain's Covenant, which he made on the Mississippi River. Brothers Blaugett and Read passed our Camp about 4:00 P.M. One of their Company, John M. King's Wife, reported to the Captain that she was in a destitute situation, so he gave her 8 pounds [of] flour to help her, so that they should not say we would not help her. Night was rainy.[47]

Monday 23 November 1846—When the cattle were found, Savary's Steer was missing again. At 9 o'clock I ordered another general hunt for it, but without success. The brethren are getting more dilatory every day. I feel mad at being delayed day after day when the Doctor and the Twelve are wanting me at Camp in order to proceed with the Church History. Wrote a letter to Wm. Meeks, to remove his Company to the West Fork of [the] Ishna Botna, and about a bag of Flour which is said to be concealed in Wm. Gray's Wagon. John Nebeker, Jesse Sanborn, and Amos Stoddard camped near us at 4:00 P.M. Another beautiful day lost. The weak teams, ten in number, [were] sent on to Keg Creek, while we hunted for Savary's Steer. Harmon caused this delay by taking the Steer with him.

Tuesday 24 November 1846—Severe frosty night. After the cattle were hunted up, Savary's Steer was missing again, but at 9 o'clock we started, with the understanding that Savary is to return for it, after arriving at the Council Bluffs; he has been idle, careless, and indolent all the journey, seldom going out of sight of Camp in search of cattle and satisfied when he had found his. At 9 o'clock we started, Savary calling out to the Captain to take care of his Wife. We crossed the West fork [of the Nishnabotna], and travelled over a beautiful Country for farms and mills, [and] over prairies, one of which was on fire, on our left hand. Crossed Keg Creek and ascended a hill, where we encamped in a wood about 4 P.M. This was a very cold day, freezing and blowing all the way. 10 miles.

---

[47] This note is inserted in the text: "Dec: 5. The Captain obtained positive proof that Brigham Young's Steer, followed Harmon 'till they met a Company going to trade in Missouri, and was sent by them; this caused us two days loss in hunting for him, and at present the loss of the Steer also."

Wednesday 25 November 1846—Severe frosty night, which froze a running creek. When [we were] prepared for a start, Father Fisher's cattle were again missing, and were not found until about 3 P.M. We have now lost two days in going one ten mile journey, for we might as well have started from here 48 hours ago as [easily as] being here now. Samuel Smith and his family staid at this place and gave up 2 Wagons and 4 yoke of Oxen for us to deliver them up at head quarters. Brother McFate stopt also on account of his very sick wife. We then started our journey over a prairie, having now only 22 Wagons, and encamped at the Mosquito Timber about 6 P.M. I saw the Bluffs ahead which made my soul rejoice and be glad, in the prospect of soon being at home again. One of the Oxen driven by Joseph Knowles [named] "J. T." gave out. 6 miles.

Thursday 26 November 1846—Captain called us all up by day break. Another severe frost, stiff breeze. Cattle all found the first time of hunting, which in our entire journey is really wonderful. Hitched up and started at 3 minutes past 9. After a short journey where we were obliged to leave John Taylor's Oxen, the boys ran a race to the top of a hill in order to get a peep at the Missouri River. When we arrived at the Mosquito Bridge, Clement Evans ran away from the Camp, leaving his Mother and Wagon without a driver, which irritated the Captain very much. Passed by the Liberty Pole where we had a splendid view of the Missouri River.[48] A keen wind, [and a] sharp appetite and chewing pop corn[49] was my situation while driving a team, yet my soul rejoiced exceedingly in the prospect of my soon arriving at home. I felt at Liberty indeed. Passed under the Bluffs to Miller's Settlement,[50] where we staid about an hour, endeavoring to procure food for our cattle, without success. [We] then crossed over a prairie thro' the Slough, and over about a mile of new road, covered with Poles which shook us very much.[51] Came

---

[48] This was the Liberty Pole erected at the Mormon Battalion mustering grounds on Mosquito Creek, near today's Iowa School for the Deaf.

[49] Overland emigrants enjoyed popcorn as much as modern movie-goers. The earliest reference to popcorn may date to 1823, and Bartlett's *Dictionary American* defined the term in 1848. See Simpson and Weiner, eds, *The Oxford English Dictionary*, 12:115. Bullock's use of the word in 1846 is the earliest reference to popcorn on the trail known to me.

[50] Henry W. Miller founded Miller's Hollow, the location of today's Council Bluffs, Iowa.

[51] Bullock described a "corduroy" road built by laying logs across the roadbed to make the road passable (if jolting) in wet weather.

to the Missouri River where the ice was running and encamped on its bank. We then hunted for Water for our Oxen to drink and after rambling in the woods about six miles, we came to the Slough which we had previously crossed. 14 m[iles].

Friday 27 November 1846—Captain called us up by day break. Carried Water out of the Missouri River, which was about 20 feet below its bank. Hunted up the cattle [and] at 11 all were found except Father Fisher's Cow. He started off in search [and] we found them about a mile on our road in a Willow Wood, the worst road I ever travelled. My kettle was flung on the ground and run over. After about two miles of such bad road, we halted to rest our teams. [We] then went on our way to our Camping ground at Sun down, rejoicing that we were now arrived at the end of our journey for this Season.[52] 6 m[iles].

Saturday 28 November 1846—I crossed the Missouri River at about 10 A.M. in a "dug out." Went to see Dr. Willard Richards who prayed God to bless me; and he blessed me with a Father's blessing. He told me to go to work and build me a log house, as I might as well blister my hands now as at a future period. Saw an Indian Interpreter.[53] Went thro' the City, where, nine weeks ago there was not a foot path or a Cow track, [but] now may be seen hundreds of houses, and hundreds in different stages of completion.[54] [It is] impossible to distinguish the rich from the poor; the Streets are wide and regular and [there is] every prospect of a large City Being raised up here. Crossed the River again in a Skiff, where I met with Captain Allen, when I recrossed with him in a Flat boat, then made [the] report of our Camp to Dr. Richards. Shook hands with H. C. Kimball, also President B. Young who told me they would not leave me behind any more, and he would take me with him, even if he had to put me in his pocket. I felt to rejoice at our interview. After visiting several brethren, [I] recrossed the River for the fourth time, in a Skiff. Ice running fast, a beautiful day.

---

[52] Bullock had arrived at the Middle Mormon Ferry in today's Council Bluffs, Iowa.

[53] In *The Mormons*, Thomas Kane identified Joseph LaFramboise as "the interpreter of the United States," and called the Pottawattamie Chief Pied Riche "the interpreter of the nation." This man, however, was probably Logan Fontenelle, the son of Bellevue trader Lucien B. Fontenelle (who had spent years in the Rockies) and an Indian mother. He worked for the Omaha Indians as Big Elk's interpreter.

[54] Although the apostles had only selected the site on 11 September, by the end of December 1846 a ward-by-ward census counted 3,483 people at Winter Quarters, of whom only 757 were men. See Bennett, *The Mormons at the Missouri*, 73, 89.

[THE IOWA TRAIL, CAMPS AND MILEAGES]

[Date]	miles	[miles] from Nauvoo
1846 Temple to the Slough	2	
Octr. 9 drove to the Bluffs	3	5
10 [drove to] Sugar Creek	13	18
11 [drove to] Bonapart	14	32
12		
13		
14		
15 [drove to] Prairie - - - - 6	38	
16		
17		
18 [drove to] Indian Creek	4	42
19		
20 [drove to] Fox River	16	58
21 [drove to] do.	14	72
22 [drove to] Allen's hill	8	80
23 [drove to] Soap Creek	12	92
24		
25		
26		
27 [drove to] Big Spring	15	107
28 [drove to] a Wood	18	125
29 [drove to] Wild Cat Grove	12	137
30 [drove to] White Breast Creek	7	144
31 [drove to] White Oak Springs	10	154
Nov. 1 [drove to] Grand River	8	162
2 [drove to] Raccoon Fork	13	175
3 [drove to] Thomson Fork	15	190
4 [drove to] Mount Pisgah	5	195
5 [drove to] Mormon Grove	6	201
6 [drove to] last of Grand River	6	207
7 [drove to] on Big Prairie	18	225
8 [drove to] "No. 102"	14	239
9		
10		
11 [drove to] the [102] Prairie	11	250
12 [drove to] Sand Stone Springs	3	253
13		
14 [drove to] Ottawa River	9	262
15 [drove to] 3rd Fork of Ishna Botna	14	276
16		
17 [drove to] A Grove	8	284
18		
Nov. 19 [drove to] Sideling Bridge	5	289
20		
21 [drove to] West Fork of Ishna Botna	10	299
22		
23		
24 [drove to] Keg Creek	10	309
25 [drove to] Mosquito Timber	6	315
26 [drove to] Banks of Missouri River	14	329
27 [drove north to] Ferryville	6	335

50 days
33 days travelling, average 10 miles per day
17 days none [no progress]

Fanny [Rushton] told me to day that my cradle was left behind at the Little Platte River.[55] This dishonest way of dealing with my property is too bad, but I ought not to feel surprised, as it accords with the treatment I have received thro' the journey. A burnt child will dread the fire.

Sunday 29 November 1846—Frosty night, went to hunt up cattle with the Captain, then attempted to cross the Missouri River to report, but was refused a passage by Pelatiah Brown & Daniel Banan. After some time I crossed in a Skiff [and the] meeting was near over. President Benson was speaking, followed by Brigham who requested the brethren to go to work at the Mill Race in order to complete it.[56] After [the] meeting, Captain Allen told me to wait at the Doctor's until he called for me to meet the High Council, but he omitted calling. At 7:00 I went to the Council with Bishop Knight and made a report. B. Young gave Council to locate all. 28 policemen were organized and a large quantity of provisions sent for from Missouri. [We] dismissed about 9 P.M. and recrossed [the Missouri] in the Flat boat. At [the] meeting I commenced chilling and had chills all afternoon. A cold windy day.

Monday 30 November 1846—Severe frost, dull heavy day. Ice still running in [the] River. Savary, Cook & his Son, Hopkins & his Son not hunting up the cattle. The rest of the brethren [were] engaged. In the afternoon I had a very heavy chill, [and was] obliged to go to bed. I was crossed over the River in my Wagon in the night.

Tuesday 1st. December 1846—Severe frost. I was on the Omaha side of the River, heavy fog over the River. [We] made a fire, when several Indians came to warm them by it. Heavy clouds rolling from the SW. About 11:00 I drove my team up to the Doctor's yard and was immediately seized with a heavy shake, which with the Fever confined me to my Wagon till dark. Father Richards came and laid his hands on me and I was considerable better afterwards and at evening he commanded me to arise, which I did, [and] went to his tent and took some Quinine.

Wednesday 2 December 1846—I was some better, fixed and nailed down my Wagon Cover and nursing. A severe cold day.

Thursday 3 December 1846—I was digging a Saw pit, covering Doc-

---

[55] Bullock's cradle may have been a frame designed to support work, part of a scythe, or simply Willard Richards Bullock's bed.

[56] This was the troublesome flour mill on Turkey Creek that generated much controversy at Winter Quarters. Despite great effort and expense, the Mormons were unable to get the mill into operation until early spring. See *Ibid.*, 115.

tor's house with dirt, [and] delivering out Salt to go with the cattle. [I] went with Dr. Levi Richards to drive cattle on to the Prairie. My cows would have gone at the same time, if they had been this side of the River, but they were not, on account of the negligence of the brethren not passing them over on the first. They were driven up to the Ferry with the cattle, but because [I] was not there to see to it myself (being shaking in bed) they would not do it for me. I will here remark that when my other cow was lost, not a man was sent after it, but when other men's cows had strayed away, the whole Camp had to wait till it was found. I saw an Ox pulled out of the Mire by Chains. We returned by the Mill Race. On my return home saw Captain Allen who told me to record, "no man helping to hunt up the Oxen and Cows and all the Men come to this side of the River, contra to Brigham's Counsel." Very cold day, ice running fast. Isabella Alice Rushton, daughter of John and Margaret Rushton, died between 11 and 12 at night, aged 14 months.

Friday 4 December 1846—I hauled Water with Oxen, carried Straw out of the house, fetched [a] Wheel-barrow from the Mill, [and] wheeled dirt into the house, &c. I had a bad cold. The day very cold and threatning like [a] Snow Storm.

Saturday 5 December 1846—I had a bad Cough, all my family do. Willard [is] reduced again almost to a mere Skeleton, but Father Richards has said he shall be well in a month, so I trust to the Lord that I shall not lose any of my family.[57] I and Wife went to the burial of John Rushton's babe. It was buried in grave No. 24. In [the] evening Father Richards let me have 12½ pounds [of] Beef. Very cold day.

Sunday 6 December 1846—While at breakfast received a notice to hunt up the 27th Quorum. In [the] afternoon I attended to it and in the evening attended a Council of the Presidents at brother Russell's when arrangements were entered into to support the 70s who were sick and poor, President Joseph Young being appointed the Commissary.[58] A Rhymy frost, Father [Richards] had a bad shake.

Monday 7 December 1846—I visited John Scott at his house, where

---

[57] Thomas Bullock later assigned blame for his infant son's death: "On our [Iowa] journey, we buried sister Joan Campbell and her babe, who died from exposure, at a time when she was least able to bear it. On the 17th of March we buried my little Willard Richards Bullock. These three deaths were decidedly caused by exposure, and the effects of persecution; and woe be unto ex-Governor Thomas Ford, for their blood will cling to his skirts in the great day of judgment." See Bullock to Richards, *Millennial Star* (15 January 1848), 29.

[58] The "Council of the Presidents" refers to the LDS Melchezidek priesthood office of Presidents of Seventies. Joseph Young was Brigham Young's elder brother.

he shewed me a spring of beautiful water. [I spent the] rest of [the] day at Father's. My cold is no better. Willard [is] getting better.[59] Cold frosty day. Father Richards let me have 12 pounds [of] Flour.

Tuesday 8 December 1846—Got water out of [the] Doctor's Well, [and] went to Scott's Spring, having wet feet at the Creek. A beautiful day. I dreamed last night among other things, that I was in a large house sitting at the left side of Mr. Richard Wassell (who is dead) and his daughters Mary and Ann [were] at his right side. He took my right hand across his breast and Mary & Ann placed each of their right hands in mine. At the same time, Mr. Wassell put one arm round my neck, and his other arm round his two daughters, and blessed us with a father's blessing, me as his Son in Law, and [giving me] his daughters as two of my Wives.[60] We were all very happy & rejoicing in each others society. I feel thankful for this dream and my fervent desire is, that in the due time of the Lord I may have them. This brings to my recollection, when I was at Common Side [near Brierly Hill, Staffordshire, England] both Mr. & Mrs. Wassell said they should like me very much, for a Son in Law.

Wednesday 9 December 1846—This morning I had a delightful conversation with H. C. Kimball for upwards of half an hour. Such visits as this are very precious to me. Between 2 and 3 o'clock this morning a party of Iowa Indians made an attack upon the Omaha Indians, [who are] settled close by our Camp. Several shots were fired. One ball entered the poor Old Chief on his right cheek below his temple, and then coming out below his eye. Another ball took off the end of his left thumb, a third entered his right shoulder and lodged there. Two other Indians were wounded, [and] one Squaw was obliged to have her arm cut off at her Shoulder. The poor Omahas scampered off as fast as they could and took shelter in President Brigham Young's house, and in the course of the day, they removed the[ir] tent close alongside of the President's house and I saw the Old Chief removed to it and his wounds were saturated with Spirits by one of our brethren.[61] Uncle John Smith visited Father Richards in his new house. About 2 P.M. in the evening removed

---

[59] Father refers to Willard Richards, and Willard is Bullock's youngest son.

[60] In his Nauvoo journal, Bullock recorded writing to "Mrs. Wassell" on 14 December 1845 and to "Mr. Wassell (England)" on 28 June 1846. In late 1847, Bullock forwarded Franklin D. Richards a copy of the "General Epistle to all the Saints" by "Mrs. Wassell's, Bramley-lane, Brierley-hill, Staffordshire." See Bullock to William, *Millennial Star* (15 April 1848), 116. There is no additional information on the sisters who prompted this most revealing journal entry.

[61] Hosea Stout saw Big Head, Bullock's "Old Chief," and noted, "I did not think he would live."

Father into his new house and he dictated a letter to Major Miller informing him of the attack on "Big head," and to inform "Big Elk" the Chief.[62] I made a copy of the letter to send. Doctor went out [and] Big Head staid in the Doctor's house all night, with his family. Beautiful day. 3 Wagons crossed over the River on the Ice.

Thursday 10 December 1846—I was assisting at Doctor's, [this] being washing day. Doctor got up about noon, [and] was about the house all day. Between 6 and 7 P.M. G. A. Smith and A[masa] Lyman came in with [the] Doctor. Several letters were read, letters written to Wm. Crosby and John Brown giving them the route to our next intended location on the head waters of the Yellow Stone River.[63] Also wrote a letter to W. H. Rodgers of Savannah [Missouri] to open a trade with him in Wheat and Corn. President Young came in, letters were read and a very interesting conversation was carried on until near midnight. Beautiful day.

Friday 11 December 1846—Severe frost in the night. Doctor arose about 9 o'clock, wrote a postscript to W. H. Rodgers to purchase beans at 50[¢] per Bushel there. The letters were delivered to James M. Flack, to take to the Post office, also 26 letters from the Post office, to be put in the United States Post office. Uncle John Smith called at 20 minutes to 1. Conversed with Doctor. I assorted the letters and papers in the Writing desk and endorsed them. Doctor [worked] about his house. Out in the evening, fine day.

Saturday 12 December 1846—Doctor arose between 8 and 9. Delivered to James Flack 50 feet [of] wire for Wm. Gardiner. Major Miller [the] Omaha Agent, Mr. Fontenelle the Omaha Interpreter and H. G. Sherwood called to consult, and make enquiries respecting the shooting of Big Head. After Major Miller had left, Doctor had his Map drawn

---

[62] Major Miller was John Miller, "the Council Bluffs agent" for the Omaha, Otoe-Missouri, and Pawnee tribes. Big Elk was the principal chief of the Omaha nation who negotiated the 28 August 1848 agreement at Cutler's Park that let the Saints settle on Indian land. (All the Mormons' Indian treaties were illegal, since Federal law prohibited anyone but the government from treating with the tribes.)

[63] John Brown received this letter shortly after his return to Mississippi on 29 October 1846. James Emmett and George Miller strongly supported establishing a waystation at the confluence of the Tongue and Yellowstone rivers, but Brigham Young gave the plan only tentative support, viewing it as a challenge to his authority by the Council of Fifty. Joseph Holbrook reported that the buffalo had "entirely eat out" the feed on the Niobrara and that the Sioux and Ponca would not tolerate a road through their country. Early in 1847, Young rejected the plan. See Bennett, "Finalizing Plans for the Trek West," 306–13.

by Mr. Grosclaude[64] out, when I took the following notes from Mr. Fontenelle's Conversation:

> The Soil about Tongue River is red and yellow Clay and you cannot raise crops on it. After you have travelled on the So ha quo 70 miles to the foot of the mountains the road is good. From the Pimca to the Oregon Trail is a broken country, [and] between the divides are Swamps. The creeks that run into the Running Water[65] are not miry, but it is a rough Country. The nighest way for you is to strike the Platte, [over] a level prairie and [it is a] good sound road to the Mountains. You will have to cross Otter Creek, Ash Creek and one or two simple branches, where there is no use of bridging. The Loup is Quick sand, none beyond Fort Laramie. Go up the South side of the Platt to the Black Hills, [for if you go] up the Running Water you will see trouble and may break your Wagons. There are two large Butes 290 miles from the Mouth. I would not undertake to go up that River, there are rushes up the river for about 200 miles, then prairie grass. [The] Month of March is very rainy and the streams raise. The rains commence about [the] 1st March and continue to the 15[th of] April. It is not bad to travel on the Platte during that time, the road being Sandy. The worst road is from the Horn [Elkhorn River] to the Platte [which is] about 10 miles. Start from the Old Council Bluffs [and] the road leads to the Ferry. You had better go back to the Spring and build a little boat, it will do you more good than a bridge. [The] Horn is a large stream and sometimes overflows its banks. I hardly believe the abutments [for a bridge] will stand, the river being full of quick sand. The stream will always wash the abutments away. There are more rushes on the Platte than on the Running Water, at any rate as far as Grand Island, [and] there is enough on the bottoms for cattle. The Buffalo grass is fine and plenty on the head waters of the Yellow Stone. A stream strikes above the two forks of Tongue River. The Winter sets in there about the 1st of November [and] lasts till [the] last of March, [with] not much difference in the Snow there and here. The climate in the Mountains is nearly always the same, the deepest Snow being about three feet. The Kansas River is a fine Country for raising Crops. The South side of Salt Lake has the best Soil.[66]

At about 1 o'clock Brigham Young, H. C. Kimball, W. Richards, O. Pratt, E. T. Benson, Major Miller, Omaha Agent, Logan Fontenelle Interpreter, Dr. Levi Richards, Dr. Sprague and myself sat in Council

---

[64] Swiss-born Justin Grosclaude had sixteen years of service with the American Fur Company when he met the Mormons, whom he offered to guide over the mountains for $200.

[65] This is the Niobrara River, which the French called "*l'eau qui court*," literally translated as water which runs, or more loosely as running water.

[66] Fontenelle offered excellent advice to Brigham Young, urging him to ascend the Platte and not the Niobrara River.

with Big Elk, Big Head, Mary and 8 other Indians. It was counselled for the Indians to remove lower down the River and the Saints would build them a strong house for them to live in. About 7 P.M. a Frenchman named La Fras came in and informed us thro' the Interpreters that about 100 Sioux had fallen on the Omahas about sixty miles North of here last night and killed about 40 of them, about 8 escaping.[67] [We] wrote a letter to his Father in Law, A. P. Sarpy Esqre,[68] to inform him of it, which was signed by Brigham Young, who then went to his house, where Willard Richards, G. A. Smith, [and] E. T. Benson had gone a few minutes previous to see Luke Johnson who had arrived here this evening. Doctor [was] about the house and neighborhood all day. Fine mild day.

Sunday 13 December 1846—I was at Doctor's all day. About noon there was a meeting at the Stand. Brother Cornelius P. Lott preached and then President B. Young told the Sisters that they ought not to grumble & complain about the Twelve for not having a sufficiency to live on, for their dear husbands who were in the Army had only sent them about 5,000 dollars out of 22,000 they received at Fort Leavenworth, reserving to themselves only [$]17,000 for the Grog Shop, Ball room & card Table; the Twelve then sent a Special Messenger after them to Santa Fe when they let their *dear* Wives and children and the Camp of Israel have about [$]4000 more, thus shewing their great love for their Families, but their greater love for the pleasures around them.[69] At 6 P.M. the Municipal High Council met at Dr. Richards' round house,[70] present B. Young, H. C. Kimball, W. Richards, G. A. Smith, W. Woodruff, O. Pratt and E. T. Benson of the Twelve; & the Bishops. After the general business had been disposed of, President Young told the High Council that the Bishops were under their control and that they ought to meet together at least once a week to consult together and if the Bishops will not do their

---

[67] Following the attack on 9 December, Brigham Young allowed the uninjured Omahas to pitch their lodges next to his house. When they learned of the slaughter of their hunting party, Hosea Stout reported, "they made such a noise that President Young had them stopt."

[68] Frontier baron Peter A. Sarpy operated the American Fur Company post at Bellevue, a few miles above the mouth of the Platte River and some twenty miles south of Winter Quarters.

[69] Brigham Young's management of part of the $5,000 of the battalion's clothing allowance generated much ill-will in Winter Quarters. Battalion veterans later complained that Young failed to fulfill his promise to provide for their families while they were in the army. As Bullock noted, Young returned this disapproval with contempt. See Bennett, *The Mormons at the Missouri*, 124–25.

[70] Often called the "Octagon" because of its shape, Willard Richards' log house also served as an office, hospital, and post office. For a drawing of the building, see the Journal History, 31 December 1846.

duty, drop them. It never will do for this people to go into the Wilderness without serving their God. We had better have a division & see who will serve God. He had gleaned his knowledge every where, if he had been more intent on getting riches some one else would have stood in his place. The Bishops ought to be able to tell what every man is doing in his Ward. You can lead a man to do his duty. See that every man woman & child has something to eat. When a man is found to be a thief, he will be a thief no longer—cut his throat & thro' him in the River, & prayed that the time might soon come that all iniquity would cease. He wanted the Bishops to organize their several wards & watch over them with a fatherly care & see that they have work & have schools in their Wards. He then called on the Twelve, the High Council & 22 Bishops to bring a log each & put up a Council house. He also wanted the brethren to complete the Mill Race. After the Council had dismissed, the Twelve remained in conversation till about 10 at night. Dr. Richards in a conversation with me said that I had now the run of his business & that I must be at his side writing from this time, henceforth & for ever. A delightful day. Luke Johnson told the Council of 12 that Carnot Mason is the only man alive out of between 25 and 30 who tarred, feathered and poisoned Joseph at Hiram, Portage County, and Mason dragged Joseph out by the hair of his head. Dr. Denison prepared [the] Viol of Aqua Fortis.[71]

Monday 14 December 1846—Snow on the ground, an inch thick which dissolved in the P.M. East wind. I assorted my books papers & records. In the evening I commenced a School for my Children, which I pray my heavenly Father to bless me in my labors, & enable me to instruct them well, & make them useful in building up His Kingdom on the Earth. Doctor went across the river between 11 and 12 and returned about 1. [We] commenced his office about 4. President Young & E. T. Benson went to look out a location for the Omahas, about 6 miles South & returned by Sunset. Thawing, East wind. Doctor let me have one sack of meal.

Tuesday 15 December 1846—More snow fell during the night. I regulated my books and papers, [and] in [the] afternoon boiled a quantity of Staves to make barrels with. Very cold day & commenced snowing, which continued thro' the evening. At 6 P.M. attended the municipal

---

[71] On 24 March 1832, a mob tarred and feathered Joseph Smith at Hiram, Ohio, and tried to force "a phial, supposed to contain aqua-fortis" into his mouth, "but broke it in his teeth." See Roberts, *Comprehensive History*, 1:281. Early Mormons relentlessly monitored the fate of the murderers and persecutors of their dead prophet.

Court & took minutes of proceedings in the Doctor's journal. President Young taught that the Bishops make a report of their several wards & said if we cannot humble this little Camp at a jump how can we manage millions? The whole of the Reports ought to be read over in 44 minutes. Their books ought to be systematically alike and correct. He also requested one more day's work for the Mill Race that it may be completed. H. C. Kimball related his dream that he & President Young were flying in the air & dropt in a valley where there was a great many Snakes coiled up. They were not hurt by them but it took them some activity to escape, & shewed that his dream alluded to this people. President Young told them if the people will do as I say, they will be saved. He was ready to night to render an account of his conduct to his Heavenly Father in regard to the goods & he should cry out "Hallelujah my work is done." He asked if he was to blame because goods rose in price in St. Louis?— or because of the low state of the River the freight had risen from 75[¢] to [$]2.25 per hundred.[72] If the brethren had done as he told them in Nauvoo, we should have been at the Rocky Mountains long ago. Fontenell brought word that there were 73 Omahas killed instead of 40 as reported on the 12th.

Wednesday 16 December 1846—A dull day. I made out reports for Bishops Fairbanks (2nd), Lutz (17th) & Robinson (7th) to present to Municipal High Council. The Mill Race was completed this evening.

Thursday 17 December 1846—I made a map of Winter Quarters.[73] [Drafted] Reports for Bishop's Rolfe ( ) Levi E. Riter (3rd.) A. Everett (21) John Vance (18th) for [the] High Council. Joshua L. Miller arrived with a letter from Punca Camp which was read in the Council at 6 P.M.[74] I took minutes of the meeting in Doctor's Journal. Dr. Richards spoke of the bushels of papers that were in his possession & not yet filed & the necessity of having a place to keep them & preparing for future history. W. Woodruff said he felt a great interest in this history being a book of

---

[72] Young used part of the Mormon Battalion clothing allowance to purchase goods at wholesale prices in St. Louis; only part of his markup at Winter Quarters could be attributed to freight charges. Young may have used this money to help pay for the flour mill, which operated only briefly. Some of the Saints complained when the prices of some goods at Winter Quarters were higher than at Sarpy's nearby trading post. See Bennett, *The Mormons at the Missouri*, 115, 127, 284, for a discussion of the controversy and a comparison of prices.

[73] This may be the map in Thomas Bullock, Plan of Winter Quarters, LDS Archives. For a facsimile from the Thomas L. Kane Collection at Brigham Young University, see *Ibid.*, 75.

[74] This letter was from George Miller's camp at the Ponca village on the Niobrara River.

Books, & the one he should have to be judged out of. O. Pratt said that 5 or 6 weeks ago a motion was made to dispose of the Church property to support the historian & now moved that a sufficient per centage be levied upon the property to support the historian for his services. [Motion] carried. During [the] Council [meeting] Snow fell an inch deep, dull day. Wife sick.

[END OF THE POOR CAMP JOURNAL]

Chapter 3

"THE CELEBRATED PLATTE— THE HIGHWAY OF OUR FUTURE JOURNEY"
The Camp of the Pioneers to the Oregon Trail, April 1847

Brigham Young faced tremendous challenges as he struggled to organize the trek west in 1847. Through the preceding winter, the Saints had debated who should go west and had even revisited the question of where they should settle. George Miller and James Emmett of the Council of Fifty argued strongly for a route up the Niobrara River that would avoid the Platte River road, "the thoroughfare where all the slime and filth" from Missouri and Illinois would pass by a Mormon settlement.[1] On 19 January 1847, Young released his only official revelation, "The Word and Will of the Lord," to counter this challenge to his authority. The revelation clearly stated that the emigration would be organized "under the direction of the Twelve Apostles."[2] George Miller complained that he was "greatly disgusted at the bad composition and folly of this revelation," but a large majority of the Saints accepted it without reservation.[3] Young set about defining a plan that would move most of the Saints west as quickly as possible. By the end of January, he had selected the Platte road as the best route west and had determined to push through to the mountains, rather than attempt to establish waystations and plant crops along the way. As early as January, he recognized that it was "very uncertain whether the pioneers will leave here before April," but he set a departure date of 22 March.[4] The apostles spent some six weeks organizing the Mormon settlements into traveling companies, and the projected size of the lead party—the pioneer company—was reduced from 300 members to a little less than half that

---

[1] Miller to Young, 17 March 1847, cited in Bennett, *The Mormons at the Missouri*, 158.
[2] *Doctrine and Covenants*, 136:3.
[3] Bennett, "Finalizing Plans for the Trek West," 312–13.
[4] Ibid., 317, 318.

size. The March departure date slipped by, but before the first week of April was over, the lead elements of the pioneer company headed west. Initially, the Pioneer Camp was to be a picked company of 144 young men, but fate reduced the number to 143, and three women and two children ultimately joined the party that was to select a new site for Zion.

Who were these men and women? The pioneer company was not, as William Mulder noted, "a ragged band of refugees but the best prepared of all western overlanders in terms of purpose, knowledge of the country, organization, and equipment."[5] They included scholars and carpenters, accountants and farmers, blacksmiths and wagon makers, lumberjacks and doctors, and "mechanics of every kind." Its members were surprisingly young—at forty-six, Brigham Young and Heber Kimball were among the expedition's several patriarchs—and "they were possessed of the natural exuberance natural to youth" that came alive with the freedom of the plains and sometimes got them into trouble. They were picked primarily for their abilities and frontier skills, not for their piety—and a surprising number of them would ultimately abandon Utah and the LDS church completely. B. H. Roberts allowed that these youths were not above "checkers, some card playing for amusement, scuffling, wrestling," and even "the telling of humorous stories of doubtful propriety."[6] In addition to its youthfulness, the "Camp of Israel" was not nearly as monochrome as might be assumed. The company included three African-Americans, one of whom, Green Flake, belonged to Brigham Young and had been baptized into the LDS church in 1844.[7] Two more blacks, Oscar Crosby and Hark Lay, were slaves from Mississippi sent ahead to prepare homes for their masters. Hark Lay lived out his life in Utah but never seems to have joined the LDS church; Oscar Crosby was baptized shortly after he arrived in Salt Lake.[8] Two or three other members of the party were not even Mormons. Brigham Young's brother Lorenzo insisted on taking along his asthmatic wife, Harriet Page Wheeler Young, and her two sons, Isaac Perry Decker and Lorenzo Zobieski Young. As Harriet needed female company, the Mormon leader decided to take her daughter, Clarissa Decker Young, one of the many Mrs. Brigham Youngs, and to permit his right-hand man, Heber Kimball, to include his wife Ellen Sanders Kimball in the company.[9]

As the Saints at Winter Quarters prepared for their move west, Thomas Bullock spent the first days of April making "a sketch of Captain Fremont's topographical map of [the] road to Oregon for the use of the Pio-

---

[5] Mulder, *The Mormons in American History*, 10. [6] Roberts, *Comprehensive History*, 3:181, 183.
[7] Jenson, ed., *Latter-day Saint Biographical Encyclopedia*, 4:703.
[8] Coleman, "A History of Blacks in Utah, 1825–1910," 34. [9] Kimball, *Heber C. Kimball*, 150.

neers."[10] On 5 April, Brigham Young dispatched Heber C. Kimball with six wagons to form an advance camp for the pioneer company near Cutler's Park, about three miles west of Winter Quarters. Kimball moved forward by stages another thirty miles to the banks of the Elkhorn River where he established the rendezvous known as the Camp of the Pioneers. Back at Winter Quarters in the log meeting house that sheltered the seventeenth annual conference of the church, on 6 April Brigham Young was sustained as president of the church and president of the Twelve Apostles—but the Twelve did not authorize him to form a First Presidency, and so he led the 1847 exodus merely as president of the Quorum of the Twelve Apostles. With this important business settled and with the sun breaking through the clouds, Young cut short the conference and set his followers to packing.

Emigration was a complicated business and the pioneer camp made several false starts, beginning with Kimball's and continuing on 7 April when four parties—led by Wilford Woodruff, Orson Pratt, Brigham Young, and Willard Richards, accompanied by Thomas Bullock—set out. Brigham Young backtracked to Winter Quarters the next day to meet Parley Pratt, who had just returned from the British Mission with good news and much-needed donations. On 13 April John Taylor arrived with $500 worth of scientific equipment, including sextants, a circle of reflection, artificial horizons, barometers, thermometers, and telescopes.[11] Armed with a shopping list drawn from Frémont's *Report*, Taylor had purchased the instruments in England for Orson Pratt. Young spent several days briefing Pratt and Taylor about the situation at Winter Quarters. He also outlined his plans, apparently not too clearly, for the great second division that would take the bulk of the initial immigration—some 1,553 Saints—over the trail in 1847. It was the ides of April before Young gathered all the loose ends of church business together and the pioneer trek began in earnest.

At the Platte River on 18 April, Young laid down the Laws Regulating the Camp of Israel: the bugle sounded at five o'clock, "a signal for every

---

[10] History of Brigham Young, cited in Roberts, *Comprehensive History*, 3:161. For the Frémont maps available to the Mormon pioneer company, see Donald Jackson's "Map Portfolio" in Spence and Jackson, eds., *The Expeditions of John Charles Frémont*. Map 2, "Map to illustrate an exploration of the country lying between the Missouri River and the Rocky Mountains, on the line of the Nebraska or Platte River," accompanied Frémont's 1843 report on his second expedition. Map 3, "Map of the Exploring Expedition to the Rocky Mountains in 1842 and to Oregon and California in the years 1843-4 by Capt. J. C. Frémont," is a much larger version of the 1843 map and accompanied Frémont's 1845 *Report of the Exploring Expedition to the Rocky Mountains in the Year 1842, and to Oregon and North California in the Years 1843-'44*. In 1846, the Senate published seven detailed maps that are reproduced in seven sections as Map 4 in Jackson's "Map Portfolio." All these maps were the work of the brilliant cartographer Charles Preuss.

[11] Kimball, *Heber C. Kimball*, 150. These instruments are on display at the Church Museum of History and Art in Salt Lake City.

man to arise and attend prayers before he leaves his wagon." The camp had two hours to attend to "cooking, eating, feeding teams &c." Men were required to get the permission of their officers to leave their wagons, and under "hostile appearances" wagons were to travel in three parallel columns (reduced the next day to two columns)—a formation that became a favorite for Mormon overland companies. The original orders directed the men to march "with their loaded guns in their hands or in their wagons where they can get to them in a moment," but after several horses were shot, the orders were modified—for as the Saints were to learn from hard experience, accidental gunshot wounds were the leading killer on the trail, after cholera and drowning. At night, the wagons formed a circular camp with "the horses to be all retired inside the circle when necessary"—that is, when Indians threatened to steal them. At 8:30 the bugle sounded and at 9:00 it was lights out.[12] Forty-eight men under Stephen Markham were organized "into four night watches to be on duty half the time."[13]

The pioneer company departed almost a month before there was enough grass on the prairie to sustain their teams; as John Brown recalled, "as there was no grass yet, we had to haul grain for feed."[14] The Indian practice of burning off the prairie in the spring to improve the range meant that securing adequate feed for the Mormons' over-burdened stock remained a critical problem through the first weeks of the journey.

At the outset of their odyssey, the Mormons had to cross the traditional lands of the Pawnees. For 300 years, three bands of the tribe had roamed from Texas to South Dakota, but a devastating smallpox epidemic in 1838 and brutal warfare with their traditional tribal enemies had left them between a rock—the Lakota Sioux—and a hard place—the swelling advance of overland emigration. The Pawnees responded by alternately extracting a toll from the immigrants (which the travelers typically regarded as begging) or stealing their stock. Their warriors, who plucked their eyebrows, painted their faces, and shaved their heads except for a narrow strip of hair that stood up like a horn, impressed and intimidated white overlanders.[15]

One of the Pawnee's favorite ploys was to catch small parties of whites and strip them—literally—of everything they owned. In 1847, the Pawnees employed this technique when they captured a party of hunters, with a slight modification—they let the hunters retain their hats and boots. Such actions earned the tribe a reputation as "grand rascals." Oregon pioneer Loren Hastings called them "the greatest thieves I ever saw," and con-

---

[12] Smith, ed., *An Intimate Chronicle*, 300; and Unruh, *The Plains Across*, 345. See Appendix B for Bullock's copy of the "Laws Regulating the Camp of Israel." [13] Roberts, *Comprehensive History*, 3:164.
[14] Brown, *Autobiography of Pioneer John Brown*, 73. [15] Kimball, *Heber C. Kimball*, 157.

cluded, "the best way I think to civilize or Christianize Indians is with powder & lead."[16] After the Mormons failed to win over the Pawnee chief, identified as Shefmolan by B. H. Roberts, with gifts of powder, lead, tobacco, salt, flour, and "some trinkets," the Saints had a similar reaction. They increased their guard, limbered up their cannon, and fired guns "to serve notice on their red brethren that the camp was watchful." As the Mormons discovered farther up the trail, it would take more than watchfulness to discourage the Pawnees from stealing their animals.

The Saint's relations with America's native peoples had a complex history long before they set out across the plains. The *Book of Mormon* tells the story of the struggles of the Nephite and the Lamanite peoples, descendants of the prophet Lehi who led his family from Israel to America at the time of the Babylonian captivity. According to LDS belief, the Lamanites annihilated the Nephites about 421 A.D. and become the ancestors of the American Indians. Early Mormons believed that when they joined the LDS church they were literally transformed into "the blood of Israel," and they felt a special kinship with Indians, whose ancestry made them, like the Saints, children of Abraham.

According to Joseph Smith's prophecies, the redemption of the Indians would be among the first signs of the second coming of Jesus Christ. The "remnant of the house of Jacob" would attack those who rejected the new gospel as "a young lion among the flocks of sheep, who, if he goeth through both treadeth down and teareth in pieces, and none can deliver." The righteous Lamanites would "beat in pieces many people; and I will consecrate their gain unto the Lord . . . And they shall be a scourge unto the people of this land." "Lamanites," "Cousin Lemuel," "the remnant of Jacob," "the stick of Joseph," and the "Tribe of Manasseh" were all names the Mormons used to refer to Indians.

Naturally these beliefs were not popular on the American frontier, and they were a key source of the continual conflict between the Mormons and their neighbors. As they moved west, these convictions occasionally prompted the Saints to treat the tribes they encountered with special respect and consideration. As Bullock's journals show, fear of the hidden raiders who continually threatened their stock soon proved a more compelling teacher than theology. In Utah, Brigham Young carefully selected neutral ground between the powerful tribes of the Great Basin, and soon concluded that an entirely new generation of Indians would have to be raised up to fulfill Joseph Smith's prophecies. Ultimately, the fate of the

---

[16] Unruh, *The Plains Across*, 183–84.

tribes in Mormon Country was no different than their grim destiny in the rest of the American West.

The pioneers "left a very good trail behind us. As good as 73 teams, seventeen cows, and one hundred and forty-three men would make."[17] As early as 1813, the returning Astorians had come down the Platte, and Stephen H. Long's 1820 military reconnaissance set out up the north side of the river from Council Bluffs. In 1844, the Stephens-Murphy-Townsend company, the group Caleb Greenwood helped become the first party to take wagons to California in a single season, followed the north side of the Platte, but such limited use meant the trace was not yet a trail, let alone a wagon road. The care the Saints took in building a road sets them apart from previous overland companies, whose sole purpose was to get on with their journey. The Mormons, by contrast, were looking to the future of their communal enterprise, and as its name indicates, the job of the Pioneer Camp of the Saints was to pioneer the road—in its original military sense, as those who go before, preparing the way for others to follow.[18]

The main challenges of the trail from Winter Quarters to Grand Island were the river crossings, including the difficult passage of the Elkhorn and the treacherous fording of the Loup. In between, the pioneers reached "none other than the celebrated 'Platte,'" which Bullock correctly identified as the highway of their future journey. After ascending the Loup Fork to establish the ford that became known as the upper crossing, the pioneers packed down a road across the quicksand bottom of the river. The company returned to the north side of the Platte about midway between present Grand Island and Central City, Nebraska. By 30 April, the Saints camped across the river from the point where the Oregon Trail from Independence reached the south side of the Platte. The pioneers were now into the treeless prairie, but they had also reached buffalo country, which presented them with a new set of challenges and adventures. Against the cold wind that howled through camp that night, Luke Johnson built a fire of buffalo chips, using a buffalo skull for a chimney.

---

[17] Snow, "Journey to Zion," 121.

[18] For a look at the pioneer company trail and its markers in Nebraska, see Kimball, "The Mormon Trail Network in Nebraska, 1846–1868," 323.

Journal of the Pioneer Camp of the Saints, from Winter Quarters, in Search of a Location for a Stake of Zion
Kept by
Thomas Bullock

1847 ~~March~~ 7 April 1847—Doctor [Willard Richards] gave orders at 1 P.M. for me to get ready & start with his teams this afternoon to the Camp of the Pioneers, to transact the business & write the instructions to be left for the brethren at Winter Quarters. Made up a mail of between 3 & 400 letters to go to the Battalion,[19] packed up his papers, hunted his cow, & about 5 P.M. made ready & started by the new & old Burying grounds, & encamped for the night on the prairie, without wood or water—a keen North Wind blowing all the time. Cold night.

~~March~~ 8 April 1847—At Sunrise started for the camp & arrived there at 10 minutes to 10 A.M. & there found Orson Pratt & Wilford Woodruff of the Twelve, 3 carriages & 28 Wagons.[20] President Young left the Camp for his farm, with Isaac Morley, John Young & Brother Grant in his carriage & at ½ past 9 A.M. Luke Johnson & A. P. Rockwood started at the same time for Winter Quarters. The Palm Tree[21] [is] in beautiful bloom, Grass springing in all directions. Clear Sky. Keen North wind & a flock of 33 Cranes flying high in the air, round the Pioneer encampment. Several wagons joined the camp thro the day. The President returned from his farm about 5:00, Amasa Lyman having met him & brought the news of the arrival of P. P. Pratt at Winter Quarters. O. Pratt started for home & in half an hour after was followed by President Young & Lyman, also John Young, Isaac Morley & several others.[22] At the same time Brown, Crosby & co., from Mississippi,[23] passed over

---

[19] By April 1847, most of the Mormon Battalion was stationed in Los Angeles and San Diego, California, but three sick detachments had wintered at present Pueblo, Colorado.

[20] Woodruff noted that on this morning the camp killed its first game—a squirrel—which was presented to Brigham Young for breakfast.

[21] Bullock's reference to the "Palm Tree" is a mystery. It may have been a willow or a Balm of Gilead tree that blossomed early, but it certainly was not a tropical palm.

[22] The pioneer company had set out on 7 April and was camped on the eighth at the large Mormon farm west of Winter Quarters, but Brigham Young and other members of the Twelve returned to hear Parley Pratt's report of his mission to England.

[23] John Brown and William Crosby were leaders of the "Mississippi Saints" previously described. Two slaves, Henry Brown and "Bankhead's negro," had died on the journey from Mississippi, and Brown took "the two black boys [Oscar Crosby and Hark Lay] that survived the trip, [and] David Powell and Mathew Ivory, and joined the Pioneer camp." See Brown, *Autobiography*, 72.

the hill, in 7 Wagons, to the next Point en route for the Horn.[24] Elder Woodruff returned from shooting as the Sun set. I killed a Mosquito.

~~March~~ 9 April 1847—Pleasant day, fresh Breeze from the West. The brethren danced one cotillion to wile away the time. W. Woodruff & a many of the brethren left the Camp to go to Winter Quarters. At 10 minutes to 2, G. A. Smith, Luke Johnson & others arrived in Camp, bringing the intelligence of the Presidency being on the road & that they would soon be here. Orders were given by O. Pratt to hitch up & be ready, which infused cheerfulness into every man. They went to work with alacrity. Immediately afterwards Presidents Young, Kimball & Richards arrived, & as quick as the teams were got ready they commenced rolling up the hill. At 3 o'clock most of the teams had started from their encampment, [and we] travelled over a very broken country, crossed one very bad miry place. Two or three of the teams only required doubling & with the assistance of about 30 of the brethren towing them thro' [we] got over without much difficulty 64 Wagons & carriages. Continued our route and encamped at half past 7 P.M. in a valley, where there was no Wood, but Water & a pretty sprinkling of Grass. B. Young, H. C. Kimball & W. Richards went to cutting grass for their cattle with knives & afterwards inspected teams to see that all was right.

Saturday 10 April 1847—A Skin of ice on the Water. The brethren cut hay, which the cattle were fond of. The grass is in pretty good condition, Water plenty. Attended to their cattle & at 20 minutes past 7 the teams began to roll up the hill, having a delightful morning to start with & a slight NE wind. [We] travelled on the divide of a rolling prairie, crossed the creek "Tapion"[25] and also a marshy creek, at both which places the "Mormon team" was called into requisition.[26] On the banks of this last marsh the Camp halted to feed the cattle. T. B. gathered a Snow Drop, saw a Dragon fly; delightful. At noon, after stop[p]ing about an hour, we again rolled. 5 teams arrived at "the Horn" about 6 o'clock, where the brethren were busily engaged Rafting over the Wagons. On our arrival we found that the River we had seen in the distance was none other than the celebrated "Platte," the highway of our future

---

[24] Here the "Horn" refers to the Elkhorn River, assembly point for the pioneer company; elsewhere it refers to the bugle used to awaken or assemble the company.   [25] That is, Papillion (Butterfly) Creek.

[26] The "Mormon team" referred to the men who banded together to pull a wagon out of a tight spot. See Bullock's entry for 29 September 1847.

journey, which caused joy & rejoicing in my Soul to my Heavenly Father. Cotton Wood Trees in full blossom, Slippery Elm Trees in leaf, also Willows. Elder Woodruff's teams crossed over [at] ½ past 6. In consequence of Indians prowling about, a Guard of eight men were detailed for night duty.

Sunday 11 April 1847—A smart breeze from the South, which turned into a very warm morning. All the teams belonging to the company were crossed by 20 minutes to 10, on a Raft, when President B. Young, H. C. Kimball, and Bishop Whitney drove up, & immediately afterwards some of the Wagons of the second part of the Pioneer Camp came in sight, when they were continued to be crossed over, and at 20 minutes to 4 the 72nd Wagon was rafted over, thus making 69 Pioneer Wagons, 3 return Wagons (72), 3 return men, 136 Pioneers, 2 Women & 2 children. When they were crossed over, they immediately started to their place of rendezvous, close to a timbered part of the banks of "the Horn." This morning I was informed by Orson Pratt that he last night took an observation by the Pole Star, & he found that our encampment was 41° 16 minutes North Latitude.[27] On the arrival of the last portion of the camp I learnt that Dr. W. Richards had his lead mare either strayed or stolen by the Indians. Present of the Twelve in Camp—B. Young, H. C. Kimball, W. Richards, O. Pratt, W. Woodruff, G. A. Smith, A. Lyman & E. T. Benson.[28] At dark President Young called for a vote of the brethren whether they would go 14 miles on their journey tomorrow morning, when the feeling was to go ahead.

Monday 12 April 1847—The night Guard called the brethren up by day break. When the bustle of camp life commenced, the brethren prepared their teams to go on their onward journey & commenced rolling out, while the Twelve & several others started out on their return home. At [blank] crossed "the Horn" at [blank].[29] Presidents Kimball & Young passed us. We staid at the old camping ground an hour to feed our team,

---

[27] As scientific officer of the Pioneer Camp, Orson Pratt used meridian observations of the Sun and the star Sirius in combination with the "altitude of the North Star" to make generally accurate readings of latitude. Lacking a chronometer, Pratt's few longitudinal readings made using a sextant were usually incorrect, as were those of the better prepared John C. Frémont. See Kimball, ed., *The Latter-Day Saints' Emigrants' Guide*, 15.

[28] Of the remaining four apostles, John Taylor and Parley P. Pratt were at Winter Quarters, Orson Hyde was on a mission, and the renegade Lyman Wight was in Texas.

[29] According to trail expert Gail Holmes, the Saints crossed the Elkhorn south of where Highway 36 now crosses the river. Erastus Snow reported he used "the old crossing" and that "Brigham Young and the rest of the company camped five miles up the river."

and at 20 minutes to 6 W. Richards & T. B. arrived at the office in Winter Quarters. After attending to our family duties Presidents Brigham Young, Heber C. Kimball, Willard Richards, Orson Pratt, G. A. Smith, Ezra T. Benson, and Parley P. Pratt (who had lately returned from his Mission to England) also Newel K. Whitney, Joseph Young and T. Bullock met in council in the Recorder's Office. Parley P. Pratt reported 469 Sovereigns were in possession, from England.[30] It was motioned that it be left entirely to the disposal of President Young—seconded & carried. Instructions were given concerning the return of American Elders who were on missions to England, several questions asked and answered, then President Young said "I want Thomas Bullock to go with the Pioneers, to keep history, and come back with the Twelve in the Fall," which all the Council confirmed by saying I [aye]. Other business was transacted, particulars of which, see the minutes (filed). At 20 minutes to 11 Council separated.

Tuesday 13 April 1847—All the Twelve (who were Pioneers) were very busy preparing extra teams to return to the Pioneer Company which were ready to start about 5. At 20 minutes to 5 T. B. left Winter Quarters (his Wife & children sick) with W. Richards' extra team, by way of the mill, thro' the Wood & encamped on the prairie in company with David Grant, at the Cross Roads in the dark. Pleasant Day. John Taylor arrived in Winter Quarters about [blank].

Wednesday 14 April 1847—A slight sprinkling of rain in the early part of the morning. Arose at daylight, fed the cattle, and while in the act of hitching my cattle to the Wagon, Four Omaha Indians came rushing down upon us, waiving their standards covered with Turkies Feathers, hallowing and yelling like Savages, which frightened my cattle [so much] that they broke away from the tongue & ran as if they were mad two or three miles in direction the of Winter Quarters. I [ran] after them at full rate, succeeded in heading and turning them back, after the loss of about another hour, during which time one drew his bow & arrow, threatening to shoot one of my oxen & another showing his gun. We had to allay their excitement by giving them our bread. They were not satisfied with that, but demanded more to take with them. After that was given them, one had the boldness to come to my Wagon & attempt

---

[30] Along with the consecrated wealth of the Saints and Mormon Battalion money, this contribution of the English Saints represented all the hard cash available to finance the 1847 Mormon emigration.

to take the front of my Wagon Cover to make him a head dress, but I repelled him & he went away in anger.³¹ We then hitched up & started on our journey. In about an hour afterwards we had a very pleasant light rain. Continued our route till we stopt to feed at the old camp ground about an hour, when we started crossed the "Papion" River, which bottom was covered with flowers.³² After another halt, we continued our route to the second creek where we encamped for the night. Directly afterwards, brother Rockwood & Lorenzo Young passed in the boat,³³ & we again hitched up to follow them to the Timber where we were told to camp. The President, H. C. Kimball, & E. T. Benson passed us about 6. When they encamped they made signal lights to guide us to their camp, where we arrived about ½ past 8. [We] drove our teams down the hollow & staid the night in peace. Pleasant day with a North Wind. Made a fire in the dry grass.

Thursday 15 April 1847—Severe frost in the night, skim of ice on the Water. About 8 we started again on our journey, arrived at the "Elk Horn," ferried over at 11 & commenced our journey to the Platte. Came to a patch of grass where we halted about an hour to feed, then started again. Crossed a bad mud hole where G. A. Smith's & my Wagon Stuck. Doubled teams, assisted each other out & arrived at camp 20 minutes to 5. After travelling about 20 miles [we camped] close to a Cotton Wood grove & a beautiful sand bank to take our cattle on to the Water. Professor Orson Pratt reports [blank lines].

At 20 minutes to 8 President Young mounted the front of his Wagon & called aloud "Attention the Camp of Israel" when the brethren assembled at his wagon & he addressed them in a short speech (see the minutes on file). Dismissed with benediction at 3 minutes past 8. A pleasant day. *From Winter Quarters 50 miles.*

Friday 16 April 1847—Attended to cattle, and other duties; at [blank] the brethren assembled together at the rear of the President's Wagon, & were addressed by G. A. Smith, H. C. Kimball, N. K. Whit-

---

[31] The Omahas had many and varied reasons to be upset with the Mormons. See Coates, "Cultural Conflict: Mormons and Indians in Nebraska," 293–96, for a summary of their grievances.

[32] Bullock again referred to Papillion Creek.

[33] This boat was called the Revenue Cutter and was "a skiff of sole leather which had been the property of Ira Eldredge, who carried his family outfit across the Mississippi and Missouri rivers in it." The pioneers named it (probably humorously) and used it from Winter Quarters "as a wagon box." See the Journal History, 9 May 1847. The Revenue Cutter was the boat Brigham Young spoke of on 7 May. He used it as a speaking platform for many of the camp meetings.

[THE NIGHT GUARD]

Thomas Tanner Capt.
Tarlton Lewis
Stephen H. Goddard
Seeley Owens
Thomas Woolsey
John G. Luce
Horace Thorrington
Jacob D. Barnham
Sylvester H. Earl
George Scholes
Rufus Allen

William Empey
John Holman
George R. Grant
William P. Vance
James Craig
Datis Ensign
William Dykes
John Dixon
Samuel H. Marble
Artemas Johnson

Norton Jacob
Addison Everett
William Wadsworth
John W. Norton
Francis M. Pom[e]roy
Lyman Curtis
Horace M. Frink
Erastus Snow
Hans C. Hansen
William A. O. Smoot

Barnabas L. Adams
Rodney Badger
Charles Burk
Alexander P. Chessley
Appleton M. Harmon
David Powell
Joseph Matthews
John Wheeler
Gilbert Summe
Matthew Ivory

Edsom Whipple
Conrad Klineman
Joseph Roder
Nathaniel Fairbanks
Ozro Eastman
Andrew S. Gibbons
William A. King
Howard Tanner Captn
John Eldridge
Hosea Cushing
John H. Tibbetts.
see May 4th.

ney, & B. Young (minutes on file). They were formed into a circle round the President & counted off 143 Pioneers. Stephen Markham and A. P. Rockwood were appointed captains of 100s; the Captains of 50s & 10s also. Stephen Markham then drew out for the night Guard 50 men.

The meeting then separated. Afterwards W. Richards dictated his Family Epistle & Presidents B. Young, W. Richards, & W. Woodruff heard read the Epistle to the Saints at Winter Quarters, which was signed by B. Young & W. Richards & sent by Bishop Whitney to President John Smith.[34] A Wagon passed the camp en route to the Pawnee Village belonging to the traders. [They] report that the Pawnees were within 40 miles of us, they had removed their village to that place. The

---

[34] For the text of this letter, which gave instructions on the organization of the companies that would follow the pioneers "as soon as grass is sufficient to support the teams," see Brooks, ed., *On the Mormon Frontier*, 247–250.

Warriors had returned from their hunt about 15 days [ago] & were about 4000 Strong. Professor Orson Pratt reports [blank lines].

Presidents Young & Richards sent to G. D. Watt (Scotland) for 200 ~~50~~ Phonotype (copy on file).[35] At 2 o'clock the Camp removed from their location, removed up the Platte about 4 *miles* and encamped again at 10 minutes to 4 near a Cotton Wood Grove, where there was a pretty good sprinkling of green grass, which the cattle ate with avidity. Also some rushes[36] that were in the timber, on the river bank & Island. Pleasant day.

Saturday 17 April 1847—In the night there was a very strong Wind, accompanied with Frost. When I arose found the ice on inch thick in the Water Buckets. The Guard complained much of the severity of the Weather & the brethren generally wrapt themselves in their Buffalo Skins & Blankets. After attending to cattle, orders were given to travel in companies of Tens. At 5 minutes past 9 the teams were hitched up & H. C. Kimball's Division led the road. [We] travelled over a deep sandy plain, surrounded on each side by Willows, high Weeds, & dry grass, and after travelling 8 miles we came to a halt at 12 o'clock, formed a line from North to South fronting a Cotton Wood grove on the West, all in line, at 12 minutes past 1. In the afternoon a bed of rushes was discovered, to which the cattle were driven & kept there until eve. Luke Johnson reported to me that he had seen some large mounds, as if there had been a great battle fought & the slain buried in them, about a mile from camp. One of the brethren found a nest with 4 Eggs in it, the birds pretty near hatched, which shows that Spring was getting advanced, also gathered some Kennekenek[37] & Prickly Ash. An Indian was seen on the South side of the River. The bugle was sounded about half past 5 [and] the brethren assembled round the President, when they fell into a Regimental column under their Captains of Tens, when it was *voted* that we act as one Regiment, [with] Stephen Markham, Colonel; John Pack & Shadrach Roundy, Majors; Brigham Young, General &c; Albert P. Rockwood, Aid, and Wilford Woodruff 1, Ezra T. Benson 2, Phinehas H.

---

[35] Clerk George D. Watt, the first LDS convert in the British Isles, introduced the Saints to a system of shorthand known as phonography; both its phonetic alphabet and type were called "phonotype." See Watt, "Sailing 'The Old Ship Zion,'" 56. This letter requested "that you procure 200 lb. of phonotype...to print a small book for the benefit of the saints." It continued, "we shall have a printing press and all common fixtures" at Winter Quarters. See the Journal History, 16 April 1847. This was the press the Mormons later used to print their Kanesville newspaper, *The Frontier Guardian*.

[36] Rushes provided excellent fodder for cattle.

[37] Kinnikinick or kinnikinic is a red willow bark mixture smoked by Indians.

Young 3, Luke Johnson 4, Stephen H. Goddard 5, Charles Shumway 6, James Case 7, Seth Taft 8, Howard Egan 9, Appleton Harmon 10, John S. Higbee 11, Norton Jacobs 12, John Brown 13, & Joseph Matthews 14, to be Captains of Tens.[38] Council was given the brethren (see minutes) & then dismissed. I hunted up & hitched all Doctor's cattle. After Supper W. Richards dictated a letter to G. D. Watt.

Sunday 18 April 1847—A slight frost in the night, thin skin of ice on Water. Cloudy until about noon when it cleared up. In the morning W. Richards dictated [a] letter to Robert Campbell & also to his family. I copied [a] letter to G. D. Watt which Presidents Young & Richards signed. I wrote to my Wife,[39] sent all the letters by Ellis Eames, a brother who was returning on account of his health.[40] About 10 [o'clock] Seven teams passed our camp loaded with peltry belonging to the traders who were returning from their trade with the Pawnees. Wind in the South East & cool—in afternoon clear & wind [from the] South West. Pleasant. The brethren kept this day as a day of rest & attending to their cattle.

About 5 o'clock P.M. as brother James Case was cutting down a Cotton Wood Tree, a sudden gust of wind blew it in a contrary direction, & in falling, one of the branches knocked the right eye out of an ox's head belonging to John Taylor. About ½ past 6 Presidents Young, Benson, & Captains of Companies met in the Grove when directions were given that at 5 A.M. the Horn should be blown & every man then arise & pray, attend to their cattle, & have every thing done, in order that all may start by seven o'clock. That each extra man should travel on the off side of his team,[41] with his gun loaded over his Shoulder; that each driver shall have his gun so placed that he can lay his hand on it in a moment; that every gun shall have a piece of leather over the nipple, or in the pan of his gun, having their caps & Powder Flasks ready for a moment's warning. The brethren will halt for an hour to have dinner,[42] which must be ready cooked. When the Camp comes to halt for the night, the front of every Wagon shall be outwards where the fires shall be built; the horses to be

---

[38] A monument in Fremont, Nebraska's Barnard Park commemorates the pioneer company organization.

[39] This note is not in the Henrietta Rushton Bullock collection at the LDS Archives.

[40] Some of the Saints interpreted Eames' withdrawal less charitably. According to Benjamin F. Stewart, Heber C. Kimball prophesied that Eames would "die spiritually" if he left the pioneer company. Eames was later the first mayor of Provo, but in 1852 he moved to San Bernardino where he kept "a saloon and gambling house." See B.F.S., "A Prophecy," 63.

[41] That is, oxen were to be driven from the left (or "off") side of the team.

[42] In the nineteenth century, dinner was the midday meal we now call lunch and supper was the evening meal.

all secured inside the circle. At ½ past 8 the Horn will be blown when every man must retire to their wagons & pray, & be in bed by 9 o'clock, except the night guard; all fires to be put out at bed time. All the Camp to travel in close order. These orders to continue in force until further orders. The Captains were also instructed to drill their men. At ½ past 8 the Horn was blown & each man is to retire to his Wagon.[43]

Monday 19 April 1847—The camp was aroused at 5 by the blowing of the Horn. The brethren went to prayers. Arose on a clear blue morning, but hazy in the horizon. Attended to cattle, at 7 hitching up & at ½ past 7 the Camp was mostly travelling. After leaving our encampment about a mile, we came to where a large battle had been fought among the Lamanites. For the distance of about a mile we walked thro' a compact mass of graves & apparently a fourth of a mile wide. On the outside ran a ridge of Earth on which were also a number of graves; some of the brethren report that while travelling yesterday they found a high entrenchment as if made to fortify themselves inside from the attack of some other people, & no doubt that this was the battle field. We continued our route over a level prairie, in some places very sandy. We passed several pools where the brethren enjoyed themselves in shooting Ducks & other Wild Fowl. The banks of the Platte [are] lined with Cotton Wood Trees, the South side of the Platte [is] hilly. We camped at 20 minutes to 2 on the Banks of the Platte to feed our teams [and] received a mail of 30 letters [brought] by John C. Litke & Porter Rockwell from Winter Quarters which were soon distributed to their owners. Porter Rockwell also brought W. Richards' mare which he had found with a Omaha Tug round her neck.[44] At ½ past 2 started again, when George A. Smith reported the death of Nancy Adelid, daughter of George & Nancy Smith, at Winter Quarters on Saturday 17th instant at 12 o'clock at night. We had a Warm afternoon, travelled *20 miles* & camped at ½ past 6 on the banks of the Platte. Attended the cattle until after it was dark. Lightning in the East.

Received a letter from G. D. Grant of 17th instant respecting Major Miller & the Omahas.[45]

---

[43] Bullock formally recorded these "Laws Regulating the Camp of Israel" at the end of Journal I, following the 18 June 1847 entry. See Appendix B.

[44] The "Omaha Tug" indicated the mare had been taken by Indians.

[45] Indian Agent John Miller disputed the Mormons' right to stay on Indian land. Grant's letter perhaps relayed Hosea Stout's report that he saw Omahas driving away Mormon cattle.

Tuesday 20 April 1847—Very strong wind the latter part of the night. Horn was blown at 5 to call up the camp [and] the cattle [were] turned loose to graze. At ½ past 6 gathered up the cattle, at ¼ past 7 the Camp started & soon passed an Indian mound, saw some Buffalo Grass. Crossed Shell Creek, where [there] was Timber on both sides. Then travelled over a level road, the ground pretty well covered with Green Grass. Halted at noon to feed, when the Wind changed to the West. In about an hour we started from the Pool & feeding place & continued to travel until 4 minutes past 6 when we again halted on the Platte [having traveled] 18 miles. Very little wood on the banks, the Timber being principally on the Islands. This was a warm day & made dusty travelling. I washed &c & then tended the cattle. After blowing Horn for bedtime, Doctor dictated a letter to Major Miller & another to Daniel Spencer & Daniel Russell in answer to a letter to Robert Campbell & G. D. Grant to President Young, which were taken to the President for approval, who on reflecting at the insulting letter of Major Miller to him, considered it not worth the while to write to him but gave orders for the other to be copied which was got ready for his & the Doctor's signatures. Doctor also gave orders for me to write a letter to Wm. Kay, which was done.

Jesse C. Little was appointed aid to Colonel Markham & sanctioned by President Young.[46]

Wednesday 21 April 1847—Doctor came & woke us up before the hour was blown to attend to cattle. I got up, herded, & attended to all the cattle. A cold East Wind, cloudy morning. At the second horn, the ox teams started, and in about two miles travel, we met the first Pawnee riding on his pony. Immediately afterwards several others came up & appeared friendly. They shook hands & so continued from Wagon to Wagon. A little rolling eminence was met with every now & then in the Prairie; at 25 minutes after 12 came in sight of the Pawnee Village, where the Pawnee Souixs [sic] were assembled with A. P. Sarpy & others,

---

[46] On 20 April, Bullock wrote to his wife Henrietta saying he had "washed my shirt and sox in the wilderness fashion." He complained, "Driving a 2 yoke oxteam is a different kind of work than I am used to and having to tend to the cattle myself, leaves me little time to read," but he reported that Brigham Young "has ordered me to ride as much as possible. I have just been in his carriage and a very comfortable place he has got and I am glad for it." See Carter, ed., "Thomas Bullock, Pioneer," 8:238. Bullock's respect for Brigham Young's privileges reveals the great deference the Mormons showed to their leader.

bartering their Buffalo Robes &c for Tobacco &c.[47] About 1 we found nearly a half circle round a bend of the River, to feed & Water our cattle, & during our halt for an hour, the Chief & a great many Indians came in. President Young gave the Chiefs some Powder, Lead, Caps, Tobacco, Flour, meal &c but the Chiefs were not satisfied; we hitched up our teams & came away.[48] My oxen were very much scared at the Indians & were very unruly, as was also some other cattle & horses. About 2 Thunder was heard, which was soon followed by lightning & rain, & continued to descend very prettily until about 4 o'clock, when a strong East wind arose & assisted to blow us forward on our journey. We had several sudden hollows & rises to pass in the prairie. We camped at 5 minutes to 6 at the North of the Looking Glass Creek,[49] as it runs into the Loup Fork, having travelled 15 miles. Immediately afterwards the brethren were called together & 100 called out to form a Guard for the night. President Young, Kimball, Benson, & the rest of the Twelve [were] on Guard [in] the fore part of the night.

Thursday 22 April 1847—I was called up at ½ past 12 & went on the morning guard. Cold morning. At the sound of the Horn, the Guard [was] relieved, when a beautiful morning came up with a North East Wind. A many Swallows flying this morning, also. Saw an Eagle's nest. Fetched up oxen, fed, hitched up. At ¼ past 7 the ox Teams started [and] in about 1½ miles we crossed the Looking Glass Creek, rolled over several small hills & hollows, passed over a high mound, on the top of which was an Indian Grave. This was a pretty view of the country on all sides; [we] then travelled over a level country covered with dry Buffalo grass & camped for the noon on Beaver Creek.[50] Presidents Young, Kimball & several other brethren went to work at grading the hill. At 10

---

[47] Here the Mormons met the legendary Peter A. Sarpy of the American Fur Company and encountered their first Pawnee Indians. After the Sioux burned one of their old villages in 1846, the Pawnee moved to this site on the Loup Fork west of present Columbus, Nebraska. The Mormons followed the Loup away from the Platte, returning to the river near Grand Island.

[48] The Mormons encountered the Grand Pawnee and Tappas (or Tepage) bands. The Pawnee chief Shefmolan was dissatisfied with these gifts and refused to shake hands with Brigham Young. He "said the whites would drive away their buffalo, and that the camp should go back, and not go on." See Roberts, *Comprehensive History*, 3:170.

[49] To the Pawnees, this was Quitooquataleri, "Water that Reflects Your Shadow." When the Mormons crossed it, the well-timbered Looking Glass Creek was sixteen feet wide and two feet deep.

[50] Near Beaver Creek the Saints established a trail station in 1857 that they called Genoa, the name the present town retains.

minutes after 2 [we] crossed the creek [and] travelled over a prairie; up a steep hill, & camped at the "Pawnee Mission" house formerly occupied by "Revd. J. Dunbar" having travelled about 20 miles.[51] Halted in the yard at ½ past 5, fed our cattle on Hay & corn Fodder, which the cattle seemed to think was very good for a change. About 6 P.M. as George A. Smith was watering his horse, he sprang suddenly, throwing George against the bank, the horse having his hind foot on G. A.'s foot, & his fore foot on G's breast, in which situation he continued until the brethren took the horse off him. It was very fortunate that the place was muddy, so he escaped with only a few bruises, having his life lengthened out & spared to him, for further usefulness. *We are now 133 miles from Winter Quarters.*

Thomas Tanner drilled his company with the cannon, putting them thro' their evolutions. Thomas Tanner, Stephen H. Goddard, Seeley Owens, Thomas Woolsey, John G. Luce, Horace Thorrington, Charles D. Barnhum, Sylvester H. Earl, George Scholes, & Rufus Allen form the Gun detachment.[52]

Friday 23 April 1847—Attended to my cattle & then filled up my Journal on the Hay Stack. Compared distances, Thomas Bullock & Horace K. Whitney making it 133 miles, William Clayton & Albert P. Rockwood calling it 134 miles (when this history is written out, get their Journals[53]). A delightful Spring morning: President Young & several others went to discover the proper place to ford the [Loup] River.

---

[51] Presbyterian John Dunbar spent the winter with the Pawnees in 1834 and established the Pawnee Mission near Plum Creek's confluence with the Loup Fork. Lakota raiders attacked the Pawnee village (located west of the mission) in 1843, killing chief Blue Coat and sixty-six of his followers. While the Pawnees were on their summer hunt in 1846, the Sioux returned to burn their village (then inhabited only by the sick and elderly), which forced Dunbar to retire to Bellevue on the Missouri River. See Jensen, "The Pawnee Mission," 301–310. One member of the pioneer company, James Case, had worked at the mission, and as he had not been paid by the government, Brigham Young allowed the company to confiscate items of value, provided they compensated Case. See Roberts, *Comprehensive History*, 3:171–73. For the troubled history of the Pawnee Mission in the mid-1840s, see Morgan, ed., *Overland in 1846*, 1:220–223.

[52] The pioneer artillery had charge of an 1812-period naval carronade mounted on a wagon box that was said to have been captured from the Missouri militia. The Saints called this short iron cannon the "Old Sow" in honor of the pig that discovered its hiding place. It is now on display in the Museum of Church History and Art in Salt Lake City.

[53] This comment reflects how clerks in the Historian's Office used primary sources to write Mormon history. The history of the 1847 pioneer company was ultimately "written out" after 1856 as part of the fifty-seven-volume Manuscript History of Brigham Young, now preserved in the LDS Archives. Clayton's journal has been widely published in several editions, while Rockwood's diary is in the LDS Archives, with excerpts published in Curtis, ed., *Compiled and Assembled History of Albert Perry Rockwood*.

They returned about 11 when all the Spare hands were called for, with Spades, Shovels &c to go & grade the hill down to a creek. I had now time to see the place. It [the Pawnee Mission] consists of two double log houses and six single smaller houses with pig pens & ashes cribs to each set, also two ricks of good hay, & a yard to enclose corn Fodder, several yards to enclose Horses & cattle, two fields fenced in with Posts & Rails where corn had grown last year. Also fruit trees & a beautiful little creek of Soft Water running behind the same, the whole making a very pleasant retired spot for a farm & where "Revd. J. Dunbar" Missionary at the Pawnee Mission had lived. We left this place at 10 minutes past 12 [and] crossed the creek.[54] (Very bad place.) In a short time we passed a large corn field without any fence to protect it, & directly afterwards left the Pawnee town with its corn gardens, descending a table land, crossed another creek, travelled on to the Loup Fork where several Pioneers were wading it, to find a proper place to cross our Wagons. Orson Pratt's carriage, H. C. Kimball's Wagon, Wilford Woodruff's carriage, & Wadsworth's Wagon crossed over as an Experiment but it was so very bad that we had to decline it for the night, so it was concluded to encamp for the night & make a raft.[55] The teams were again reloaded & started a short distance, when they fell in order of encampment at 10 minutes to 6 P.M. at a Bluff opposite the crossing place. A beautiful day & travelled about 6 miles. In the evening W. Richards reported that he rode thro the Pawnee Town about half a mile West of us & had counted the remains of about 175 houses which had been burnt to the ground by the Sioux Indians, while the Pawnees were on their hunting expedition, [and] also great numbers of holes that had been used for cashing their corn &c. About 8 P.M. the Presidency with the Captains of Tens assembled on the edge of the Bluff at the sound of the horn to take into consideration the propriety of making a raft to carry over the goods; when President Young suggested that there be two rafts built which was made a motion of by W. Richards & carried. It was then voted that Tarlton Lewis & Thomas Woolsey manage the two rafts.

Voted that Tarlton Lewis pick 10 men out of First Division to manage it.
Voted that Thomas Woolsey pick 10 men out of Second Division ditto.

---

[54] Cedar Creek flows into the Loup east of Fullerton, Nebraska.

[55] Treacherous currents and quicksand made the Loup Fork the worst river crossing on the north side of the Platte. The Mormons forded the river east of where Highway 14 crosses the Loup near Fullerton. In his 14 May letter to his wife, Bullock complained he had lost the sole of his boot "wading thro' Loup Fork."

[THE 1847 BRIGHAM YOUNG PIONEER COMPANY]

1st. Ten
Wilford Woodruff
John S. Fowler
Jacob Burnham
Orson Pratt
Joseph Egbert
John M. Freeman
Marcus B. Thorpe
George A. Smith
George Wardle
9

2nd Ten.
Thomas Grover
Ezra T. Benson
Barnabus L Adams
Roswell Stevens
Amasa Lyman
Starling Driggs
Albert Carrington
Thomas Bullock
George Brown
Willard Richards
~~John~~ Jesse C. Little
11

3rd Ten
Phinehas H. Young
John Y. Green
Thomas Tanner
Brigham Young
Addison Everett
Trueman O. Angel
Lorenzo Young
Bryant Stringham
Albert P. Rockwood
Joseph S. Scofield
10

4th. Ten
Luke Johnson
John Holman
Edmund Ellsworth
Alvarus Hanks
George R. Grant
Mellen Atwood
Samuel Fox
Tunis Rappelyee
Harvey Pierce
William Dykes
Jacob Weilar
11

5th. Ten
Stephen H. Goddard
Tarlton Lewis
Henry G. Sherwood
Zebedee Coltrin
Sylvester H. Earl
John Dixon
Samuel H. Marble
George Scholes
William Henry
William Empey
10

6th. Ten
Charles Shumway
Andrew Shumway
Thomas Woolsey
Chancy Loveland
Erastus Snow
James Craig
William Wordsworth
William Vance
Simeon Howd
Seeley Owen
10

7th. Ten
James Case
Artemas Johnson
William A. Smoot
Franklin B. Dewey
William Carter
~~Franklin~~ John G. Loose
Burr Frost
Datus Ensign
Franklin B. Stewart
Monroe Frink
Eric Glines
Ozro Eastman
12

8th Ten
Seth Taft
Horace Thornton
Stephen Kelsey
John S. Eldredge
Charles D. Barnham
Almon M. Williams
Rufus Allen
Robert T. Thomas
James W. Stuart
Elijah Newman
Levi N. Kendall
Francis Boggs
David Grant
13

9th. Ten
Heber C. Kimball
Howard Egan
William A. King
Thomas Cloward
Hosea Cushing
Robert Byard
George Billings
Edison Whipple
Philo Johnson
Carlos Murray
10

10th. Ten
Appleton M. Harmon
William Clayton
Horace K. Whitney
Orson K. Whitney
Orrin Porter Rockwell
Nathaniel Thomas Brown
Jackson Redding
John Pack
Francis M. Pomeroy
Aaron Farr
Nathaniel Fairbanks
11

11th. ten
John S. Higbee
John Wheeler
Solomon Chamberlain
Conrad Klineman
Joseph Rooker
Perry FitzGerald
John H. ~~Tibbetts~~ Tippetts
James Davenport
Henson Walker
Benjamin Rolfe
10

12th. Ten
Norton Jacobs
Charles A. Harper
George Woodward
Stephen Markham
Lewis Barney
George Mills
Andrew Gibbons
Joseph Hancock
John W. Norton
9

13th. Ten
Shadrach Roundy
Hans C. Hanson
Levi Jackman
Lyman Curtis
John Brown
Matthew Ivory
David Powell
Hark Lay ⎱ (Blacks)
Oscar Crosby ⎰
9

14th. Ten
Joseph Matthews
Gilbert Summe
John Gleason
Charles Burke
Alexander P. Chessley
Rodney Badger
Norman Taylor
Green Flake   Black
8

Clarissa Decker Young
Ellen Sanders Kimball
Harriet Young
Perry Young ⎱ Children
Sabriski Young ⎰

1 Cannon ⎫
1 Boat   ⎬ 73
71 Wagons ⎭
143 Pioneers
3 Women
2 children
93 horses
52 mules
66 Oxen
9 cows
17 Dogs

Voted that Stephen Markham manage the Stock & Teams in crossing, & the meeting then broke up. [See table on page 130.]

Saturday 24 April 1847—All up at the Sound of the Horn, when it was discovered that a favorite horse belonging to ~~Phineas H.~~ President Brigham Young & driven by John Y. Green was dead, it having fallen into a small ravine & the chain by which it was fastened to the post drawn tight round his neck, which had caused suffocation. The Captains with their men went to work to make the two Rafts in accordance with the votes of last night, while others unloaded some of the Wagons, carrying the load on their Shoulders down the cliff to the Boat which was then rowed over; the light loaded teams at the same time crossing the River at the lower crossing place. I was tending the cattle. Went thro' the remains of the Town which was about half a mile long. I will here observe that the entrance to these houses were invariably fronting the East ~~an assurance that they have a knowledge Masonry~~. Each house had its stable & 1, 2, or 3 Cachet holes close by.[56] The whole was surrounded by an embankment & outside of that a deep wide ditch as an entrenchment; some of the brethren went thro' their burial ground & saw about 40 Skulls & bones scattered about, no doubt dug up by the Wolves. I went up the high hill about a mile North & went round several graves on the highest tip.[57] There were also graves scattered about on the sides of the hill. From the top of the highest hill I had a very extensive view & could distinctly trace the bendings & course of the Platte [Loup Fork] for many miles; returning down the hill saw a beautiful butterfly. On my return drove in the cattle, fed, & hitched up. The brethren continued rowing the goods over the River in the Boat, while the light loaded wagons continued crossing at the Ford, until a pretty good road was made on the Quicksand, or more properly now called Pressed Sand; one of the Rafts floated down the River a few minutes before the last team forded the River. The last Wagon crossed over at 20 minutes to 3, thus passing our greatest obstacle on our route without any accident for which blessing from our Heavenly Father all the camp felt to render thanks & praise

---

[56] Bullock's "Cachet holes" were storage pits for corn.

[57] Vermont-born Randall Fuller crossed the plains five times between 1849 and 1860, in addition to participating in the Colorado and Montana gold rushes. In 1876, following the transfer of the Pawnees to Oklahoma, Fuller purchased seven quarter sections of land and established his ranch headquarters on this very hill near the town that bears his name, Fullerton, Nebraska. See Martin and Hunt, eds., "The Diary of Randall Fuller," 2–3.

to the Lord, & rejoicing at the prosperity of our journey to this place. Allowed the teams time to graze & again started on our route, passing the remains of a number of Wicka ups, travelling over green grass, & encamped on the South side of the Loup Fork at 30 minutes after 5 having a long pool & Wood on our right & a thick wood on our left. Travelled about 4 miles. A beautiful day.

Sunday 25th April 1847—The Camp arose at the sound of the Horn, attended to their cattle, and observed it as a day of rest, for meditation, prayer & praise. All was harmony, peace, & love, and an holy stillness prevailed throughout the day. The principal sounds heard were the tinkling of the cow Belles & the screams of Wild Geese as they flew past our camp. The Sky was beautiful with a South Wind.

About 5 P.M. the brethren were called together to worship the Supreme, when President Young called on the choir to sing "This land was once a garden place" followed by H. C. Kimball making prayer to our Heavenly Father; several of the brethren then spoke their feelings, & while G. A. Smith was relating the Prophet Joseph's instructions not to kill any of the animals or birds, or any thing created by Almighty God that had life, for the sake of destroying it, a large Wolf came out of the Wood on our right hand & walked very leisurely within about 50 rods past our camp; as much as to say the Devil & I are determined to prove whether you will practice what is now taught.[58] All the brethren saw it, but the meeting continued, & President Young gave some useful instruction (see the minutes on file). Dismissed at Sundown. At moonlight met again to organize a company of Buffalo hunters, when Thomas Woolsey [was chosen] the Captain—John Brown, John S. Higbee, O. P. Rockwell, Thomas Brown, Joseph Matthews, Amasa Lyman & Wilford Woodruff were chosen for the Horsemen—and Phinehas H. Young, Tarlton Lewis, John Pack, Joseph Hancock, Edmund Ellsworth, Roswell Stevens, Edson Whipple, Barnabas L. Adams, Benjamin F. Stewart, Jackson Redding and Eric Glines were chosen for footmen. It was then voted that the Twelve go & hunt when they please.

Monday 26 April 1847—The Camp was awoke this morning at ½ past 3 by the blowing of the Horn & firing of Guns, an alarm being

---

[58] The Saints used the term "wolf" to refer to both coyotes (*Canis latrans*) and wolves (*Canis lupis*), sometimes distinguishing coyotes as "prairie wolves." Bullock never refers to either coyotes or prairie wolves, but called both species wolves—though the "large Wolf" mentioned here is clearly *Canis lupis*.

made that Indians were near us; which turned out to be that John Eldridge, Levi Kendall, & Stephen Kelsey of the Guard were the persons who saw them. John Eldredge says he thought he saw a couple of Wolves coming to the Camp within four rods & determined to have some fun, run as if to chase them, when they rose up on their feet & turned out to be two Indians. He levelled his pistol but it did not go off. He then called to Kendall & Kelsey who fired their Guns, four other Indians having jumped up & run. A general alarm being raised nearly all the men were found to be at their posts, under their commanders of Tens who continued on Guard till Sunrise. The Horn was again blown at 5 for all to get up. Herded the oxen until horn blew. Drove in, fed & hitched up. The Camp was all started by ¼ past 8, the horse teams going first, ox teams last, making an entire new road, on the South side of the Loup Fork. Travelled over a Prairie covered with dry Grass & great many Prairie Daisies scattered about, both blue & White. The face of the country is now beginning to change, we had to cross many Sloughs & small ridges. The large trees disappear & instead thereof have small stunted scrubby trees & willows on the margin of the River. Halted at noon by one of the Sloughs where were a many small Fishes. In about an hour started again, having a West Wind & Blue Sky, a very pleasant day; in the afternoon small White clouds floating in the West. On our left hand is a continuous ridge of high land about two miles distant. On the other side of the River is a similar ridge. John Y. Green's team tired out in evening. During the afternoon crossed 98 trails leading to the river. ~~some conjecture them to be~~ Indian trails ~~but when they~~ in some places 28, 18, 13 in a bunch. ~~I conjecture them to be Buffalo trails going to the River to drink— as Captn. Fremont (I believe) reports such things very common on the Platte River.~~ We camped for the night on a clear stream of Water down in a ravine.[59] *17 miles.* In the neighborhood [we] discovered Buffalo tracks, hair, & dung. Some horses straying away too far from Camp, President Young called to the brethren to attend to their horses: he has frequently called on the brethren [to] "take care of your horses, they are straying away," &c. I herded cattle, & also assisted in driving in ten horses & mules. About 8 o'clock another alarm was given that an Indian was riding away a horse; the brethren flew to arms & horses, & several went in pursuit. They having returned unsuccessful,

---

[59] The Saints camped on Elk Sand Creek.

Presidents Young, Kimball, Lyman; and Thomas Grover, Joseph Mathews, Luke Johnson, John Brown, & about half a dozen others mounted their horses & went in pursuit. After travelling some distance, they also returned unsuccessful at ½ past 10.

Tuesday 27 April 1847—Early in the morning P. Rockwell, Jos. Matthews, J. Eldredge & Thos. Brown went on horseback to track the two lost horses, discovered both trails; where one had been tied up in a Willow Bed & pawed away the Earth some 6 inches. Followed the trail to within about 1½ miles of our Saturday night's camping ground; when Porter Rockwell thought he saw a Wolf, determined to shoot it, descended from his horse, levelled his gun to fire, which brought up the resurrection of 15 Pawnee Indians, who [were] running to seize his & Mathews' horses;[60] Rockwell first jumped on his horse & levelled his Pistol, which caused them to draw back. The 15 Indians were armed with Bows & Arrows & Guns, [and were] Ready for fight, but were bluft by the 4 brethren. The Indians got enraged, retreated about 50 yards, & fired 6 Guns at the brethren, sending the balls whistling close by their heads. Not being able to gain the two Stolen horses, they returned & fired the Prairie to purify it by fire. The Camp started at 8. Horse teams, then Second Division ox teams, & last First Division ox teams, crossed the [Elk Sand] creek, & then the dividing ridges of hills. In the middle saw some Aloes growing, also the prairie daisey & a many pink flowers. Found a small Chamelion, a pretty little harmless reptile. Pursued our journey next over some ridges of Land, not a tree to be seen, & at length was gladdened by a halt at ½ past 2 in the bottom where [there] was a plenty of green grass. The brethren set to work & dug three wells, getting to water which has a very copperas like taste. Having halted an hour, again pursued our journey until we arrived on the banks of goose Prairie Creek[61] [at] 6 P.M. where there was the best green grass we have yet come to on our journey. Turned our cattle to feed on the rich herbage. I caught a Mud Turtle with my hands. Directly afterwards a Storm came on—the wind blew very hard. All hands had to lock Wagon Wheels. The lightning flashed, the thunder rolled, but not much rain came. The Wind then changed from West to NE, the Storm going round the Camp towards the South. After Rockwell & Matthews had given the result of their mission;

---

[60] Norton Jacob wrote that the Mormons recognized these "15 naked Pawnees" as "some of the very fellows who came around where we halted down at the first Pawnee village."

[61] This watercourse is now known as Prairie Slough.

Colonel Markham came to tell President Young that one of his team was shot in the leg. It turned out that Captain Brown in pulling his coat out of his Wagon, pulled at the same time his Gun which discharged itself thro' the hind end of the Wagon, shooting the horse belonging to Barney in the near fore leg, the ball breaking the bone & lodging in the flesh. It was then reported to me that Presidents Young & Kimball chased an Antelope, which Captain Brown wounded, then Wilford Woodruff shot it, & which was finally killed by Roswell Stevens about 3 P.M.

(I had omitted in its order,) altho' making a new road, a deal of dust was raised & the Wind blowing from SW sent it along the line.[62]

After the horse teams had camped for the night at 5, President Young returned with several horses & mules to assist forward the ox teams which arrived at 6:30 P.M. 18 miles.

Wednesday 28 April 1847—Herded, Watered cattle, filled up my Journal. Pleasant NE wind—clouds in the East drawing vapor from the Earth. The grass is in good condition, 6 or 8 inches high, several violets & butterflies seen. The brethren engaged in grading the hill down into the creek, to ease the teams in crossing over; so that at about 9 o'clock the teams began to cross & be pulled over. Left at this place a small board giving particulars of our Camp to any who may hereafter pass this way; while the teams were crossing, Joseph Matthews shot the horse belonging to Lewis Barney thro' the heart, to put it out of its misery. It died almost instantly. About ¼ to 10 the camp started from this creek, taking a South Westerly direction, along very level ground, having the sight of Grand Island Timber all the way,[63] & came to its banks, to refresh our teams at ¼ to 3. Staid an hour, & then continued our route until 20 minutes past 6 when we camped for the night, a short distance from the Water, having travelled about 18 & 16 miles. Luke Johnson gave T. Bullock a bunch of 12 rattles, taken from a Snake which he shot yesterday afternoon, measuring about 4 feet in length & several inches in circumference. The Rattle Snake was preparing for a Spring when Luke so unceremoniously prevented him. The oil was taken out, rubbed on Zebedee Coltrin's Black Leg,[64] which did it a great deal of good. Presidents Young & Kimball

---

[62] Bullock again reported the company was breaking a new trail—"making a new road."

[63] This night's camp was several miles from the foot of Grand Island, which was covered with the last healthy stand of timber the pioneers would see on the prairie.

[64] This was the first of many Prairie rattlesnakes (*Crotalus viridis viridis*) the pioneers encountered. Coltrin's "Black Leg" was scurvy.

with several others rode on horseback ahead in order to pick the best Road; as usual—and altho' making an entire new road, the road was very dusty.[65] I can say the most dusty day we have had.

Thursday 29 April 1847—The camp arose at the sound of the horn to hitch up our teams & remove to where we could get better feed. At Sunrise [we] started on our journey & travelled a couple of miles when we halted to feed our cattle on the green grass. A beautiful morning. South West Wind—many bunches of the Prickly Pear growing about this place.[66] After staying about an hour, we travelled again about two miles when the Camp crossed Wood Creek, President Young directing the crossing.[67] There [we] saw fruit trees in bloom & Cotton Wood & other trees in leaf. [We] continued our journey over a prairie covered with dry grass. Saw a natural amphitheatre & an Antelope [and] came to a camp on green grass at 10 minutes past 1 where we staid an hour. On resuming our journey, some of the brethren put fire to the dry grass in several places to burn it; that those who follow after may have green grass for their cattle. There were showers on our right & left, & yet none with us. In the afternoon the Wind veered round to the North, which then blew pretty boisterous. The Camp came to a halt about 6 P.M. on the banks of the River Platte where we found a plentiful supply of rushes, the Cotton Wood & other Trees being in leaf. Travelled 20 miles.

Friday 30 April 1847—Camp arose at the sound of the horn, finding a cold North Wind but clear. Attended to cattle, hitched up & started at ¼ to 9 travelling over an uneven Prairie & with little grass on it. Came to a halt at noon on a clear little Stream, which, with having by far the best grass on its banks, may be truly called "Grass Creek"; it is pretty well supplied with Water Cresses, which are the first I have seen in this country.[68] A gravel bottom makes it about as pretty a place to camp as any we have had. The Hunters report having seen the tracks of Buffalo this morning. The Camp started again about 1:30 P.M. travelling in a Westerly direction over a more broken country: a very Strong North Wind blowing, & being dark, caused the Camp to halt for the night at 6

---

[65] This is Bullock's third reference to blazing a "new road."

[66] Although cornfields have replaced much of the natural vegetation of the prairie, prickly pear cactus can still be found in central Nebraska.

[67] The Mormons crossed Wood River about five miles west of present Grand Island, Nebraska.

[68] This watercourse has apparently been replaced by the Kearney Canal.

P.M. under a small Bluff without either Wood or Water.[69] The brethren dug 3 Wells & procured a dark colored Water for the cattle. Dug small trenches, used Willows & Buffalo Dung for fuel. One of the trenches most useful in this Shape: ▽‾fire‾▽

The fuel burnt well in these shaped holes. At Luke Johnson's fire I saw a Buffalo Skull made ~~for~~ a chimney—the smoke coming out at two holes between the horns, combined the useful & ludicrous. Here were found tracks, indicating that Buffalo have passed very lately, also calves' tracks. President Young gave liberty for the brethren to have a dance & enjoy themselves, as they had neither wood to warm, nor good water to drink; which they improved to their satisfaction. When they had warmed themselves, the brethren retired to bed. 16 miles.

---

[69] This camp was about five miles east of present Kearney, Nebraska.

Chapter 4

"The Tracks of Buffalo"
Kearney, Nebraska, to Fort Laramie, May 1847

The vast herds of bison that greeted the pioneers on their road up the Platte River elated the company and replenished their slim stock of food. The men reveled at hunting the beasts. "Several of the brethren mounted their horses, went several miles in pursuit of a band of sixty-five and then gave chase in splendid style along the mountain side in full view of our camp," Bullock later wrote. "The way they raised a dust was a caution to fox hunters—they were soon enveloped in a cloud, now and then a straggler was singled out and became a victim, and the sport was not ended until they had killed and secured eleven bulls, cows and calves."[1]

Modern agriculture has transformed the Nebraska prairie dramatically from the open plains of the nineteenth century. Vast reaches of corn have replaced the buffalo grass and prickly pear, and farms, ranches, and cities now occupy the sites of former prairie dog towns. Rows of trees create "shelter belts" that break the endless view, and irrigation has redirected and reduced the flow of the shallow, meandering rivers. The route of Interstate 80 closely follows the trail of the Mormon pioneers from present Kearney to Brady, Nebraska, where Highway 30 then tracks their route to North Platte. From Lewellen to Bridgeport, Highway 26 traces the trail closely, and picks it up again from Scottsbluff, Nebraska, to Fort Laramie, Wyoming.

The prairie fires the Indians set to freshen the grass for the buffalo left the Mormons with scorched pastures—and when the spring growth came on they found the vast bison herds quickly stripped the grass their animals desperately needed. As the Saints approached the forks of the Platte, "the prairie was literally a dense black mass of moving animals; that day I saw something like one or two hundred thousand buffalo."[2] By the middle of May the buffalo thinned out and sand hills pushed the company away from the river.

---

[1] Bullock to William, *Millennial Star* (15 April 1848), 116.   [2] *Ibid.*, 117.

Bullock began writing a letter to his wife, Henrietta, on 14 May that contains vivid details of the journey. The proud clerk reported, "brother Benson tells me I make a good oxdriver" and he was pleased to have "heard brother Kimball tell brother Brigham, 'Tommy has too much to do.'" He wrote, "my clothes are all getting worn out . . . Both my pantaloons have been ript from stem to stern." He reported, "This is the coldest, & most dusty journey I ever travelled; I wash my hands & face, some days twice, & three times, & yet I have been as dirty as a Sweep in two hours." Bullock also described the quality of the game that formed a large part of his diet: "I sometimes eat dried buffalo meet without bread, but if I do not lose some of my teeth it will do a good job. Buffalo meat, fresh, is far better than Beef—and Antelope is very good meat—having two Cooks, J. C. Little & G. Brown, we get a variety every day, & both being professed Cooks, we have it done up nice."[3]

During this time the Mormons devised a "mileage machine" to measure the distance their wagons traveled. Differing estimates (such as the ones Bullock noted on 23 April) demonstrated to William Clayton the need for an accurate way to record mileages. On 19 April Clayton discussed the problem with Orson Pratt "and suggested to him the idea of fixing a set of wooden cog wheels to the hub of a wagon wheel, in such order as to tell the exact number of miles we travel each day." Three weeks later Clayton tied a piece of red flannel to a wheel, counted the 4,070 rotations it made that day—a task he found "somewhat tedious"—and knowing that exactly 360 rotations equaled one mile, he was able to calculate that the company had traveled "eleven and a quarter miles—[with] twenty revolutions over." On 10 May, at the request of Brigham Young, Orson Pratt designed "a double endless screw" that was "simple in its construction and of very small bulk," and by the twelfth Clayton with the help of "the mechanical genius of" Appleton Harmon had constructed a "roadometer" and attached it to a wagon wheel. "We have now," noted Erastus Snow, "the distance counted off to us like clock work."[4] Although not a Mormon invention—"viameters" had long been used in Europe, Lt. George Stevens had used one to measure distances to the Rio Grande for the Army in 1845, and an Oregon-bound Quaker, Henderson Lewelling, had one on the trail in 1847—the device gave the Saints a way to describe the route with precision and accuracy.[5]

---

[3] Thomas Bullock to Henrietta Bullock, 14 May 1847, Henrietta Bullock Collection, LDS Archives.

[4] Snow, "Journey to Zion," 121.

[5] For a discussion of overland trail "mile machines," see Wright, "Odometers: Distance Measurement on Western Emigrant Trails," 14–24.

Despite the Indians, prairie fires, and buffalo—all said to be less troublesome on the southern side of the Platte—the Mormons chose to sacrifice convenience for privacy. The Saints continued to build their road on the north side to support their vast migration, despite the encouragement of a band of trappers they met on 4 May to cross the river and take advantage of the better grass and the easier, established road. Wilford Woodruff noted in his journal that the Saints preferred to "let the river separate the emigrating companies that they need not quarrel for wood grass or water." As B. H. Roberts commented, "the making of a new trail on the north side of the Platte was not a difficult thing" across the flat and dry Nebraska prairie, "and often the camp moved two and sometimes even four or five wagons abreast for the sake of moving in compact form."[6]

On 24 May the Saints encountered a band of Sioux, who Norton Jacob thought were "noble looking fellows." For people who had mostly grown up in wet climates and verdant countries, the land must have grown increasingly alien and strange; as they approached and crossed the hundredth meridian, the country was transformed before their eyes. They began to pass the great landmarks of the trail—all on the opposite side of the river: Ash Hollow on 20 May; Courthouse Rock and its attendant Jail Rock (which the Mormons mistook for Chimney Rock) on 25 May; and Scotts Bluff on the 27th.

As might be expected of a company of single young men, the pioneers were rowdy. By 28 May, Brigham Young had had enough and gave the company a tongue-lashing, which he continued the next morning. "For a week past," he complained, "nearly the whole camp has been card-playing, and checkers and dominoes have occupied the attention of the brethren, and dancing and 'hoeing down'—all this has been the act continually. Now," the president announced, "it is quite time to quit it."[7] Young blamed this behavior on the influence of the six non-Mormons in the band (exempting Benjamin Rolfe, but noting especially "those negroes [who] want to dance"), but he expected his pioneers to be worthy to find "a resting place for the saints where the standard of the kingdom of God would be reared, and a banner unfurled for the nations to gather unto."[8]

By the first of June, the pioneers had reached the Laramie River, where they would cross the Platte, visit the famous fur trade post at Fort John, and unite their way with the Oregon Trail. They were half the distance from Winter Quarters to the Salt Lake basin.

---

[6] Roberts, *Comprehensive History*, 3:168–69.   [7] *Ibid.*, 3:184.
[8] Jacob, eds., *The Record of Norton Jacob*, 52–53; and Roberts, *Comprehensive History*, 3:185.

May Saturday 1st—Commenced with a very cold morning, the wind blowing from the North. S. Markham being sick, John Pack directed the Camp to go by Tens, the Captains of Companies leading. Started by 5:30 A.M. About 7 saw three Buffalo's to our right, on the Bluff; when Luke Johnson, O. P. Rockwell & Tom Brown started in pursuit of them. The Camp continued their journey until ½ past 8 when they again camped on the bank of the Platte River. At the same time saw a herd of Buffalo about 6 miles ahead on the side of the Bluffs. Willard Richards counted 65, William Clayton counted 72, & Orson Pratt 74 by the assistance of their Telescopes. After refreshing our cattle, at 10:45 Camp started again. At noon crossed the mouth of a Slough, or rather the mouth of a creek where the Water had sunk into the Earth, [with a] considerable quantity of Willows growing on the sides. Immediately afterwards Johnson & Rockwell returned, reporting that Johnson had shot one thro' the Spine, but it escaped into the herd; & owing to the rugged country they were unable to follow it. About 1 P.M. saw another herd of Buffalo to the West of us, grazing at the foot of the hill. When the Camp arrived opposite the herd, a halt was called, when 11 hunters mounted their horses & got to the Eastward of them. At the same time one of the brethren shot at an Antelope, when a dog run it straight among the herd of Buffalo, which alarmed them, and away they went, raising a cloud of dust behind them, running along the side of the hill in a Westerly direction, then galloped the hunters down & along the hill in full chase; all enveloped in one cloud of dust. H. C. Kimball then started from the camp, joined the hunters, & shot down one of the cows previously wounded; now was a time of great excitement—every glass was in operation to see the chase, & every man was intensely anxious for the success of our raw hunters; this being their first chase. Still the Buffalo fly, still the hunters are in their midst & the dust rises in clouds above them, when some of the Buffalo rise the hill. Three are detached from the herd, which take to the plains. These are headed by one of the brethren, one stops suddenly, then pursues its course, followed by two hunters, who finally succeed in saving one of them. The chase on the side of the hill ceased about 4. The hunters returning to the Camp about 5, having killed & secured one Bull, Three Cows & Six Calves, being a good day's work for a set of inexperienced hunters. The entire

Camp were very glad & felt thankful to our Heavenly Father for a supply of food, which came at a very acceptable time, many being without meat. The Camp halted for the night about 6:30 P.M. & unloaded several teams to go & fetch in the meat. This day many Flocks of Geese were seen & we travelled thro' a large "Prairie Dog Town," suppose about 3 or 4 miles long & could not see the width of it. One of the brethren succeeded in securing one of these timid animals. I felt very sick—the severe cold Weather afflicted me much. 15 miles. Attended to the cattle, went to bed without supper, afterwards got some composition [tea]. The Wagons returned with the Buffalo meat which was cut up into portions, to be divided amongst the several Tens.

Sunday 2 May 1847—The North Wind still continues, cold, the Sky clear. Another Buffalo Calf was killed last night. It approached very near the camp & one of the Guard killed it. Brother Joseph Hancock returned to camp this morning reporting that he had killed & secured one cow. Some Wolves smelling the blood come to get some of it. One coming too near Hancock to be social, he shot it. After fencing it in with Stakes he started for the Camp but could not find it. He lay down on the Prairie for the night & came in this morning: all the brethren glad to see him safe. A Wagon was sent for the cow. This is the 12th killed. The meat being divided & distributed, the Camp was enlivened by the appearance of the Shambles.[9] The meat was cut up in strips & part dried over the fire to preserve it for future use. The hides were cut up into ropes & thongs & stretched between Stakes. The hair on the Bull's head was about a foot long & the hide about 1 inch thick. O. P. Rockwell had fired a ball at his head, which only made him shake it once or twice. On examination after he was killed, it was found that the outer Skin was broken & that was all—which is a convincing proof that to fire at the head of a Buffalo is only to waste Powder & Ball. About 11 President Young & several others went to search out another & better camping place; returned about 1. At ½ past 2 the teams were all hitched up & started. Crossed a ravine, then thro' another Prairie Dog Town. Travelled 2 miles & camped at the mouth of a small creek as it empties into the Platte River. Here we have plenty of good Water & feed for cattle, the Sky cloudy. Prairie set on fire by the Indians within two miles a head of

---

[9] "Shambles" is an English term for meat market or butcher shop.

us. This morning one of the Hunters saw a Buffalo, he was within 8 rods of it, but did not shoot it, because President Young gave orders not to shoot on the Sabbath day.

Monday 3 May 1847—As I arose up at break of day, saw three Buffalo pass the camp, on their way to the Bluffs. Sharp frost in the night. The Sun arose with a gentle breeze from the West. About 7 a very large Wolf passed the camp. Orders were given for 20 men to go out on the hunt, & 15 to go & search out a road & another camping place, while some were appointed to watch the cattle; & all the rest were ordered to stay in camp. The cattle were driven out, the Sentries placed. The hunters & others started on their journey, while the remainder attended to Washing [and] drying meat. Two Blacksmiths fixed their bellows & anvils, & repaired Wagons &c. Presidents Young & Richards in council in Doctor's Wagon. The Heavens began to be very cloudy and threaten like rain, which came over the camp at ½ past 12 in a gentle shower. At 2:20 the Exploring Company returned & reported that about 10 or 12 miles off, a drove of Antelope galloped by. When Brother Empy galloped round to head them, one took towards the River. Empey while in hot pursuit, turned his head in the same direction & looked down a Ravine & saw a War party of Indians about 2 or 300 in number: some mounted on their horses, the remainder ready to mount their horses. He immediately wheeled his horse, galloped to the brethren, who then retraced their steps to the Camp. On their arrival & making known their report, President Young called the men together, ordered them to gather up all their horses & go to the hunters; that they may return to the Camp in safety, which was done. The hunters returned about Sunset having Shot 2 Calves, 2 Antelopes, 1 Wolf. Hark Lay shot a Prairie Dog, given to T. B. In consequence of seeing the Indians, the Cannon was fired about 9 o'clock, to warn them we were prepared. West Wind.

Tuesday 4 May 1847—The cannon was fired again at 4 o'clock which awoke the entire camp. On rising found the Frost had whitened the grass, also a dew fell at Sunrise which made Wet Shoes. A gentle breeze from the South West. Several horses straying away, some horsemen had a gallop to bring them back. At ½ past 7 the brethren were called together, where James Case, ~~Stephen Markham~~, George Brown, William Carter, Marcus B. Thorpe, Jack Reddin, Carlos Murray, Albert

Carrington, John Y. Green, Alva Hanks, & Hark Lay volunteered to be the 6th Company of Ten for night Guard; & Green Flake & Oscar Crosby to fill the places of John H. Tibbets in 5th Ten, & afterwards President Young counselled the brethren not to leave the Camp 20 rods, without orders from their Captains. He stated that this Camp had travelled to this place with the best of feelings & told them all they had to do was to find out what was right & then do it. No man feels as he should do, unless he feels that we are as one family & feels for his brethren as for himself. We are all Stewards over the property committed to us & I am to see that my property does not go to waste, but convert it to a good use. We are not to indulge a man in Idleness, for there are some men who would not lift a finger or do a chore between this place & the Rocky Mountains if other men would do their work for them. Have a prudent, industrious Spirit & you will do [well]. I see the hand of Providence in our journey to this place, that no man has been hurt. Mind my Word for it, if the brethren will combine to straggle away from the camp, some of you, if not killed, will be stript & robbed & come naked to the Camp, or be kept prisoners by the Indians. You are sure to be ill used if not killed. Let every man have his guns & pistols in perfect order and the Tens all keep together. Is this right? (All said right.) The historians & clerks have been so busy that I have not yet seen a copy of the rules of the Camp. Have them read at least on Sundays. Now I want you all to recollect—don't leave the Camp without instructions from your Captains. The Pawnees would steal all our horses & use us up if they could. I want the cannon to go without the box—put the box on another wagon & divide the load in other wagons. The meeting then separated. W. Richards wrote on a board instructions for the next Camp. Saw many antelopes & several Indians. At 20 minutes past 9 started across the creek[10] & there halted until the cannon was put in condition & brought over, when the Camp moved off by Platoons. The 1st Company First, or all abreast, the 2nd ditto & so thro' out, the cannon bringing up the rear. When all the Camp was in order, President Young called out attention the Camp of Israel. First Company forward—& away they went in close column regimental style. A Camp was seen on the opposite side of the River. At noon we were called to a halt, Charles Beau-

---

[10] The company forded Elm Creek near the present town of the same name.

mont having come over & kindly offered to take letters;[11] when President Young ordered a letter of directions written to the Saints at Winter Quarters, which President Richards wrote & T. B. copied, signed by Young & Richards & directed to Mr. John Smith, or Alpheus Cutler (copy filed) [at] Winter Quarters.[12] I also enclosed a note to my Wife.[13] Made up a mail of 54 letters to Winter Quarters & sent [it] by Mr. Beaumont, who was going to Council Bluffs. Bread, Meat, Sugar, & coffee was given to him. He was very thankful, said he would not take 20 dollars for his presents & frequently begged not to be over loaded as he had got enough. Brother Woolsey, Brown & Pack went with him over the River to see the other traders. The Camp continued their journey over a burnt prairie, crossing a Slough where the cattle were watered, and at ½ past 3 made a halt where there was a little grass. Several antelopes seen in the distance. Colonel Markham drilled several companies of the brethren in Military tactics. Afterwards President Young called the brethren together to hear report of Brown, Pack, & Woolsey. Brown reported that Pappa [Pierre D. Papin] said the grass was good on the South side & [the Indians were] firing the prairies on the North side. If we continue on the north side we must ferry the North Fork. Brown has a knowledge of the road on the South side to within 12 miles of Fort Laramie. We can go on the north side as far as Fort Laramie, but the Black Hills stop progress on [the] north side. President Young motioned that we continue our journey on the north side, seconded & carried. He said if we crossed the River here, in order to get good feed for ourselves, when the next company comes it will be high water, they could not cross & would feel bad about it. At 10 minutes to 6 we started again. Saw a Buffalo flounder in the River; many Snipes & Geese. Travelled over a burnt prairie, having a South wind & halted on the banks of a Creek[14] at 7:15 having travelled about 11 miles. Fine evening.

---

[11] Pierre Didier Papin, Charles Beaumont, and seven other traders left Fort Laramie with three wagons and 1,100 packs of buffalo robes and furs on 20 April 1847. For Papin, see Goff, "Pierre Didier Papin," in Hafen, ed., *The Mountain Men*, 9:305–20. Although both William Clayton and Bullock believed Papin was going to Council Bluffs, the traders arrived on the Missouri frontier in mid–May, with six of the men arriving in St. Louis on 24 May. They estimated the total non-Mormon 1847 emigration at 400 to 500 wagons. See Barry, *The Beginning of the West*, 684.

[12] For this letter, see the Journal History of this date.

[13] This note is not in the Henrietta Rushton Bullock collection at the LDS Archives.

[14] Heber Kimball dubbed this Buffalo Creek, the name it bears today.

Wednesday 5 May 1847—On rising in the morning, saw one of the Doctor's cattle loose, which was fetched up. Saw a band of Buffalo in the West. A cool but pleasant morning, gentle breeze from the SW. At ½ past 7 the Camp started, crossed the creek, travelled over a burnt prairie, saw several Sloughs, & halt at ½ past 11 on a part of the prairie only partially burnt, opposite an ~~Brady's~~ Island. A very strong wind blowing from the South. Two Buffalo Bulls being a short distance from the Camp, Captain Grover & I went to look at them in their Native wildness. They allowed us to approach to within 40 or 50 rods, when they rolled off. At 5 minutes past 1 started again; when a band of Buffalo being ahead, the hunters gave chase & succeeded in securing 1 cow & 5 calves dead & President Kimball & O. P. Rockwell succeeded in capturing a fine Bull Calf alive, which will be taken to the Mountains.[15] Continued our route until we came to the Prairie that was burning like a roaring furnace. Presidents Young & Kimball thought it was wisdom to turn back a mile, to Camp & in the morning we can pursue our journey early. The teams then turned round & the Wind blew the ashes of the burnt grass in all directions which soon caused us to look like Sweeps. However by washing, after our halt, we were enabled to discern each other again. Travelled about 13 miles & 1 mile back again. Fine day.

Thursday 6 May 1847—A Shower of rain fell about 4 A.M. which damped the grass & partly extinguished the fire. The Wind also changed into the West. Our Camp started about 5 [and] passed thro' between the fires, once more getting on the grass, & a pleasant morning. After travelling about 3 miles, came in sight of a large herd of Buffalo. I had a shot at an antelope which brother [Jack Redden] secured & brought to Camp. Halt to feed a little before 7. In about an hour again start over dry grass, seeing many antelopes & about 10 or 15,000 Buffalo. A calf followed Luke Johnson into Camp & at noon halt it was placed in sight of its mother, by order of President Young that the mother might get it, but George Brown & another brother very foolishly went in sight, close to the old cow, when she started off & left it. The calf was afterwards seen caught by a Wolf & killed. At ½ past 1 Camp again move, seeing immense droves of Buffalo. 7 Buffalo run thro' the midst of the Camp.

---

[15] The buffalo calf was tied to a stake; it was dead by morning. Bullock later wrote, "We caught several calves alive; remember, catching a buffalo calf and a domesticated calf are two different things." See Bullock to William, *Millennial Star* (15 April 1848), 117.

In the evening we came to a cow lying down & tired. Many of the brethren went up & touched her. She had a very Wild eye, but had not strength to get away. I touched her back. The brethren got her up several times & she continued to lie down, when President Young told them to come away & leave her alone. The South side of the River is very green & [has] much better grass than on the north side, but we had rather go a little slower & continue making a new road on the North side for the future use of the Saints. Pleasant day. Travel about 9 miles [and] Camp opposite an Island about ½ past 6, hearing Wolves & seeing antelopes.[16]

Friday 7 May 1847—Arose at dawn of day, her[d]ed cattle, & on Guard until 10. Cold West Wind. When I was relieved [as] Guard by G. A. Smith, he reported there had been a meeting about the cannon when President Young had occasion to talk pretty severe to Erastus Snow, & requested that not more than one man should ride on the cannon instead of half a dozen. President Richards reported ¼ to 9. The brethren assembled at Head Quarters. President Young said there were are horses wanted to draw the cannon. I have procured a Boat & am taking it along for the benefit of the Camp, & have furnished most of the horses for the cannon, until my teams are so worn down that I have need of them all, & I want the brethren to feel a common interest in the welfare pertaining to the whole; & those who have horses that they can spare, to put them in to draw the cannon. When we left Winter Quarters there were four horses attached to the cannon; & I supposed that the Teams had been fitted up according to my instructions & was going thro' the Journey; but the horses have been since taken away & it has fallen on my hand & I want the brethren to furnish some horses to draw the Cannon.[17] Colonel Markham will put on a driver that will not let the men ride on it & kill the horses.

Let the Buffalo & Game alone & kill no more till we need it. I feel we shall want for Game if we don't take this course & the Camp voted unanimously that they would kill no more Game until they needed it to eat. I want to know if the Camp will take care of the cows, or whether every man shall take care of his own; or what they intend to do about it.

---

[16] The Saints camped near the foot of Willow Island, between present Cozad and Gothenburg, Nebraska. On this day, the pioneer company crossed the hundredth meridian near Cozad.

[17] Brigham Young's problem was quickly addressed, but his complaint shows how much the pioneers suffered from a severe shortage of draft animals.

Yesterday there was no one with the cows & they started twice to go to the Buffalo & I had to run my horse twice to bring them back, in doing which I lost a good telescope. I did not know then that Erastus Snow was the drover for that time. If I had, I should have known that he would not go out of his road one rod, he is so lazy.[18] I expect some of the boys will get caught by a Buffalo on the Prairie & get badly hurt if not killed, before the brethren will stop going after them. Don't dare the Buffalo, but let them alone; if the Buffalo should come in the night & scare our cattle & they brake loose & run they will follow the Buffalo & we shall lose them in all probability. The brethren must guard against this thing. Erastus Snow said that he had furnished some team for the cannon, had a team of his own to drive, that he had no cow in the herd—that after this, men might drive their own Cows & if any man could fix a charge of laziness upon him, or anything else wherein he had not done his duty, they might do it & welcome; & if I can't throw it off, I will bear it. President Young then said brother Snow was to drive the cattle yesterday. Snow replied, Yes, I volunteered to do it. The Camp voted yesterday unanimously that Erastus Snow was not in the line of his duty in not taking care of the cows. President Young said I will warrant the best man in Camp that undertakes to stick up his nib against the authorities that he will slide off like Warren Parish & Sylvester Smith.[19] Brother Snow apologized. At ¼ to 11 the Camp started on their journey, Doctor leaving another board of directions for future emigrants. We were in sight of Buffalo & continued in sight all day.

At 10 minutes past 1 a band had a race round the camp, first 7 then 4 & then 4, exactly as if racing for a Sweepstakes for a considerable amount, but after they had run round the Camp, within 15 or 20 rods of it—seeing it they halted to look at us with astonishment. The Camp had made a halt in order to see the end of their gambolling. At the same time some of the brethren caught another calf but let it go again. Green Flake walked up to within two rods of a fine Buck Antelope, before the Buck got up. I wondered why he did not kill it, but the meeting held this morning was a sufficient reason for not killing it. About 1 the Camp

---

[18] Snow believed Brigham Young's lost telescope was the cause of the "regular built dressing" here described. When Snow attempted to exonerate himself, "I drew from him a severer chastisement." Snow wrote that it was the first rebuke he had had in his fifteen years in the church, and "I hope it may last fifteen years to come." See Snow, "Journey to Zion," 117.

[19] A nib was the point of a quill pen, and Parish and Smith were noted apostates.

came in view of thousands upon thousands & thousands of the Lord's cattle yea the cattle on a thousand hills as the Scriptures speak of— surely the Fat Bulls of Bashan are here. At 3 the Camp halted close to an Island, where we found pretty good feed for the cattle, having travelled about 7 miles. The evening was very dull, cold & chilly & had a slight sprinkling of rain. Wind from NW.

Saturday 8 May 1847—Wind in the north West, very pleasant & clear. The cattle grazed. The brethren cooked & attended to their business & duties. I was on Guard until ½ past 8. One of the brethren caught a young Hare alive & brought it into Camp. After exhibiting it to the brethren it was again allowed its liberty. At 9 o'clock the Camp started thro' a prairie of deep dry grass for several miles. On the South side of the River the Buffalo was in one dense mass, several miles in length, covering the plain & marching towards the Mountains. Many of the brethren expressed their thankfulness that we were on the north side of the River, out of the midst of such an intense drove, but in a short time the Camp turned a sudden round of a hill & there were the thousands & thousands of Buffalo ahead of us, marching directly in our Path & going the same way as the Camp. There were such a mass of living blackness that the Van Guard could not see the Prairie beyond them. When the Van got up to them they marshalled themselves into one immense Regiment & had to kill a young cow (of course the best) that the report might scare them away & allow the Camp a passage thro'. At 5 minutes to 1 the Camp halted to feed. Between 2 & 3 William A. Smoot's horses ran away for the second time this week thro' negligence. Presidents Young & Kimball rode out & Thomas Grover & John Brown put their horses full speed to overtake them. They had run more than a mile in the midst of a large band of Buffalo before Grover & Brown could overtake them. They succeeded in recapturing the horses & bringing them safe back to Camp. Smoot had been told to hobble his horses by one of the brethren, or they would run away, when Smoot replied "dam you its none of your business if they do go." About ½ past 3 the Camp was again in motion & went over a country where the Grass was all eat up by the Buffalo & came to a halt at the foot of a Sand hill on the brink of a Precipice of Sand [running] to the River about ½ past 5 [having] travelled about 12 miles. The Bluffs here rise in a broken sharp pointed ridge with a very uneven ascent, scarce any grass & not a Tree or Shrub on the banks. In the small Islands there are some small Trees just coming into leaf. The Bluffs on the South side of the River are getting very precipitous & broken—they appear about three miles from the River. The plains being covered with Buffalo, about ¼ to 7 the Camp was all in Circle for the night. Cold Wind from the East.

Sunday 9 May 1847—Clear morning accompanied with a Cold South East Wind. Attended to cattle. At 20 minutes past 8 the camp start from this bare place, travel over a Sandy ridge, descend to the River bottom, where Luke Johnson, Edmund Ellsworth & 2 others caught a four year old Buffalo Bull & took him to the River to water him, Edmund Ellsworth driver & guided by the Tail by Johnson. After watering him [they] let him go, as he was not fat enough to kill. The Camp travelled 4 miles & camped on the bank of the River where was some dry grass & the Wood on the Island easy to procure. President Richards dictated a letter to Porter Dowdle, President of Saints at Pueblo & I copied same, when the Twelve met with Woolsey, Tibbets & Stevens & after a short conversation it was agreed they would continue with the Camp to Fort Laramie.[20] [At] ½ past 3 the brethren assembled round the Revenue Cutter, opened by singing "Come all ye Sons of Zion." Prayer by Amasa Lyman. W. Woodruff, Pratt, Lyman & Benson spoke (see minutes on file). Afterwards T. Bullock read the laws regulating the Camp & benediction by W. Woodruff. Afterwards I went within 20 rods of 4 Buffalo Bulls to look at them—[they] did not appear very wild. Made out an Epitome of this Journal for the benefit of the Saints who follow after (on file).[21]

Monday 10 May 1847—Very cold wind in the night from the West. Made out a copy of the Epitome also the laws regulating the Pioneer Camp, for the benefit & comfort of the Saints who follow after. Read same to President Young, who said, "that's Scripture." President Richards wrote a few words in addition, then sealed it up & enclosed it in a box, which was then attached to a twelve foot pole.[22] On the outside

---

[20] Roswell Stevens brought Mormon Battalion pay back from Santa Fé with John D. Lee and Howard Egan. Thomas Woolsey and John Harvey Tippets had left Pueblo in December 1846 and brought money and mail from the sick detachments to Winter Quarters. The Twelve were trying to decide what to do with Woolsey, Tippets, and Stevens, who were still enlisted in the army.

[21] The "Sketches from the journal for the benefit & comfort of the Saints that follow after," summarizing Bullock's journal from 14 April to 9 May is the first item in MS 1385, Folder 5, LDS Archives.

was written in Red Chalk "open this & you will find a letter"; on the reverse "look in this—316 miles from Winter Quarters—bound Westward—Pioneers"; on the Post "Platte Post Office." Close by the side of the post was left a Currier's Shop.[23] The letter was directed to C. C. Rich. At 9 o'clock the Camp start, 2nd Company of 1st Division leading. Went over an uneven prairie bare of grass, then crossed a small creek & came in the midst of an abundance of dry grass & a good size. When a Wild horse passed thro' our Camp, ~~Prest. Young~~ Thomas Brown & Porter Rockwell went in pursuit but were unable to run him down. At noon the Camp halted to refresh teams & tarried until ¼ to 2 when we left. [We] set fire to the Prairies, that the next company may have some green grass for their cattle. Crossed a couple of Sloughs & camp at ½ past 4 because the oxen in President Young's Wagon gave out. Travelled about 10 miles. This is a pretty camping place, the trees on the Island being in leaf, the grass just springing [up] gives a pleasing appearance. The Bluffs on the South side are getting sharp & rugged in appearance & destitute of vegetation. A fine young Buffalo killed & divided, also two Deer killed. One was run down by Trip, a dog belonging to President Richards, which was killed by P. H. Young & J. S. Higbee. A NW wind, gentle but cool. I was on guard from the time of halting to ½ past 7 when I was relieved by Dr. Richards.

Tuesday 11 May 1847—On rising found South breeze, pleasant, a dew on the grass. While attending cattle some of the brethren dug out a den of Wolves. There were 4 fine cubs in it which were brought out alive, but afterwards killed, to make caps. Dr. Richards found a Buffalo horn filled with a Hornet's nest and brought it to camp. He afterwards rode to the Island with an axe, cut off a patch of bark on a large tree & wrote an inscription for the benefit of the Saints who follow after. Brought up the cattle & at ½ past 9 start on our journey over the prairie with a short sprinkling of Grass upon it. Pass several Islands with Cedar & other Trees on them; halt on the brink of the River by a Steep Sand Precipice, in order to Water the cattle & rest a short while. When we continued our journey, turned the Bluffs, turning towards the North fork, over a Sand

---

[22] The sketch covering 14 April to 10 May in the Bullock journals collection has this note by Willard Richards at its end: "Let no man disturb this but the Saints for whom it is intended."

[23] A currier dressed leather after it was tanned or curried horses; what the pioneers left as a "Currier's Shop" is a puzzle, but it was perhaps a pile of uncured buffalo hides.

Road & camped on the Prairie without Wood or Water at 3 o'clock, but with much better grass for the cattle than we have seen the past week.[24] The brethren dig several Wells & get good Water. A. Lyman found a Skull, where could be seen the Arrow Shot, the blow of the Tomahawk & the Scalping Knife marks, which A. P. Rockwood exhibited to the Camp. Cloudy evening, South West Wind. I attended cattle & Tailoring. Travelled about 9 miles.

Professor Orson Pratt took an observation at noon & reports Lat 41°.7m. 44sec. North. Barometer stood at 27.125. Attached Thermometer 71°. Detached Thermometer 70°. Clear Sky. Moderate South Wind.

Wednesday 12 May 1847—At 5 A.M. Barometer stood at 27.136. Attached Thermometer, 44°. Detached Thermometer, 41°. Clear Sky, South Wind. Cattle grazed until 9 o'clock when the Camp started, going over a dark colored soil, with many patches of Saline deposit, more so than any place we have yet seen. After about two miles came to Sandy ground again. Watered the cattle again & proceeded on our journey. At ½ past 1 Camp halted opposite three small Islands in the North Fork of Platte River, where we found a pretty good sprinkling of Grass for the cattle, also a large nest in a tree, measuring about 27 inches in Circumference inside rim, which would fill a bushel basket outside. [At] ¼ past 3 Luke Johnson & Phinehas H. Young returned from Shooting, bringing the news of Indians being in the Neighborhood, they having counted 100 large Buffalos dead & Skinned, some having the Sinews cut out of the Flesh, other having had the thigh bones cut out & broken for the sake of the marrow & the Flesh left to rot. They left off counting at 100. Also saw a great number of dead Calves Skinned—a great waste of animal life.[25] Also saw Poney tracks & Indian & Children's tracks without number. These signs have been made very recently. At ½ past 3 the Camp start again, cross two creeks and camp at 20 minutes after 5 opposite several small Islands, finding a pretty good Sprinkling of Grass. Nothing but Willows on the Islands. Travelled 12 miles, according to William Clayton's Roadometer, attached this morning.[26] The val-

---

[24] The pioneers had passed the forks of the Platte near the present city of North Platte, Nebraska.

[25] Bullock's observations contradict the old and untrue platitude that Indians never killed more than they could eat.

[26] The "roadometer" and the accurate mileages it produced gave the Saints a tremendous edge when it came to managing overland travel. Odometer carpenter Appleton Milo Harmon saw a similar device attached to the wagon of the Quaker nurseryman Henderson Lewelling on 10 July at the Mormon Ferry on the North Platte.

ley thro' which we have this day travelled may aptly be called the Valley of Dry Bones from the immense number of Bleached Buffalo Bones. A young Buffalo [was] killed & brought into Camp. Lightning in the North West—Dark Clouds.

Thursday 13 May 1847—Very Cold, Wind all night. Horn was blown before 4 A.M. Got up, cold & raw. Cattle being loose had gone to graze. I then went up & travelled thro' the remains of a Sioux Town, it is supposed there were 4 or 500 lodges. Meat, remnants of Buffalo Skins, Mocassins, Halters &c were left behind, as if they had been recruiting with new & casting away the old. Found a pair of Mocassins in pretty good condition.

At ½ past 8 I assisted gathering up the cattle. At 9 the Camp start with a North East Wind cross the creek, travel over a loamy soil. At 11 A.M. halt to feed the cattle by the side of a Slough. Start again at about ¼ to 1 crossing the Slough & in some places [we found an] uneven road, with but little grass until we came to a wide River, full of Quicksand.[27] Three Wagons stick, but by doubling teams & the brethren assisting, they were pulled thro' with a little delay & welling themselves. The Camp was formed in nearly a Semi Circle at 20 minutes to 4. Cattle turned loose upon pretty good feed, after travelling 10¾ miles by brother Clayton's Roadometer. Presidents Young & Kimball rode ahead & searched out a road for the Camp to go over the Bluff,[28] tomorrow morning. Four of the hunters went in pursuit of a band of 10 Buffalo, but they getting the scent escaped from the hunters.

N.B.[29] Altho this is a river about 10 rods wide, there is no mark on the Maps, shewing that such a river flows.

In picking up Buffalo Dung this morning, I discovered a very pretty green snake, which I played with, on the end of a thin Stick. I was afterwards told that it was one of the most poisonous of Snakes.[30]

Friday 14 May 1847—Thundering in the distance, slight rain between 5 & 6, dull, cold, cloudy morning. Several bands of Buffalo run[n]ing from West to East. Brother Higbee reports having seen 32

---

[27] Brigham Young named this watercourse North Bluff Fork, but as the Journal History noted, it "is now called Birdwood Creek."

[28] This is site of the Sand Hill Ruts, an imposing obstacle north of present Sutherland, Nebraska.

[29] *Nota bene*—note well.

[30] Bullock had encountered a Green Racer (*Coluber constrictor*), which is non-venomous, but aggressive.

Indian Poneys over the West ridge of hills. About 7 a thunder shower coming on, the horn was blown to fetch in the cattle. I got nearly wet thro'. All took to their Wagons for shelter until it was over.[31] When the Shower subsided, the horn was blown again to gather up the cattle that had strayed away; went out again, hitched up, and started about 10 o'clock during the rain. Camp went round a hill, passing through a vale, Wild Sage seen on our route, also the Prickly Pear; turned round towards the River, going between the ridges, over a Sandy Road, & camped on the other side of the hill, at ¼ after 1 to refresh our teams for an hour by the side of a pool. Here were seen a curious grass—ring streaked, alternate yellow & Green—& also a deep blue grass.[32] There were many shells of mud Turtles scattered about. We again continued our route, dragging thro' some very heavy Sand spots & camped at ¼ after 4. After waiting about an hour, the Camp began to form for the night, intending to make an Eschalon, but thro' a little mistake, they formed the figure of, as near as possible, Ursa Major, or the Great Bear. Travelled 8¾ miles. Hunters kill an a Buffalo, Two Antelopes, & a Badger. President Richards gave me a Pen Knife. Wind changed from West in the morning, to South East in the evening. The 32 Indian Poneys as reported this morning were our own horses, that a few of the brethren had taken over the hill to graze. Saw a New Moon.

Saturday 15 May 1847—Rodney Badger having reported that while on Guard, he saw something moving, watched it for some time, and seeing it move quicker towards a Span of Mules that were chained together, close by; the Mules pricked up their ears & snorted. He then fired, when a man jumped up & ran away. Colonels Markham & Rockwood immediately called up those brethren who had horses or mules, to see that they were fastened inside the circles, which was done. The Wind blew cold from the North West, heavy clouds covering the Sky. I attended to the cattle. A cold rain commenced about 8 o'clock. The teams were fetched up and started at 10 minutes to 9, taking a winding course through a Mountain of Sand, which was hard pulling for the oxen. Where we descended from it was steeper than most house roofs and went with almost a jump. Here we found the most grass of any place this

---

[31] While waiting out the rain, Bullock wrote a letter to his wife, Henrietta, now in the LDS Archives.

[32] Dominant grass species on the mixed-grass prairie of the North Platte are Little bluestem (*Andropogan scoparius*) and Side-oats grama (*Bouteloua curtipendula*).

journey. Halted the Wagons & turned the cattle out to graze at 10 minutes to 10, the rain falling all the while. Staid until 20 minutes after 12 when it ceased raining & the Camp again pursued its journey over the bottom, arriving at a camp ground at 20 minutes after 4. We had to Camp here because the Explorers report that the Buffalo have eat up all the grass ahead. The brethren dig several wells from 3 to 4 feet deep & procure water. Many Buffalo seen. Cloudy, Wind from the North, cold. The Buffalo killed last night was divided into 14 Portions & distributed before the Camp started this morning. Another Buffalo [was] killed and brought into Camp this evening. 7 miles.

Sunday 16 May 1847—At Cock Crow, the Horn blew, arose; cold morning, but pleasant. Wind in the north, clear Sky. Ice seen in several places. An antelope killed this A.M. This day was a day of purifying, nearly all the brethren were engaged in Washing. In afternoon rather cloudy. At 4 P.M. a Band of Buffalo being seen coming from the Bluffs among the horses, Eric Glines went out to drive them away & shot a fat one. He afterwards shot three successive times at him. After he was Skinned it was discovered that the first ball had passed thro' the heart, the ball falling inside the bag. While the brethren were skinning him the time for meeting had come; I having seen him, being a fine old bull, weighing about 800 pounds. The hair on his forehead was about a foot long and very shaggy—[the men] then returned to camp & found Stephen Markham exhorting the brethren to their duty; followed by A. P. Rockwood on the same subject. Then Elder Kimball got into the Boat & testified that he had travelled in many Companies; that he was in the Zion's Camp that went up to Missouri in 1834,[33] but he never was in a Camp or company that behaved themselves better than this Camp. These Pioneers were like clay in the hands of the Potter; they could be made into any thing that the Potter wanted to make of them; and said that the Lord was blessing us, and would bless us on this journey; that His Angels went before us & guided & directed us. After he had finished I read the laws to regulate the Camp. Afterwards brothers Markham & Rockwood made a few remarks on them & the congregation was dismissed by Brother Rockwood giving the benediction. The cattle were

---

[33] "Zion's Camp" was a Mormon paramilitary organization that marched from Kirtland, Ohio, to Missouri in 1834. Although the effort to support LDS interests in Missouri was a failure, many future church leaders, including all of the original Twelve Apostles, were drawn from those who participated in the march.

then brought to the Camp and tied for the night. Cold, frosty morning, NW wind.

Monday 17 May 1847—Horn blown at day break, arose, loosed the cattle; cold frosty morning, NW wind. Copied the extracts from Journal for the benefit and comfort of the Saints that follow. Appleton Harmon made a letter box, Elder Richards made up the mail & directed it to "C. C. Rich & Compy." On the reverse "North Fork Letter Box" May 17, 1847 ½ past 7 AM" & fixed it in the ground,[34] at which time the Camp again resumed their journey, over a black loamy soil, until we came to the Bluffs of Sand. Crossed "Spring Creek" named by President Young. At the crossing place, the brethren had graded both sides of the Ravine, thro' which it ran. On ascending the West side of it I gathered a bouquet of Sweet smelling flowers for President Richards. Went thro' a vale round the Bluffs, in which were several deep ravines & holes & descended by a couple of Gates, or steep jumping places; came to the bottom where was good grass & clear water, watered the cattle, & continued our journey over an uneven bottom until 20 minutes to 12 when the camp halted & refreshed teams. Warm day, Clear Sky. Roswell Stevens caught a young Fawn, which Lorenzo Young will endeavour to rear. A horse belonging to Phinehas H. Young got mired, the brethren got ropes and after some difficulty, they got him out. The cattle had good grass at this place. Saw a large Water Snake. At 20 minutes to 2 the Camp again pursued their journey, crossing two or three creeks and marshy places. At 20 minutes to 4 the Camp halted to divide 2 Buffalo & an Antelope & send on the Revenue Cutter to bring in more Buffalo. Presidents Young, Kimball & others went on ahead to explore a road for the Camp. The cattle were turned loose to eat, the meat was skinned & divided, and at 25 minutes to 5 the Camp started again. Went under the foot of the Bluffs, crossing several Water courses & Mud holes, pulling thro' two Sand hills. The rest of the journey [was] over a Black Loam surface, and halt at 10 minutes to 6 in a circle, about a mile from the River, having travelled 12¾ miles. A Warm afternoon, clear Sky. At our camping place, we found plenty of good grass for feed & some Water about a ¼ of a mile North of the Camp. The brethren dig 3 Wells & get excellent Water at 4 feet deep. The Soil is rich for about two feet, then a

---

[34] For extracts (or a copy) of Bullock's journal left at the "North Fork Post Office" on this date, see MS 1385, Folder 5, at the LDS Archives.

hard pan, (white) in some places, & gravel in others. At Sundown the Revenue Cutter brought in another Buffalo & Antelope.

Tuesday 18 May 1847—A beautiful morning and Clear Sky. The cattle were grazing and did well. At 25 minutes past 8 the Camp continued its line of March, going towards the River. Crossed two small creeks, travelled over a dark colored Soil with a short distance of a Sand ridge. On the South side of the River, the Bluffs come close to the River and were dotted with Pine trees and Cedars. The River then crosses over to the North Bluffs and we halted for noon near the Bluffs. About 11 o'clock clouds began to gather & about ¼ to 12 Showers were seen to fall ahead of us, moving from SW to NE at noon thundering with light showers. While crossing a Shallow Creek (opposite Cedar Bluffs) this morning President Young rode a short distance up it on horseback, heard a snake's rattle, his horse stept a little on one side. Brother Thomas Woolsey following on foot, the Snake made a jump at him, and reached to within a few inches of his foot. Brother Young then told brother Higbee to fire, which he did, cutting off the Snake's head. It measured about 4½ feet & had on seven rattles, and one had fallen off. He then kicked the snake into the creek; when President Young named it "Rattle Snake Creek."[35] After the cattle had grazed about an hour, they were hitched up & the Camp again pursued its journey by the side of the River & then again steering in the direction of the Bluffs. Several Buffalos seen each side of the River & a Stork wading in the River near some small Islands. The Camp crossed over and halted for the night at ¼ to 6 on the junction of two small creeks of beautiful Water, having travelled 15¾ miles. Immediately afterwards Orson Pratt & William Clayton met in Dr. Richards' Wagon, and a consultation took place about delineating the Pioneer Road on the Topographical map sent by Colonel Kane[36] to President Young, when it was decided that brother Clayton should get Professor Pratt's observations that he had taken; then the course of the Road by brother Clayton's measurement showing the Bluffs & each creek as we found them, in order; also affix the names that should be given to the different creeks & prominent places. Professor Pratt reports that at noon, by an observation of the Sun, we were in Latitude 41° 13' 44"

---

[35] This creek and the section of the Mormon trail that crossed it is now buried beneath the waters backed up by Kingsley Dam to form Lake McConaughy.

[36] This is Thomas L. Kane, ally of the Saints.

North & brother Clayton reports that we are now 69½ miles from the Junction of the North and South Forks—according to measurement by his Roadometer. 333 miles from W.Q. [to the] Junction: Total 402½ miles this night.

The cattle were gathered up at dusk & immediately the brethren were called together to the centre of the ring & were addressed by Colonels Markham & Rockwood. In order to get the brethren to do as they would be done by a man & put away the selfish principle of a man bringing up his own cattle & leaving his brother's horse or ox, for fear of walking ten rods, to save his brother one, two, or three miles journey after it—when it was unanimously voted that from this time the brethren would drive in all the cattle and horses at one time, and it was also voted that four out of each ten should go at the Sound of the Horn for that purpose. President Young then stated that the Captains of Tens ought not to leave their companies, without appointing a man to act in his absence & that they must travel by companies; & then dismissed the brethren telling them to go and behave themselves.

I was informed that President Young called the Captains together about ½ past 7 (I was on guard) & reproved all the brethren who had been wasting their shot & Powder & reproved the horsemen for wasting the strength of their horses, without benefiting the Camp. Some had been murmuring about their meat, while at the same time a great deal had been wasted & ordered that no more Game be killed until it was needed.

Wednesday 19 May 1847—Rain [a]bout midnight till morning, horn was blown at ½ past 4 to arise. Found a dark cloudy morning. Easterly wind. The grass very wet; not being much feed, the cattle were gathered up and at ½ to 6 started iggledy piggledy, or in no order thro' tall dried grass, until 25 minutes past 6 when the Camp halted near several small Lakes and Streams of Clear Water. Some places were marshy—many ducks about on the ponds &c on the South side of the River, several Trees, & very green Shrubs are growing luxuriantly. The Explorers go to search out a Road thro' the Bluffs. After their return, the cattle again gathered, in a shower of rain, and at 10 minutes to 9 start over a Sand plain. At ¼ to 10 cross "Wolf Creek" in two places (it was called Wolf Creek from the circumstance of several Wolves chasing

Elder Kimball while searching out a road for the camp) and commence ascending the mountains, which was the most difficult of any to cross over. Pass a circuitous route thro' it and again descend to the bottoms, where the Camp crossed another creek. Found some grass and at 11 minutes to 11 halt & turn out cattle to graze, the rain continuing all the time. ~~at 3 o'clock~~ The rain ceased, when the cattle were again hitched up, & at 3 o'clock the Camp was again under way, in order to find good feed. At ¼ past 4 halted for the night on the bank of the River & a creek running at our rear. I then made a tracing of Fremont's route & the North Fork, from the Junction to beyond Fort Laramie.[37] Travelled 8 miles. Swallows flying.

Dr. Richards read game of Chess with Buonapart to B. Young, H. C. Kimball, A. Lyman, W. Woodruff & E. T. Benson in Doctor's Wagon, at dark.

Thursday 20 May 1847—Cloudy morning with a North Breeze. I was on guard part of the morning. The cattle were gathered up and at 10 minutes to 8 Camp again moved on their journey. Crossed a creek and a Slough as they empty into the Platte opposite an Island. Continued our course a short distance from the River. In some places the ground was very Springy, rocking like a Cradle, in other places firm ground, with a thin tall sprinkling of grass. At ¼ past 10 passed a lone Cedar Tree having in it the body of an Indian Child. It was wrapped in a thin wrapper of Straw, then a wrapper of deer Skin—also a second deer Skin covered with a Buffalo Robe, & lashed to the Tree with Raw Hide bands. It had two Spoons, a Horn & Shot Pouch attached to it. A very cold morning. I suffered much from the effects of the cold Weather. At 25 minutes to 11 halted for noon on a patch of tall grass, thinly scattered. On the South side the Bluffs begin to have a Rocky appearance & are more Bold than they have been and have Cedar & Pine Trees scattered about on the sides: & directly opposite our halting ground in a Wide Chasm [were] several White Ash Trees. Three Islands a little to the West have Cedar Trees on them. The Revenue Cutter went over with L. Johnson, J. Brown, A. Lyman & O. Pratt & brought back branches of Mountain Cherry; &

---

[37] Early in 1845, Stephen Douglas sent the Saints Frémont's *Report of the Exploring Expedition to the Rocky Mountains in the Year 1842, and to Oregon and North California in the Years 1843–'44* and its map, but Bullock apparently used the seven-part "Topographical map" provided by Thomas Kane that the Senate issued in 1846. William Clayton had tried to record the pioneer company route on it the day before, but found that Frémont's map did "not agree with my scale nor Elder Pratt's calculations." Neither Pratt nor Frémont were able to calculate longitude accurately.

a Medicinal Shrub, a canker medicine; in flowers, the Wild Currant with fruit on, Rose tree with berries on, a branch of the blue Bells and also report it to be the Ash Valley where the Oregon trail comes down to the North Fork.[38] They saw a large quantity of grape vines in blossom & the grave of an Oregon Emigrant that brother Brown assisted to bury last year.[39] The Rocks are a Soft Limestone & abrupt. At 10 minutes to 2 the Camp again pursued its journey, nearly following the course of the River. About 5 [we saw] several Showers ahead of us. We crossed a large stream of Water & named it "Castle Bluff River,"[40] passed full of Quicksand, but the brethren rushed the teams thro' at a rapid rate and in quick succession, thereby getting thro' safely & making the road better for the last teams. Then came upon a road having sweet smelling herbs on it. The Rocks on the South side have much the appearance of Castellated Towers and look very handsome and romantic. One was expressed to be like Solomon's Temple and are named "Castle Bluffs." [At] ½ past 5 a Shower passes over the Camp and at ¼ to 6 the Camp came to a halt for the night, near the River, having plenty of water, feed and wood. During the formation of the Circle I saw a large striped Snake, which was thrown out of our road, and out of the reach of harm.[41] Travelled 15¾ miles.

Friday 21 May 1847—Opened with a very pleasant morning, scarce any Wind, & that in the South. Clear Sky. I commenced making a Synopsis of the Pioneer Journal for Dr. Richards, at 7 minutes to 8 halt. Camp started in nearly the centre of the Valley [with] the Bluffs on the South side of the River running very near the River. Many Swallows and other birds flying about. Crossed some marshy places. The remainder of the road appears clayey. At 20 minutes after 11 the Camp halts to feed the teams in pretty good grass. While Presidents Young & Kimball were riding a head, they saw five cub Wolves, succeeded in killing two, while three escaped to their den. When the camp halted, the brethren went to dig them out, but were unsuccessful. At 35 minutes after 1 Camp again

---

[38] The main branch of the Oregon Trail, which left the South Platte at California Hill, reached the south side of the North Platte at Ash Hollow.

[39] John Brown left no account of this emigrant's demise in his autobiography.

[40] The Sioux called Blue Water Creek (now sometimes simply called Blue Creek), west of present Lewellen, Nebraska, Mini-to-Wakpala. Near this spot in 1855, General William S. Harney earned the sobriquet "Squaw Killer" for leading the assault that killed eighty-six Brule Sioux in revenge for their part in the Grattan "massacre" of the previous year.

[41] This was likely either a Common garter (*Thamnophis sirtalis*) or a Plains garter (*Thamnophis radix naydeni*) snake.

pursues its course, principally thro' dry grass, in some places deep. This afternoon we had several Frog Symphonies in different Sloughs as we passed along. Went over a gentle Bluff, then crossed a dry Creek where Dr. Richards found a petrified Bone of some large animal. T. Grover reports it the Bone next to the Shoulder Bone & must have belonged to an animal much larger than the Elephant. Directly afterwards two Indians of the Sioux nation rode up to Camp—several others were seen peeping over the edge of the hill. At ½ to 6 the Camp halted for the night having travelled 15½ miles. Small clouds in the horizon, pleasant day. After Sunset a full Frog Symphony, full of music & variety. The Prairie set on fire by the brethren.

Forenoon 7¾ [+] P.M. 7¾ [=] 15½.

Saturday 22 May 1847—Very Pleasant morning, clear Sky [with a] gentle breeze from South East. Dr. Richards measured the Bone 17¼ inches long, 11 wide, 6 thick, inferior 5, weight 27 pounds. He then buried it, placing beside it a board written "Mammoth Bone Encampment 21 & 22 May 1847 Pioneers" [and] on the reverse "All well, Sioux Indians seen here."[42] Left this camping ground at ¼ past 8. After travelling a short distance passed thro' a large patch of dry weeds about 7 feet high, then [at] 9:20 [crossed] over a dry creek. Continued our road near the Bluffs and passed thro' a "dry creek" about 3 rods wide [and] continued our route nearer to the Bluffs. About 11:50 o'clock crossed another shallow creek about 20 or 25 or 30 feet wide, then travelled within a fourth of a mile & called [the site] "Crab Creek" [where we] camped near a bold Bluff.[43] On the South side of the River on the top of the Bluffs was a Grove of Trees, appearing to be Cedar or Pine. We camped in two different divisions on account of feed being rather scarce. At 11:37 staid for our noon halt until 1:45 when the camp again got under motion, continuing our route near the Bluffs, passing thro' a very large patch of Artemesia Southern Wood, succeeded by a great quantity of the Prickly Pear, then pulled over several ridges and valleys of Sand; then commenced ascending a high hill, between two Pyramids, the nearest to the River called "Gravell Point," during which time there was a

---

[42] Willard Richards' identification of the fossil shows the surprising scientific knowledge and sophistication of the Saints. Fossils of the remarkable prehistoric fauna of the Platte Valley are displayed at Scotts Bluff and Agate Fossil Beds national monuments.

[43] Named by the Mormons, Crab Creek flows through present Lisco, Nebraska.

Hare Hunt parallel with our line of March. Elder A. Lyman ascended a large steep Rock on horseback, exactly [im]personating Napoleon Buonaparte crossing the Alps, & the teams pulling up the steep hill, much represented the crossing of "the Great St. Bernard" in Europe.[44] After a toilsome march, [we] succeeded in getting over without doubling teams. Then was presented to our view a splendid view of some Rocks, having the appearance of Round & Square Towers, Castles, Obelisks, Chimneys, & all the appearance of Ancient Ruins which we named Ancient "Bluff Ruins" was given to the Rocks by President Young.[45] At the same time there was a thunder & lightning, [and a] shower of rain passing in the distance from South to North. On rounding and descending the Bluffs, came in full view of the "Chimney Rock" on the South Side of the River, several miles to the West of us.[46] I killed a Rattlesnake with seven rattles on, then descended a Sand hill, twice crossing the Sandy Bed of a River about three rods wide, coming to the bottoms again within 20 rods of the River. About 5:50 [we] continued along the bottom until 6 P.M. when the Circle was forming for the night, between "Ancient Ruins" and the River. George R. Grant caught on the top of one of the apparent Square Towers and brought into Camp a young Grey Eagle, measuring 46 inches between the tips of his Wings. The nest on the top of a Cedar Tree he said was more than 3 feet in diameter. He saw the two Old Eagles flying about. Luke Johnson killed 3 Rattle Snakes having 4, 8, & 12 rattles on [and] gave them to me. Dr. Richards then had the bunch of 12 rattles. At Sunset another heavy thunder Shower approaching the camp from the South East, the lightning being vivid & forked. A terrible yellow looking cloud threatens hard what we are to expect, but it passed a little East of the Camp.

Sunday 23 May 1847—Opened with a clear Sky and very warm morning. I was on guard till 10 when the horn was blown to gather in the cattle. When they were taken in, I found that all of the Twelve had

---

[44] Lyman was mimicking the famous painting "Napoleon on Mount St. Bernard" by the French artist Jacques-Louis David (1748–1825).

[45] The site about five miles southeast of Broadwater, Nebraska, is still so-named and can be viewed from a historical marker about a mile and a half east on U.S. 26.

[46] Earlier in the day, Porter Rockwell climbed Indian Lookout Point to catch the first glimpse of what he thought was Chimney Rock. Rockwell was actually looking at Courthouse and Jail rocks, some eighteen miles west of Ancient Bluff Ruins, a mistake that Bullock later corrected in his journal when he sketched an accurate drawing of Chimney Rock. Mormon journal keepers, including William Clayton, seem to repeat the error.

started on an exploring excursion to the mountains. At 9:24 they visited several of the Bluffs, before they arrived [at] "Observation Bluff" at 10:05 where there was a Cedar growing on the South East end of it. Professor Pratt took an observation by which he found it was 235 Feet higher than the River.[47] Several of them engraved their names in the bark, or wrote them on the White of the Bark. [They] rolled down some large Stones from the top, and returned to Camp at 11:05. As brother Nathaniel Fairbanks was descending from one of the Bluffs he was bit on the left side of the calf of his left leg by a very large yellow Rattle Snake, but before his companions could return to kill it, it had again returned to is hole & escaped. By the time that he could return to Camp & procure medical assistance (about ½ past 9) his tongue was dry, leg swollen, pain in his belly & eyes dimmer. Luke Johnson immediately applied a corn meal mush Poultice, with Tincture of Lobelia and No. 6 and at the same time giving him a Lobelia Emetic, and then another.[48] Fairbanks complained much of the pain in his belly.

At ½ past 12 Meeting was opened by the President calling on the brethren to sing a hymn, he then made prayer. Another hymn sung, when Erastus Snow spoke a few minutes & was followed by President Young & G. A. Smith. Meeting dismissed at 2:30 P.M. (See TB's minutes on file.) Dried off the articles found & lost. After meeting Luke Johnson & I went to the top of "Observation Bluff" in order that I might engrave on the Cedar Tree the altitude, under Professor Pratt's name. While I was on the very top of the bluff, a rattle snake challenged for battle. His rattles startled me. I sprung over him, calling to Luke, he turned round, and said "If that's the way you fight my friend, I take his part in the battle." The Snake continued shaking his rattles, when Luke put his rifle to his Shoulder, & wong went the Snake's head & cutting his body in two. He had 7 rattles pieces.[49] I then engraved "235 Feet" under O. Pratt's name [and] writing our names, descended from the Bluff. Found a Mammoth bone imbedded in the soil, one portion of it was bare, while the remainder was covered with 7 or 8 feet of soil. We succeeded in digging out a

---

[47] By a "barometrical measure," Pratt "ascertained the height" of the bluff "to be 235 feet above the river, and 3590 feet above the level of the sea."

[48] William Clayton wrote that the lobelia—also called Indian Tobacco—"soon vomited him powerfully." Whether Fairbanks survived due to or in spite of this powerful frontier remedy is left to the reader.

[49] Bullock saved the rattles from this snake and sent them to his wife, Henrietta.

portion of it. At 3 P.M. it was a lovely day, but it suddenly changed to a severe storm of Wind. The clouds gathered very dark & before we could return to Camp, it blew almost a hurricane of Wind, succeeded by rain, hail, thunder & lightning which continued till after Sunset. The cattle were all tied up for the night. At this place W. Woodruff saw a perfectly Square Snake, which coiled itself up in a fighting attitude and vomited out about a table spoonful of blood at him. He had heard of such a Snake in these quarters & if the wind blew from the Snake towards a man he could be poisoned by it. Fortunately for Elder Woodruff he received no accident.[50]

Monday 24 May 1847—Cold Cloudy morning, with North wind. This morning brother Fairbanks was a little easier in pain, but his leg was considerably swollen. Made out another "Sketches from Journal no. 3" [and] making another Post Office, sealed it up endorsing it to "C. C. Rich or any member of the Camp of Israel," [and] put the Letter Box in the ground having endorsed it "Ancient Ruins Bluffs." At 8:20 left this Encampment, and took almost a strait course towards the Chimney Rock, passing a rock very much resembling an Ancient Sacrificial Altar, about two miles from [our] starting point. Continued our route until 12:45 when camp had passed over a small rise of ground and halted near the River. Two Sioux Indians came to our Camp whom we fed with bread, meat, beans, & coffee; they gave signs that they were Camped on the South side of the River. When they crossed the river, our Camp again resumed its journey at 2:52, pursuing a strait course towards the Chimney over a level road, and when approaching the River, saw a drove of Indians on the gallop on the opposite side of the River, riding in the direction of our Camp; which caused a Messenger to be sent a head, to cause the forward teams to halt; and commenced forming the Circle for defense.[51] At 5:45 it was nearly formed, but could not be completed for more than half an hour after, in consequence of John Pack, O. K. Whitney & 3 other teams having loitered behind. The Indians waved a flag on

---

[50] Like Brigham Young, Wilford Woodruff believed a variety a rural folk-tales and traditions. This was possibly a non-venomous Bull snake (*Pituophis melanoleucus*), which may imitate a rattlesnake when molested, but lacks the ability to poison from afar. The snake may have appeared "perfectly Square" due to a recent meal.

[51] Perhaps due to the excitement of the Indian encounter at this spot, Bullock failed to mention Courthouse and Jail rocks, which were across the river south of present Bridgeport, Nebraska. These rocks are the first massive formations of the Wild Cat Range, which extends up the North Platte and culminates at Scotts Bluff.

the opposite side of the River, which we answered by sending the "White Flag of Peace," & hoisting it on our side the River with Colonel Rockwood & H. G. Sherwood to receive them & learn their intentions. The Indians crossed the River, being 35 men, women & children who brought two letters of recommend written in French, one was given to "O Wash to cha ou belle Journie" and signed by "G. D. Papie"; the other was to "Louis Brave or the Brave Bear" and signed at "Fort John December 24, 1846." The Chief "O Wash te cha" had a large medal hung round his neck, having inscribed on one side "Pierre Chowteau Jr. & Co. Upper Missouri outfit" with the bust of a man in the center. On the reverse the "Brave Bear" held in his hand a flag bearing the Stripes and Eagle with "E. Pluribus unum,"

but no Stars were on the Indians Banner, which is emblematical of America scourging the Indians but giving no Star of glory to the Sons of the Prairie.[52] The recommends were partially deciphered by brother Carrington and several Indians visited the camp. Five of the principal men were escorted round the camp, shewing them several Six Shooters and Fifteen Shooters,[53] and the Cannon Company were put thro' their evolutions, which brought out the exclamation "Wash te" or good. Tobacco was given them. When the Five smoked round, giving the Pipe to President Richards to smoke, they conversed by signs until after the Guard was set. One of them with his Squaw slept in a tent, within our Guard's watch—the remainder slept a short distance outside our Guards.[54]

Tuesday 25 May 1847—A severe frost thro' the night. Some damp clothes that were left out were covered with a thick hoar frost called Black Frost. The Indians were in and round the Camp from Sunrise to

---

[52] Inexplicably, Bullock's description does not match his sketch of the medallion.

[53] Mormon gunsmith John Browning designed and made both the six-shooter (which was probably one of his revolving rifles) and the "15 shooter." His son, John Moses Browning, founded the firearms company that bears the family name. The popular "15 shooter" used an interchangeable harmonica-shaped clip that held five to twenty-five ball-and-powder charges. See Rockwell, *Pioneer Guns and Gunsmiths*, 10.

[54] The 24 May camp is marked by a cobblestone monument erected in 1938 by the Utah Pioneer Trails and Landmarks Association just across the Platte from Bridgeport, Nebraska.

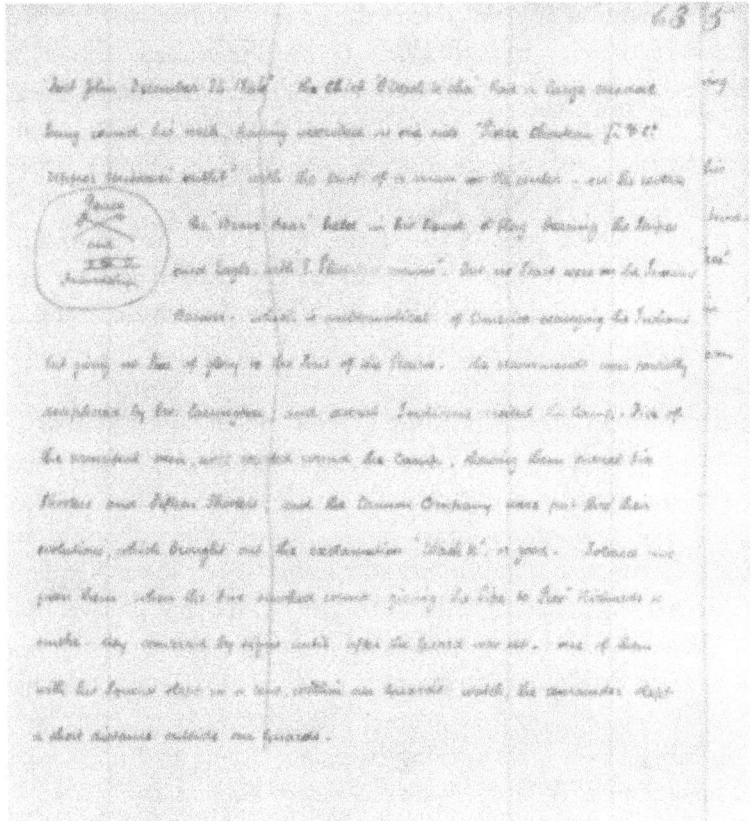

This page from Thomas Bullock's Journal Number I of the Pioneer Camp of the Saints shows Bullock's drawing of the medal carried by Lakota chief Wash-te-cha. *Courtesy LDS Archives.*

the time of Starting, going about just as their curiosity led them, some to get bread & other things, some trading Moccassins, Blankets, Horses &c. One of the Chiefs "Wash te ha" was very pressing for a written paper, when I wrote the following: "This is to Certify that Wash te ha of the Dacotah tribe of Indians, with Wash te cha the principal Chief, and thirty three other men, women and children, visited our Camp, on the 24th and 25th May 1847, behaved themselves civilly and peaceably; we gave them bread. They were very friendly to us, and the best behaved

Indians we have yet seen. W. Richards. Thomas Bullock—Scribe." After this certificate was given to Wash te ha, the Indians shook hands, mounted their horses and rode away to the River where they crossed yesterday.[55] The cattle were gathered up as the Indians were leaving the Camp and we started on our journey at 8:10 going round a large Sand hill, Dr. Richards being the Pioneer, on foot. At 9:23 stopped to bait[56] on a green patch of grass. I was so sick that I went to bed in Doctor's Wagon, Brother Little driving my team for me. Started again at 11, taking a strait course and again halting at 1:20 to refresh the teams. Staid till 2:45 when I got up to drive my team. Doctor gave me some tea & cayenne Pepper to warm me up. I took 3 doses during the day. We started on almost a strait line, the Doctor picking out the road all the way, until within half a mile of the camping ground. The teams turned round to the right hand, instead of the left where the Doctor was and halted at 5:30 in good dry grass, but [on] a wet sloppy bottom, having travelled 12 miles. The Camp halted NE by North about 5 miles from the Chimney Rock, having had a warm day [with a] SW breeze. Hunters kill 2 Wolves & 2 Antelopes. While Dr. Richards was picking out the road, he saw a Rattlesnake in his path. He fired at it 3 times with his pistol, but the Snake dodged each time. The 4th time he fired at the body, cutting him in two. This evening President Young had his Supper on bread baked by his Wife, in his own Oven, in Nauvoo last January [and] 12 months.[57] It was still very good. Very few men can say like unto it. The brethren dig 3 wells about 5 or 6 feet deep.

Wednesday 26 May 1847—Was another delightful Spring morning. While I was engaged filling up the Doctor's Water Bottle, my Ink Bottle fell out of my pocket into the Well, there being about four feet of Water in it. I went to work, emptied the Well, descended, and after groping some time in the mud bottom, I again found it safe & sound. The camp started at 8 o'clock, again taking a strait course. When opposite the Chimney Rock, Professor Pratt took an observation & reports his result at 41° 45' 58" North Latitude and the height, as near as he could

---

[55] As this encounter shows, until 1854 when the Sioux became embroiled in a dispute over a Mormon's cow at Fort Laramie that led to the Grattan Massacre, the Sioux in general and the Lakota in particular regarded themselves as firm friends of the whites.

[56] In its archaic use, "to bait" meant a stop for rest or food during a journey.

[57] That is, the bread was baked in January 1846.

get it from where he was, 260 feet high. Variation of compass 12°. The shape of the rock is nearly[:]

Immediately afterwards the horse that Colonel Markham had from the Indians started off in full gallop with the traces & Single tree banging behind him. His fright started five teams out of the ranks in different directions, the Cows dingling their bells, and the Dogs barking in all directions, [and] made a scene of confusion for a few minutes. Soon they got into order again & continued until 12:03 where we halted near green grass and Water, [with] 3 abrupt bluffs, one like an immense brick kiln, nearest the river, the next more like a Pyramid & much smaller. All the Bluffs on the South side are abrupt. At 2:15 the Camp again started in a strait line, until near time to halt, when the Camp steered towards the River and formed a circle at 5 P.M. where [there] was pretty good green grass. I may have observe[d] that away from the River feed is very poor & no wood, but on the banks the feed is better & [we] can pick up drift wood. 7¼ [+] 5 [=] 12¼ miles. A warm afternoon. 4 Antelopes & [a] Wolf killed. About 7 the Wind commenced blowing from the South West.

Thursday 27 May 1847—A delightful Spring morning. Colonel Markham's Indian horse strayed away. The Colonel went after him, and with some difficulty again secured him. While I was out gathering up the oxen, I saw two Parrots or Parroquets with their yellow breasts chattering away. At 7:50 Camp started away, taking nearly a strait course for Scotts Bluffs.[58] Very little grass on the route. Staid a short time to water the cattle & then continued our journey until 11:40 when Camp came to noon halt opposite a steep bluff resembling a large fortress, having towers & bastions in clear, distinct & bold appearance. The small trees scattered about upon it are not bad representations of the men in a fortress. Before leaving the Camp I planted three seeds of White Corn near the Doctor's Wagon to shew the next Camp of brethren Indian Corn growing on the Prairie, by orders of the Doctor. At 1:40 Camp again moves off over a barren level road, with scarce a blade of grass for about 4 miles. Nothing save the Prickly Pear growing, then descended to

---

[58] Scotts Bluff, now a national monument, was named for American Fur Company clerk Hiram Scott, who died there in 1828.

a bottom where [there] was some green grass. [We] continued on that until 4:40 when the Camp halted for the night, having travelled 13¾ miles 8 A.M. [+] 5¾ P.M. Turned out the cattle on a blue grass to feed. About 6 it commenced to rain. 4 Antelopes killed and brought into Camp by the Hunters.

Friday 28 May 1847—A dull cloudy morning. Many flowers similar to Wild Roses in bloom. Cold East Wind. An unpleasant mizzling rain commenced about ½ past 6 which was the cause of Colonel Rockwood calling the Camp together, round the Cutter, and after a few observations it was voted to remain in our present place until the rain subsided. All the brethren then dispersed to their Wagons. I went into the Doctor's Wagon, and Inked our route on a map, [and] also made another tracing of the North Fork from the Junction to Fort Laramie. The rain having subsided, the horn was blowed to gather up the cattle: the wet grass wet me thro'. At 10:56 started from our encampment, over barren plain. About noon, passed "Trout Book," a small clear stream, which had its origin in a Spring. There were many Speckled Trout, and other Fish in it, also a Beaver House & Dam across it. Several of the Brethren declared that they were the first Trout they had seen since they left the Eastern States. Continued our route over a barren level for several miles; then descended a gentle steep & travelled on a marshy bottom, where the Saline deposit made its appearance again. On our journey saw several trees on the Islands which was like old scenes to us. Travelled 11½ miles. At 4:50 Camp halted for the night about ½ mile from the River where we found plenty of drift wood, in addition to two large trees, which have been cut down by some persons previously: & one large tree blown down. I went for a load & was tired out & after beginning my Journal had to lay it down as usual, George Brown coming for me to fetch him the cow. (Note I have had more hard words & insolent behavior from him than any other person since I left Nauvoo.[59] Having to assist him, attend to cattle & drive a team is the cause that I have so little down in my Journal. I could wish to have had the best & fullest Journal of this Mission, but am sorry I cannot do more; may the Lord accept what I have written & done in this Journey. Amen.) A dull cloudy

---

[59] Bullock confided in a note to his wife, "I shall be glad when I change both my bed and my bedfellow... George Brown is my bedfellow, & the most uncomfortable one I ever slept with—if it was night only I could pull thro', but he is a disagreeable, saucy, idle fellow by day." See Thomas Bullock to Henrietta Bullock, 14 May 1847, Henrietta Bullock Collection, LDS Archives.

day, with a North East Wind. At 9:20 President Young called H. C. Kimball, W. Richards, W. Woodruff & E. T. Benson to his Wagon.

Saturday 29 May 1847—Was a miserable mizzling rain; the 3rd & 4th Tens not having any Guards out, the cattle strayed away between 3 & 4 miles. When the rain subsided, the horn was blowed to gather up the cattle. I went out about 2 miles & got very wet about my feet. After all the cattle were hitched up, the brethren were all collected inside the circle. I called over all the names of the men in camp. Brothers Joseph Hancock & Andrew Gibbons absent, all the rest present at 11:45 when President Young addressed them severely on their levity, dancing, checkers, cards, Swearing, &c. When the Priesthood was called into ranks, of the Twelve 8, High Priests 19, Seventies 78, Elders 8 who severally covenanted with the uplifted hand, to serve the Lord, humble themselves, repent of their sins, cleave unto the Lord & renew their former Covenants.[60] (See TB's minutes.) It was a very solemn & impressive meeting. Dismissed at 20 min to 2 1:20 and at 1:30 the Camp pursued their journey. Take a strait line to where the Bluffs & River meet. Passed thro' & halted on a level spot of barren ground near a Creek at 5:30 having travelled 8½ miles.[61] On the Islands in the River were several trees in very green leaf, which was a pleasing sight. It commenced raining about 5 & continued thro' the evening.

Sunday 30 May 1847. Fast Day[62]—A cool pleasant morning. At 8 A.M. the brethren assembled on a green dry spot near the Camp, for the purpose of prayer, praise, & confession of Sins. Bishop Tarlton Lewis taking the lead of the meeting commenced by singing "The spirit of God like a fire is burning." Many of the brethren prayed, spoke and sung; which continued until 10 minutes after 10, when meeting was dismissed to gather up the cattle preparatory to Sacrament meeting at 11. After the cattle were all gathered up, the brethren again assembled at the same place for prayer and Sacrament. The rain commencing as soon as the cup had been passed round brought the meeting to a close sooner than intended. Dr. Richards reports "12:30 The Twelve, Rockwood,

---

[60] See the Woodruff and Clayton journals for this harangue. On 28 May, Young received a revelation, warning that unless the men repented, they would "not have power to accomplish your mission."

[61] The Saints camped for the next two days at Prayer Circle Bluffs, about two miles east of the present Nebraska-Wyoming state line near present Henry, Nebraska. On nearby Horse Creek, 10,000 Plains Indians gathered in 1851 to sign the Fort Laramie Treaty.

[62] Mormons observe one Sunday every month as a day of fasting and prayer. That day's "fast and testimony" meeting is dedicated to taking the sacrament and bearing personal testimonies of the gospel.

Shumway, P. H. Young, Snow, Clayton, Pack," went to a Valley in the bluffs & prayed, while Rockwell & Carrington watched.[63] "Thomas Bullock could not be found. 1:30 returned." I confess, I have not been 45 yards from Camp, nor out of sight since last night. After [this] morning's meeting returned to my Wagon & back from Wagon to the Sacrament meeting. I was not the tenth part so grieved, to leave My Wife and all my children sick, one near the point of death in Winter Quarters as I am now grieved, that yesterday I covenanted to serve the Lord and to day I am reported "Thomas Bullock cannot be found" when I have prepared every thing for the meeting [and] was perfectly ready & in sight of my Wagon, all the time, for a moment's notice. I have been deprived of one of my greatest & sacred privileges. O my God look down upon my tears & suffering & have mercy on me. Wherein I have offended thee, make it manifest to me, that I may repent, whatever it may be. In a short time the rain left off & cleared up for a fine afternoon. In the evening J. C. Little gathered some Prickly Pears & stewed them in Sugar. I tasted of them, they were good. At ½ past 5 another Shower of rain passed over Camp.

Monday 31 May 1847—A very fine day, clear sky. Gathered up cattle & started at 8:10 over a barren country yet abounding with Prickly Pears. I was taken very sick with Auge and Fever, & was obliged to relinquish driving my team to Conrad Klineman. The brethren kill 1 Rattlesnake. Camp halts at 12:20 on the top of a Sand hill, a considerable distance from the River. The brethren dig a Well 4 or 5 feet deep & get excellent water. At 2:45 again start, Dr. Richards having removed me into his Wagon & administered Composition Tea &c. J. C. Little drove my team in the afternoon. Passed several Trees & Bushes, travel over a very heavy Sandy road & camp at 6:30 having travelled 10 [+] 6¾ [=] 16¾ [miles]. [We camp] on "Raw Hide Creek."[64] The Hunters kill 1 Deer. In the evening Doctor administered a Lobelia Emetic & attended me through the operation.

---

[63] Clayton reported that this was actually a meeting of all "the Council of F[ifty] or Kingdom of God in the Camp except Thomas Bullock…Out of sight, we clothed ourselves in the priestly garments and offered up prayers to God…We all felt well and glad for this privilege."

[64] Rawhide Creek flows into the North Platte east of present Lingle, Wyoming. William Clayton noted that the Saints had learned the creek's name from Justin Grosclaude. The creek (or a tributary of the Elkhorn by the same name) was said to be named for a man who shot and killed a nursing Indian woman and was subsequently skinned alive for the crime.

Chapter 5

"TO THE TOPS OF THE MOUNTAINS"
Fort Laramie to South Pass, June 1847

"No person," Thomas Bullock wrote in 1848, "can help noticing the sudden transition from level and sandy roads to the mountain roads" west from Fort Laramie. Even today, leaving the irrigated cornfields of Nebraska and a similar slice of eastern Wyoming for the sage-clad high desert of the arid West is a dramatic change. Here the Camp of Israel began its journey "over hills and mountains" to the crossing of the Rocky Mountains at South Pass. As Bullock later wrote, at Fort Laramie "commences a 500 mile journey through the eternal sage from six inches to ten feet high."[1] After crossing "an immense Park," the Saints chose the "Mountain Route" over the Black Hills, where the trail left the north fork of the Platte River. The vast dry grasslands of the Platte grew increasingly barren, and the Mormons watched the conifers and junipers that give the Black Hills their name thin out and soon found that timber on trail west was confined to the banks of streams and creeks. William Clayton advised "you will find rough roads, high ridges, and mostly barren country." The road that followed the Platte was "represented as being as near, and much better traveling if the river is fordable," but the Saints took the high road.[2]

After their long odyssey across the plains and a winter at Pueblo on the front range of the Rockies, an advance party of the "Mississippi Saints," seventeen people chiefly from the Crow and Therlkill families, at last rendezvoused with the mother church when the pioneer company arrived at Laramie. Robert Crow of Illinois, whose family would be plagued by accidents as they journeyed west, led the group, and mountaineer Lewis B. Meyers acted as guide. They brought no definitive word about the plans of

---
[1] Bullock to William, *Millennial Star* (15 April 1848), 117.
[2] Clayton, *Emigrants' Guide*, 23. Clayton's guide described two routes from Fort Laramie to present Casper, Wyoming: a Mountain Route (also called the Hill Road or the Bluff Route), which the Mormons used to cross the Black Hills; and a River Route, which was a river route in name only. Clayton incorrectly wrote that the River Route required fording the Platte in three places; it actually stayed in the hills to avoid the canyon of the North Platte west of Guernsey. Both routes merged five miles west of LaBonte Creek.

the 150 men in the Mormon Battalion's sick detachments, who had also spent the winter at Pueblo. Brigham Young dispatched Amasa Lyman and a small party to intercept the soldiers and direct them to the mountains, and Young authorized Lyman to replace the officers if they refused to follow orders—his orders.

As they crossed the Black Hills, the Mormons met other emigrant companies that included a number of their old enemies from Missouri. The encounter made both parties nervous, but they maintained an uneasy truce while they raced and sparred for the best campsites. Curiosity got the best of the Missourians, and on 6 June one party dropped by to see the Mormon's odometer. On the ninth, Young out-maneuvered the Missourians by dispatching a party of forty-nine picked men to forge ahead and secure a bull boat left hanging in a tree at the crossing of the Platte by a party of east-bound trappers the pioneers met on 8 June.

Altogether, the mountain road with its excellent feed favored the pioneers and they set mileage records. Whatever time they gained on the trail was lost in the five days the company spent crossing the North Platte at the site of present Casper, Wyoming. While Bullock lay sick, the Saints ferried some of the Missouri parties across the river. Seeing the windfall of fees (paid in supplies) the operation produced and sensing its future commercial possibilities, Brigham Young left Thomas Grover and eight men behind to establish the "Mormon Ferry." This enterprise pointed the way for a flourishing business the Mormons developed providing services on the overland trail, but the halt at the river proved to be the longest delay of the journey. In their initial crossings at the ferry, the Saints collected 1,295 pounds of flour and "beans, soap and honey" and two cows.[3] Bullock got to collect the ferry tolls from the Missourians.

The pioneers had their first encounter with a true western desert on their three-day crossing of the barren country between the ferry and the Sweetwater River. This was much the worst section of the entire Mormon Trail. Again they passed a series of noted trail landmarks—Independence Rock, Devils Gate, Split Rock, the Great Stone Face, and Castle Rock—and on 25 June the Saints found snowbanks on the margins of the road, which they used the next day to cool the milk they got from the cow Lorenzo Young had insisted they bring along. Like most overland journal keepers, Bullock expressed his amazement at finding snow in the high country in summer, it "being a rarity in the longest days." Both children and

---

[3] Roberts, *Comprehensive History*, 3:196.

adults engaged in snowball fights. Bullock described this strange new country: "The rocks now are very bold like the roaches, only higher; the roads very sandy; the sage bushes more plentiful."[4]

The Saints crossed South Pass on a momentous day: Sunday, 27 June, the third anniversary of the murder of Joseph and Hyrum Smith. The ascent of the continental divide was so gradual that Bullock reported, "You will not know you are in the south pass until all of a sudden you will find the water running in the opposite direction—that is, towards the west." This marked the beginning of "several heavy days' drive without seeing water," but Bullock recalled, "you will be rejoicing that every day brings you nearer home."[5]

June Tuesday 1—I continued with a great deal of Fever through the day, still continuing in the Doctor's Wagon. Camp start at [9:00] crossing the "Raw Hide" Creek, seeing many trees on the banks of the River, having on our right very Sandy Bluffs and Rocks. Pass 4 bodies of Indians tied up in Skins and fastened to the Trees; this being a preferable manner of disposing of the dead, to burying them in the ground for the Wolves to dig them up again and devour them. The noon halt was opposite the place where a trading house formerly belonging to J. Richiau stood, but which has since been burnt to the ground.[6] Continued our route and in a short time heard the cry of "I see Fort Laramie,"[7] when all were anxious to see an habitation once more. Came into a very pretty vale, turned round a point of timber & camped on the banks of the River opposite "Fort John."[8] [We came] 12 miles. Before we could form

---

[4] Bullock to William, *Millennial Star* (15 April 1848), 117.   [5] *Ibid.*

[6] This is John Baptiste Richard (1810–1872), who in 1846 guided the Mississippi Saints from Fort John to Pueblo while on his way to Taos to buy liquor. In late 1845 Richard occupied Joseph Bissonette's abandoned Fort Bernard, some eight miles east of Fort John, and competed successfully with the American Fur Company in 1846. The following winter, the fort mysteriously burned to the ground. See John Dishon McDermott's sketch in Hafen, ed., *The Mountain Men*, 2:289–304.

[7] Fur traders Robert Campbell and William Sublette founded Fort William in 1834 near the confluence of the Laramie and Platte rivers. The American Fur Company bought the stockaded post in 1836 and rebuilt it with adobe walls in 1841 about a mile upstream as Fort John; despite the official names, both establishments were universally called Fort Laramie. The government purchased the post in 1849. It was a strategic location in the Indian wars, and was a waystation for the Pony Express, transcontinental telegraph, and overland stage. The government abandoned the post in 1890, but it is now a national historic site.

[8] The Saints were across the river from the abandoned Fort William, located near the iron military bridge on the North Platte River.

the Circle two brethren came to us, Robert Crow & George W. Therlkill,[9] who told us the man on the look out reported that he saw 500 Wagons coming up the North side which Brother Crow knew to be [the] brethren. They have been at the Fort 16 days, came from the remainder [of the] Mississippi Camp at Pueblo. The [rest] of the brethren there would start about 1st June for this place; the Battalion would be furnished with 3 months provisions &c. At 8:55 the Council & Captains met at the President's Wagon when it was decided that 2 men out of each 10 should watch the cattle. The Blacksmiths should burn coal to repair Wagons. Colonel Rockwood should charter the Boat in order to ferry over all the Wagons, the Water being too high to ford, & that all Wagons should be overhauled &c. James Case, Shadrach Roundy, & Seth Taft were appointed a committee to overhaul and select Plows. Council closed at 9:50.

Wednesday 2 June 1847—Opened with a very pleasant morning, clear sky. At ¼ past 9 the Twelve—B. Young, H. C. Kimball, W. Richards—with A. P. Rockwood & T. Bullock [and] several others started for Fort Laramie. Crossed the River which is 108 yards wide, first visiting Fort Platte in ruins.[10] Wm. Clayton & Thos. Bullock measured it: 144 by 103.2 outside; the door at the East side 9 feet 9 inches; height of walls—11 feet; the door way on South side 10.6 wide. All the walls were about 30 inch thick; round the inside of the Walls were 15 rooms. The one on the SW corner appeared to have been a store. These small rooms [were] 16x15 [feet] surrounding [a] yard 61 feet 9 inches by 56 feet. On the Chimney piece of the second room on the West side were paintings of a horse & a Buffalo but little defaced. On the North side was the yard for horses: 98 feet 9 inches by 47 feet inside, having on the NW Corner a square tower with holes to shoot thro' on the sides, which was 9 feet 3 inches square. On the NE Corner was an attached building 29 feet 4 inches by 19 feet 6 inches outside dimensions. See the lower plat on next page.

The Oregon trail runs one rod from the SW Angle of the Fort, running [along] the River Road, under the Bluffs. The building was

---

[9] These men were leaders of an advance party from the Mississippi Saints who followed John Brown to Fort Laramie and Pueblo in 1846.

[10] Lancaster P. Lupton (1807–1885) began building Fort Platte in 1839 as competition for Fort William, but had not completed the post when he sold it in 1845. The fort closed in 1845, but the close attention of the Mormons suggests they were interested in the commercial possibilities of the site.

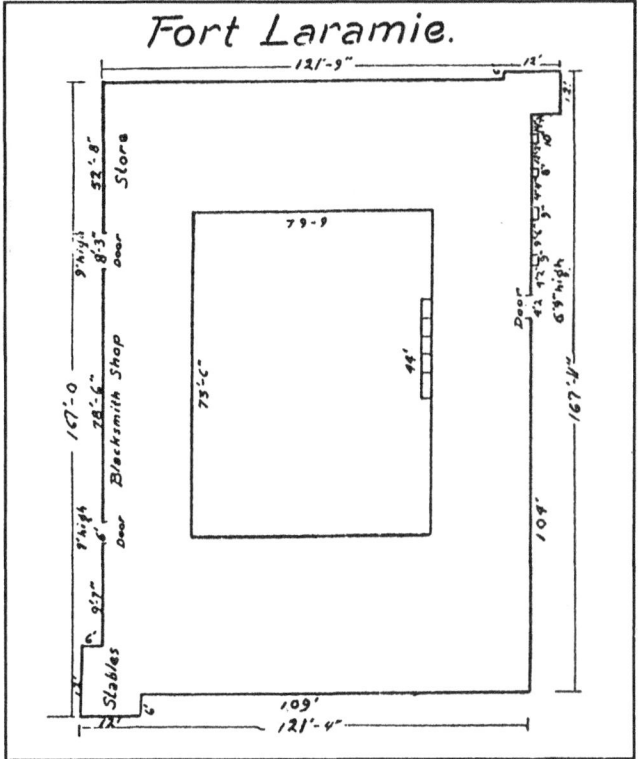

Thomas Bullock's drawing of Fort Laramie as reproduced in Hafen and Young, *Fort Laramie and the Pageant of the West, 1834–1890*.

made with bricks & had been white washed. We then went to Fort Laramie, arriving at 10:15. We were shown up a flight of stairs, into a large room where we found Seats, Bedstead, Desk, a fiddle, some Pictures: J. Bourdeaux[11] the principal man in the Fort answered all questions that were put to him. After staying a short time here [we] then visited the Store & had a short conversation with the Store keeper. Professor Pratt took an observation at noon.

---

[11] James Bordeaux (1814–1878) was born near St. Charles, Missouri, and began working in the fur trade at age twelve. He visited the Great Salt Lake country in 1837 and had been associated with Fort Laramie since 1836. Known to his in-laws the Sioux as "Bear," Bordeaux' good relations with the tribe were a key to the success of the post. The American Fur Company appointed P. D. Papin factor at Fort John in 1845, but Bordeaux remained in practical command of the post until it was sold in 1849. See John Dishon McDermott's sketch in Hafen, ed., *The Mountain Men*, 5:65–80. For $15, Bordeaux rented the Mormons the flatboat they used to ferry the Platte.

Snow was distinctly seen on the top of Laramie Peak with the naked eye, which is upwards of 100 miles distant. We were informed there had not been any rain here for two years & we are informed it is 350 miles to Fort Bridger. At ¼ to 1 a company of Indians came to pay a visit to the Fort, one of the Men having an Indian Wife & these were her relatives. Not only were the horses loaded with Tent poles, but a dog had also some attached & dragging.[12] At 1:13 the brethren got into the Boat on their return trip to Camp, had a pretty sail down Laramie River, arrived at the Platt 1:57. The brethren drew up the Boat & returned to Camp 2:16. On our descending Laramie River, saw a Bald Eagle perched on the top of a Stump. He was alarmed at our approach & flew away.

A short distance from Fort John was an Indian Corpse raised upon Poles & Cross Poles. Found many mushrooms, much mustard & Pig Weed about. At the Store Sheeting, Shirting, Calicoes & Cottons are [$]1.00 per yard; Butcher Knife [$]1.00; Robes from [$]3 to [$]5.00; Buck Skins [$]2 to [$]5.00; Mocassins [$]1.00; Cows from [$]15 to [$]25.00; Horses & Ponies [$]40; Flour 25[¢] per pound.

Thursday 3 June 1847—A dull cloudy morning. Commenced ferrying the Wagons over at Sunrise and continued all day, except during the thunder shower in the afternoon, which commenced at ¼ to 2.[13] Thundering, Lightning, Rain & Hail and continued about an hour. Many of the brethren were busy picking Beads out of the Sand the Hills, which were made by the ants, & they gathered Beads & small Stones to preserve their habitation from being blown away.[14] In the forenoon I made a duplicate of the letter to Captain [James] Brown for Elder Lyman. The President wrote a note in pencil to send at same time. Presidents Young & Richards signed Elder A. Lyman's authority letter & duplicate to Captain Brown & [a] letter to Elder Dowdle, both at Fort Pueblo.

Made up the Mail of 349 letters to the Battalion. Gave it to Thomas Woolsey appointing him Deputy Postmaster.[15] Doctor instructed him

---

[12] Bullock had, of course, encountered a *travois*, which was invented for use with dogs.

[13] The Saints crossed the North Platte about 600 feet above the present highway bridge, nearly opposite the site of Fort Platte.

[14] Gathering beads from anthills "which were lost by the Indians and collected by these indefatigable little workers" became a favorite occupation of children on the Mormon Trail. See the Autobiography of Mary Jane Mount Tanner, quoted in Kimball and Kimball, *Mormon Trail, Voyage of Discovery*, 39.

[15] As noted, Thomas Woolsey had carried mail from the Mormon Battalion sick detachments to Winter Quarters with John H. Tippetts during the winter of 1846–47, experiencing bitter weather and a narrow escape from the Pawnees.

to bring back all the letters that he did not deliver to the brethren. At 11 A.M. Presidents Young, Richards, Kimball and Pratt accompanied the brethren A. Lyman, Thomas Woolsey, Roswell Stevens & John H. Tibbets to the Ford of Laramie River & took Seats on a large Tree fallen on the banks of the River. President Young read some instructions, which he had previously written to the brethren, and gave them to Amasa Lyman. He told the brethren that they had accomplished their designs in getting the Battalion to Mexico but the brethren at Pueblo must not follow Brown to Mexico, but go to California. If the officers will not do right, he instructed Amasa to call out the men & choose officers who would do right. If the Battalion are at Santa Fe these brethren [are] to go there & bring the Battalion on also & if the Pueblo Command is gone there to pursue them and bring them back, and if General Kearney is there & objects to their returning, according to our agreement, tell him we are bound for California, and throw all the Gentile officers out of the Battalion when you come up to it.[16] Brother Young said he was very angry with the President when he learned that his orders were not to enlist more than ⅓rd Mormons in his Army on any consideration.[17] The brethren all kneeled while President Young led in prayer. He then blessed the brethren, who arrived on the opposite bank at 11:27, who went on their way & council returned to camp. Phinehas Young & Tunis Rapplleyee were present also. The brethren were 11 minutes in crossing a Wagon & returning. West Wind. I went to the Fort with Brother Little & returnd before 6 when it again rained.

Friday 4 June 1847—A fine morning. I wrote a letter to C. C. Rich giving him instructions regarding our journey. (Copy on file.)[18] Took same to Fort Laramie, in company with Presidents Young, Kimball & Richards, also A. P. Rockwood, who settled for the Boat. Dr. Richards wrote a note to Winter Quarters & left same with J. Bordeaux Bordo.[19]

---

[16] By California, Young meant today's Great Basin. There was much confusion over the sick detachments' orders, arising from the belief that they must go to California to be discharged and paid. Captain James Brown resolved the problem when he marched his command north to Fort Laramie.

[17] Young's bitter response to President Polk's political calculation that it would be disastrous to give the Saints effective control over the balance of military power in California expressed the Mormon leader's contempt for the Battalion's military orders.

[18] This document is in the Thomas Bullock Journals, MS 1385, Folder 5, LDS Archives.

[19] On 12 August 1847, Mary Haskin Parker Richards wrote that Thomas Bullock "has sent back to his wife a journal of their travels from this city to Fort Laramy...which was read last T[hurs]day at the evening meeting it was very interesting." See Carr, *Winter Quarters*, 176.

J. B. remarked to Brother Rockwood that there never had passed Fort Laramie such a company as this, for this people would not go any where without first asking liberty to go & they felt a pleasure in seeing us & showing us thro'. When any company of only 10 or a dozen Wagons came along, they would run & peep into every room & every thing & they (of the Fort) had plenty to do to watch that the people did not Steal any thing. When Ex Governor Boggs[20] passed thro, he was all the time railing about the Mormons being bad people. But he was told that the Mormons could not be worse than that company, for they were fighting every, or every other night, but the people of the Fort several times expressed their great pleasure at seeing us, expressing themselves that we were the best behaved Company that had passed there & stated their intention of visiting us when we get settled. Dr. Luke Johnson attended some of them in his medical capacity, they paid him mocassins, skins, &c. He gave T. B. a pair of mocassins. After visiting their corral, Store &c, the Presidents returned to Camp, when all the brethren who were there followed to Camp, when the teams were gathered up & the Camp started from this place at 12 o'clock, taking the road under the Bluffs.[21] At 1:15 having come to good grass, Camp came to a halt to feed the cattle; at 2:27 moved again, continuing [up] the road by the River. We moved thro' an immense quantity of Grasshoppers during a Warm afternoon. The scenery is altogether different to what we have had of late—bold ragged bluffs, speckled with Cedar and Pine Trees. The river bottom was interspersed with Cotton Wood Trees & Wild Choke Cherry bushes. There were some conical hills on the north side covered with Cedar Trees; which is quite a variety & change of scene for the eye. The road is very irregular & uneven. We came to a very steep bank of Sand where the teams had to halt several times. A Mr. Archibald Litle [Lytle] (a new comer this day) ill used his oxen very bad, striking them on the head & body with the butt end of his Whip.[22] Presidents Young & Richards & 6 or 7 of the brethren went to assist him with his team, but he treated their assistance with contempt, all the time thumping away at the oxen. The brethren then left him to get up, himself; President Young remarking that there had been more abuse of cattle in those

---

[20] In 1846, former Missouri Governor Lilburn Boggs led a company in the overland emigration to California.

[21] The Saints took the "River Road" from their camp near Fort Platte, following the river bottom for several miles until it reached a sharp bend in the North Platte. Here they turned due west to climb a long sandy slope to the benchland, where in a mile and a half it merged with the "Bluff Route."

[22] This incident probably took place where the river road leaves the North Platte east of Mexican Hill.

few minutes than by all the brethren since they left Winter Quarters. After the ascent, continued our route by the River. We had a very steep hill to descend between 4 & 5. We not only locked Wheels, but had attached ropes to the hind end of the Wagons [with] the brethren holding back [at] the same time.[23] In about 2 hours we got safely thro' & halt for the night at 5:20 in the bottom, near the River, having travelled 8¼ miles.[24] A thunder shower passing over at the time from [the] North directly afterwards [and we] saw two perfect rainbows in the heavens and an Eagle flying in the Air.

[THE ADVANCE GUARD OF THE MISSISSIPPI SAINTS]

This day [arrived] Robert Crow with 5 Wagons
Elizabeth Crow
Benjamin B. Crow
Harriet Crow   1 cart
Elizabeth Jane Crow   11 Horses
John McHenry Crow
Walter H. Crow   12 yoke of Oxen
Matilda Jane Therlkill
George W. Therlkill   22 cows
Milton Howard Therlkill
James William Therlkill   7 Calves
William Parker Crow   3 Bulls
Ida Vinda Exene Crow
Ira Minda Almarene Crow
Archibald Litle   joined our camp at leaving Fort Laramie
James Chesney   Laramie
Lewis B. Myers
= 17 Persons[25]

In the evening I visited the entire Camp and found:

Men	148	Oxen	90[26]
Women	8	Cows	43
Children	5	Calves	9
Wagons	79	Bulls	3
Horses	96	Dogs	16
Mules	51	Chickens	16

---

[23] This was Mexican Hill, where the trail descended from benchland to the river bottom of the North Platte.

[24] The Saints camped near Register Cliff, the "very bold Bluffs of Plaster of Paris" south of Guernsey, Wyoming.

[25] The integration of the Mississippi Saints subtly changed the composition of the company, increasing the number of women by five and children by three. It also added the pioneer company's only true mountain man—Lewis B. Meyers, who is probably the model for character LeBonte in George Frederick Ruxton's *Life in the Far West*.

[26] Note that the total of 237 draft animals for seventy-nine wagons equals exactly three animals per wagon—an extremely low ratio.

Saturday 5 June 1847—Cloudy morning with a gentle South breeze. 4 Eagles flying round about. On gathering up the cattle, several yoke were missing; another hunt took place when they were discovered on an Island, straying among the young cotton wood shrubs. At 8:29 the Camp started, passing under same very bold Bluffs of Plaster of Paris. At 9:20 the weather cleared up. On coming to the hills we had a very difficult spot to ascend, pass thro' & again descend to a prairie.[27] Then turned from the River to the left up a gravel bottom & halt at 11:50 near the "Warm Spring."[28] Went to visit it & drink of the Water. It was a beautiful clear Spring, slightly warm & in sufficient quantity to turn a mill Wheel. While at this place a Camp of 11 Wagons pass by [on] the Mountain route with a guide or Pilot.[29] At 1:35 our Camp starts again, passing thro' a narrow defile & then ascending a steep hill; on reaching the top came on a beautiful undulating prairie, taking a circuitous route to the 20 miles post, then descend a hill to a dry gravel bottom and pass round the hill during a pleasant Shower from the West which produced a double rainbow. Pass the other camp & halt at 6:30 having travelled 17 miles. On "Bitter Creek" we found good feed for our cattle.[30] G. A. Smith & I went to the top of the Bluffs, being the Guard in that direction & there found Presidents Young, Kimball & Richards, viewing the country with their Telescopes; we could clearly discern Snow on the top of the Laramie Peak. An antelope killed. At dark it commenced raining heavy with lightning & thunder.

Note. On our return this fall, after ascending the Steep Hill, & shortly before coming to the 20 mile Stake pass to the right, taking a strait line to the centre cluster of Trees will save about 2 miles in the distance.

Sunday 6 June 1847. Fast Day—A cloudy morning. Heard a young child cry, which is quite a Novelty to us, in the Pioneer Camp of Israel; the Gentile Camp passed ours about 8 & as soon as they were clear away from our cattle, the Horn was blown for the brethren to assemble themselves to prayer meeting. Opened by singing & prayer; then the brethren

---

[27] This is Deep Rut Hill at present Guernsey, Wyoming.

[28] Marked on Frémont's map, this 70° spring was known as "The Emigrant's Washtub."

[29] The trail today called the Plateau Route stayed on top of the bluffs for the twelve and a half miles from Fort Laramie until it descended into Warm Springs Canyon one quarter mile beyond the spring; this is the route the "Camp of 11 Wagons" used to pass by the Mormons.

[30] This is Cottonwood Creek, which today flows into the Guernsey Reservoir.

spoke their feelings & experience. A very good & lively meeting was continued until ½ past 10. The rules I read & the President adjourned the meeting to assemble again in an hour. At ½ past 11 the horn having blown the brethren met again, while thunder was rolling in the distance & increasing in violence. Orson Pratt called on the choir to sing, when the hymn on 95th page "With all my powers of heart & tongue" was sung, followed by E. T. Benson offering prayer to the throne of grace. President Young seeing the van of the next Emigrating Company approaching our Camp, gave orders to Colonel Rockwood to see that our cattle were got out of their way, & as a Storm was commencing, directed that the meeting should be dismissed, which was done by Elder Pratt. The brethren had scarce got to their Wagons before the Storm passed over the Camp & the 2nd Gentile Camp passed ours at the same time. There being a long journey to Horse Shoe Creek & more than would be well for our cattle, it was thought the best way to go a short distance this afternoon; accordingly the teams were gathered up & at 2:35 our Camp again pursued their journey, along the banks of "Bitter Creek" going thro' a grove of Cotton Wood & Willow Trees, which is a rarity on this journey. Passed thro' a small quantity of very good grass, then took a sudden bend to the left, round a Ravine, & again crossed over "Bitter Creek," then halted for 40 minutes, while our Exploring Company go to search a place for the night. On their return, the Camp again moves on & passes the other camp coming to a halt for the night at 5:22, having travelled 5 miles. A North wind, pleasant afternoon. Here we found plenty of grass for the cattle. Travelled by the most Timber this day than any where since we left Grand Island.

In the evening President Richards having heard that he could send a letter to San Francisco, he wrote a letter to Mr. Samuel Brannan, giving him particulars of the situation of the Saints, which I copied, & afterwards read in President Young's Wagon; to Presidents Young, Kimball, Richards & Woodruff, who were satisfied with it.[31] Presidents Richards & Woodruff returned to R's Wagon, made an addition, & closed by W. Woodruff being mouth in prayer.[32]

---

[31] This revealing letter gave a short history of the Saints over the last year, but apparently was never sent. Richards informed Brannan, "The camp will not go to the West Coast or to your place at present, they have not the means."

[32] In early Mormon terms, a "mouth" spoke the words to be repeated by the members of a prayer circle.

Monday 7 June 1847—A Pleasant morning with a South West Breeze. The 2nd Camp passed thro' our Circle, numbering 19 Wagons, 2 Buggys, 25 Horses, 73 yoke of oxen, & about 100 Cows. The Horn was then blown to gather up our teams & at 7:15 we made a start, leaving a letter to C. C. Rich in a Box "To Fort John 30¼ miles," [and] on the Reverse "W.R." & go to the dry bed of a creek, which we travel along, go up twice, & cross 6 times being in a valley between gentle undulating hills, when we arrived at a small Spring. Halted at 11:20 to Water & feed, when another Camp of 13 Wagons, 14 Horses, 64 Cows, & 43 yoke of oxen pass us. At 12:45 start. We then ascended some hills skirted & dotted with Pine Timber; when at the top we had view of a most beautiful country, being in two directions like an immense Park, without any fence, & dotted with Pines. On the other side had a full view of Laramie Peak, covered with Timber & tipt with Snow.[33] We then commenced our descent, the brethren having to grade the hill in some places. Had to lock the Wheels twice. Descended to the bed of a creek[34] & again made another steep ascent, which after crossing came down to the Horse Shoe Creek. Saw all the three camps at one view a head of us, finding most Excellent Grass [and] the most beautiful Spring of Water yet seen on this route,[35] and an abundance of Timber. We halted at 3:50 when a Heavy Thunder Shower of Hail & rain descended.[36] Killed 2 Deer & an antelope. Found in this place plenty of Sweet Sicily, Pepper mint, & Yarrow. President Richards all day engaged [in] picking Stones out of the way of the Teams & preparing a better road. In the Evening a very strong Wind, but our Camp was sheltered by the Timber. Travelled 13 miles.

Tuesday 8 June 1847—A fine morning. Gather up teams & start at 7:20 crossing the Horse Shoe Creek taking a bend to the left. See a Buffalo capering on the Prairie & then ascend the steepest and most difficult hill yet seen on our route.[37] Many of the teams were under the

---

[33] At 10,272 feet, Laramie Peak is a looming landmark visible for miles as the trail in Wyoming arches north around the mountain.

[34] This is today's Middle Bear Creek.

[35] This is Heber's Spring of Clayton's *Emigrants' Guide*, which said the spring "lays a little to the right of the road, at the edge of the timber." Heber C. Kimball found it near Horseshoe Creek and named it after himself. According to Mrs. Clayton Russell, whose family has owned the site for some 100 years, the spring washed out in a severe flood many years ago. Randy Brown to editor, 1 March 1996.

[36] This night's camp was on Horseshoe Creek, which today flows into Glendo Reservoir.

[37] William Clayton called this ascent of the Horseshoe Creek bluffs "the worst we have ever had."

necessity of doubling in order to get up, which all did without any accident. I left a Buffalo Skull written on "Pioneers,—Double Teams—8 June 1847. Camp all well. Hail Storm last night fine morning. T. Bullock. No accident."[38] On the top of the hill had a splendid view of the country on each side for I should suppose 80 or 100 miles. On the left side of our Road saw the hills & peaks rising to a great distance, then descended from our elevation having to lock Wheels. About 11 o'clock Sister Harriet Crow got on the Wagon tongue to get a drink of Water. As she was jumping down, her coat caught by the Wagon Hammer & she fell to the ground; her husband seized her, pulled her body from under the Wheel, but her coat being still entangled on the Wagon Hammer could not clearly extricate her, before the front Wheel passed over her left thigh & ancle. Fortunately no bones were broken. She was much bruised, had great pain, but before night was considerably easier.[39] Crossed a creek where we watered our cattle & again pursued our journey until 11:55 when we halted on pretty good grass. Found some Thistles at this place. At 1:40 Camp again started ascending and descending hills all the afternoon. Between 4 & 5 a very Strong Cold Wind commenced blowing from the West. The clouds hung very heavy & threatened much for Snow or Rain. President Richards [was] with A. P. Rockwood, Albert Carrington, Jacob Weilar, James Craig & Horace Thornton all day, H. K. Whitney & Burr Frost in the forenoon & Artemas Johnson in the afternoon, clearing the road of the Stones that were on it, & preparing the way for the camp to follow. The Camp halt at 6:10 on "La Bonte" Creek,[40] where we found Cotton Wood & Black Ash Trees & the Choke Cherry Shrub, in a pretty camping place. 6¾ A.M. [+] 8¾ P.M. [=] 15½ miles. Hunters kill 2 Deer & an antelope. Immediately after camping William Tucker & another Trapper paid a visit to the Camp. Tucker was sick with the chills & Fever. Dr. Johnson administered to him. James H. Greive was the principal of the Men,

---

[38] B. H. Roberts described the Saints' "Bulletin of the Plains" and provided an engraving of an annotated buffalo skull, but noted the "false date and false statement" of the skull's forged inscription, which credited the pioneers with traveling fifteen miles on 3 June, the day they crossed the Platte at Fort Laramie. See Roberts, *Comprehensive History*, 3:177–78.

[39] Harriet Crow's experience is one more example of one of the many hazards of overland travel—wagon accidents. The long dresses (and in this case, a coat) dictated by fashion and modesty in the 1840s were an all-too common cause of wagon accidents. This was only the first of many disasters to strike the Crow family.

[40] LaBonte Creek enters the North Platte southeast of Douglas, Wyoming, about two miles from this campsite.

[with] William Tucker, American & James Woodrie, James Rouvoir & 6 other Frenchmen with 2 Squaws.[41] 2 Wagons, 3 Carts &c made up the Camp 1½ mile from us. President Richards & TB went to visit the traders & were joined by President Woodruff. They reported [it is] about 50 miles to the crossing of the Platte. Good feed on our route. Mr. Bridger [is] at home about 300 miles from here; can ride to Salt Lake in two days from Bridger's.[42] Utah country a beautiful country— have to go down & in Green River some distance. On return met Presidents Young, Kimball, & others who returned with us to Camp.

Wednesday 9 June 1847—The feed getting scant here, Camp arose by day break. Hitch up and remove at 4:40. Sunrise along the River & remove 1¼ miles to get good feed for our cattle. Halt [at] 5:13 for breakfast, the birds singing delightfully. I wrote & sent a letter to my Wife by Mr. James H. Grieve, who will take it to Fort Pierre & forward it to P. A. Sarpy Esqre.[43] These traders having left a Bull Boat in a Tree at the Platte for brother Crow's Co. & Myers, they were sent ahead.

Our Camp start at 7:45 taking a turn to our left & in a short distance, the brethren had to grade a hill, & after ascending out of the vale, again descended a valley full of Red Sand & Red Stone [that] may be properly called "the Red Valley." Came to a very clear & pretty creek.[44] Again graded its sides, crossed over & took a circuitous route, passing a Pyramid of Stones almost the shape of a Sugar loaf,[45] & having hills on our left hand about ½ mile from the road, continuing towards NW until 11:45 when we halt on the Bed of a Dry creek;[46] finding on our route

---

[41] In Colorado in 1843 a James Grieves joined Charles A. Warfield's unsuccessful expedition to New Mexico along with Rufus Sage. Francis Parkman mentioned "that fellow Tucker" in his *The Oregon Trail*, but the identity of these "trappers from the mountains" (as Bullock called them in his 9 June letter to his wife) remains obscure.

[42] William Clayton measured the distance between Fort Bridger and the Salt Lake Valley as a mountainous 113 miles, so this would be a hard, but not impossible, ride.

[43] Bullock wrote that he was gathering buffalo hair to make "a softer bed" and reported, "We are now about 300 miles from Fort Bridger, but where we go, we know not." He said he was reading the Bible and had reached 119 Psalms. He wrote he was "up before the sun every morning praying for you, & long to clasp you feverently in my arms again." Thomas Bullock to Henrietta Bullock, 9 June 1847, Henrietta Rushton Bullock Collection, LDS Archives.

[44] This was Wagonhound Creek, which many emigrants mistook for a tributary of LaBonte Creek.

[45] The trail passed directly in front of this strange formation, today called Grindstone Butte or Knob Hill. In 1860, Richard Francis Burton "saw on the left of the path a huge natural pile or burrow of primitive boulders, about 200 feet high and called 'Brigham's Peak.'" See Burton, *The City of the Saints*, 150.

[46] This was Bed Tick Creek.

some mountain Flax, a deal of Artimesia & many crickets. There were an immense number where we halted. At 2:10 start again, ascended a hill, & found a very good road for several miles about ¼ mile from the hills. Saw 2 Prairie Dogs—heard them bark. Then crossed a creek twice,[47] went down it a short distance, then ascended a hill, & on our descent saw the Pioneer Expedition about 2 or 3 miles ahead ascending a hill. Halt for the night at 6:00 on "R. a la Prele" finding plenty of Cotton Wood, Ash & Timber—plenty of feed, a Swift current of Water about 7 yards wide, & a beautiful place having travelled 1¼ [+] 10 [+] 8 [=] 19¼ miles.[48] Presidents Young, Kimball, Woodruff &c riding a head, the brethren clearing the road of Rocks. Shortly after we had camped, 6 men & 15 horses (reported to me) passed our camp. Some of them [were] lately arrived from Santa Fe. Report the Battalion gone to California, that General Kearney had had an engagement with the Mexicans, was Wounded in three places by a Spear, & was doubtful whether he would recover, &c.[49] The Mormons at Pueblo were much dissatisfied & many of them talked of returning to the States to their families. They are now about 15 days march from that place towards Fort Laramie. The Hunters kill 2 Antelope [and] 1 Deer. A Beautiful day. Starling Driggs also kills 1 Antelope [and] 1 Deer, arriving in Camp at 10 at night. I made a tracing of Fremont's Map from Fort Laramie to Deer Creek.

Thursday 10 June 1847—Opened with a lovely morning. The place I had to stand guard was on a hill where I had a beautiful view & delightful company, the Birds were singing merrily. The country looked Green. I could see a great distance in some directions. A solemnity prevailed near me & altogether to praise their Creator. Two Deer galloped by in their happy manner & "the Brook murmured by" in its course to the Father of Waters. A few rods from the Camp was a Grave, several Stones piled on it; on one of which was written the name "J. Umbree 1843."[50] Gathered up teams & at 7:20 start. Crossed "La Prele" River taking a North then West & again North course. On ascending a hill, at 5:30 saw

---

[47] This was Sand Creek, which is almost always dry.
[48] The Saints camped near Ayres Natural Bridge on LaPrele Creek.
[49] On 6 December 1846, California lancers badly wounded General Stephen Watts Kearny at the Battle of San Pasqual, but he survived. With the support of the Mormon Battalion, Kearny was able to wrest power from an insubordinate John C. Frémont and assert his presidential appointment as governor of California.
[50] This was the grave of six-year-old Joel Hembree, who was run over by a wagon. See Reg Duffin, "The Grave of Joel Hembree," 6–16.

Platte River & one of the Emigration Companies about 3 miles a head. After crossing 2 small creeks[51] & ascending & descending 2 or 3 hills, came to a halt at 1:15 on the "Fourcher Boisee" to water, feed & rest our teams.[52] Some good grass on the banks of the River. Also Stunted Cotton Wood & other Trees & Willows. All the country covered with [the] "Artimesia" of Fremont. Some of our brethren call it "Southern Wood,"[53] intermixed with a slight sprinkling of tall grass. At 1:30 Camp again start in nearly a strait line, about West by North, over a good road. In about 4 miles travel arrived again on the Platte [at] ¼ past 3. Having a steep descent, obliged to lock Wheels. On the opposite side of the River is a very pretty grove of Cotton Wood Trees; we then nearly follow the course of the Platte, on the route killing a Viper & Rattlesnake. Crossed over Deer Creek, a very pretty clear stream of Water about 50 feet wide & about 20 inches deep. We then halt on the opposite Bank, or West side, at 5:30. This is the prettiest place we have yet camped at, finding plenty of grass [and] a beautiful Timber spot consisting chiefly of Cotton Wood, Ash, Box Alder, Choke Cherry & Willows.[54] Two beds of coal were found, one a few rods from Camp, the other about ¼ mile. Specimens were brought to Camp, Albert Carrington bringing a canal coal & G. A. Smith bringing a Bright Black Coal. Several brethren went a fishing with rods & lines & caught many Fish of the White sort. Many Deer & antelope were seen on the route. 4 antelopes were killed & brought to Camp. The Whip poor will & Red breasts enlivened the Grove. While the Twelve go to meet on the banks of the Platte, Presidents Young, Kimball, Woodruff & Smith ride ahead, while six brethren follow picking the Stones off the road & clearing a better way for the Wagons. A fine day, very warm in the evening. Travelled 8¾ [+] 9 [=] 17¾ miles.

Friday 11 June 1847—I wrote on a Skull directions for the next Saints, planting it near my Wagon, also planted a hill of corn as usual. A lovely morning & birds singing in a pretty grove of Timber. Onions grow in plenty about here & on all this day's journey, also the mustard in

---

[51] These were West Cottonwood and Little Box Elder creeks.
[52] This halt was on Box Elder Creek.
[53] This was clustered broomrape (*Orobanche fasciculata*), or perhaps simply sagebrush (*Artemisia*).
[54] Erastus Snow agreed with Bullock, calling Deer Creek "the most delightful place we have seen since we left the states." The Saints would establish a waystation here in 1857, despite the protests of the Indian Agents who had given the site to a Sioux band. The pioneer company camp was near present Glenrock, Wyoming.

patches. At 7:30 Camp starts from Deer Creek & soon comes to an ugly pitch in a gulley, which we got thro' safe.[55] Follow the course of the Platte nearly in a strait line & passing a couple of ravines. On descending a hill, halt at 11:40 in the bottoms, near some Cotton Woods & plenty of mustard & Grass. I found several mushrooms on our road. At 1:30 the Camp again start, come to a rapid muddy creek about 15 or 20 feet wide & two deep.[56] Water the cattle, cross it & then travel on generally a level road. Cross another very small creek, ascend a hill, passing strait across it; come in sight of two of the camps at halt ahead, when we turn down to a Cotton Wood grove, and halt at 5:30 about ½ mile from them where President Richards had previously been to explore a good place for the night.[57] Presidents Kimball, Woodruff, Benson & Smith ride ahead, & report [a] crossing place 10 or a dozen miles from this place.[58] Hunters kill antelopes. 9¼ [+] 7¾ [=] 17 Miles. The rugged bluffs have disappeared from our course. They are now more gradual & at the top of some bluffs, about 7 miles off, patches of Snow are still left. The two camps half a mile off make more noise by ten times than all our Camp put together. I clearly hear their caroling while writing this. There is a Woodpecker taping a hollow Cotton Wood Tree, over my head. Some of the men in next Camp brought down a ball of Snow, which A. P. Rockwood held in his hand. Elder Kimball saw it. The Snow was several feet deep on the drifts.

Saturday 12 June 1847—A beautiful morning, clear sky & Pleasant breeze. The Emigrants [are] crossing [the] River above us. After closing up my journal, I went to pack away the goods in my Wagon to be in readiness for starting, when George Brown said, the Captain's orders were to see after the cattle, that they were all safe. I told him I would go myself as quick as I could put the things away; which took me about 5 or 10 minutes at the outside. I then started after the cattle, saw them all, & then met G. Brown & told him I had seen them all. He asked why I had not gone when he told me, "instead of idling & fooling away your time half an hour." I replied "O Good God, what a lie, if you say I have

---

[55] This "ugly pitch" can still be seen in a ravine about a mile west of Glenrock.

[56] Naturally enough, this was present Muddy Creek.

[57] The Mormons camped on the southeast point of the big bend in the North Platte at the site of today's Edness Kimball Wilkins State Park, about five miles east of today's Casper, Wyoming.

[58] The scouts found the site of their next day's camp where the Saints built the first Mormon Ferry across the North Platte.

been idling or fooling half an hour." He said you were idling, & if you say that again I'll strike you. He went a short distance & came back & said "did you say I lied?" I replied, "If you say, I either idled or fooled away half an hour, for I was not 10 minutes about the Wagon." He then struck me with his Whip saying, "I am ready for a fight, for I'd as leave fight as not." I said, "You shall hear of this again, for I shall tell the Doctor." He up with his fist to strike me, saying, "You may tell the Doctor as soon as you like," but I got out of the reach of his arm, & so avoided another blow. George Brown has lied to and about the Lord's anointed many times. I have been more abused & reviled by him than any other person. He has now Struck me with his Whip and I now pray that the Lord God of Israel may reward him according to his evil deeds & punish him until he [shall] repent & forsake his evil ways.

Saturday 12 contd. The teams were gathered up & 2nd Company, 1st Division leads at 8:07 passing thro' a steep gully and hill, following the course of the Platte. Cross a small creek & in a short distance after, the brethren made a bridge over another creek[59] & continued our course until we came to an old Ford where Colonel Markham & brother James Case forded it, finding that the Water came as high as the middle of the horses' sides. The Camp went on & halt on a ridge near the River at 11:45 where the River was again examined, but it would not do for us to cross. During our halt, the brethren grade the hill, so as to make a better road, to go down, & reascend the opposite side of the Gully. At 1:45 the Camp started again, taking nearly a strait line. About 4 P.M. we crossed a swift muddy creek,[60] about 6 feet wide & 2 or 3 deep, & halt for the night at 4:15 [after] travelling 7¼ [+] 4 [=] 11¼ miles.[61]

The Hunters kill 4 antelopes. Seeley Owens also kills a Big Horned Mountain Sheep. Some of the brethren bring in Specimens of coal from a bed about 10 feet thick, also of Brown Mica, Micaceous Sandstone, Calcareous Sandstone, Whitish Compact Limestone, & Granite Quartz.

Artemas Johnson was out all day hunting without leave, and Tunis

---

[59] Clayton called Bullock's "steep gulley" Deep Gulf; highway construction has destroyed the trail through this area. The two creeks are Claude Creek and Elkhorn Creek, which Clayton called Muddy Creek.

[60] The Saints crossed Garden Creek in present west Casper.

[61] The pioneer camp on the North Platte was located within the city limits of Casper, "but the exact location has yet to be found and probably never will be." See Franzwa, *Maps of the Oregon Trail*, 120. Bullock's distances support the belief that the first Mormon Ferry was located near today's reconstruction of Fort Caspar, which displays a replica of the ferry boat.

Rappelyee went without leave to the mountains after we had halted to get a Snow Ball, supposing the distance only about 3 miles. Neither of them having returned at dark, the brethren began to fear for their safety, as there are the appearances of many bears in this country. Colonel Markham went out with a detachment of Sidney A. Hanks, John Y. Green, Phinehas H. Young, Harvey Pierce, John Holman, James Craig, & Samuel Fox in search of them. The Bugle was sounded in different directions round the Camp, at distances, from ½ past 8 to ½ past 12. Guns were fired at intervals, and a large fire was kindled as guides for the brethren. At 11 minutes to 11 Rappelyee returned, & it was not 'till ½ past 12 that Johnson was found & brought back to Camp. Rappelyee said he would not go another such a journey after a Snow Ball for 100 dollars. Johnson had got tired out & sat down on the hills. Although the hills appear only about 3 miles, they are actually about 6 or 8 to the top. There is Snow in many places on the top & the sides are covered with Pine & Cedar Trees.

I was very sick, & feeble all day, from the effects of a severe bowel complaint. Doctor administered some Composition Tea at night to warm my System.

Sunday 13 June 1847—I continued sick, in my Wagon all morning. Doctor made me more Composition Tea & Boiled Milk & Flour, which did me good. There was a meeting in the morning. Presidents Young, Kimball, & Pratt spoke. John S. Fowler took notes of the Speeches. Afterwards the Twelve and Captains met at the President's Wagon, to take into cons[ideratio]n the manner of crossing the River in the best way, when the companies joined two or three together to effect that purpose. Each company thus united went with Teams to the Pineries for trees to construct their rafts, while Presidents Young, Pratt, Smith & Benson with Lorenzo Young & Edmund Ellsworth rowing the boat, [went] to ascertain the depth of the River. It varies from 4 to 6 feet deep. While Luke Johnson & James Case ford the River in other places on horseback, the brethren tow a yoke of oxen over the River for the Emigrants.

The Pioneer Company of 17 Wagons & Cutter that came ahead on the 9th have killed 3 Buffalo, very fat, 5 Antelopes and 4 Bears. The Paw of a She Black Bear measured 10 inches between the Spread of the

Toes—7 inches long, 5½ wide [and] the Claws 2¾ inches long, [which] will give any man an ugly clutch, or the ball of his foot would give a man a very ugly box on the ear, & may the Lord preserve me from such animals. They also saved the life of a young man belonging to the Emigrating Company & ferried over 24 Wagons at [$]1.50 each receiving in pay Flour at [$]2.50 per 100 pounds, Meal at [$].50 per Bushel, & Bacon at .6[¢] per pound. They also did some Blacksmithing for the Emigrants who were chiefly from Jackson, Clay, & Lafayette & Davies[s] Counties Missouri.[62] When the brethren first commenced ferrying for them, they were armed with Bowie Knives & Pistols, but before the brethren had finished their work the men had put them all away and having put away their fears also, were very civil and kind to the brethren, often inviting them to take coffee & biscuits; & when the job was finished made quite a feast of Tea, coffee, Biscuits, Butter, Meat & the good things. Mr. Bowman the leader of the lower Company, told Colonel Markham that he was the Father of Bill Bowman, who had custody of Joseph Smith at the time he escaped from Missouri. His Son was rode to death on a Bar of Iron.[63] Obadiah Jennings was the leader of the Mob who did it (Jennings was also at the Haun's Mills Massacre of the Saints) either in 1841 or 1842. The old man says it would not be good for him to see any of the mob, but he tries to keep it out of his mind as much as possible. He also said Morgan the Sheriff is in Oregon. Brassfield & Pogue he did not know; Markham last heard they were in the South East of Missouri. Bowman, Morgan, Brassfield & Pogue all divided alike.[64] The Flour & Meal was divided amongst the brethren [with] 6 pounds of Flour and 2 pounds Meal to each person, which is

---

[62] These were the Missouri counties where the Mormons first settled in 1831, and were close to Caldwell County, where most of the Missouri Saints settled after being driven from Jackson County in 1834.

[63] William Bowman was the first sheriff of Daviess County, Missouri, before the 1838 Mormon War. He swore an affidavit for Joseph Smith's arrest in August 1838, but a mob correctly believed he later collaborated in Smith's escape from Liberty Jail and dragged Bowman by his hair across the town square. Daviess Sheriff William Morgan was said to have died at the hands of the same mob from the affects of a ride through town on an iron bar, but the older Bowman's account puts him in Oregon. See Roberts, *Comprehensive History*, 1:532; and LeSueur, *The 1838 Mormon War in Missouri*, 244.

[64] *The History of Caldwell County* called William O. Jennings "the Hector of the fight"—which was actually a massacre—at Haun's Mill. As a militia colonel from Livingston County, Jennings had "entered into a treaty of peace" with the Saints in Caldwell County, but treacherously assaulted them two days later, perhaps in response to Governor Boggs' "extermination order." See Roberts, *Comprehensive History*, 1:481–83. Along with William Bowman, John Brassfield and John Pogue guarded Joseph Smith in Daviess County. See Smith, *History of the Church*, 3:309.

quite a blessing to the Camp. Pleasant day. East wind. At 10 minutes past 7, the 3rd 10 brought a small dog raft to carry the goods over which Presidents Young, Kimball, Richards, Smith & several brethren haul on Shore.

Monday 14 June 1847—Arose by day break. The 1st Company (1st & 2nd tens) ferry over the first boat load of goods at 4:20 [and] got steering poles trimmed & 4 Wagons unloaded sooner. After 5:00 I was out on Guard. Heard a rushing noise behind me, turned round & saw a cloud passing over & enveloping the tops of the Mountains in White mist, which in a short time cleared away again. A great deal of Wild Sage, Camomile, & other herbs about the country and an immense quantity of Crickets & Grasshoppers. A very laborious day for the brethren who were getting over the River. 23 crossed to land safely & 2—John Pack's & the Cannon Wagon box—roled over several times, breaking some of the boys & losing several articles. The Wagons were afterwards got to shore [and] the goods were put across in the Cutter safe. I was better to day & was out on guard all day, until about 4 when a very heavy thunder shower came on, the rain and hail pouring down in torrents, beating thro' most of the Wagon Covers. The river rose very rapidly after the Storm subsided. I hunted up & milked the cow & then crossed the River to the North side, the Sun about an hour high. SE Wind until the Storm when it changed to the West.

Tuesday 15 June 1847—A very strong West Wind made it very difficult for the brethren to Cross over their Wagons. Many horses were swam over when as one drove was swimming over, a horse belonging to Robert Crow, having a Larryat on it, got loose, when the horse got his foot entangled in it [and] drawing his head under water, he got drowned. Doctor had all his Seeds & bedding out of both Wagons having the benefit of the Sun shine. Joseph Scofield killed a very large Rattle snake. Doctor Got the Oil out of him. After he was skinned, cut open, & his fat taken out, he writhed about, until the Doctor found his heart & cut it through with his knife. I watched the oxen thro' the day, at one time sitting under a very large Eagle's nest which appears about 6 feet deep and about 5 feet wide, made of dry twigs & resting upon three branches of a tall cotton Wood Tree. Many onions scattered about our camping ground. New Moon this evening visible.

Wednesday 16 June 1847—A very fine morning, South West Wind. I commenced washing my Clothes and dried same. A Storm passed over the hills South of the River, but a slight rain came to our Camp. Jacob D. Burnham gave me a coat for which I am very thankful.

Doctor went out between 10 and 11, crossed the river, went down to the President's encampment and dined with him. President Young had sent a four horse team to get timber to make a good raft, in addition to the timber already on hand, which arrived about 10; when President Young stript himself and went to work with all his strength, assisted by the Doctor and the brethren, and made a first rate White Pine and White Cotton Wood Raft. The Presidents also sent two 6 horse teams down the River after timber to make 2 Canoes. Doctor returned at 6:30. A Camp of 10 Wagons, 10 horses, & 33 yoke of Oxen pass up the South side of the River & will give [$]1.50 for each Wagon to be ferried over & [$]5.00 Extra if they are ferried over to night. There is another Camp a little below & one about 5 miles below who wish us to ferry them over. 3 men arrive in Camp, who had crossed below about 5 miles, they wish they had known of our Ferry & they would have had their 24 Wagons crossed over by us. The President will leave several men here to ferry over all the Companies that come along, until the brethren who come from Winter Quarters; after ferrying them over, then to come along with them.[65] Very windy evening. 1 antelope killed.

Thursday 17 June 1847—The mosquitoes have been very plaguy the past night; they are more numerous here than any other place on our route. Frosty night, Pleasant day. The brethren still continued ferrying over the River. The Cannon was passed over about ½ past 2 when the brethren commenced ferrying over the next Camp. The new raft was in operation all day & worked well. Some of the brethren made two Canoes to leave with a few of the brethren who will stay 'till the next Camp of Saints from Winter Quarters arrives here. About 1 P.M. President Young gave orders for the Pioneer Camp to come together & form the Circle. I

---

[65] The Mormon Ferry on the North Platte was the first commercial ferry operation in the Rocky Mountains. By 23 June the ferry company—Thomas Grover, John S. Higbee, William A. Empey, Appleton M. Harmon, Edmund Ellsworth, Luke Johnson, Francis M. Pomeroy, James Davenport, and Benjamin F. Stewart—moved the operation some eight miles downriver to where the trail met the North Platte near the pioneer camp of 11 June. Here they ran the ferry until the bulk of the non-Mormon emigration had passed; the party then dispersed, some waiting at the ferry or going down the trail to join their families in the second division, and some returning to the States. See Morgan, "The Mormon Ferry on the North Platte," 111–12.

gathered up my team & drove up both of the Doctor's Wagons. In the course of this day I travelled about 24 miles after the oxen & was very tired at night. Fastened the 2 yoke to the Stakes & went to bed, after dark. Saw many thistles in my travels & onions in flower.

Friday 18 June 1847—I was awoke by dawn of day, arose, & found the oxen loosed from the Stakes; leaving no signs of being there thro' the night. This is the 2nd time Doctor has ordered me to tie up the cattle this week & each time they have been turned loose in the night. I was sent on Guard & waded thro' the Wet Grass about 5 or 6 miles to drive in a drove of stray cattle, among which were two that I tied up last night. It was thro' getting wet feet that brought on the Auge before; & this morning's jaunt will, I am afraid, bring it back again. A cold morning, keen West Wind, Clear Sky. I can only see one man on guard beside myself. The brethren resumed crossing the Emigrant Camp; gathered up teams, when I went with Rockwood to receive pay from the two Camps already crossed. Kept an account while Rockwood weighed & received it. Afterwards Captain Ashworth invited us to breakfast with him, on Bacon, Warm Biscuits, & light fried Biscuits, good coffee with Sugar & then milk. Eating a good breakfast from a Woman's Cooking is a remembrance of past times & renews the desire for such times to come again. In a short time afterwards Colonel Rockwood & T. B. crossed the River in a Boat to receive the pay from Captain Kerls' Company. At ¼ to 2 assisted to put on the new raft, which went across well. Then went to look at a cow which we rece[ive]d with other things from Captain Kerls' Company & recrossed the river with the provisions about ½ past 3. Pleasant day. The brethren make 5 Wharves in different places besides crossing teams. Doctor dictated instructions to Thomas Grover & Company who were going to stay here, after which President Young took them & a few others a short distance from Camp, gave them good instr[ucti]ons, & then preached a Sermon on Plurality of Wives. Would not council Glines to stay, & those who were staying voted that they did not want Glines to stay.[66]

---

[66] Against counsel, Eric Glines stayed at the ferry, "but repenting of his disobedience," he followed the pioneer company, camping alone and with a Missouri company—"a dangerous undertaking" that earned a reprimand from Brigham Young when Glines rejoined the Camp of Israel on 26 June. See Jenson, *LDS Biographical Encyclopedia*, 4:704.

Here Bullock completed Journal No. 1. For the accounts, lists, tables, and the "Laws Regulating the Camp of Israel" at the end of the journal, see Appendix B.

No. 2
JOURNAL OF THE TRAVEL OF THE PIONEER CAMP OF ISRAEL, FROM WINTER QUARTERS, IN SEARCH OF A LOCATION FOR A STAKE OF ZION
KEPT BY
THOMAS BULLOCK
CLERK OF THE PIONEER CAMP

1847 June Sunday 27—I commence to fill up the notes I have taken on the route, as it is utterly impossible for me to do justice in writing a Journal. Having besides a team to drive, to run after the cow, fetch Water, hunt up and carry Wood, look after the oxen, stand guard over the cattle, load and unload my Wagon of its contents, and run to do every job that is wanted, & when I pick up items not allowed time to fill them out. Almost every man in Camp has more or less time to spare, but I have not *now* spare time allowed to fill up the Journal, to fulfil the very office I was brought out to fill—namely, keep the Camp Journal.

Thomas Bullock

So I commence.

Saturday 19 June 1847—I made copy of instructions to Grover & Company who are going to stay. Presidents Young & Richards sign both copies also Grover, Johnson, Davenport, Empy, Stewart, Pomeroy, Higbee, Harmon, & Ellsworth, copy on file. Other given to Luke Johnson. Eric Glines stays without council. Camp starts to ascend some hills to the right. Cross a large plain then descend the hill.[67] See a Camp ahead. Halt opposite "Red Buttes" about ¾ hour, no water, pretty good feed.[68] Hitch up, go half a mile & Water cattle, then start at [blank] over gravel

---
[67] This is the descent from Rim Rock.

[68] The name Red Buttes was a legacy of the fur trade that described the hills flanking the North Platte between Coal and Bessemer mountains. Here on 26 July 1865 Cheyenne and Sioux warriors overran a circled Army wagon train and annihilated Sergeant Amos Custard and some twenty men after ambushing and killing Lieutenant Caspar Wever Collins, for whom Casper, Wyoming, is named.

road. Leaving a row of hills on the left come to a natural wall.[69] Descend a gully by zig zag uneven road & very bad. Turn to the right [and] halt in a hollow at [7:40]. Bad water, saline deposit, scanty grass, no wood, but some Artimesia.[70] I ascend [a] steep hill with Professor Pratt [and] find green & divers colored Stones. Fine view of the country, it being a very steep high hill. O. P. Rockwell kills 1 Buffalo. Travelled NW then SW 11¼ A.M. [+] 10 P.M. [=] 21½ miles. Wind NW. President Young told me "I had proved faithful. I should enjoy better health & this journey would prove as good as a little fortune to me." We then examined Fremont's Map. 1 Deer & 3 Antelopes killed. At night used Sage to cook with.

Sunday 20 June 1847—Several cattle getting mixed, orders given to gather up at day break & start at 5:17 over a good road. [After] about 3 miles [we] halt at 7:04 in [the] road by [a] clear streamlet and good grass. See Camp ahead. Doctor cooks breakfast by Artimesia fire. Many Thistles, fine bed of mint. Start at 10:10. Presidents Young & Kimball [go] ahead on horses thro' narrow vale [and] ascend a hill. Pass Willow Springs at 11:20—clear, beautiful water—where cattle were watered.[71] [We] again ascend [a] hill [and] on the summit see Snow on mountains, the Sweetwater, Rocks, Hills, & Plain.[72] Presidents Young, Kimball, & Richards examine Map, then descend the hill. One place very steep. Cross several small runs of Water, Slight grass. Halt at 2:50 near a creek & good grass. Start at 4:56 over generally level road. Cross small River, crooked & rapid, 3 yards wide. See mark of a Bears Paw, 10 inches long in sand, ball 7 inches, claws 3 inches. The Sun set behind the Mountains. Camp halt at 7:40 on a hill, by a Stream & good feed.[73] Saw many Flowers & Thistles, Artimesia all over the country. Sandy road. Wind SE, clear day. I was sent on Guard till late at night. Elder Woodruff &

---

[69] Instead of the Emigrant Gap trail, the pioneers took a northern variant of the River route, later known as the Telegraph or Military Road, west from present Casper. The "natural wall" was also known to emigrants as the Devil's Backbone, Rock Avenue, or Avenue of Rocks.

[70] Many of the Saints regarded this camp at Poison Spring Creek as the worst campsite on the entire journey. Ironically, as a local joke it bears the name of William Clayton Slough, despite his advice that it smelled bad and "ought to be avoided as a camping ground."

[71] Willow Springs was later a Pony Express station.

[72] This was 400-foot Prospect Hill, which gained its name from the expansive view of the Sweetwater Mountains from its summit.

[73] To emigrants this was Sage or Greasewood Creek, but today it is known as Horse Creek.

Thomas Brown absent from Camp. Fearing that they might be lost, a large fire of Sage was kindled, & the Cannon fired at 12 o'clock, to let them know our whereabouts. Travelled 3¾ before breakfast, 9 [miles before our] noon halt, 7¼ [by] Night [for a total of] 20 miles. Warm day. Sandy road.

Monday 21 June 1847—Fine morning. Clear Sky. Woodruff & Brown not returned cause much anxiety for their safety. At 8:45 Camp starts, Presidents Young & Kimball's Wagons going first. Go back to the road, then South along a level Sandy Road, pass a big rock.[74] Go between two Lakes & over a bed of Saline matter. The Gad Flies begin to plague oxen. Saw a small Lake to the left, of Saleratus. Sent G. Brown to get a sample, which Sister Lorenzo Young tried with Sour Milk also Vinegar, it being better than the Saleratus they had from the States.[75] Brother Young & G. Brown returned to the Lakes to fill two Buckets. I drove both teams the while. They returned to Camp loaded. Halt on the Sweetwater at 12 o'clock. Brother Young having tried the Saleratus to make light Cakes & answering well, many brethren return to the Lake to fill their Buckets. I am thankful to the Lord that I have been enabled to do so much good. Elders Woodruff & Brown returned to Camp.[76] I went to the top of Independence Rock, found Presidents Young, Richards, Smith, Woodruff & others, who went over & round it.[77] President Young gave orders while on the Rock to gather up teams. When Camp start at 2:50 a smart Shower passed over. [We] then pass Independence Rock. Saw many names written on it.[78] Cross the Sweetwater—6 rods wide, a very

---

[74] This was Steamboat Rock.

[75] Saleratus is sodium bicarbonate, commonly known today as baking soda. Bullock advised Griffith William, "About four miles east of Independence Rock is a small saleratus lake on the left of the road, where I would advise you to gather one or two hundred pounds weight for family use; this stuff is what you will rise your bread with, and the soda in the same lake is excellent to wash with. Remember this." See Bullock to William, *Millennial Star* (15 April 1848), 117.

[76] Woodruff and Brown had visited Independence Rock and spent the night with the Missourians.

[77] The granite dome of Independence Rock was the most noted trail landmark west of Fort Laramie. William L. Sublette of the Smith, Jackson & Sublette fur company named "Rock Independence" when he camped there on 4 July 1830. Surveyor F. V. Hayden measured the rock's circumference as 1,552 yards in 1870. See Morgan and Harris, eds., *The Rocky Mountain Journals of William Marshall Anderson*, 118.

[78] Hundreds of emigrant names are still scratched and painted on Independence Rock. Robert Spurrier Ellison's *Independence Rock: The Great Record of the Desert* recorded some 600 of these names in 1930; the Wyoming chapter of the Oregon-California Trails Association currently has located more than 1,300 names. Project leader Levida Hileman reported the survey crew located "Norton Jacob 47" inscribed on the top of the north end of the rock. Letter to Will Bagley, 16 January 1996.

crooked River. Ascend hill to the Road. Saw another Camp in our rear. Pass "Devil's Gate." Presidents Young, Kimball, Woodruff, Pratt, Smith, brother Little & others go inside one portion of it. I and several others then clambered over the hill. Saw two places where men had camped on the top. Also blood, near the houses of Pine brush, [and] the tracks of Bear. Pine, Cedar, Gooseberry & other Trees. Very romantic Spot. Descend on opposite side. Altogether a romantic Spot.[79] The rocks overhang the River 4–5– or 600 feet high & make a man dizzy to look up. The roar of Water deafening. Camp halts on West side at 6:30 near a creek.[80] Warm day. 7½ [+] 7¾ [=] 14¼ miles [sic].

Tuesday 22 June 1847—I was called up to Guard at 3 A.M. by the Doctor's orders [and] guarded cattle until horn blew to gather up. A good place, plenty of grass, many Flowers, Dandelions, Thistles, Mosquitoes, and much Grease Wood. Also many Snipes & an immense quantity of Crickets. (I gave up the Journal to Doctor, as he said if I must Guard, the Camp must do their own writing. I took it up again on 26th to record Notes, & do as well as I can, & try my best to fulfil what the President wanted me for; but I have so many commanders; it is hard for me to do every thing.) Camp start at 7:15. Cross the creek, the most crooked I ever saw, about 12 feet wide & Swift. Presidents Young & Kimball ahead. Warm morning, Clear Sky, very Sandy road. Grade two places [and] make a bridge. Cross another creek about =20= feet wide. Travel over some beautiful prairie, then over uneven road, thro' Grease Wood, & past much Saline deposit. [We] halt on the Sweetwater at 11:50 [with] good grass. Bathed in river. A clear Sky & travel thro' romantic scenery. Camp of 10 Wagons pass us. Report Columbus Dustin from Morgan County, Illinois, drowned at the Lower Ferry. Also several other camps behind them. Good grass at this place. Lorenzo Young broke the Axle Tree of his Wagon this A.M. Presidents Young, Woodruff & Benson return to his assistance.[81] Camp start at 2:15 [and]

---

[79] "By a barometrical measurement," Orson Pratt determined the walls of Devil's Gate rose 400 feet above the river, "which here cuts through a granite rock, forming a chasm about 900 or 1000 feet in length, and 130 feet in breadth." (The gate is actually 370 feet deep and 1,500 feet long.) Devil's Gate remains one of the most beautiful spots on the trail.

[80] The Mormons camped on the site of today's Sun Ranch.

[81] Harriet Young, who kept much of the journal attributed to her husband, recorded "one of our axeltrees broke on the naked prairie without a sticke of timber or anyone to help us." She assigned the events to 23 June, when Charles Harper finished fixing it. See Young, ed., "Diary of Lorenzo Dow Young," 162.

ascend a steep, long Sand hill. Descend it on opposite side by 3 steep places. Pass another Saleratus Lake. Grade the hill to a creek 5¾ miles from start, then cross it. After another hill, [we] pass the Camp at halt on Sweetwater. Cross another small creek, & halt near a high, steep hill at 8 o'clock—a pretty place, beautiful grass & camping spot. Warm day, dusty road. 10 [+] 10¾ [=] 20¾.

Wednesday 23 June 1847—I Bathed before Sunrise with Brother Little. Clear sky, warm morning. Camp start at 7:25. Pass a Grave "Matilda Crowley B. July 16, 1830. D. July 7, 1846."[82] [We] see Rocky Mountains covered with Snow. Cross a Shallow creek 6 feet wide. Presidents Young & Kimball's Wagons going first, they on horses, over [a] Sandy Road, but good travelling. At 10:30 came to River & halt at 11:10 on good grass, near bold rocks, with a few stunted trees on. Here were the remains of some Indian Wicka Ups. Many mosquitoes, some mint, much Flag. At noon commenced being cloudy. Start at 1:15 leaving the River, going thro' very heavy Sand. A Deer passes thro' Camp a few yards before Doctor's team. Very bold rocks. Travel thro' much Grease Wood & Artimesia, but very little grass. Get a fine view of the Wind River chain of Mountains. Came to the River at 4:43 & halt at 5:45 on good grass.[83] A Warm day. Slight Wind in afternoon from South. Travelled 8½ A.M. [+] 8½ P.M. [=] 17 miles.

Thursday 24 June 1847—Camp start at 6:15. I was very sick in bed, Brother Little driving my team. At 11:30 reached top of bluff. Pass 10 Wagons at noon resting in the road. No wood, water or grass along the road, which was Sandy, yet good travelling. [We] descend the hill & Camp on the Sweetwater at 3:35.[84] A company of Emigrants [was] crossing the River at the time. [We] travelled 17¾ miles; here we find plenty of grass, water, & wood. The Company of 10 Wagons camped below us. A Warm day. The Sweetwater Mountains are disappearing, the Rocky Mountains coming into plainer view. This evening while driving

---

[82] Trouble dogged the Crowley family; a fourteen-year-old daughter later died 18 October 1846 on the Applegate Cutoff, and her grave near Grants Pass gave the name to Grave Creek. See Morgan, *Overland in 1846*, 1:185, 2:764.

[83] The Deep Sand Route let the Mormons avoid the three crossings of the Sweetwater to reach this camp beyond the fifth crossing of the Sweetwater, about seven miles northwest of present Jeffrey City, Wyoming.

[84] This night's camp was at the sixth crossing of the Sweetwater. Between the fifth and sixth crossings, the pioneers discovered an "Ice Spring" (probably at the site now called Ice Slough), consisting of ice still frozen beneath the prairie from the previous winter.

up the cattle, John Holman [was] carrying his Gun. It accidentally went off, shooting President Young's "John" Horse in the belly. He lingered till night when he died. This is the 3rd horse killed thro' accidents.[85] Presidents Richards & Woodruff laid hands on me, to rebuke my sickness, brother Woodruff, mouth.

Friday 25 June 1847—Camp called up by day break, several brethren cross the River to fetch up our cattle that had mixed with the Missourians herd. When they started, we hitched up and started at 6:45 with a pleasant morning but a dusty road, the wind being ahead, the other Camp of 10 Wagons & 33 yoke of Oxen following in our trail. Camp crossed the Island in the Sweetwater and then ascended a high hill. Descending again to the River, then took a bend to the right over a steep hill of sand, the dust flying in a perfect cloud & almost suffocating.[86] Crossed two small Sloughs, then continued up the valley by the river side, until we crossed a small beautiful creek when Camp came to a halt on a beautiful bottom of excellent grass, with plenty of wood, and surrounded by high hills, at 11:15. Here we found plenty of dandelions, White flowers called Pickpockets, Onions, Gooseberries, a Strawberry Vine & a Mineral Spring.

[We] leave this place at 1:30 continuing thro' a very narrow vale. At the end of it, [we] pass Captain Ashworth's & Smith's Companies at halt, when we ascended a long steep hill, finding many Daisies which was a pleasant sight for me.[87] Brother Wordsworth brought me a ball of Snow which I ate; quite a treat for the Anniversary of my Wedding day.[88] On arriving at the top saw 3 small lakes on the plain on our right.[89] Dr. Richards clearing away the Stones out of the Road, then travelled over a level, hard road, for several miles. Cross a creek & halt on the banks of another creek where we find many Strawberries in flower.[90] G. A. Smith brought in a branch of the "Aspen Poplar" from the Grove on the hill &

---

[85] Norton Jacob noted that this stallion was "the best horse in the camp, cost $150.00."

[86] By climbing this "steep hill of sand," the Mormons avoided the seventh and eighth crossings of the Sweetwater. Trail expert Randy Brown notes that the deep ruts on this hill are the only trail remnants in this section of the Sweetwater Valley.

[87] The company entered the "very narrow vale" of Sweetwater Canyon to avoid the usual climb to Rocky Ridge. They then climbed its south slope, the "long steep hill," to scale Rocky Ridge.

[88] Bullock had married Henrietta Rushton on 23 June 1838.

[89] These were the Lewiston Lakes. The pioneer company stayed south of the lakes and rejoined the main trail a mile or two west.

[90] Not surprisingly, this is today's Strawberry Creek.

reports it a beautiful grove. White Clover in flower, but little grass & form in circle at 7:15. One of the brethren brought into Camp two solid lumps of Ice, gave one lump to the Doctor and Sister Lorenzo Young gave him about ⅓ pound of Butter (the largest lump the Doctor has had for about 3 months) which he put some Ice to, making it hard and cold and having some light bread made, had a perfect feast in the ~~Little~~ Wilderness. Brother Little brought the Doctor a fine Specimen of Sandstone Grit, which he brought from a bed while ascending the Steep hill, the best that has been seen on our journey. The Wind River chain [was] in view several times during the day, covered with Snow. A very cold day, which caused the Warmer Clothing to be put on by the brethren. 8¾ A.M. [+] 11½ P.M. Total 20¼ miles.

Saturday 26 June 1847—Severe Frost in the night. Ice in the Buckets of Water. A Pail of milk in Brother Rockwood's Wagon frozen solid. Morning clear and cold. Fetched up cow & in going after the oxen saw many Strawberry Vines in Flower, Gooseberries, also Willows on the banks of the River. Got Wet. Kicked three times by cow, while milking. Assisted brother Little cooking. Camp starts at 7:40. [We] pass 3 small Groves on [the] left, one on the right. Ascend some gentle hills. On a Sudden come to the Sweetwater in a deep ravine with many Willows & Shrubs on its banks.[91] Cross it at 9:45, about 15 yards wide. Ascend a hill, see another camp in our rear, continue over a very good road in a line to Table Rocks[92] & descend a gentle inclined Plane to the main branch of the Sweetwater. Cross it. Some of the Wagon boxes had to be raised higher, the Water being deep & swift. Cross it & halt on the South bank at 12:50. Plenty of grass, wood & water. Here was a very large Snow Drift, about 10 feet deep. The boys & girls Snowballing each other. The Doctor & I had a regular turn at it for some minutes, being a rarity in the longest days. Eric Glines returns to Camp. Left the brethren at the Ferry well on Wednesday morning, the river had fallen about 18 inches & the Ferry was removed about 8 miles lower. Camp starts at 2:30 [and] ascend a very steep hill, travel over a level gravelly road seeing many antelopes on our route, also Daisies, Pinks, Onions, Artimesia [and] many Curious & Clear Stones. Had a Warm & Dusty afternoon, white clouds flying in the air. A Pleasant day's journey. Turned off the

---

[91] This was actually Rock Creek.   [92] These were the Oregon Buttes.

road, to halt again on the Sweetwater at 7 P.M.—a good camp ground.[93] Travel 11 A.M. [+] 7¾ P.M. [=] 18¾ miles. Presidents Young, Kimball & Woodruff riding a head. O. Pratt, G. A. Smith & others saw a Company returning to the States camped about 6 miles further & staid with them all night, reading Oregon & California Papers & conversing all night.[94] We kindled a fire as a Signal where we are at camp.

Sunday 27 June 1847—Fine morning. Clear Sky. The ox teams start first this morning at 8:20 shortly after met a Company of 8 Emigrants with mules returning from Oregon to the States with Pack mules.[95] Send letters by them. Pass the Dividing Ridge.[96] Descend West side of the South Pass. At the Springs met Mr. Harris, a Mountaineer, where G. A. Smith & O. Pratt had staid all night reading the Oregon newspapers & conversing all night. Intended staying here, but the place being very miry, [we] had to pursue our journey. Went to a creek where were many small Fish, but very little grass & halt at noon. The Artimesia 5 or 6 feet high & very thick. Start again at 2:40 over a level, barren, Sage country with but little grass, over a near gravel road, and halt for the night near a bed of Quick sand, having travelled 6¼ [+] 9 [=] 15¼ miles.[97] A Warm and dusty day. Mr. Moses Harris encamped with us & lent 7 Oregon Papers to read. Ezra T. Benson taken very sick. Anniversary of the Martyrdom of Joseph & Hyrum Smith.[98]

June 27—[written upside-down beneath the 22 June 1847 entry:] Moses Harris informs us that if we come from the States in Winter &

---

[93] From this campground the Saints left the Sweetwater River, which had brought them to within ten miles of the continental divide.

[94] Pratt camped at Pacific Springs and conversed with Major Moses "Black" Harris, a renowned mountaineer, who "intended to act as a guide to the emigrant companies if they wished to employ him." Pratt noted that Harris "had acquired an extensive and intimate knowledge of all the main features of the country to the Pacific." For Harris, see Peltier, "Moses 'Black' Harris," in Hafen, ed., *The Mountain Men*, 4:103–117.

[95] Levi Scott guided this party, which left Oregon City on 5 May, to Fort Hall via the Applegate Cutoff. They arrived at St. Joseph, Missouri, on 28 July, and included 1846 emigrant R. H. Holder and men identified only as Shaw and Thompson. See Barry, *The Beginning of the West*, 707–08.

[96] With four words Bullock noted the crossing of the continental divide at South Pass, which Robert Stuart and the returning Astorians discovered in 1812. South Pass remained unknown until 1824, when Jedediah Smith crossed it with a party of trappers. The gradual ascent to 7,750 feet made the pass a natural wagon road. Captain Benjamin Bonneville brought the first wagons over the pass in 1832.

[97] The Mormons camped on the Dry Sandy.

[98] The pioneer company considered marking this anniversary with fasting and prayer, but as William Clayton explained, "the gentile companies being close in our rear and feed scarce, it was considered necessary to keep ahead of them."

[find] the ground covered with Snow when we "arrived 3 miles above "Devil's Gate" on the Sweetwater, look to your left; you will see an open space in the Mountains; go thro' it. Then let your course be West, till you top the hill out of the Great Plain. Then look to the South and you will see a Square But[t]e. Leave it to the left. Go on and cross Green River, then let your course be West to Bridger's Fort, by the road." We can travel along Snake River, almost any time in Winter [and] find grass, little Snow, & free from Indians.

Chapter 6

"THE COUNCIL ON LITTLE SANDY RIVER WITH MR. BRIDGER"
South Pass to Green River, June 1847

After crossing the continental divide, the pioneers began a remarkable series of encounters with some of the most knowledgeable and colorful veterans of the great fur trade era—the mountaineers. At Pacific Springs they met Moses "Black" Harris—who William Clayton thought "appears to be a man of some intelligence,"—coming east from Oregon with copies of Samuel Brannan's *California Star*. Harris "spoke unfavorably of the Salt Lake country" for a settlement and recommended that the Mormons consider Cache Valley. The next day, on the Little Sandy, the pioneers met Jim Bridger, who gave them a more encouraging description of their planned destination. "Old Gabe" was kind enough to share his vast knowledge of the intermountain country, but the skeptical Saints were still greenhorns and discounted most of what Bridger told them. Later the company met Miles Goodyear, whose trading post and garden on the Weber River encouraged the belief that the Great Basin would support permanent agricultural settlements.

Some days later the pioneers had a different sort of encounter with a mountaineer. An advance party of thirteen Mormon Battalion soldiers from the sick detachments under the command of Sergeant Thomas Williams met the pioneer company at Green River. The soldiers were in pursuit of Tim Goodale, a mountaineer from Pueblo who had absconded with some of their livestock. Brigham Young was able to diffuse a confrontation between Williams and Goodale at Fort Bridger, but this encounter foreshadowed the course of Mormon-Mountaineer relations: their interests were fundamentally incompatible.

At their camp on Green River, the Saints had another surprise visitor from the West, the mercurial Samuel Brannan, who had crossed the Sierra in April with three companions to report the success of his mission to California and to find out what had happened to Brigham Young. Brannan had passed the Donner camp at Truckee—now Donner—Lake on his eastbound journey and had met several of the Donner party survivors. He told the pioneers horrific tales of the disaster, contributing to the widespread myth among the Mormons that the party had consisted largely of their old enemies from Missouri. Brannan lobbied hard with Brigham Young to take the Mormons on to California, but with no success.

Few of the pioneer company's experiences have become more encrusted in myth than their meeting with the legendary Old Gabe, Jim Bridger. In 1847, Bridger was "the most celebrated trapper in the Rocky Mts."[1] Thomas Bullock, Albert Carrington, and William Clayton took notes of the meeting between Bridger and the Mormons, but generations of scholars have relied on William Clayton's diary for details.[2] Clayton's version of events—while much expanded over Bullock's telegraphic minutes—is so cloudy in several particulars that Bullock's minutes give us a much more accurate record of the interview.

Other members of the pioneer company recorded their impressions of the interview. Howard Egan reported:

> Soon after we encamped the Twelve and some others went to Mr. Bridger to make some inquiries about the country. I understand that it was impossible to form a correct idea from the very imperfect and irregular way he gave his description…After I ate supper I went down to where Mr. Bridger was encamped, and from his appearance and conversation, I should not take him to be a man of truth. In his description of Bear River Valley and the surrounding country, which was very good, he crossed himself a number of times. He said that [Moses] Harris knew nothing about that part of the country. He says there is plenty of timber there; that he made sugar for the last twenty years where Harris said there was no timber of any kind. But it is my opinion that, he spoke not knowing about the place, that we can depend on until we see for ourselves.[3]

Norton Jacob took a more charitable view of Bridger's conversation:

> He was very obliging and gave all the information in his power concerning the country. He has explored the Great Basin more than any other white man living. The Twelve had a council with him. The information concern-

---

[1] Morgan and Harris, eds. *The Rocky Mountain Journals of William Marshall Anderson*, 267, quoting Lieutenant Theodore Talbot.

[2] For Carrington, see The Journal of Amasa Lyman 1847, Utah State Historical Society, 38.

[3] Egan, ed., *Pioneering the West*, 87–89.

ing the Utah country was most encouraging. [It is] 3 to 4 hundred miles from here. Twenty days travel from here, south through a sandy desert, he found a country, the best he ever saw. It is bordering on the range of mountains that constitutes the southern boundary of the Great Basin. He crossed that desert in the month of January and found the sand was so hot as to burn his horses' feet; and was obliged to travel nights and lie by daytimes where he could find water. A great portion of the country is yet unexplored, and [there are] many tribes of Indians. Those he saw were engaged in cultivating the earth. There is a tree peculiar to that country that produces a very delicious fruit about the size of a plumb. The Indians pound it and make bread of it, which has a spicy taste like ginger cake.[4]

The Mormons' skeptical reaction to Bridger's account reflects a problem that dogged the mountaineer all his life—listeners believed his stories were wildly exaggerated, when in fact they were generally accurate descriptions of western landscapes or real-life events that were simply fantastic. A cynic might view much of the information Bridger gave the Saints as self-serving but prophetic: did Bridger recommend a location far to the south in today's Arizona to decoy these religious zealots into a country outside of his immediate neighborhood? The veteran mountaineer (at forty-three, "Old Gabe" was three years younger than Brigham Young) must have instinctively known that these people, come to settle and put down roots, could only spell trouble for the current residents of the Rockies—and it was probably immediately apparent that he would never make much profit off these sharp Yankees. However cordial their initial encounter might have been (some Mormon writers suggest that Bridger's conversation was fueled by whiskey), conflict between the Saints and the mountaineers was inevitable, and by 1853 relations between Bridger and the LDS church had broken down completely. The conflict was economic and political: through the Utah Territorial Legislature (whose jurisdiction extended into the southwestern corner of today's Wyoming), the Mormons claimed the right to operate ferries on the Green and Bear rivers, while the mountaineers held to their long-established tradition of making money in the mountains any way they could. Both sides accused the other—accurately it seems—of recruiting and arming Indian allies. The bad blood between Brigham Young and Jim Bridger came to a climax in 1853 when the Mormons revoked Bridger's trading license and sent a posse to arrest him. Bridger fled and the Saints built a post of their own near his fort that they called Fort Supply; Bridger returned to the mountains in 1855 and seems to have sold his fort to the

---
[4] Jacob, eds., *The Record of Norton*, 63-64.

Mormons, who used it until 1857 when it was burned to deny its shelter to the advancing U.S. Army. At that time, Bridger was acting as a guide to Johnston's Army, claiming the Mormons had forced him from his property and stolen his fort.

This chapter begins with Bullock's journal entries for the last days of June 1847 and then presents "T. B's minutes" of the "meeting in the grove." Jim Bridger's description of (in Orson Pratt's words) "the great basin and the country south" jump from subject to subject, probably reflecting the questions the Mormons directed at the trapper. For almost 150 years, this document has been buried in the General Church Minutes at the LDS Archives. In contrast to Bullock's journal entries, the transcription of these minutes is reproduced with minimal editing to represent the original document as closely as possible.

Monday 28 June 1847—The cattle not being fond of the Wire grass & Rushes, [they] scattered abroad [and] were gathered together a second time & yoked up. Mr. Crow's Bull gores an ox in the bowels until they protrude. His bulls are Savage creatures, having gored many of the oxen. Mr. Harris [was] trading his Skins for Guns, Caps, Lead, Shirts &c. He partook of breakfast with President Young. Camp start at 7:45 & left him [Harris]. Presidents Young & Kimball [go] ahead on the Boat Wagon. Came to a Cross Road at 10:30.[5]

[It is] 297½ miles to Fort John where Dr. Richards puts up a guide board to Oregon & California. We turned the left road in a SW direction over a level road [and] go round a Sand Bluff on our right. Travel over a Sandy Road, seeing much Artimesia, Daisies & Dog Daisies & camp on the "Little Sandy" at 1:30. [It is] a deep, rapid, muddy stream of Water with many Willows, Gooseberry & Rose Trees on its banks [and] pretty good grass. A Warm morning, blue Sky with small White round clouds floating in the Air, a Dusty morning. Many yellow and

---

[5] This was the Parting of the Ways, some 9½ miles west of the False Parting of the Ways on Highway 28. Here the Greenwood Cutoff (later called the Sublette Cutoff) went directly west to bypass Fort Bridger on the original Oregon Trail; though shorter, the route required a long dry crossing of the desert west of Green River. While Richards identified the Fort Bridger route as the California road and the Sublette Cutoff as the road to Oregon, after 1848 most travelers on both routes went to California.

blue flowers, also Mosquitoes. [We can] see the Bear River Mountains covered with Snow. Father Case wades the River to ascertain [the] best crossing place. Start across the River [that is] about 3 rods wide & deeper than the axle Trees. In about ½ hour after [we] met Mr. James Bridger with 2 men going to Fort Laramie.[6] Called a halt, looked for a good camping place & came to a halt for the night at [the Grove]. Mr. Bridger returned to Camp with us & in the evening held a meeting in the Grove (see T. B's minutes). He supped with the President. E. T. Benson [is] sick. I found a petrified piece of Cotton Wood by the road Side. Artemas Johnson carried it to Doctor who buried it near the bank of Little Sandy. [We should use the] right hand side on our return journey. 13′ A.M. [+] 1¾ P.M. [=] 15¨ miles.

Bullock's Minutes of "The Council in the Grove"

June 28.1847   Little Sandy River[7]

B. Young, H. C. Kimball, O. Pratt, W. Woodruff, G. A. Smith, W. Richards, E. T. Benson

Mr. Bridger

Mr. Bridger has been sent for to Fort John. they want to take advantage of me − we make contracts for our Peltries & r [are] furnished by the Upper Gentry −[8] we may have some peltry to go to the States in the Fall. It costs 4 or $5000 a year to keep up this place.[9]

they [?] and the Black Fork−then a little South of West − under the mountain. ~~where~~ the Green River runs thro' it about 400 miles in some places / rocks 5000 feet high − nothing can go down safe − persons have been [down] both sides of the River over the mountains, but cannot by

---

[6] According to Kimball, *Heber C. Kimball*, 166, when Bridger met the pioneers he "was so 'likered up' he could hardly sit on his horse."

[7] The minutes were tri-folded so they could be placed in the slots designed to hold documents in the early LDS church offices. This was written on the back fold: "Council in the Grove on Little Sandy River with *Mr. Bridger*"; and this note in pencil follows: "gave some scattering ideas scattered   big exaggerations   no opinions as I found it—A. J." [Andrew Jenson, LDS church assistant historian.]

[8] That is, the traders at Fort Laramie furnished Bridger supplies in exchange for his furs.

[9] This estimate seems high for the upkeep of Bridger's ramshackle establishment, but it is decidedly too low for the cost of running Fort Laramie.

[10] Bridger referred to William Ashley's descent of the "Seeds-ka-de" (the Green River) in buffalo-hide boats in 1825, and possibly to other trapper adventures on the river, including voyages such as D. Julien's in 1836. Bridger probably knew of other river expeditions for which no accounts survive.

the water[10]   it is a level high country above – full of crevices – a black rock glazed c [and] rings like Pot metal – would destroy horses feet.[11]

About the middle of the Rocks, comes in the Rio Colorado—[12] it winds & twists round – look like old castles burnt, nothing but brush grows [and] the Soap Weed & Prickly Pear – we call them Lancers – it is covered with musqeet, some willows– until about 200 miles of Tide Water [above the mouth of the Colorado] then Cotton Wood, musqeet – Tallow weed. The Mescal grows there –[13] to go by the way of Hastings about 100 miles – I've been thro' 50 times – it leaves at my Station – goes to Weavers River – Crosses Red Fork & Bear River[14] – then to Lake   heavy timber – like Poplar– Oak, Sugar Tree, Cotton Wood – Pine – Sugar Maple in hollows – plenty of the finest Pine – no timber on the Edge of the Lake. Little Streams r [are] well timbered. outlet of Utah [Lake] – 30 miles from Lake to Lake – no timber on it   three [level?] creeks put into the river, well timbered – best soil – blue grass, White & Red clover – this on the S.E. of the Salt Lake – a good smart current – low banks.[15] Salt Lake does not rise much by freshets – the boys sd. it was 550 miles in going round – they were 3 months[16] – Utah Lake about 15 miles long. Ute Indians – & Root Diggers – where they can get something to eat– they live – Weaver River is larger than Bear River – the Indians round Utah Lake will strip a man, if they dont kill him[17] – the Root Diggers use Bow & Arrows – r very wild – you can see their Smoke & backs & that is all –   ~~Mr. Miles~~ Mr. Wells an Englishman is there alone, in charge of the whole –[18] the Snow lies close. the

---

[11] Bridger described the country along the upper Green River.

[12] The junction of the Green and the Colorado in today's Canyonlands National Park was not officially discovered until the 1869 Powell Expedition.

[13] Here Bridger's tale abruptly jumped from the Colorado country to describe the trail west from his fort.

[14] Bridger listed the river crossings in reverse order; the Hastings companies crossed the Bear River, Echo Creek ("Red Fork"), and the Weber River in succession.

[15] Bridger described the "Utah Outlet," the trapper's name (along with "Provo River") for the stream the Mormons soon named the "Western Jordan"—today's Jordan River.

[16] The "boys" were James Clyman and three companions—probably Louis Vasquez, Moses Harris, and Henry G. Fraeb—who circumnavigated the Great Salt Lake in skin canoes in the spring of 1826.

[17] This information did much to persuade the Mormons to settle in Salt Lake Valley, a traditional neutral territory between the Utes and the Shoshoni.

[18] "Captain" Wills, Welles, or Wells and others told Edwin Bryant in 1846 that he had held a commission in the British Army and had fought at the battles of Waterloo and New Orleans. He was Miles Goodyear's partner at Fort Buenaventura on the Weber River in present Ogden.

only danger is of its being killed by Frost.[19] I know of several [better] places – the South end of the Basin is a good country – they empty into the Lakes on the East side – close to the Calafornia mountains   you can cross into the Sacramento in 5 or 6 places – this is on the S.E. [*sic*] of the Basin as shown by Fremont – he can only give a description of 10 or 12 miles each side [of the Oregon wagon road][20] – Coal is very Common. the Streams r well timbered – Ive seen plenty of Oak, Walnuts, Hackberry &c   I could go 300 miles S. of the Lake without stopping. S. of the Utah Lake is a barren Sandy Desert – a valley of 40 or 50 miles extends clear to the Gulf – you will find Sheep & vegetation – there is a tribe of Indians that farms, that nobody knows any thing about & it is in the same vicinity –[21] S.E. of the Colorado – if there is a promised land – thats it –[22] the muscalaras Indians r very wild   the mohavey Indians live on a mountain[23] – there is a tree, like a cedar, produce[s] like a juniper berry – yellow – a small seed the Indians grind – a spicy taste – you may gather 100 Bushels off one tree – you can eat twice the full of your hat[24] – there r the finest streams & well watered[25] – a man may go with Pack Animals in about 20 days – a very hilly country – but a great part of the country [has] nothing for animals to live on – [on] a little branch of the Ely [Gila] River is a copper mine – a whole mountain of it – a good Quicksilver mine there – Coal & Iron Ore – & timber enough – good Farming Ground– the Wild Squash grows there– & Wild Grapes –

---

[19] This single sentence summarized a longer discussion of northern Utah's prospects as a farming country— a subject of vast interest to the Mormons, who later sent a party to the Weber River to check out Miles Goodyear's garden. If, as legend has it, Bridger informed Brigham Young he would pay $1,000 for the first bushel (or, perhaps, ear) of corn grown in the basin (or Salt Lake Valley), the remark escaped comment by all the contemporary scribes—except perhaps Willard Richards. His 28 June journal entry is quoted as saying, "Bridger considered it imprudent to bring a large population into the Great Basin until it was ascertained that grain could be raised; he said he would give one thousand dollars for a bushel of grain raised in the Great Basin." See the "Manuscript History of Brigham Young," 95, cited in Snow, "Journey to Zion," 270.

[20] Wilford Woodruff reported that Bridger "was ashamed of the maps of Fremont, for he knows nothing about the country, only the plain traveled road."

[21] Dale L. Morgan surmised these Indians were the Hopi. See Morgan, *The Great Salt Lake*, 192–93.

[22] Bridger's "promised land" seems to be in today's central Arizona.

[23] Bridger referred to the Athapaskan-speaking Mescalero Apaches and to the Yuman-speaking Mojaves.

[24] William Clayton essentially repeated Bullock's description of this mysterious fruit, which was perhaps juniper berries or persimmons: "There is a kind of Cedar grows on it which bears fruit something like Juniper berries of a yellow color about the size of an ordinary plum."

[25] This perhaps referred to the Kaibab forest in the Arizona "strip" north of Grand Canyon.

No Grapes about the Utah Lake– but plenty of Choke Cherries – but could gather immense quantities – also acorns for Hogs – the Utah Lake & South of it is the best land – that good land runs to where the Snow will not lie – you can go 200 miles South of the Lake, well timbered – all kinds of Fish – the Timber runs close to the mountains– Timber all round the Utah Lake – not so much Sage – it grows in patches – then meadows.[26] Flax grows in the Valleys – July 1845[27]– Showering 2 or 3 times a day – sure of 1 or 2 Showers very heavy thunder – not much Wind – if you go S of Utah Lake 50 miles you strike Surveyor [Sevier] Lake – in one day I could make a map to all [page 2] you go down Green River about 5 miles[28] – goes up the hill to the old houses – then 18 miles without water – then up creeks 4 or 5 miles – then + [to] Ham's Fork a pretty valley – it is more than half way to the Fort – it is you go down Green River 5 miles then +18 miles to the River – Big Sandy is Flat & Shallow – Mr Hastings trail goes S E of the Salt Lake. they have to go down Weaver River about a mile – but you can avoid that – it is about 2 miles from Mr. Miles house[29] – the only difficulty is thick Oak Saplings – in the Utes Land you must not stick a Stake. all they r fit for is Slaves[30] – there r 10 Indians on the West side of the mountains, to 1 on the East side   only 200 miles S of the Utah [Lake] they raise corn wheat Peas &c[31] – I have bought & eat it myself – they r wild as Beasts – they r outrageous against White People, because the Spaniards killed many, & stole their children[32] they cultivate it with a wooden hoe – Corn grows pretty, as in Old Kentucky; & the best wheat I ever saw – when you get to the Utah, you can go strait to it – the Cattle Winter themselves – the grass cures itself – it is a different kind

---

[26] Bridger described both the high country of the Wasatch Plateau in central Utah and, in contrast, the drier valleys to the west.

[27] Clayton's notes suggest that Bridger now described his return from California in 1845.

[28] The minutes now described the trail west from the Little Sandy, beginning with directions to the first Fort Bridger ("the old houses"), the post on Green River that Bridger founded in 1840–41 with Henry Fraeb. The waterless eighteen-mile crossing ended at Blacks Fork at exactly the distance below Hams Fork that Bridger indicated.

[29] Bridger apparently described Devils Gate at the mouth of Weber Canyon, which the Mormons avoided by using "Reed's Road" across the Wasatch Mountains.

[30] Again, Bridger warned against settling in the Utes' country.

[31] This refers to the Southern Paiutes who raised crops along the Santa Clara River.

[32] The Southern Paiutes had little use for their neighbors, the Utes, and even less for the Spanish and Mexicans. Both groups raided the Paiutes and, as Bridger says, enslaved their children. The Southern Paiutes, called "Piedes" by the Mormons, had equally difficult relations with fur traders and explorers.

of grass — a second growth — it rains at the Salt Lake all times of the year, but not so much as in the old country[33] — on Green River, 50 miles below the trail — can get plenty of coal — burn like a candle & Ashes White — the whole country is Iron Ore I believe — I know a lead mine in the Black Hills — it runs in the cracks of the mountains — I see it every time I go to Laramie — It is called the Big Timber Creek[34] — a little branch that runs into it.

[*End of Bridger Minutes*]

Tuesday 29 June 1847—Immediately after Sun rise, President Young came to me to write an introduction for James Bridger to take to Captain Grover [at the Mormon Ferry on the Platte], which B. Y. signed & gave Mr. Bridger. After a short conversation Mr. Bridger left the Camp. Gather up teams & start at 7:30. Presidents Young & Kimball ahead on the Boat Wagon. [We take] a SW course over a Sandy road, thro' dwarf Artimesia. See the Bear River Mountains tipt with Snow, also Butter Cups, Daisies & Flags. A Warm morning, Clear Sky. Halt on "Big Sandy" at 10:45. Good camping, plenty of Willows & Artimesia. I was sent to gather Dandelions, then pick them—this instead of writing a Journal. Camp starts at 1:25. Cross the river about 6 rods wide. Then, generally level road, some hills, stony road in portions. President Young a head as usual. Returned & directed the brethren to quicken their pace as we had a long distance yet to travel to a good camping ground. Descended the hills, then [took] a level road. Sun set behind the hills. On the bottom, a great dust from Saleratus [that] smelt very disagreeable. Continued on till we arrived at the River at 9:05, having travelled 6¾ A.M. [+] 17 P.M. [=] 23¾ miles.[35] Morning Warm, P.M. Cloudy, Evening cold.

June 30 June 1847—Clear Sky. Very Pleasant morning. Handsome camp ground [with] some large Cotton Wood Trees, the largest timber since we left the North Fork Ferry. Some Shrubs, a Wide River & plenty of grass. Camp starts at 8. Very warm over a level gravel road. Barren

---

[33] Bridger was born in Virginia in 1804 but spent his youth in Missouri, which is probably his "old country."

[34] "Big Timber Creek" was an early name for LaBonte Creek, but the location of Bridger's lead mine remains a mystery.

[35] This day the pioneers made the best distance of the entire journey, traveling twenty-four miles in thirteen and one half hours. They camped about five miles west of Farson, Wyoming, near the Big Sandy River.

country. Leave some bluffs on our right hand [and] continue over a gravel & Pebbly Road in a SW course until we halt at Green River at 11:40 having travelled 8 miles.[36] Here is a good camping ground, tolerable grass, plenty of Cotton Wood & other Trees, [the] largest we have seen for upwards of 200 miles. President Young gave orders to Tarlton Lewis to build a raft to ferry over the First Division of the Camp.[37] President Kimball also gave orders for a raft to ferry over the second Division. Lewis completed his before dark. About 3 P.M. brother Samuel Brannan arrived from San Francisco bringing intelligence from that part of California, also files of "The California Star";[38] also [news] that the "Mormon Battalion" were at Pueblo de los Angeles well in health, but having had a hard journey, most of the Animals being worn out. He gave a description of his visit to the unfortunate Cannibal Emigrants from Independence Missouri, who were at Truckers lake & Neighborhood;[39] also of his route to this place. I have Eight sections of maps to copy, besides bringing up the arrears of notes in this Journal—and yet I was sent out on Guard. In running after the Animals, sweating, & then sitting down to map brought on sickness again. I write this to show the difficulties I have to encounter even in doing this fragment of a Journal. Several of the brethren are taken sick, with Fevers. Pains in the head & back. Warm day. Mosquitoes very troublesome.

[36] The Green River—the Verde of unknown Spanish traders and the Siskadee Agie (Prairie Chicken River) of the Crow and the mountaineers—is the main branch of the Colorado. It derived its name from "a greenish tinge from the shales which compose its bed" on its upper course and "the thin ribbon of green its banks flaunted through a waste of rock." See Morgan, *Jedediah Smith*, 93, 389-90.

[37] The pioneer company crossed the Green near today's Lombard Buttes, close by the site of the modern Highway 28 bridge. (The name Lombard, often applied to this ferry, dates from the settlement era, about 1880.)

[38] Samuel Brannan and the ship *Brooklyn* arrived in the San Francisco Bay on 31 July 1846, only three weeks after the U.S. Navy seized the port—much to his lasting disappointment. He began publishing the *California Star* early in 1847 and was deeply impressed by the country's potential.

[39] The Mormons seem to have heard vague rumors of the disaster that overtook the Donner party as early as April 1847, when Brigham Young wrote, "we are credibly informed that thirty Saints of the original emigrants perished in the mountains with hunger the last season." See Young to Brethren, 16 April 1847, Brigham Young Collection, LDS Archives.

Chapter 7

"HURRA, HURRA, HURRA, THERE'S MY HOME AT LAST"

Green River to the Salt Lake Valley, July 1847

At the crossing of Green River, the three elements of the Mormon emigration reunited. As noted, Samuel Brannan, leader of the *Brooklyn* Saints, arrived from California on the afternoon of 30 June, and on the Fourth of July an advance guard of the Mormon Battalion sick detachments joined the pioneer company. George A. Smith rode into the mountains and gathered snow that was mixed with sugar to create a concoction that was used to celebrate the reunion.

Following Jim Bridger's directions from Green River, the pioneer company made a waterless crossing over a desolate landscape to Blacks Fork, where they camped near present Granger, Wyoming. After crossing Hams Fork, the pioneers again reached the winding Blacks Fork and Fort Bridger. While the Mormon pioneers generally expressed disappointment with the simple corral, log huts, and stockade that made up the renowned trading post, Bullock found Fort Bridger to be "a delightful camping place."[1]

A strange illness that the Saints called "mountain fever" had afflicted some of the party from Green River, and it numbered Bullock among its victims. This malady has been identified as altitude sickness, Rocky Mountain spotted fever, and high-altitude mosquito-borne malaria, but most likely it was Colorado tick fever—though it is worth noting how often Bullock mentioned mosquitoes and sickness in the same sentence.[2] The illness laid low many of the pioneers, including Brigham Young. Several sufferers were rebaptized to restore their health, but no one died and most of the sick recovered after four or five days.

"Between Fort Bridger and the Valley," Bullock recalled:

---

[1] Bullock to William, *Millennial Star* (15 April 1848), 117.
[2] Schindler, *Orrin Porter Rockwell*, 161; Kimball, *Heber C. Kimball*, 166; and the research of Dr. Jay Aldous.

the mountains are very high; the road winds through the valleys, some of which are very narrow—not more than ten yards wide, while the rocks overhang the road; the dividing ridge that we have to go over is about 7300 feet above the level of the sea; on this ridge you will see "the twin peaks" covered with eternal snow; those peaks run into the valley, and when you see them, you will sing out, "I shall soon be at home now." There is no fear of your travelling far out of your way, for we are hemmed in by mountains on each side. After crossing a small creek twenty-one times in about five miles, and between mountains near a mile high, on making a sudden bend in the road, you come in full view of the Great Salt Lake, and a valley about 30 miles by twenty.[3]

Here the pioneer company divided into three parties: an advance guard of about forty-two men under Orson Pratt, the bulk of the company under Willard Richards and George A. Smith, and finally, the small group that remained in the rear to nurse Brigham Young and his fellow sufferers back to health. Bullock entered the valley with the middle group on 22 July 1847.

Early in 1848, Bullock recalled the excitement of the first view of the valley: "You will be sure to say, 'Thank God I am home at last.'"[4]

Thursday 1 July 1847—A fine warm morning. The brethren commence ferrying Wagons over the River, but were obliged to desist in the afternoon on account of Strong Wind. Only ferried over 9 of the First Division & 1 of the Second Division, total 10. The raft for 2nd Division being too heavy, had to cut it to pieces & make a new one. Most of the cattle were swam over. I was sick in bed from over exertion. Doctor gave me orders not to do the like again for any man, or Saint, King, Lord, or Devil. I was warmed up by Tea & chewing Ginger Root. William Clayton, Ezra T. Benson, G. A. Smith, G. Wardle, and others sick.[5]

Friday 2 July 1847—Continued Ferrying the Wagons over the River. Commenced at daylight. Passed over Presidents Young, Kimball & Richards, & 44 other Wagons, total 47. I was ordered to plant a patch of

---

[3] Bullock to William, *Millennial Star* (15 April 1848), 117.

[4] *Ibid.*

[5] Norton Jacob also fell sick and described how he "suffered excessively with pain in the spine, joints, and head, with a high fever through the night." Jacob and others ascribed the affliction to a sudden change of climate, perhaps repeating mountain lore that it was a "fever of acclimatization." See Schindler, *Orrin Porter Rockwell*, 161.

corn. Doctor came & assisted at a few hills [and we] planted 3 patches of Early Yellow & White corn. Crossed over the River about 11 A.M. Warm day. Cloudy in evening. Slight wind.

E. T. Benson, G. A. Smith, W. Clayton, T. Bullock, G. Wardle, M. Ivory & several others sick. The Mosquitoes in great numbers, very plaguing.

At 2 P.M. Presidents Young, Kimball, Richards, Woodruff, Pratt, Smith & Benson with Lorenzo Young, T. Bullock, & Samuel Brannan met in the Grove and decided to send messengers to the camps in our rear & Pilot them thro', when O. P. Rockwell, P. H. Young, Eric Glines, & Geo Woodward were chosen for that purpose. Each of the Twelve were instructed to write their views & hand them to the Doctor, previous to writing the letter.

Samuel Brannan stated that he had a large box of Doctrine & Covenants, also Pratt's Almanacs & other Mormon Books, but refused to sell one, altho' he had had more than 50 applications.[6] There are 7 months rainy Season & 5 dry in California, the dry Season commencing in April. Very Windy.[7] Barley [grew with] no hull on it. [The farmers] don't cultivate Oats, they grow wild. Clover [grows] as high as the horse's Belly. Wild Horses scattered all over the Plains. Geese in abundance. Salmon in the River San Joaquin weigh 10 or 12 pounds. Oysters very small, no Lobsters, Crabs, [or] Whales, & but few small Fish in the bay. The meeting then adjourned. Saw a heap of nine Buffalo Skulls in one place.

Saturday 3 July 1847—Cold morning. I was some better. Brethren ferry over 19 Wagons, when a very strong West Wind arose. Presidents Young & Kimball ride out to look out another Camp ground. Immediately on their return, it commenced raining; thundered & lightned several times. Gathered up teams. Camp starts at 3:15 & removes down by the River Banks, to a good Camp ground, 3 miles.[8] Halt at [blank]. Doctor wrote a letter to Elders Amasa Lyman & C. C. Rich, which I

---

[6] In May 1845, Parley Pratt tried to arrange with the Twelve to print the *Doctrine and Covenants*, a LDS scripture, in New York. How Brannan carried a "large box" of books across the Sierra and the Great Basin is not explained in any source.

[7] Brannan, of course, had been living in Yerba Buena, today's San Francisco.

[8] This site provided better grass for the Mormons' animals, but had even more mosquitoes than the previous camp.

copied. William Clayton made out a table of distances between creeks & Camp grounds. T. B. made out a Synopsis of Journal from Fort John to Green River, then combined both together, a troublesome job. President Kimball said it could not be bettered.[9] The Twelve met in the Doctor's Wagon, when both papers were read to them, & observations made in the margin. Then a meeting was held [at] (dark) to find out who wanted to return to the next Camps & Pilot them thro', when Phinehas H. Young, Aaron Farr, George Woodward, Rodney Badger & Eric Glines (5) agreed to go. President Young lent them his light Wagon & 2 horse harness. I then commenced copying the condensed table of distances. Sat up as long as I could keep awake. William Clayton very sick, the other brethren some better. Passed a Mosquito manufactory, immense swarms of them. Warm P.M., West breeze. President Young with a number of others, went to make a good road about ½ mile beyond our Camp Ground, so as not to stop on Monday morning.

Sunday 4 July 1847—Arose by day break to continue copying the condensed Synopsis & table of distances, which I completed for Elders Amasa Lyman & C. C. Rich. Signed it officially, and obtained signatures of Presidents Young & Richards. Gave both to P. H. Young. The 5 brethren left Camp at [blank], accompanied by Presidents Young, Kimball, Richards, Woodruff and several others. They arrived at the Ferry about ¼ past 11 and met 13 of the Battalion, who had placed their goods on the raft, preparatory to ferrying over the River. It was decided that one of them should return with our 5 men. The Presidency & brethren came to camp at ¼ past 2 [and] formed a line. President Young spoke a few words; the Camp gave 3 Cheers for their return, when he proposed glory to God for their safe return, all crying out "Hosanna, Hosanna, Hosanna, Give glory to God and the Lamb, Amen," then dismissed, to receive congratulations of the brethren.[10]

A meeting in Camp all morning, led by the Bishops. Singing, praying & speaking. An ox poisoned by eating some Weeds belonging to brother Crow [was] brought out of the River into Camp where it died. About 4

---

[9] This document was probably the genesis of Clayton's *Emigrants' Guide*.

[10] This was Thomas Williams' advance guard of Mormon Battalion men from Pueblo. They were pursuing Tim Goodale and other traders who had stolen horses from the Mormons. William Walker returned with the party under Phinehas Young in hopes of meeting his family in the second division. Williams reported Captain James Brown had left the Mormon Ferry on the North Platte on 30 June.

Presidents Young, Kimball, Richards, Woodruff, Smith, Pratt, & Benson with T. Bullock met in the Doctor's Wagon and had read a letter from Amasa Lyman, also one from Captain James Brown, Commander of the Battalion from Pueblo, and Councilled thereon.

Brothers Clayton, Egan, & Fowler very sick. Remainder getting better. Clear, Warm day. Mosquitoes troublesome. West breeze. President Young counselled brother Brannan how to proceed in California, for the best. A full belly seldom thinks of the hungry—Proverbs.

Monday 5 July 1847—Not having had any sleep brought on a severe head ache. Went after cattle, hitch up, and start at 8 A.M. down the River banks about 3 miles when we Watered the cattle. Left the River, ascended a steep Pebbly hill to a level Table Land, then about SW round a steep Bluff on the left of the road. Descend this hill, to another valley [and] come to a steep bank of a dry creek. Go up it ¼ of a mile, down opposite side. President Young orders a new & better road made across it. Saves going round it, which was done. Dust flying in two contrary directions. Shortly after a slight portion of a heavy thunder shower passed over us. A level S.S. [soft sandy?] road to the River, and halt on the banks of "Black's Fork" at 4:45 [with] tolerable grass, best camping spot since start.[11] 20 miles. Some Shrubby trees on the banks, Tallow Weed plenty. Warm morning, Cloudy in afternoon. Rain in distance in several places. A gravel and a sandy, dusty road all day. Chiefly West Wind. See Prickly Pear in Flower, some yellow, others Red. Several of the brethren continue sick.

[THE BATTALION ADVANCE PARTY]

Thomas S. Williams	Samuel Gould
John Buchanan	Benjamin Roberts
Allen Compton	James Oakley
Joel J. Terrill	George Clarke
Francilias Durfee	Thomas Bingham
Andrew J. Shupe	William Casto

[*Written sideways to the right of names:*] 12 of the Battalion travelled with us this day. William Walker returned with the Five brethren at the Ferry.

---

[11] This camp was about three miles east of present Granger, Wyoming.

Tuesday 6 July 1847—A clear Sky, pleasant morning. Gather up teams and start at 7:40 thro' a gulley, then a South by West course for about three miles, when [we] crossed "Kanes Fork" [which is] about four rods wide.[12] Some Willows and Grass, a pretty good camping Place. [The stream is] rapid. Then up a hill in a strait line towards some high bluffs. In about 2 miles crossed "Black's Fork" about 8 rods wide in a slanting direction (plenty of Artimesia here). Continued over a tolerable good road, but very barren. Saw many dog daisies and many beautiful blue flowers, also red flowers. Go round the high bluff in the form of a semi circle,[13] leaving it on our left, then descend to the bottom again in a strait line, until we reach Black's Fork[14] which we again cross in a slanting direction, about 8 rods wide, when we camp on the West side, in a pretty good camping place, tolerable grass, some blue grass [and] many Thistles; & Mountain Flax the best we have seen on our route. Travelled 18¼ miles without stopping. Halt at 4:20. Hard gravel road. Dr. Richards sick in his Wagon. All the rest of the sick better.

Wednesday 7 July 1847—Strong Wind from NW early in the morning. Cold. In gathering up teams see plenty of beautiful Flax, currants &c. Start at 25 minutes to 8 in a Westerly direction towards the North end of the Snowy Mountains. In 2½ miles again crossed "Black's Fork" [with] plenty of grass, flax, & pretty flowers. In about 2 miles further forded a branch starting downwards, swift current, then rise a hill leaving some Bluffs on our right. About noon we halted on tolerable grass on the banks of a creek. At 20 minutes to 2 again start over an uneven pebbly road. Turning round a bluff on our left hand saw 9 Wicka ups in a beautiful vale, also many horses grazing in a beautiful camp ground. [We] cross over 4 creeks of clear water, running very rapid over large pebble bottom, halt for a short time near Fort Bridger. Then pass it, & 6 more Wicka ups, crossing over three other small streams and halt in a beautiful vale where grass is "knee deep, and deeper." Water very clear, excellent mill sites, Timber plenty, the Scene lovely & delightsome to look at. Several Speckled Trout were caught which did my eyes good to look at once more. Travelled 9 A.M. [+] 8¾ P.M. [=] 17¾. Some parts of the road very dusty.

---

[12] This was Hams Fork, near its confluence with Blacks Fork in present Granger.
[13] This was the formation known as Church Butte.
[14] Blacks Fork, a tributary of the Green, rises in the Uintah Mountains. The Mormons crossed Blacks Fork four times on their way to Fort Bridger.

Bridger's Fort is 397 miles from Fort John. There are two Log houses & a large pen for horses made of upright poles. [It] is situated 41°.19'.13" North Latitude by Professor Pratt's observation & [is] 6665 feet above the level of the Sea.[15]

Thursday 8 July 1847—Camp staid here all day. Several brethren go to make trades with the French & Indians, but few succeeded, as they could not obtain sufficient for their goods. I went out with Sergeant Thomas Williams & worked my passage back on Erastus Snow's mare on bare bones. A Warm day. Doctor dictated a letter to Amasa Lyman, which T. B. read to Presidents Young & Kimball.[16] Two alterations were made, I then copied it. Also wrote a letter to Robert Campbell in Winter Quarters giving the results of our journey so far, news from Battalion & San Francisco &c which Doctor sent by Colonel Findley, who was going to the States.[17] Made a copy of Hastings' directions from Bridger's Fort to the Settlements in California also a map of the route, returning the originals to brother Brannan.[18]

In the evening George Mills preferred a charge against Andrew Gibbons for Assault & abuse. (Minutes on file.) It appeared both used abusive language. After close both begged to be forgiven. It was then voted that we pursue our journey in the morning. Sergeant Williams seized a horse belonging to Tim Goodale,[19] for a mule stolen by one of his men at Pueblo, [and] gave a receipt to Goodale, settling the business, leaving Goodale to recover from his man. Mr. Goodale appeared very anxious that no other man should come upon his man for it. The receipt satisfied him. Mosquitoes very troublesome. The sick getting better. Presidents Young & Kimball traded & got Hunting Shirts, Pantaloons &c & H.C.K got 20 good Skins to cover their boys with.

Friday 9 July 1847—Elder Brannan & Sergeant Williams return to Battalion with the Letter to Amasa Lyman which was signed by Presi-

---

[15] Few of the pioneers were impressed by Bridger's ramshackle fort, which nonetheless had been a main supply and rest stop on the overland trail since its founding.

[16] For this letter to Amasa Lyman from "Bridger's Fort," see the Journal History for this date.

[17] William Findlay, an 1845 emigrant to Oregon, left the Dalles on 31 May 1847 and reached St. Joseph, Missouri, about 20 August. See Barry, *The Beginning of the West*, 710.

[18] For Bullock's transcriptions of two Lansford Hastings waybills and the copy of his map, see Korns, ed., *West from Fort Bridger*, 241-250.

[19] Tim Goodale came west in 1839 and settled at Greenhorn near the Arkansas River headwaters about 1843. Bullock gives as a good an explanation of this horse-stealing episode as any source. Goodale did considerable business on the overland trail, selling horses at Fort Laramie with Kit Carson in 1850 and running a Green River ferry from 1854–56. He settled in the Bitterroot Valley in 1864, and died there some years later.

dents Young & Richards. The other brethren from [the] Battalion go on with us. Camp started at 8 A.M. [and] crossed the beds of 3 creeks, also many Gooseberries, Buttercups, Willows, Roses, Meadow Butes, Pink & Blue Flowers, also several beds of mint. (President Young gave the horse back to Goodale in the neatest, quietest, prettiest way possible; for which Goodale expressed his thankfulness to "Captain Young.") Ascended a steep hill, having a plenty of Cedar Trees & Artimesia on it, going in a Westerly direction towards a Square Bute;[20] went to the foot of it. Leave it on our left. Came to a Spring & small Stream of Water (6¼ miles) where we halt, & water our cattle, a tolerable camping ground.[21] Then ascended a hill & descended to a small creek in a gully. Then ascended a very steep & long hill. Gathered some Poplar. Went on a bank of Snow about 120 feet long & several deep. Made two Snow balls, a refreshing bite at this time of year. Many Flowers at this place. Continued on the top of [the] hill[22] some distance thro' the Artimesia, then descended by a ravine, where we had to lock [wheels, the descent] being very steep into a beautiful valley having grass on the sides of the hills. Cross "Muddy Creek" about 3 P.M., a beautiful clear stream of Water with a Pebbly bottom & camp on the West side at [blank].[23] Travelled 6¼ [+] 6¾ [=] 13 miles, a Pleasant day. This is an entire change in country. The Grass, or rather Wild Wheat, is about 4 feet high, which the cattle like. Plenty of short grass, Willow, Flax & Flowers. A pretty Camp Ground. W. Woodruff [was] taken very sick today. Made another Copy of "The Word & Will of the Lord" for "President" Brigham Young. He was very much pleased, & told me to make a copy for myself. Several beds of Excellent Grindstone found by Elder Carrington who brought in 5 Specimens. The brethren singing hymns for the President—a delightful evening.

Saturday 10 July 1847—A beautiful morning. Elder Woodruff much better. T. B. unwell. Assist cooking &c instead of writing, as usual. Gather up teams and start at 8 o'clock going along by the river side, a Copperas Spring on the left hand, where we ascended the hill. Passed thro' some Artimesia, descended, turned to the right. Had to halt &

---

[20] This was Sugarloaf Butte.
[21] This was Cottonwood Creek.
[22] This hill was Bigelow Bench.
[23] The camp on Muddy Creek was about one-half mile south of present Interstate 80.

make a new road [over] a deep pitch in the mountain, leaving on our right a high bold bluff. Again had to cut away part of a hill to descend, Presidents Young & Kimball assisting the brethren made a road wide enough for the Wagons to pass; locked wheels, & descended into a beautiful valley with good grass.[24] On the hills [are] Cedar Trees. [We] then took a sudden turn to the left up another valley[25] with plenty of grass, leaving at the high bluff. Pass up some distance & halt at ¼ to 2 opposite a "Gunpowder Spring," the Water bubbling up clear, tasting like Gunpowder & smelling like rotten Eggs. A little further was a Copperas Spring staining the soil a deep red for some distance. Mr. [Lewis] Myers caught a young "War Eagle" & brought it into Camp to look at. It measured 6 feet between the tips of its wings. A little after 3 start again up the valley, pass over a small hill & then ascend the "dividing ridge" by a zigzag road. Elder Pratt reports [7,700] feet above the level of the Sea.[26] A She Bear & two cubs were seen by brother Cloward going over a high hill on our left hand. Descended by two steep pitches, almost perpendicular, which on looking back from the bottom looks like jumping off the roof of a house to a middle story, then from the middle story to the ground & thank God there was no accident happened. Presidents Young & Kimball cautioned all to be very careful & locked the Wheels of some Wagons themselves. It was a long, steep, & dangerous descent. Then went thro' a Valley, hemmed in by high mountains.[27] Travel to the end, which was the foot of a steep, high, bold bluff. Then took a very sudden ~~shoot~~ chute to the left, round another point [and] ascend a hill thro' Artimesia. W. Clayton put down "30 miles to Fort Bridger" near a large bed of onions. Continued to ascend the hill & then a long gradual descent, thro' Artimesia, between high bluffs. Crossed a shallow creek about 10 feet wide & camp on West bank at ¼ to 8 having travelled 9 A.M. [+] 9 P.M. [=] 18 miles.[28] Here is a clear cold Spring which runs

---

[24] The camp climbed Soda and Ash (or Williams) hollows and descended a slot canyon to this meadow.

[25] This was Pioneer Hollow on Antelope Creek.

[26] This was "the rim of the basin" at Aspen Mountain; its elevation of more than 8,300 feet made it the highest point on the pioneer trek. Here the Saints left the Colorado drainage and entered the Great Basin of North America, from which no water flows to any ocean. Encompassing parts of six states, this arid region reaches from the Bear River divide in eastern Wyoming to the crest of the Sierra Nevada in California.

[27] This was Stowe Creek, near present Altamont.

[28] After crossing the divide between Stowe Creek and Sulphur Creek, the Saints camped on the south bank of Sulphur Creek about a mile and a half east of the Bear River, near the now-abandoned Beartown.

thro' the centre of our Circle. A Pleasant day, a mountainous day's journey.

Sunday 11 July 1847—Ice on the Water Buckets. A Pleasant morning. Mr. Miles Goodier came into Camp. He lives on Weber River [and] gives a very favorable account of the country. Has a garden planted with all kinds of vegetables. He reports Mr. Wells an Englishman living on his place.[29] After conversing with President Young, he went with brothers Little, Matthews & Brown to shew them a new road & nearer. He made a map of the route & gave it the brethren.[30] At the foot of the mountain near the Camp was discovered a Sulphur Spring having flour of Sulphur floating on the top of it and about 1½ mile on the South road was discovered a tar Spring, where several brethren take their tar buckets to fill, to grease their Wagons with.[31] It burned bright like oil. Here are Pure Water Springs, a creek, a Sulphur Spring, & a Pitchy or Greasy Spring within 1¼ miles of Camp. It appears as if Nature herself had separated her different productions for the especial use of the Persecuted Saints on their journey. As I lay in my Wagon sick I overheard several of the brethren murmuring about the face of the country, altho' it is very evident, to the most careless observer, that it is growing richer & richer every day: grass grows luxuriant; Cedars are beginning to flourish; Pines are seen on the Mountains; Cotton Wood Trees on the River banks. Flowers are getting very numerous. Herbage is getting richer all over the country & the Artimesia disappearing. After dusk, the brethren were called together & decided to take the new, or northern route which Miles Goodier spoke of.[32] A warm P.M. To me this has been the stillest day I have had being sick, neither speaking or spoken to. The brethren had a singing meeting this P.M.

Monday 12 July 1847—A cool, cloudy morning, threatning rain.

---

[29] Miles Morris Goodyear (1817–1849) of Connecticut had just come east across the Hastings Cutoff with a band of California horses when he encountered the Mormon pioneers. Goodyear came west in 1836 with Marcus Whitman and accompanied William Drummond Stewart to Green River in 1843. In the fall of 1846, Goodyear and "Captain Wells" founded Fort Buenaventura on the site of present Ogden. Goodyear sold his establishment to the Mormons in late 1847 for $1,950 and died on the Yuba River in California.

[30] Bullock's copy of this map was preserved in the LDS Archives and is printed in Korns, ed., *West from Fort Bridger*, 247.

[31] Later famous as the "Brigham Young Oil Well," the Mormons used Norton Jacob's "fountain of petroleum" to lubricate their wagon wheels.

[32] The Mormons followed the north fork of two branches of the road, choosing Heinrich Lienhard's route over the longer southern alternate the Donner-Reed party used in 1846.

Continued sick in my Wagon all day, Horace Thornton driving for me. Camp start at ¼ past 7 taking the right hand road.³³ Pass thro' a bed of Willows, ascend a steep hill & descend to Bear River which we crossed, a rapid stream about 6 rods wide, water up to the axle Trees. Plenty of Cotton Wood on the banks, also Willows, a good camping ground. Ascended over a ridge & descended to a long level valley covered with grass strait towards a bold Rock³⁴ & halt near it, at 10 minutes past 12, [on] a small Spring & stream of Water running thro' the Gap.³⁵ Rested about 2 hours, when Camp again started (except Presidents Young & Kimball's Wagons), President Young having been taken very sick. Went thro' the Gap, the mountains looking ready to fall on us. Passing thro' a bed of Willows, cross the creek, turn to the left, & cross the bed of a creek,³⁶ which the brethren had mended with Willows & dirt. Then ascend a gentle hill in a Southerly direction with many flowers on [it], & descend a winding course between hills to a beautiful vale. Camp at 6 P.M. 6¾ P.M. [+] 9¾ A.M. [=] 16½ miles. Here is a small creek and Spring of good Water.³⁷ Plenty of grass, about 12 Antelope killed.

In the evening a slight shower of rain, with Thunder & Lightning passed over the camp & country, the first "Pacific Thunder Shower" we have had. Elders Pratt & Carrington laid hands on me to rebuke my sickness. The brethren visit a cave a short distance from Camp.

Tuesday 13 July 1847—A Pleasant morning. Another beautiful Spring found a short distance from Camp. I was some better, visited the "Swallows" Cave,³⁸ which is 36 feet by 24 feet & about 4 to 6 feet high. Many of the brethren have engraved their names on the sides. There are about 50 Swallows nests attached to the Roof. Upon close inspection they are swarming with bed bugs. About noon Elder Kimball arrived in Camp and reported President Young some better. The brethren were called together to consult what was best to be done, when a Shower came on. Presidents Kimball, Richards, Pratt, Woodruff & Smith took shelter in Doctor's Wagon & held a consultation. After the Thunder Shower had

---

[33] This was the road Lienhard took in 1846 from Sulphur Creek to Yellow Creek on the advice of Lansford Hastings. It crossed Bear River about seven miles south of Evanston and followed Coyote Creek.

[34] This was the Needles.

[35] This was Coyote Creek.

[36] This was Yellow Creek.

[37] The pioneers spent three days at this camp about three miles inside today's Utah state line.

[38] Also called Redden's Cave, and now Cache Cave, this site was one-quarter mile from the Mormon camp.

[Orson Pratt's Advance Company, 13 July 1847]				
O. P. Rockwell	Robert Crow	John Brown	Joseph Mathews	Seth Taft
Jack Redding	Ben. B. Crow	Shadrach Roundy	Gilbert Summe	Horace Thornton
Nathaniel Fairbanks	John Crow	Hans C. Hanson	Green Flake	Stephen Kelsey
Joseph Egbert	W. H. Crow	Levi Jackman	John S. Gleason	James Stewart
John M. Freeman	Walter Crow	Lyman Curtis	Charles Burke	Robert Thomas
Marcus B. Thorpe	G. W. Therlkill	David Powell	Norman Taylor	J. D. Burnham
	James Cheney	Oscar Crosby	A. P. Chessley	John S. Eldredge
		Lewis B. Myers	Hark Lay	Elijah Newman
				Francis Boggs
				Levi N. Kendall
				David Grant
First Division	7 Wagons	15 Men		
Second Division	16 "	27 "		
Total	23 "	42 "		

passed over, brethren again met, when it was voted that Orson Pratt be commander over the Expedition to look out a road, instead of going thro' the Kanyon [and] that Stephen Markham be Aid.[39]

The teams were gathered up & the Company left the Camp at ½ past 2. President Kimball dined with President Richards & T. B. and then returned to his Camp, accompanied by George A. Smith, who returned in the evening saying the President was very sick & would not be able to move for a day or two. A Cloudy Pleasant Evening. President Richards had a Well dug nearer the Camp, the Water has a Sulphury taste with it. With this rest, T. B. was enabled to bring up his arrears of Notes, [but] being too weak, was very fainty at night. Brother Clayton very sick to day. Our Camp was stiller to night than [it] has been since we left Fort John.

Wednesday 14 July 1847—T.B. felt some better. Sat in the Cave all day (with S. H. Goddard). Made another copy of "The Word and Will of the Lord" [and] endorsed it "Thomas Bullock," according to President Young's directions. Warm day. The brethren generally out hunting—kill several antelopes. President Woodruff & ~~Albert Carrington~~ Barnabas L. Adams went to visit the President. Several Antelopes gal-

---

[39] With Brigham Young indisposed, the apostles decided to send Orson Pratt ahead with a picked company to explore the road and decide whether to follow the road of the advanced Hastings parties down the wilds and narrows of Weber Canyon or to follow "Reed's Road" over the mountains.

loping near the Camp. The Swallows very busy, attending to the wants of their young. Clouds floating about in the afternoon. A little after dusk brothers Woodruff & Adams returned, reporting the President some better, but A. P. Rockwood is very sick and delirious. A meeting of the brethren was called round the Doctor's Wagon when it was voted to hitch up and remove the Camp a short distance in the morning. After the horn had blown, many of the brethren sat up as usual, when a Shower of rain came on to send them to their Wagons & remind them of the 5th law of the Camp.[40]

Thursday 15 July 1847—Immediately after breakfast Elder Woodruff went out with his carriage to carry President Young & A. P. Rockwood into Camp. About noon he returned. President Young & Brother Rockwood being much better, the 8 Wagons that had been left behind returned at the same time. Morning cloudy but pleasant. When the cattle were gathered up & commenced Harnessing, a Shower passed over. Camp start at [1:30] over a pretty good road. Pass a Spring in about 2 miles, then descend to the ravine, continue until about past 3 when [the] Circle was formed, near a beautiful Spring between some bold hills on all sides.[41] Travelled 4½ miles [and] had 3 Showers during the day, two of them accompanied by thunder, afterwards a Pleasant evening. Good camp ground; seven varieties of pretty flowers gathered within twenty yards of my Wagon. T. B. very sick. Doctor gave some Pills, made me vomit.

Friday 16 July 1847—Two Thunder Showers before starting. I was some easier. Thomas Cloward drove my team. At ¼ to 9 Camp start down a narrow ravine, hemmed in by high mountains,[42] crossed a steep pitch, many had to double teams to get out. Crossed the creek several times during the day. At one place William Smoot broke the reach of his Wagon, unloaded it [and] the brethren removed the Wagon box & Wheels & repaired the reach, while others made a new road across. At ¼ past 12 the Camp came to a halt at 6¾ miles near a Spring. O. P. Rockwell arrived from O. Pratt's advanced Camp. Reports the Canion about 20 miles distant. They had found the cut off & were to ascend it to

---

[40] "The fifth law of the camp" set a curfew at nine o'clock.
[41] The pioneers camped about one-half mile east of Castle Rock in Echo Canyon.
[42] This was Echo Canyon, today the route of Interstate 80. The color of the dramatic rocks that form the canyon led the mountaineers to call it Red Fork.

day.⁴³ At [1:40] start again thro' a narrower way, many times appearing blocked up by the Rocks. Some places could not see two Wagons ahead. Many beds of Willow passed thro'. To my great joy, as well as others, found Hops flourishing, a pretty good proof of the absence of severe frosts & shews a mild climate. Also Elder in Flower, Gooseberries ripe, Roses in full bloom, many Flowers, Wild Wheat, plenty of grass & many Springs of good Water. Continued down this vale, between very high rocks, until [6:45] when formed a circle having travelled 9½ miles: total 16¼ miles. Fine day.⁴⁴

Saturday 17 July 1847—The blacksmiths repaired Solomon Chamberlain's Axle Tree, which he had broken last night, when [we] gathered up teams [and] started at 20 minutes to 10. In about one mile turned round a high bold rock,⁴⁵ to the right, following the course of the "Weber River" & camped on the East bank at [blank].⁴⁶ Travelled 2½ miles. The banks are covered with thin tall Cotton Wood and other Trees; & Shrubs. In some places scarce possible for men to creep thro'. The Water is very Clear & has some fine speckled trout in it. The brethren caught some fine ones during the afternoon. Warm, clear day. Presidents Young, A. P. Rockwood, & several others very sick. Mosquitoes plenty. About 2 P.M. H. C. Kimball, W. Richards, E. T. Benson, G. A. Smith, John Pack, H. Egan, T. Bullock, E. Snow, & Lorenzo Young, & A. Carrington, ascended a very high & steep hill, & prayed to God for the Sick to be healed, the Camps to be prospered, the Saints to be blessed &c &c. They amused themselves by rolling large rocks down the hills.⁴⁷ Afterwards Elders Kimball, Smith & Egan visit the Kanyon & did not return until 10 at night, which caused some uneasiness to the Camp.

Sunday 18 July 1847—Warm clear day. President Young very sick. About 8 o'clock Elder Kimball called the brethren together at the Doctor's Wagon & stated his wish that the day should be spent in prayer, instead of

---

[43] Pratt's advance guard had located the head of the Donner-Reed trail at present Henefer, Utah.

[44] The Saints camped about a mile above the mouth of Echo Canyon.

[45] In the late 1930s a spectacular explosion demolished Pulpit Rock during road construction at the mouth of Echo Canyon.

[46] Brigham Young had rejoined the main company at Cache Cave. Clayton wrote that the camp traveled only a short distance because Young "being so very sick found he could not endure to travel further." The Saints camped on the Weber River near present Echo, Utah.

[47] Rock rolling was a favorite if destructive pastime of Mormon wagon parties, as noted by Abner Blackburn and Henry Bigler.

scattering all over the country, when it was decided to assemble at 10. The brethren went to work transplanting the tops of trees & built a beautiful bowery; in one of the trees was a bird's nest. At 10 o'clock the brethren met pursuant to agreement.[48] Elder Kimball again spoke. He proposed to the brethren that all the Camp (except 8 or 10 Wagons) should proceed on their journey in the morning, look out a place to plant Potatoes & seeds, as the time had come to plant which was agreed to. Several of the brethren prayed & expressed their feelings & adjourned to 2 P.M. At 2 they again assembled [and] the Bishops administered the Sacrament. The brethren enjoyed a good day. Near the close of the meeting Elder Kimball reported that President Young was much better, that our prayers were answered, which caused all hearts to rejoice. A very warm day. Made out a table of distances for Amasa Lyman & Charles C. Rich.

Sent table of distances for Elder Lyman & Rich, by a Soldier.

Monday 19 July 1847—Warm morning. President Young much better. Camp gather up & start, but two Steers being missing, Dr. Richards could not start until ¼ to 8, when President Young removed down the river about 2 miles, where we left him with Elders Kimball, Woodruff, Benson & 8 or 10 other Wagons. We then crossed over Weber River [which was] about 5 rods wide & as deep as the Axle Trees. Elder Snow was waiting to guide us to the cut off, where we found a guide board "Pratts Pass, to avoid the Kanyon.[49] To Fort Bridger 74 miles." We then passed thro' a heavy patch of Artimesia to the foot of the hill, then ascended a hill by a winding course, mending a bridge. Elders Kimball, Woodruff, Smith, and Howard Egan passed us on horseback, and again met them when near the top of the hill. Descended in a sideling direction. G. A. Smith's Wagon Wheels gave way going down the hill. After travelling 10½ miles we watered our cattle in a ravine, then turned suddenly to the right up a ravine, and passed over a high hill. After descending a considerable distance we crossed "Kanyon Creek" and came to a halt in a thick patch of Willows.[50] 13¾ miles. Here we found many Cur-

---

[48] All except John Wesley Norton, who, according to Norton Jacob, "manifested a spirit of contention with the brethren and instead of attending meeting went to bed."

[49] That is, Weber Canyon and the narrows at Devils Gate.

[50] The pioneers ascended Main Canyon from present Henefer, crossed the Hogback Summit, and descended Dixie Hollow before climbing a final hill to their camp at the site of the East Canyon Reservoir. "Kanyon Creek" is today's East Canyon Creek.

rants and Gooseberries just ripening. Several accidents occurred thro' the day, which caused Frost to put up his Blacksmith's shop to repair the Wagons. Warm, dusty day, very cold night.

Tuesday 20 July 1847—Frosty night, Ice in Water Buckets. The Blacksmiths repair the Wagons which delayed the Camp until near 1 o'clock. Brothers Sherwood & Dewey & Case being very sick, they staid with their Wagons &c at this place. The remainder started up "Kanyon Creek," crossing it several times, repairing the road over it & thro' the Willows all the way. Brother Crow returned to Camp bringing word that their Camp is about 9 miles ahead & were ascending a very steep hill. When we had travelled about 4 miles [we] halted to water & refresh teams, until the rear came up. Again started up the ravine, clearing the Willows, repairing the road all the way. We could not find a room for the Camp until we had travelled about 7 miles. Here is a very large Spring of Cold Water but tolerable grass.[51] This has been a crooked & rough day's journey & hard driving thro' the Stumps & Stones. One place we passed thro' many tall Cotton Wood Trees, the remainder of the road [went] thro' Willows, Aspen, Gooseberry bushes & briars. At this place Elder Pratt left a letter of directions, having explored the country ahead (on file). I made copy of same for benefit of President Young, Amasa Lyman and Charles C. Rich, & fixed it in the crotch of a Stick.

Wednesday 21 July 1847—Doctor dictated a long letter to Elder Orson Pratt in reply, which I copied [and] read to Doctor & G. A. Smith, which they signed, & then sent it by Erastus Snow.[52] Gathered up teams and start at ½ past 6. Crossed the Kanyon Creek once more then turned to the right, ascend the mountains by a gradual ascent up a ravine, clearing away the rocks & repairing the road.[53] Pass several Springs of cold water [and] go thro' quite a forest of Aspen, Balsam of Fir, & Cotton Wood. As we ascended higher the road became steeper until we reached the highest point & immediately commenced a very

---

[51] Heber Kimball's detachment fought their way up East Canyon Creek, having to "cross this creek thirteen times, besides two bad swamps," camping at the foot of Big Mountain near present Mormon Flat.

[52] Snow delivered the letter to Pratt, and later that day the two men became the first of the pioneer company to enter the Salt Lake Valley.

[53] As Clayton's guide noted, the Saints now had "to ascend the highest mountain you cross in the whole journey." To climb Big Mountain, the Mormons followed and improved the road the Donner-Reed company pioneered up Little Emigration Canyon.

rapid descent, many teams having to lock both wheels.[54] The road lay thro' a very thick forest of Aspen [and] Poplar Trees with an immense growth of Weeds & Flowers. The brethren led by W. Richards & G. A. Smith cut out the Stumps of Trees & made a very good road. One Wagon was upset in the ditch but got out without any damage.[55] Watered our cattle at a small run of Water & then proceeded on until we came to a good sized creek, made a better bridge over it, crossing several times. Travelled thro' thick Willows, some Oak, Black Birch & Maple, scarce room to pass thro'. Then out into an open country. Found a good Spring of Water, then turned to the right to avoid a rough Kanyon, ascended a long steep hill. At the top could see the next Camp [and] descended to another run of Water which is muddy. Passed two or three ugly places & camped in a bed of Wild Wheat at [7:30 having] travelled 14 miles in 13 hours.[56] Colonel Markham came to superintend our camping. The Cannon & Brother Frost's Wagon were left behind. Warm, dusty day.

Thursday 22 July 1847—Many rushes by the sides of the creeks. Elder Pratt came up to our Camp & consulted with W. Richards & G. A. Smith, when it was decided that O. Pratt, G. A. Smith with several others should go ahead & look out a place to plant; while W. Richards was to take the lead of the Pioneers in preparing the way thro' the Kanyon. Gather up and start at 9. Soon passed the other camping ground [and] went through a heavy Willow bed. Overtook the last teams [and] graded the hill [on] each side the creek, when teams halted while extra hands go to repair the roads, then crossed over & entered the Kanyon; which required much hard work to make a road thro'. At this point the Emigrant Company of last year got tired of cutting trees [and] turned to the left over a very steep hill which appears almost impossible.[57] [We] succeeded in getting thro' the narrow spot of the Kanyon about 4 o'clock, when we turned round the hill to the right & came in full view of the

---

[54] The pioneers had reached "Pratt's Pass," today's Big Mountain Pass on Highway 65, which is 7,400 feet above sea level. They immediately began the steep descent to Clear Creek and Mountain Dell Canyon.

[55] Joseph Rooker's wagon overturned while trying to cross a bridge built by Pratt's party.

[56] The main company avoided the rough and narrow Parley's Canyon, and climbed over Little Mountain from Mountain Dell to reach their camp in Emigration Canyon.

[57] Tired of cutting a road through tangled underbrush, the Donner-Reed party climbed what is now known as Donner Hill to escape Emigration Canyon.

Salt Lake in the distance, with its bold hills on its Islands towering up in bold relief behind the Silvery Lake. A very extensive valley burst upon our view, dotted in 3 or 4 places with Timber. I should expect the valley to be about 30 miles long & 20 miles wide. I could not help shouting "hurra, hurra, hurra, there's my home at last"—the Sky is very clear, the air delightful & all together looks glorious; the only draw-back appearing to be the absence of timber, but there is an Ocean of Stone in the Mountains, to build Stone houses & Walls for fencing. If we can only find a bed of Coal we can do well & be hidden up in the Mountains unto the Lord. We descended a gentle sloping table land to a lower level where the Soil & grass improve in appearance. As we progressed down the Valley, small clumps of dwarf Oak & Willows appear [and] the Wheat Grass grows 6 or 7 feet high. Many different kinds of grass appear, some being 10 or 12 feet high. After wading thro' thick grass for some distance, we found a place bare enough for a camping ground, the grass being only knee deep, but very thick; we camped on the banks of a beautiful little Stream which was surrounded by very tall grass.[58] In digging a place down to the Stream, cut thro' a thin bed of Clay. After about a foot depth of rich soil; then rich soil again. Many mosquitoes about in the evening; a rattle snake killed near the Camp. A Scorpion [was] seen by young brother Crow. Many of the brethren met in the evening round the Camp fire to hear the report of O. Pratt, G. A. Smith & several others who had been out on an Exploring Expedition on horseback. They report having been about 20 miles north. About 4 miles north from this Camp ground are two beautiful Streams of Water with Stony bottom.[59] Beyond that is a Saline country & about 50 mineral Springs. One will do for a barber's Shop & the largest Spring rushes out of a large rock having a large Stone in the middle; [it] would make a first rate Thomsonian Steam House. They explored about 20 miles North. They have picked out a place for a permanent Camp ground. Doctor dictates a long letter to President Young.[60]

Pratt's Pass is 35 miles from where it enters the mountains on Weber River, to the outlet of the Kanyon, opening into the Valley of the Salt

---

[58] Bullock's first camp in the Salt Lake Valley was near today's "Woodruff Villa" at 500 East and 1700 South.

[59] This was City Creek, which divided into two streams near today's Temple Square.

[60] For this letter, see the Journal History for this date.

[Distances from Winter Quarters to Salt Lake Valley]		
From Winter Quarters to Junction of Forks	333 miles	(guessed)
Junction to Fort John	227	—
Fort John to Fort Bridger	397	measured
Fort Bridger to The Farm	116	—
From Winter Quarters to Location	1073 miles	

Lake. Saw a Magpie, several Sand Hill Cranes, a Hawk, the Wandering Milk Weed & other herbs.

Friday 23 July 1847—Clear Sky, warm morning. I copied the long letter to President Young, which was read to & signed by Presidents O. Pratt, G. A. Smith, & W. Richards. I also made out a table of distances & [the] route from Weber River to this place. Gave both to Major Pack, who went back to the President. Camp gathers up & starts about 7. Took the back track about a mile, then a strait road to a small Grove of Cotton Wood Trees—a hare crossed the road, two Wagons ahead of me—on the banks of a beautiful Stream of Water covered on both sides with Willows & Shrubs. Here is very rich land, deep grass & the intended location for a farm. W. Clayton allows that we are about 2 miles further from Winter Quarters than last night's Camp.

About ½ past 9 the brethren were called together & after a few introductory remarks by Elder O. Pratt. O. Pratt made prayer to Almighty God, returning thanks for the preservation of the Camp; their prosperity in the journey; safe arrival in this place; consecrated and dedicated the land to the Lord; & entreated his blessings on the seeds about to be planted; & on our labors in this valley. After a few remarks by Elders Pratt & Richards, a Committee of Five—Shadrach Roundy, Seth Taft, Stephen Markham, Robert Crow, & Albert Carrington—were appointed to look out a place for planting Potatoes, Corn, Beans &c, who left meeting for that purpose. It was then voted that Charles A. Harper, Charles Shumway & Elijah Newman be a committee to Stock Plows & Drags & to call those men to their assistance that they want. It was also voted that Henson Walker, William Wadsworth & John Brown be a committee to superintend the moving & rigging up of Scythes. Stephen Markham was appointed to attend to the Teams & see that fresh sets were hitched up every four hours. It was motioned that every man plant his own potatoes & seeds as he pleased, and also motioned that Almon Williams oversee the making of a Coal Pit. Dr. Richards advised that no man leave the Camp, but attend to his seeds & put them in. G. A. Smith recommended the brethren to gather out the dead timber & leave the live timber standing & to use as little wood as possible in their cooking. About ½ past 11 [the] Committee reported they had staked off a piece of fine ground 40 rods by 20 for Potatoes, also a suitable place for beans, Corn & buck wheat. The soil is fertile, friable loam, with fine gravel. At 12 o'clock the first furrow was turned by Captain Taft's Company.[61] There were 3 Plows & 1 Harrow at work most of the afternoon. Taft's Plow got broke. At 2 o'clock the brethren commenced building a dam & cutting trenches to convey the water, to irrigate the Land. At 4 o'clock other brethren commenced mowing the grass, to prepare a turnip patch. About 6 heavy clouds & a thunder shower passed over the Camp, a South West wind. At dark Major Pack reported that President Young was this side the Mountain, camped on the creek a few miles back & were all better. Regulations were entered into about the Teams & Plow men to work from 4 A.M. to 8 P.M. coursing by turns of 4 hours each.

---

[61] In typical fashion, the pioneers immediately set to work upon arriving in the Salt Lake Valley. This field was between 200 and 300 South and State Street and 200 East.

Chapter 8

"THE GREAT SALT LAKE CITY OF THE GREAT BASIN"
Salt Lake Valley, July–August 1847

Contrary to popular belief, the valley the Mormons entered in 1847 was no desert wasteland. The mountaineers had long loved the rich and fertile basin, renowned among the fur traders as the "Oasis of the Wasatch." Jedediah Smith wrote fondly, "I had traveled so much in the vicinity of the Salt Lake that it had become my home in the wilderness."[1] With the big game hunted out by the firearms of Indians and trappers, the benches were covered stirrup-deep with rich grasses. Rather than desolation, Wilford Woodruff described the "vast rich fertile valley" that was clothed "with the Heaviest garb of green vegetation [sic]." The valley—or more accurately, the basin—was "abounding with the best fresh water springs rivulets creeks & Brooks & Rivers."[2]

The valley was also in Mexico. Mexico had never exerted any government control over its territories in the Great Basin, and the American victories of the summer of 1847 would forever foreclose that possibility. The treaty of Guadalupe Hidalgo in 1848 formally transferred the land to the United States, forcing the Mormons to again deal with the government that they compared to Babylon. But the government was far from the valleys of Utah, and in the shadow of the Wasatch Mountains it was easy for the Mormons to dream of independence. The Saints had found their refuge in the mountains, the spot where they would plant a new stake of Zion and raise the standard of the Kingdom of God. "Cry it aloud," wrote Bullock. "Come, ye poor afflicted people, come and live; come and worship the Lord God of Israel, and let your years be many on the earth."[3]

---

[1] Brooks, ed., *The Southwest Expedition of Jedediah S. Smith*, 193.
[2] Staker, ed., *Waiting for World's End*, 122.
[3] Bullock to William, *Millennial Star* (15 April 1848), 117–18.

In less than a month, the Saints planted eighty-four acres in corn, potatoes, beans, buckwheat, turnips, and "garden sauce"; surveyed and irrigated the town site; laid off "a ten acre block for a fort, where about 160 families can winter"; manufactured 125 bushels of salt; and explored the valleys to the west, north, and south. They

> surveyed and laid out a city, with streets running east and west, north and south, in blocks of ten acres, divided into eight lots of one and a quarter acre each; the streets will be eight rods wide, having two sidewalks of twenty feet each, to be ornamented with shade trees; all the houses are to be built twenty feet in the rear of their fence, with flower gardens in the front; one block is reserved for a temple, and three for public grounds, [and] promenades—having fountains of the purest water running through each square and ornamented with every thing delightful.

The Mormons accomplished all this, Bullock happily noted, with "no lawyers."[4]

The Saints quickly adapted to their new home. Battalion veterans had seen practical irrigation in New Mexico, and the pioneers turned water onto fields and plowed them up even before Brigham Young arrived in the valley. Sam Brannan reported that he had raised a newspaper office in California in a week using mud bricks—adobes—and the practical Saints immediately adopted the technique to build their fort.

The Mormon Battalion sick detachments and the remaining wagons of the Mississippi Saints arrived in the valley in the last days of July. The church leaders had long been concerned about how to separate these veterans—whose terms of enlistment ran out on 16 July 1847—from the United States Army, and, more importantly, how to get the pay still due to the troops. A flash flood in Emigration Canyon that damaged some of the detachments' wagons provided a good excuse not to send the entire body to California for discharge. Young sent a small party to California under Captain James Brown and Samuel Brannan to settle the battalion's affairs and collect their back pay. He also used this opportunity to send a scouting party to Fort Hall to procure much-needed supplies and to open trading relations with the powerful Hudson's Bay Company. The busy Mormons also dispatched exploration parties south to Utah Valley, west to the Tooele Valley, and north to Cache Valley. By the time the "Returning Pioneers" turned their course to the Missouri, the Mormon

---
[4] *Ibid.*, 118.

leaders had an excellent understanding of the physical geography of their new home.

There was no rest in store for Thomas Bullock, or for the majority of the members of the pioneer company. On 17 August, Bullock tallied the number of men and wagons dispatched under Tunis Rappleye, Shadrach Roundy, and battalion officer William Willis; this first party was powered by ox-teams that the Mormons incorrectly assumed would travel more slowly than the second company that used horse and mule teams. In the waning days of August, Bullock set out with the return to Winter Quarters, where the pioneers would tell the story of their success, form a new First Presidency to lead the church, and prepare in the next spring to conduct the body of the church to their new Zion in the Rocky Mountains.

Saturday 24 July 1847—A warm morning, clouds flying. The brethren very busy, Plowing, Stocking Plows, & cutting ditch to irrigate the Land. About noon the 5 acre potatoe patch was plowed, when the brethren commenced planting their seed potatoes. Amasa Lyman's Plow got broke. The brethren then planted some Early Corn. The Plowers continued at work on the South of the Potato Patch. When the ditch was completed, the Water was turned on to irrigate the Potatoe Patch, which answered very well. About 2 o'clock President Young, his Company, and the rest of the sick arrived in Camp. All were rejoiced to see them, especially as they are all better in health and may the Lord grant that all who are sick may soon be made well and attend to their duties as Pioneers of Israel. In the evening a light shower passed over Camp, which continued some time. A stiff breeze from the West accompanied it. President Young rode in W. Woodruff's Carriage & Colonel Rockwood was on horseback.[5]

Sunday 25 July 1847—A warm morning, Clear Sky. At 10 A.M. the

---

[5] In 1880 Wilford Woodruff claimed that it was from this carriage that Brigham Young looked at the Salt Lake Valley for the first time and said, "This is the right place, drive on." Although the main elements of the pioneer company entered the Salt Lake Valley on 22 July, the arrival of Brigham Young on the twenty-fourth established "Pioneer Day," the holiday first celebrated in 1849 to commemorate the arrival of the Saints in Salt Lake. While the men were generally pleased with their prospects, Harriet Young recorded different emotions in her journal for 24 July: "my feelings were such as I cannot describe every thing looked gloomy and I felt heart sick." See Young, ed., "Diary of Lorenzo Dow Young," 163.

brethren assembled round the Cannon. After singing & prayer Elder G. A. Smith preached about the House of the Lord being established on the tops of the Mountains, followed by Elder Kimball & E. T. Benson, and all expressed their gratification at the prospects before us & referred to the blessing of God on our journey, that not a man, woman or child had died & not an animal lost only by carelessness, except brother Crow's ox which was poisoned. In the afternoon the brethren were addressed by W. Woodruff, O. Pratt, W. Richards & President Young who stated that he approved of what the brethren was doing this fall, that another Spring every one would have his inheritance & he must cultivate it. He told the brethren to cheer up their Spirits, as the brethren reported plenty of timber in the mountains, & also on two large streams higher up the valley towards the Utah Lake, there was plenty of Timber and requested those brethren who had found any thing to bring it forward, to restore it to its owner, for rest assured if any one found a thing & did not restore it to the owner, it would one day Leak out and it would be a curse in his nose all the days of his life. I was sick & unable to sit up & report.

Monday 26 July 1847—The brethren busy plowing, planting corn, & Irrigating. Warm day. About 12 o'clock Presidents Young, Kimball, Richards, Smith, Woodruff, Benson; [and] W. Clayton & Albert Carrington ascended a steep hill of the Mountain named "Ensign Peak" in sight of Camp, then separated into two exploring Companies. Dr. Richards recommended me to go with Solomon Chamberlin to the hot Mineral Spring to bathe for the benefit of my health. Saddled a couple of his mules [and] went past a many Mineral Springs to the largest which rushes out at the foot of a large rock, having a large Stone in the mouth to stand on, as if purposely placed there. The Water was so very hot that I was unable to bear [keeping] my fingers in four or five seconds. This Spring with the other small Springs forms a deep lake & runs off with a rapid current, by a course about 4 or 5 feet wide & I deep into a large lake 2 or 3 miles long, upon which are several thousands of Plover or Snipes. We returned to the nearest hot Spring & bathed in it. It was very warm & smelt very bad.[6] After washing we returned to Camp

---

[6] Bullock traveled several miles north of the pioneer camp to the now-destroyed "Hot Sulphur Springs," located near the junction of US 89 and I–15 and later known as Beck's Hot Springs, whose runoff formed the also-vanished Hot Springs Lake. He then returned south to bathe in the Warm Spring located near today's Children's Museum of Utah.

when I had a sweating. President Young gave directions to have a Tree sawed & make a boat.⁷

Dr. Richards reports, we the Council ascended a portion of the Mountain on the North by the West side, President Young naming it "Ensign hill" from whence they had a splendid view of the Salt Lake, Islands thereon & the surrounding valleys, descending by the East side, in the Stream.⁸ After quenching our thirst we went up to the Warm Spring, returned very tired. O. Pratt was planting Corn.

Tuesday 27 July 1847—A warm fine morning. At ½ past 8 Amasa Lyman, R. Badger, R. Stevens & S. Brannan joined the Camp & report leaving the Battalion on Weber River & they will be here in a day or two. they A. Lyman & S. Brannan joined the Council who were just starting on an Exploring Expedition, 16 in all. (Doctor reports the Council took a Westerly course, President Young in brother Woodruff's Carriage, [and] crossed the river Jordan. About 1 o'clock arrived at the foot of a mountain on the West side, where was a large spring of Water, a little brackish. Here we dined & refreshed our horses, then went round a point of a hill to the Salt Lake, supposed to be 22 miles from Camp. Here is a perpendicular rock about 40 rods within circle of the shore, of considerable height.⁹ From thence [Black Rock] extended into Lake where were fragments of rocks which made it passable 20 rods further. President Young first arrived at this point. All bathed in the Lake which they found so very Salt, that no man could sink in it, & so warm that no one had a desire to retreat from it; a man could sit in it as in a Rocking Chair. On their way thither after dinner P. Rockwell went over a hi bluff on the left in search of Game & ascended to a considerable height in pursuit of

---

⁷ This describes the genesis of the *Mud Hen*, which Albert Carrington used in April 1848 to explore the Great Salt Lake. See Van Alfen, "Sail and Steam: Great Salt Lake's Boats and Boatbuilders," 199.

⁸ That is, the party ascended Ensign Peak and crossed present Capitol Hill to descend into City Creek Canyon. Wilford Woodruff wrote that a select party "went onto the top of a high Peak in the edge of the Mountains which we considered a good place to raise An ensign upon which we named ensign Peak or Hill." Bullock sheds no light on a long-standing controversy over whether the exploring party raised a flag—perhaps the standard of the Kingdom of God—on Ensign Peak. Young certainly recalled the prophesy of Isaiah 11:12 that the Lord "shall set up an ensign for the nations, and shall assemble the outcasts of Israel, and shall gather together the dispersed of Judah from the four corners of the earth." Contrary to later tradition, which held that the knob was a landmark shown in a vision to Brigham Young so he could identify Salt Lake Valley as his destination, the name referred to the gathering of Israel in the Last Days as foretold in Isaiah 5:26: "And he will lift up an ensign to the nations from afar, and it will hiss unto them from the end of the earth: and, behold, they shall come with speed swiftly." For more, see Walker, "'A Banner is Unfurled': Mormonism's Ensign Peak," 71-91.

⁹ Black Rock still stands at the Point of the Mountain on the southern shore of the Great Salt Lake.

a flock of Mountain Sheep, which arose from the valley, while the Doctor rode on the top of a small Bute on the right. At the same time Elder Kimball & others rode into a Cave underneath, supposed 60 feet long.[10] After bathing gathered a cup of beautiful White Salt from the rocks & discovered a fresh water Spring, somewhat brackish, near the Shore of the Lake. The party then proceeded west about 3 miles when the road was Stony for Carriages, when President Young & most of the party returned to noon encampment. O.P., W.R., & G.A.S.[11] went 1¼ mile further to the opening of another valley, about 10 miles in diameter, opening thro' mountains on the South, & of considerable ascent on East side.[12] Returned to noon camp about 10 P.M. where they camped for the night. After supper they had prayers & sweet sleep on the Earth, Presidents Young & Kimball excepted. The Brethren continued plowing and planting. Burr Frost had a Blacksmith's Shop put up & did the work at the Plows &c. Two Utah Indians came to Camp & trade away two ponies for a rifle & musket. In the evening other Indians come to "Swop" buckskins &c, the brethren giving 20 charges of powder & ball for a single Skin. The traders generally give from three to six charges. This is a foolish beginning by the brethren. Some of the brethren bring in a handsome Pine tree 14 feet long, 20 inch thro', to saw into Planks for a boat. President Young & Kimball's Wagons are removed to the intended site of the city. My Wagon was also driven up.[13] Jackson Shupe & T. Bullock cleaned out the Spring this evening.[14]

Wednesday 28 July 1847—Fine Warm day. The Indians remained about the Camp all night & appear very peaceable & are desirous to barter. At ½ past 3 President Young & Explorers return from Salt Lake, bring with them samples of pure, white salt. [They] report that a Gallon of Water will make 3 pints of pure Salt. (Doctor reports [that] about 8 Elder Brannan left for Camp, while the remainder went a Southerly course, ascended the rise of the valley on the West side, so as

---

[10] In 1985, road material excavation buried the mouth of Black Rock Cave (sometimes called Clinton's Cave), but the entrance to this lake-scoured tunnel can now be seen from the rest stop at Black Rock on Interstate 80.

[11] That is, Orson Pratt, Willard Richards, and George A. Smith.

[12] The men viewed the Tooele Valley.

[13] These wagons were moved from the block immediately northwest of the present City-County Building to the vicinity of South Temple and Main streets.

[14] This is the Warm Spring.

to overlook the opening of hills on the South & could see the Watercourses on the East side of the valley. But [they found] no pure Water on the West. At 11 o'clock turned homewards, arrived at the Ford between 1 & 2, took refreshment, & several bathed.) Joseph Hancock & Lewis Barney return from a two days' hunt in the mountains & report plenty of Timber, fir, balsam & poplar, many sticks making 2 good logs. The brethren dig a saw pit for the Sawyers to go to work at the Pine log.

The MOTTO: "It is expected that every man will do his duty."[15]

Wednesday 28 July 1847—(Continued.) At 5 o'clock in the evening Presidents Brigham Young, Heber C. Kimball, Willard Richards, Orson Pratt, Wilford Woodruff, Amasa Lyman, George A. Smith, Ezra T. Benson, and Thomas Bullock walked from the North Camp to about the centre, between the two creeks, when President Young waived his hands and said, "Here is the forty acres for the Temple lot."[16] The spot runs up to a small ridge on the East side & is midway between a cluster of Trees on the South & a few trees on the north creek. President Young requested Orson Pratt to tell Father Sherwood how many degrees of variation of compass there is at this spot, so that the City may be laid out perfectly Square North & South, East & West.[17] Ezra T. Benson then told Howard Egan (who was passing at the time) to notify the brethren to meet on the Temple Square at 8 o'clock this evening. President Young stated that he wanted the room for the Baptismal Font to be 20 feet high and the Basement Story to be 10 feet above the level of the Ground. Orson Pratt remarked that Nature could not possibly form a more beautiful Spot than this for Mountain Scenery. President Young said, In all my life I never felt the warm gushes of air come from the North or NW before this place, & this is caused by the Salt Sea. On this place we can lay out a City two miles East & West, and as large as we have a mind to North & South. I want the rushes and grass on the bottoms to be left for our cattle.

---

[15] The motto was derived from Lord Nelson's battle signal at Trafalgar: "England expects that every man will do his duty."

[16] As Bullock noted, on 4 August the temple lot was reduced to ten acres. It is today Temple Square, whose southeast corner marks the origin of local addresses.

[17] Although Brigham Young is credited with planning Great Salt Lake City, he simply implemented the design of Joseph Smith's "New Jerusalem, City of Zion," originally intended to be built in Jackson County, Missouri. See Bigler *et al*, eds., "'O Wickedness, Where is Thy Boundary?'" 28. This design became the pattern for the hundreds of villages the Saints established throughout the West.

Orson Pratt motioned "that the Temple be built upon this Spot of ground, and the 40 acres be between the two creeks." Amasa Lyman seconded [and] carried. President Young said we have room enough here to have lots as large as we please and Streets as wide as we please and have three blocks of ten acres each for public Squares, on the North, West, & South. We can put our Streets 8 rods wide and our lots 10 rods by 20, independent of streets.

O. Pratt motioned "that the lots contain one acre and a quarter each, independent of the Streets, 20 rods by 10." H. C. Kimball seconded. Carried.

W. Richards motioned "That the Streets be 8 rods wide." G. A. Smith seconded. Carried.

B. Young motioned "that the side walks be 20 feet wide." President Young said he wanted the houses to be put so far from the line of his Neighbor's lot & 20 feet from the front of the Street, so that if one house gets on fire, it does not endanger another.

H. C. Kimball motioned "that they be placed 20 feet back." O. Pratt seconded. Carried. G. A. Smith said he thinks it better to lay out places, or Squares, for markets. B. Young thinks it better for any man who wants a market to have it on his own lot & let each man cultivate his own lot. In regard to Schools I shall have a School for my own children & the people on a block can choose a School for themselves. Let the children be kept out of the Streets, keep them on the lots or in the houses. We will have our bathing places directly, and in three years we shall not know what sickness is. All said "Amen."

G. A. Smith motioned "that we have four public Squares for play ground & walks." E. T. Benson seconded. Carried.

At 8 o'clock the brethren assembled on the Temple Square. After several of the brethren had expressed their feelings, it was voted without one dissenting voice that this is the place to build the Temple and lay out a City.[18] It was also voted that a Committee superintend the management of laying out the City and that the Twelve be that Committee, with power to call for what assistance they need.

President Young then addressed the brethren on the order of building the City, its regulations for cleanliness & being supplied with pure Water, his determination of having order, and righteousness in all things. He stated Joseph Smith's views of coming to this valley—that he would have still been alive, if the Twelve had been in Nauvoo when he recrossed the River from Montrose to Nauvoo. He reviewed the driving of the Saints from place to place & stated the only way that Governor Boggs, General Clark & Lucas, & the leaders of the Missouri mob could have been saved; but now will be eternally damned.[19] [Young] also damned President Polk—stated the numerous petitions to all the Governors & Presidents, all refusing aid. That when the Saints were driven from Illinois, Polk's tyranny in drafting out 500 men to form a Battalion, in order that the women & children might perish on the Prairies. In case he had refused their enlisting, Missouri was ready with 3000 men, to have swept the Saints out of existence on attempting to cross the Missouri River.[20] He next made a discourse on the duties of men and women, that men should find out & then do the will of the Lord & the women should observe and do the Will of their husbands. It is their duty to rear the children from their birth until they are old enough to go under a master. He stated the objections of some men to the plurality of Wives and that the Elders would marry Wives of every tribe of Indians, and showed how the Lamanites would become a White & delightsome people & how our descendants may live to the age of a tree & be visited

---

[18] According to Norton Jacob, after the vote Young told the pioneers he was confident that if he concluded "this is the spot, they would be entirely satisfied if it was on a barren rock."

[19] Young referred to generals John B. Clark and Samuel D. Lucas of the Missouri militia, and to Governor Lilburn Boggs, all participants in the 1838 Mormon War. Young probably suggested that the men could have escaped damnation only by forfeiting their lives.

[20] The Mormon leader believed Senator Thomas Hart Benton had struck a deal with President Polk to permit the annihilation of the Saints if they refused to serve in the Mexican War—an allegation for which there is no evidence.

& hold communion with the Angels; & bring in the Millenium.[21] He hoped to live to lead forth the armies of Israel to execute the judgments & justice on the persecuting Gentiles & that no officer of the United States should ever dictate him in this valley, or he would hang them on a gibbet as a warning to others. He showed the spot where the Ensign would be hoisted & never have any commerce with any nation, but be Independent of all. If we want any thing we cannot get here, let the Elders of Israel gather it when they are on Missions preaching the Gospel. He made a most powerful & impressive discourse & did not conclude until 5 minutes past 10 when he dismissed the Meeting.[22]

A very strong wind blew all night from ENE.

Thursday 29 July 1847—I bathed in the Warm Spring, after sunrise [and] by myself cleared the pool of its scum. Felt wearied by the journey. About 9 Presidents Young, Kimball, Richards, Smith, Lyman, Woodruff, Benson, & 5 others rode out on horseback to meet the Battalion. At noon a very refreshing thunder shower passed over the Camp. A few of the Soldiers came to Camp & reported that the leading Wagon had broken down in the Kanyon, which delayed the whole Camp there. (The brethren very busy irrigating, plowing, harrowing, and planting the Farm and Garden.) The Council met a detachment of the Battalion* at the Garden, who returned with them to the Kanyon. While in the Kanyon a very heavy Shower passed over which caused them to turn back. A tremendous roaring was behind them & suddenly a rise of about 3 feet of water rushed in a perfect head down the Kanyon, washing away the bridges we had made.[23] William C. Smithson's team had just descended into the Kanyon, [seeing] apparently but little water, when the rush came so tremendous that it reached his Wagon bed, near 4 feet high. He had to wade up to his breast, while he lashed a Cable round his steers to prevent their overturning the Wagon. Several Wagons were

---

[21] This sentence encapsulates the Millennial role of the American Indian in LDS belief, which would have enduring consequences in Mormon-Indian relations in Utah Territory. The phrase "white and delightsome" is from the *Book of Mormon*, but the LDS church has removed it from recent printings.

[22] Young's vision of the apocalypse would have dramatic consequences in 1857, when the Mormons challenged the authority of the federal government and raided a U.S. Army expedition ordered to Utah by President James Buchanan to enforce federal law.

* Here Bullock inserted this note: "Captn James Brown's & Lieut Wesley Willis's and Captn. Nelson Higgins detachments of sick–left on the Arkansas."

[23] The battalion veterans experienced a classic flash flood of the sort that still occurs in Emigration Canyon.

under the necessity of staying on the other side of the Kanyon; while the Battalion & Council with 3 of the Mississippi Wagons came in Military order: Council & Officers first, Infantry next with martial music, then followed the Cavalry with the Baggage Wagons bringing up the rear. Passed the first Camp, crossed the creek & camped between the two creeks at 3 P.M. They report that the Camp from Winter Quarters will be here in a fortnight or 20 days. The brethren were very much rejoiced at getting once more among their friends & a general congratulation took place.

Friday 30 July 1847—A fine warm morning. At 10 minutes to 9 the Council met with the Officers of the Battalion. [They] meet in the Tent. A long conversation ensues & Council [is] given (see the Minutes on file). Afterwards they rode up to the Warm Spring. Several bathed & visited the other Springs. I gathered out Doctor's Garden seeds [and] in [the] afternoon sowed & planted several sorts. Warm day with Gentle breeze from NW. Notice was sent out to the different Camps to assemble at 8 o'clock at the Upper Camp at which time & place they met. A Wagon being prepared [as a speaking platform], President Young made a few preliminary remarks, when praise to God for [the] safe return of so many of the Battalion was given by shouting "Hosanna, Hosanna, Hosanna, give Glory to God & the Lamb, for ever and ever, Amen, Amen, and Amen." He then made some very pointed remarks, stating that the battalion saved the people by going into the Army. If they had not gone, Missouri was ready with 3000 men to have wiped the Saints out of existence. [Young] reiterated his feelings towards United States Officers, [and] also [described the] plan & order of the City similar to Wednesday evening. He requested the battalion to build a bowery on the Temple lot, tomorrow, which they agreed to. He did not close his remarks until about 10 when he ceased, being very hoarse.

Saturday 31 July 1847—Strong wind from SSE. The Battalion make a Bowery 40 by 28 to preach in. In the course of the day many Utahs with Squaws visit Camp. I was told that one Indian had stolen a horse from another Indian & traded with one of our brethren for a Gun, refusing to give up to the owner either his horse or Gun; that he took the Gun from him & broke the Stock over his head. Directly afterwards the same man stole a 2nd horse [and] galloped away towards the Utah Lake. He was pointed out to the other Utah who gave chase, overtook & killed him & the horse, which shews that thieving from each other is not allowed, but quickly punished. These Indians had a quantity of dried crickets in a bag, to eat. They will trade a pretty good horse for a musket. In the evening Colonel Markham reported that the brethren have wooded 13 Plows & 3 Harrows this week & broke 3 lots of land containing 35 acres, ⅔rds of it planted with Corn Oats Buck Wheat &c. 8 acres are planted with Corn Beans Potatoes [and] 10 acres with all manner of Garden seeds & there are about three acres of Corn up 2 inches above the ground; also beans & potatoes are up—all this being done in 7 days labor. A Warm day.

President Young was sick in the night.

August Sunday 1st—A cold strong wind in the night. President Young very sick with Diarrhea. Clear pleasant day. NW breeze. At 10 in the morning the brethren assembled in the Bowery. All of the Twelve except President Young present. Choir sung "On the Mountain Tops Appearing." Elder Kimball, Pratt, & Richards addressed the brethren. WR also read "Orders No. 1" (on file) from the Lieutenant Colonel of the Mormon Battalion.[24] T. Bullock read a letter from Captain Jefferson Hunt to Captain Brown. Meeting adjourned at ¼ to 1. (See TB's minutes.) In P.M. Sacrament meeting, when President Richards read "The Word and Will of the Lord" given 14 January 1847, which the brethren received & said they were willing to observe it. H. C. Kimball, A. Lyman & W. Richards spoke.

Afterwards it was voted "that all the companies be formed into one."

——"that the officers be a Committee to form the Caral."

——"that the Caral be formed tomorrow."

——"that it be carried out in the same order that the Pioneers travelled."

——"that we build a Stockade of houses."

W. Richards "I motion that the order of the Kingdom be carried out in this as in all other business." Seconded & Carried.

Samuel Gould & James Dunn were appointed lime burners. Sylvester

---

[24] In these famous orders of 30 January 1847, Philip St. George Cooke congratulated the Mormon Battalion and noted, "History may be searched in vain for an equal march of infantry." See Tyler, *A Concise History of the Mormon Battalion,* 254–55.

H. Earl, Joel J. Terrill, Ralph Douglas, & Joseph Hancock brick makers (see minutes on file).

Monday 2 August 1847—Cool night, some rain. Bathe by myself. Fine warm morning. The three camps move into one caral. Doctor dictates a letter to C. C. Rich which was approved, then copied [and] signed by President Young & Richards, [and] given to E. T. Benson who left Camp about noon with O. P. Rockwell & 3 Soldiers to meet the Saints from Winter Quarters. O. Pratt & H. G. Sherwood commence surveying. The brethren continue sowing buck wheat & plowing, others making moulds for Dobies.[25] Warm day, NW breeze.

T. Bullock with Jackson Shupe & Dimic Huntington take 2 Spades & 1 Hoe to make a good job of "Bullock's warm bathing Spring." Tear down the embankment, dig it deeper. ~~before~~ I had scarce made "the pillow" when W. Richards, W. Woodruff & G. A. Smith came up. W. R. went "to bed," while we continued to dig the bath deeper & make a Stone embankment. When we damd it up, all bathed & were satisfied with the improvement.[26] When I & Shupe returned on foot, we found a delightful Cold Spring. I dug out a hole while he cut away the tall grass & called it "Jackson's Spring." Wm. Clayton informs me that he is to return with the ox teams & I to stay till horse teams go. The ox teams [are] to dry Buffalo meat & wait for the horse teams at Grand Island, if they get there first.[27] He will commence fixing a new Roadometer directly.

Tuesday 3—Fine clear morning. Starling Driggs & 3 other hunters go with 2 Wagons to fetch Meat. Albert Carrington goes to hunt for limestone & finds it. The Surveyors run out the base line and commence surveying the 40 acre Temple Square & also run out the chain to the Dobie Square which is 3 Blocks South by 3 West from the Temple Square.[28] I

---

[25] Adobe bricks.

[26] "About one and a half mile north of the Temple Block," Bullock wrote Franklin D. Richards from Winter Quarters, "is a beautiful warm sulphur spring, which I dug out and made a most beautiful bathing place of. The brethren were pleased to name it after me, on account of my labor. It is 100 degrees Fahrenheit. About two miles further, is a hot spring, 120 degrees, and about fifty other springs, mineral and warm." Bullock to Richards, *Millennial Star* (15 January 1848), 30.

[27] Most of the Mormon leaders returned to Winter Quarters to fetch their families and prepare for the 1848 emigration. As Bullock notes, the returning companies were organized into ox and horse companies—a strategy that created much bad feeling on the return journey.

[28] The "Dobie Square" became the site of the "Old Fort," located at today's Pioneer Park, where the Mormon settlers wintered.

retire to the Bowery and make 2 Copies of "Orders No. 1," also a Copy of Captain Hunt's letter (both on file). I also Make a plot of the City, when President Young came into the tent & orders me to rest, and take care of myself. That I must not worry myself so much about the business, but preserve my health for future usefulness. I feel thankful for his kind attentions to me. Very warm day.

In the evening I received a citation "Gribble v Tubbs" [and] Gribble & Brown & [was] requested to attend bowery at 8 in the morning.

Wednesday 4—At 8 A.M. I was in the Bowery. All of the Twelve being present I called the parties before [the] Court: William Gribble v. William Tubbs, Sophia Gribble & Harriet Brown (TB's Minutes on file). In [the] afternoon Tubbs came before Young, Kimball, Richards, Pratt, Lyman & TB in [the] tent [and] makes a partial Confession (on file).[29] Council afterwards decided there has been much wickedness in the Battalion & it will be the best thing to baptize all of them.[30] Also to reduce the Temple lot from 40 acres to 10. Spoke of Joseph's views regarding the Garden. The largest city to be on the opposite side the Valley towards the Utah Lake. To send Gribble to California. The Twelve then went to the Dobie Yard. S. Brannan & J. C. Little go to Utah Lake to explore. The Surveyors run a line on the NW & NE Corner of Temple Block also some Streets on [the] North side. The brethren continue plowing, planting, gardening, & bringing logs to the Square. John Dixon planted Locust seed & Peach Stones for me, in his lot.

Thomas Tanner & Burr Frost build their Blacksmith Shop. Fine Clear Warm day. In the evening I rode to the Spring with John S. Fowler. Delightful ride & bathe. On my return I found the 70s gathering in the Bowery when they were addressed by A. P. Rockwood [and] President Young about what had been done in Winter Quarters for their Wives & families [and] their future prospects, advocating honesty, integrity & virtue. [Young] preached [the] doctrine of husbands and wives [and] called on them to fix the bowery & prepare a baptizing place for Sunday.

---

[29] The records of the Gribble-Tubbs matter are not available, but a note in the Journal History for 4 August indicates Tubbs was accused of "improper conduct with Harriat [sic] Brown" and adultery with Sophie Gribble, which led to her subsequent divorce from William Gribble.

[30] Although the practice is no longer followed, nineteenth-century Mormons were often rebaptized to renew their covenant to the church and to obtain remission for their sins. See Bullock's entries for 7 and 8 August for an account of these ordinances.

Thursday 5 August 1847—A warm clear day. At 9 o'clock Elders Kimball, Richards & Lyman found a place which would be made to do to baptize in, on the North Creek. At 10 B. Young, H. C. Kimball, Richards & Pratt met in Tent, councilling on the Temple lot Surveying [and] General business in the Valley. The brethren are set to work to build a dam across the creek so as to make a good place to baptize in. D. B. Huntington brought a Wart from a Rose bush, very red, handsome & curious. President Young signs a receipt to James Brown 2 for [$]20.00 on Subscription Paper for Council. Also to D. B. Huntington for 10$, 5 being for the poor & 5 for the Council. Brothers Clark & Owens return to Camp & report having seen a beautiful valley 20 miles from this beyond the Salt Lake having considerable timber & beautiful little Springs & Streams running thro' it.[31] They came to a Village of Utahs [Goshutes] 3 or 400 in Number. The women & children ran away in all directions, while the men put themselves in a warlike attitude with Bows & Arrows; but one man who had been at our Camp recognized them, came out, shook hands with [them], & took them in to their village. They report the Children were a perfect swarm.

Professor Pratt went South 6 or 7 miles, ran a base line of 300 rods & measured the 2 highest peaks on the East side of Valley. A lone peak SSE from camp is by a probably Air line at the distance of 18 miles & 6319 feet high. The twin peaks, southern one, is, distance from camp 15 miles & 6619 feet high, bearing SE by East.[32] He also measured by a base line of 100 rods, the Sugar Loaf Peak or Light House, at the North End of West range 16½ miles air line.[33] The brethren finish sowing Buck Wheat & make 1600 Adobies.

Friday 6 August 1847—Clark Stillman and Lodema his Wife having differences between them, Presidents Young, Kimball & Richards went to the Tent of Thos. Williams, when it was decided they should be separated. In the after noon Doctor dictated the "Disolution of Marriage" which T. B made 3 copies for Signatures. In evening Presidents Y. K. & R.[34] went again procured their signatures to the papers. Original on file.

[31] George Sheffer Clark and Seeley Owen seem to be the men who explored the Tooele Valley.
[32] Lone Peak and the Twin Peaks south of Salt Lake City still bear these names.
[33] This describes present Kessler or Farnsworth peaks at the north end of the Oquirrh mountain range.
[34] That is, Young, Kimball, and Richards.

Duplicate & triplicate given to [the] parties. Samuel Brannan reports that he, Lieutenant Willis, J. C. Little & another left camp on [the] fourth taking the left hand trail towards the Utah [Lake], after crossing 6 creeks (12 miles); at the Junction of another trail found the bodies of two Indians who were killed the last Monday by the Indians. Here we see the Indian law against Stealing carried out with rigor, as a warning to others. They continued their course by the left trail crossing two more creeks and then came to a Kanyon where a creek ran thro' from a high land.[35] Here they had a view of the Utah Lake on the right hand having seven Streams running in from the left side thro' a good land, at which place they camped for the night. The next day they took a Westerly course by the side of the Salt Lake, over a good land, having good grass on it. On their right was a table land & behind it the Light House mountain. After crossing several miles in a strait course they came to the two mouths of the Utah Lake [the Jordan River] which run out to the Salt Lake. Here they bathed. The Lake here takes a sudden turn to the South at the Fork of the Dark Mountains, having Trees scattered along its banks. They then turned to the East, keeping along the edge of a bluff, which they came to several Springs of hot Water, three of them being about 25 yards across. They further report that two or three of the Lakes do not appear to have any bottom to them, for they could not see the bottom. The Water is pure & so very hot they could not bear their fingers in it for more than 4 or 5 seconds at a time. In coming along the side of the hill they could see the bottom of the River & say that it is a good valley. They then took a NE trail to where it joins the other trail & returned home last evening about dusk. 400 Square miles arable.

 I sorted & took account of the different seeds that were in the Doctor's Wagon which had a regular cleaning out. I also took out an assortment of seed for Elder Brannan. Took my bathe in the evening. After return hunted for the cow & got very tired. Four Wagons went to the Woods to fetch logs to make a house for the Doctor [and] returned in [the] night. A warm day, breeze from South. Thermometer at 2 P.M. 98°.

 Presidents Young, Kimball, Richards, Pratt, Woodruff, Smith, Lyman, & Benson are baptized & confirm each other soon after dark at

---

[35] Brannan and his party had reached the "point of the mountain" of the Traverse Range where the Jordan River enters Salt Lake Valley.

THE GREAT SALT LAKE CITY

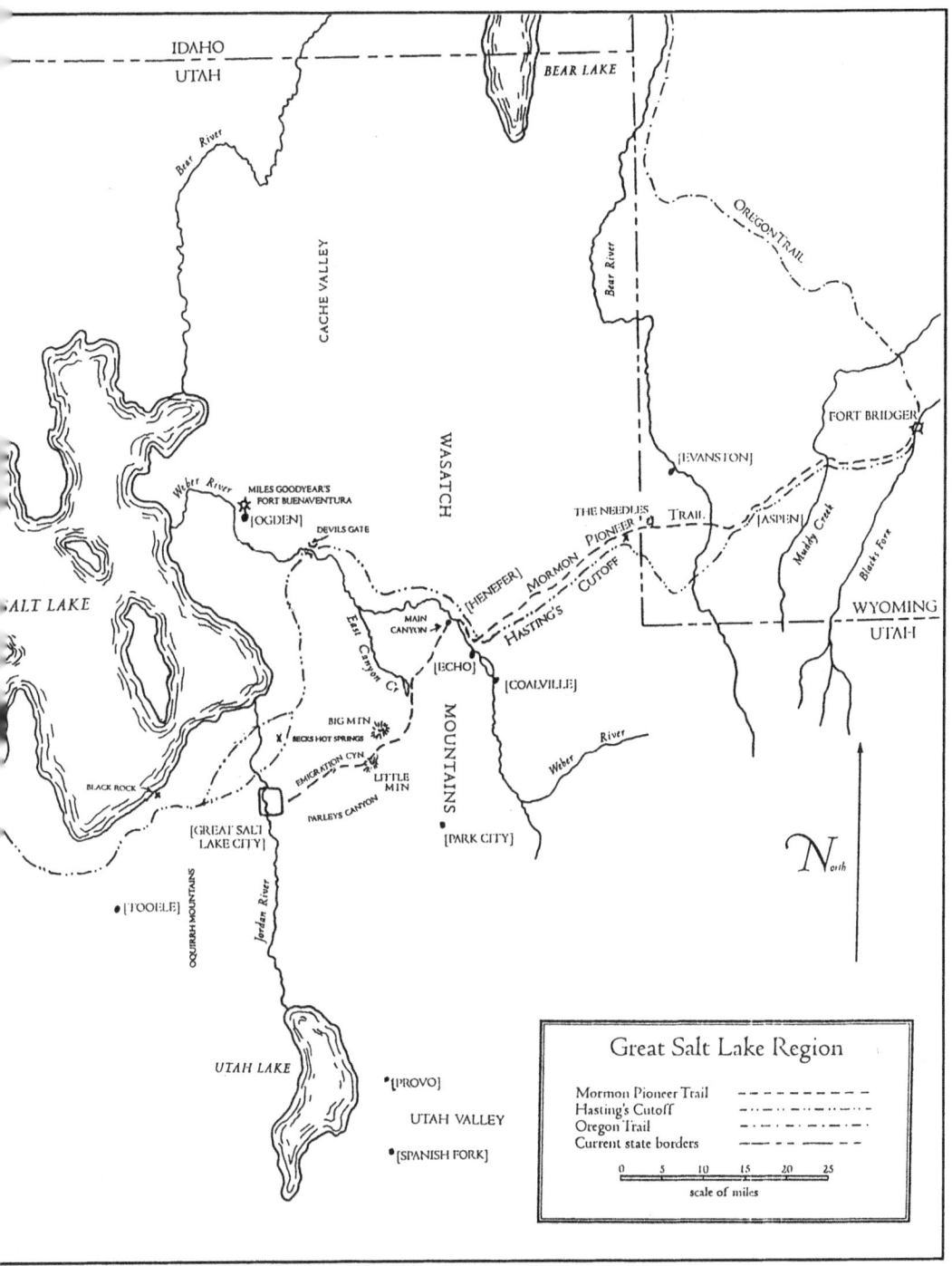

the NE baptizing place. A whirlwind passes thro' the camp in the evening pulling off one Wagon cover & the Grass from several boweries before the tents.

The wind often commences in the East in the morning then [switches] to South, then West, North & back to East in the course of the day & small whirlwinds seen nearly every day in some portion of the valley.

Saturday 7th. August 1847—Clear Sky, pleasant morning. The brethren dig a trench into the creek & dam the creek up, then plow a gutter thro' the Camp, so as to Irrigate each side. After cutting 8 or 10 Gutters & daming up the creek the Water was turned in & flowed thro' & around the Camp. Dr. Richards & T. Bullock about 2 P.M. went up to [a] tree on the left creek [and] under its shade, spread a robe. Doctor dictated a very long Epistle to the Saints in California, also a long letter to Captain Hunt of the Battalion (on file).[36] [We] returned shortly before Sundown, having named "the Clerk's Bank" upon it. Read letters to President Young, made copy of a letter from Elder Hyde of 5th September 46 to Elder Brannan.[37]

At dark President H. C. Kimball goes into the Water & baptized 56 of the brethren & are confirmed by Presidents Young, Woodruff, Lyman & Pratt—for fuller particulars see the records.[38] Between 9 & 10 Council met at the Doctor's Wagon when it was agreed that Tarlton Lewis, Charles Shumway, Erastus Snow, Stephen H. Goddard & Addison Everett should baptize in the morning [and] Wilford Woodruff, Heber C. Kimball, Orson Pratt, Amasa Lyman & G. A. Smith should Confirm & Thomas Bullock, Albert Carrington, Jesse C. Little, John Smith & Lieutenant Willis be Clerks & to commence at 6 o'clock in the morning.

---

[36] These two important letters, addressed "An epistle of the Council of the Twelve Apostles of the Church of Jesus Christ of Latter-day Saints to the Saints in California under the Presidency of Elder Samuel Brannan," and "To Capt. Jefferson Hunt and the officers and soldiers of the Mormon Battalion" defined LDS church policy in California. The first confirmed Samuel Brannan's leadership and the letter to Hunt advised battalion veterans to "come directly to this place, where you will learn particularly who is here, who not. If there are any men who have not families among your number who desire to stop in California for a season, we do not feel to object; yet we do feel that it will be better for them to come directly to this place." It directed the men to retain "arms, equipments, camp equipage, etc." See the Journal History, 7 August 1847.

[37] This letter contained general information and one very interesting sentence that suggests Brannán took a flag of the Kingdom of God to California: "The standard which you took with you, do not exhibit, till the council of the church have approved of it." See Orson Hyde to Brannan, 5 September 1846, LDS Archives.

[38] The ledger listing those baptized is part of Record of Members Collection in the LDS Archives.

Sunday 8 August 1847—I prepared papers for the different Clerks. At 6 o'clock, Wilford Woodruff, Tarlton Lewis & Thomas Bullock repaired to the Upper pool & attended to the ordinances of baptism & confirmation to 99 persons. The other brethren attended to 126 persons, making a total of 289 persons, who went forward & renewed their Covenant to serve the Lord. At ¼ past 9 the Council met in [the] Office Tent to hear the letters to the Saints in California & to the Battalion which was finished at ¼ to 11 [and] read. Then repaired to the bowery when Choir sung "Come thou to whose all searching eye," were addressed by H. C. Kimball & W. Woodruff & dismissed at ½ past 12. At 2 P.M. again assembled to administer Sacrament. Afterwards 76 men volunteered to work on Dobie yard. Then voted that one side of the Square be built with logs. Also voted to have 4 Gates to the Stockade. President Young then made some remarks & dismissed them with a benediction at 20 minutes past 5 (minutes on file). In the morning light rain, evening clear & pleasant.

Monday 9 August 1847—About one hour before day break Catherine Steele Wife of John Steele was safely delivered of a daughter named Young Elizabeth by Ruth Abbott.[39] Made up a Mail of 252 letters to [the Mormon] Battalion [and] gave same to Captain Brown to take, also a letter to Captain Jefferson Hunt signed by B. Young & W. Richards. They also signed a letter to Elder Brannan which he took.[40] J. C. Little J. S. Fowler, Wm. Gribble accompanied him to San Francisco. J. C. Little, Lieutenant Willis, J. Matthews, J. Brown & J. Buchanan accompanied them [and] go with them to Bear River, to explore the Valley. Presidents Young, Kimball & Richards met with Wm. Gribble & Huldah Sophia his Wife, when it was decided to separate them, making 3 copies of Dissolution of Marriage which was signed at noon. Original on file. Ebenezer Hanks, Thomas Williams, & Edd. Dalton go to Fort Hall for provision for Soldiers. Captain James Brown, Jesse S. Brown, Wm. Squires, W. Gribble, Lisander Woodworth, Gilbert Hunt, & [Abner] Blackburn go as a detachment to Battalion in California, to get dis-

---

[39] The proud father noted, "my wife was safely delivered of a fine little girl who was named Young Elizabeth Steele, in honor of President Young and my sister Elizabeth." She was "the first white child born in the valley." See Steele, "Extracts from the Journal of John Steele," 18. Ruth Abbott (1810–1903) was the wife of battalion veteran Joshua Chandler Abbott.

[40] This was the 7 August letter that confirmed Brannan's authority as leader of the Mormons in California.

charges &c.[41] Stephen H. Goddard, Chesley, Loveland & Zebedee Coltrin go to Salt Lake to make Salt. 30 men work at 7 moulds & make about 2,600 Adobies, previously made, about 1500. Warm clear day. About 5 all of the Council meet in Tent, examine [the] map which I finished while they were present.[42] Marked out the Blocks for the Council. Decide to build the Council house on the Block South of Temple at [the] NE corner. Also decided to call the City "Salt Lake City, Great Basin, North America." After meeting was over, they went down to the Adobie yard. Rufus Allen prepared & fixed up a Grind Stone brought from the Mountains. It is a hard stone, works well.

Tuesday 10 August 1847—Warm day, clouds floating. Presidents Young, Kimball & Richards went down to measure out ground to erect log houses. Sent men at 9 A.M. to the Dobie block to work preparing logs for building. Commenced laying the logs for same. [There was a] cool breeze from West at noon. Thermometer 93°. Starling Driggs & Simeon Howd return from 8 days hunting, killing 1 Hare, 1 Badger, 1 White Wolf & 3 Sage Hens. [They] had a frost every night. The lowest temperature since we have been in Valley is 42°. B.Y. & H.C.K. in Tent about 2 P.M. [to] consult about building a mill on the creek, making a Park & enclosing Deer, Antelope, Elk, Sheep, Mountain Ram & Goats. Glad hunters do not find much Game as it will not encourage others to hunt. It is better to drive cattle here than hunt.[43] After staying about an hour, they went to the Dobie Yard. Clouded Sky. Distant thunder & Showers all afternoon. Strong South Wind in evening. Professor Pratt reports yesterday he went 1 mile up the creek & found the fall of Water to the meeting ground on Temple Block [to be] 251 feet fall. At 2 miles 569 feet [and] at the foot of Ensign rock to where carriages can go 862 above Temple Block. At the top of Ensign rock 1081 above [Temple Block]. The 2nd hill NE of Ensign Rock about ¾ mile [is] 1510 feet. The mountain on the NEast [is] 1859 feet. [These figures were] taken as Barometric Observations.

---

[41] Young sent James Brown to make sure the sick detachments were properly discharged and, most importantly, to pick up their pay, which the Saints used to purchase Miles Goodyear's fort. For an account of this interesting venture, see Bagley, ed., *Frontiersman: Abner Blackburn's Narrative*, 63–120.

[42] The LDS Archives contains three Bullock "Plats" of Great Salt Lake City. See Appendix A for a list of these maps.

[43] The hunters' lack of success shows how quickly the introduction of firearms resulted in the near-extermination of large game in northern Utah. Brigham Young was determined to create an agrarian society in the Great Basin, and later opposed mining just as he had hunting.

President Kimball laid the foundation of 5, Young 4 & Richards 1st log houses on the East side of the Dobie Block & commenced the 2nd tier of logs. About 4000 Dobies made this day.

Wednesday 11 August 1847—Clear Sky, Pleasant morning. About 8 o'clock A.M. thermometer stood at 79°. President Young reported Father Sherwood's Survey of City runs 15 Blocks North & South by 9 East & West. Many Wagons taken to Burr Frost's Blacksmith Shop to have the Tire[s] set.

Norton Jacobs, John Wheeler, John Norton, Joseph Hancock, Lewis Barney, Thomas Brown, Richard D. Smith, James Oakley, David Perkins, William E. Bexted & Isaac Carpenter being out of provisions & returning to the hunting grounds with 4 Wagons, President Young gave me directions to write a letter of instructions to them, which when done, I read to Young, Kimball & Richards. Then copied same for Signatures, which was signed & delivered to Jacobs (Copy on file).[44] They then walked down to the Dobie Yard. A great number of Utahs come in a body to our Camp, many of them are entirely naked & all armed with a bow and arrows. About 4 o'clock Milton Howard Therlkill, Son of George W. Therlkill & Matilda Jane his Wife, was drowned, age 3 years 8 months 26 days. He fell into the river on the South East of the Camp & before assistance could be rendered he was quite dead. Means were used to revive him, if possible, but all was of no avail. This is the first death in this Valley.

Solomon Chamberlain reports gathering a great quantity of Salt on a rock which he called "Chamberlain's Rock" [and] collected bags to send after a Wagon load. S. H. Goddard & Z. Coltrin report they had gathered 4 barrels of Salt from this place before Chamberlain came & he has no right to the name but ought to be called "Goddard & Coltrin's Salt bed," for they drained it. The Boat finished this afternoon & put into the Creek to float it before the boy was drowned. The brethren commence putting up the Walls of Dobies on the North side. Professor Pratt reports the altitude of Temple Block to be 4309 feet above the Sea.[45]

Thursday 12 August 1847—Warm day, temperature about 9 A.M. &

---

[44] See Jacob, eds., *The Record of Norton Jacob*, 78, for his instructions.

[45] The marker on the southeast corner of Temple Square sets the altitude at sidewalk level as 4,327.27 feet above sea level. It marks the Great Salt Lake Base Meridian at Latitude 40° 46' 04", Longitude 111° 54' 00". On page 115 of Journal No. 2, Bullock recorded Orson Pratt's "Latitude of Great Salt Lake City 40° 45'.50" Temple block" and a different altitude: "Profr. Pratts—Temple Block 4360."

½ past 4 [is] 94°. Cloudy in the distance with a Storm on the top of the high peak on the left. About 10, H. C. Kimball & W. Richards go down to the Dobie Block. B. Young & A. Lyman come into my Office tent [and] converse about the lots in the City, the importance of punctuality & the way to create confidence in each other. Afterwards they go to Tanner & Frost's Blacksmith Shop, where they were shoeing oxen that are going to return. About noon I ride on brother Richardson's horse up to Warm Spring [and] bathe. Then to the farm. Some Corn, Potatoes, Beans & Buck Wheat looking well. Then to Garden, very little produce up. Then to Dobie lot [to] find about 60 men at work, some making Dobies, others putting up the North outside wall. Have run out about 80 feet & about 4 feet high. Others squaring, hewing, & preparing house logs, while the remainder were busy building same, among whom was A. Lyman, G. A. Smith & W. Woodruff. Saw the funeral of the drowned boy coming & witnessed its lowering to Mother Earth. O. Pratt made prayer & followed by some remarks on the Visitation & morn of the resurrection, exhorting the Father to be baptized & the family to lead holy lives. About 3 P.M. on my return met B. Young, H. C. Kimball & W. Richards going down to the Dobie Yard.

Friday 13 August 1847—Clear Sky, cool wind from South. S. H. Goddard, Z. Coltrin, C. Loveland & [?] return from Salt Lake having prepared 125 bushels of White Salt & boiled down 4 Barrels of Salt Water, making 1 Barrel of the finest White Table Salt.

Saturday 14 August 1847—Clear Sky, warm day. About noon Lieutenant Willis, J. C. Little & others return from Cache Valley reporting it a most beautiful valley, having seen the most timber of any place explored. From 9 miles to 17½ miles from Camp are 12 Streams running thro a good country to the Salt Lake. At Goodyear's garden Spanish Corn in Silk, Yankee Corn as long as they could reach, planted 9th June. Beans ripe, Carrots a foot long, Cabbages looking well, Radishes &c [left them] satisfied that this country will produce well, if planted in proper season. Had a large flock of Goats [that] looked well, some Sheep wanted shearing bad. Mr. Wells the man in charge was very friendly.

About Sundown A. Carrington & Co. returned from Utah Lake. Could not get the Wagon Boat over the mountain. They came down the outlet, a very rapid Stream, [its] Banks thickly fringed with Willows.[46]

---

[46] Today's Jordan River was known to the mountaineers as the Utah Outlet.

Only caught 4 fish. Faint traces of Ore in the creek & River banks. Also some bog ore. About 3 John Sunderland Eldredge was ordained to the Office of a Seventy under the hands of Albert P. Rockwood & [blank].

About 8 P.M. Matilda Jane, Wife of George W. Therlkill, was safely delivered of a daughter, Harriet Ann, by Dr. McIntyre.

Sunday 15 August 1847—Cloudy, warm day. Breeze from NNW. At 10 o'clock meeting in the Bowery opened by singing "The glorious day is rolling on." Prayer by H. C. Kimball, when President Young made an excellent discourse on the Patriarchal Priesthood & remarks on the death of Mrs. Therlkill's little boy (see TB's minutes). At 2 o'clock Sacrament meeting I was copying the table of distances, observations &c by W. Clayton from Winter Quarters to Great Salt Lake City (on file). At 6 the Choristers met in the President's tent & sung "the Prodigal Son" and other pieces. Afterwards the brethren who are going to return tomorrow were called into two ranks & were addressed by President Young.

The Soldiers were told their Guns must be left here & not taken to the States and appointed tomorrow morning to receive the remainder which are not yet delivered in. It was voted that Shadrach Roundy & Tunis Rappelye should be the leaders of the Company, when the brethren were exhorted to faithfulness & were dismissed with the blessing of the Lord.

This day the first four chickens in the "Great Salt Lake City" were hatched by a hen belonging to Stephen H. Goddard.

Monday 16 August 1847—Cloudy & cool. The ox teams began to start on return route. [They] rendezvouz in the Kanyon very early in the morning, while the remainder of the Soldiers who had not returned their Guns to head quarters brought them in. (See list.)

About noon Presidents Young Kimball Pratt, Woodruff & Smith met in the President's Tent and after consultation voted to name the Streets round the Temple Block "East Temple Street," South Temple Street, West Temple Street, North Temple Street, and to Number the remainder of the Streets "First South Street" "Second South Street" &c [as] suggested by President Young.[47] Motioned by O. Pratt, seconded by H. C. Kimball. An alteration was also made in the order of numbering

---

[47] So was born the street naming convention still used in Salt Lake City today. East Temple is today's Main Street, but the other street names remain unchanged.

lots in the alternate blocks, so as to have all uniformly beginning at the SE Corner of the Block.

T. B. made another new map. Four more Chickens hatched this day (8). President Young instructed me to write a letter to Shadrack Roundy & Tunis Rappelye, which I did.[48] Read same to W. Richards, O. Pratt, W. Woodruff, G.A. Smith & A. Lyman in WR's Wagon, at dusk, (on file), also numbering the blocks they wanted for their families, in pencil, on the map.[49]

The Wagon I drove here, having returned about 3 P.M. with Thos. Richardson & Joseph Shipley, I slept with Doctor.

Heavy thunder shower in the night with strong wind.

Tuesday 17 August 1847—T.B. copied letter to Shadrack Roundy & Tunis Rappelye for Signatures. Was called on by Colonel Rockwood & Captain Higgins to ride over to Camp, to take number of Men &c returning & to get receipts for Government cattle &c. About 7 we started for that purpose, travelling slowly. As soon as we arrived I commenced numbering them & found 24 of the Pioneers [and] 46 of the Battalion with 34 Wagons. 92 yokes of oxen, 18 horses, 14 Mules returning, namely:

Pioneers	[THE OX COMPANY OF RETURNING PIONEERS]				
	Battalion	Wagon	Yoke of Oxen	horses	mules
	Thomas Richardson	1	3	–	
	Joseph Shipley				
	Henry W. Sanderson	1	1	–	–
	Miron Tanner				
Norman Taylor		1	3	1	–
John S. Gleason					
George Wardle		1	6	–	
	Clark Stillman				
	William Bird	1	2	1	–
	Samuel Badham				
	George Cummings	4	1	–	
	James Cazier				
	Erastus Bingham				
	Lorin E. Henney				
	Luther W. Glazier	1	3	1	–
	Daniel Miller				

[48] In this letter, Young cautioned Roundy and Rappleye to "not give way to an over anxious spirit, so that your spirits arrive at Winter Quarters before the time that your bodies can possibly arrive there." See the Journal History, 4 August 1847.

[49] This may describe Thomas Bullock, Plat of Great Salt Lake City, 1847, LDS Archives. A facsimile is on display at the LDS Museum of Church History and Art in Salt Lake City.

THE GREAT SALT LAKE CITY

Pioneers	Battalion	Wagon	Yoke of Oxen	horses	mules
	Benjamin Roberts				
	Francilias Durfee				
	Jarvis Johnson	1	3	1	–
	Albert Clarke				
	Jackson Shupe				
	John Calvert	1	–	1	5
	James Hendrixon				
	Allen Cumpton	–	1	5	–
	John Bybee				
	Philip Garner	1	5	–	–
	David Garner				
Charles Burke					
	James Stewart	1	3	–	–
	William McLellin				
	John G. Smith				
	Franklin Alle				
	Judathan Ever	12	–	1	
	Barnabas Lake	1			
Robert Byard		1	2	–	–
Ben W. Rolfe		1	2	–	–
Thomas P. Cloward	Lisbon Lamb	1	2	–	–
John Pack	William H. Carpenter	1	2	2 –	–
	John H. Tippets				
	Lyman Stevens	1	2	–	–
	Francis T. Whitney				
Samuel H. Marble					
George Scholes	Lorenzo Babcock	1	2	–	–
Zebedee Coltrin		1	2	–	–
Chaney Lovland		1	–	1	2
	William Bird	1	1	–	–
	Josiah Curtis				
	Charles Hopkins				
	Harmon Persons	1	3	–	–
	Solomon Tindal				
	Roswell Stevens	1	3	–	4
Artemas Johnson	Joseph Skeen	1	4	1	–
Sylvester H. Earl		1	4	1	–
Seeley Owens					
John Eldredge		1	2	1	
Horace Thornton					
Francis Boggs		1	2	–	–
Shadrack Roundy		1	2	1	–
	Lyman Curtis	1	1	1	–
Tunis Rappelye		1	4	–	–
	James Dunn	1	2	–	–
	Bailey Jacobs	1	2	–	–
William Clayton					
Jackson Redding		1	–	1	2
Rufus Allen					
Almon. M. Williams		1	–	2	–	-
Total 24 Pioneers	46 Soldiers	34 Wagons	92 Yoke of Oxen	18 horses	14 Mules

After attending to different duties, hearing that President Young was not coming out, we despatched a messenger to Camp for the letter of instructions. The Camp moved on its way & we went to the Service berry gathering. Staid about an hour [and] returned to Camp. Called to order by H. C. Kimball & W. Richards, when I read the letter to Roundy & Rappelye & the Company were then addressed by H. C. Kimball exhorting them to their duties, advising them to dedicate themselves, their Wagons, their all, to the Lord to obey Council & they should be blest and warned them strongly that if one of them, thro' the Spirit of revenge or hatred, should betray his brethren & cause trouble, that the curse of God would rest upon him. W. Richards then confirmed his statements & blessed them in the name of the Lord. Captain Higgins then addressed the detachment telling them they were detailed to go the States after provisions & would be under the command of Lieutenant Willis & exhorted them to be faithful. H. C. Kimball dismissed them with the blessings of the Lord. The Camp then moved on its way & H. C. Kimball, W. Richards, A. P. Rockwood, T. Bullock, S. H. Goddard, H. Egan & N. Higgins returned towards Salt Lake City, after partaking of Bread & Water in the Kanyon. It was agreed to go over the ridge where the Emigrants of last year went, Kimball & Richards leading their horses. I rode the one I was on clear to the top, while the remainder led theirs up. [It was] a terrible steep ascent & when [we] arrived at the top, President Kimball remarked that he never in the course of his life saw such presumption as to attempt to take Wagons up it. Here the Emigrants Camped.[50] We had a most splendid view of the Valley & the Great Salt Lake. Then descended to the bottom on the opposite side. Had to plunge into Grass by a descent 14 or 16 feet steep. President Kimball on horseback, I on the ridge could not see him, the grass being so much taller. I rode down it & leaped my horse over the creek safely. I am not afraid now but that by a little practice I could make a good Equestrian & thank the Lord for my improvement. We waded thro' this tall grass not seeing one yard before, at the sides, or behind us until we emerged on the opposite side. President K. & I returned to Camp while the remainder rode to the Garden & Farm & report the Corn, Potatoes,

---

[50] Bullock and Kimball climbed Donner Hill at the mouth of Emigration Canyon. The Donner-Reed company spent an entire day hauling their wagons one-by-one out of the canyon to reach a camp at today's Donner Park.

Beans & Buck Wheat looking splendid. We returned to Camp ½ hour before Sundown when I went to take my daily bath in "Bullock's Bathing place" with S. H. Goddard. Pleasant day cool breeze. Showers in the distance.

About 8 o'clock Elder Orson Pratt reported that he had married William Tubbs and Sophia Smith for time only[51] in the presence of Daniel Brown and Harriet Brown, in their tent (see minutes of August 4 to August 9th). Windy night.

Wednesday 18 August 1847—Dull cloudy morning. Presidents Young, Kimball & Richards at the Dobie Yard & building log houses. President Young has 4 & Kimball has 5 log houses up, ready for receiving the roofs. The West side of Doby Wall commenced this day, the North being left for the present about 5 feet high. Presidents Kimball & Pratt fixing their relatives and friends on different Blocks & lots. Three thunder showers pass over the Valley during the day. President Richards squaring timber, marking logs & preparing to put his house up tomorrow. In digging a ditch 3½ feet deep came to an excellent Spring of cold water.

T.B. writing on "the Clerk's bank."

Thursday 19 August 1847—Cloudy & Cool morning. About 7 A.M. Stephen Markham baptized Joshua Abbott & Ruth Abbott & were Confirmed by Stephen Markham & Thomas Bullock about noon. Much anxiety was manifested by the report of the Express from Winter Quarters Camp being in sight: which turned out to be Six Indians & Half breeds from Fort Bridger with Pack Mules. They passed the Camp towards the Salt Lake & which proved a great disappointment to many.

Dr. Richards built his house 6 logs up & prepared Timber for his other house. Presidents Young, Kimball, Woodruff, Smith & Lyman with many of the brethren very busy with their houses. Many at work on the Dobie Yard. Pleasant day.

Friday 20 August 1847—About 8 A.M. hearing that Ivory, John Freeman, Joseph Egbert & M. B. Thorpe were riding to Salt Lake I procured a saddle & went with them to catch their horses. [We] crossed the River Jordan [and] in a few miles came to the Sage country. At the foot of the hills [are] several brackish Springs. On the banks of the creek at the foot of "Rattle Snake Caves" I & Thorpe killed an old [snake?].

---

[51] Today LDS marriages can be "for time"—until the death of one spouse, or "for eternity." For a discussion of LDS temple marriages in Bullock's time, see Kimball, *Heber C. Kimball*, 93–94.

G. A. Smith while heaving a heavy log of timber off the Wagon, with brother Woodruff & another man, got knocked down by it hitting him on the head. A mercy he was not killed. [At] ½ past 8 P.M. A. Carrington, J. Brown, W. W. Rust, & A. Calkins started out to go to the Twin Peaks SE by South from Camp [and they] rode to near the base of the mountain by midnight & Camped.

Saturday 21—Presidents Young & Kimball commenced removing their Seeds & goods that they were going to leave here into their houses.

President Richards part covered his house. He & his assistants have built 3 houses in the last 3 days.

The remainder of the Council & many of the brethren very busy building log houses, making Dobies & the Doby Wall.

Warm day. Cloudy in evening. Mr. Wells an Englishman from Weber River, visits the Camp, City, Farm & Garden.[52]

At 8 A.M. [the men at Twin Peaks] began to ascend the mountain, Carrington with Barometer & Brown with Thermometer. Near the highest line of vegetation [they found] red raspberries & red gooseberries. Saw 16 fine fat mountain sheep. Carrington, Wilson & Rust reached top of West peak of twins at ½ past 4 P.M. Air very hazy, plenty of Snow. At 5 P.M. thermometer 55°. Started back [at] ½ past 5 [and] passed red raspberries, gooseberries, quaking asp, fir balsam, Spruce Pine, Norway Pine—green & thrifty very tall & strait, uniform size [with a] gradual taper, small to 2 feet thro'. At 10 P.M. Carrington & Brown lay down on gravel to sleep.[53]

Sunday 22 August 1847—Doctor dictating letter & TB writing until after 2 o'clock when we retired to rest. About 9 Doctor & TB went up to Warm Spring. Found W. Woodruff & another there. While in the Spring Mr. Wills (the Englishman settled on Weber's River) passed us on his return home. On our return to Camp Doctor continued the dictation of the Epistle to the Saints in the Great Salt Lake City, T.B. writing. There was a meeting at the Stand, A. Lyman preaching. As soon as meeting was dismissed, the Council assembled under "the Old Oak Tree" & heard read the Epistle to the Saints. Several alterations were suggested. They also took into consideration the matters of business to be brought before the Conference to be held in the afternoon.

---

[52] Again, this is the mysterious Captain Wells of Fort Goodyear.

[53] Albert Carrington, John Brown, "and others" climbed Twin Peaks above present Sandy, Utah. See Brown, *Autobiography*, 82–83 for their adventures.

At I P.M. Conference commenced by singing "The Spirit of God like a fire is burning." President Kimball brought the business before the meeting with a few preliminary remarks when President Young [said] "I move that the brethren fence in the City, or such portion as they've a mind to in sections, & cultivate it." D. B. Huntington seconded. Clear vote.[54]

B. Young "I move that there be a President to preside over this place. D.B.H. seconded: Clear vote.

[B. Young] I move that there be a High Council. [D.B.H. seconded: Clear vote.]

[B. Young] "I move that all other officers that are necessary be appointed for this place." T. Lewis seconded. [Clear vote.]

[B. Young] "I move that we call this place "The Great Salt Lake City" of the Great Basin North America. D.B.H. [seconded: Clear vote.]

[B. Young] "I move that we call the Post office "The Great Basin Post Office." T.B. [seconded: Clear vote.]

H. C. Kimball "I move that we call the River "The Western Jordan." [Seconded: Clear vote.]

[H. C. Kimball] "I move that Colonel Rockwood be honorably discharged from the duties as Overseer of the Stockade. Seconded & carried. (contd next page)

H. C. Kimball "I motion that Tarlton Lewis be appointed to that office. Seconded. Clear vote.

President Young then addressed the Conference & wanted to engage 50,000 Bushel of Wheat @ [$]1.25 & 50000 Bushel of Corn @ 50[¢] per bushel & 20,000 Bushel of oats @ .25[¢] per Bushel for next year & spoke of growing all that they could for the Emigrating Companies.

B. Young "I motion that this creek be called "the City Creek." T. Lewis seconded. Clear vote.

[B. Young] "I motion that the large creek about 8 miles South be called "Mill Creek." T. Lewis seconded. Clear vote.

[B. Young] "I motion that the little creek a little South is called "Red Bute Creek." T. Lewis seconded. Clear vote.

[B. Young "I motion that the] next is called "Kanyon Creek." T. Lewis seconded. Clear vote.

---

[54] "Clear vote" meant the motion passed unanimously.

[B. Young "I motion that the] next can be called "Big Kanyon Creek." T. Lewis seconded. Clear vote.⁵⁵

[B. Young] "I want to know if the people are satisfied with the labors of the Twelve."

Tarlton Lewis "I motion that we give them our approbation, that we are satisfied with their labors and give them our blessing." T. Bullock seconded. Clear vote.

President Young then requested to know who are going back to Winter Quarters (rose up).

[President Young then requested to know of those who] stay if you will finish the Doby Wall (up).

[President Young] "I move that brother McIntyre be Clerk & keep an account of the Public labors." Seconded. Clear vote.

[President Young] "I move that we adjourn this Conference to Oct. 6, 1848 at 10 o'clock at this place. D. B. Huntington seconded. Clear vote.

About 6 P.M. Presidents Young, Kimball, Richards, Pratt, Woodruff, Smith, Lyman, T. Bullock, and Lorenzo Young met in H. C. Kimball's Log house. President Young prayed, then President Kimball led in prayer. Dedicated the land, ourselves, our all to the Lord & prayed for his protection & blessing on our return journey, our wives, & all we had & to come again in peace & safety to this place. Elder Orson Pratt baptized James Albert Campbell for the remission of sin in River Jordan. Confirmed by O. Pratt & Robt. Crow. Clear Sky, Warm day.

Wilson got to the Camp at 2 A.M. having gone to [the] top [of Twin Peaks] & returned to Camp in 18 hours travelling as fast as he could. Carrington & Brown arrived at ½ past 7, & Rust at 9. As they were riding to the City some Sage Hens frightened our horses & broke one tube of the Barometer by the sudden start. Arrived at the City ½ past 2 P.M. For particulars about the Quarries of Stone see Carrington's Journal.⁵⁶

---

⁵⁵ City, Mill, and Red Butte creeks still have the same names. Kanyon Creek is now Emigration Creek, while Big Kanyon Creek is now Parley's Creek.

⁵⁶ According to his son, Calvin Carrington, Albert Carrington's "diary was burned at his express order, in his old age." See Kelly, *Salt Desert Trails*, 166. Carrington, however, wrote Amasa Lyman's journal, and its 20 August 1847 entry described the expedition to and the geology of the Twin Peaks. See the Journal of Amasa Lyman, 1847, Utah State Historical Society, 50.

Monday 23 August 1847—Clear Sky, Warm day. Thermometer about 4 P.M. 89°.

This morning James T. S. Alred commences a rope factory of Buffalo hair. Sergeant [Thomas] Williams, Sergeant [Ebenezer] Hanks & Ed. Dalton returned from Fort Hall about 3 P.M. They got some Flour at [$]20.00 per 100 pounds & Beef cattle .10[¢] per pound.

The Council & Others very busy about their houses all day. In evening Presidents Young & Kimball visited Camp to procure a Beef to kill on Wednesday eve preparatory to start on Thursday morning, & making arrangements about [the] return Company. The brethren have succeeded in building 29 log houses between 8 & 9 feet high and generally 16 or 17 feet by 14 feet & Eleven of them covered in with Poles & Dirt.

Tuesday 24 August 1847—This morning commenced operations to remove Doctor's seeds & goods to his house. Removed the first load about 11 [and] returned for the other load, when a heavy thunder shower came on, wet many papers, bedding, clothing & some seeds. Stephen Markham seeing their exposed situation had most of the goods removed into the house for security. [We had] the heaviest shower in the Valley. Many of the brethren go to the Salt Lake, preparatory to their return to Winter Quarters. Presidents Young, Kimball, Richards, Woodruff & many brethren very busy about their new houses. W. Woodruff & H. C. Kimball filling up lots and blocks in City Plot.

Doctor examined all his seeds while T. B. Took an account of same, [and] let Lorenzo Young have a variety of seeds & Peach Stones. Paid Thomas Tanner [$]10 for Blacksmith work. In the night the Wolves were very annoying, keeping up a continued howling.

Wednesday 25 August 1847—Light dew, very cold morning, when Sun rose [into a] clear Sky. Warm day. Doctor busy packing up goods & seeds to stay in his house, also those goods that were going to be carried back. Assisted by T. Bullock, Daniel Brown & Benjamin Richmond assisting at his house. Emptied the Doctor's Wagon of every thing in it & cleaning every thing. President Young let the Doctor have 50 pounds Flour & 18 Shorts. He had only 6¾ pounds [of] Flour before & was a seasonable supply.

President Kimball, Young, & Smith, had lots placed [for their] families on [the] City Plot. All the brethren return from [the] Salt Lake during the day.

Made an Inventory of the Doctor's seeds & effects, & packed them away in the Upper part of the house for safe keeping. Made a fire in the house in the evening which reminded me of olden times.

Chapter 9

"THE BEST & NIGHEST ROAD"
The Returning Pioneers, Great Salt Lake City to Winter Quarters, August–October 1847

When Brigham Young organized two companies for the return trip to the Missouri River in August 1847, the "Ox train of returning pioneers" and the "horse and mule train," he anticipated that the equine company would travel faster than the bovine-powered party. Young sent a party of hunters under Norton Jacob to press through to the buffalo country and lay in a supply of meat, and on 17 August he dispatched the ox train of thirty-four wagons under the command of Tunis Rappleye, Shadrach Roundy, and Lieutenant William W. Willis. Lacking discipline and leadership, these men arrived at Winter Quarters "not as austerely disciplined companies but as a rabble of backbiting stragglers."[1]

After spending thirty-three days in the Salt Lake Valley, Young's camp of 107 men, including Thomas Bullock and seven of the Twelve Apostles, departed on 26 August. The camp included no women; both Heber Kimball and Brigham Young left their wives behind.[2] On 29 August, the returning pioneers met Ezra Taft Benson, who was coming from the Second Division and reported that the first of its nine companies had reached Independence Rock on 22 August. Young's company met Daniel Spencer's party on the Big Sandy on 3 September and encountered Parley P. Pratt and the main body of the Second Division on the next day.

The popular Pratt's leadership of the Second Division had earned the wrath of Brigham Young "for disorganizing all the Winter's Work" by ignoring Young's marching orders, "The Word and Will of the Lord," which, as Wilford Woodruff noted, were "governed by revelation." In addi-

---
[1] Stegner, *Gathering of Zion*, 184. Stegner summarized the return journey of the ox company from Clayton's journals.
[2] Lorenzo Young's wife Harriet also stayed behind. Harriet Young and Ellen Kimball gave birth during the winter, but both infants died. See Kimball, *Heber C. Kimball*, 173.

tion, Pratt had failed to organize the emigration into two divisions based on the adopted families of Young and Heber Kimball because several of the leaders Young had assigned were not ready to depart with the Second Division. As an apostle, Pratt felt that in Young's absence, he held equal authority—"All the 12 are alike in keys, power, might, majesty and dominion"— and was free to reorganize the emigration as necessity dictated. "The time is now when we have to go," he responded to critics on 15 June, "& the theory is not what we will see now so much as the practical."[3] At South Pass, Brigham Young did not look kindly on such pragmatic reasons for failing to implement his plans. Pratt resisted at first, but quickly "humbled myself, acknowledged my faults, and asked forgiveness."[4] In such a way did Young deal with a possible rival for leadership of the church—and by sending Pratt and John Taylor on to the valley, he effectively silenced the two men most likely to oppose his hopes to form a First Presidency.

Two days later, the returning pioneers encountered snow on the Sweetwater River. Apostle John Taylor lightened the mood with a surprise feast "which was royally served." On 9 September they met the rear guard of the Second Division under Jedediah Grant. During the night, disaster struck in the form of an Indian raiding party that escaped with fifty much-needed horses. A raid on 21 September further weakened the return company with a loss of eight to ten more animals.

The horse and mule train was plagued by blizzards, skunks, Sioux (or perhaps Crow) horse raiders, hunger, exhaustion, and general misfortune. The company had left most of their provisions in the valley where the remaining pioneers were nonetheless reduced to surviving on roots and hides. The returning pioneers were forced to live off the country on their return; as they made their way east the Saints found that all the fat was gone off the land.

To the immense aggravation of the rear guard, they were unable to overtake the ox train. In early October Young sent Amasa Lyman ahead to overhaul the advance party, but despite his promise to "overtake them, if it is at Winter Quarters," Lyman abandoned the pursuit at Grand Island. He reported he was "perfectly satisfied that the Ox teams were running ahead at 25 miles a day—perfectly reckless of their promises & determined to leave us at the mercy of the weather." The Saints now learned through hard experience that oxen "made the better team." They could go more than twenty miles per day "and often gain in strength with no other feed than the grass of the plains and the brouse and grass of the hills," while horses and mules bred as farm animals slowly starved without grain.[5]

---

[3] Pratt, "Parley P. Pratt in Winter Quarters and the Trail West," 383–86.

[4] Roberts, *Comprehensive History*, 3:295-96.

As Bullock's account demonstrates, the return company made great efforts to improve and shorten the route, continually trying to find the "best & nighest road." His journal contains many memoranda for the "Spring journey," suggesting routes that "will save a considerable distance."

A fuming Brigham Young arrived at Fort Laramie to find that the Sioux raiding parties who had given him such grief at South Pass were comfortably camped near the fort with the Mormons' horses. Despite the assurances of James Bordeaux, the fort's management did nothing to help the Saints regain their livestock, and the Mormons were forced to struggle across the plains with few supplies and exhausted animals. On the road down the Platte, Bullock suffered a final indignity when Willard Richards decided "to load up his Wagon with Skins & make me walk all the way home." A relief party under Hosea Stout met the return company on 18 October and brought much-needed food and spirits. A larger party under Newell K. Whitney joined them on the Elkhorn. On the last Sunday in October, a mile from Winter Quarters, Brigham Young assembled his ragged band and gave them his simple praise:

> I wish you to receive my thanks for your kindness and willingness to obey orders; I am satisfied with you; you have done well. We have accomplished more than we expected. Out of one hundred forty-three men who started, some of them sick, all of them unwell, not a man has died; we have not lost a horse, mule, or ox, but through carelessness; the blessings of the Lord have been with us...You are dismissed to go to your own homes.[6]

The Camp of Israel made its return trip to Babylon in nine weeks and four days. Bullock left no account of his reunion with his families, but we must assume it was, as Hosea Stout noted on 30 October, "a most joyful meeting and a very happy time."

Thursday 26 August 1847—Up by day break. A Beef Creature being killed for the return Company, Doctor gets 102 pounds & 8 pounds Tallow, paying Captain Higgins 7$.12ct for it. H. C. Kimball kindly lending the Clerk a Horse to ride, he went thro' the Camp to borrow a Saddle, but could not get one, thus evincing that none but the Twelve evince much regard for a correct history of the Journey of the Camp of the Saints. At 10 o'clock President Young shouted "Good-bye all who

---
[5] *Ibid.*, 3:293.
[6] Heber C. Kimball Journal (kept by Horace Whitney), cited in Kimball, *Heber C. Kimball,* 175.

tarry," "I feel well" &c. At 5 minutes past 10 Doctor's team started. [We] go by the Farm which looks in a very healthy condition [and] also the Garden, but many of the seeds had not grown. Many large birds flying about. In a short time [we] continue our journey [and] see the Salt Lake for the last time this Season. Sky blue, Atmosphere hazy & enter the Kanyon passing many rushes, Sunflowers & Hollyhocks, much Oak brush, many Sugar Maple & Balm of Gilead Trees. In crossing "Last Creek" for the 4th Time the reach in the Doctor's Wagon broke in two. [We] go to work & cut a Maple Tree to make another. While making another, Presidents Young & Richards rode up, when a plan was made to splice the old one. [We] get a couple of Strong ropes, fastened them to the reach at the hind end, underneath the Wagon, [and] to the fore axle tree. [We] then got a small Maple Stick, twisted both ropes together & lashed all to the old Reach. When completed again pursued our journey. Crossed "Last Creek" 19 times more, then ascended a high mountain on the right thro' Service Bushs, Scrub Oak, Choke Cherries & over a rough road, a mile in length. Immediately on ascending the top, commenced our descent on the East side with Wheels locked—a dusty journey. When we came to the creek, [we] took a sudden turn up the Valley to the left & continued by the creek until we arrived at the "Willow Springs" [and found] good Water & tolerable camping.[7] Doctor sick & wearied, rode in W. Woodruff's Carriage. President Young & Kimball well. Northerly Wind [and] not a cloud seen all day. The brethren eat many Service Berries, Choke Cherries & Haws.

Friday 27 August 1847—Very pleasant morning. Charles Shumway makes a new reach for the Doctor's Wagon, which when completed & the things packed snugly away, we started on our journey at 8:12 continuing our course by the side of & crossing the creek 7 times. Plenty of Willow, Birch & Balm of Gilead. Then took to the left up a Forest of Aspen Poplar, all the way up the hill. On arriving at the top, took the last view of the Salt Lake Valley, and descended on the Eastern side of the Mountain among a forest of Balsam of Fir, Quaking Asp & Poplar & many Box Trees.[8] Here the Doctor & T. B. gathered a small quantity of the

---

[7] The returning pioneers ascended Emigration Canyon, crossed Little Mountain, and climbed Mountain Dell Creek to their camp at the site of Little Dell Reservoir.

[8] The company climbed Big Mountain and descended Little Emigration Canyon to East Canyon Creek. Little Emigration Canyon remains much as Bullock described it.

Essential Oil of Balsam of Fir, by picking the blisters & catching with a Spoon. President Young rode up & examined the Box Wood which is to beautify the Temple of the Lord & prayed that the time would soon come that every man, woman & child would have as much food to eat as they needed & expressed his fears that some persons would be wasteful & so bring down the displeasure of the Almighty. Rode down the hill until we came to "Kanyon Creek," crossed it & halted on our old Camp ground at 1:34 having had a dusty journey. At 4 past 3 Camp starts down the "East Kanyon Creek" thro' a heavy mass of Willows, Rose bushes, & some Cotton Wood Trees, crossing the creek 9 times & camp on its banks amongst a good patch of Musqeet grass at 4 past 5. Presidents Young & Richards on horseback a head of the Wagons. President Young was talking of having these rough roads put in good order for travelling & thinks [$]1000.00 would cover the expence. It is much warmer than when we were here before. The Prickly Pears begin to make their appearance on this creek.

Saturday 28 August 1847—A Slight rain in the night. Cloudy, pleasant morning. Horses stray away but again caught. At 21 minutes past 8, President Young starts driving his own team. Still down the River, thro' Willows, Rose, & Gooseberry bushes, in open ground Sage & Saffron & very stony in some places. We cross the river 4 times more & (East) then ascend a very steep hill on our right. After continuing some time up it took a sudden turn down, to the right again (South) until we came to a Cold Spring. (Memorandum: Presidents Richards & Woodruff riding on horse back rode strait from the river to this spot & report that 15 or 20 men with Spades & hoes could in one hour make this a better road for Wagons, than any portion of the road our Wagons travelled between the River & this place & save 1 or 2 miles.)[9] Then sudden turn to left up the hollow by Willows & Cotton Wood Trees. On the top, took a last view of "the Twin Peaks" tipt with Snow & descended in nearly a strait line to Weber River leaving the high red bluffs on our left. After crossing Weber River, halted at ½ past 12. [We] found a Beef belonging to [the] U.S. which was killed & distributed among the brethren.[10] In about 2 hours start again up, by the Weber, pass by "the Supplication hills" &

---

[9] The pioneer company had avoided the mouth of Dixie Hollow by climbing over Bullock's "very steep hill"; the suggested shortcut followed the line of the present road, Highway 65, as it leaves East Canyon reservoir.

[10] This steer had escaped from the Mormon Battalion sick detachments.

our old Camp ground at the entrance of the Red Fork.[11] Some of the brethren saw & heard a Bear but did not kill it, having plenty of Fresh meat by them. Large rocks of Red Sand or Pudding Stone on our left which we turn round, close by "the four tier of pulpits,"[12] up the Red Fork, still thro' a thick bed of Willows. Gathered Service Berries, Gooseberries, Cherries; & a beautiful wreath of Hops, which did my Soul good to see & gather.[13] We crossed the "Red Fork" 3 times & halt at 6, all in a line in the road ready for [the] morning start. Tolerable good camping & grass. Cleared up at noon, very dusty travelling. Doctor heard the chattering of a Red Squirrel which he was delighted to hear.

Sunday 29 August 1847—Cool morning before Sun rose. Cloudy. At 7 the Camp again start, President Young leading up the Ravine, the creek all the way up fringed with Willows & the mountain sides covered with Cedars. After crossing the creek three times & [passing] several small Springs, halt to Water our horses at a beautiful Spring of Cold Water. As we keep ascending, the ravine gets wider & the Rocks diminish in size. They are generally either Pudding Stone or Sand stone [and] there is good grass all thro' this valley. Near the top of the valley you cross a deep ravine & ugly for heavy loaded wagons. We again halted at the Spring on our right to water our teams. At the end of the valley the road makes a sudden twist in a gulley. Ascend some red hills & halt opposite "Swallow Cave" at 24 minutes to 1.[14] (On next Spring journey examine if not a good & strait road on the right, down the valley.)[15] We had not been long here before we hailed Ezra T. Benson on his return from the Saints from Winter Quarters. He reports he had to go within 40 miles of Fort John, met the Saints in 9 Camps, brought lists from them. Left the nighest Camp at Independence Rock this day [last] week. The remainder of the Camps were within 100 miles behind. He brought with him a Mail of 102 letters & bundles of letters & a bundle of Newspapers which the Doctor & TB in a very short time sorted &

---

[11] The name Red Fork was applied to both Echo Creek and Echo Canyon. This night's camp was near Echo, Utah.

[12] Although Pulpit Rock is gone, David L. Bigler observes that Bullock's "four tier of pulpits" still stand at the mouth of Echo Canyon. The phrase suggests the formation was named after the tiers of pulpits at each end of the Kirtland and Nauvoo temples. See Andrews, *The Early Temples of the Mormons*, 46, 76.

[13] Bullock's repeated fondness for hops suggests he enjoyed the beverage brewers make from the plant.

[14] The Saints camped near Cache Cave.

[15] Bullock suggested investigating Chalk Creek Canyon as a possible roadway.

delivered to the anxious brethren. Made up a Mail of 22 letters for the Great Salt Lake City. T. B. wrote a letter to the Saints giving brother Benson's intelligence which was undersigned by President Young, Richards & Benson. Delivered same to John Young, Son of Lorenzo Young, who went on with Captain Higgins to the City. In about 2 hours we again started up the ravine. On the summit of the hill saw Snow on "the Twin Peaks" & other mountains. Descend on the East side hill and cross a small creek fringed with Willows. In a short time again cross the creek at the foot of some bold ragged rocks & halt at dusk.[16] After Supper the Council met in the Doctor's Wagon & heard read the papers & letters from Robert Campbell, Reuben Miller, G. P. Dykes. Also the letters from Presidents P. P. Pratt & John Taylor. Continued in Council until between 10 & 11.

Monday 30 August 1847—During the night [there was] frost which made Ice [a] tenth of an Inch thick on the water. TB visits the brethren to obtain Number of Wagons horses & mules & had reported to him 36 Wagons, 108 Men, 42 Horses & 35 Mules with which, on consideration, is an incorrect return & will have to go thro' again on account of the wilfulness of some of the brethren to mislead.

At 7:24 the Camp again starts towards the East, up the Valley which in a few miles descended to Bear River, which we crossed & halted at 20 minutes past 10 on tolerable grass. (Memorandum: heavy loaded Wagons after crossing the River had better go round the point of the hill on West side.) T.B. read the names of the 6 first Companies Emigrating hear. Took 25 minutes. At 25 minutes past 11 Camp again starts, ascend steep pitch & then over another hill. Cross the creek where we camped coming up.[17] Several brethren gather grease for their Wagons while we Water the Teams. Then took a sudden turn up a narrow gulley full of luxuriant Sage, then descend the hill, at the bottom took a very sudden bend to the left & in about 100 yards another short turn over a creek (dry now) to the right up another valley. Pretty good grass, but little water. Continue to the top of the Valley then pass over the dividing ridge.[18] Presidents Young & Richards cleared the lower pitch of Stones

---

[16] This camp on Yellow Creek was close to the formation called the Needles near today's Utah-Wyoming border.

[17] This was the camp of 10-11 July on Sulphur Creek.

[18] The company crossed Aspen Ridge and left the Great Basin.

& T. B. the Upper ascent. Very steep, also steep descent on East side. At the foot tolerable grass. Pass over another small hill, by a good spring & camp at 3:40. A slight shower passed over Camp. At Sundown all the brethren were called together & after a few words addressed by President Young on the subject of organization.

A. P. Rockwood motions "that we organize in the same way, as we came up." J. Scofield Seconded. Carried.

B. Young (——) "that Col. Markham be Captain of the 100." —— H. C. Kimball seconded. do.

H. C. Kimball (——) "that Barnabas L. Adams be Captain of 50." B. Young (seconded.) do. (do.) do.

B. Young (——) "that Joseph Matthews be Captain of 50."

H.C. Kimball (do.) do. do. do (motioned) that Brigham Young be Captain of 10. 7 of the Twelve Rockwood, Scofield & Goddard be the 10, with those with them. do.

B. Young motioned "that John Brown be Captain of 10." A. Lyman seconded – Carried.

H.C. Kimball —— "Howard Egan be Captain of 10.

S. Markham	– do.	– do.
George Clarke	– do.	– do.
George Wilson	– do.	– do.
Erastus Snow	– do.	– do.
Thomas Tanner	– do.	– do.
Charles A. Harper	– do.	– do.

H. C. Kimball motioned "that we travel in order." A. P. Rockwood seconded. —— do.

Afterwards T. Bullock read the names of 7th, 8th, & 9th Emigrating Companies. Dark came on. Meeting was dismissed.

After Supper all the Council assembled in the Doctor's Wagon. Some Newspapers read, also letters from Colonel Kane, Captain Jefferson Hunt, Levi Hancock, J. M. Grant, I. Morley, W. Major, Wm. S. Muir, Mary Shepherdson.[19]

After considerable conversation on the different copies Council adjourned. (Memorandum: from this Spot, on going West, keep up a

---

[19] Kane was Thomas Kane; Hunt, Hancock, and Muir were Mormon Battalion members; Grant was Jedediah Grant; Major was artist William Warner Major; and Morley was Isaac Morley.

gradual rise on the right hand & descent much better on the West side than the present.)

Tuesday 31 August 1847–Cold night, succeeded by a Pleasant day. At 6:30 Camp again start, in an organized state. Down the Valley several miles, then turn to the right & ascend a long hill towards the South, descend on the East. Continue along a valley & ascend another long hill, then descend to "Muddy Fork" which is dry.[20] Cross over it, keep to the right & ascend a steep hill. Continue some time on the top of the divide [and] took a straight course towards the center of two Butes.[21] Descend to a Spring where Camp halts at 1:10 to refresh the horses & again started at 2:20 in a direction of East by North. Passed over a low hill & descended thro' the Sage, having Cedars on the left, down to Bridger's Fort where we halted for a Short time. Saw some Indians gambling, a woman (Squaw) was scraping the hair of[f] a Deer Skin, another Squaw was Smoking Skins. The Council go to trade with the people of the Fort. They were lower in price than when we came before. Again started on our journey. We crossed 4 Streams with only ⅓rd Water than before & the remainder of the creeks are dry. The grass is also getting very scanty & dry. Camp halts about 6 P.M. in a Circle.

After supper W. Woodruff & G. A. Smith in Doctor's Wagon reading News.

September Wednesday 1st.–Cool pleasant morning. A great many horses & mules Missing, delays the Camp for starting. Receive a Mail of 48 Letters from Fort Bridger to go to the States. When delivered to the Postmaster, remember & get a receipt. An ox belonging to U.S. being found, it was killed & distributed among the Soldiers. Mr. Bridger visits Camp. Latitude of Bridger's Fort 41°.19'.13" above the Sea 6665 feet. The horses found & Camp starts at 7:45 towards East, in strait line, some rough road, then beautiful road several miles, having hills on our right & on the North side of the River. About noon arrived at a Stream 2 rods wide, 1 foot deep, where we water our horses.[22] Crossed it [and] continued on the South side of the River. Went up a hill [and] saw 5 Antelopes. In about 2 miles crossed Blacks Fork [which is] about 18 inch deep. Ascend the hill and halt at 1:35 to feed. A NW breeze. Some

---

[20] This was today's Muddy Creek, where the pioneer company had camped on 9 July.
[21] The divide was Bigelow Bench, while the "two Butes" were Bridger and Sugarloaf buttes.
[22] This was Blacks Fork.

parts of the road full of Bo[u]lder Stones, the rest good travelling. At 3:07 Camp again starts, cross Black's Fork again. In 2 miles come to small creek which was dried up, or only small pools of Stagnant Water, then a gradual ascent to the top of the hill, having a beautiful amphitheatre of rocks on our left shaped in turrets, pinnacles & towers & an imitation of St. Paul's Cathedral.[23] Then branched out another beautiful amphitheatre. Continued our route over a beautiful road. Descended the hill, passing other "fancy work" on left. Crossed Black's Fork, very shallow; watered our horses, ascended hill on East side & descended to Ham's Fork where we camped for the night at 6:40.[24] Good roads & a pleasant day, NW breeze. 13 miles [with] no water or grass. Several hornet's nests discovered. [They] sting 2 or 3 horses bad.

[THE RETURNING PIONEERS][25]

	Wagons	Horses	Mules		Wagons	Horses	Mules
1st. Ten				2nd. Ten			
Brigham Young				John Brown			
John Y. Green	1	4	1	Barna S. Adams			
Trueman O. Angel				Thomas Karren	1	3	–
A.P. Rockwood				Samuel Gould			
Joseph S. Scofield	1	–	2	John Gould			
Stephen H. Goddard				Jabez T. Nowlin			
H. C. Kimball	1	–	4	James W. Stewart	1	2	2
Hosea Cushing				Robt. T. Thomas			
Orson Pratt	1	–	2	M. B. Thorpe	1	2	1
Joseph Egbert				Joel J. Terrill			
Willard Richards				10	3	7	3
Thomas Bullock	1	1	4				
Harvey Pierce							
Benjamin Richmond				3rd. Ten			
				Thomas Tanner			
Wilford Woodruff	1	2	1	Addison Everett	1	2	–
Dexter Stillman				Melen Atwood			
George A. Smith	1	2	2	Sidney A. Hanks	1	–	2
Amasa Lyman				John G. Luce			
Albert Carrington	1	4	–	John Hollman			
A.P. Chesley				G. R. Grant	1	5	1
Ezra T. Benson				D. T. Laughlin			
Matthew Ivory	1	4	–	W. Dykes			
David Powell				D. Grant	1		
23	9	17	16	10	4	7	4

[23] This was Church Butte.

[24] The party camped near Granger, Wyoming, after making thirty-one miles from Fort Bridger, the longest day's travel of the returning pioneers.

[25] This lists members of the returning pioneers on 1 September 1847. Many of these men, including Porter Rockwell, returned to the Salt Lake Valley with the second division.

	Wagons	Horses	Mules		Wagons	Horses	Mules
4th Ten				7th Ten			
G. S. Clarke				Orson K. Whitney	1	2	1
Hayward Thomas	1	4	—	Horace K. Whitney			
Thomas Woolsey				Stephen Markham			
Samuel Fox				George Mills	1	3	1
Charles Shumway	1	1	3	Conrad Klineman			
Andrew Shumway				William Terrill			
William Carter				Monroe French			
Burr Frost	1	3	—	Ozra Eastman	1	2	1
Lucus Hoagland				Levi N. Kendall			
Franklin Dewey				Isaac N. Wreston			
10	3	8	3	10	3	7	—
5th. Ten				8th Ten			
Erastus Snow				Nathaniel Fairbanks	1	—	1
George Brown	1	3	1	Perry Fitzgerald	1	2	1
Wm. Mcintyre				O. P. Rockwell		11	2
John P. Wrieton				Sol. Chamberlin	1	1	2
Charles Barnum	1	2	1	William Gifford			
Stephen Kelsy				Peter I. Meshich	1	—	2
William Wordsworth	1	—	4	William Roe			
Datus Ensign				Caritad C. Roe			
John Dixon	1	2	2	James Davis	—	1	1
Simeon Howd				James Cawkins			
10	4	7	7	10	4	5	8
6th Ten				9th Ten			
Howard Egan				George Wilson			
Wm. A. King	1	5	1	Arza E. Hinckley			
Carlos Murray G				John Brimhall			
Andrew Gibbons				Wm. W. Rust			
George Billings				Jesse W. Johnston			
Ralph Douglas	1	—	4	Rodney Badger			
Ed. Holden				James Camp	1	1	2
Thurston Lawson				William A. Park			
James Case				Joseph Matthews			
Abel M. Sarjent	1	—	2	Green Flake			
James C. Earl				Benjamin Stewart	1	—	2
Judson Person				John Crow			
12	3	7	4	12	3	6	4

	Men	Wagons	Horses	Mules
1st. Ten	23	9	17	16
2nd. Ten	10	3	7	3
3rd. Ten	10	4	7	4
4th. Ten	10	3	8	3
5th. Ten	10	4	7	7
6th. Ten	12	3	7	4
7th. Ten	10	3	7	—
8th. Ten	10	4	5	8
9th. Ten	12	3	0	4
	107	36	71	49

Thursday 2 September 1847—The brethren gather many beautiful black Currants on the banks of Hams Fork. Pleasant morning. Camp starts at 8:15 [and] crosses the River; Presidents Young, Kimball, Pratt, Woodruff, Benson, Smith, Lyman & others on horses, ahead. Took an Easterly course over a hard level road for several miles, then bent towards NE & ascended a steep long hill. The horsemen rested some time & then continued their route leaving a high bluff of green colored stone or clay. Then descended to a table land which we travel over barren sage country, no grass. Then descended to the bottom land, watered our horses in Green River, continued our route up by Green River & camped in a bend of the river near our old ground.[26]

At 4:36 [stopped at] a good camping place [and] found many fine Black Currants. In evening strong cold wind & slight shower, lightning in NE.

Doctor dictating & T. B writing Doctor's family Epistle two hours after [the] rest of Camp were in bed.

Friday 3 September 1847—Some Geese fly over Camp towards South at day break. Cold cloudy morning. Gathered currants while on Doctor's Poney, off a Currant Bush 14 feet long, pulled up by Captain Adams. Camp starts at 6:37. Pass our old Camp ground,[27] ascend to the table land, then turn to the left in a Bend of the river. Ford at the new or lower ford, about 18 inches deep, then ascend a hill, take a bend to the left, over a level barren land, gravelly. Join the old road at the Bluff & continue to the right of the hills until we came to our Camp on Big Sandy, which is very shallow. Grass pretty near all eat up. (Memorandum: In Spring journey keep to the left on the hill, down by the Sandy & will save a considerable distance.) Camp halts at 10:27 & stays until 1:25 when it again starts in NE direction leaving the River, over three hills & Vales, the rest a level plain. Some parts of the road rough loose rocks, the rest very good road. Sun set & in a few minutes after came to a halt, after crossing "Big Sandy," on the South of Captain Spencer's Company.[28] Visiting the brethren, all rejoicing together. In evening 4 tents were put up & the brethren filled them full. (See T.B.'s minutes on file.) Continued talking until about 11 when they separated.

---

[26] This was the camp where the pioneer company spent 3 to 5 July 1847.
[27] This was the mosquito-plagued camp at the ferry on Green River.
[28] Daniel Spencer was leading the first party in the second division.

Saturday 4 September 1847–Sent a Messenger ahead to P. P. Pratt's Company requesting him to stay at his encampment until we should come to him. Afterwards O. Pratt started ahead for same purpose. Continued visiting with the brethren, all feeling well. T. B. obtained from Staines his minutes & reports. Found minutes of a meeting of 25th June last; which fully corroborates the President's views of last night. Afterwards Presidents Young, Richards, Pratt & Benson met in Doctor's Wagon while I read them, which brought forth much conversation on the subject. About 8 A.M. Daniel Spencer's Company started & before they all started our Return Camp started East. A pretty sight to see the Wagons rolling out of the Earth, as it were (not being able to see the Camp Ground) & going each way. Cool morning. Continued up by Big Sandy about 2 miles, then a strait course towards the Bluff. East of "Little Sandy," saw P. P. Pratt's Company at or near our old camp ground. Turned off road & halt at [blank]. Found Pratt, Captain Rufus Beach, Clerk, John Smith Patriarch & a number of old friends visiting them. I took an account of Men, Souls, Wagons, Horses, Mules, Oxen, Cows, Pigs, Sheep, & Chickens. Then Presidents Young, Kimball, Richards, Pratt, Woodruff, Smith, Lyman, Benson, and P. P. Pratt & John Smith Patriarch, with T. Bullock, Scribe, met on the banks of the River, when President Young reproved P.P.P. very strongly for disorganizing all the Winter's Work of the Quorum of the Twelve.[29] He at first manifested a contra Spirit, but afterwards repented. The Spirit & power of God was poured out. Much instruction was given and it proved a most glorious meeting to all (see TB's minutes on file). O. Pratt & T. B. supped with P.P.P. & family. Then went to a public meeting by the fire of a great Patch of Willows. O. Pratt, W. Richards, & others addressed the people (T.B.'s minutes filed), then called to President Young's Wagon to read over the list of all the Men in the Camps to Presidents Young & Kimball, to enable them to select out High Council for the Great Salt Lake City.[30]

Sunday 5 September 1847–The brethren engaged in visiting with P. P. Pratt's Company mutually gratified at the opportunity & such good feelings existed that we did not separate until 9. Pioneer Camp start at

---

[29] Wilford Woodruff reported that Pratt had "done wrong by disorganizing the two divisions & Companies" that the Twelve had spent the previous "whole winter in organizing." Pratt had "mixed the companies all up." See Staker, ed., *Waiting for World's End*, 133.

[30] The stake high council, a Mormon religious body, governed Great Salt Lake City until the return of Brigham Young in the fall of 1848.

9:45 & took a new route direct to the East end of the Bluff. Cross the little Sandy. (Memorandum: When you cross the last ravine, in going West, bear to the left towards a Cluster of Trees & cross the creek at last night's camp ground & will save a considerable distance.) Continued in a NE direction till we came to the Oregon Road, then turned East.[31] Crossed "Dry Sandy" [and] passed over the hill & came in view of three Camps on the small creek.[32] Crossed the small creek & formed in line close to the West Camp. Found they were A. O. Smoot's, G. B. Wallace, & C. C. Rich's Companies. All in good health & spirits & rejoicing. (T.B. supt with G. B. Wallace.) Meeting in Centre Camp addressed by G. A. Smith, W. Woodruff, P. Pratt, & B. Young, (see minutes on file). President Young wanted the horses secured & a good guard kept up all night on account of the Indians. Voted that all the Camps lay here tomorrow, officers to meet at 8 & Companies at 11. Hazy day. Wind from South yet Pleasant.

Monday 6 September 1847—Cold Wind from West. Cloudy morn. The Council & officers of the Camps met at the South of the Camps. Conversed about the City, its plan & future operations, [and] about the wrong organization at "the horn," General Kearney & the Guide boards, the breaking down of the mill dam at Winter Quarters,[33] but had to adjourn on account of wind & dust. Put up a tent inside the Circle. All the brethren seem satisfied with the Valley & the labors of the Pioneers & glad to meet us. At 11 the brethren assembled at the Center Camp & were addressed by Erastus Snow & others. while the Council of the Twelve, Captain C. C. Rich, A. O. Smoot, G. B. Wallace & several others met in Council in the Tent & nominated the President, High Council & Marshall of "Great Salt Lake City" (minutes on file). After adjournment T. B. copying W. Richards' family Epistle & Epistle to the Saints in Great Salt Lake City. In evening Council & A. O. Smoot met on banks of creek, when Smoot made a statement about John Taylor, John Benbow & Agnes his Wife, and requested an Appeal from the Hi Council at Winter Quarters to the Quorum of the Twelve; several votes were taken on the subject (T. B. minutes on file). It was severely cold &

---

[31] At the Parting of the Ways, Bullock again identified the Sublette Cutoff as the "Oregon Road."

[32] This was North Pacific Creek, which the trail crossed between the Dry Sandy and the False Parting of the Ways.

[33] This again refers to the flour mill at Winter Quarters that was "plagued with problems." See Bennett, *The Mormons at the Missouri*, 114-15.

threatened Stormy Weather. At night the Council met in the Doctor's Wagon & again heard read the Epistle to the Saints in the Great Salt Lake City. Afterwards Doctor dictated & T. B. wrote an addition to the same. TB continued copying till after midnight during which time Snow, Hail & Sleet fell accompanied with a Cold boisterous wind.

TB also numbered the Men & families. Also Wagons, Horses, Mules, Oxen, Sheep, Pigs, & Chickens.

Tuesday 7 September 1847–Cold morning. At day break continued Copying the Epistle to the Saints in the Great Salt Lake City. Received many letters to carry to the States. Despatched two Messengers to get the next camps to stay on the Sweetwater till we came to them. The Twelve & Pioneers visiting with the brethren of the Three Camps, some of whom gave us some Buttermilk which is a rarity in this cold region & when we see all the hills tipt with Snow & feel the chilling blasts of Winter, causes me to feel anxious for the safe & speedy journey of the Saints to their respective homes. After witnessing the departure of many, we started at 9:35 & directly afterwards we had a Snow Storm which continued until 4 P.M. We passed over the Dividing ridge[34] & Camped on the Sweetwater at 1:20 between Horn & Hunter's two fifties. Received a bag of Newspapers from John Taylor which T. B. read to the Twelve under Taylor's tent.

In the evening the two Companies prepared a supper in a Willow Grove for the Pioneers which was furnished with Roast & boiled Beef, Veal (they had killed the fatted Calf to make merry), Pies, Cakes, Biscuits, Butter, Peaches, with coffee, Tea, Sugar, Cream & a variety of the good things of life.[35] About 60 sat down to the Table first time, the remainder at the second spread. Also the 3 Frenchmen who have travelled with us from Fort Bridger & who are going to the States in our Company.[36]

Afterwards the brethren & sisters tript "the light fantastic toe" in the

---

[34] Bullock again quietly noted crossing South Pass.

[35] Some 130 guests joined this "banquet of the desert," prepared as a surprise by the John Taylor and Joseph Horne companies. "The Pioneers knew nothing of what had taken place until they were led by Elder Taylor through a natural opening in the bushes fringing the enclosure, and the grand feast burst upon their astonished vision." See Roberts, *Comprehensive History*, 3:297.

[36] Bullock later mentioned "Joseph the Frenchman," but his two companions remain nameless, a typical practice in overland journals. Skilled frontiersmen, these men provided expert help to the Mormons. On 7 October, one of them apparently joined a California-bound party that included Joseph R. Walker.

dance, making a large fire in the Willow Patches; which they kept up until about 10 or 11 o'clock.

Nine of the Twelve met in Vinson Shirtleff's tent, held a Council until next morning. The Epistle was read. Votes were taken to seal Mary Brochway to Vinson Shirtleff [and] release widow Thompson[37] from her engagement with J. Taylor. Empower President J. Smith to seal her to a good man holding the Priesthood; to release Agnes Benbow from John Benbow; & seal her to any good man. [The Twelve] related their feelings about the disorganization at the Horn & several other matters (see TB's Minutes). A severe frost, freezing tents & Wagon covers.

[Journal pages 99–101 blank].[38]

Saturday 11 September 1847–Pleasant morn, some hazy. Camp starts at 8:30 [and] in a short distance crossed the Sweetwater to the South side & soon again to the North, thus missing the Sand Hill.[39] Ascended a long hill & then descended about 3 miles, again crossing the Sweetwater.[40] Watered teams, made a short halt. Saw an ox, very lame. Passed 2 dead carcasses, then ascended the high bluff & continued about 10 miles nearly due East thro' a barren Sage country, road tolerably hard, some parts Sandy. Made a short halt at the Ice Spring, but a horse getting mired immediately, Camp continued its journey to the Sweetwater which we again crossed[41] [and] continued down its banks near a mile & then halted on its banks [with the] Wagons forming 2 sides of [a] Stockade, the River the other side, at about 5 o'clock. [At] ½ hour after Sunset saw New Moon of yesterday. West Wind, hazy day. T. B. bathed in the River. (Memorandum: going West, it is said a much better road might be made from the "Ice Spring" by continuing down the Valley on the left clear to the River.)

~~Saturday~~ Sunday 12 September 1847–In the night, Camp was

---

[37] Possibly R. Thompson, 35, of Joseph Mount's Ten in A. O. Smoot's Hundred, who was accompanied by an unnamed nine-year-old child.

[38] Bullock apparently reserved these three blank pages for the 9 and 10 September entries, but never used them. On 9 September, the returning pioneers met the Jedediah Grant company, the last of the 1847 Mormon parties. During the night, Indians ran off some fifty head of horses, including thirty belonging to the pioneers. Scouts retrieved five horses, but as B. H. Roberts noted, "the loss materially weakened both encampments."

[39] The returning pioneers used the eighth and seventh crossings of the Sweetwater, which they had avoided on the trip west by climbing the "Sand Hill" on 25 June.

[40] This was the Sixth Crossing of the Sweetwater.

[41] This was the Fifth Crossing of the Sweetwater. Lower water levels may have persuaded the Mormons to use the crossings they avoided on the trip west.

alarmed by firing of a Gun by some person or Indian & one of our Guard ([William] Dykes) fired his off, without any orders; [Barnabas] Adams, Captain of [the] Guard, wheeled out of the Corral to the North side & distinctly heard the tramping of several horses & some voices, but could not understand what they said. They appeared to be going West. One horse [was] missing in the morning. Frost in night, made an Ice on the Water. Beautiful morning, tho' hazy. Camp starts at 8:30 taking a chute between two ridges of bold rocks, then bearing to the left under some bold rocks, nearly strait for the River. Saw many Ducks on it. We crossed the Stream twice [and] came between the ridges of rocks & made a halt at 11:22. By taking this route we evaded the heaviest Sand road on the South of the River & travelled over a good hard road, also a nigher cut.[42] At 12:52 Camp again starts, keeping [to] the South Side of the River. In some places very Sandy. Visited a rock perforated by an innumerable host of small yellow Wasps on our left hand [and] then crossed "Bitter Cotton Wood Creek" perfectly dry; came in view of a herd of 10 Buffalo. At 3:30 a number of brethren go on foot in pursuit. W. Woodruff on horseback goes to head them from turning the point. They finally managed to drive them up a ravine & killed three bulls, allowing the remainder to escape. When we halted on the banks of the river at 4:48, Presidents Young & Benson went to their assistance & shortly afterwards two wagons were sent to fetch in the Meat. John Brown shot a Mountain Sheep on the rocks, brought it home & divided among the brethren. Its head is a perfect Sheep (or Ibex of Scripture), body covered with hair like an Antelope. On close examining can discover Wool. It was a young one & weighed about 100 pounds. Warm hazy day. 9 Indians seen by the brethren. Slight breeze from South. Saw very many Antelopes.

Monday 13 September 1847–Cool cloudy morning, East breeze. Distributed the Buffalo meat then Camp starts at 8:45. Cross a dry creek, also "Sage Creek," dry. Went over a high hill, descended past a Lake[43] which was also dry & made our noon halt on the banks of the River about ½ past 11 where we found tolerable picking for our cattle. At 1:15 again started, the wind blowing very Strong from the SW. [We]

---

[42] The company used the route through Three Crossing Canyon, which they avoided on the trip west by taking the Deep Sand route.
[43] This was Soda Lake, nine miles west of Devil's Gate.

passed along down the valley going over 2 Dry creeks [and] thro' a small creek with good grass on its banks, then a pretty long level prairie covered with good feed. Crossed over 2 creeks having [a] pretty well of Water in them, then went thro' the Mountains close by "the Devils Gate," where we turned off the road to the left [and] descended to the Banks of the Sweetwater which we crossed being very Shallow & formed a Semi circle on the North Bank in the midst of some Excellent grass at 5:45 & where our Teams can fill themselves.[44] The Wind continued very strong & heavy Clouds in the South. We passed 9 dead carcases of oxen this day. Part of the travelling was Sandy, the remainder a good hard road.

Tuesday 14 September 1847–Being a good place for feed, President Young determined that the horses should stay & eat as long as they would. T. B., J. Egbert & several others walked (about 10 miles) ahead to fill our bags with Saleratus at the Lake. The Lake had dried up & left a solid Ice of Saleratus from ½ to 3 inches thick which we cut out with hatchets, axes & knives. I gathered about 50 pounds & was satisfied. Many Carts might have been filled with it, if we had needed. In a short time afterwards 12 Wagons drove up for a portion & then proceeded on our way. (We had passed Independence Rock & went on it, a very swift wind blowing at the time & examined two other Lakes of Saleratus.)[45] The road is very Sandy, the Plains covered with Saline Deposit & Sage wood, but very little grass indeed. After travelling 18½ miles come to a halt on the banks of a small creek at 3 o'clock.[46] Not much grass. The clouds have been gathering all day & threaten a Storm. At 7 minutes to 4 the first rain of a thunder Shower commenced, which passed from West to East chiefly on the Sweetwater Mountains, the lightnings flashed & the rain descended fast. In about an hour after Presidents Young, Kimball & the remainder of the teams came up. It was showery thro' the night. Plenty of Tall Sage here.

Several Buffalo seen in different parts of the Valley.

About 3 miles West of Independence Rock is a Lake of Borax.[47]

---

[44] The Saints camped on the site of the present Dumbbell Ranch.

[45] For the location of some of these deposits of baking soda, see Franzwa, *Maps of the Oregon Trail*, Maps 55 and 56.

[46] The Mormons camped on Horse Creek.

[47] This is now called Soda Lakes, about three miles north of Devil's Gate.

THE BEST AND NIGHEST ROAD

Wednesday 15 September 1847—Several showers in the night, at break of day hitched up the Teams & started on our route in search of better feed & continued until 7 when Camp halted in the road & the horses were taken to a Stream about ¼ mile to the right.[48] Staid until 9:45 when Camp again started on its route, most of the brethren walking a head. The roads were hard but ascending. [We] passed over the Slough, then ascended to the Summit of the hill where we took a last view of the Sweetwater Mountains for this Season.[49] Sky being clear [we] had a good view of them. To our front we were gladdened by a long view of the Platte Valley & hills dotted with Cedars. Many Buffalo in small Groups seen scattered over the Plains. The grass is nearly all eat away by Buffalo and Emigrating Camps, which gives our teams but a poor chance. Descended the hill, passed "Willow Springs" [and] after crossing 3 small ravines came to a halt in the road & turned the horses & mules out to the banks of the "Small Creek" to pick what feed they could. At ¼ past 4 Camp again started over a good hard road, passed the "Poison Springs" where we discovered the tracks of our horses & Mules which had been stolen at the Pass [and] evidently taken to Fort John. Ascended the hill, kept to the right of "the Wall,"[50] then descended several miles in NE direction & halted on the banks of "the Lake" about ½ past 8 having seen both the Sun and Moon set behind the hills.[51] West wind, pleasant day.

Thursday 16 September 1847—West Wind, Cold, Clear Sky. Found best picking since we left Independence Rock at this place; at 8:35 the Camp again resumes its journey [and] ascends a long hill on the right. Presidents Young, Kimball & others walking ahead. On the top, President Kimball, Rockwood & Bullock continued their walk over a level plain [and] saw many Buffalo scattered about. Then ascended another hill & descended to the Upper Ferry on the Platte, conversing on Plurality, the rationality of man, & the resurrection.[52] It was a delightful walk to me. At 10 minutes to 2 the Camp came up, crossed the North Fork & encamped on the South side. We found some very good feed &

---

[48] This was Fish Creek.
[49] Bullock had climbed Prospect Hill.
[50] This was the Avenue of Rocks, also known as the Devil's Backbone.
[51] The returning pioneers used the Emigrant Gap route instead of the River route they took on the trip west.
[52] The company arrived at present Casper, Wyoming, site of the Mormon Ferry on the North Platte in June 1847.

determined the cattle should have a rest & recruit themselves. (T. B. bathed in the River, put on Clean Clothes sent by his Wife, & blessed her for her kindness. Doctor shaved & cleaned up; then we drank Soda Water Draughts, partook of Ginger, Dried Prunes, Peaches, Dried fruit, & finished with a lump of Sugar, sent as presents to the Doctor by his family. Our Souls rejoiced & were exceeding glad for our treat in the Wilderness.) A Pleasant day. The Wolves kept up a great howling in the night.

Friday 17 September 1847–A lovely warm morning, Clear Sky, not a breath of Wind stirring. Several brethren turn out to hunt Buffalo, while the Camp lies by to refresh our teams. At 11:35 Camp starts & crosses a small creek. In about 3 miles cross 2 deep Ravines near the 120 mile board, then cross 2 other very small muddy creeks. Presidents Kimball & Woodruff walking. President Kimball continued his conversation on the subject of the resurrection which was truly edifying to me. When I was with President Woodruff each of us related our Experience, then come to a very deep Ravine & descended a gentle sloping hill to our old camping ground of the 12 June & came to a halt at 4:15.[53] A beautiful day, Clear Sky. Here the Grass is pretty well eaten up, the horses beginning to ramble after better feed. We were 42 days going from this Spot to Great Salt Lake City, including stoppages. We are 23 days coming from Great Salt Lake City to this place, including stoppages or *19 days* quicker on return journey.

This day passed the Grave of the man who was drowned at the Ferry last June. After dark, Doctor dictated a long letter to Reuben Miller, also the Fable of the Lamb & the Beasts (filed).[54]

A magpie crossed our path.

Saturday 18 September 1847–Pleasant morning, Clear Sky. The Horses being in pretty good feed, the Camp did not start until 9 o'clock when it pursued its course down the South side of the River which is very Shallow in many places. The Cotton Wood Trees are beginning to look yellow, giving the Fall appearance to the scenery. Crossed "Muddy Creek," very Shallow. In about 2 hours crossed "Crooked Muddy Creek" at a new crossing, better than the old one. Here we watered our Teams, then went on to the Grove on the River Banks, but the Grass was

---

[53] This was the pioneer camp of 11 June 1847 at the big bend of the North Platte.

[54] For the letter to Miller, see the Journal History for this date.

all gone. Then took a sudden bend to the South, passing several dangerous places, which requires much caution in passing. Afterwards came to a Deep Ravine where we had to lock the Wheels, steep banks on both sides. Then went over a high hill & descended to "Deer Creek," which we crossed, not more than one foot deep & encamped on the East side in a bend of the River [at] 3:50, where we found some excellent green grass, which our horses & mules ate with avidity. Pleasant Warm day, Clear Blue Sky. Many young Frogs in the Streams [and] Many Buffalo seen. A Frenchman kills 1 Bull. 3 Magpies seen.

A Spring was discovered near this place by one of the brethren. I went to examine it. It lies on the banks of the Platte & in a high stage of Water is *non est inventus*.[55]

Presidents Young, Kimball, Richards, & Benson & Bullock went to search for the Coal bed & in about 1 mile up Deer Creek President Kimball gave a Signal for silence for he discovered a Grizzly Bear & two cubs. Y.K.B.&B. crept up near them. Benson's Gun would not go off, tried 3 times, Young fired his pistol 3 times. He knocked one of the cubs over, but did nor kill it. K. fired once. The way the Old Bear danced was amusing. At one time she ran towards the Bushes where we were & challenged fight when it was prudent for us to get on a rock out of danger. At which time they gave us the slip, round a rock, into the woods. T. B. ran to the Camp for the Dogs & returned piloting men & Dogs to the Thicket, but it was getting dark & the President thought it wisdom not to pursue any further, but adjourn until tomorrow morning at daylight.[56]

Sunday 19 September 1847–Several of the brethren go to kill a Buffalo cow if one could be found, while Presidents Young, Pratt, Woodruff Kimball, Benson, Lyman & Smith, T. B. & several others go hunt the Grizzly Bears. They beat all the Woods on each side of "Deer Creek" but without success. Hearing the report of several Fire Arms higher up the River, we concluded that Sir Grizzly was found when Young, Kimball, Benson, Bullock & 2 others started up in that direction, but were disappointed. On arriving at the spot we found some of the brethren

---

[55] Not discovered/found.

[56] By most accounts, *Ursus horribilis* won this encounter. There is no more dangerous animal in the American West than a mother grizzly bear. As this bear defended her cubs, the Mormon hunters beat a hasty retreat up the rocky side of Deer Creek near present Glenrock, Wyoming. The site is now called Mormon Canyon.

had been shooting at Geese—truly they were a glorious set of Grizly Bear Hunters, so to waste their Powder & Ball & with the knowledge of their near proximity. So we gave up the chase & returned to Camp. Captain Adams reports having killed 1 Buffalo cow (perhaps 2) & 2 Deer. Despatched 3 Wagons to fetch the Meat while the Camp started at 3 minutes to 2 down the Valley, cross the dry bed of a creek, ascend & pass over two hills & then descend to the "Fourche Boisee." Cross over about 1 rod wide, 6 inches deep & Encamp on the SE side at 5:42. Found some young green grass. Dr. Richards reports about 1 mile up the River is Splendid grass. Plenty of Box Elder on the Banks of this Stream [which] begins to put on its autumnal appearance, Yellow leaves & Empty boughs. A beautiful day. Blue Sky, West breeze (when any). Many Grasshoppers about, also young Frogs. The 3 Wagons did not return until the morning guard was on duty. In hunting for the Bears we found a fine bed of beautiful coal, running partly under the River. It is as pretty a looking Coal as I ever saw.

T. B. [dreamed he was] with his family. Also an increase in his family. Felt very well.

Monday 20 September 1847–A lovely morning. Breeze from the [blank] causes a Gentle Shower of the Yellow Leaves. Distributed the remains of the Buffalo cow & 2 Deer among the brethren. The Frogs are singing. Camp starts at 9:30 taking a bend to the South, going up & down hill, crossing 2 very small creeks & several small Gulleys.[57] The Trees [are] looking very like Autumn.

Tuesday 21 September 1847–Dull Cloudy morning, looks the appearance of rain. H. C. Kimball & S. H. Goddard go to hunt for Judson Persons & succeeded in finding him. He had slept in a hole all night & his stupidity caused a deal of anxiety & trouble to the Camp. At the time orders were given to start at ½ past 8, the men were just going to fetch their horses & mules, when the firing of several guns was heard & immediately the cry of "look to your horses," "the Indians are upon us," "to arms," &c &c, when several of our horses rushed up the hill followed by two or three Indians, followed by another lot of horses & Indians & a 3rd & 4th lot taking different directions up the hills. The brethren took to arms, others ran up the hill to head some of them. I was in one

---

[57] Bullock seems to refer to Little Box Elder and West Cottonwood creeks, but he failed to mention the larger LaPrele and Wagonhound creeks that the Saints crossed on the way to their camp on LaBonte Creek.

Company that succeeded in heading & turning one company of horses & brought them safely into Camp. This enabled a few of the brethren to mount their horses & go in pursuit, while at the same time Indians after Indians came pouring into sight & sweeping thro' the valley like a torrent. When after a scene of great confusion & excitement, the Indians discovered that the horses belonged to a camp of White men & shouted most discordantly to our ears. After a while one of their Chiefs came down to us, on foot & thro' the Frenchman informed us they thought the horses belonged to a War party of Snakes or Crows, but as they belonged to White people, they would bring them back again to us. We shortly afterwards saw "Wash te cha" & several of the Indians who visited us on the 25th of May last & we found our old acquaintances of the Dacotah tribe. They again appeared friendly, telling us thro' the Frenchman that we should have all our horses again & several of the Indians were sent after them. Several of their principal men came in front & sat down to smoke the pipe of peace, while 200 sat & or stood behind. Wash te cha from the hill, shouted to the Indians & then disappeared over the hill. All who remained behind behaved civilly, many sat down in rows. Presidents Young & Richards were smoking the Pipe of Peace with their principal men when the Galloping of horses was heard. The Indians were alarmed, running in different directions, some ran up.[58]

Tuesday 21 September 1847–(continued.) hill, others jumped into the River, while Presidents Kimball & Benson, bareheaded, galloped up to us. They reported they were unsuccessful in getting any of the horses, that wherever they went Indians were on the tops of every hill & estimated their number between 3 & 500. They were informed that the Chief had promised to return us our horses & had sent after them when they joined the Peace Circle & the Pipe was again passed round. In a short time after ~~Laime~~ Laime (Lamme) the old Chief came & made a talk, shaking hands with many of the brethren. He then requested our Chief to go up to his Village & he promised to restore us our horses. President Young being too unwell, President Kimball & Woodruff with Stephen Markham & Joseph Matthews, also Joseph (the Frenchman)

---

[58] Here ended the text of Bullock's Journal No. 2 from 1847. He continued the account of the returning pioneers in an unbound, handsewn set of sixty-two pages. See Appendix C for tables and lists from the end of Journal No. 2 and from the beginning of the Returning Pioneer Journal.

went up taking several Bushels of Salt with them as presents to the Indians. The old Chief and many others went with them while the remainder of the Indians had "a smoke" [and] visited round our camp & went away, a few at a time, apparently friendly. The camp being entirely cleared from Indians about ½ past 12, President Young thought it wisdom to remove the Camp to a more open spot where we could have a better chance for defence. Accordingly at 1 P.M. Teams were made up & removed the First Division of the Camp down the River about half a mile & then sent up Teams to bring down the remainder of the Camp. This closed up an entire circle of about Six rods in Diameter. After all was enclosed, Presidents Young, Richards, Pratt, Smith, Lyman & Benson met in the Doctor's Wagon when T. B. read Honorable Thomas Corwin's Speech in the Senate of the U.S. on the cause of the Mexican War (on file). While the reading was going on, brother Clark came into camp bringing 5 of the Stolen mules. In a short time after brother Matthews brings in a horse & a message from H. C. Kimball for men to go out who can Identify the missing animals. Accordingly a company of 6 men go out for that purpose, the President instructing them to be back before dark. A little before Sundown B. B. Richmond returns, leading in two mules, one of the Doctor's & one of H. C. Kimball's, & at dark H. C. Kimball returns with another mule & the remainder of the brethren.[59] We have still lost 2 horses, one belonging to John Brown, the other to A. P. Chessley. The afternoon was very cloudy. Strong wind from NW denoting a Storm. At dusk it commenced raining and continued all evening.

Wednesday 22 September 1847—Gentle rain all night. At day break all the horses & mules were driven up to the same place where the Indians drove them away yesterday morning. At the same time a Strong guard went up to protect them. I went up as one of the Guard. In about ½ hour, orders came to bring them down and harness up. At 8:07 camp started, retracing our steps to the road. Then went up the bed of a dry creek & commenced ascending the range of hills. When we had travelled about 4 miles, the rain changed to a Sleety Snow Storm which continued for near two hours when it cleared up. We kept ascending &

---

[59] Kimball reported the Sioux camp consisted of 100 lodges and a horse herd of 1,000 animals, including some of the animals stolen on 9 September. The Sioux claimed they had captured these animals from a Crow raiding party. See Kimball, *Heber C. Kimball*, 174.

descending all morning. At 11:43 we made a halt on the 2nd creek until 12:56 when we again resumed our journey, again ascending and descending hills, and crossing 4 creeks which were all dry. Then went over a long hill & descended the Steep Bluff. The creek was running. Continued to our left along the bottom, descending to and crossing over "Horse Shoe Creek" which was dry at the crossing place, but about ½ mile below it was about a rod wide & 6 inches deep. Continued on to "Heber's Spring" where we halted at 3:40. The Spring is nearly dry, full of large frogs and covered with scum.[60] The Grass has nearly all been eaten up by the Emigrating Companies & we find a difficulty in procuring feed for our horses & mules. The Sky is cloudy, air cool, West breeze.

The Caral not being quite closed, the brethren go to work. Cut down large Trees and fence up the vacancy of about 4 rods in a substantial manner.

After dark Presidents Young, Richards, Pratt, & Lyman met in Doctor's Wagon. T. B. read the letter to Reuben Miller. Also some newspaper tales. Sung the return song of the Pioneers.[61] All felt well.

Thursday 23 September 1847—Severe frost in the latter part of the night (Equinox 3 A.M.). At break of day hitched up the teams & started as the Sun rose. A beautiful Sky & cold morning. Took a strait line up a valley, ascending all the way until we had passed over a high bluff. Here we have a most beautiful view of the surrounding country for a very great distance. Laramie Peak on our right has Snow on it. We can also see a fog rising in the valley along the North Fork of the Platte, which has a very pretty appearance. The hills are all tipt with Fir over an undulating country making altogether a handsome Park of immense size. Then descended the hill on the South side passing thro' many Spruce Pines of a handsome size & appearance. At the Spring the Grass was all eat up, so we only stopt to get a little water. Pursued our journey, finding some good dry Buffalo grass. Halted for breakfast at 8:40 staying until 11:40, when the Camp again resumed its journey down the Valley. Near the bottom made a cut off to the left to the 30 mile post, finding signs of the Crow Indians being in this neighborhood. Continued up by the side of the creek until we crossed it, about 4 yards wide & 4 inches

---

[60] Such was the seasonal transformation of "the most beautiful Spring of Water yet seen" on the westbound trip.

[61] This song does not survive in any of the published collections of Mormon folk songs.

deep.[62] Watered the Teams, then took the sudden bend in the road (South) and coming in sight of good green grass made a halt at 2:05 to allow the animals to fill themselves. Beautiful clear Sky. West Wind.

At [blank] we again start down the valley [and] twice cross the dry bed of Bitter creek. At our old Camp ground the Spring was dry also.[63] After continuing down [the] valley some distance turned to the right up another valley, then ascended a high hill, passing "Porter's Rock" on our right hand.[64] The Sun had set & we now travelled by the light of a full moon. Continued over the long level (the cut off at the 20 mile board not being made). At the end of the Table land, waited until all the Wagons came up, then descended the steep stony pitch [with] locked wheels. Then turned to the left down to the "Warm Spring" [where we] watered the teams [and] filled our bottles. The Water is much warmer than when we were here in the Spring. Afterwards turned off to the Southern route. Went up about mile & camped in a bend at 9:45. Fine cool night, this has been a clear day, blue Sky & very pleasant.

Friday 24 September 1847–Pleasant morning, blue Sky. When the teams were hitched up & all ready to start, the brethren were called into the circle. The Captains of 10s called their men into rank. T. B. called the rank roll, when President Young enquired if every man was going to gad round the Fort on our arrival there without any regularity, or shall we go like respectable men? President Kimball "I motion that we all behave ourselves like Gentlemen & mind our own business." W. Richards seconded it. President Young said you have all seen all that is to be seen & I don't want 40, 100, or 5 men to get our horses that have been stolen. It will cost us something. It is not wisdom to take them by force. If they are Gentlemen at the Fort they will use their influence to get them for us & then enquired, Who is there that will obey your officers? & Who will revolt?

David Grant "I motion we all obey our officers." Saml. Gould seconded. President Young then took the vote by tens. All voted. He then enquired, "Officers if you are in favor of H. C. Kimball's motion, walk out & signify it by the uplifted hand." Done. I want you to do as you are

---

[62] The camp returned to Big Cottonwood Creek just east of the point where Interstate 25 crosses it today.

[63] This was the camp of 7 June on Horseshoe Creek.

[64] Located about five miles west of present Guernsey, Wyoming, this rock was named on the outbound journey for Orrin Porter Rockwell.

told. I want the Officers to keep better order after leaving the Fort. I don't want a man to take his Gun to the right or left without orders. If my Council will be adhered to, we can travel 1000 years without any accident. Not one accident has occurred since we left Winter Quarters by the persons following our Council. When we lost our horses it was the only night that I did not go & see after the Guard. That night we had the Mail to make up, the Epistle to finish, my family, & provisions & changing teams to look after and then every Officer & every man went to sleep & it was every man take care of his own horses. E. T. Benson tied his own, all were perfectly unconcerned about it. Did I ever manifest such a Spirit? We are now going to the States, there are men now before me when they get to the States will turn round & God dam B. Young, I'm free from you now. If there is a man who has been wronged, now tell me of it, that I may rectify it. If there is another man that murmurs about the Guard, he shall take 39 lashes well put on & you shall carry the marks on your backs & I'll do it when I get to W. Quarters & you may run & tell of it & I ask no favors. John Crow is one of them that dams the orders & Benjamin Stewart is another. You shall receive civility & good treatment while you are with us, but keep your Slack until you get away from us [and] we'll feed you & tote your things you poor Devils you. I tell you would be made slaves of yet, you won't be worthy to black the shoes of those who you now curse. Monroe French lost his horses. Dr. Richards let him have his riding poney & Sharpe being sick, French won't let him ride. Now the Wagon & every thing else don't belong to him. Stop your growling & whining. G. R. Grant sings out going past a Wagon, why dam you, if you don't take care of that horse, I'll take it out of the harness. (Grant denied, Atwood affirmed.) George, I know you did say so & I do know you took my Saddle without leave; the next morning I told Markham, take his horse & put it in the harness. If Grant refuses, shew him his way. This was to learn him a lesson not to take any thing again without asking for it. Away with your snarlish & petulent Spirits; why take a course to make yourselves obnoxious? Never do it! Ingratiate yourselves with your superiors: be mild & learn to be ruled before you rule. Practice that which you know. It's our business to administer Salvation to the children of men. Now begin to go in order. Captains set the Examples yourselves. I say may the Lord bless you all.

(½ past 9.) At 9:40 the Camp started, taking the Southern road.[65] Went over a gentle hill, then over a long level prairie. Descended another gentle hill & come to the SW Corner of Fort John (this is decidedly the best & nearest route & over a very good road). Passed Fort John, crossed [the] North Fork, then down the River about 2 miles & Camped near a Grove of Cotton Woods at [blank]. A delightful day. Saw many Prickly Pears [and] gather the Fruit.

In the evening S. Markham, A. P. Rockwood, J. Brown, G. Brown, B. L. Adams, S. Chamberlin, J. Matthews, A. P. Chessley, H. Egan, S. A. Hanks, J. Terrill & S. Gould were chosen to go after the horses & 38 others to follow in small Companies on their trail. All met round the Doctor's Wagon, when E. T. Benson was voted to be Captain of the 2nd Company. President Young wants the reinforcement ready in morning & the 2 Captains to have an understanding about it.

E. T. Benson expects the men to have confidence in their officers & leave grumbling behind. We want as many horses as they have taken away. If we go in the name of the Lord, we'll come back well horsed.[66]

B. Young. I feel to bless you in the name of the Lord. We are kicked & cuffed by our enemies. There are great & glorious things in store for the faithful & the Saints can see them by the Spirit. We have an eye on futurity after dissolution of our bodies, then is the time for man to enjoy; that's what we are Mormons for; all Creation is against us now, but all Israel will know who are their friends. They are now ignorant & darksome, [but] we shall approximate to the Station from which we have fallen: even the Elders of Israel can swallow up all the religion in the world & yet they have not peeped into the things of futurity. There never was a Company of men on the face of the Earth from Enoch[67] 'till now that have gone on as easily as we have. Moses could not find them even in Israel. There is nothing so obnoxious to an Holy Being as a nasty, lit-

---

[65] The camp took the Plateau Route, avoiding Deep Rut Hill and Mexican Hill to follow the divide between the North Platte and Laramie drainages to reach the Laramie River valley about a mile west of the fort.

[66] Distrustful of assurances from the Sioux that they would return any remaining Mormon stock at Fort Laramie, the Saints devised a plan to recover their animals by negotiation or force. Erastus Snow attributed the failure of the plan to James Bordeaux, who at first offered and then refused to supply an interpreter to help the Mormons: B. H. Roberts wrote, "Whether he was sincere in his counsel and advice or whether he was afraid of injuring his influence and trade with the Sioux, or whether he was in league with them in their robberies, is more than I can determine." See *Comprehensive History*, 3:309.

[67] The Old Testament prophet Enoch was translated to heaven; see Genesis 5:18–24. Joseph Smith often used the name Enoch to identify himself in revelations.

tle, petulent, fault finding Spirit. It has been said of old, all the world is a Goose & a man is a fool who has not some picking of the Feathers. I ask, can an honest man go & live in the world? No! They would fleece him of all he has. Every man must have benevolence & do as you would be done by & I know by the God of Abram, Isaac & Jacob that that people is destined to be rich. I never have put my hand to any thing since I've been in the Church but I've prospered. All the men in this Camp know more than they practice. Many manifest a heedless careless Spirit. Every man's interest is the temporal & spiritual salvation to the Four Quarters of the Earth. I have an interest for all of you. I want you all to have an interest one for another. No man was more sorry than I was when Joseph was taken away. The Savior & the Apostles were plagued with dishonest men same as we are. He then blest the brethren in the name of the Lord.

S. Markham made a few remarks & testified before God that no accident has befallen us, thro' following the Council given us, but when we have disobeyed Council, we have catched it.

Saturday 25 September 1847–The Company start to the Fort for the Interpreter. Presidents Young, Kimball, Benson & others also go to the Fort. At 10:20 the Doctor & T. B. start on 2 mules [and] on their arrival met all the brethren there. They buy robes from [$]1.25 to [$]2.00, Antelope Skins from [$].75 to [$]1.50, Tea @ [$]4.00 per pound, Flour .25[¢] per pound. Afterwards Presidents Young, Richards, Kimball, Benson, A. P. Rockwood & Bullock dine with Mr. Bords [Bourdeaux] on Roast & Boiled Buffalo, very good, flat cakes, fried cakes & milk, which is a delightful treat to me. About 3 P.M. I returned with the mules, then gathered some Pears. In the evening the remainder of the brethren return bringing the news of Luke Johnson, J. C. Little, Commodore Stockton & a Company of troops from California will be at the Fort this evening.[68]

A fine day. West Wind, in eve changed round to East. In the evening Professor Pratt reads a long paper to Presidents Young, Richards, Woodruff, & T. Bullock on theological matters until about 10 P.M.

---

[68] Commodore Robert Field Stockton's inept administration of California following its conquest succeeded in stirring the *Californios* to revolt and encouraged John C. Frémont to be insubordinate to his military superior, Stephen W. Kearny. Stockton was returning overland to the states with a large party to testify at Frémont's court-martial.

Sunday 26 September 1847–A Pleasant Clear morning. While many of the Camp were at their breakfast, brothers Luke Johnson, Jesse C. Little & two others return to us with 9 horses & all were glad to meet again. They had heard of our loss of horses by the Sioux at the South Pass & thinking we were so crippled as to be unable to proceed on our journey, they started to render us what assistance they could.[69] They went up the River Road on Monday last. On arriving at the mouth of the ~~Horse Shoe~~ "Big Timber"[70] they heard the reports of rifles [and] felt satisfied it was our Camp. [They] took a Bee line to the place & were surprized by finding themselves in the midst of about 200 Lodges of Indians. They were immediately surrounded. Many Indians headed their horses, but Luke Johnson made motions to them to get out of the way or he would fire upon them. They were very noisy & made many gestures & appeared violent and saucy. They cleared the road in a disappointed mood. The brethren then saw the tracks of Wagons, loose horses &c & a few miles ahead saw a couple of Wagons &c &c. They then felt satisfied they had caught our rear Guard, pushed on & again disappointed. This Company turned out to be Commodore Stockton & about 40 others from California. Yet this was good [news] to them at this critical time, or they would have lost all their horses by the same Indians & perhaps their lives. They then continued their journey together, receiving respectable & kind treatment from them & arrived at the Fort last night.

Camp were called together when it was "motioned that we proceed on our journey, a few miles, in the afternoon, to get better feed." Seconded & carried. President Young & several others again go up to the Fort, returning about 3 P.M. At 3:40 the Camp again resumes its journey down the River Road [and] over a Prairie; which seems good to us, who have been so long accustomed to Sage Bushes, Ravines, Rocks & mountains. Saw many Prickly Pears, which many brethren gather & eat. Travel over generally a Sandy road & halt when we came to a small Grove 4 or 5 miles down the River. Not much grass on our route. Many Sand Burrs.

Afterward T. Bullock & S. H. Goddard gather many Pears. Presidents

---

[69] Johnson and Little learned on 14 September "that a party of Sioux warriors have got the brethrens horses 17 in number on the Raw Hide" and met Stockton's party from California while investigating. On the same day, William Clayton and the Ox company "concluded to go on as fast as circumstances will permit to Winter Quarters." See Smith, ed., *An Intimate Chronicle*, 388.

[70] This was LaBonte Creek.

Young, Kimball, Richards, Benson, with T. B & Luke Johnson met in Doctor's Wagon. Johnson related his Grizzly Bear Hunts & other occurrences since we parted. Heard of an Apple Orchard on the Powder River, about 70 miles North of the Upper Ferry in the Crow country.

Monday 27 September 1847–At day break, the teams are hitched up & Camp resumes its journey, travelling about half a mile before the Sun arose. Many brethren gather Prickly Pears, which are a very pleasant fruit to eat, after they are disrobed of their Coat of Pricks. They are troublesome to get; as my hands were stuck pretty full with their needles & getting many in my lips, tongue, mouth &c is a drawback to eating this fruit, but still I gathered sufficient to satisfy my hunger, as did also other brethren. We travelled over a Sandy road thro' a Prairie country. Not having much Sage on it, is much pleasanter to travel over than the last half of our route & again it looks more like going home to our Wives and Families. Crossed the "Raw Hide" which was dry & halted for breakfast at 9:40 near a Grove of small Cotton Woods on the North side of the North Fork of the Platte in the midst of a patch of dry grass & some rushes.[71] Again starting at 12:30, taking [a route] near the centre of the valley. Much of the road is thro' a barren or very short dry grass. On the banks of the River is a scanty fringe of Cotton Wood bushes bordered by a band of dry grass. Our Pioneers found a patch of Excellent grass to which place we turned out of the Road, and came to a halt at 5 P.M. After our horses were turned out, the brethren mowed a considerable quantity & carried it inside the Caral so that our Animals might eat all night. Stephen Markham, Albert P. Rockwood & Thomas Bullock went round the Camp taking an account of the Arms & then organized them into a Military body (see 1st page of this Journal–total 85 Rifle Shots 20 Musket shots, 145 Pistol shots, 250 Shots or 3 to a man).[72] Afterwards Presidents Young, Richards & Benson, & Bullock met in the Doctor's Wagon & conversed until 9 o'clock stating the difference of administering the laws in England & United States & what the laws ought to be. Also about another Mission to England &c.

At 9 visited the Guard. Doctor cut more Grass for his mules & Horse.

Tuesday 28 September 1847–At break of day the teams were hitched

---

[71] The pioneer company had camped at Raw Hide Creek, today's Rawhide River, on May 31.
[72] For this list of the returning pioneers' "Military Organization," see Appendix C.

up & Camp starts at 5:55 going back to the road then taking a course South of East. The Sun rose in Splendor as we wended our way under the bluffs, travelling over a good hard road, thro' a prairie covered over with good grass in most places, the remainder of the land covered with a short stunted grass 2 or 3 inches high and many Prickly Pears, but no fruit growing on them. Continued downwards until we came to some Low Sandy Bluffs near the River when Camp halted at 8:45 in another patch of good green grass about foot long. Clear blue sky, warm morning. We had not been long on this spot before a body of mounted Indians on the South Side of the River were seen, which we presumed was the Lodge that was at Fort John when we were. In a short time we discovered they were on the move towards the East. After breakfast all the brethren were called out in military organization & reviewed, finding 85 Rifle Shots, 20 Musket Shots, 145 Pistol Shots, total 250 Shots without any reloading. Instructions were given by B. Young when it was voted "that we all obey the orders of our officers" & were then dismissed.

We have halted opposite "The Boat Rock."[73] At 11:37 Camp again started taking nearly an East by South line over a very good road, then over a bottom land thro' tall grass (or about 2 feet). We watered our teams at the River, then ascended to a table land of barren land [with] a little very short grass scattered about. Seeing a quantity of good dry Muskeet grass on the banks of the river, we turned out of the road & camped at 3:23 having the river bank as one side of our Caral.

As we were about coming to our halt a band of Antelope ran between us & the River, running the Gauntlet of the Wagons. One was killed, the remainder escaped to the bluffs. One of these was afterwards killed.

Very pleasant day. West breeze, blue sky, but few small clouds in East. Mowed grass & gave to the animals in addition to the good quantity growing inside caral. T. B. bathed in the river & went across the River for Fire Wood.

Wednesday 29 September 1847—At break of day, the teams were hitched up & made a start at 5:47. Came to a miry Slough, could not cross it well. Tried 3 places. Two wagons got mired, which the brethren pulled out with ropes (the Mormon Team). While crossing, the dogs killed a Skunk, a small black animal which stunk in a dreadful manner.

---

[73] This distinctive formation near present Henry, Nebraska, has been destroyed by railroad or highway construction.

The dog then leaped into 2 other Wagons, which it did not belong to, and kicked up a bad stink by rubbing itself against the clothes. On being put out, it went into the River to wash itself. As the Sun rose we wended our way thro green short grass, passing along "Spring Creek." Bent to the South to Scott's Bluffs where we found a heavy bottom of grass, then took a Strait line for "Chimney Rock," ascending to a barren table land having many Prickly Pears, but no fruit on them; & Thistles. Here we went at a pretty good pace for several miles, until we came to the bend in the river when we halted at 8:45 having travelled about 11½ miles. Turned out our animals on good & fine grass & prepared our breakfasts.

Very clear sky, warm morning, gentle South breeze. [The] Platte looks [like] a Stream of Silver. An alarm of Indians being seen on the opposite side the river, the Teams were all brought up close to the Wagons. The Indian camp still continuing its course towards the River, it was thought prudent to hitch up & remove from here. Accordingly at 12:05 we again resumed our journey over a good road, with short Buffalo Grass all over the country. Seeing some Buffalo's on our left, Luke Johnson went out and shot a Bull, many brethren thus getting a portion of meat to eat. The Indians on arriving at the River put up their Wicka ups on the South Banks. We continued our route, seeing many Antelope & Buffalo & formed our caral about 5 miles west of Chimney Rock at 4:20 having plenty of short Buffalo Grass for our animals.

A Warm day. Part of the road dusty, very still breeze from South. Saw Laramie Peak when at Scotts Bluffs. Several Geese & Ducks flying about.

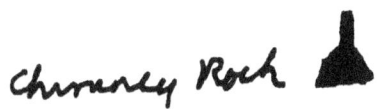

Thursday 30 September 1847—An Indian discovered by the Guard at 3 A.M. prowling about the Camp, but kept his distance. Shortly after 4 President Young got up to see if the Guard was all on duty. At ½ past 4 all the brethren were called up. Hitched up teams & at 5:32 Camp started, crossing several roads in order to travel in the road nearest the bluffs, which Professor Pratt considered the best & nighest road, he acting as Pilot. Saw another Skunk which "Trip" seized behind, but immediately released his hold again on account of its offensive odor, which

stunk all the neighborhood. President Benson killed another Skunk. Many Buffalo & Antelope roaming over the Prairie. The droves of Antelope look really handsome as they gallop past, one following after the other. This morning many Flocks of Geese & Ducks are flying about which keeps the mind continually active watching their movements. We continued in nearly a strait line from "Scott's Bluffs" to a Bluff on the East of us; passing by three Lakes of Water & several dry Lakes which have left a Saline deposit behind on the drying up of the Waters. We see the Prickly Pears in many places but no fruit on them. There is a short Buffalo Grass all over the country. In some places the Grass is waist deep, but every where there is a plenty of Grass. Our course was nearly East about 2 or 3 miles from the River until about 10 when, as we neared the River, we turned off to its banks & halted at 10:30. Found good feed. Beautiful morning, blue sky, very gentle breeze from SW. At 1:55 we again started taking a line to the Sand Bluffs [over a] sandy road. Crossed over the Sand Ridge, heavy pulling. On the top a young Wolf crossed our path. On the East side came in view of several Wicka ups on the South side of the River, then took a strait road East. When opposite the Wicka ups, we learned from a White man, who had a fat Buffalo cow on a mule, that Mr. Rashiaw[74] was there. When we turned Square down to the River & Camped at 5 P.M. precise on the North side, here we learned that all the Ox teams started from here 5 days ago, the first Company having waited for the last Camp. President Richards & several others go over the River to trade with Rashiaw. On their return President Young stated that it will be best for us to tarry here tomorrow and kill some meat. Orders were given that no man leave the Camp in the morning without orders.

Friday 1st. October 1847–Cold night, cool pleasant morning. Several Squaws came to Camp to trade meat for knives. Some Indians also come & start on the hunt, but owing to some misunderstanding between Colonel Markham & Mr. Rashiaw our brethren did not go until 12 o'clock & returned again at 3 P.M. without having found either Indians or Buffalo Cows & proving an entire disappointment to all the brethren.

About 4 Commodore Stockton & his Company arrived in sight. After watering their horses, they drove them into our Caral. Luke John-

---

[74] This was trader John Richard, guide of the Mississippi Saints in 1846. Richard seems to be located near Courthouse and Jail rocks, which again escape mention in Bullock's journal.

son went out to meet them. When he returned he reported that the Commodore wished to have our Company, also some of our Wagons, to carry his sick men. The Indians returned about Sunset & appear to have killed about a dozen buffalo. Several Swaps & trades were made by our brethren with the Indians, Traders & others. Several horses thus exchanged hands, also several brethren cross the river to Swap Salt, Knives &c with the Indians. Rashiaw asks [$].10 per pound for dried Buffalo Meat [and] from 2 to 8 dollars for robes.

Pleasant day, Blue Sky, slight breeze from West.

Saturday 2 October 1847–The Doctor having bought a cow, TB went out as the cow driver. Calf Skin the father of the two men who stole our horses being in Camp, President Young told him thro Mr. Rashiaw that we should return next Spring with 3000 [people] & should make them cry, if our horses were not given up. He burst out crying & pledged himself that every one of them should be given up to Mr. Rashiaw. The President told him we had seen about 25 of them & could have taken them, but we wanted to get them peaceably. An order was drawn out authorizing Mr. Rashiaw to receive & take them into his charge; & get a copy of the particulars from Fort John.

At 9 o'clock Camp started, going over a tolerable road until they came to the Buffalo cow which Thos. Woolsey shot, when they halted at 11:30. While I was driving the cows I saw a Buffalo bear down to the River & as it appeared to be gaining on Woolsey. I rode the poney & headed it. It then turned to an Island in the River & halted a short time, during which time Woolsey came up, took aim & shot him down in the River. The Stream was soon "a river of blood." I then pointed out a herd of Buffalo cows & Woolsey went in pursuit.

Luke Johnson & Stephen Markham kill & bring to the Road a fine calf. At 1 P.M. Camp again started taking a line for Ancient Ruins Bluffs, where they arrived & halted at 3:30 in a patch of tall grass on the banks of the River.

Immediately after the caral was formed President Kimball, Jos. Matthews & T. B. go to shoot a cow. They crept up among the Bluffs [and] saw a Bull which had been killed by Woolsey. We might have killed several Bulls, but would not shoot them. We were near enough to one Bull to stone it. Joseph Matthews was within 5 rods of another. We came upon 3 droves of Bulls, but they were not molested & returned to Camp at Sunset. A large black cloud covering the West while the Sun appeared to throw up red glares of flame as from an immense furnace. Fine day, clear sky.

Sunday 3 October 1847–Very warm night, T. B. sweat much. The Wolves kept up a continual yelling & howling all night. A rather dull morning, clouds floating & appear to draw rain. When [the] teams were ready to start, President Young went round to see that all the fires were put out. After water was put on all of them, then Camp started about 9. Had a good road to the foot of the Cobble Hills, when instead of going over the Camp went down the River about one mile. The foremost teams waited until the last Wagons came out of the Water, then started again, crossing 3 beds of dry Streams, when W. Woodruff having killed a Buffalo cow, the Camp halted about noon while the Buffalo was skinned, dressed, brought in & cut up & divided. [We] then resumed the journey at 5 minutes to 2 [and] went over a good road when news came in that Amasa Lyman had killed another cow, which again caused the Camp to halt. [We] then turned down to the River near a mile & halted at 3:15. President Kimball came to Doctor's Wagon & said "I move that the Twelve Apostles be the Hunters on the Sabbath Day." President Richards said "there was no occasion to make that move, as they already prove themselves." We have now travelled about 21 miles in 3 days, the first day [we] spend our means in buying Buffalo meat at [$].10 per pound, the two last [we] kill 3 cows, 1 Bull, 1 calf. We are now delaying time [and] losing the fine weather, loading up our Wagons & do not know but that the Severe Weather may overtake us before we can get to Grand Island where we might & could shelter our animals & ourselves & procure plenty of meat. Morning very hot, afternoon Cloudy & strong Wind from West. A large herd of Buffalo gallop close past our horses, then get scared & ascend one of the Bluffs in regular line, a pretty sight.

Monday 4 October 1847–In dividing out the Meat, Dr. Richards was entitled to about 2 Quarters, to make him equal with the remainder. When he went & choose one Quarter the nearest to him, Colonel Markham objected to it. In the evening he sent down to the Doctor's Wagon 35 pounds Bone, 3 Shin Bones forming a part of his allowance. Last night some thief stole a Buffalo Tongue hanging on the Doctor's

Wagon. T. B. drove all the 4 cows on foot, [a] tiresome morning's drive. Camp starts about 8 over a good road until we came to some Sand Bluffs, which we pass over and halt on the East side, on the bank of the River, with plenty of grass at 12:35. The Frenchmen have killed 3 of the Fattest cows that have been brought into Camp. Four Sioux Indians came to the Camp and cook their dinner at the camp Fires. One of them give T. Bullock a fine Buffalo tongue. Camp again starts at 2:15 & takes a line to Castle Bluffs. A badger being seen, Presidents Young & Kimball with Captain Adams & Matthews race after it & kill it with Sticks. Herds of Buffalo are seen in all directions.

The Horizon is hazy all day, the Zenith a pale blue. South Breeze. Camp halts at 5:25 on the Bank of the River on the West Side of Castle Bluffs. At night President Young requests a Company of Footmen to go as Express to the Ox Teams, to order them to hold up, recruit their teams, kill & dry Buffalo & wait our arrival, when Amasa Lyman, Luke Johnson, John Brown, Alexander P. Chessley, Ezekiel Kellogg, William Roe, Newton Wreston, Stephen H. Goddard, Joseph Rooker, William Park (with 2 others who did not go) went as the detachment. Guns & mocassins were provided for those who have not them, when a letter was written for the brethren to take (on file) [and] copied for Signature. Signed in behalf of the Council. The detachment to start by break of day.

Tuesday 5 October 1847–Amasa Lyman & escort start at day break on foot.

Hazy morn. Sun rises nearly blood red, the Zenith of a Pale Blue. East South wind. T. B. [was a] cow driver in [the] morning. Camp starts at half past 8 thro' near the center of the prairie over a pretty good road [through] two short lengths of Sand, pass on the right of a Sand Bluff and halts on a beautiful patch of Buffalo Grass about 11:00 near the bend of a river, having travelled thro' a large Prairie Dog Town. Saw several hundreds of the timid animals running about who kept a continual barking until they popt into their holes.

Also saw several very large bands of Buffalo, several thousands at one view [and] many flocks of Geese flying about. T. B. bathed in the Platte.

Camp again starts at 1:15 and in a short time cross "Castle Bluff Creek"[75] which was near the same size as when we crossed it on the 20th

---

[75] This was Blue Water Creek near present Lewellen, Nebraska.

May last. Pass two small Islands with Timber on it. Also pass "Ash Hollow," then turn off the road & form a Semi circle on the bank of the River at 4 P.M. This day we have seen a tolerable plenty of Buffalo Grass on our entire route. SE Wind.

Doctor told me that on the 3rd he prophecied that "if we don't lay in plenty of Buffalo meat soon, we shall go home with hungry bellies." Most of the brethren say we shall have plenty of Buffalos as far as Grand Island.

The Sun sets with a great appearance for Windy Weather. A Bat is seen flitting about the Camp, after Sun set. This Creature has been seldom seen on our journey. At night we have a Grand Solo, Quartete & Chorus from the throats of a very musical band of Wolves, the Serenading being continued thro' the entire night.

Wednesday 6–[No entry.]

Thursday 7 October 1847–T.B. very sick, unable to keep up with [the] Teams. Howard Egan brought me a mule to ride up to H. Kimball's Wagon & then ride in Egan's stead. Crossed a creek, had much difficulty in coming up to the Wagons; which had halted, because Mr. Pappan of Fort John, Captain Walker and others who were going to California, had rode up to camp.[76] Doctor wrote while TB copied [a] letter to President John Smith & Saints, Great Salt Lake City, [and] Saml. Brannan, San Francisco Bay, [and] Mr. Rashiaw, (trader) (all on file).[77]

The letters [were] all signed by Presidents Young & Richards, also delivered letters to Appleton Harmon at the Fort & Edson Whipple [at] Salt Lake City. After hearing the news of the day, Mr. Pappan told us, if he had been at the Fort, he should have sent an Interpreter to the Indians & we should have had our horses. He promised to do all he could to assist us. After chatting some time, Camp resumes journey, crossing

---

[76] Mountaineer Joseph R. Walker, who opened the wagon road to California in 1843, left Westport, Missouri, on 2 September with Frank McClelland and five others, including his brother Samuel Walker and his nephew, James T. Walker. See Barry, *The Beginning of the West*, 715. Salt Lake High Council minutes report Walker wintered on Green River. On 23 January 1848, five or six Saints volunteered to go with him to California in the spring.

[77] The letter to Brannan from the "Return Pioneer Camp of Israel" was dated 6 October 1847 and read: "Sir, We drop you a line by Capt. Walker whom we have met this [day] en route for California. We have lost many horses by the Indians [and] have regained some and expect to get the remainder. Our camp is in good health & spirit. We met the emigrating camps between Green & Sweet water well and before this they are directly safe at the valley. They had 566 waggens & souls in proportion well provided with bread, and very happy. The weather is very fine. The Lord bless you & all the brothers in your region for the council." Young to Brannan, Brigham Young Collection, LDS Archives.

"Crooked Creek" & 2 other very small creeks & halt at 11:40. A Cloudy Morning, many geese flying South, denotes that cold Weather is fast approaching. While travelling this morning a Buffalo Bull stood in the road [and] would not stir out of it until 3 dogs went at it & slowly drove it away to the mountains. Camp again starts at 1:35 travelling all the afternoon thro' a long coarse grass & halt on the West side of Rattle snake creek at 4 P.M. Here our messengers found the first letter from Wm. Clayton dated "Friday morning Octr. 1" from which it appears they have made up their minds to go on to Winter Quarters & not wait for us, altho they are aware of our heavy loss of animals at the South Pass & have "considerable anxiety" about our not having reached them.

Appended was a note from Amasa Lyman saying they were going ahead & "we shall overtake them, if it is at Winter Quarters," dated Wednesday evening. P.M. was clear and Warm. T. B. very sick.[78]

Friday 8 October 1847–Rather hazy morning. Very large herd of Buffalo seen on the Bluffs, like a small Forest when they descend. Camp gathers up & starts at about ½ past 8 and in about 1 mile cross the Rattlesnake Creek,[79] which is nearly as large as it was in the Spring. On the East bank, W. Clayton's letter was found.[80] He is 7 days ahead & A. Lyman is supposed about 40 miles ahead of us. In a short time we pass our Encampment of 17th May.[81] After following the course of the River some distance, Camp crosses three very small creeks, which came from several small pools of Water. Going over some heavy sand for about ½ mile, [we] then halt at noon. No sooner had some of the animals been loosed from the Traces, than the cry of "brethren, gather up your horses, a band of Indians is coming on us." On close examination, it proved to be a large herd of Elk coming down the hill behind us. The

---

[78] A loose sheet inserted between pages 36 and 37 and the 21 and 23 October dates of the Return Pioneer Journal may describe the contents of this note. It listed Lyman's party—Amasa Lyman, John Brown, Alexander P. Chessley, John Buchannan, Ezekiel Kellog, William Roe, Luke Johnson, Newton Wreston, Joseph Rooker, William Park, and John Crow—marked with two sets of undefined check marks, perhaps indicating which men were armed. The sheet contains these notes: "5 want fire arms &c"; "give state of Camp"; "lots of leaves"; "teams breaking down"; "15 or 20 miles a day"; "Stop till we come, kill & dry Buffalo"; "Take Amasas council: Don't go or write for wood." These notes are written sideways on the list: "to overtake one learns—they to halt & recruit   will we come up   stick up notes."

[79] Brigham Young named Rattlesnake Creek, which is probably today's Whitetail Creek. See Kimball, ed., *The Latter-Day Saints' Emigrants' Guide*, 55.

[80] The discovery of this letter was reported in the Journal History for 7 October. Bullock made no entry for 6 October and the following entries seem to be one day in advance of the events they describe.

[81] This camp was about two miles east of present Keystone, Nebraska.

hunters turn out, the Elk scent them. 2 Frenchmen gallop round the hill and head them and kill one, which they bring to Camp.

About 2 P.M. Camp again starts passing over "Elk Stream," a shallow rapid stream of clear Water. Travel on a Sand road about 1 mile, then cross a creek about 6 feet wide, excellent cold water. In about 1 mile further came to a muddy creek which forms quite a large Slough on our right. A Buffalo Calf descended from the hill [and] was shot at by Wm. King, who missed it, and it escaped very leisurely to the river. [We] then passed over two very small creeks and ascended a very heavy Sand Bluff, very heavy pulling for the animals. [We] then wound round & descended to the East side of the Bluffs, crossing over "Spring Creek," a beautiful little Stream of clear water. Here I saw a very large herd of Buffalo several miles ahead. Camp on the Banks of the river at 5:30 P.M. Hazy horizon, Zenith pale blue. Pleasant day.

Saturday 9 October 1847—New moon 8:37 A.M. (Full 23rd, 6:06 P.M.) A boisterous SW wind early in the morning which ceased about 8, afterwards very fine day. Camp starts at 8:10, taking a strait line towards the Bluffs, crossing "Bluff Creek" with a good supply of clear cold Water. Wind round to the right of the road being [a] much easier ascent, yet it was tedious, then a gradual descent to the East side of the Bluffs. Here is a great supply of tall coarse grass, but being too far from the River, we continued our route until we come to the West side of the next Sand Bluffs, where we halt at 12:45, Presidents Kimball, Richards, Woodruff, Smith & T. B. walking ahead conversing on several principles. H. K. remarked that where a man following his file leader, sees him go out of the road, he ought not to go out of the road because his file leader had done wrong, but continue straight forward in the right road, giving it as a word of caution. In the same conversation he remarked that the God of Abram, Isaac & Jacob was always leading the mind of man to the things that are right, yet man did not always see it and he had to learn the things by what he suffers. He also prophesied in the name of the Lord that the day would come, in *that* valley that a man who had been oppressed, his bonds would be broken, and every man have a chance to prove himself & the glory of God would shine on him.

At 2:45 Camp again starts taking a large bend to the left, round the Sand Bluffs. In crossing over [we] saw 2 Rattle snakes which escaped into their den. Presidents Young & G. A. Smith, H. C. Kimball, W. Richards & TB walking ahead again in continuation of the principles & on Foreign Policy.[82] After descending from the Bluffs, continued an Easterly course to the "Junction Bluff Creek" where we halt at 5 P.M. [83] Fine day, clear Sky.

In the evening Doctor was sick and we had a "Grand Concerto" by wolves. O. Pratt & W. Woodruff conversing (*inter alia*)[84] on distributing 20,000 Copies of the Epistle from the Twelve Apostles to the Members of Parliament, Clergy, the Universities & the Learned thro' the United Kingdom & the enquiries for debate made. It will be the means of doing much good there.

Heard of a new dish of Cookery, viz "Fried Watches" in Butter.[85]

Sunday 10 October 1847–It was determined by the Council to let the horses have a rest today so many of the brethren bathe in the River & cleanse themselves. T. B. bathed again. Presidents Young, Kimball, Richards, Pratt, Smith, Woodruff, Lyman [?] & Benson went to the bank of the River, prayed & conversed. Joseph Matthews went a head to look out a camping place about 3 miles further. Gather up teams about 1 and Camp starts at 1:45 taking a straight East line to the camping place, where they halt about 3. Many Geese flying about. T. B. discovered a small herd of Buffalo cows, pointed them out to the two Frenchmen, who went in pursuit. [They] succeeded in killing a young cow. A hazy, warm day, breeze from SE. This day is so very calm, the brethren are very still, which gives a quiet solemn Sabbath stillness.

At night many Wolves approach close to the Camp & keep up a great howling.

Monday 11 October 1847–Heard Thunder a few minutes after 12 followed by light rain from 3 to 5 with some Thunder, also strong East Wind. Morning [was] very hazy.

Camp starts at 8:30 A.M. [and] soon passes the Ox Company Camp ground. [We] found a letter from Amasa Lyman & Company, who left

---

[82] The discussion of "foreign policy" among these members of the Council of Fifty shows that they already regarded the Kingdom of God as an independent political entity.

[83] This camp was about ten miles west of North Platte, Nebraska, near today's Sand Hill Ruts at the mouth of Birdwood Creek.

[84] Among other things.

[85] Bullock's reference to fried watches has stumped many trail experts. It was perhaps a dish made of buffalo testicles.

here on Saturday morning at day break. [We] then cross a bad Slough or muddy creek where two Wagons had much difficulty in getting thro'. [We] then took a strait line for some Islands in the River, passing over an uneven road & a small Sand ridge. Saw two large herds of Buffalo on the hill [and] the hunters go out & kill a cow. T. B. rode with President Young in his carriage. Found an Antler of a Deer having a prong growing on the opposite side of where they generally grow.

At 11:45 A.M. Camp halts opposite several small Islands having a thick bed of Willows & a few short Cotton Wood Trees on them with plenty of the Rosin Weed, other Weeds, & coarse grass on the prairie. Hazy atmosphere, East Wind. This is our old Camp ground of 12 May last.

At 8 minutes to 2 Camp again starts and in about 1 mile cross a small creek or Slough, not much water in it. See 3 bands of Buffalo & many Geese. Camp halts at 3:15 P.M. opposite the "Eagle's nest" [with] not much feed. We get along at a slow pace of late, or rather since Captain Matthews & the Two Frenchmen have joined hands. Question: Is it to get a supply of Fat Buffalo meat to retail to the Saints at Winter Quarters at exhorbitant prices? Time will shew. Atmosphere hazy, few clouds floating about, Easterly breeze. Frogs sing to tell us of rain soon coming. [We see] large flocks of Geese flying South in the evening.

At night Wind blew very strong from NW, the strongest breeze we have had on our return journey.

Joseph Egbert killed a cow & calf. The brethren went out for the meat, it being 3 miles from Camp. [They] did not return until late in the evening. We had to exalt lights, shout &c to guide them to Camp, having to pass many marshy places.

Tuesday 12 October 1847–Shortly after midnight the Wind began to cease until it died away into a cold morning with a NW breeze. About 8 the brethren began to gather up teams & at 8:30 Camp started over a good road close by the banks of the River, then took a strait line for some Timber ahead, thro rank deep grass. Cross a creek several feet wide & about 1 deep, then travel over a Sandy patch a short distance & halt at 12:30 on the banks of the river having [in view] several Islands covered with Willows & small Cotton Wood Trees. There has been Wood in sight all the morning & altho' the Sear & Yellow Leaf has made its autumnal visit, still it is cheering to see Timber so close to us. Saw several small Bands of Buffalo this forenoon.

About noon it was much warmer & pleasanter, light clouds flying about in different directions. The mountains on the South side are abrupt & broken, being a miniature representation of the mountains hemming in the Great Salt Lake Valley, while the Timber gives an improving appearance to it.

At 25 minutes to 2 Camp again resumes its journey, but instead of the route of last Spring, we bore away to the left up to the Bluffs & round the head of 4 Sloughs. The entire "bottom" to the river appears covered with a tall coarse grass. Many Geese rise up out of its midst. Our road is considerable Sandy part of the way. At 20 minutes to 5 Camp halts on the side of a Slough, where the Ox Company appears to have Camped.[86]

Dexter Stillman kills a Buffalo cow, W. Woodruff's Carriage goes for it. A mild and pleasant evening. The Animals appear fond of this grass. The New Moon made her appearance in a Clear Blue Sky this evening. In the evening E. T. Benson [spoke] with Doctor in Doctor's Wagon. In talking about the Ox Teams the Doctor said they were rebellious & if they did not think they were, they had only to look at their instructions, which they had in their pockets. Doctor also said we might see one herd of Buffalo more, but that would be all, as we passed the bulk 10 days ago. The Water in the Slough was black & unpleasant & [we] had nothing but Buffalo Dung to cook with. This has been our fuel the way from Fort John & makes but a poor fire.

President Young is sick.

Wednesday 13 October 1847–Cold night, strong NW breeze. The brethren have to assist "Jacob," "Moses" and 2 or 3 other horses who are nearly worn out to get on their feet every morning. We have several horses that are obliged to be driven loose every day & several are very weak, [so] that we are afraid [they] will "give out" almost every day.[87] The Teams were turned loose out of the caral directly after 4 o'clock. Again gathered & Camp starts at 8:10, going very near a Bluff & mak-

---

[86] Bullock failed to mention that the returning pioneers had passed the confluence of the North and South forks of the Platte River.

[87] As noted, being accustomed to eating grain, the horses were weakened by their restricted diet of grass. The teams of the ox company, by contrast, thrived on this regimen.

ing a great Semi circle to the creek, going round the head of 2 Sloughs & crossing a creek of cold Water about 8 feet wide & one deep, thro' pretty coarse grass. [We] then Sweep round to the River keeping near the bank of the creek (Memorandum: when you come to this creek in the Spring, go strait ahead to the point of Timber ahead [following] the old Pioneer Road [for a] better chance to Camp & nearer road.) [We] then turned East to the bend of the River & halted at 11:40 near some Islands [with] not much grass, few rushes. Staid until 1:40 when Camp again starts towards a Sand Bluff, which we pass over; this was much heavier pulling for the Animals than we had on going over the bed of the River in the Spring & some little further journey. [We] then went over a prairie with a good road to a small Island, where we Camp at 4:50 [with] not much grass, yet more than we had in the Spring.

Saw between 2 and 3,000 Buffalo this afternoon. We had 5 bands a few hundred yards from where we camped. Tom Woolsey walks up to a band & kills one. The Frenchmen kill [blank]. Clear Sky, Pleasant evening, Easterly breeze.

T. B. is the cow Driver this day.

President Young a little better at Sundown.

Doctor told T. .B. this evening that he intended to load up his Wagon with Skins & make me walk all the way home. He told me to get what skins I could & he would carry them on halves, but T. B. can not get a robe, a Skin of any description, a tongue, a bladder, or any thing to take home to his family, or to keep him or his family warm the coming Winter. But I pray the Lord to open up the way for me at Winter Quarters or some where else that I may be able to earn a comfortable fit out for next Spring.[88]

Thursday 14 October 1847–Frost in the night, very cold morning, East breeze. Camp starts about 8:07 taking the most northerly road, the grass nearly all eat up by the numerous Buffalo about here. Turned off the road to the river to halt about noon, going about a mile by an Island through long coarse grass where we staid until about 2, when President Young & T.B. went ahead to search out a crossing place over a bad Slough ahead. Saw a Mud Turtle & several Ducks in it, crossed over at the entrance into the River, and then bore away to the left to our old

---

[88] Having now learned he will have to complete the last two hundred miles of his journey afoot, Bullock seemed almost resigned to his fate.

road. Passed a Camp ground [and] continued round the Slough & came to a halt at ¼ to 4. [We] found a bed of rushes on one of the Islands which our animals like, also some young Cotton Wood Trees, which they relish.

Saw many Buffalo dotted all over the Prairie. T. B. killed a large Snake. Camp passed thro' a small Prairie Dog Town. The brethren kill two. Clear Blue Sky, SE Breeze.
Doctor fleshing Buffalo hides.

Friday 15 October 1847–The Wolves appear to be in greater abundance here by their tremendous howling all night. Pleasant morning. [We] take horses & mules on the Island to the rushes. At 8:15 Camp starts again on their homeward journey, over a prairie with small uneven patches in it, covered with the small Buffalo Grass, again seeing many Buffalo in the distance, but having a strong Westerly wind blowing from us towards them. They were at a considerable distance from us. Came to a halt at 11:30. T.B. washes in the River, when Solomon Chamberlin sets the Prairie on fire. He has shown much selfishness & disobedience of the regulations for some time & altho' orders are often given to be very cautious about the fires, yet he built his fire in the midst of the dry grass & before he attempted to quench the flame away it went jumping & crackling through the dry grass. About 40 of the brethren went & thro' much activity succeeded in putting it out before it had burnt many rods, which I trust will prove a strong lesson of caution to all. About 1 o'clock Camp again started, and again took a strait line towards the East, thus saving some distance, instead of following the River Bank, & halt at 3:30. See many Buffalo thro' the day [and] kill one and bring it to Camp. Pleasant evening.

On the banks of the River where we camped found plenty of tall grass and wood for fuel. The Buffalo Dung is now going out of use.

Colonel Markham gave orders this afternoon that for the future the Wagons should travel in two Columns; every man must go close by his Wagon; all Meat that is killed must be brought in and divided by the Commissary, as we are now approaching the Pawnee country and it is not wisdom for any man to scatter from the Camp.

Saturday 16 October 1847–Cool night & morning.

Camp gathers up and starts at A.M. taking a strait line across the

Prairies, instead of following our road of last Spring. Going thro' two Prairie Dog Towns, [we] saw many of the timid animals as they ran to their holes. When they got to their holes, they would bark, wag their tails & then pop down out of sight in two moments. "Trip" and "Louder" chased a Wolf, but he was too great a match for them. They ran away from him & he went on his road.

Saw many signs of the ox teams having gone this route. Came to a halt on the bank of a creek having Ash & Red Elm Trees on it. The creek being dry, the Camp had to resume the journey. When they crossed the dry creek, turned round to the right & camped on the bank of a Slough as the Sun was setting in the middle of a patch of dry grass. Here Amasa Lyman & Company (except Goddard & Kellogg, who continued their Mission) again met us, reporting that they had been down to Grand Island & there discovered evidences of the Ox Teams being several days ahead, last Tuesday. That they were perfectly satisfied that the Ox teams were running ahead at 25 miles a day, perfectly reckless of their promises & determined to leave us at the mercy of the weather. That it was impossible to overtake them before they got to the Pawnee Mission. That if they had pursued their journey & stopt them there, they would be out of the Buffalo country & could be using up their means; indeed we are now out of the Buffalo range, having seen the last band of cows for this year. That it would be necessary for us to halt here & kill so much meat as would carry us to Winter Quarters & send hunters & teams back several miles after that. Accordingly it was decided to go to the banks of the Platte & halt until we could get the Buffalo meat & then pursue our journey as we best could.

Sunday 17 October 1847–Leek Wakes Sunday.[89] Warm day, Clear Sky. The Hunters–John Brown, Luke Johnson, Amasa Lyman, Thomas Carns, Ralph Douglas, William Park, Wilford Woodruff, George Billings, Joseph Egbert, A. P. Chessley–go at 9 A.M. to kill Buffalo. Woolsey could not go because he had got no Tobacco (Pshaw). The Teams are gathered up & Camp removes at 9:13 down by the side of the Slough until we arrived at the mouth & our old camp ground of 2nd May last[90] [at] 10:17 having by taking nearer & straiter courses, [which] saved 13 miles of road between here & the Junction. Immediately after

---

[89] "Leek Wakes Sunday" may refer to a local holiday in Bullock's hometown, Leek, in Stratfordshire.
[90] This camp was near Elm Creek, Nebraska.

forming the caral, W. Woodruff's carriage followed the Hunters, also 3 Wagons.

Doctor at work dressing Raw Hides, also H. C. Kimball & Howard Egan, President Young & T. B. assisting shoeing President Young & Doctor's cows. About 4 P.M. the Wind blew strong from the North. Many brethren wash in the River.

Plenty of Tall dry grass close to the River Banks. The Slough is hemmed in with Willows & instead of being deep, as it was on 2 May, both it & the River are very shallow.

The Prairie back from the River is one immense Prairie Dog Town. Some of the brethren go to kill some of them.

In the afternoon 4 Wagons (with 10 or a dozen men) very heavy loaded go up the South side of the river. They are going to build an opposition Fort a few miles this side of Fort John.[91]

At Sundown the Wind commenced blowing a perfect hurricane & continued until Sunrise next morning. The Wagons rocked like a Ship in a Storm, the Wind roaring terribly.

Monday 18 October 1847—As the Sun rose, it was very cold, but the Wind has in a great measure subsided.

It being decided that we had better resume our journey, Tom Woolsey was sent to the Hunters to order them to return to Camp to night with what meat they had got. We went to work to hunt up the teams.

[A]bout 9 o'clock it was found that the Black mare belonging to President Young & driven by John G. Luce was missing. It had been watched by Atwood till breakfast time, who wanted Luce to watch but he refused. Several went to hunt over the ground that Luce said he had hunted, where they found it mired. President Young, Kimball & Benson, with Captains Markham, Adams & others go & pull her out. When she is brought to Camp, [we] hitched up and teams start at 10:45 over & thro' a Prairie Dog Town of several miles, when to our great joy we saw 3 Wagons & a number of horsemen coming towards us, when they stopt with the first wagons & proved to be 16 brethren from Winter Quarters (see their names at the bottom of this page) together with Stephen H. Goddard, one of our Express, & Jackson Redding, one of the Ox Team

---

[91] This was the John S. Shaw and Robert Wilson party of twelve men; the "venture was later reported a profitable one." See Barry, *The Beginning of the West*, 719.

Company who turned back at the Loup Fork.[92] The Ox Company were putting ahead about 20 or 25 miles a day, thus not only breaking their Covenant at the valley, but also the letter left by Wm. Clayton at Rattlesnake Creek. After saluting, hugging & blessing each other for some time, we continued our route thro' the Dog Town & camped on the banks of the Platt at [blank] having plenty of grass, wood & water. Fine day, cool breeze from West.

Woolsey on his return reporting that he had seen from 3 to 500 Pawnees on the South side of the River about 5 miles above our Camp, putting up their Wicka ups, President Young thought it wisdom to send up a company to put them on their Guard & return to our Camp this night, when Hosea Stout, Wilber F. Earl, Wm. D. Huntington, Wm. Martindale, Jackson J. Redding & Jos. Mathews went on the Express at 7 P.M. A fine night.

Geo. W. Langley very sick. Administered composition & Lobella.

All of the Twelve in Camp meet in Doctor's Wagon. T. B. reads the newspapers to them.

Tuesday 19 October 1847–Severe frost. Ice nearly covered the creek. Camp lays by all day. Fine day, SW wind. The animals generally on the rushes on the Islands. Several brethren wash Clothes.

Several go to the Island to kill some Buffalo that have been seen there last night.

Others go to hunt Prairie Dogs. Generally a still quiet day.

T. B. suffers much head ache & W. Richards & O. Pratt lay hands on him to rebuke his sickness.

A Sun Dog was seen when the Sun was about an hour high. About 9 P.M. the Express & Hunters returned, bringing 3 Wagons loaded with meat, having the Carcasses of nine Buffalos & Woolsey's report of Indians is all fudge; there being no signs of Indians or Wika ups for several miles round. President Kimball & Company returned to Camp having

---

[92] On 6 October, the High Council at Winter Quarters learned that troops had been dispatched from Fort Kearny to Grand Island. As Hosea Stout noted, "we were not certain as to their intentions towards us so the council thought best to send me with a company of men to meet the pioneers and put them on their guard and also assist them in case they need us." Stout and his men met Jack Redding on 15 October and discovered Stephen Goddard "lying by the road fast asleep" the next day. Stout found the pioneer company "strung along the road some on foot & some a Horse back for three or four miles....They were worn down with fatigue and hunger with many an anxious thought on home and the welfare of their families & the church. Many of their animals had to be lifted up every time they laid down." See Brooks, ed., *On the Mormon Frontier*, 1:278, 282–283.

[Hosea Stout's Relief Party from Winter Quarters]			
Hosea Stout	21 Shots	Wm. Martindale	1
Geo. D. Grant	11	Wm D. Huntington	8
Gardiner Potter	1	Luman H. Calkins	9
Wm. Kimball	21	Jas. W. Cummings	15
Jacob Frazier	1	Lum. L. Thornton	1
Geo. W. Langley	3	Levi Nickerson	6
Wilber F. Earl	6	Jas. H. Glines	1
Wm. Meeks	3	Chancey Whiting	<u>3</u>
		<u>16</u> Persons	<u>111</u> Shots

killed one cow. President Young divided a Canteen of Spirits among the brethren [and] visited the Guard to see that they were on duty, as usual.

Wednesday 20 October 1847–Cold, raw, dull cloudy morning. SE wind. Luke Johnson gave T. B. a tongue to take to his family & I do sincerely hope that I can preserve it from the fingers of the thief who stole his & the Doctor's tongues.

Thursday 21 October 1847–Very cold day, keen wind from NE. T. B. riding Doctor's poney.

After cooking breakfast, Teams were gathered up. Dull cold cloudy morn. Camp starts at 9:35 keeping the lower or bottom road, until we had passed the "Big Camp" ground, when we turned to our left to the open ground where the short Buffalo Grass admitted of a much better road. Then continued in nearly a strait course towards the "Wood River," which, instead of crossing, we turned off the road to our right & camped in the Dry Bed of part of the Platte River, near the entrance of Wood River.[93] As the Wind still continues to blow very strong, our animals will be pretty well sheltered. Here we found an excellent bed of rushes which all the animals are very fond of. Some of the brethren in going after a flock of Turkies reported that he had discovered signs of Indians having been here recently, which caused many of the brethren to go into the wood and watch their animals.

Thro' the very severe weather TB caught a violent inflamation in his eyes. Wilford Woodruff [was] mouth at laying on of hands to rebuke [the] complaint. Willard Richards had a very narrow escape from Palsy. He was so very much enfeebled that "I could not remember the name of

---

[93] The party camped near present Central City, Nebraska. From here, they left the Platte and turned north to the Loup.

that boy (T. B.) who has been close to my elbows for the last five years." The wind moderated about 8 P.M. when it became much milder. James H. Glines fixes a new front to the Doctor's Wagon to make it warmer.

Full Moon 6:06 P.M. Sharp Frost.

Saturday 23 October 1847–Arose at 3 A.M. to watch the mules, went on Guard, by myself [and watched] the Aurora Borealis appearing very beautiful, changing red & white streaks alternately, sometimes brighter, at other times very faint & continued in sight until Sunrise. When the moon set, it went down in the most curious way possible. Altho' [a] full moon this evening, the upper half was entirely square & the lower part, next the Earth, like 2 small wings supporting the half Globe. Professor Pratt declared he never saw such a sight before. At Sunrise the Camp was ready to start, which Professor Pratt requested might be recorded, as the first instance that the Camp was ready to start at the time appointed.[94] They then attempted to cross the Prairie creek, Levi Nickerson grading the upper bank, but in consequence of the difficult crossing, many of the Wagons went about a mile lower down & found a good crossing. A dead bough was stuck up here by some of the former Saints as a guide to the place. [We] then took a northerly course over a great succession of small hills [following] generally a good road, not much sand, until we had passed the highest ridge when the Road bears away towards the East over a good road & level prairie, until we descend to the Loup Fork; going thro' dry Prairie Grass all the way until we came to a small Island, having small Cotton Wood Trees & brush on it & on the banks, where we halt at ½ past 3 & form our Circle on the South Bank.[95]

A Clear blue Sky. Westerly breeze.

Doctor some better. Such was the great hurry for me to get up at 3 A.M. to watch mules that when I was on duty, B. Richmond went to bed again. I shall rejoice when I finish this journey that I may be a little more my own master.

Sunday 24 October 1847–Sharp frost thro' night. Hunted up cows & Poney & did all the chores about the Wagon. An attempt at crossing was made about 9 o'clock. Levi Nickerson & 2 others in crossing on

---

[94] Orson Pratt's ironic observation reflects today's "Mormon Standard Time," which runs five to ten minutes behind other clocks.

[95] The party had reached the Loup Fork.

horseback to shew the way; Nickerson & [blank] fell down & floundered in the Water. Then led their horses across. Four Wagons rushing in, before they were ordered, stick in the Sand & Mud. Markham by doubling Teams gets out & comes to shore. George D. Grant's Wagon getting fast & the Water about 6 inches in the Wagon box, Presidents Kimball, Lyman & several brethren wade in & pull it out. T.B. taking in a rope, it was hitched to the tongue of another Wagon & the brethren pulled that out, without any horses attached. When all were out of the Water, President Young distributed a canteen of Spirits to them. The Wind blowing very severe, it was deemed prudent to remove down to Cotton Wood Grove for shelter & rest for the Sabbath & accordingly the Camp removed down about a mile. Several brethren climb the Trees & cut off the Limbs for our animals to eat. There is plenty of tall dry grass about this place. The Weather continued very severe all afternoon.

Doctor Washing, T.B. very busy fetching water & boiling & fifty other things. Amasa Lyman with Doctor in the Wagon, eating Pop corn, reading "Library of Useful Knowledge" &c &c. Brother Lyman is going Express to Winter Quarters to ease their minds about our safety & welfare as soon as we are safe on the other side of the "Loup Fork."

A large Circle round the moon. Geese flying South.

Monday 25 October 1847–About 11 last night a Snow Storm commenced & continued thro' [a] great part of the night. Many geese fly in the night [and] keep up a continued chatter. After breakfast Presidents Young & Kimball call for volunteers to go & search out a fording place & when they had succeeded, they stuck stakes to guide the Teamsters through. The second Wagon stuck in the Sand, but was soon released again, also E. T. Benson's. All the [other] Wagons get thro' in perfect safety. T.B. drove the Cows thro' [and] got wet like the rest. Levi Nickerson found an ox on the North bank, which was sent from some of the Battalion to assist up Joseph Young next Spring. When all the Wagons were on the hill, T.B. called the Roll to see that all were safe, when the Wagons filed off in due order going along the Bluff, crossing upwards of 60 Pawnee trails in different groups. [We] went across two ravines, crossing a small muddy creek, going over a bottom land & then ascended to the remains of "old Pawnee Town" where we found excellent green grass. Our animals here filled well. [We] also saw many Geese, Ducks,

Prairie hens & other birds. It being deemed advisable to send our Express to Winter Quarters to quiet the fears & anxieties of the Saints concerning us, Doctor dictates & TB writes a letter to the Saints there, which is read to the President & approved, then copied & signed. [We] make up a mail of 8 letters & gives same to [blank].

[*No entries for October 26 and 27. Bullock left pages 41 and 42 blank.*]

Thursday 28 October 1847–Severe frost in the night. Strong Wind blowing from the South East kept up a continued roar among the Trees, but as we had got a well sheltered camping spot, [we] did not suffer much from the cold. The brethren cut down more Cotton Wood Trees & feed to the animals. Camp starts at ¼ to 8 & soon passes the place where we saw the Pawnee Village last April. It appears that the Loup Fork enters the Platte a short distance below this Point. Continue down about ½ mile from the River in an Easterly direction in nearly a strait line, until we came to the banks of a Slough. Continued down by its side until we came to the mouth, when we halted to water the animals [and] then passed over two small mounds of sand, which when we had got over we took a strait line, over an excellent road, to the "Shell creek" where we camped for the night at ¼ past 3, [having] travelled 7 hours at a good pace [for a total of] 25 miles. The Grass all the way is perfectly dry. Strong breeze from the South all day & the prairies being on fire on the South side of the River, we are in a cloud of Smoke all day, which gives all the brethren a very dirty appearance.

At this place there was beautiful feed when our brethren passed, but the ox team company appears to be determined we should not have any of it for what they did not eat, they set fire to, leaving us a prairie of burnt ashes. The Doctor says "the ox team company have gone on like a parcel of Geese: they eat all before them and shit on all behind them."[96]

[*End of the 1847 Trail Journals*]

---

[96] Here ends Bullock's 1847 trail journal in the camp on Shell Creek. On 30 October, a second relief party from Winter Quarters met the returning pioneers, who enjoyed a "perfect feast." Hosea Stout noted, "Many of the pioneers lately had subsisted on buffalo meat entirely for months and when this supply came in hardly knew when to quit eating." See Brooks, ed., *On the Mormon Frontier*, 1:286. The company reached Winter Quarters on Sunday, 31 October 1847.

AFTERWORD
The Triumph of Brigham Young and the Road to Great Salt Lake City, 1848

Brigham Young had won a bruising fight for leadership of the Mormon church in Nauvoo in 1844, but even as late as the fall of 1847 his position was still ambiguous. Although church conferences had repeatedly and unanimously sustained him as president of the Council of Twelve Apostles and even as president of the church, he had not been authorized to completely fill the second office. The First Presidency, the prophet and his two counselors who stood at the apex of the Mormon power structure, had not been reorganized since the death of Joseph Smith, and it was as leader of the Twelve Apostles that Brigham had directed the emigration. The return journey of the 1847 pioneers to Winter Quarters was in many ways a gamble—getting to the Salt Lake Valley with as few animals and supplies as the Mormons had was an audacious achievement in itself—but the overland march back to the Missouri of August to October 1847 posed as severe a test of Young's leadership as anything in his career—excepting, of course, his war with the U.S. government ten years later. During the return journey the Mormon leader delicately inquired of his fellow apostles "concerning one of the Twelve Apostles being appointed as President of the Church with his two Counsellors." Wilford Woodruff told him that he felt that such an act would require a revelation, but agreed, "whatever the Lord inspires you to do in this matter I am with you."[1] Young's bedraggled but triumphant return to Winter Quarters enforced his claim to undisputed power. He met with nine of the apostles on 30 November to make the

---
[1] Staker, ed., *Waiting for World's End*, 134.

proposal to the Twelve, and at a meeting of the quorum on 5 December 1847, Young overcame his reluctant colleagues. The apostles unanimously sustained Brigham Young as president, with Heber C. Kimball and Willard Richards as his counselors. The Saints met in conference on the twenty-seventh, after building a "Log Tabernacle" at Kanesville that Norton Jacob called "the biggest log cabin in the world." "The time has come," Orson Pratt said, to form a First Presidency "to defeat the adversary." The church membership sustained the new First Presidency without a dissenting vote. Although Brigham Young always denied that he was Joseph Smith's legal successor, merely referring to himself as "an apostle of Jesus Christ and Joseph Smith," he now wielded utlimate power over the LDS church.[2]

Two weeks before Young's confirmation the last of two companies of Mormon Battalion veterans had straggled into Winter Quarters, "having suffered much on their return from cold and hunger, with no provisions part of their way, but a little horse flesh of the worst kind." Andrew Lytle had led one party of veterans from the Sacramento to Great Salt Lake City; and following the tracks of P. C. Merrill's party, Lytle's band left the valley in mid-October for the Missouri.[3] The battalion veterans encountered no buffalo and weather so bad it froze the tips off their mules' ears.

With the largest concentration of Latter-day Saints gathered on the Missouri River and the remainder of the church scattered from the Mississippi valley to the Rocky Mountains, Young and his associates began organizing the 1848 emigration. From Winter Quarters Young issued a "General Epistle to the Saints throughout the Earth," a resounding call for a gathering to prepare for the exodus to the Rocky Mountains, "bringing their money, goods, and effects" and all the stock they could gather to the Missouri by the first of May. Young directed the Saints in Great Britain "and adjacent islands and countries" to "come immediately and prepare to go West." He asked them to bring "all kinds of choice seeds, of grain, vegetables, fruits, shrubbery, trees, and vines— every thing that will please the eye, gladden the heart, or cheer the soul

---

[2] Bennett, *The Mormons at the Missouri*, 211–14; and Quinn, *The Mormon Hierarchy: Origins of Power*, 251.

[3] *Millennial Star* (15 March 1848), 83. Fifteen men arrived at Winter Quarters on 11 December, while "in all about thirty" of the "pennyless and destitute" battalion veterans arrived on 18 December. See Little, *From Kirtland to Salt Lake City*, 160–62.

of man." He called for "the best of tools of every description" and all types of machinery and farming utensils "such as corn shellers, grain threshers and cleaners, smut machines, mills, and every implement and article within their knowledge that shall tend to promote the comfort, health, happiness, or prosperity of any people."[4] Young's call reflected the euphoria of his recent triumphs, but it was at least partly motivated by the need for the Saints to leave Winter Quarters, which stood on Indian land.[5]

"On the last day of May," Bullock wrote from the trail at the beginning of the 1848 trek, "Our beloved President, Brigham Young, commenced organizing the people" into their tens, fifties, and hundreds on the west bank of the Elkhorn. The "gathering up of Zion" was organized into three great companies led by Brigham Young, Heber C. Kimball, and Amasa Lyman and totaled 2,408 people in 923 wagons. Surprisingly, the parties included twenty-four black pioneers.[6] Bullock felt that if someone asked the question, "Is Mormonism down?" simply seeing "such a host of wagons...would have satisfied him in an instant that it lives and flourishes like a tree by a fountain of waters; he would have seen merry faces, and heard the song of rejoicing, that the day of deliverance had surely come." On the first of June, Young dispatched Lorenzo Snow's company to the Liberty Pole on the Platte, and the hundreds of Zera Pulsipher and William Perkins followed on Friday and Saturday. On the fifth, 1,220 people, 397 wagons, and 2,251 animals in "President Young's company took up their line of march." The Saints now began "their journey into the wilderness, over these immense prairies, barren sage plains, sterile lands, and Rocky Mountains; that they might gather into the valley, which is hidden up in the bosom of the mountains, in the tops of the everlasting hills."[7]

There were fundamental differences between the pioneer company of 1847 and the mass migration of 1848. First, this expedition was made up of families, so the bachelor atmosphere of the 1847 adventure was

---
[4] *Millennial Star* (15 March 1848), 84–85.
[5] See Trennert, "The Mormons and the Office of Indian Affairs: The Conflict over Winter Quarters, 1846–1848," 381–400, for an excellent discussion of the problems surrounding the Mormon settlement. The stake high council formally decided to abandon Winter Quarters in January 1848.
[6] Kimball, *Heber C. Kimball*, 149, 280.
[7] Bullock to Richards, *Millennial Star* (15 October 1848), 313–14.

gone, making Bullock's 1848 journal a much more typical overland narrative than his 1847 account. Much of Bullock's 1848 journal was very prosaic, containing many comments on daily routine and trail life, illustrating that an overland trek was in many ways an extended camping trip. Details about managing animals consumed a surprising amount of space and showed the tremendous importance of the stock that powered a wagon train.

The Saints also now had the advantage of "the most complete and reliable guide available for any strand of the Overland Trail," William Clayton's remarkable *The Latter-Day Saints' Emigrants' Guide*.[8] The book was based on his journal and odometer readings, and Clayton had 5,000 copies of this useful guide printed in February 1848; it sometimes retailed on the trail for as much as $5.00 a copy. Bullock contributed much to the guide, providing several "epitomes"—summaries—of the company's mileages and camps and sharing his journal with his fellow Englishman. On 3 July 1847, Bullock had noted that he combined Clayton's table of distances with his own "synopsis Journal"—which he called "a troublesome job." Bullock even sold the book at the Mormon camps, but Clayton's extremely popular guide, which was occasionally pirated and regularly plagiarized, contained no acknowledgment of the contributions of Orson Pratt, Willard Richards—or Thomas Bullock.[9]

In 1848 Bullock traveled most of the way to Salt Lake with the Brigham Young company instead of joining the party of his adopted father, Willard Richards. Bullock may have been directed to keep Young's official journal—or he may simply have resented the fact that Richards had ejected him from his wagon the previous fall to make room for hides to trade, forcing the long-suffering scribe to walk down the Platte to Winter Quarters.

The Mormon Trail west in 1848 followed the main course of the 1847 route, with improvements made and shortcuts taken where possible. "I, Thomas Bullock (the Church Scribe)" oversaw management of the "Big Wagon" the wagon that carried the precious records of the LDS church part of the way to the Salt Lake Valley. Bullock also brought both his wives

---

[8] Clayton's guide was published in St. Louis in 1848. For its complete title, see the Bibliography. The comment is from Stegner, *Gathering of Zion*, 199.

[9] See Kimball, ed., *The Latter-Day Saints' Emigrants' Guide by William Clayton*, for a recent edition.

and their families, noting that Lucy Clayton Bullock sometimes drove his team, helped hunt up lost stock, and gathered firewood and berries.[10] He only once mentioned his first wife, Henrietta Rushton Bullock, reporting on 12 September 1848, "Henrietta sick."

Bullock's 1848 journal chronicled the journey up the Platte Valley and the crossing of it tributaries, the Papillion and Elkhorn, and the ascent of the Loup and the passing of Shell, Looking Glass, Beaver, Plum, Ash, and Cedar creeks. West of Chimney Rock, Brigham Young divided the companies on 16 July to handle the drier trail conditions. Bullock and his family were assigned to Isaac Morley's fifty, but on the Sweetwater on 24 August, Young ordered Bullock to rejoin his company "to be on hand to do the writing." In the last days of summer, the Camp of Israel arrived at Big Mountain. Here Bullock rejoiced: "on reaching the Summit & again seeing the Valley my Soul could not refrain crying out Hosanna to God & the Lamb for ever, Amen." Thomas Bullock, his families, and his religion had found Zion, their refuge in the Rocky Mountains.

The Saints did not long enjoy the isolation Brigham Young was seeking. As Young learned on the trail west in 1848, the gentile leader of a Mormon work party at Sutter's Mill had discovered gold in California, and the news launched one of the largest migrations in history, the 1849 gold rush. Many of the tens of thousands of Americans who went west over the next two years visited Great Salt Lake City, helping to insure the survival of the struggling settlement. The existence of the first city between the Missouri and Sacramento Rivers would transform the very nature of wagon travel and America's overland trails forever. Instead of finding solitude, the Mormons would build their new Zion at the crossroads of the West.

Bullock ended his trail journal on 21 September 1848, and later that day the clerk and his families arrived in Great Salt Lake City. Bullock made no entries in his journal again for another week, but on Friday, 29 September, he recorded, "Henrietta, Wife of Thomas Bullock, safely delivered of a fine daughter, 9 pounds, at Sunrise by Mrs. Singley"—his first mention of his wife's pregnancy in his journal. The daughter, Mary Elizabeth Bullock, lived until 1930.

---

[10] Thomas Bullock, 1848 Journal, 7, 9, and 12 August 1848, LDS Archives.

A GALAXY OF MORMON PIONEERS
Biographical Sketches

These biographical sketches provide information about most of the Latter-day Saints mentioned in Thomas Bullock's Mormon Trail journals. I supply more detail on the obscure stars in the Mormon constellation than I give for their more famous companions. Related individuals are listed as families, but the grouping by immediate families only begins to suggest the complicated kinship patterns that existed among the early Mormons. Each of the people in the 1847 Brigham Young company is identified as a "member of the 1847 pioneer company," although this term reflects the composition of the party when it arrived at Fort Laramie, and some of its members, such as William Empey, did not actually make it to the Salt Lake Valley in 1847. Towns not identified by state are in Utah. Unless otherwise noted, quotations and information are from Andrew Jenson, ed., *Latter-day Saint Biographical Encyclopedia*. These initials identify other sources:

WB	Will Bagley, ed., *Frontiersman: Abner Blackburn's Narrative*.
DB	Davis Bitton, *Guide to Mormon Diaries & Autobiographies*.
SEB	Susan Easton Black, *Early Members of The Church of Jesus Christ of Latter-day Saints* (InfoBases LDS Collectors Library CD-ROM).
JB	Juanita Brooks, ed., *On the Mormon Frontier: The Diary of Hosea Stout*.
DUP	Daughters of Utah Pioneers, *The First Company to Enter Salt Lake Valley*.
FE	Frank Esshom, *Pioneers and Prominent Men of Utah*.
RH	Corrected dates provided by Robert K. Hoshide.
SBK	Stanley B. Kimball, *Heber C. Kimball: Mormon Patriarch and Pioneer*.
GK	Greg R. Knight, ed., *Thomas Bullock Nauvoo Journal*.
CL	Carl V. Larson, *A Data Base of the Mormon Battalion*.
DLT	Dan L. Thrapp, *Encyclopedia of Frontier Biography*.
HS	Harold Schindler, *Orrin Porter Rockwell: Man of God, Son of Thunder*.
GS	Gene A. Sessions, *Mormon Thunder: A Documentary History of Jedediah Morgan Grant*.

Barnabas Lothrop Adams (1812–69). A member of the 1847 pioneer company, Adams was born in Canada. He became "accustomed to river work when floating logs down the Mississippi River from Iowa to St. Louis." He furnished timber for the Salt Lake Tabernacle, the theater, and other public buildings. Adams died suddenly at his home in Salt Lake.

Orval Morgan Allen (1805–93). Born in Pike County, Missouri, Allen was a "lineal descendant" of Revolutionary War hero Ethan Allen. His father disinherited him when he joined the LDS church in 1838. He was a member of Joseph Smith's Nauvoo bodyguard and pushed through to the Missouri with the first of the 1846 companies. Captain of the 1846 "Poor Camp" during its crossing of Iowa, Allen did not go to Utah until 1852, when he led a company across the plains. He settled at Springville, Spanish Fork, and Toquerville, and served as a probate judge in Kanab, Utah. At seventy-five, he pioneered Pima, Arizona, where he died, the father of fifteen children. FE.

Rufus C. Allen (1814–87). A member of the 1847 pioneer company and a returning pioneer, Allen was born in Connecticut. Allen served as the first president of the Southern Indian Mission and eventually settled in Ogden.

George Alley (1792–1859). A shoemaker born in Massachusetts, Alley joined the LDS church in 1842. An 1848 pioneer, Alley settled in Bountiful. SEB.

The Allreds. James Allred (1784–1876) was a member of Zion's Camp and came to Utah in 1851 to become one of the first settlers of Sanpete County. His son, James Tillmon Sanford Allred (1825–1905), served in the Mormon Battalion. His brother, Isaac Allred (1788–1870), was a member of the 1847 second division and was known as Father Allred. His sons, Redick Newton Allred (1822–1905) and James Riley Allred (1827–71), served in the Mormon Battalion. The entire family settled at Spring City, Utah. GS.

Truman Osborn Angell (1810–87). A member of the 1847 pioneer company, Angell was a brother-in-law of Brigham Young. As church architect, he designed the Salt Lake Temple, the Tabernacle, the St. George Temple, and "many other important public buildings." He served as patriarch in Salt Lake City.

Millen Atwood (1817–90). A member of the 1847 pioneer company, a returning pioneer, and a member of the 1848 Brigham Young company, Atwood was born in Connecticut. From 1852–56 he served a mission to Great Britain and "suffered much when he returned with the Willie handcart company." At his death he was a bishop in Salt Lake City.

Almon W. Babbitt (1813–56). Babbitt was born in Massachusetts and was a member of Zion's Camp and president of the Kirtland Stake in the 1840s. He came to Utah in 1848 and served as territorial secretary from 1853. The Cheyenne killed Babbitt as he was returning from Washington. GS.

Rodney Badger (1823–53). A member of the 1847 pioneer company, Badger was born in Vermont. He was a member of the Nauvoo Legion, a special agent of the Perpetual Emigrating Fund Company, and deputy sheriff of Salt Lake County. He accidentally drowned in the Weber River trying to save an emigrant family bound for California.

John Bair (1810–84). Born in Pennsylvania, Bair joined the LDS church in 1834. He was a leader of the Poor Camp and had arrived in Utah by 1850, where he built the first ferry on the Bear River and the first saw mill in Davis County. SEB.

Robert Erwin Baird (1817–75). A member of the 1847 pioneer company, Baird was born in Londonderry, Ireland. He settled in Weber County and served as justice of the peace and city councilman in Ogden.

Lewis Barney (1808–94). New Yorker Lewis Barney joined the LDS church the spring of 1840. He crossed Iowa in 1846 and was a member of the 1847 pioneer company. In Utah he was noted as an Indian fighter. Barney died at Mancos, Colorado, leaving a large family.

Charles David Barnum (1800–94). A member of the 1847 pioneer company, Barnum was born in Canada and was baptized in 1836. He lived at Nauvoo where he quarried rock for the temple. He returned to his family at Winter Quarters in 1847, but they refused to accompany him west. Barnum returned to Utah in 1850 and died in Salt Lake City.

Rufus Beach (1795–1850). A native of Connecticut, Beach was a merchant at Winter Quarters and had a son born shortly after reaching Utah in the fall of 1847. He died in California. SEB, FE.

Ezra T. Benson (1811–69). An apostle, a member of the 1847 pioneer company, and a returning pioneer, Benson was born in Massachusetts and joined the LDS church in 1840. He returned to Salt Lake in 1849 and served in the Utah territorial legislature. Benson died unexpectedly in Ogden.

John M. Bernhisel (1799–1881). Born in Pennsylvania and trained as a medical doctor, Bernhisel was Utah's territorial representative to Congress for eight turbulent years in the 1850s.

The Billings. A captain in the 1848 emigration, Titus Billings (1793–1866) was born in Massachusetts and joined the LDS church in Kirtland in 1830. He fought in the Battle of Crooked River in 1838 and lived in Nauvoo. He married Diantha Morley and died in Provo. His son, Alfred Nelson Billings (1825–81), led the Elk Mountain Mission that founded Moab, Utah. Alfred's daughter, Diantha Billings, was a midwife and member of the 1848 emigration. Titus' son George Pierce Billings (1827–96) was born in Kirtland and was a member of the 1847 pioneer company. He left Utah for California, but later filled a LDS mission to Carson Valley, Nevada. He finally settled in Manti, Utah. SEB.

Abner Blackburn (1827–1904). A veteran of the Mormon Battalion, Blackburn accompanied James Brown to California and back in 1847. He helped found Mormon Station in Carson Valley in 1850 and settled in San Bernardino in 1851.

Curtis Edward Bolton (1812-1890). Among the last Saints to leave Nauvoo, Bolton had joined the LDS church by 1842. He apparently came to Utah in 1848 and was called to serve in the French Mission with John Taylor in 1849. He translated the *Book of Mormon* into French and returned to Utah in 1853. Bolton died at Marysvale, Utah.

Francis Boggs (1807–89). Boggs was born in Ohio. A member of the 1847 pioneer company, he returned to Winter Quarters with the ox teams and later served a term in the Utah territorial legislature. Boggs settled at Washington, Utah, where he died, the father of eleven children.

Samuel Brannan (1819–89). Born in Maine, Brannan led some 230 Mormons around Cape Horn to California in the ship *Brooklyn* in 1846 and met the pioneer company at Green River in 1847. His attempt to lure Brigham Young to California failed and Brannan apostatized in 1849. Brannan acquired great wealth and influence in the gold rush, but ultimately died in poverty.

James Brown (1801–63). Born in North Carolina, Brown joined the LDS church in 1838 and settled at Nauvoo. He served as captain of Company C in the Mormon Battalion and conducted the sick detachments from Santa Fé to Pueblo and Salt Lake. In the fall of 1847 he collected the battalion's back pay in California; Samuel Brannan wrote to Brigham Young to accuse Brown of defrauding the government while on the trip. The Saints used the battalion pay to purchase Miles Goodyear's claim and Brown settled at Ogden, where he died in an accident involving a molasses mill. JB, WB.

John Brown (1820–97). A member of the 1847 pioneer company, Brown was born in Tennessee and led the Mississippi Saints to Fort Laramie and Pueblo in 1846. In 1847 he was a member of Orson Pratt's advance company. A first-rate frontiersman, Brown crossed the plains thirteen times. He served as bishop and patriarch of Pleasant Grove.

The Browns. A member of the 1847 pioneer company, Nathaniel Thomas Brown (?–1848) returned to Winter Quarters and was accidentally shot at Council Bluffs in February 1848. Brigham Young said that Brown's old shoes were worth more than the whole body of the man who killed him. His son, George Washington Brown (1827–1906), was born in Ohio and was Thomas Bullock's "bedfellow" and critic during the 1847 trek. He returned to Winter Quarters in 1847 and went to Utah with his mother, a brother, and a sister in 1850. He settled at Charleston, Utah, where he died. SEB.

Harrison Burgess (1814–83). A member of Zion's Camp, Burgess was born in New York and was baptized in 1832. He was bishop of Pine Valley, where he died.

Charles Allen Burk (1823–80). A member of the 1847 pioneer company, Burk was born in Kirtland. He "endured persecutions with the saints in Missouri, and was forced to vacate his home in Nauvoo." He was active in pioneer enterprises and died at Minersville.

Jacob D. Burnham (1820–50). A member of the 1847 pioneer company, Burnham was born in New York. "He remained only a short time with the saints in the Salt Lake Valley" and died in California.

Robert Walton Burton (1826–?). A blacksmith and member of the Poor Camp, Burton was born in England and was endowed in the Nauvoo Temple on 6 February 1846. He married Elizabeth Marriott. In 1870, Burton was living at Bear River City, Utah. SEB.

Robert Taylor Burton (1821–1907). Born in Canada, Burton joined the LDS church in 1838 and two years later moved to Nauvoo, where he was a bugler in the legion. He was one of the first to cross the Mississippi after it froze in February 1846, and was bugler for Brigham Young's 1848 company—though Bullock made no mention of him. He served as a territorial marshal, as a major-general in the Utah militia, and as sheriff of Great Salt Lake County. He led a savage assault against the "Morrisites" in

June 1862, but became a bishop in Salt Lake and was a legislator and university regent.

The Cahoons. An 1848 pioneer, a native of New York, and a veteran of the War of 1812, Reynolds Cahoon (1790–1861) was one of the first settlers in Ohio, where he joined the Mormons in 1830. In May 1845, Cahoon commented "with his usual sneer" on Bullock's reliance on the Temple Store, where the clerk was paid "in kind" for his services. Bullock wrote, "I can not bring myself to like that man—his ways do not suit me—why he should act so—God only knows—I do not recollect having done any thing to cause it." His son, Andrew Cahoon (1824–1900), was later the bishop of South Cottonwood. GK.

Robert Lang Campbell (1825–72). A Scotsman and close friend of Thomas Bullock, Campbell was selected as a member of the pioneer company but was detained as a clerk at Winter Quarters. He explored southern Utah in 1849 with Parley Pratt, was chief clerk in the LDS Historian's Office, and served as superintendent of schools in Utah territory.

Albert Carrington (1813–89). A member of the 1847 pioneer company, Carrington was born at Vermont and claimed to be a Dartmouth graduate. He joined the LDS church in Wisconsin in 1841. He was Brigham Young's representative with the Stansbury Expedition and was one of the first editors of the *Deseret News*. Carrington was made an apostle on 3 July 1870, but "on account of transgression" he was temporarily disfellowshipped in November 1885. He rejoined the LDS church before his death in Salt Lake City.

William Carter (1821–96). A member of the 1847 pioneer company, Carter was born in Ledbury, England. He came to Nauvoo in 1841, where he married Ellen Benbow. After serving six months in the Utah Territorial Penitentiary for illegal cohabitation, he received a medal in 1888 for plowing the first furrows in the Salt Lake Valley.

James Case (1794–1858). A member of the 1847 pioneer company, Case was born in Connecticut and worked at the Pawnee Mission in 1846. He settled in Sanpete Valley in 1851 and represented the area in the territorial legislature. He died in Sanpete in 1858 after returning from "a successful mission to the Cherokee Indians, in Oklahoma."

Solomon Chamberlain (1788–1862). Chamberlain was born in Connecticut. A member of the 1847 pioneer company, "he had a full suit of buckskin with a wolf skin cap, tanned with the ears on to resemble that animal which he used as a disguise when engaged in secret missions, and which gained for him the name of 'old buckskin.'" The pioneers voted him the most even-tempered man in the camp—"invariably cross." He died at Washington, Utah.

Alexander Philip Chesley (1814–84). A member of the 1847 pioneer company, Chesley was born in Virginia. He served as constable in Provo and filled a mission to Australia in 1856–57. Later he lived at Fillmore and represented Millard County in the territorial legislature. He was a farmer and stockman and died in Orange, Australia.

James Albert Chesney (1824–64?). Although a native of Missouri, Chesney was among the Mississippi Saints who entered Salt Lake Valley on 22 July 1847. He settled in southern Utah and died at Panaca, Nevada.

George Sheffer Clark (1816–91). A sick detachment veteran and a captain of ten in the returning pioneers, Clark was one of the founders of Pleasant Grove, Utah. CL.

William Clayton (1814–79). Thomas Bullock's brother-in-law, Clayton was born at Penwortham, England, and was one of the first LDS converts in England. He emigrated to Nauvoo in 1840 and in 1842 succeeded Willard Richards as clerk to Joseph Smith. He wrote the famous hymn "Come, Come, Ye Saints" in 1846 and created what is arguably the best journal of the 1847 pioneer trek. Clayton accompanied the ox train on its return to Winter Quarters in 1847 and compiled and published his famous *Latter Day Saints' Emigrants' Guide* during the winter. He came west again in 1848, after which he lived in Great Salt Lake City, where he served as treasurer of ZCMI, territorial recorder of marks and brands, and auditor of public accounts. He died in Utah, survived by a large family.

Thomas Poulson Cloward (1823–1909). A member of the 1847 pioneer company, Cloward was born in Pennsylvania. He returned to Winter Quarters in the fall of 1847 and did not come back to Utah until 1852. He was a shoemaker and is said to have made the first pair of fine shoes in the territory. He located in Provo and in 1862 moved to Payson, where he died.

Zebedee Coltrin (1804–87). A member of Zion's Camp, the 1847 pioneer company, and a returning pioneer, Coltrin was born in New York and was one of the seven presidents of Seventy. Coltrin returned to Utah with his family and settled at Spanish Fork, where he was patriarch.

Henry Lyman Cook (1803–69). A New Yorker, Cook was baptized in 1837 and was a member of the Poor Camp. He came to Utah in 1850 and died in Iron County.

James Craig (1821–68). Craig was born in Ireland, and the Museum of Church History and Art displays the instrument he used as "Bugler of the Pioneers." He located for a time in Mill Creek and in 1854 was called on a mission to Great Britain where he served as president of the Preston Conference and labored in Ireland. He crossed the plains with Thomas Bullock in 1858. In 1861 Craig was called to settle southern Utah. A successful cotton farmer, he died at Santa Clara, Utah.

Oscar Crosby (1815–70). One of three African-Americans with the 1847 pioneer company, Crosby was born in Virginia and was a slave of William Crosby, a wealthy convert from Mississippi. Crosby, John Brown, John H. Bankhead, and William Lay each sent a slave west in charge of John Brown, accompanied by a "family or two" of Saints. En route two of the four blacks died, but Oscar Crosby and Hark Lay "accompanied the Pioneers on their journey rendering good service on the way." Crosby died in Los Angeles.

The Crows. Robert Crow (1794-?) and his wife Elizabeth Brown Crow (cousin of John Brown) joined the LDS church in Illinois in 1838; they were part of the Mississippi Saints that joined the pioneer company at Fort Laramie. Their daughters, Matilda Jane Crow (wife of George Threlkill), Elizabeth Jane Crow, and twins Ida Vinda Exene Crow (?-1851) and Ira Minda Almarene Crow (?-1860) and sons, Benjamin B. Crow (1824-1897) and his wife Harriet Blunt, Walter Hamilton Crow (1826-1906) and wife Mary Jane Stewart (1817–82), John McHenry Crow (1830-1894)—a rebellious member of the returning pioneers—and William Parker Crow were not considered official members of the 1847 pioneer company, but arrived in Salt Lake Valley on 22 July 1847. SEB.

Lyman Curtis (1812–98). A member of Zion's Camp, the 1847 pioneer company, and a returning pioneer, Curtis was born in Massachusetts and was baptized about 1833. He followed the Saints from Missouri to Illinois and Winter Quarters. Curtis brought his family to Utah in 1850. In 1853 he went to southern Utah and was said to have picked the first cotton raised in Utah. He settled in Utah County as one of the pioneers of Salem, choosing that name to honor his birthplace. He died there, father of a large family.

Hosea Cushing (1826–54). A teamster with the 1847 pioneer company and a returning pioneer, Cushing was born in Boston, Massachusetts. He returned to Great Salt Lake City with his wife, Helen Janet Murray, in 1848 and died there of consumption, or perhaps from the effects of an ordeal experienced during the Walker War. DUP.

James Davenport (1802–85). A member of the 1847 pioneer company, Davenport was born in Danville, Vermont. He died at Richmond, Utah.

Daniel C. Davis (1808–92). Born in Massachusetts, Davis joined the LDS church in 1845. He was the man Bullock saw "baptized" by a mob in September 1846. Davis worked as a laborer, served a mission to England from 1856–57, and died in Bountiful, Utah.

Daniel Coon Davis (1804–50). A New Yorker, Davis was captain of Company E in the Mormon Battalion. He led the company that reenlisted in California for six months' service. He settled near Farmington, and died at Fort Kearny while attending to personal business. Davis County, Utah, was named for him.

The Deckers. Two sons of Isaac Decker and Harriet Page Wheeler (later married to Brigham Young) came to Utah in 1847. Charles Decker (1824–1901) was a member of the Poor Camp relief and came to Utah in the Jedediah Grant company. He was a lieutenant in the Utah War and died at Vernal. One of the two boys in the 1847 pioneer company, Isaac Perry Decker (1840–1916) was born in Illinois. He remembered "the invasion of the crickets and the providential arrival of the sea gulls." He settled in Provo and "died of infirmities incident to his age."

Benjamin Franklin Dewey (1829–1904). A member of the 1847 pioneer company, Dewey was born in Massachusetts and was baptized by Wilford Woodruff at Winter Quarters in the spring of 1847. Dewey returned east with Brigham Young as far as Pacific Springs, where he met his family in Abraham O. Smoot's company. In 1849 he accompanied Jefferson Hunt to California and returned to Utah in 1850. He filled a mission to the East Indies in 1852–54, worked as a miner, and died in Chloride, Arizona.

John Dixon (1818–53). A member of the 1847 pioneer company, Dixon was born in Cumberland County, England. In 1850 he accompanied George Q. Cannon on a mission to the Hawaiian Islands. Indians killed Dixon and John Quayle on 17 August 1853 as they were hauling wood to Snyder's Mill near Parley's Park.

Absolom Porter Dowdle (1819–?). Ecclesiastical leader of the Mississippi Saints who had wintered at Pueblo, Dowdle was president of the Australian Mission in 1856–57.

Sterling Graves Driggs (1822–60). A member of the 1847 pioneer company, Driggs was born in Pennsylvania. Bullock's consistent phonetic spelling of his name as "Starling" gives some idea of the broad Yankee accent common among Mormon pioneers. He joined the LDS church in Ohio and moved to Nauvoo in 1840. In 1851 he helped found the settlement at San Bernardino. He married Sarah Rodgers in Great Salt Lake City 29 May 1855, and returned to California, remaining at San Bernardino until 1857 when he settled at Parowan. He died there in a threshing machine accident.

George Parker Dykes (1814–88). Born in Illinois, Dykes was a lieutenant in the Mormon Battalion. While German mission president from 1851–54, he helped John Taylor translate the *Book of Mormon*. Dykes died in Arizona.

William Dykes (1815–79). A member of the 1847 pioneer company and a returning pioneer, Dykes was born in Philadelphia. He was a Seventy in Nauvoo and lived in Great Salt Lake City as late as August 1856. He died in Nebraska.

The Earls. A member of the 1847 pioneer company, Sylvester Henry Earl (1815–72) was born in Ohio and was baptized in 1837. He settled in Nauvoo and moved with the Saints to Winter Quarters. He served a mission to Great Britain and in 1861 settled in Pine Valley, where he ran a saw mill and raised stock. Earl died at Middleton, survived by seven children. Mormon Battalion private James Calvin Earl (1827–71) was his brother. CL.

The Eastmans. James Eastman (1786–1847) fitted out a wagon at Winter Quarters in 1847 and "was very anxious that his son Ozro should become a member of the pioneer company." Ozro French Eastman (1828–1916) was born in Vermont. His parents joined the LDS church in 1843, but Eastman was never baptized, yet "bore a strong testimony to Brigham Young and Heber C. Kimball." A member of the 1847 pioneer company and a returning pioneer, Eastman took his widowed mother and sister to Salt Lake Valley in 1848 where he established the first harness shop. In 1855 he married Mary Whittle and became the father of ten children. He settled in Idaho, worked as a saddler, and died at Idaho Falls.

Howard Egan (1815–78). Famous as "a frontiersman who was a stranger to fear," Egan's journal, *Pioneering the West*, is one of the best accounts of the 1847 pioneer company. Born in Ireland, he came to Canada as a child and married Tamson Parshley. In 1842 Erastus Snow converted the couple. In Nauvoo, Egan was a policeman and a major in the Nauvoo Legion. In 1846, Egan was sent with James Pace and John D. Lee from Winter Quarters to Santa Fé to collect Mormon Battalion pay. He led parties across the plains in 1848 and 1849. Near Cache Cave in 1851, he killed one James Monroe for seducing his wife, but following "the established principles of justice known in these mountains" and a jurisdictional technicality, a jury found him innocent. Egan held many civic offices, was a Pony Express agent, and "enjoyed success as a missionary to the Indians." DLT.

Joseph Teasdale Egbert (1818–98). Born in Indiana, Egbert was one of Orson Pratt's advance company in 1847. He returned to Winter Quarters in the same ten as Thomas Bullock and brought his family to Utah in 1849, settling Kaysville, where he established a hotel and held public offices. He later drove LDS church teams across the plains "to assist emigrants" and died at Ogden.

The Eldredges. An 1848 pioneer, Horace S. Eldredge (1816–88) joined the LDS church in 1836 and served as the emigration agent in 1852. His brother, John Sutherland Eldredge (1831–73), was a teamster with the 1847 pioneer company and was born at Brutus, New York. He was among the first to plow land in Great Salt Lake City and served a mission to Australia from 1852–56. He died suddenly while plowing at Charleston, Utah, and was survived by a large family.

Edmund Lovell Ellsworth (1819–93). A son-in-law of Brigham Young, Ellsworth was born in New York and joined the LDS church in 1840. He crossed Iowa in 1846; in 1847 the pioneer company left him at the North Platte to ferry emigrants across the river. Ellsworth arrived in Great Salt Lake City on 12 October 1847. He filled a mission to England in 1854–56 and took command of the first handcart company to cross the plains—"quite successfully." In 1880 Ellsworth moved two of his families to Arizona to avoid indictment for polygamy, but he was arrested in Prescott, served a short prison term, and paid a fine of $300. Ellsworth died at Show Low, Arizona, survived by a large family.

James Emmett (1803–?). A Kentuckian who joined the LDS church by 1832, Emmett was a corporal in the Nauvoo police and one of the men Joseph Smith called in February 1844 to "to explore Oregon and California, and select a site for a new city for the saints." Emmett led twenty-five families from Nauvoo across Iowa in late 1844, eventually taking them to the Vermilion River where the expedition floundered. He and his followers rejoined the Saints at Council Bluffs in 1846. Emmett went to Utah in 1848, but joined Jefferson Hunt's party in 1849 and moved to California, where he died at San Bernardino sometime between 1852 and 1855.

William Adam Empey (1808–90). A member of the 1847 pioneer company, Empey was born in Canada. He settled in Nauvoo and Winter Quarters. Empey kept a journal of his work at the North Platte ferry and returned to Winter Quarters that fall. Empey and his family came to Utah in 1848. From 1852–54 he served a mission to England. Empey settled at St. George and died there, survived by a large family.

Horace Datus Ensign (1826–66). Ensign was born in Massachusetts. His parents joined the LDS church in 1843 and moved to Nauvoo in 1846 but were soon forced to Winter Quarters, where Ensign's father died in September. Ensign was a member of the 1847 pioneer company and that fall met his family in Daniel Spencer's company on the Big Sandy. With them he returned and settled in Ogden with Captain James Brown. He was active in the Utah War, fathered six children, and died in Ogden.

David Evans (1804–83). A member of Zion's Camp, survivor of the Haun's Mill Massacre, and bishop of Nauvoo, Evans came to Utah in 1850. He was mayor and bishop of Lehi and served as a colonel in the territorial militia.

Addison Everett (1805–85). A member of the 1847 pioneer company, Everett was born in New York and was baptized in 1837. He settled in Nauvoo and was a bishop at Winter Quarters and Great Salt Lake City. In 1861 he settled in southern Utah, where he died at St. George.

Nathaniel Fairbanks (1823–53). A member of the 1847 pioneer company, Fairbanks was born in New York and settled at Nauvoo in 1844. He returned east with Brigham Young in 1847, but met his family in Daniel Spencer's company and returned to

Great Salt Lake City. Fairbanks went to California during the gold rush, where he drowned in a river near Sacramento.

The Farrs. Born in Vermont and baptized in 1832, Aaron Freeman Farr (1818–1903) and his family moved to Kirtland in 1836 and in 1842 settled at Nauvoo. He was one of five men who left the pioneer company at Green River to guide the second division. He arrived in Salt Lake Valley on 20 September 1847 with Daniel Spencer's party. In 1852–53 he served a mission to the West Indies and succeeded Horace S. Eldredge as president of the St. Louis Branch. Farr made his home in Ogden, where he practiced law and served as U.S. Deputy Marshal. In 1856 he filled a mission to Las Vegas, Nevada, and in 1859 was elected probate judge of Weber County. He died at Logan, survived by three sons and two daughters. His brother Lorin Freeman Farr (1820-1908), was a member of the 1847 second division and founded Farr West, Utah. SEB.

Pliny Fisher (1775–1860). A member of the Poor Camp relief, Fisher was a high priest. He died in Utah. SEB.

Perry Fitzgerald (1814–89). Born in Pennsylvania, Fitzgerald joined the LDS church in Illinois in 1842. He was a member of the 1847 pioneer company and helped build the Old Fort in Great Salt Lake City. In 1849 he located at Mill Creek, finally settling in Draper, Utah. He fought in the Walker Indian war and was the father of twelve sons and eight daughters. RH.

The Flakes. James M. Flake seems to have had postal duties at Winter Quarters and was a captain of 100 in Amasa Lyman's division in 1848. After his baptism in 1844, Flake (whom Bullock called "Flack") gave his slave Green Flake (1828–1903) to Brigham Young. One of the three African-Americans in the 1847 pioneer company, Green Flake was born in Anson County, North Carolina. He came with the James Flake family to Nauvoo. Green Flake resided for some years in Union, Utah, before moving to Idaho Falls, where he died.

John Sherman Fowler (1819–60). A member of the 1847 pioneer company, Fowler was born in New York City. He received a patriarchal blessing from Asahel Smith at Nauvoo in February 1846 and was a Seventy. He accompanied Samuel Brannan to California in 1847 to meet his wife, Jerusha H. Fowler, who had gone west with their children in the *Brooklyn*. During the gold rush, Fowler established the City Hotel with Brannan in Sacramento and joined a filibustering expedition to Hawaii with him in 1851. WB.

Samuel Bradford Fox (1829–post 1870). Born in New York, Fox served as a teamster for Brigham Young in the 1847 pioneer company. He went to California in 1850 where, the following year, he suffered a severe attack of smallpox. He said that his friends in Utah should never see him in that disfigured condition; he was last reported to be living in Oregon.

John Monroe Freeman (1823-1850). A member of the 1847 pioneer company, Freeman was born in Connecticut and lived for a time in Nauvoo, where he became a Seventy. He helped found Mormon Station (now Genoa, Nevada) in the Carson Valley in 1850, dying there of cholera.

Horace Monroe Frink (1832–74). A member of the 1847 pioneer company, Frink was born in New York. He returned to Winter Quarters in the fall of 1847 and died in San Bernardino, California.

Burr Frost (1816–78). Blacksmith for the 1847 pioneer company, Frost was born in Connecticut. He was "at all times ready to protect the settlers against marauding Indians." He filled a mission to Australia from 1852–54 and died in Salt Lake City, survived by a large family.

Andrew Smith Gibbons (1825–86). A member of the 1847 pioneer company and a returning pioneer, Gibbons was born in Ohio. As an infant, his family gave him to relatives of Joseph Smith. He married Rispah Knight, a daughter of Bishop Vinson Knight, in Nauvoo. He returned to Utah in 1852 with his family and settled in Davis County. In 1854 he was one of the Indian missionaries called to Iron County. In 1861 he settled in St. George, where he was elected sheriff of Washington County. In 1880 he moved to St. Johns, Arizona, where he died, a member of the Eastern Arizona Stake High Council.

John Streater Gleason (1819–1904). A member of the 1847 pioneer company, Gleason was born in New York and helped build the Old Fort in Great Salt Lake City. He married Desdemona Chase and settled in Davis County, where he served as county commissioner, justice of the peace, and county clerk. In 1873 he moved to Pleasant Grove, where he died.

Eric M. Glines (1822–81). An independent-minded member of the 1847 pioneer company, Glines was born in New Hampshire, "but little is known of his history." On the trek to Utah, Brigham Young reprimanded Glines for his refusal to follow orders. He committed suicide in Santa Rosa, California.

Stephen Hezekiah Goddard (1810–98). A member of the 1847 pioneer company, Goddard was born in New York. He was leader of the Tabernacle choir when it sang in the Old Tabernacle. Goddard died at the home of his daughter in San Bernardino, California.

The Goulds. At sixty-nine, Samuel Gould (1778–1869) served as a private in one of the Mormon Battalion sick detachments and was a member of the returning pioneers. He died in Parowan, Utah. His son, John Calvin Gould (1821–50), was born in West Virginia and served with his father as a private in the battalion. He died in California.

The Grants. Most of the children of Joshua Grant (1778–1865) and Athalia Howard Grant (1786–1853) followed their parents into Mormonism after they joined the LDS church in 1833. George D. Grant (1812–76) was a member of Hosea Stout's 1847 relief party from Winter Quarters and an 1848 pioneer. He settled at Bountiful and was a prominent officer in the Utah militia. His brother, Jedediah Morgan Grant (1816–56), led a detachment of the 1847 second division. Jedediah brought the body of his wife, Caroline Ann Van Dyke, from Bear River to Great Salt Lake City. Jedediah Grant succeeded Willard Richards as second counselor to Brigham Young in 1854 and died after fanning the flames of the Mormon Reformation. GS.

David Grant (1816–68). A member of the 1847 pioneer company, Grant was born at Arbroath, Scotland, and was one of the early LDS converts in England. He was ordained a priest in Nauvoo in 1840 and joined the Saints at Winter Quarters. Grant was a returning pioneer and came back to Utah in 1848. He filled a mission to England from 1852–56, crossing the plains with Edward Bunker's handcart company. In 1862, Grant was called to southern Utah, but he returned to his home in Mill Creek, Utah, where he died.

George Roberts Grant (1820–89). A member of the 1847 pioneer company and a returning pioneer, Grant was born in New York. "He probably returned with Brigham Young in 1848" and settled in Kaysville by 1852. From 1855–58 he was a Salmon River missionary. He died in California.

John Young Greene (1826–80). Brigham Young's nephew and a teamster in the 1847 pioneer company, Greene was born in New York. In 1857 he served in the Scandinavian Mission, where he "gained many friends among the warmhearted Danish people, but returned to Utah in 1858, on account of the Johnston army troubles." Greene died in Salt Lake City.

Thomas Grover (1807–93). Born in New York and a ferryman by trade, in 1847 he was assigned by Brigham Young to manage the North Platte ferry. He died in Utah on 4 July 1893.

The Hancocks. Joseph Hancock (1800–93), a member of the 1847 pioneer company, was born in Massachusetts and was baptized in Ohio in 1830. As hunter for Zion's Camp, Hancock was known as "Joseph's Nimrod"; "he was taken sick with cholera, but was healed under the hands of the Prophet." Hancock returned to Winter Quarters in 1847 but went back to Utah in 1852. He "liked a roving life and spent much of his time traveling back and forth between Utah and California." He died at the home of his nephew, George W. Hancock, in Payson, Utah. His brother, Levi Ward Hancock (1803–82), was only a fifer and private in the Mormon Battalion but acted as its senior spiritual leader. RH.

The Hankses. Sidney Alvarus Hanks (1820–70), a member of the 1847 pioneer company, was born in Ohio, a son of Benjamin Hanks and Martha Knowlton Hanks. From 1852-60 he was a missionary in the Society Islands. On 1 June 1862, he married Mary Ann Cook, who became the mother of one son and two daughters. His family settled at Snyderville, where he froze to death searching for a cow. His brother Ephraim Knowlton Hanks (1826–96) served in the Mormon Battalion and ran a Pony Express station at Mountain Dell.

Hans Christian Hansen (1806–90). A sailor since boyhood and a member of the 1847 pioneer company, Hansen was born in Copenhagen, Denmark, and was baptized in Boston in 1842. He was an expert violinist and entertained Salt Lake with his music. He never married and settled at Salina, where he died.

The Harmons. Jesse Pierce Harmon (1795-1877) was born in Vermont and joined the LDS church in 1838. He was a member of the Poor Camp and Heber Kimball's 1848 company. In Utah, he was a colonel in the Nauvoo Legion and died at Holden. His son Appleton Milo Harmon (1820–77) was born in Pennsylvania and married Elmeda Stringham in Nauvoo. He was the "mechanical genius" of the 1847 pioneer company who built "the famous roadometer." Harmon was one of the men left at the ferry on the North Platte. He filled a mission to England from 1850–53 and helped build sawmills across Utah. He finally settled at Holden, where he died, survived by several sons and daughters.

Charles Alfred Harper (1816–1900). A member of the 1847 pioneer company and a returning pioneer, Harper was born in Pennsylvania. He was a college graduate and joined the LDS church at Nauvoo. He returned to Winter Quarters in 1847 and brought his family to Utah in 1848. He pioneered southern Utah and Arizona but finally located in Cottonwood, where he died, survived by a large family.

Alpheus Peter Haws (1825–1906). Born in Canada, Haws was a member of the Council of Fifty and a sergeant in the Mormon Battalion. He ran a ranch at Gravelly Ford on the Humboldt River in the 1850s and died in Berkeley, California.

William Henrie (1799–1883). A member of the 1847 pioneer company, Henrie was born in Pennsylvania. He remained in Salt Lake in 1847 and helped built the Old Fort. In 1849, he explored Utah Valley. He settled at Bountiful, where he died, survived by a large family.

Joseph Leland Heywood (1815–1910). Heywood converted to Mormonism in Illinois, served as one of the trustees assigned to dispose of Mormon property in Nauvoo, and witnessed the Battle of Nauvoo in September 1846. He came to Utah in 1848 with the Willard Richards company and served as Salt Lake's first postmaster and as federal marshal. He laid out Nephi, helped settle Carson Valley, and "lived on rawhide" while winter-bound at Devil's Gate in 1856. Heywood settled in St. George and served as patriarch.

Nelson Higgins (1806–90). A New Yorker, Higgins was captain of Company D of the Mormon Battalion. Perhaps because his wife and eight children accompanied him, on 18 September 1846 Higgins was assigned to conduct battalion dependents to Pueblo, Colorado, where he was joined later in the year by the Brown and Willis sick detachments. Higgins died in Sevier County, Utah. JB.

The Higbees. Leader of an 1848 company, Isaac Higbee (1797–1874) was born in New Jersey and joined the LDS church in 1832. He ran the ferry at Winter Quarters and led the settlement at Provo. His brother, John Summers Higbee (1804–77), was a member of the 1847 pioneer company. Born in Ohio, J. S. Higbee was a cabinet maker and was baptized in May 1831. He moved to Jackson County, Missouri, and served as assessor of Caldwell County. Like his brother, he was a bishop at Nauvoo. In 1847, he was one of the men left at the ferry on the North Platte. He started east to meet his family on 10 August and arrived in the Salt Lake Valley 26 September 1847. From 1849–52 he filled a mission to England. In 1865 he moved to southern Utah and died at Toquerville. His son, Major John Mount Higbee, was the senior militia officer present at the Mountain Meadows Massacre in 1857.

John Greenleaf Holman (1828–88). A member of the 1847 pioneer company and a returning pioneer, Holman was born in New York and was baptized when eight years old. He moved with his parents to Kirtland. He returned to Utah in 1850 with his wife, Nancy Clark, whom he married in 1849. Holman lived at Pleasant Grove and Santaquin and in 1883 moved to Rexburg, Idaho, where he died.

Simeon Fuller Howd (1823–62). A member of the 1847 pioneer company, Howd was born in New York. He was called in 1851 to settle Iron County and in 1856 was appointed the first presiding elder of the new settlement at Beaver, where he died. RH.

The Hydes. Orson Hyde (1805–78) was a member of Zion's Camp and one of the original apostles. He was left in charge of Winter Quarters from 1847 to 1850. Heman Hyde (1788–1867) was a captain of fifty in Lorenzo Snow's 1848 company. Heman's son William Hyde (1818–74) was a sergeant in the Mormon Battalion. SEB.

Mathew Hayes Ivory (1800–85). A member of the 1847 pioneer company, Ivory was born at Philadelphia. He settled at Beaver, Utah, and served a mission to New Jersey in 1879. He was an expert mechanic, but in 1885 he was killed while setting up the mill stones in a grain chopper at Beaver. The name he carved in Cache Cave in 1847 is still visible.

Levi Jackman (1797–1876). A member of the 1847 pioneer company, Jackman was born in Vermont. He died a patriarch at Salem, Utah, survived by a large family.

Norton Jacob (1804–79). A member of the 1847 pioneer company, Jacob was born in Massachusetts. He kept one of the best journals of the 1847 journey. In 1848 Norton returned to Utah with his wife, Emily Heaton Jacob, and family, acting as captain of the guard. He was foreman of the carpenters and joiners employed on public works, designing the Weber River bridge in 1855. He settled at Heber City and was appointed justice of the peace in 1862. Jacob fathered seventeen children and died at Glendale, Utah.

Artemas Johnson (1809–?). A hunter with the 1847 pioneer company and a returning pioneer, Johnson was born in New York. He was ordained an elder at Commerce, Illinois, in 1839. He is believed to have returned to Utah.

Luke Samuel Johnson (1807–61). A member of Zion's Camp and physician to the 1847 pioneer company, Joseph Smith baptized the Vermont-born Johnson in 1831. According to Brigham Young, "When the Quorum of the Twelve was first chosen, Lyman Johnson's name was called first, Brigham Young's second, Heber C. Kimball's third, and so on." Johnson was excommunicated for apostasy at Far West, Missouri, in 1838, but was rebaptized in Nauvoo. He settled at St. John, Utah, and served as bishop. Johnson died at the home of his brother-in-law, Orson Hyde, in Great Salt Lake City.

Philo Johnson (1814–96). A member of the 1847 pioneer company, Johnson was born in Connecticut. Brigham Young "appointed him to manufacture" highly praised hats. He settled in Payson where he worked as a gunsmith. RH.

Stephen Kelsey (1830–1900). A member of the 1847 pioneer company, Kelsey was born in Ohio. He was not baptized until he returned to Winter Quarters in 1847 to find that his mother and sister had died. He returned to Salt Lake Valley in 1848 with his mother's family. In 1850 he went to California and panned $500 worth of gold in four months. He returned to Utah and married Lydia Snyder, who bore him eleven children. They settled at Brigham City in 1856, but in 1864 Kelsey moved to Bear Lake Valley. He died at Paris, Idaho.

Levi Newell Kendall (1822–1903). A member of the 1847 pioneer company and a returning pioneer, Kendall was born in New York. He lived at Nauvoo and filled a mission to Michigan in 1844. Kendall returned to Utah in 1848 and married Elizabeth Clemmons in Salt Lake City in 1851. In 1856 he moved to Springville, where he built canyon roads and irrigation canals. In 1861 he went to the Missouri River with John R. Murdock "to bring poor saints" to Utah. Kendall died at Springville, Utah, survived by a large family.

Conrad Kleinman (1815–1907). A member of the 1847 pioneer company, Kleinman was born in Germany and emigrated to America when quite young. In 1856 he filled a mission to New York and in 1861 was called to southern Utah. Kleinman was ordained a patriarch in September 1891 and died at St. George, the father of thirteen children.

The Kimballs. An apostle, Heber Chase Kimball (1801–68) was a member of the 1847 pioneer company and a returning pioneer. Kimball was born at Sheldon, Vermont, and was baptized in April 1832. At Winter Quarters in December 1847, Kimball was set apart as first counselor to Brigham Young. He married forty-three wives and had sixty-five children. A popular and plain-spoken leader, Kimball died in Great Salt Lake City. His wife Ellen Sanders Kimball, née Aagaat Ysteinsdatter Bakka (1823–71), was one of the three women in the 1847 pioneer company. She was born in Thelemarken, Norway, a daughter of Ysten Sondrasen. The family emigrated to America in 1837 and settled in Indiana. She joined the LDS church in 1842 and became the mother of five children, three of whom died in infancy. She died in Salt Lake City. Kimball's wife Sarah Ann Whitney Kimball (1825–73) was a widow of Joseph Smith, Jr. and was mother of a son who died at Winter Quarters and of David Chase Kimball, who was born on the trail on 26 August 1848. Kimball's oldest son, William Henry (1826–1907), was a member of the Poor Camp relief, an 1848 pioneer, and was owner of a stage station at Parley's Park near today's Park City. He was the "Danite" Mark Twain described in *Roughing It*. RH, FE, SEB, SBK.

William A. King (1821–62). A member of the 1847 pioneer company and a returning pioneer, King was ordained a Seventy in Nauvoo. It is not known if he ever returned to Utah; he apparently died in Boston, Massachusetts.

Charles Lambert (1816–92). An Englishman, Lambert joined the LDS church in 1843 and married Mary Alice Cannon in 1844 at Nauvoo. A stone mason and stone cutter, he worked on the capstone of the Nauvoo Temple and fought in the Battle of Nauvoo. A mob seized and forcibly immersed him in the Mississippi River "under the most hideous oaths and blasphemies imaginable." He was a member of the Poor Camp and built a small house in Winter Quarters. Lambert crossed the plains to Utah in 1849 and died at his farm in Granger, Utah.

Asahel Albert Lathrop (1810–71). Born in Connecticut, Lathrop joined the LDS church in 1836. He was a captain of ten in Jedediah Grant's 1847 party. SEB.

Hark Lay (1825–90). One of the three blacks in the 1847 pioneer company, Lay was a slave of William Lay, a wealthy member of the LDS church from Monroe County, Mississippi. Hark Lay was apparently an independent spirit, for Amasa Lyman, Jr., claimed, "Hark was always hard to manage." Lay remained in the West and died at Union, Utah. JB.

Tarlton Lewis (1805–90). A member of the 1847 pioneer company, Lewis was born in South Carolina. He moved to Kentucky in 1809 and married Malinda Gimlin in 1828. In 1836, he was baptized by his brother, Benjamin Lewis, who was killed in

1838 at Haun's Mill. He was one of the founders of Parowan, where he served as bishop until 1858, when he was called to settle Minersville. In 1877 he was appointed a bishop in Sevier County. He finally moved to Teasdale, where he died. His daughter, Matilda, was an 1848 pioneer.

Jesse Carter Little (1815–93). Adjutant of the 1847 pioneer company, Little was born in Maine. He served as president of the Eastern States Mission in 1846. Assisted by Thomas L. Kane, Little negotiated the agreement with President Polk that authorized the Mormon Battalion. Little returned to Winter Quarters in 1847 and again served as president of the Eastern States Mission; he did not return to the Salt Lake Valley until 1852. In Utah, he was a U.S. Marshall and ran a hotel at the Warm Springs. Little was involved in an unsuccessful Mexican land speculation with Sam Brannan in the 1880s and died in Salt Lake City.

L. O. Littlefield (1819–88). Editor of the *Hancock Eagle* in Nauvoo, Littlefield carried a letter from the LDS church leaders to the Poor Camp. Littlefield was a founder of Logan, Utah, where he edited the *Utah Journal*.

Franklin G. Losee (1815–?). See John G. Luce.

Chauncey Loveland (1797–1876). A member of the 1847 pioneer company and a returning pioneer, Loveland was born in Connecticut and lived at Carthage, Illinois. He joined the LDS church after the death of Joseph Smith. He settled at Bountiful, Utah, where he died.

John G. Luce (1817–?). Almost nothing else is known about Luce except that he was born in Maine, became a Seventy at Nauvoo, married Harriet N. Luce, and was a member of the Nauvoo Fourth Ward. He was listed as Franklin G. Losee on most pioneer company rosters. Despite "intensive research," Losee also remains obscure. He was born at Belmont, Maine, and is said to have died at Lehi, Utah. DUP.

Amasa Mason Lyman (1813–77). An apostle, member of the 1847 pioneer company, a returning pioneer, and captain of a division of the 1848 emigration, Lyman was born in Lyman, New Hampshire, and was baptized in 1832. A member of the Council of Fifty, in 1851 he established San Bernardino, California, with Charles C. Rich. Lyman developed an interest in spiritualism and "advocated false doctrines and was excommunicated" in 1870. He died in Fillmore, Utah. RH, WB.

John Lytle (1803–92). A Nauvoo policeman and Poor Camp blacksmith, Lytle was among those arrested for the destruction of the *Nauvoo Expositor*. He was an adopted son of Brigham Young and a bishop in Salt Lake. SEB.

James McFate (1804-1865). A wagonwright, McFate was born in Pennsylvania and was baptized at Nauvoo in 1845. A member of the Poor Camp, McFate moved to Mississippi before coming to Utah in 1850 or 1851. He died a patriarch at St. George. SEB.

Samuel Harvey Marble (1822–1914). A member of the 1847 pioneer company and a returning pioneer, Marble was born in New York and joined the LDS church at Nauvoo. He settled at Manti, Utah, and eventually moved to Round Valley, Arizona, where he died.

Stephen Avon Markham (1800-1878). "Colonel" of the military organization of the 1847 pioneer company and a returning pioneer, Markham was born in New York and was baptized in July 1837. He visited Carthage jail the day Joseph Smith was killed. While breaking steers for the 1847 journey, Markham had his forefinger ripped from his hand. He returned to Utah in 1850 in charge of an overland company and was sent "to preside over the infant settlement of Palmyra, Utah." In 1856 he established Fort Supply near Fort Bridger. During the Walker Indian war Markham was a colonel in the Nauvoo Legion. He died at Spanish Fork.

Joseph Matthews (1809–86). A member of the 1847 pioneer company, Matthews was born in North Carolina and worked on the Nauvoo Temple. He was one of Orson Pratt's advance company and explored southern Utah in 1849 with Parley P. Pratt. In 1851 he moved to San Bernardino, but returned to Utah in 1857. He moved to Arizona in 1880 and died at Pima.

William Meeks (1815–77). A member of the Poor Camp, Meeks married Mary Elizabeth Rhodes and settled in Indiana before crossing the plains to Utah in 1852. SEB.

George Miller (1794–1856?). Born in Virginia, Miller joined the LDS church in 1839 and was presiding bishop in Nauvoo and a charter member of the Council of Fifty. He led the vanguard of the Mormon emigration into Nebraska in 1846 and wintered on the Niobrara River. Miller rejected Brigham Young's leadership and was "cut off" from the church in December 1848. He joined James Strang in 1850 and died on his way to California. SEB.

Reuben Miller (1811–82). A native of Pennsylvania, Miller joined the LDS church in 1846, crossed the plains in 1849, and served as bishop of the East Mill Creek ward.

George Mills (1787?–1854). A member of the 1847 pioneer company, Mills was born in England. He died of cancer in Utah after Dr. Samuel L. Sprague performed an unsuccessful operation.

Carlos G. Murray (1829–55). A member of the 1847 pioneer company and a returning pioneer, Murray was born in New York. He was Heber Kimball's nephew. In 1855 Jules Remy described him as "a young man rather under-sized, a fresh ruddy complexion, and an almost red beard"—and called Carlos Murray "a dangerous assassin." He returned to Utah in 1848 and was said to be killed by Indians on the Humboldt with "his wife and a man named Redden." RH.

Lewis B. Myers (1812–93). The mountaineer who was the likely model for LaBonte, hero of Ruxton's *Life in the Far West*, Myers was born in Pennsylvania. He guided the advance party of the sick detachments to Fort Laramie and was the first to explore Utah Valley. In 1848, Myers settled briefly at Brown's Fort, the future Ogden, Utah. He reached California early in 1849 where he set up a canvas restaurant and opened a store in El Dorado County. He bought the Chimney Rock Ranch, where he lived until his death. WB.

Elijah Newman (1793–1872). A member of the 1847 pioneer company, Newman was born in Virginia and joined the LDS church in 1832. He built the gates for the Old Fort and settled at Parowan, where he served as justice of the peace and died. DUP.

John Wesley Norton (1820–1901). A hunter for the 1847 pioneer company, Norton was born in Indiana. From 1854–57 he filled a mission to Australia. He settled in southern Utah, residing for a time at Panaca, Nevada. He died at Panguitch, survived by several children.

Seeley Owen (1805–81). A member of the 1847 pioneer company and a returning pioneer, Owen was born in Vermont. He married his cousin, who died at Winter Quarters. Owen returned to Utah by 1854 and settled at Provo. He was killed in a railroad construction accident near Flagstaff, Arizona.

John Pack (1809–85). A member of the 1847 pioneer company and a returning pioneer, Pack was born at St. Johns, Canada, and was baptized in 1836. Pack returned to Utah in 1848 with his family. In 1856 he settled in Carson Valley. He died in Salt Lake City.

Henry Miller Parker (1807–87). Born in England, Parker joined the LDS church in 1838 and traveled to Winter Quarters with the Poor Camp in 1846. He came to Utah in 1850 and died in Wellsville. SEB.

Hezekiah Peck (1820–50). Oliver Cowdery baptized Peck as one of the first members of the LDS church in June 1830. He apparently never went farther west than Iowa and died in Missouri.

Eli Harvey Peirce (1827–58). A teamster in the 1847 pioneer company, Peirce was born in Pennsylvania and was baptized in 1842 by Joseph Smith. In the fall of 1847 he traveled to California with Jefferson Hunt. He became the second bishop of Box Elder, now Brigham City. He was an 1857 handcart missionary and journeyed to Utah with Thomas Bullock in 1858, dying shortly after his return in Great Salt Lake City. DUP.

Stephen Chadwick Perry (1818–88). A member of the Poor Camp, Perry was born in New York, joined the LDS church in 1833, and was one of Joseph Smith's bodyguards in Nauvoo. He came to Utah in 1850, fought in the Indian wars, and died at Springville. SEB.

The Piersons. Brothers Harmon D. Pierson (1818–91), Ebenezer Pierson (1821–92), and Judson A. Pierson (1827–?) served as privates in the Mormon Battalion sick detachments. Judson Pierson was a returning pioneer.

William Pitt (1813–73). Captain of the pioneer brass band, Pitt was born in England and joined the LDS church in 1840. He came to Utah in 1850. SEB.

Francis Martin Pomeroy (1822–83). A member of the 1847 pioneer company, Pomeroy was born in Connecticut and learned Spanish as a shipwrecked whaler in South America. In Utah, he operated a saw mill and served as a missionary to the Indians. Pomeroy pioneered Bear Lake in Idaho and died at Mesa, Arizona. DUP.

Gardner Godfrey "Duff" Potter (1820-1857). After following James Emmett across Iowa in 1844, Potter was a member of the 1847 party that left Winter Quarters to relieve the returning pioneers. Potter went to Utah in 1848 and was killed with Orrin Parish in a sensational murder at Springville, Utah. FE.

David Powell (1822–83?). A member of the 1847 pioneer company and a returning pioneer, Powell was born in South Carolina and lived in Nauvoo. He returned to Utah in 1853 with his wife, Ann, and son, David. He settled in California and died near Santa Rosa. DUP.

The Pratts. Parley Parker Pratt (1807–57) was an apostle and leader of the second division of 1847. His brother and fellow apostle, Orson Pratt (1811–81), was a leader of the 1847 pioneer company and a returning pioneer. He was born in New York and led the advance company into the Salt Lake Valley. Early Mormonism's leading intellectual, Orson Pratt published widely and made the public announcement of polygamy in 1852. His 1847 journal, serialized in the *Millennial Star*, is one of the best accounts of the pioneer company. Both brothers were charter members of the Council of Fifty.

Tunis Rappleye (1807–83). A member of the 1847 pioneer company, Rappleye was born in New York and joined the LDS church in 1832. He married Louisa Cutler, who bore him eight children. Rappleye led one of the advance parties of the 1847 return to Winter Quarters. He worked for three years as Brigham Young's head gardener and was an overland teamster. Rappleye died at Kanosh, Utah. DUP.

Return Jackson Redden (1817–91). A scout with the 1847 pioneer company and a returning pioneer, Redden was born in Ohio. He was a bodyguard to Joseph Smith and lost a wife at Winter Quarters. He "discovered a curious cave now known as Cache Cave," which was originally named for him. He returned to Utah in 1848 with his family and accompanied Amasa Lyman to California in 1849. He settled in Carson Valley for two years and later lived in Tooele and Summit counties in Utah, serving as a justice of the peace in both. He died at Hoytsville, Utah, survived by a large family. DUP, RH.

Charles Colson Rich (1809–83). Commander of the Nauvoo Legion in 1844, he led one of the parties in the 1847 second division. Appointed an apostle in 1849, he settled San Bernardino and Bear Lake.

The Richards. Willard Richards (1804–54) was an apostle, a member of the 1847 pioneer company, and a returning pioneer. Thomas Bullock's adopted father was born in Massachusetts and was baptized by his cousin, Brigham Young, at Kirtland in 1836. In the 1820s, he toured with an "Electro Chemistry" show before developing an interest in herbal medicine and taking a six-week course with Samuel Thompson that made "Doctor" Richards a "Thompsonian" physician. He became Joseph Smith's secretary in 1841 and kept the prophet's private journals. Richards was wounded in Carthage Jail and was made second counselor to Brigham Young on 27 December 1847. He led one of the divisions of the 1848 emigration and was postmaster of Great Salt Lake City and LDS church historian. His brother, Dr. Levi Richards (1799–1876), married Sarah Griffiths and was a correspondent of Thomas Bullock. While living at Winter Quarters in 1848, the couple was called on a mission to England; on Brigham Young's advice, they sent their son, Levi Willard Richards (1845–1914), to Utah with his uncle. SBK, DB.

Levi Evans Riter (1805–77). A member of Jedediah Grant's 1847 company, Riter was born in Pennsylvania and joined the LDS church in 1846. He oversaw Mormon Battalion families at Winter Quarters. Riter journeyed to California in 1848 in an unsuccessful attempt to retrieve goods shipped to California with Samuel Brannan. A gunsmith, he pioneered Carson Valley and settled at Great Salt Lake City.

Orrin Porter Rockwell (1813–78). Born in Massachusetts, baptized in 1830, he was a distant cousin of Joseph Smith and Abraham Lincoln. By legend he was Smith's "Avenging Angel"; by occupation he was Smith's bodyguard and factotum. Rockwell wounded former Missouri Governor Lilburn Boggs in May 1842 and spent eight months in jail for the crime but was never tried. He planned to go west with Joseph Smith in 1844 and carried word of the Prophet's death to Nauvoo. In the 1847 emigration, "Orrin Porter Rockwell rendered signal service as a hunter. He was one of Orson Pratt's advance company. He had considerable influence with the Indians." Rockwell ran a saloon in California in the gold rush, commanded 100 guerrillas in the 1857-58 Utah War, and participated in the brutal murder of the Aiken party, but he later served as a mail contractor and deputy marshal of Salt Lake City. When he died, *The Salt Lake Tribune* said "he killed unsuspecting travelers...fellow Saints who held secrets...Apostates who dared to wag their tongues...and he killed mere sojourners in Zion merely to keep his hand in." One thousand people attended his funeral, where Joseph F. Smith conceded, "He had his little faults." DLT, HS.

Albert Perry Rockwood (1805–79). Brigham Young's first adopted son, a member of the 1847 pioneer company, and a returning pioneer, Rockwood was born in Massachusetts and was baptized in Kirtland in 1837 by Brigham Young. He commanded Joseph Smith's bodyguard and was a general in the Nauvoo Legion. Rockwood returned to Utah in 1849 with three wives and was warden of the territorial penitentiary for fifteen years, served in the legislature, and was director of the Deseret Agricultural and Manufacturing Society. He died in Salt Lake City. DUP.

Benjamin William Rolfe (1822–92). A member of the 1847 pioneer company and a returning pioneer, Rolfe was born in Maine. His father, Samuel, joined the LDS church and moved to Kirtland in 1834, but Rolfe did not join the LDS church until after 1847. His father was selected to go with the pioneer company, but Rolfe took his ill father's place. In 1848, Rolfe carried mail from the emigration to Great Salt Lake City. He served in the Salmon River Mission and helped to establish Fort Supply. He worked as a carpenter and "was of a retiring disposition and was esteemed for his honesty and general straightforwardness."

Joseph Rooker (1818?–95?). A member of the 1847 pioneer company, Rooker resided for a time at Black Rock on the Great Salt Lake. He left Utah about 1857 and died in Oceanside, California.

Shadrach Roundy (1789–1872). A member of Orson Pratt's advance guard in 1847, Roundy was born in Vermont. He served as a legislator and bishop in Great Salt Lake City and crossed the plains five times. Roundy died in Salt Lake City on 4 July 1872.

The Rushtons. Thomas Bullock was the son-in-law of Richard Rushton (1780–1842) and Lettice Johnson Rushton (1784–1846). They had ten children born in Leek, England, including Frederick James (1806–71), Richard, Jr. (1814–84), Mary Olivia (1820–71), Fanny (1821–81), and Edwin (1824–1904), all of whom emigrated to Nauvoo after the entire family converted to Mormonism in 1840. Lettice, Frederick, and Edwin Rushton lived in St. Louis until they crossed the plains to Utah in 1851. Richard's nephew John Rushton (1821–50?) and his wife, Margaret, were with the Poor Camp and buried a daughter at Winter Quarters. They also moved to St. Louis, where John Rushton died. GK.

Samuel Savery (1814–?). Born in Rhode Island, Savery joined the LDS church in 1842. A member of the Poor Camp, Savery became a farmer in Provo.

George Scholes (1812–57). A member of the Poor Camp, the 1847 pioneer company, and a returning pioneer, Scholes was born at Chadderton, England, and was baptized in 1839. He arrived at Nauvoo in April 1841, where he built a brick house and cultivated an orchard. His wife and three children died at Nauvoo. Scholes returned to Great Salt Lake City in 1850 with his new wife, Mary Spencer, and settled at Cottonwood, where he died, leaving four children.

Joseph Smith Scofield (1809–75). A teamster with the 1847 pioneer company, Scofield was born in New York and was a carpenter by trade. He pioneered southern Utah and died at Bellevue, "respected and loved by all who knew him."

Henry G. Sherwood (1785–1862). Oldest member of the 1847 pioneer company, Sherwood was born in New York and was city marshal at Nauvoo and commissary general for the pioneer company. He made the first survey of Great Salt Lake City and served on its High Council. In 1852 he moved to San Bernardino to survey the settlement. He returned to Utah in 1857 and became Salt Lake agent for the Pony Express. He died in San Bernardino.

The Shumways. A member of the 1847 pioneer company and a returning pioneer, Charles Shumway (1808–98) was born in Massachusetts and joined the LDS church about the 1840. He was a member of the Nauvoo police and was the first to cross the Mississippi River in February 1846. His wife, Julia Ann Hooker Shumway, died at Winter Quarters. Shumway pioneered Manti, Utah, in 1849, and served in the territorial legislature. He settled in southern Utah and in 1880 erected a grist mill at Shumway, Arizona. He died at Johnson, Utah. His son, Andrew Purley Shumway (1833–1909), also a member of the 1847 pioneer company and a returning pioneer, was baptized by Joseph Smith in Nauvoo. He filled a mission to Great Britain in 1856–57 and was a teamster with Thomas Bullock's 1858 overland party. In 1858 he married Amanda Graham and settled at Mendon, serving as bishop from 1859–72, when he filled another mission to Great Britain. In 1874 he moved to Franklin, Idaho, where he died. RH.

The Shupes. Brothers Andrew Jackson Shupe (1815–77) and James Wright Shupe (1823–99) operated a Nauvoo blacksmith shop with their father and entered the Salt Lake Valley in July 1847 as privates in the Mormon Battalion sick detachments. Both men are buried in Ogden. CL.

The Smiths. Joseph Smith, Sr. (1771–1840) was born the second son of Asahel Smith and Mary Duty Smith in Massachusetts. He married Lucy Mack (1776–1855) and was the father of Hyrum Smith (1800–44) and the LDS prophet Joseph Smith, Jr. (1805–44). Mary Fielding Smith (1801–52) was a member of the Poor Camp and widow of Hyrum Smith. Their son, John Smith (1823–1911), accompanied his mother (who married Heber C. Kimball) to Utah in 1848 and was ordained LDS church patriarch at age twenty-two. "Uncle" John Smith (1781–1854), brother of Joseph Smith Sr., was born in New Hampshire and served as leader of the Salt Lake Stake High Council during the winter of 1847–48. His son, George A. Smith (1817–75), was an apostle, a member of the 1847 pioneer company, and a returning pioneer. George A. was known as the father of southern Utah and died in Salt Lake City.

Samuel Trunkey Smith (1817–98). A farmer, Smith joined the LDS church in 1841 and was a member of the Poor Camp relief. He married Mariah McFate in Nauvoo. Their children's birth dates suggest they came to Utah in 1849. The family settled at Cedar City and Camp Floyd.

The Smoots. Leader of a party in the 1847 second division, Abraham Owen Smoot (1815–95) was born in Kentucky and joined the LDS church in 1835. He served as mayor of both Provo and Salt Lake. His adopted son, William Cockran Adkinson Smoot (1828–1920), was a member of the 1847 pioneer company. Along with Benjamin Franklin Dewey, William Smoot was "placed under the immediate direction" of Wilford Woodruff. He spent the winter of 1847–48 in the North Fort and later settled in Sugar House. William Smoot was the last survivor of the 1847 pioneer company.

The Snows. Willard Snow (1811–53) was a captain of fifty in the 1847 second division. His brother, Erastus Fairbanks Snow (1818–88), was a member of the 1847 pioneer company and a returning pioneer. Erastus Snow was born in Vermont and was baptized in 1833. Sharing a horse with Orson Pratt, he descended Emigration Canyon to be one of the first two men to enter Salt Lake Valley. He returned to Utah in 1848 and became an apostle in 1849. Snow was "spiritual leader" of southern Utah for years and died of diabetes at Salt Lake City. DUP.

Eliza R. Snow (1804–87). Widow of Joseph Smith and wife of Brigham Young, Snow crossed the plains in 1847. Her brother, Lorenzo Snow (1814–98), was a captain in the 1848 emigration and became fifth president of the LDS church.

The Spencers. Daniel Spencer (1792–1868) was born in Massachusetts and served as mayor of Nauvoo. He commanded the lead party of the 1847 second division. His brother, Orson Spencer (1802–55), graduated from Union College and joined the LDS church in 1841. He served as president of the British Mission and came to Utah in 1849. He became sick on a mission to the Cherokees and died in St. Louis.

William Carter Staines (1818–81). An English convert who eventually became emigration agent for the LDS church, Staines accompanied George Miller west in 1846 and spent six months with the Ponca Indians. He traveled to Utah with the 1847 second division and farmed in Davis County.

Roswell Stevens (1808–80). A member of the 1847 pioneer company and a returning pioneer, Stevens was born in Canada and was baptized in 1834. He served on the Nauvoo police and enlisted in the Mormon Battalion. He traveled with his company to Santa Fé, where he returned to Winter Quarters with John D. Lee and Howard Egan. Stevens died at Bluff, Utah. RH.

Benjamin Franklin Stewart (1817–86). A member of the 1847 pioneer company, Stewart was born in Ohio. He was left at the North Platte ferry, meeting his wife and children and going on to Salt Lake Valley. He was a founder and mayor of Payson, Utah, where he had a nail factory. Benjamin, Utah, was named in his honor. He died there, "being struck by lightning." DUP.

James Wesley Stewart (1825–1913). A member of the 1847 pioneer company, Stewart was born in Alabama. He was left at the North Platte ferry and recalled eating cowhides and sego roots in Great Salt Lake City. He later married Jane Grover, daughter of ferry boss Thomas Grover. Stewart lived in Farmington and Morgan County and died in Cokeville, Wyoming, at the home of his daughter.

Dexter Stillman (1804–52). A private in Company B before he was assigned to a Mormon Battalion sick detachment, Stillman was a returning pioneer. His wife, Barbara Redfield Stillman, gave birth to a son who died at Winter Quarters in July 1847. CL, SEB

Briant Stringham (1825–71). A member of the 1847 pioneer company, Stringham was born in New York. He was appointed probate judge of Cache County in 1856, but was renowned as a stockman and had charge of the LDS church's tithing stock for fifteen years. He ran the militia commissary department during the Indian wars.

Hosea Stout (1810–89). An 1848 pioneer and captain of the police at Nauvoo and Winter Quarters, Stout led the relief to the returning pioneers in 1847. In Utah, he was a prominent attorney and was one of the founders of St. George. His journals, edited by Juanita Brooks, are among the most useful sources on early LDS history.

Gilbard Summe (1802–67). A member of the 1847 pioneer company, Summe was born in North Carolina. He pioneered San Bernardino and died at Harrisburg, Utah.

Seth Taft (1796–1855). Captain of the eighth ten in the 1847 pioneer company, Taft was born in Massachusetts. He returned to Winter Quarters with the ox teams and became a bishop in Great Salt Lake City, where he died a patriarch. DUP.

Thomas Tanner (1804–55). A blacksmith with the 1847 pioneer company and a returning pioneer, Tanner was born in Bristol, England, and emigrated to America in 1831. He spent the winter of 1846–47 at Winter Quarters and in 1848 returned to Salt Lake with his family. He was foreman of the LDS church blacksmith shop until his death from a fall.

John Taylor (1808–87). A member of the Council of Fifty and a leader of the 1847 second division, Taylor was an apostle and survived the wounds he received while present at the murder of Joseph Smith in 1844. He became LDS church president following the death of Brigham Young.

Norman Taylor (1828–99). A teamster with the 1847 pioneer company and a returning pioneer, Taylor was born in Ohio. He returned to Salt Lake Valley with his wife, Lurana Forbush Taylor, and in 1850 married her sister, Lydia. He returned to Utah from San Bernardino in 1857 and died at Moab.

The Therlkills. George W. Therlkill (who with his incessant questions at Pueblo so irritated Francis Parkman that he appeared in *The Oregon Trail* "as a sample of the loutishness of western emigrants") and his wife, Matilda Jane Crow Therlkill, daughter of Robert Crow, lost their son, Milton Howard Therlkill (1843–47), in the Salt Lake Valley on 11 August, when he drowned. Three days later, Matilda gave birth to Harriet Ann Therlkill.

Robert T. Thomas (1820–92). A wagonwright with the 1847 pioneer company, Thomas was born in North Carolina. He was an early settler and justice of the peace at Provo, where he died. RH, DUP.

Horace Thornton (1822–1914). A hunter with the 1847 pioneer company and a member of the ox team return company, Thornton was born in New York. He was one of Orson Pratt's advance guard. He lived throughout Utah and died at Manti.

Marcus Ball Thorpe (1822–49). A member of the 1847 pioneer company and a returning pioneer, Thorpe was born in Connecticut. He returned to Utah in 1848 and the following year went to California to get money to bring his family to Utah. He left California with his savings in a money belt in 1849, but fell overboard on the voyage round the Horn. His body and money were not recovered. RH.

John Harvey Tippets (1810–90). A member of the 1847 pioneer company, Tippets was born in New Hampshire and was baptized in 1832. He joined the Mormon Battalion and on 23 December 1846, he and Thomas Woolsey started from Pueblo for Winter Quarters with money and mail for the Saints. He died a patriarch at Farmington.

William Perkins Vance (1822–1914). A member of the 1847 pioneer company, Vance was born in Tennessee and was baptized in 1842. He lived for a time in the home of Joseph Smith. He explored southern Utah with Parley P. Pratt and was one of the first settlers of Iron County. He died at Lund, Nevada.

Henson Walker (1820–1904). A hunter with the 1847 pioneer company, Walker was born in New York and was baptized in 1840. He became bishop and mayor of Pleasant Grove, Utah, where he died, the father of twenty children.

George Benjamin Wallace (1817–1900). A captain of fifty in the 1847 second division, Wallace had been Nauvoo's undertaker. He served a mission to England from 1849–52 and was president of the Salt Lake Stake from 1874–76.

George Wardle (1820–1901). A member of the Poor Camp and the 1847 pioneer company, Wardle was born in Cheddelton, England, and was baptized in 1839. He was the husband of Thomas Bullock's sister Fanny. With the Bullocks and Rushtons, he emigrated to America in 1843. He was a talented musician and played at the laying of the cornerstones of the Salt Lake Temple in 1853; his cello is displayed at the Museum of Church History and Art in Salt Lake. He settled at Vernal, Utah, where he died.

William Shin Wardsworth (or Wordsworth) (1810–88). A member of the 1847 pioneer company, Wordsworth was born in New Jersey and was baptized in 1841. He died at Springville, Utah.

Jacob Weiler (1808–96). A member of the 1847 pioneer company and a returning pioneer, Weiler was born in Pennsylvania and was baptized in 1841. In 1847, he met his family in the second division and returned to Utah. He served as a bishop in Salt Lake City for nearly forty years and died there, a patriarch. RH.

Daniel H. Wells (1814-1891). A member of the Council of Fifty, Wells served as commander of the Nauvoo Legion in Utah territory, as mayor of Salt Lake, and as Brigham Young's second councilor from 1857–77.

John Wheeler (1802–?). A member of the 1847 pioneer company and a returning pioneer, Wheeler was born in South Carolina. He returned to Utah in 1848 where he was a noted stockman. After 1861 he moved to California and "became lost to the knowledge of his former friends."

Edson Whipple (1805–94). A member of the 1847 pioneer company, Whipple was born in Vermont and was baptized in 1840. His wife, mother, and daughter died near

Winter Quarters. He drew the plan for Parowan, Utah, and built the first thresher there. He died at Colonia Juarez, Mexico. DUP.

The Whitneys. The 1847 pioneer company included two sons of presiding bishop Newel K. Whitney (1795–1852). Both returned to Winter Quarters with Brigham Young. Horace Kimball Whitney (1823–84) was born at Kirtland and married Heber C. Kimball's favorite daughter, Helen Mar. He was "an expert mathematician and an accomplished musician" and learned the printer's trade in Nauvoo. Whitney set type for the first issue of the *Deseret News*. He was the father of apostle and historian Orson F. Whitney. Orson Kimball Whitney (1830–84) was born at Kirtland and "took part in numerous expeditions in connection with Indian depredations and was a daring and adventurous frontiersman." DUP.

James Whitehead (1813–98). An English clerk, Whitehead served as William Clayton's assistant in the Nauvoo recorder's office from June 1842. He refused to issue an order for Bullock to cross the Mississippi during the evacuation of Nauvoo.

Benjamin Whitehead. Among the wounded in the Battle of Nauvoo, Whitehead served as blacksmith for the Poor Camp.

Almon Mack Williams (1807–84). A member of the 1847 pioneer company and of the returning ox team company, Williams was born in New York. He apparently never returned to Utah. RH.

Thomas Stephen Williams (1826–60). A sergeant in the Mormon Battalion, "the notorious" Tom Williams was born in Tennessee and "made his brag that he had stolen [everything] from a hen on her [nest] to a steamboat engine." Williams joined the gold rush and became a prominent Salt Lake lawyer and merchant. He apostatized when his daughter eloped with Heber C. Kimball's son and his business interests clashed with Brigham Young. Williams settled briefly in Missouri, but returned to Utah in 1858 and became involved with the crusade against the LDS church in 1858-59. Williams was killed on the Mojave Desert in mysterious circumstances. WB.

Wilford Woodruff (1807–98). An apostle, member of the 1847 pioneer company, and a returning pioneer, Woodruff was born in Connecticut. He kept one of the best pioneer company journals. As fourth president of the LDS church, Woodruff renounced polygamy with the Manifesto of 1890. He died while visiting friends in San Francisco.

George Woodward (1817–1903). A member of the 1847 pioneer company, Woodward was born in New Jersey and was baptized in 1840. He pioneered southern Utah and was a prominent citizen of St. George, where he died.

Thomas Woolsey (1806–97). A member of the 1847 pioneer company and a returning pioneer, Woolsey was born in Kentucky and was baptized in 1838. He joined the Mormon Battalion and returned to Winter Quarters from Pueblo with mail. He returned to Utah in 1852 and died at Wales, the father of 27 children. RH.

The Youngs. The sons of John Young (1763–1839) and Abigail Howe (1766–1815) were prominent among Utah pioneers. Joseph Young (1797–1881) came to Utah in 1850. Phinehas Howe Young (1799–1879) was born in Hopkinton, Massachusetts, and worked as a printer, saddler, and contractor. He was captain of the third ten of the 1847 pioneer company and served missions to Canada and to England before dying in Salt Lake City. Brigham Young (1801–77) was born at Whitingham, Vermont, and was baptized in 1832. He led the 1847 pioneer company as president of the Twelve Apostles. He served as governor of Utah territory and directed the settlement of more than 300 towns. Clarissa Decker Young (1828–89), a plural wife of Brigham Young, was born in Freedom, New York. One of the three women in the original pioneer company, she stayed in Great Salt Lake City while her husband returned to Winter Quarters, "and was an example of patience and industry to the pioneer women." Joseph Angell Young (1834–75) was the son of Brigham Young and his second wife; he came to Utah about 1848 and "figured prominently in emigrant affairs." Brigham Young's brother, Lorenzo Dow Young (1807–95), was born in New York. His wife, Harriet Page Wheeler Young (1803–71), was born in New Hampshire and was one of three women in the original pioneer company. She was the mother of Clarissa Decker Young and Isaac Perry Decker. Joseph Watson Young (1829–73) and Lorenzo Zobieski Young (1841–1904) were sons of Lorenzo D. Young by Persis Goodall. Joseph Watson came to Utah in the 1847 second division, while Lorenzo Zobieski arrived with his father and Harriet Young as the youngest member of the pioneer company. His odd name was said to trace from John III, king of Poland. Like his father, Zobieski, as he was generally called, loved horticulture. He died at Shelley, Idaho, survived by several children.

Henry Isaac Young (1798-1885). A second cousin to Brigham Young and a LDS church member from 1842, Young married Temperance Jolley and managed the Nauvoo Temple during the last days of the Mormon city. He carried the temple key with him to Utah, where he died in Juab County. DUP.

Appendix A
THOMAS BULLOCK PAPERS AND JOURNALS

This appendix describes the location of some of the diaries and papers of Thomas Bullock and provides a physical description of Bullock's Mormon Trail journals from the 1840s.

PAPERS

The LDS Archives, the Harold B. Lee Library at Brigham Young University, and the Daughters of Utah Pioneers have collections of Thomas Bullock's papers. "Thomas Bullock—Pioneer," in Volume 8 of Kate B. Carter, ed., *Our Pioneer Heritage*, 20 vols. (Salt Lake City: Daughters of Utah Pioneers, 1961–77), includes the text of one of the notes Bullock sent his wife in April 1847. The files at the Daughters' Pioneer Memorial Museum contain several Bullock family biographies. Additional papers may be in the possession of the Bullock family.

Orval M. Allen Diary, 1846. MS 307, LDS Archives. This "Camp Journal" of the 1846 Poor Camp is in Bullock's handwriting and appears to have been dictated by Orval Allen and composed by Bullock.

Thomas Bullock, Letter to Willard Richards, 10 September 1846, MS 5213, Folder 1, LDS Archives.

Henrietta Rushton Bullock Collection, 1836–1914, MS 5404:1-3, LDS Archives. Folder 1 contains letters from Thomas Bullock to his wife, beginning 23 December 1836 and ending 22 August 1839. Folder 2 begins with an 8 October 1846 letter from Willard Richards at Winter Quarters to Thomas Bullock. Items 3, 4, and 5 are letters written from Thomas Bullock to Henrietta Bullock dated 10 May, 14 May, and 9 June 1847.

Thomas Bullock Journals 1843–49, MS 1385:1-5, LDS Archives. These are Bullock's 1846–48 trail journals. Folder 1 contains the Poor Camp journal. Detailed daily accounts of his journey with the pioneer company to the Salt Lake Valley are contained in two journals in folder 2, both with indexes. Folder 3 contains the journal of the returning pioneers, and folder 4 holds the 1848 journal. Folder 5 is a catch-all of wonderful trail documents. It contains several "Sketches from the journal for the benefit & comfort of the Saints that follow after"; minutes of a meeting at Fort Laramie; a table of distances from Fort Laramie to Green River; Bullock's transcription of a Lansford W. Hastings waybill; and a hand-sewn manuscript guidebook of the "Pioneers return from G.S.L. City."

The Edyth Jenkins Romney typescripts of the Thomas Bullock journals are in MS 2737:22, LDS

Archives.

Thomas Bullock Papers, 1844–81, MS 12475:1-8, LDS Archives. This collection includes manuscripts, blessings, broadsides, poems, lyrics, a "Geographical and Historical Catechism of Utah Designed for Schools by Thomas Bullock," and an autobiographical obituary composed in September 1876.

Thomas Bullock Collection, Vault MSS 772, Special Collections & Manuscripts, Harold B. Lee Library, Brigham Young University. See David J. Whittaker, Errin Parker, and Chris McClellan, *[Register of the] Thomas Bullock Collection*, Harold B. Lee Library, 1993. This includes Thomas Bullock's 1845 Nauvoo journal, which was donated to BYU in December 1987 by a branch of the Bullock family in Colorado and which is published as Greg R. Knight, ed., *Thomas Bullock Nauvoo Journal*.

Thomas Bullock, Winter Quarters Minutes. LR 5613 21, LDS Archives. This leather-bound notebook contains records of the 11th ward at Winter Quarters in the handwriting of Bullock and a second unidentified clerk. It includes a list of ward members, tithing accounts, a "Wood Account," listings of "Contributions to Sisters whose husbands are in the Army," and cash "Paid to the Widows and Sisters whose husbands are in the Army."

Thomas Bullock, A Mormon Trail Journal of Thomas Bullock, May–June, 1858, transcribed by La Jean Purcell, typescript by Rita Bowers, Manuscripts Division, Harold B. Lee Library, Brigham Young University.

Maps

The LDS Archives has these Bullock maps of Winter Quarters and Great Salt Lake City:

Thomas Bullock, Plan of Winter Quarters. MS 8774, LDS Archives.

Thomas Bullock, Plat of Great Salt Lake City, 1847, MS 9118, Folder 2, LDS Archives. This folder contains Bullock's rough plat of the city and assigns land to members of the Twelve in Great Salt Lake City. Its 9x11-inch block plat covers 400 North to 600 South and 300 East to 500 West. A replica is on display at the LDS Museum of Church History and Art in Salt Lake City.

Thomas Bullock, Plat of Great Salt Lake City, ca. 1847 or 1848, MS 9118, Folder 2, LDS Archives. This folder contains a 9x15 block plat of Great Salt Lake City in brown ink, slightly run throughout. It covers 500 North to 900 South and from 300 East to 500 West, showing the Fort and public squares. One square is assigned to J. Ferguson and A. O. Smoot, who were not in Great Salt Lake City with Bullock; most other names are of apostles in Salt Lake in 1847. The map is drawn on heavy paper glued on a canvas backing.

Thomas Bullock, Plat of Great Salt Lake City, ca. 1848, MS 9118, Folder. 3, LDS Archives. Photocopy of map/plat showing blocks and property assignments. It was labeled Utah-SLC/1847, but contains the names of 1848 pioneers, including "H. Stout" and "A Nëbaur."

Published Letters and Speeches

Thomas Bullock, "Letter from the Camp to Elder Franklin Richards," *Latter-day Saints' Millennial Star*, 10 (15 January 1848), 28–30.

Thomas Bullock, "Letter from Thomas Bullock [to Griffith William]," 4 January 1848, *Latter-day Saints' Millennial Star*, 10 (15 April 1848), 116–19.

Thomas Bullock, letter to Levi Richards, 10 July 1848, in "Letters from the Camp of Israel," *Latter-day Saints' Millennial Star*, 10 (15 October 1848), 313–15.

Thomas Bullock, letter to Levi Richards, 24 August 1848, in "Glorious News from the Salt Lake," *Latter-day Saints' Millennial Star*, 10 (15 December 1848), 369–71.

Thomas Bullock, "Celebration of the Twenty-Fourth of July at Great Salt Lake City," *Latter-day Saints' Millennial Star*, 11 (1 December 1849), 353–59.

Thomas Bullock, "Letter from Elder Thomas Bullock to Elder John O. Angus," 18 December 1851, *Latter-day Saints' Millennial Star*, 14 (3 July 1852), 298–300.

Thomas Bullock, "Oration," *Latter-day Saints' Millennial Star*, 14 (23 October 1852), 546–51.

"Thomas Bullock, Pioneer" in Kate B. Carter, ed., *Our Pioneer Heritage*, 8: 229–96, contains a number of Bullock letters, including a 20 April 1847 note to his wife, Henrietta. (Although Carter edited the series, *Our Pioneer Heritage*, the actual author of this study is unidentified.)

THE TRAIL JOURNALS

Six physical journals constitute Bullock's 1846 to 1848 trail diaries and all are now in the Library-Archives of the Church of Jesus Christ of Latter-day Saints. They are composed in Bullock's tiny and meticulous hand, and all show the wear and tear of their origin.

THE POOR CAMP JOURNAL

The 1846 "Poor Camp" journal is a simple, hand-sewn collection of 116 pages measuring 19.5 cm by 8 cm. The journal has no cover or binding. The first page is covered with odd notes, and the journal proper begins on the first interior page. The journal text runs length-wise, while the occasional tables are on separate pages and cross the shorter dimension. Daily entries end on 15 December 1846 with the entry "wife sick." Some twenty-five pages, including blank pages, accounts, a list of items collected from the Poor Company for sale, a summary of the party's food supplies, and a twelve-page census of Winter Quarters, follow. The journal ends with an index.

THE 1847 JOURNALS

Bullock's 1847 account of the "Pioneer Camp of the Saints" consists of three journals, The Pioneer Camp of the Saints, Journal No. 1; The Pioneer Camp of the Saints, Journal No. 2; and the Return Pioneer Journal 1847. The first two documents are a matched pair of commercially manufactured journals bound in light-brown leather that measure 17.7 cm by 11.7 cm (7 inches by 4 ⅝ inches). The covers are worn and are pulling away from their end-sheets. Paper labels are pasted to the spine and read "Bullock's Pioneer Camp Journal," plus the journal number: "No. 1" and "No.

"No. 2." The labels' text is now almost invisible from wear. Both journals are composed in a very dark brown ink, which contrasts with a darker black ink used to write the indexes at the back of the journals. The pages have faint blue lines and are divided by four vertical red lines.

The Pioneer Camp of the Saints, Journal No. 1

In "No. 1," the first page reads: "Journal of the Pioneer Camp of the Saints, from Winter Quarters, in search of a location for a Stake of Zion kept by Thomas Bullock." Three blank pages follow and the journal begins on the first numbered page with the entry for 7 April 1847. The text ends with the 18 June entry on page 102, with the words, "those who were staying voted that they did not want Glines to stay." Page 103 lists accounts for the ferry at the North Platte; pages 104–07 are blank, short notes for 16-18 April and the "Laws Regulating the Camp of Israel" follow on pages 108–09. A list of camps and mileages follow on pages 110–111, and a brief record of a birth attended by Patty Sessions is on page 112. A three-page index begins on page 113. Pages 116–17 are numbered but blank; two more blank pages follow. The last page contains notes from the Mormon Ferry and the name of "La mie friend / The old chief of the Ogolallahs" and "2nd 50. Samuel Russel's Co. 16 sheep 4 Pigs 57 (Poultry)."

The Pioneer Camp of the Saints, Journal No. 2

Journal "No. 2" starts with a brief complaint and then proceeds to the entry for 19 June 1847. Except for wear and content, the journal is physically identical to its predecessor and begins with these words on the title page: "Journal of the Travel of the Pioneer Camp of Israel, from Winter Quarters, in search of a location for a Stake of Zion kept by Thomas Bullock Clerk of the Pioneer Camp." Page numbers begin as page 1 on the fourth page, and journal entries run to page 112, ending with the 21 September 1847 entry. Page 113 lists camps and dates, while pages 113–17 are blank, except for one short sum: 382/513/895. A five-page index begins on page 118.

Return Pioneer Journal

Bullock filled his two commercial journals and apparently improvised the Return Pioneer Journal 1847. It is a hand-sewn and unbound set of sixty-two numbered pages. Thomas Bullock is written on the front sheet in blue ink, but not in Bullock's handwriting. "Return Pioneer Journal, 1847" is written below the name, in Bullock's handwriting. The journal measures

16 cm by 9.5 cm. The first interior page is numbered 2 and lists the "Military Organization" of the returning Brigham Young party, while the third page lists the members of the "Traveling Organization" and their stock. The journal proper begins on page 4, with a continuation of Bullock's 21 September 1847 entry. The last entry is on page 43 on 28 October 1847, with Willard Richard's remarkable complaint about the ox teams. Pages 44-59 are blank while the remaining pages are blank to the index, which runs from pages 60–62.

THE 1848 JOURNALS

Two 1848 journals complete the set of Thomas Bullock's trail diaries in the LDS Archives. They are physically similar to the 1847 journals, except the blue-lined pages are not divided into columns. The first journal, "Camp Journal No. 1," covers May to September 1848. "Camp Journal No. 2, 1848" covers September 1848 to January 1849.

Appendix B

BULLOCK'S NOTES AT THE END OF JOURNAL NO. 1, 1847

These notes are appended to "The Pioneer Camp of the Saints, Journal No. 1," following the entry of 18 June 1847.

[FERRY ACCOUNTS ON THE NORTH PLATTE]

Received of Christopher Ashworth's Co.
    1 Bushel of Beans ——— 1.25
    1 — do. ——— 1.20
    1' do.— meal 75
    153 lbs Flour - 2' — 3.82'
    Sack ——— 20
    Heifer ——— 7.00
    Cash ——— 6.55} 6.80
    Discount ———.25__
') 14 Wagons @ 1.50   21.02'
<u>7</u>
21.00

Received of Captn. Smiths' Company
    5' Bushel meal 1.75
        05
    916 lbs Flour @ 2' 22.90
    Peck of Beans ——— 31
    Honey ——————— 1 —
18 wagons at 1.50   27.01
<u>9</u>
27.00

received of Captn. Kerl's Company
    226 lbs Flour @ 2' <u>5.65</u>
    92 Shorts 1" 1.15
    117 Soap .10 11.70
    6 Pulgs Tobacco .25 1.50
    Cow ——— <u>10.00</u>
20 Wagons at 1.50   30.00
<u>10</u>
30.00
        21.00
        27.00
        <u>30.00</u>
    Total <u>78.00</u> from 3 camps

Cash
Tobacco
Flour
Meal
Beans
Soap
Delivered to
Lorenzo Young for Iron   2.00
Ed Ellsworth. night work   5
Luke Johnson   — do. — 5
Melen Atwood   — do. — 0 61
A. Gibbons   — do. — 0
J. Norton   — do. — 30
J.S. Higbee   — do. — 5
Discount   ——— 25
    B. Young .10
        6.80√
H.C. Kimball———.50.167
B. Young——— .75
John S. Fowler———————.25 20
        1.50√
W. Richards ————————— 9
O. Pratt ————————— 5
E.T. Benson ————————— 5
G.A. Smith ————————— 5
W. Woodruff ————————— 5
P. H. Young ——————}167 ——— 5
T. Tanner ———————— ——— 5
A. Everett ——————95 ——— 6
John Y. Green ———————— 6
O. P. Rockwell ——————— 100 <u>118</u>
Hanks & Fox ——————— 68 —
Zebedee Coltrin ——————— 13 —
H. C. Kimball ——————— 2 B?? —
Jacob Weiler ——————— 1' Peck —

J. G. Holman	— 2 —		Epitome delivered out	
Rockwood & Scofield	—41 2 —	cash	— 6.80	
Lewis Barney	— 33 —	tobacco	--- 1.50	
Andrew Gibbons	— 15 3/4 —	195.5 lbs	T. Co —32.37'	
Norman Taylor	— 18 —	92 Shorts	— 1.15	
James Craig	— 1' —	TB. meal	— 3.50	
Brigham Young	~~894~~ 401 1" 5	2" Beans	— 2.87	
	√√ ~~1788~~ 712.97	118 ℔ Soap	— 11.80	
	1295	2 cows	— 17.00	
	Prest. Young 2 cows 17.00	Honey	— 1.00	
	Honey 1.00		77.93	
	92 ℔ Shorts 1.15		.20	
			78.13	

increase on soap .10 } 13'
fractions 3' 1.50

Laws Regulating the Camp of Israel

1st. After this date, the Horn shall be blown every morning at 5 o'clock when every man is expected to arise and pray–then attend to his cattle, get breakfast, and have every thing finished, so that the Camp may start by seven o'clock.

2nd. Each extra man to travel on the off side of the Team, with his Gun over his Shoulder, loaded; and each driver have his gun so placed, that he can lay hold of it at a moments warning. every Gun must have a piece of Leather over the Nipple of his Gun, or if it is a flint lock, in the pan–having caps, & Powder Flask ready.

3rd. The brethren will halt for an hour, about noon, & they must have their dinner ready cooked, & not detain the Camp for cooking.

4th. When the Camp halts for the night, Wagons to be in a circle, where the fires shall be built; the horses to be all retired inside the circle when necessary.

5th. The Horn will be blown at ½ past 8 when every Man must retire to his Wagon & pray (except the night Guard) and be in bed by 9 o'clock, at which hour, all fires must be put out.

6th. The Camp to travel in close order, and no man to leave the Camp, 20 rods without orders from his Captain.

7th. Every man to feel as much interest, in taking care of his brother's cattle and preserving it, as he would of his own– and Indulge no man in Idleness.

8th. Every man have his Guns and Pistols in perfect order.

9th. Let the Tens keep together–and the cannon bring up the rear, the company organized to attend it, travel along with it–and see that nothing is left behind at each stopping place.

[CAMPS AND MILEAGES, 1847]
[Journal pages 110–111]

	1847 April	miles					
				Tuesday	18	15¾	
				Wednesday	19	8	
Tues	13	6		Thursday	20	15¾	
Wed	14	22		Friday	21	15½	
Thurs	15	20		Saturday	22	<u>15½</u>	
Fri	16	4					83 ¼
Satur	17	<u>8</u>		Monday	24	16½	
		in a week 60		Tuesday	25	12	
Mon	19	20		Wednesday	26	12¼	
Tue	20	18		Thursday	27	13¾	
Wed	21	18		Friday	28	1½	
Thur	22	20		Saturday	29	<u>8½</u>	
Fri	23	6					74½
Sat	24	<u>4</u>		Monday	31	16¾	
			86	June			
Mon	26	17		Tuesday	1	12	
Tue	27	18		227 miles from Junction			
Wed	28	16		___ to Laramie			
Thur	29	20		560 to Winter Quarters			
Fri	30	16					
	May			[sideways] From Fort John Total to Winter			
Sat	1	<u>15</u>		Quarters 560			
			102	June			
Sunday	2	2		Friday	4	8¼	
Tuesday	4	11		Saty.	5	<u>17</u>	
Wednes	5	13				25¼ (54 this week)	
Thurs	6	19			6	5	
Friday	7	7				17	
Saturday	8	12				<u>11¼</u>	
			64			1	98¾
	1847				19	<u>21½</u>	
	May	312	312				22½
Sunday	9	4		[Many of the June dates are illegible.]			
Monday	10	16		day	20	20	
Tuesday	11	7		day	21	15¼	
	2 <u>333 miles to Junction of N & S Forks</u>			day	22	20¾	
Wednes	12	12		day	23	17	
Thursday	13	10¾		day	24	17¾	
Friday	14	8¾		day	25	20¼	
Saturday	15	<u>7</u>		day	26	<u>18¾</u>	
			61½				129¾
Monday	17	12¾					836¼

day	27	15¼	Tuesday	6	18"	
day	28	15¼	Wednesday	7	17¼	397 miles from Fort John to Bridger
day	29	23¾				
			Friday	9	13	
[*Sideways between columns*]			Saturday	10	18	87
From Winter Quarters to Junction of Forks 333 miles			Monday	12	16½	
			Thursday	15	4½	
Junction to Fort John ——————— 227			Friday	16	16¼	
Fort John to Fort Bridger ———— 397			Saturday	17	2½	39¾
Fort Bridger to Farm ——————— 116			Monday	19	13¾	
From Fort John From Winter Quarters			Tuesday	20	7"	
		330	Wednesday	21	14	
	June		Thursday	22	7¼	
Wednesday	30	8	Friday	23	2½	44¾
Saturday	July 3	3	Total		1073	
		65¾				
Monday	5	20				

NOTES AT THE END OF JOURNAL NO. I

"I *Patty Sessions* delivered *Rebecca*, Wife of *Jonathan C. Wright*
"of A Son, named *Enoch*, born Novr. 16 {1846} 8 o'clock A.M."
[113–115 Index]
[116–117, blank pages]
[118 copy]
by Pole Star

	Wagons	Buggy	Horses & Mules	Y. of Oxen	Cows	
Monday 6 1st. Emigrating Co.	10	1				
Tuesday 7 2nd. ———————	19	2	25	—	73	100 we ferried over
3rd. ———————		13	—	14	—	43 64
9 4th. ———————	6 men	—	15		—	
16 5th. ———————	9	1	10	—	33	—
17 6 ———————		21			—	—

[bottom of page, upside down]
La Mie
La mie Friend
The old chief of the Ogalallahs

2nd. 50. *Samuel Rusell's* Co. 16 Sheep 4 Pigs 57 (Poultry)
[End of Journal I]

Appendix C

Notes from the Returning Pioneer Journals

These notes and tables appeared at the end of Bullock's "The Pioneer Camp of the Saints, Journal No. 2," following the entry of 21 September 1847.

In three weeks 376 [miles] From Great Salt Lake City 426½

Thursday 26	14¾	Willow Springs
Friday 27	14¾	Kanyon Creek
Saturday 28	20¾	Red Fork
Sunday 29	23½	Ragged Rocks
Monday 30	20¾	East side of Divide
Tuesday 31	21½	Fort Bridger
September		
Wednesday 1st.	31¾	Black's Fork
		147¾
Thursday 2nd.	23¾	Green River
Friday 3	26	Big Sandy
Saturday 4	8½	Little Sandy
Sunday 5	24½	Pacific Springs
Tuesday 7	12	Sweetwater
Wednesday 8	11	Small Creek
		107¾
Friday 10	15¾	N. side Sweetwater
Saturday 11	21¼	N. side Sweetwater
Sunday 12	20¾	S. side Sweetwater
Monday 13	19½	E. Side Devil's Gate
Tuesday 14	18½	creek
Wednesday 15	24¾	Spring & Lake
		128½
Thursday 16	12	Upper Ferry
Friday 17	12½	S. side N Fork. Platte
Saturday 18	16¾	Deer Creek
Sunday 19	9	Fourche Boisee'

In three weeks 376 √
From Great Salt Lake City 426¼√

Monday 20	28	La Bonte
Tuesday 21	——	——
Wednesday 22	15½	Heber's Spring
		93¾
Thursday 23	28½	Warm Spring
Friday 24	<u>14¾</u>	Fort Laramie
		<u>513 miles</u>
Sunday 26	7	down Platte
Monday 27	17	— " —
Tuesday 28	19	— " —
Wednesday	29	S. Chimney Rock
		108¼
Thursday 30	23 mi	Sand Bluffs
October		
Saturday 2	15	Ancient Bluffs Ruins
Sunday 3	8	w. two hills on N side of :
Monday 4	18	mi. W. end of Castle Bl
Tuesday 5	14	opposite Ash Hollow
Wednesday 6	15	Camp Creek
Thursday 7	12	West side of Rattle snake C
Friday 8	15	East side of Spring Cree
Saturday 9	17	Junction Bluff Fork
Sunday 10	3	opposite an Island
Monday 11	12	Eagle's Nest
Tuesday 12	15	Bank of a Slough 227
		5 <u>232</u>
Wednesday 13	16	near an Island
		90
Thursday 14	12	— do. —
Friday 15	14	Platte

Saturday 16	21	Slough	Tuesday 26	20	Pawnee Mission
Sunday 17	2	Slough	Wednesday 27	27	Slough
Monday 18	10	Grand Island	Thursday 28	25	Shell Creek
Wednesday 20	21	Grand Island	Friday 29	24	Platte
Thursday 21	15	Wood River	Saturday 30	13	Elk Horn
Friday 22	13	Prairie Creek	Sunday 31	<u>26</u>	Winter Quarters
Saturday 23	23	Loup Fork			525
Monday 25	8	Old Pawnee Town			

[page 114 blank]

Latitude of Great Salt Lake City 40.°45'.50" Temple block
Thomas Bullock
New York City Hall 40° 42' 30"
     Nauvoo   40 36   by Quadrant
Stephen H. Goddard
Rufus Beach
Harvey Pierce
Charles A Harper
Levi N. Kendall
Arza E. Hinkley
James Lawson
John O. Angus
James Hawkins
Stephen H. Goddard
Fremont's Barometer height of Salt Lake 4200 feet
Profr. Pratts ––––– Temple Block 4360–
Barometric height of West Peak of the Twins
Observation by Carrington 11.219–
Height of said Peak above Temple Block 6919–
rough calculation
Hot Spring 126° 15°45'50"
TB Warm Spring 109° variation
New York Agriculturalist
Nassau Street
between John & Spruce

2.94	Wm. Roe	
10.00	Thos. James	Fort John
8.00	J. J. Terril	

[side ways]
Albert Sharpe Scipio Cuyahoga Co. New York 21st Septr. 1828
[bottom of page upside down]
[page 118–121 index]

Thomas Bullock Return Pioneer Journal 1847
Military Organization[1]

Independent Company	First Ten	Second Ten
Brigham Young	Howard Egan Captain	Thomas Tanner, Captain
Heber C. Kimball	Dexter Stillman	Stephen Kelsey
Willard Richards	Stephen H. Goddard	Thomas Karron
Orson Pratt	Trueman O. Angel	John F. Wreston
Wilford Woodruff	George Clarke	Isaac N. Wreston
George A. Smith	Albert Sharpe	Samuel Fox
Amasa Lyman	Joel J. Terrill	John G. Luce
Ezra T. Benson	A.P. Chessley	George R. Grant
Albert P. Rockwood	Norman Taylor	David Grant
Stephen Markham	Samuel Gould	Milton How
Thomas Bullock	10	10
11		

Third Ten	Fourth Ten	Fifth Ten
Luke Johnson Captain	Charles A. Harper Capn	George Wilson Capn
Thomas Woolsey	Ralph Douglas	William Roe
William Baldwin	Orson K. Whitney	James W. Cawkins
Pliny Fisher	Ezekiel Kellogg	Jesse Johnstone
Samuel Bird	John Buchanan	John Crow
Jesse C. Little	Ozro Eastman	William A. Park
Abel M. Sarjent	William Miles	Arza E. Hinkley
Andrew S. Gibbons	Judson Persons	John Brimhall
George Duncan	William W. Rust	Joseph Matthews
9	9	9

[These arms are shown by military company:]
   [ind] 27 Rifle Shots
   13 Musket shots
   105 Pistol shots
   [1] 17 Rifle Shots
   02 Pistol Shots
   [2] 01 Rifle Shot
   08 Pistol Shot
   [3] 13 Rifle Shots
   01 Musket
   12 Pistol
   [4] 2 Rifle Shots
   3 Musket
   3 Pistol
   [5] 01 Rifle
   01 musket
   01 Pistol

---

[1] As noted in that day's entry, Bullock compiled this list on 27 September 1847.

Teamster Company

Barnabas L. Adams	Melen Atwood	George Billings
Hosea Cushing	Alvorus L. Hanks	Horace K. Whitney
Benjamin Richmond	John G. Holman	William Terrill
David Laughlin	William Dykes	Horace M. French
George Brown	Hayward Thomas	Joseph Rooker
Joseph Egbert	Charles Barnham	Solomon Chamberlin
John Brown	Erastus Snow	Caritad C. Roe
Peter Meshech	William King	Benjamin Stewart
Matthew Ivory	James Camp	
26		

24 Rifle Shots
02 Musket Shots
14 Pistol Shots

[Returning Pioneers] Traveling Organization

	horses	mules		horses	mules
Brigham Young	4	–	John T. Wreston		
Trueman O. Angel			Isaac N. Wreston		
Albert P. Rockwood	1	1	Erastus Snow		
Stephen H. Goddard			George Brown		
Heber C. Kimball	1	4	10	3	
Hosea Cushing			Thomas Tanner	2	–
Orson Pratt	2	–	Millen Atwood		
Joseph Egbert	5		Sidney A. Hanks		
Willard Richards			John G. Luce		
Thomas Bullock	–	3	John Holman		
Ben. Richmond	5		George R. Grant	5	
Wilford Woodruff	2	1	9	4	7
Dexter Stillman			David Laughlin		
George A. Smith	2	2	William Dykes		
Amasa Lyman	2	–	David Grant		
A.P. Chessley			Haywood Thomas		
Ezra T. Benson			George S. Clarke	2	1
Matthew Ivory			Thomas Woolsey		
	18	9	Samuel Fox		
John Brown			Charles Banion	3	
Barnabas L. Adams	1	2	Samuel Bird		
Thomas Karron			Pliny Fisher		
Samuel Gould			William Bolden		
Joel J. Terrill			Millon Howe		
Peter I. Meshek	2	1	9	?	23

	horses	mules			horses	mules	
Howard Egan				Joseph Rooker			
William A. King	I	–		Judson Persons			
Andrew Gibbons				Solomon Chamberlin	2	I	
George Billings				Ezekiel Kellogg			
Ralph Douglas				William Roe			
Abel M. Sargent	2			Cartad C. Roe	2	I	
John Hart				James Cawkins			
Charles L Hart				8	3	6	I
Albert Sharp				George Wilson			
9	2	3		Arza E. Hinckley			
Orson K. Whitney				John Brimhall	2	I	
Horace K. Whitney	–	2		William W. Rust			
Stephen Markham	2	I		Jesse W. Johnston			
William Terrill	2			James Camp			
Monroe Frink				William A. Park			
Ozro Eastman	I			Joseph Matthews	2	I	
William Miles				Benjamin Stewart			
7	3	3	3	John Crow			
Charles A. Harper	2	I		10	2	4	2

BIBLIOGRAPHY

BOOKS

Allen, James B. *Trials of Discipleship: The Story of William Clayton, A Mormon* (Urbana: Univ. of Ill. Press, 1987).

────── and Glen M. Leonard. *The Story of the Latter-day Saints* (S.L.C.: Deseret Book Co., 1976).

Anderson, Maybelle Harmon, ed. *Appleton Milo Harmon Goes West* (Berkeley, CA: Gillick Press, 1946).

Andrews, Laurel B. *The Early Temples of the Mormons: The Architecture of the Millennial Kingdom in the American West* (Albany: State Univ. of N.Y. Press, 1978).

Arrington, Leonard J. *Brigham Young: American Moses* (N.Y.: Alfred A. Knopf, 1985).

──────, *Charles C. Rich: Mormon General and Western Frontiersman* (Provo: Brigham Young Univ. Press, 1974).

Bagley, Will, ed. *Frontiersman: Abner Blackburn's Narrative* (S.L.C.: Univ. of Utah Press, 1992).

Barry, Louise. *The Beginning of the West: Annals of the Kansas Gateway to the American West, 1540–1854* (Topeka: Kansas State Hist. Soc., 1972).

Bancroft, Hubert Howe. *History of Utah, 1540–1886* (San Francisco: History Co., 1889).

Barney, Lewis. "Excerpts from a Journal of the Trek," in L. J. Arrington, ed. *Voices from the Past: Diaries, Journals, and Autobiographies* (Provo: Brigham Young Univ. Press, 1980).

Bashore, Melvin L. and Linda L. Haslam. *Mormon Pioneer Companies Crossing the Plains (1847–1868) Narratives: Guide to Sources in Utah Libraries and Archives* (S.L.C.: Hist. Dept., The Church of Jesus Christ of Latter-day Saints, 1989).

Beecher, Maureen Ursenbach, ed. *The Personal Writings of Eliza Roxcy Snow* (S.L.C.: Univ. of Utah Press, 1995).

Bennett, Richard E. *The Mormons at the Missouri: "And Should We Die..."* (Norman: Univ. of Okla. Press, 1987).

Benton, Thomas Hart. *Thirty Years' View; or, A History of the Working of the American Government for Thirty Years, from 1820 to 1850*, 2 vols. (N.Y.: D. Appleton and Co., 1856).

Bieber, Ralph P., ed. "Cooke's Journal of the March of the Mormon Battalion, 1846–1847," in *Exploring Western Trails, 1846–1854*. Southwestern Hist. Series, VII (Glendale, CA: Arthur H. Clark Co., 1938).

Bigler, David L., ed. *The Gold Discovery Journal of Azariah Smith* (S.L.C.: Univ. of Utah Press, 1990).

Bitton, Davis. *Guide to Mormon Diaries & Autobiographies* (Provo, UT: Brigham Young Univ. Press, 1977).

Black, Susan Easton. *Early Members of the Church of Jesus Christ of Latter-day Saints, 1830–1848*, 50 vols. (Provo: Religious Studies Center, Brigham Young University, 1993).

Brodie, Fawn. *No Man Knows My History: The Life of Joseph Smith the Mormon Prophet* (N.Y.: Alfred A. Knopf, 1945. Second Edition, 1973).

Brooks, Juanita, ed. *On the Mormon Frontier: The Diary of Hosea Stout*, 2 vols. (S.L.C.: Univ. of Utah Press, 1964).

Brown, John. *Autobiography of Pioneer John Brown, 1820–1896* (S.L.C.: Stevens and Wallis, 1941).

Bryant, Edwin. *What I Saw in California* (N.Y.: D. Appleton & Co., 1848. Reprinted Palo Alto: Lewis Osborne, 1967).

Burton, Richard F. *The City of the Saints and Across the Rocky Mountains to California*, Fawn Brodie, ed. (N.Y.: Alfred A. Knopf, 1963).

Carter, Kate B., ed. *Heart Throbs of the West*, 12 vols. (S.L.C., Daughters of Utah Pioneers, 1955).

————. *Our Pioneer Heritage*, 20 vols. (S.L.C.: Daughters of Utah Pioneers, 1961–77).

————. *Treasures of Pioneer History*, 6 vols. (S.L.C., Daughters of Utah Pioneers, 1955–60).

————. "Thomas Bullock—Pioneer," in *Our Pioneer Heritage*, 8:229–96.

Chittenden, Hiram Martin. *The American Fur Trade in the Far West*, 2 vols. (Lincoln: Univ. of Neb. Press, 1986).

Clayton, William. *The Latter-Day Saints' Emigrants' Guide: Being a Table of Distances, showing all the springs, creeks, rivers, hills, mountains, camping places, and all the other notable places, from Council Bluffs to the Valley of the Great Salt Lake. Also, the latitudes, longitudes, and altitudes of the prominent points of the route. Together with remarks on the nature of the land, timber, grass, &c. The whole route having been measured by a Roadometer, and the distance from point to point, in English miles, accurately shown* (St. Louis: Mo. Republican Steam Press—Chambers and Knapp, 1848). Reprinted S. B. Kimball, ed. (St. Louis: Patrice Press, 1983).

————. "The Journal of William Clayton," in *Heart Throbs of the West*, compiled by Kate B. Carter, 12 vols. (S.L.C.: Daughters of Utah Pioneers, 1945 and 1994) 6:197–312.

Cleland, Robert Glass and Juanita Brooks, eds. *A Mormon Chronicle: The Diaries of John D. Lee 1848–1876*, 2 vols. (San Marino: Huntington Library, 1955. Reprinted S.L.C.: Univ. of Utah Press, 1983).

Cooke, Philip St. George. *The Conquest of New Mexico and California* (Albuquerque: Horn and Wallace, 1964).

Curtis, Luceal Rockwood, ed. *Compiled and Assembled History of Albert Perry Rockwood* (S.L.C.: 1968).

Daughters of Utah Pioneers, *The First Company to Enter Salt Lake Valley* (S.L.C.: Daughters of Utah Pioneers, 1993).

———. *An Enduring Legacy*, 12 vols. (S.L.C.: Daughters of Utah Pioneers, 1979).

Davies, J. Kenneth. *Mormon Gold: The Story of California's Mormon Argonauts* (S.L.C.: Olympus Pub. Co., 1984).

DeLafosse, Peter, ed. *Trailing the Pioneers* (Logan: Utah State Univ. Press, 1994).

DeVoto, Bernard. *The Year of Decision, 1846* (N.Y.: Houghton–Mifflin Co., 1943).

Doctrine and Covenants of The Church of Jesus Christ of Latter-day Saints (S.L.C.: LDS Church, 1921).

Egan, William M., ed. *Pioneering the West, 1846 to 1878: Major Howard Egan's Diary; also Thrilling Experiences of Pre-Frontier Life Among the Indians...and Part of Autobiography, Inter-Related to His Father's, by Howard R. Egan* (Richmond, UT: Howard R. Egan Estate, 1917).

Ellison, Robert Spurrier. *Independence Rock: The Great Record of the Desert* (Casper: Natrona County Hist. Soc., 1930).

Esshom, Frank. *Pioneers and Prominent Men of Utah* (S.L.C.: Western Epics, Inc., 1966).

Flanders, Robert Bruce. *Nauvoo: Kingdom on the Mississippi* (Urbana and Chicago: Univ. of Ill. Press, 1965).

Franzwa, Gregory M. *The Oregon Trail Revisited* (St. Louis: Patrice Press, 1972; Fourth edition, Tucson, 1988).

———. *Maps of the Oregon Trail* (St. Louis: Patrice Press, 1982; Third edition, 1990).

Frémont, John C. *Report of the Exploring Expedition to the Rocky Mountains in the Year 1842, and to Oregon and North California in the Years 1843–'44* (Washington: Gales and Seaton, 1845). Reprinted as Allan Nevins, ed. *Narratives of Exploration and Adventure by John Charles Frémont* (N.Y.: Longmans, Green & Co., 1956).

Golder, Frank Alfred, Thomas A. Bailey, and J. Lyman Smith. *The March of the Mormon Battalion from Council Bluffs to California, Taken from the Journal of Henry Standage* (N.Y.: Century Co., 1928).

Hafen, LeRoy R., ed. *The Mountain Men and the Fur Trade of the Far West*, 10 vols. (Glendale, CA: Arthur H. Clark Co., 1965–72).

——————— and Francis M. Young. *Fort Laramie and the Pageant of the West, 1834–1890* (Glendale, CA: Arthur H. Clark Co., 1938).

Hallwas, John E. and Roger D. Launius. *Cultures in Conflict: A Documentary History of the Mormon War in Illinois* (Logan: Utah State Univ. Press, 1995).

Hammond, George P., ed. *The Larkin Papers: Personal, Business, and Official Correspondence of Thomas Oliver Larkin, Merchant and United States Consul in California*, 10 vols. (Berkeley: Univ. of Calif. Press, 1951–68).

Hartley, William G. *My Best for the Kingdom: History and Autobiography of John Lowe Butler, A Mormon Frontiersman* (S.L.C.: Aspen Books, 1993).

Hanson, Klaus J. *Quest for Empire: The Political Kingdom of God and the Council of Fifty in Mormon History* (East Lansing: Mich. State Univ. Press, 1967).

Harlow, Neal. *California Conquered: War and Peace on the Pacific 1846–1850* (Berkeley: Univ. of Calif. Press, 1982).

Hastings, Lansford W. *The Emigrants' Guide, to Oregon and California; Containing Scenes and Incidents of a Party of Oregon Emigrants; A Description of Oregon; Scenes and Incidents of a Party of California Emigrants; and a Description of California; with a Description of the Different Routes to Those Countries; and All Necessary Information Relative to the Equipment, Supplies, and the Method of Traveling* (Cincinnati: George Conclin, 1845).

Jacob, Edward and Ruth S., eds. *The Record of Norton Jacob* (S.L.C.: Norton Jacob Family Assoc., 1949).

Andrew Jenson, ed. *Latter-day Saint Biographical Encyclopedia*, 4 vols. (S.L.C.: Andrew Jenson History Co., 1901. Reprinted S.L.C.: Western Epics, 1971).

Johnson, Clark V. *Mormon Redress Petitions: Documents of the 1833–1838 Missouri Conflict* (Provo: Bookcraft, 1992).

Journal of Discourses, 26 vols. (London: Latter-Day Saints Book Depot, 1854–86).

Kane, Thomas L. *"The Mormons." A Discourse Delivered Before the Historical Society of Pennsylvania, March 16, 1850* (Philadelphia: King and Baird Printers, 1850).

Kelly, Charles. *Salt Desert Trails* (S.L.C.: Western Printing Co., 1930. Third edition, S.L.C.: Western Epics, 1996).

Kelly, Charles, ed. *Journals of John D. Lee, 1846–47 & 1859* (S.L.C.: Western Printing Co., 1938. Reprinted S.L.C.: Univ. of Utah Press, 1984).

Kelly, Charles and Maurice L. Howe. *Miles Goodyear, First Citizen of Utah* (S.L.C.: Western Printing Co., 1937).

Kelly, Charles and Dale L. Morgan. *Old Greenwood* (Georgetown: Talisman Press, 1965).

Kenney, Scott G., ed. *Wilford Woodruff's Journal*, 10 vols. (Midvale: Signature Books, 1983).

Kimball, Stanley B. *Historic Resource Study: Mormon Pioneer National Historic Trail* (Washington: United States Dept. of the Interior/National Park Service, 1991).

———. *Historic Sites and Markers along the Mormon and Other Great Western Trails* (Urbana: Univ. of Ill. Press, 1988).

———. *Heber C. Kimball: Mormon Patriarch and Pioneer* (Urbana: Univ. of Ill. Press, 1981).

——— and Violet T. Kimball. *Mormon Trail, Voyage of Discovery: The Story Behind the Scenery* ([Las Vegas]: KC Publications, 1995).

Knight, Greg R., ed. *Thomas Bullock Nauvoo Journal* (Orem, UT: Grandin Book Co., 1994).

Knight, Hal and Stanley B. Kimball. *111 Days to Zion* (S.L.C.: Deseret Press, 1978).

Korns, Roderic and Dale L. Morgan, eds. *West from Fort Bridger: The Pioneering of Immigrant Trails across Utah, 1846–1850.* Revised and updated by Will Bagley and Harold Schindler (Logan: Utah State Univ. Press, 1994).

Lamar, Howard R., ed. *The Reader's Encyclopedia of the American West* (N.Y.: Thomas Y. Crowell Co., 1977).

Larson, Carl V. *A Data Base of the Mormon Battalion* (Providence, UT: Kieth W. Watkins and Sons Printing, Inc., 1987).

Larson, Carl V. *Women of the Mormon Battalion* (By the Author, 1989).

Lass, William E. *From the Missouri to the Great Salt Lake: An Account of Overland Freighting* (Lincoln: Neb. State Hist. Soc., 1972).

LeCompte, Janet. *Pueblo, Hardscrabble, Greenhorn: The Upper Arkansas, 1832–1856* (Norman: Univ. of Okla. Press, 1978).

LeSueur, Stephen C. *The 1838 Mormon War in Missouri* (Columbia: Univ. of Missouri Press, 1987).

Linforth, James. *Route from Liverpool to Great Salt Lake Valley*, ed. by Fawn Brodie, illus. by Frederick Hawkins Piercy (Cambridge: Belknap Press of Harvard Univ. Press, 1962).

Little, James A. *From Kirtland to Salt Lake City* (S.L.C.: James A. Little, 1890).

Daniel Ludlow, ed. *Encyclopedia of Mormonism*, 4 vols. (N.Y.: Macmillan Pub. Co., 1992).

McCormac, Eugene Irving. *James K. Polk: A Political Biography* (Berkeley: Univ. of Calif. Press, 1922).

Mattes, Merrill J. *The Great Platte River Road* (Lincoln: Neb. State Hist. Soc., 1969).

———. *Platte River Road Narratives* (Urbana: Univ. of Ill. Press, 1988).

Mintz, Lannon W. *The Trail: A Bibliography of the Travelers on the Overland Trail to California, Oregon, Salt Lake City, and Montana during the Years 1841–1864* (Albuquerque: Univ. of New Mex. Press, 1987).

Mitchell, S. Augustus. *Texas, Oregon and California* (Oakland, CA.: Biobooks, 1948).

Morgan, Dale L. *The Humboldt: Highroad of the West* (N.Y.: Farrar & Rinehardt, 1943).

———. *The Great Salt Lake* (Indianapolis: Bobbs-Merrill Co., 1947).

———. *Jedediah Smith and the Opening of the West* (Indianapolis: Bobbs-Merrill Co., 1953).

———. *Overland in 1846: Diaries and Letters of the California-Oregon Trail*, 2 vols. (Georgetown, CA: Talisman Press, 1963).

———. *News Clippings from Iowa and Illinois, 1841–1849* (Burlington, WI: John J. Hajicek, 1992).

——— and Eleanor Towles Harris, eds. *The Rocky Mountain Journals of William Marshall Anderson: The West in 1834* (San Marino: Huntington Library, 1967; Reprinted Lincoln: Univ. of Neb. Press, 1987).

Muir, Leo. *A Century of Mormon Activities in California*, 2 vols. (S.L.C.: Deseret News Press, 1951–52).

Mulder, William. *The Mormons in American History* (S.L.C.: Univ. of Utah Press, 1957).

——— and A. Russell Mortensen, *Among the Mormons: Historic Accounts by Contemporary Observers* (N.Y.: Alfred A. Knopf, 1958).

Newell, Linda King and Valeen Tippitts Avery. *Mormon Enigma: Emma Hale Smith* (Garden City, N.Y.: Doubleday and Co., 1984).

Parkman, Francis, Jr. *The California and Oregon Trail: Being Sketches of Prairie and Rocky Mountain Life* (N.Y.: George P. Putnam, 1849).

Parmelee, Robert D. *Pioneer Sonoma* (Sonoma, CA.: Sonoma Index-Tribune, 1972).

Quaife, Milo Milton, ed. *The Diary of James K. Polk During His Presidency, 1845 to 1849*, 4 vols. (Chicago: A. C. McClurg & Co., 1910).

Quinn, D. Michael. *The Mormon Hierarchy: Origins of Power* (S.L.C.: Signature Books, 1994).

Remy, Jules. *A Journey to Great-Salt-Lake City*, 2 vols. (London: W. Jeffs, 1860).

Roberts, Brigham H. *A Comprehensive History of the Church of Jesus Christ of Latter-day Saints*, 6 vols. (S.L.C.: Deseret News Press, 1930).

L. H. Rockwell. *Pioneer Guns and Gunsmiths* (S.L.C.: Daughters of Utah Pioneers, 1988).

Ruxton, George Frederick. *Life in the Far West*, ed. by LeRoy R. Hafen (Norman: Univ. of Okla. Press, 1951).

———. *Ruxton of the Rockies*, ed. by LeRoy R. Hafen (Norman: Univ. of Okla. Press, 1950).

Schindler, Harold. *Orrin Porter Rockwell: Man of God, Son of Thunder* (S.L.C.: Univ. of Utah Press, 1966; Second Edition, 1983).

Sellers, Charles. *James K. Polk, Continentalist, 1843–46* (Princeton Univ. Press, 1966).

Sessions, Gene A. *Mormon Thunder: A Documentary History of Jedediah Morgan Grant* (Urbana: Univ. of Ill. Press, 1982).

Simpson, J. A. and E. S. C. Weiner, eds. *The Oxford English Dictionary*, 20 vols. (Oxford: Clarendon Press, 1989).

Smith, George D., ed. *An Intimate Chronicle: The Journals of William Clayton* (S.L.C.: Signature Books, 1991).

Smith, Joseph, Jr. *History of the Church*, Brigham H. Roberts, ed., 7 vols. (S.L.C.: Deseret News, 1932).

Smith, Joseph Fielding. *Doctrines of Salvation: Sermons and Writings of Joseph Fielding Smith*, 3 vols. (S.L.C.: Bookcraft, 1954, 1955, 1956).

Spence, Mary Lee and Donald Jackson, eds. *The Expeditions of John Charles Frémont*, 4 vols. (Chicago: Univ. of Ill. Press, 1970–84).

Staker, Susan, ed. *Waiting for World's End: The Diaries of Wilford Woodruff* (S.L.C.: Signature Books, 1993).

Stansbury, Howard. *Exploration and Survey of the Valley of the Great Salt Lake* (Philadelphia: Lippincott, Grambo & Co., 1852).

Stegner, Wallace. *The Gathering of Zion* (N.Y.: McGraw Hill Book Co., 1964).

Stewart, George R., Jr. *The California Trail: An Epic with Many Heroes* (N.Y.: McGraw-Hill Book Co., Inc., 1962).

Taylor, Samuel W. *The Kingdom or Nothing: The Life of John Taylor, Militant Mormon* (N.Y.: Macmillan Pub. Co., Inc., 1976).

—————. *Nightfall at Nauvoo* (N.Y.: Macmillan Co., 1971).

Thrapp, Dan L. *Encyclopedia of Frontier Biography*, 4 vols. (Glendale, CA: Arthur H. Clark Co., 1988, 1994).

Townley, John M. *The Trail West: A Bibliographic-Index to Western Trails, 1841–1869* (Reno: Jamison Station Press, 1988).

Tullidge, Edward W. *Life of Brigham Young; or, Utah and Her Founders* (N.Y.: Tullidge & Crandall, 1876).

—————. *History of Salt Lake City* (S.L.C.: Star Printing Co., 1886).

—————. *Histories of Utah Volume 2: Northern Utah and Southern Idaho Counties* (S.L.C.: Press of the Juvenile Instructor, 1889). There is no Volume 1.

Tyler, Daniel. *A Concise History of the Mormon Battalion in the Mexican War, 1846–1847* (S.L.C., 1881. Reprinted Glorieta, N. M.: Rio Grande Press, Inc., 1980).

Unruh, John D. *The Plains Across: The Overland Emigrants and the Trans-Mississippi West, 1840–1860* (Urbana: Univ. of Ill. Press, 1979).

VanWagoner, Richard. *Sidney Rigdon: A Portrait of Religious Excess* (S.L.C.: Signature Books, 1994).

Wagner, Henry R. *The Plains and the Rockies: A Bibliography of Original Narratives of Travel and Adventure, 1800–1865*, third edition revised by Charles Camp. (Columbus, OH: Long's College Book Co., 1953).

Ward, Maurine Carr. *Winter Quarters: The 1846–1848 Life Writings of Mary Haskin Parker Richards* (Logan: Utah State Univ. Press, 1996).

Wheat, Carl I. *Mapping the Transmississippi West*, 5 vols. (San Francisco: Institute of Hist. Cartography, 1957–63).

Whittaker, David J., ed. *Mormon Americana: A Guide to Sources and Collections in the United States* (Provo: Brigham Young University Studies, 1995).

Periodicals

Andrews, Thomas F. "The Controversial Hastings Overland Guide: A Reassessment," *Pacific Historical Review*, 36 (Feb. 1968).

———. "The Ambitions of Lansford W. Hastings: A Study in Western Myth-Making," *Pacific Historical Review*, 39 (November 1970).

———. "Lansford W. Hastings and the Promotion of the Salt Lake Desert Cutoff: A Reappraisal," *Western Historical Quarterly*, 4 (April 1973).

Bagley, Will. "Lansford W. Hastings: Scoundrel or Visionary?" *Overland Journal*, 12 (Spring 1994).

——— and Robert Hoshide, eds. "The Last Crossing of the River: The 1847 William and James Pace Trail Diaries," *Crossroads*, 4 (Spring 1993).

Bennett, Richard E. "Finalizing Plans for the Trek West: Deliberations at Winter Quarters, 1846–1847," *Brigham Young University Studies*, 24 (Summer 1984).

Bidwell, John. "Life in California Before the Gold Discovery," *Century Magazine*, 61 (Dec. 1890).

Bigler, David L., Donald Buck, and Merrill Mattes, eds. "'O Wickedness, Where is Thy Boundary?': The 1850 California Gold Rush Diary of George Shepard," *Overland Journal*, 10 (Winter 1992).

Black, Susan Easton. "How Large was the Population of Nauvoo?" *Brigham Young University Studies*, 35 (Spring 1995).

Brannan, Samuel. "To the Saints in England and America," *Millennial Star*, 9 (15 October 1847), 20.

Christian, Lewis. "Mormon Foreknowledge of the West," *Brigham Young University Studies*, 21 (Fall 1981).

Christiansen, Larry D. "The Struggle for Power in the Mormon Battalion," *Dialogue: A Journal of Mormon Thought*, 26 (Winter 1993).

Coates, Lawrence G. "Cultural Conflict: Mormons and Indians in Nebraska," *Brigham Young University Studies*, 24 (Summer 1984).

Duffin, Reg. "The Grave of Joel Hembree," *Overland Journal*, 3 (Spring 1985).

Easton, Susan W. "Suffering and Death on the Plains of Iowa," *Brigham Young University Studies*, 21 (Fall 1981).

Gentry, Leland H. "The Mormon Way Stations: Garden Grove and Mt. Pisgah," *Brigham Young University Studies*, 21 (Fall 1981).

Hartley, William G. "Broken Sails off Cuba: LDS Immigrants and the Voyage of the *Yorkshire*," *Mormon Heritage Magazine*, 2 (May-June 1995).

———. "Down-and-Back Wagon Trains: Travelers on the Mormon Trail in 1861," *Overland Journal*, 11 (Winter 1993).

Harvey, R. E. "The Mormon Trek across Iowa Territory," *Annals of Iowa*, 28 (July 1946).

Irving, Gordon. "The Law of Adoption: One Phase of the Development of the Mormon Concept of Salvation, 1830–1900," *Brigham Young University Studies*, 14 (Spring 1974).

Jensen, Richard E. "The Pawnee Mission," *Nebraska History*, 75 (Winter 1994).

Kimball, Stanley B. "The Iowa Trek of 1846," *Ensign*, 2 (June 1972).

———. "The Mormon Trail Network in Iowa, 1838–1863: A New Look," *Brigham Young University Studies*, 21 (Fall 1981).

———. "The Mormon Trail Network in Nebraska, 1846–1868: A New Look," *Brigham Young University Studies*, 24 (Summer 1984).

———. "Religious Beliefs were Major Influence along the Mormon Trail," *Pathways Across America*, 8 (Fall 1995).

Knight, Gregory R. "Introduction to the 1845–1846 Journal of Thomas Bullock," *Brigham Young University Studies*, 31 (Winter 1991).

Knight, Gregory R. "Journal of Thomas Bullock," *Brigham Young University Studies*, 31 (Winter 1991).

Martin, Charles W. and Thomas H. Hunt, eds. "The Diary of Randall Fuller," *Overland Journal*, 6 (Winter 1988).

Mattes, Merrill. "The Northern Route of the Non-Mormons: Rediscovery of Nebraska's Forgotten Historic Trail," *Overland Journal*, 8 (Spring 1990).

———. "Potholes in the Great Platte River Road: Misconceptions in Need of Repair," *Wyoming Annals*, 65 (Summer/Fall 1993).

Morgan, Dale L., ed. "The Mormon Ferry on the North Platte: The Journal of William A. Empey," *Annals of Wyoming*, 21 (July-October 1949).

———. "The Reminiscences of James Holt: A Narrative of the Emmett Company," *Utah Historical Quarterly*, 23 (Jan. and April, 1955).

Pratt, Orson. "Interesting Items Concerning the Journeying of the Latter-day Saints from the City of Nauvoo, Until Their Location in the Valley of the Great Salt Lake (Extracted from the Private Journal of Orson Pratt)," *Latter-day Saints' Millennial Star*, 12:2 (Jan. 15, 1850) 18–19; 12:3 (Feb. 1, 1850) 33–35; 12:4 (Feb. 15, 1850) 49–50; 12:5 (March 1, 1850) 65–68; 12:6 (March 15, 1850) 81–83; 12:7 (April 1, 1850) 97–100; 12:8 (April 15, 1850) 113–15; 12:9, (May 1, 1850) 129–31; 12:10 (May 15, 1850) 145–47; 12:11 (June 1, 1850) 161–66; and 12:12 (June 15, 1850) 177–78.

Pratt, Stephen F. "Parley P. Pratt in Winter Quarters and the Trail West," *Brigham Young University Studies*, 24 (Summer 1984).

Pearson, Carol Lynn. "'Nine Children Were Born': A Historical Problem from the Sugar Creek Episode," *Brigham Young University Studies*, 21 (Fall 1981).

Quinn, D. Michael. "The Flag of the Kingdom of God," *Brigham Young University Studies*, 14 (Autumn 1973).

———. "The Council of Fifty and Its Members, 1844 to 1945," *Brigham Young University Studies*, 20 (Winter 1980).

Simon, Jerald F. "Thomas Bullock as an Early Mormon Historian," *Brigham Young University Studies*, 30:1 (Winter 1990).

Snow, Erastus. "Journey to Zion," *Utah Humanities Review*, 2 (April and July 1948).

Steele, John. "Extracts from the Journal of John Steele," *Utah Historical Quarterly*, 6 (Jan. 1933).

B.F.S. [Stewart, Benjamin Franklin]. "A Prophecy," *Juvenile Instructor*, 17 (15 Feb. 1882).

Trennert, Robert A., Jr. "The Mormons and the Office of Indian Affairs: The Conflict over Winter Quarters, 1846–1848," *Nebraska History*, 53 (Fall 1972).

Van Alfen, Peter G. "Sail and Steam: Great Salt Lake's Boats and Boatbuilders, 1847–1901," *Utah Historical Quarterly*, 63 (Summer 1995).

Walker, Ronald W. "'A Banner is Unfurled': Mormonism's Ensign Peak," *Dialogue: A Journal of Mormon Thought*, 26 (Winter 1993).

Watt, Ronald G. "Sailing 'The Old Ship Zion': The Life of George D. Watt," *Brigham Young University Studies*, 18 (Winter 1978).

Wright, Norman E. "Odometers: Distance Measurement on Western Emigrant Trails," *Overland Journal*, 13 (Fall, 1995).

Young, Brigham. "General Epistle from the Council of the Twelve to the Church of Jesus Christ of Latter-day Saints, abroad, dispersed throughout the Earth," *Latter-day Saints' Millennial Star*, 10 (15 March 1848).

Young, Levi Edgar, ed. "Diary of Lorenzo Dow Young," *Utah Historical Quarterly*, 14 (1946).

Newspapers

(Copies of these newspapers are available at the library of the Historical Department of the Church of Jesus Christ of Latter-day Saints in Salt Lake City, UT.)

The California Star, Yerba Buena and San Francisco, California, 1847–48.

Andrew Jenson, "Day by Day With the Utah Pioneers 1847," *Salt Lake Tribune* (June, July 1947).

Joseph T. Liddell, "Restoration of blasted Clinton's Cave is still in doubt," *Deseret News* (7 July 1985).

Joseph T. Liddell, "Rubbly cave isn't getting any raves," *Deseret News* (18 October 1985).

New York Messenger, New York, New York, 1845–46.

The Prophet, New York, New York, 1844–45.

Times and Seasons, Nauvoo, Illinois, 1840–46.

The Western Adventurer: Newsletter of the Exodus Chapter of the Iowa Mormon Trails Association, (Dec. 1995).

Theses

Andrews, Thomas F. "The Controversial Career of Lansford Warren Hastings: Pioneer California Promoter and Emigrant Guide" (Ph.D. diss., Univ. of Southern Calif., 1970).

Christian, Lewis Clark. "A Study of Mormon Knowledge of the Far West prior to the Exodus," (M.A. thesis, Brigham Young Univ., 1972).

Coleman, Ronald G. "A History of Blacks in Utah, 1825–1910," (Ph.D. diss., Univ. of Utah, 1980).

Despain, C. Ward. "Thomas Bullock, Early Mormon Pioneer" (M.A. thesis, Brigham Young Univ., 1956).

Yurtinus, John F. "A Ram in the Thicket: The Mormon Battalion in the Mexican War" (Ph.D. diss., Brigham Young Univ., 1975).

Manuscripts

Allred, Redick. Mormon Battalion Experiences, Typescript A-60, Utah State Hist. Soc., S.L.C., UT.

Blanpied, Dorothy B. Thomas Bullock's Home in Nauvoo, Bullock Collection, Daughters of Utah Pioneers, S.L.C., UT.

Bullock, Thomas. Collection, Daughters of Utah Pioneers, S.L.C., UT.

Bullock, Thomas. Letter to "Cousin Thomas," 21 September 1850, typescript in the Thomas Bullock Collection, Daughters of Utah Pioneers, S.L.C., UT.

Hastings, Lansford Warren. Instructions, 1847, LDS Archives, S.L.C., UT.

Journal History of the Church of Jesus Christ of Latter-day Saints, LDS Archives, S.L.C., UT.

Lyman, The Journal of Amasa Lyman. 1847, A 661-I, Utah State Hist. Soc., S.L.C., UT.

Palmer, Amber R. History of Thomas Bullock, Jr., Thomas Bullock Collection, Daughters of Utah Pioneers, S.L.C., UT.

Polk, James K. Papers, Library of Congress, Washington, D.C.

Pratt, Parley P. to Isaac Rogers, 6 September 1845, LDS Archives, S.L.C., UT.

Steele, John. Reminiscences and Journals, 1846–98, LDS Archives, S.L.C., UT.

Utah Semi-Centennial Commission. The Book of Pioneers, Utah State Hist. Soc., S.L.C., UT. (These are the forms submitted in 1897 by 1847 pioneers for the "Pioneer Semi-Centennial.")

Whitney, Horace Kimball. Journal, LDS Archives, S.L.C., UT.

Young, Brigham. Collection, LDS Archives, S.L.C., UT.

Young, Brigham. A Discourse, 16 August 1857, in Edyth Romney Typescript Collection, LDS Archives, S.L.C., UT.

INDEX

Illustrations are referenced in italics.

Abbott, Joshua Chandler: 253, 261
Abbott, Ruth: 253, 261
Adams, Barnabas Lothrop: and pioneers, 122, 130, 226–27, 274, 276, 278, 283, 294, 313, 363; hunts, 132, 288, 303; bio, 326
African-Americans: 52, 112, 130, 321, 330, 334, 339
Allen, James: recruits Mormon Battalion, 54-55; death of, 56-58
Allen, Orval Morgan: leads Poor Camp, 65, 72, 74, 76, 78, 82, 95, 99, 101, 102; speech of, 72; buys wife, 85; diary, 351; bio, 326
Allen, Rufus C: 122, 128, 130, 254, 259; bio, 326
Allred, James T. S: 265; bio, 326
Amaranth: steamboat, 28
American Fur Company: 52, 106, 175, 177
Ancient Bluff Ruins: 163, 165, 301
Angell, Truman Osborn: 130, 276, 362-63; bio, 326
Angus, John O: 361
animals: chickens, 33, 181, 257, 258, 279, 281; cows, 45, 68, 71-73, 75, 79-80, 82-86, 89, 92, 102, 116, 130, 139, 142, 148-49, 169, 174, 178, 181, 184, 279, 301, 313, 316-17; dogs, 20, 69, 130, 169, 181, 287, 298, 305; goats, 254, 256; pigs, 33, 79, 279, 281; sheep, 75, 211, 256, 279, 281, 283; *see also* birds, insects, wildlife
Antelope Creek: 223
Arkansas River: 57
Army of the West: 54, 60
Ash Creek: 105
Ash Hollow: 141, 161, 304
Ashworth, Christopher: 195, 201, 356
Aspen Mountain: 223, 273
Astorians: 22, 116, 202
Atwood, Millen: 130, 276, 293, 313, 356, 363; bio, 326
Aurora Borealis: 316
Avenue of Rocks: 197, 285

Avery, Dr: 80
Ayres Natural Bridge: 187

Babbitt, Almon W: 69, 81; bio, 326
Badger, Rodney: 122, 130, 155, 218, 239, 277; bio, 326
Badham, Samuel: 258
Badlam, Alexander: 42
Bair, John: 72, 74; bio, 326
Baird, Robert Erwin: 130, 259; bio, 327
Baker, Benjamin: 71
Baldwin, Asher: 75, 79
Baldwin, C. N: 65
Baldwin, William: 362
Banan, Daniel: 101
Bancroft, George: 46
Barney, Lewis: 130, 135, 241, 255, 327, 357; bio, 327
Barnum, Charles David: 130, 277, 363; bio, 327
Bassett, Charles: 75
Battle of Nauvoo: 64
Beach, Rufus: 279; 361; bio, 327
Bear River: 45, 59, 210, 253, 273; pioneers cross, 225
Bear River Mountains: 209, 213
Beaumont, Charles: 145
Beaver Creek: 127
Bed Tick Creek: 186
Bellevue, Nebraska: 22, 106, 128
Benbow, Agnes: 280; divorced, 282
Benbow, John: 280; divorced, 282
Bennett, James: 75, 84, 85, 86, 89, 91, 96
Benson, Alfred G: 46, 49, 54
Benson, Arthur W: 46, 49
Benson, Ezra Taft: with pioneers, 105-07, 119-121, 123-24, 127, 130, 139, 160, 171, 189, 191, 199, 217, 219, 228-30, 241-42, 250, 276, 278-79, 289-90, 294-95, 297, 307, 309, 313, 317, 356, 362-63; hunts, 283, 287, 300; sent to meet 2nd Division,

247; rejoins pioneers, 267, 272-73; sick, 203, 209, 216-17; speaks, 101, 151, 183, 238; rebuked, 293; bio, 327
Benton, Thomas Hart: 55
Berhelow, Berkeley, Berkelow: *see* Van Burklow
Bexted, William E: 255
Bidwell, John: 46
Big Cottonwood Creek: 292
Big Elk (Omaha): 104, 106
Big Head (Omaha): 103-04, 106
Big Mountain: 230, 323
Big Sandy River: 213, 267, 278, 279
Big Timber Creek: 213
Billings, George Pierce: 130, 277, 312; bio, 327
Bingham, Thomas: 219
Bird, William: 258
birds: 72, 187, 188, 270; bald eagles, 178; black birds, 77; cranes, 117; ducks, 125, 159, 283, 299, 300, 310, 317; eagles, 127, 163, 181, 182, 223; geese, 21, 70, 132, 143, 146, 217, 278, 288, 299-300, 303, 305, 307, 308-09, 317-18; hawks, 233; magpies, 233, 286, 287; parrots, 169; prairie chickens, 77; quail, 76, 83; red breasts, 188; sage hens, 254, 264; sand hill cranes, 233; sky larks, 82; snipes, 146, 199, 238; storks, 158; swallows, 127, 160-61, 225, 227; turkeys, 315; whippoor-wills, 188; woodpeckers, 189
Birdwood Creek: 154; *see also* Junction Bluff Creek
Bissonette, Joseph: 175
Bitter Creek: 182, 183
Black Hills: 105, 146, 173, 174; Bridger's lead mine in, 213
black pioneers: *see* African-Americans
Black Rock: 239
Blackburn, Abner: 253; bio, 327
Blacks Fork: 209, 215, 219-220, 275-76
Blauger, Newman: 65, 97
Blue Coat (Pawnee chief): 128
Blue Water Creek: 161, 303
Bluff Creek: 306
boat: *see* Mud Hen, Revenue Cutter
Boat Rock, 298
boat wagon: 208, 213, 256
Boggs, Francis: 130, 226, 259; bio, 327
Boggs, Lilburn: 60-61, 180, 243, 344
Bolton, Curtis Edward: 69; bio, 327
Bonaparte, Iowa: 63, 70, 73, 78-80, 83
Bonaparte, Napoleon: 160, 163

Bonney, Wales: 52
Bordeaux, James: 177, 179, 269, 294, 295; compliments pioneers, 180
Bosley, E: 69, 77, 81
bowery: 245-46, 248, 253, 257; battalion builds, 245
Bowman, William: 192
Box Elder Creek: 188
Brady, Nebraska: 139
Brannan, Samuel: 59, and *Brooklyn*, 49-50; California scheme, 46-49; meets pioneers, 205, 214-15; and pioneers, 205-06, 217, 219, 221, 236, 239-40, 250; and adobes, 236; explores Utah valley, 248, 250; letters to, 183, 252-53, 304; *passim*, 334, 340, 343; bio, 328
Brassfield, John: 192
Brattle, J. W: 70
Brave Bear (Lakota): 166
Bridgeport, Nebraska: 139, 165
Bridger, James: 186, 206; and Mormons, 207; meets with pioneers, 206, 209-213; visits returning pioneers, 275
Brigham Young Oil Well: 224, 273; *see also* Tar Spring
Brigham's Peak: 186
Brimhall, John: 277, 362, 364
Broadwater, Nebraska: 163
Brochway, Mary: 282
Brooklyn, ship: 50, 56, 215
Brown, Daniel: 261, 265
Brown, George Washington: with pioneers, 130, 140, 144, 147, 189, 198, 277, 294, 363; and Bullock, 170, 189-90; bio, 328
Brown, Harriet: 248, 261
Brown, James: commands sick detachments, 56, 57, 58, 178, 179, 219, 246, 249, 253, 327, 333, 337; sent to California, 236; bio, 328
Brown, Jesse S: 253
Brown, John: and Mississippi Saints, 52, 57, 104, 117, 146, 161; with pioneers, 114, 124, 130, 146, 160, 198, 224, 226, 233, 253, 274, 276, 290, 294, 303, 330, 363; hunts, 132, 134-35, 150, 283, 312; climbs Twin Peaks, 262, 264; bio, 328
Brown, Nathaniel Thomas: 130, 132, 142, 152, 198, 255; bio, 328
Brown, Pelatiah: 101
Brown, Randy: 184, 201
Buchanan, John: 219, 253, 362

buffalo chips: 116, 154, 309, 311; as fuel, 137
Buffalo Creek: 146
buffaloes: signs, 133; pioneers encounter, 136, 146-58, 176, 184, 191, 197, 217, 247, 283-312, 314; captured, 147, 151; consume grass, 150, 156; called Lord's cattle, 150
Bullock, Betsy Prudence Howard (wife): 38, 35
Bullock, Charles Richard (son): 25
Bullock, Henrietta Rushton (wife): 24-25, 27, 31, *38*, 64, 68, 80; gives birth, 323; health, 72, 74, 85, 93, 109; letters to, 124, 126-27, 129, 139, 146, 155, 186; papers, 351
Bullock, Lucy Caroline Clayton (wife): *31*, 32, 35, 38, 323
Bullock, Mary Elizabeth (daughter): 323
Bullock, Mary Hall (mother): 25
Bullock, Pamela (daughter): 25
Bullock, Ralph (grandfather): 25
Bullock, Thomas: 15, *26*, 170, 253, 276; life sketch, 25-38; character, 19; appearance, 25; family, 25; conversion to LDS church, 26; meets Joseph Smith, Jr., 28; joins Masons, 29; contributions to Manuscript History, 37; and Poor Camp, 63–99; preaches, 95; arrives at Winter Quarters, 99; assigned to keep history, 120; and journal keeping on 1847 trek, 15, 17, 19, 20, 29, 108, 128, 135, 151, 157, 161, 165, 170, 189, 196, 199, 213, 218, 226; as ox driver, 72, 86, 139, 195; reads laws, 151, 156; finds fossil, 164; misses Council of Fifty meeting, 172; minutes of meeting with Bridger, 206, 209-213; and mail, 165, 185, 188, 273; plants corn, 169, 188, 216; sees Great Salt Lake, 232; makes table of distances, 218, 229, 233, 257; maps city, 248, *251*, 258; and Warm Springs, 238, 247; makes good equestrian, 260; visits Great Salt Lake, 261; hunts, 287; sick, 78, 84, 86, 143, 168, 172, 175, 191, 200, 214, 216-17, 224-25, 227, 238, 304-05, 314; counts 2nd division, 279, 281; dines at Fort Laramie, 295; forced to walk, 310; trail journals, 23, 352-355; death and obituary, 38; papers, 24, 351-355; progeny, 38
Bullock, Thomas Henry (son): 25, 64
Bullock, Willard Richards (son): 31, 34, 102, 103
Burgess, Harrison: 96; bio, 328

Burk, Charles Allen: 70, 122, 130, 226, 259; bio, 328
Burnham, Jacob D: 122, 130, 194, 226; bio, 328
Burton, Richard Francis: 186
Burton, Robert Taylor: bio, 328
Burton, Robert Walton: 71-72, 75; bio, 328
Burton, William: 69
Butler, John L: 43, 53
Byard, Robert: *see* Baird, Robert Erwin

Cache Cave: 225, 272
Cache Valley: 205, 236; explored, 256
Cahoon, Andrew: 20; bio, 329
Cahoon, Reynolds: bio, 329
Calf Skin (Lakota): 301
Calhoun, John: 30
California: 22, 40, 43, 45, 48, 50, 54, 58, 59-60, 116, 179, 187, 206, 236; as LDS destination, 30-31; Young's policy towards, 219
California Hill: 161
Calkins, Asa: 262
Calkins, James W: 277, 362, 364
Calkins, Luman H: 315
Camp of the Pioneers: 113, 117
Campbell, Brother: 74
Campbell, James Albert: 264
Campbell, Joan: 80, 102; buried, 81
Campbell, Robert (fur trader): 175
Campbell, Robert Land: 75, 124, 126, 221, 273; bio, 329
cannon: 128, 144-45, 148-49, 166, 193, 198, 238; left behind, 231
Carl, Hannah: 75
Carns, Thomas: 312
Carpenter, Isaac: 255
Carrington, Albert: with pioneers, 130, 145, 166, 172, 185, 188, 206, 225-26, 228, 233, 238, 252, 256, 276; climbs Twin Peaks, 262, 264; observations of, 222, 247, 361; bio, 329
Carter, William: 130, 144, 277; bio, 329
Carthage Jail: 30-31, 42
Case, James: 124, 130, 144, 176, 190-91, 209, 230, 277; bio, 329
Casper, Wyoming: 174, 189, 285
Castle Bluff Creek: 161, 303
Casto, William: 219
Centerville, Iowa: 63
Central City, Nebraska: 116, 315

Chamberlain, Solomon: 130, 228, 238, 255, 311; names rock, 255; bio, 329
Chariton River: 63, 87, 66
Charleston, Iowa: 77
Chequest Creek: 63
Chesley, Alexander Philip: with pioneers, 122, 130, 226, 254, 276, 290, 294, 303, 312, 362-63; bio, 329
Chesney, James Albert: 181; bio, 329
Children of Israel: 21, 33, 39, 76
Chimney Rock: 163, 165, 168, 169, 299
Church Butte: 220, 276
Church Historian's Office: 15, 36
City Creek: 232
Clark, George Sheffer: 219, 249, 274, 277, 290, 362-63; bio, 330
Clark, John B: 243
Clark, Lodema: 249
Clark, Rodman: 71
Claude Creek: 190
Clayton, William: as clerk, 28; journal of, 20; Bullock's brother-in-law, 31; composes "Come, Come Ye Saints", 63; with pioneers, 130, 142, 172, 205, 216, 223, 233, 238, 259, 348; measures Fort Platte, 176; and odometer, 128, 140, 153, 154, 158, 159, 247, 257; and Bridger meeting, 206; makes table of distances, 218; sick, 217-19, 226; message from, 305, 314; *Emigrants' Guide*, 173, 322; bio, 330
Cloward, Thomas Poulson: 130, 223, 227, 259; bio, 330
Clyman, James: 52, 210
Coalville, Utah: 37-38
Collins, Caspar Wever: 196
Colorado River: 210, 211
Coltrin, Zebedee: with pioneers, 130, 135, 254-56, 259, 356; bio, 330
Compton, Allen: 219
Condiff, Silas: 70
Cook, Henry Lyman: 83, 84, 92-93, 101; bio, 330
Cooke, Philip St. George: 57-58, 246
Copperas Spring: 222-23
Corbett, Daniel: 83-85, 89, 94
Corwin, Thomas: 290
Council Bluffs, Iowa: 52, 54, 64-65, 73, 94, 116, 146
Council of Fifty: 29, 41, 42, 44, 111, 172, 307; *see also* Kingdom of God
Courthouse Rock: 141, 163

Coyote Creek: 225
Cozad, Nebraska: 148
Crab Creek: 162
Craig, James: 122, 130, 185, 191, 357; bio, 330
Crooked Creek: 305
Crooked Muddy Creek: 286
crops: beans, 233-34, 246, 256, 261; cabbages, 256; carrots, 256; corn, 233, 246, 256; potatoes, 229, 233-34, 237, 246, 256, 260; radishes, 256; turnips, 234; *see also* plants
Crosby, Jonathan: 75
Crosby, Oscar: 112, 130, 145, 226; bio, 330
Crosby, William: 104, 117
Crow Indians: 268, 289, 291, 297
Crow, Benjamin B: 181; bio, 330
Crow, Elizabeth Jane: 181; bio, 330
Crow, Harriet Blunt: 181, injured, 185; bio 330
Crow, Ida Vinda Exene: 181; bio, 330
Crow, Ira Minda Almarene: 181; bio, 330
Crow, John McHenry: 181, 226, 277, 362, 364; damns orders, 293; bio, 330
Crow, Matilda Jane: bio, 330
Crow, Robert: 173, 176, 181, 186, 193, 208, 226, 230, 233, 238, 264; ox dies, 218; bio, 330
Crow, Walter Hamilton: 181, 226; bio, 330
Crow, William Parker: 181; bio, 330
Crowley, Matilda: grave of, 200
Cruso, John: 25
Cummings, George: 258
Cummings, James: 43
Cummings, James W: 315
Curtis, Lyman: 122, 130, 226, 259; bio, 331
Cushing, Hosea: 122, 130, 276, 363; bio, 331
Custard, Amos: 196
Cutler's Park: 71, 80, 113
Cutler, Alpheus: 44, 146

Dalton, Edward: 253, 265
Daughters of Utah Pioneers: 25, 351
Davenport, James: 130, 196; bio, 331
Davis, Daniel C: 69; bio, 331
Davis, Daniel Coon: 58; bio, 331
Davis, Mary: 75
Davis, Samuel: 80
Davison, Nancy: 75
Dawson, Patrick: 71
Decker, Charles: 83; bio, 331
Decker, Isaac Perry: 349; bio, 331
Deep Rut Hill: 182
Deer Creek: 187-89, 287, 360

Deforest, Josiah L: 75
Des Moines River: 63, 78, 88
Devil's Backbone: 197; *see also* Avenue of Rocks
Devil's Gate: 199, 204, 284
DeVol, David: 69
DeVoto, Bernard: 52
Dewey, Benjamin Franklin: 130, 230, 277, 345; bio, 331
Dixon, John: 122, 130, 248, 277; bio, 331
Donner Hill: 260
Donner party: 18, 52, 58, 206, 231, 260; Brannan describes, 214
Dorland, William: 75
Douglas, Ralph: 247, 277, 312, 362, 364
Douglas, Stephen: 160
Douglas, Wyoming: 185
Dove, steamboat: 28
Dowdle, Absolom Porter: 151, 178; bio, 331
Draper, Alfred R: 75
Driggs, Sterling Graves: 130, 187, 247, 254; bio, 331
Dry Sandy: 202, 280
Dunbar, John: 127, 129
Durfee, Francilias: 219, 259
Dustin, Columbus: 199
Dykes, George Parker: 273; bio, 331
Dykes, William: 122, 130, 276, 283, 363; bio, 331

Eames, Ellis: 124
Earl, James Calvin: 277, bio, 331
Earl, Sylvester Henry: 122, 128, 130, 247, 259; bio, 331
Earl, Wilber F: 314, 315
East Canyon: 229, 230
East Canyon Creek: 271; *see also* Kanyon Creek
Eastman, James: bio, 331
Eastman, Ozro French: 122, 130, 277, bio, 331
Eccles, Henry: 75
Echo Canyon: 227-28; *see also* Red Fork
Echo, Utah: 228
Edness Kimball Wilkins State Park, Wyoming: 189
Egan, Howard: journal of, 20, 206; with pioneers, 58, 66, 124, 130, 228-29, 241, 260, 274, 277, 294, 313, 345, 362-63; sick, 219; helps Bullock, 304; bio, 332
Egbert, Joseph Teasdale: 130, 226, 261, 276, 284, 308, 312, 363; bio, 332
1848 emigration, 321-323
El Camino Real: 58

Eldredge, Horace S: bio, 333
Eldredge, Ira: 121
Eldredge, John Sutherland: 122, 130, 133-34, 226, 257, 259; bio, 333
Elk Sand Creek: 134
Elk Stream: 306
Elkhorn Creek: 190
Elkhorn River: 105, 113, 116, 118-19, 121, 269, 321
Ellsworth, Edmund Lovell: 130, 132, 151, 191, 196, 356; bio, 333
Elm Creek, Nebraska: 145, 312
Emigration Canyon: 19, 22, 59, 231, 236; flood in, 244
Emmett, James: 40, 43, 111, 342; bio, 333
Emmett party: 53
Empey, William Adam: 122, 130, 144, 325; bio, 333
Enoch: 294
Ensign Peak, 238-39, 254
Ensign, Horace Datus: 122, 130, 277; bio, 333
Evans, Clement: 65, 98
Evans, David: 92; bio, 333
Everett, Addison: 108, 122, 130, 252, 276, 356; bio, 333

Fairbanks, Bishop: 108
Fairbanks, Nathaniel: 122, 130, 226, 277; snake bites, 164-65; bio, 333-34
Farmington, Iowa: 63
Farnham, Thomas Jefferson: 46-47
Farr, Aaron Freeman: 130, 218; bio, 334
Farson, Wyoming: 213
Findley, William: 221
firearms: 67, 145, 166, 257, 357; accidents, 114, 135, 201
First Presidency: 16, 42, 44, 113, 237, 268, 319, 320
fish: 193, 203; *see also* trout
Fish Creek: 285
Fisher, Father Pliny: 65, 79, 81, 83, 94, 96, 98-99, 362-63; bio, 334
Fitzgerald, Perry: 130, 277; bio, 334
Flake, Green: 112, 130, 145, 149, 226, 277; bio, 334
Flake, James M: 104; bio, 334
Florence, Nebraska: 23
flowers: buttercups, 222; daisies, 134, 201-02, 208, 213, 220; dandelions, 199, 201, 214; pickpockets, 201; roses, 222, 228; sunflowers, 270

Follett, King: 29
Fontenelle, Logan: 99, 104, 105, 108
Fontenelle, Lucien B: 99
Ford, Thomas: 30, 66, 81
Fort Bernard: 175
Fort Bridger: 36, 204-05, 215, 261, 281; distance from, 178, 223, 229, 233, 359; pioneers arrive at, 220; prices at, 275
Fort Buenaventura: 224
Fort Caspar: 190
Fort Hall: 236, 253; prices at, 265
Fort John: 141, 209, 272, 285, 294, 301, 304, 313
Fort Kearny: 331
Fort Laramie: 43, 52-53, 58, 105, 146, 151, 160, 170, 175, 187, 209, 269; pioneers visit, 177; prices at, 178, 295; routes from, 173
Fort Leavenworth: 54, 57, 106
Fort Pierre: 186
Fort Platte: 176
Fort Supply: 207
Fort William: 175
fossils: 164
Fowler, John Sherman: 130, 191, 219, 248, 253, 356; bio, 334
Fox River: 66, 83
Fox, Samuel Bradford: 130, 191, 277, 356, 362, 363; bio, 334
Fraeb, Henry G: 210
Freeman, John Monroe: 130, 226, 261; bio, 334
Frémont, John C: 31, 58, 113, 188, 295, 361; maps of, 112, 160, 187, 197, 211
Fremont, Nebraska: 124
Frenchmen: 186; with returning pioneers, 281, 287, 289, 303, 306-08, 310
Fried Watches: 307
Frink, Horace Monroe: 122, 130, 277, 293, 364; bio, 334
Frost, Burr: 130, 185, 231, 240, 248, 256, 277; repairs wagons, 230, 255; bio, 335
Fuller, Randall: 132
Fullerton, Nebraska: 131
Fullmer, David: 40
Fullmer, John S: 43, 74, 76

Gabbut, William: 75, 86, 96
Gabbutt, Sarah: 88
Galena, Iowa: 73

Garden Creek: 190
Garden Grove, Iowa: 63, 83, 87, 91
Gardiner, George B: 83, 86
Gardiner, William: 104
Gates, Hiram: 93, 94
Gerger, D. M: 76
Gibbons, Andrew Smith: 122, 130, 171, 221, 277, 356-357, 362-63; bio, 335
Gila River: 211
Gleason, John Streater: 130, 226, 258; bio, 335
Glendo Reservoir: 184
Glenrock, Wyoming: 188, 287
Glines, Eric M: 130, 132, 156, 195, 202, 217-18, 354; stays at Mormon Ferry, 196; bio, 335
Glines, James H: 315-16
Goddard, Stephen H: with pioneers, 122, 124, 128, 130, 226, 252, 257, 260, 261, 274, 276, 288, 296, 303, 312-13, 361-63; makes salt, 254-56; bio, 335
Goodale, Tim: 205, 221-22
Goodyear, Miles: 205, 210, 212; meets pioneers, 224; garden, 256
Goshutes: 249
Gothenburg, Nebraska: 148
Gould, John Calvin: 276, bio, 335
Gould, Samuel: 219, 246, 276, 292, 294, 362-63; bio, 335
Grand Island, Nebraska: 53, 105, 116, 135, 247, 268, 302, 304, 312
Grand River: 63, 88, 90, 91
Granger, Wyoming: 215, 219
Grant, Athalia Howard: bio, 335
Grant, David: 120, 130, 226, 276, 292, 362-63; bio, 335
Grant, George D: 126-26, 315, 317; bio, 335
Grant, George R: 122, 130, 163, 276, 293, 362-63; rebuked, 293; bio, 336
Grant, Jedediah M: 268, 274, 331, 339, 343; bio, 335
Grant, Joshua: bio, 335
grass: lack of, 114, 285, 286, 291
Grass Creek: 136
Grattan Massacre: 168
Gray, William: 75, 82, 91, 94-96
Great Basin: 18, 31, 45, 60, 115, 206-07
Great Britain: 17, 21, 24, 36, 48, 54, 120, 297, 320
Great Salt Lake: 59, 105, 232; pioneers visit, 239

Great Salt Lake City: rebaptisms at, 250, 257; named, 254; Brigham Young names, 263; High Council appointed, 280; epistle to, 281
Great Western Measure: 48, 55
Green River: 186, 204, 209, 212-13, 278; pioneers reach, 215
Green, Edward M: 65, 80, 83-85
Green, Job E: 75
Greene, John Young: 130-31, 133, 145, 191, 276; bio, 336
Greenfield, Iowa: 92
Greenwood Cutoff: 208, 280
Greenwood, Caleb: 116
Gribble, Sophia: 248
Gribble, William: 248, 253
Grieves, James H: 185-86
Grindstone Butte: 186
Grosclaude, Justin: 105, 172
Grover, Joseph: 75
Grover, Thomas: 130, 134, 147, 162, 346; hunts, 150; commands Mormon Ferry, 174, 195, 196; letter to, 213; bio, 336
Guernsey, Wyoming: 173, 182, 292
Gunpowder Spring: 223
guns: *see* cannon, firearms

Hams Fork: 215, 220, 276, 278
Hancock, Joseph: 130, 132, 143, 171, 241, 247, 255; bio, 336
Hancock, Levi Ward: 56, 58, 274, bio, 336
Hanks, Ebenezer: 253, 265
Hanks, Sidney Alvarus: 130, 145, 191, 276, 294, 356, 363; bio, 336
Hansen, Hans Christian: 122, 130, 226; bio, 336
Harmon, Appleton Milo: 122, 124, 130, 196, 304; and odometer, 140, 153; makes letter box, 157; bio, 336
Harmon, Jesse Pierce: 84-86, 89, 92, 94, 96-97; bio, 336
Harper, Charles Alfred: 130, 199, 233, 274, 361, 362, 364; bio, 337
Harris, Moses: 203, 205-06, 210; pioneers trade with, 208
Hastings Cutoff: 210, 212
Hastings, Lansford Warren: 31, 46-47, 52, 351; waybill, 221
Hastings, Loren: 114
Haun's Mill Massacre: 192, 340

Hawkins, James: 75
Hawks, Joseph V: 75
Heber's Spring: 184, 291
Hembree, Joel: grave of, 187
Henrie, William: 130; bio, 336
Henry, Nebraska: 171, 298
Herr, John P: 75
Heywood, Joseph Leland: 68, 74, 76; bio, 337
Higbee, Isaac: 68, 89, 93; bio, 337
Higbee, John Summers: 124, 130, 132, 152, 154, 158, 196, 356; bio, 337
Higgins, Nelson: 57, 258, 260, 269, 273; bio, 337
Hileman, Levida: 198
Hill, Sally: 83
Hinckley, Arza E: 277, 362, 364
Hoagland, Lucus: 277
Hodges, Curtis: 69
Hogback Summit: 229
Holden, Edward: 277
Holden, Elijah E: 84
Holman, John Greenleaf: 122, 130, 191, 201, 276, 357, 363; bio, 337
Hopkins, Charles: 259
Horn, Wm. O. H: 90
Horse Creek: 197
Horseshoe Creek: 183, 184, 291
Houghton, Reuben: 75
Howd, Simeon Fuller: 130, 254, 277; bio, 337
Hudson's Bay Company: 236
Hunt, Gilbert: 253
Hunt, Jefferson: 56, 58-59, 246, 248, 253, 274, 331, 333, 341; epistle to, 252
Huntington, Dimick B: 247, 249, 263-264, 314
Huntington, William D: 315
Hyde, Orson: 41, 252-53, 338; bio, 338

Ice Spring: 200, 282
Independence, Missouri: 48, 52, 60, 116
Independence Rock: 198, 267, 272, 284
Indian Creek: 82
Indian Town: 94
Indians: 94, 101, 119, 133, 144, 204, 280, 283, 298, 301, 315; and Mormons, 115-16; set fires, 139; disguised as wolves, 133-34, 155; waste buffalo, 153; burial customs, 160, 178, 175; false alarms, 160, 305; Bridger describes, 207, 211-12; at Fort Bridger, 275; *see also* Crow Indians,

Goshutes, Lakotas, Omaha Indians, Pawnee Indians, Ponca Indians, Pottawattamies, Snake Indians, Utes
insects: ants, 178; bed bugs, 225; butterflies, 131, 135; crickets, 187, 193, 199, 247, 331; dragonflies, 118; gad flies, 198; grasshoppers, 180, 193, 288; hornets, 152, 276; mosquitoes, 118, 194, 199-200, 209, 214-15, 217-18, 221, 228, 232; wasps, 283; wiglers, 87
Iowa: 16, 32, 50, 52, 63-64
Iowa City, Iowa: 43
Ishna Botna: *see* Nishnabotna
Ivory, Mathew Hayes: 122, 130, 217, 261, 276, 363; bio, 338

Jack Mormons: 71
Jackman, Levi: 130, 226; bio, 338
Jackson's Spring: 248
Jacob, Norton: 20, 122, 124, 130, 141, 206, 255, 267, 320; name on Independence Rock, 198; bio, 338
Jail Rock: 141, 163
Jennings, Obediah: 192
Jewell, William: 69
Johnson, Artemas: 122, 130, 185, 190, 191, 209, 259; bio, 338
Johnson, Colonel: 68
Johnson, Luke Samuel: with pioneers, 106, 107, 116-17, 118, 123-24, 130, 134-35, 142, 147, 151, 153, 160, 163-64, 191, 196, 295-97, 299-301, 303, 312, 315, 356, 362; makes chimney, 137; as doctor, 180, 185; encounters Lakotas, 296; bio, 338
Johnson, Philo: 130; bio, 338
Johnston's Army: 208
Johnston, Albert Sidney: 36
Johnston, Jesse W: 277, 362, 364
Jones, Sister: 78
Jordan River: 210, 239, 250, 261; named Western Jordan, 263
Journal History: 23, 232, 253, 305
Junction Bluff Creek: 307

Kane, Thomas Leiper: 54, 158, 274, 340; describes Poor Camp, 64
Kanes Fork: 220; *see also* Hams Fork
Kanesville Log Tabernacle: 320
Kansas River: 105
Kanyon Creek: 229-30, 271
Karren, Thomas: 276

Kay, William: 126
Kearney, Nebraska: 139
Kearny, Stephen Watts: 54, 57-58, 60, 179, 187, 280, 295
Keg Creek: 97
Kellogg, Ezekiel: 303, 312, 362, 364
Kelsey, Stephen: 130, 133, 226, 277, 338, 362; bio, 338
Kendall, Amos: 47, 49, 54
Kendall, Levi Newell: 130, 133, 226, 277, 361; bio, 338-39
Keokuk, Iowa: 72
Kerl, Captain: 195
Keystone, Nebraska: 305
Kimball, Ellen Sanders: 112, 130; bio, 339
Kimball, Heber C: 43, 55; at Winter Quarters, 99, 105-06, 108; with pioneers, 112-13, 118-23, 127, 129-30, 132, 139, 147, 150, 156, 160, 171, 176, 179, 182-83, 186, 189, 191, 193, 198-200, 203, 208, 213-14, 216-19, 221, 225-26, 228-29, 238, 240-42, 246, 248-50, 252-57, 260-70, 274, 276, 279, 284-90, 292, 295, 297, 301-07, 313-14, 317; clears road, 128, 224; scouts road, 135, 154, 157, 187-89, 197, 278, 317; hunts, 134-35, 142, 147, 161, 287; wolves chase, 160; on Donner party, 260; talks to Bullock, 103, 218; in First Presidency, 320; bio, 339
Kimball, William: 315, 339
King, William A: 131, 277, 306, 339
Kingdom of God: 29, 41, 47, 60, 235; Bullock keeps journals and minutes of, 37; flag of, 239, 250; *see also* Council of Fifty
Kingley Dam: 158
kinnikinick: 123
Kleinman, Conrad: 122, 130, 172, 277; bio, 339
Knight, Joseph: 75, 82, 84-86
Knight, Newel: 89-90, 92, 95, 101
Knowles, Joseph: 95, 98

La Fras: 106
La Mie: "old chief of the Ogalallahs," 289, 359
LaBonte Creek: 173, 185, 213
LaFramboise, Joseph: 99
Lake McConaughy: 158
Lakotas: 43, 53, 114, 129, 141, 154, 162, 165, 168, 189, 268-69, 296, 303; attack Omahas, 106; trade with pioneers, 167; surprise returning pioneers, 288

Lamanites: 115, 125; to become "white and delightsome," 243
Lambert, Charles: 69, 93; bio, 339
Lamoreaux: A. L: 75
Langley, George W: 314, 315
LaPrele Creek: 187
Laramie Peak: 178, 182, 184, 291, 299
Laramie River: 141, 178, 179
Last Creek: 270
Lathrop, Asahel Albert: bio, 339
Latter-day Saints: and history, 15; contribution to trails, 21; and persecution, 40, 80, 224; as children of Israel, 33; and Indians, 115
Laughlin, David: 276, 363
Law of Adoption: 28
Law, Wilson: 30
Laws Regulating the Camp of Israel: 113, 357
Lawson, Thurston: 277
Lay, Hark: 112, 130, 144-45, 226, 330; bio, 339
LDS Archives: 23, 24, 128, 208, 351
Lee, John D: 58
Leek, England: 25, 344
Lewellen, Nebraska: 139, 303
Lewelling, Henderson: 153; and odometer, 140
Lewis, Tarlton: and Poor Camp, 72, 74-76, 89, 93; and pioneers, 130, 132, 171, 214, 252-53, 263; bio, 339-40
Lewiston Lakes: 201
Liberty Pole: at Council Bluffs, 98; on the Platte, 321
Lingle, Wyoming: 172
Lisco, Nebraska: 162
Litke, John C: 125
Little Emigration Canyon: 230
Little Mountain: 231
Little Platte River: 101
Little Sandy River: 205, 208-09, 279, 280
Little, Jesse Carter: and Polk, 54; with pioneers, 126, 130, 179, 199, 200, 202, 224, 252, 296, 362; cooks, 140, 172, 202; drives Bullock's team, 168, 172, 200; explores, 248, 250, 253, 256; meets Stockton, 295; bio, 340
Littlefield, L. O: 91, 92; bio, 340
Locust Creek: 63, 66
Lone Cedar: 160
Lone Peak: 249
Long, Stephen H: 22, 116
Looking Glass Creek: 127
Losee, Franklin G: 340; *see also* John G. Luce
Lott, Cornelius P: 106

Loup Ford: 116
Loup Fork: 53, 105, 127, 129, 132-33, 314, 316-17, 318
Loveland, Chauncey: 130, 254, 256; bio, 340
Lucas, Samuel D: 243
Luce, John G: 122, 128, 276, 313, 340, 362-363; bio, 340
Ludington, Elam: 56
Lyman, Amasa: 59, 104, with pioneers, 117, 119, 130, 132, 134, 151, 153, 160, 178-79, 217-19, 221, 219-30, 237, 239, 243, 246, 248-50, 252, 256, 258, 261, 264, 268, 274, 276, 278-79, 287, 290-91; preaches, 262; kills buffalo, 302; leads express to ox teams, 303; writes from express, 305, 307; gives up express, 312; with returning pioneers, 317, 334, 343, 362-63; bio, 340
Lytle, Andrew: 320
Lytle, Archibald: 180, 181
Lytle, John: 65, 84, 85, 86; bio, 340

Maid of Iowa, steamboat: 28
Main Canyon: 229
Major, William: 274
malaria: 32, 64, 71, 101, 172, 195
Mammoth Bone Encampment: 162
Manuscript History: 37, 128
Marble, Samuel Harvey: 122, 130, 259; bio, 340
Marcy, William: 54
Markham, Edwin: 67
Markham, Stephen Avon: with pioneers, 114, 122, 126, 130-31, 135, 192, 226, 233, 261, 265, 274, 277, 289, 293-95, 300-02, 313, 317; as colonel, 123, 146, 155-56, 159, 169, 190-91, 231, 246, 297, 311; sick, 142; bio, 340-41
Marsh, Cyprian: 75
Martindale, William: 314-15
Mary (Omaha): 106
Mason, Carnot: 107
Masonry: 28, 132
Mattes, Merrill: 20, 22
Matthews, Joseph: with pioneers, 122, 124, 130, 134-35, 224, 226, 253, 274, 277, 289-90, 294, 307, 314, 362, 364; hunts, 132, 301, 303, 308; bio, 341
McAuley, John: 66, 70
McFate, James: 65, 83, 84, 85, 86, 95, 98; bio, 340

McFate, Lucy J: 95; sick, 98
McFate, Mariah: 345
McIntyre, William: 257, 264, 277
Meeks, William: 83-86, 90, 95-97, 315; bio, 341
Merrill, Philemon C: 320
Mexican Hill: 180, 181
Mexican War: 52, 54, 290
Mexico: 46, 48, 60, 236
Middle Bear Creek: 184
Middle Mormon Ferry: 52, 102
Milam, William: 75
Millennial Star, 24, 36, 343, 352-53
Miller's Hollow, Iowa: 64
Miller's Settlement: 98
Miller, Daniel: 258
Miller, George: 42-44, 52-53, 63, 111, 345; bio, 341
Miller, Henry W: 64, 98
Miller, John: 104-05, 125; insulting letter of, 126
Miller, Joshua L: 108
Miller, Reuben: 273, 286, 291; bio, 341
Millron, John J: 75
Mills, George: 130, 221, 277; bio, 341
miracle of the quail: 16, 33, 34, 76, 83
Mississippi River: 67, 76, 83, 89
Mississippi Saints: 52, 57-58, 173, 175, 236; advance guard, 181; pioneers meet, 176
Missouri: 39, 55, 63, 111, 156, 243; emigrants from, 174, 180, 182, 183, 184, 188, 191, 192, 195, 201
Missouri River: 64, 73, 98, 99
Montrose, Iowa: 33, 71, 74
Moreton, William D: 75
Morgan, William: 192
Morley, Isaac: 117, 274, 323
Mormon Battalion: 54, 56, 215; mail to, 117; advance party meets pioneers, 219; sick detachments, 57-59, 174, 205, 215, 236, 328, 335, 341, 345-46; arrives in Salt Lake, 246; veterans reach Winter Quarters, 320
Mormon Canyon: 287
Mormon Ferry: 174, 189, 213, 285; established, 194; men left at, 196; moved, 202
Mormon Flat: 230
Mormon Grove: 90
Mormon team: 118, 298
Mormon Trail: 16, 21-22, 24, 66, 322; in Iowa, 63-64, 66, 100; landmarks, 174; origins, 116

Mormon Trail Park: 92
Mormon Volunteers: 58
mosquitoes: *see* insects
Mosquito Bridge: 98
Mosquito Timber: 98, 100
Mount Pisgah, Iowa: 63, 66, 73, 87, 90-91
mountain fever: 215-16
Mud Hen, 239, 255
Muddy Creek: 189, 222
Muddy Fork: 275
Muir, William S: 274
Mulder, William: 112
Murray, Carlos G: 130, 144, 277; bio, 341
Museum of Church History and Art: 113, 128, 330
Musquito Creek: 93
Myers, Lewis B: 58, 173, 181, 186, 223, 226; bio, 341

Nauvoo, Illinois: 16, 28, 31, 34, 39, 42, 44-45, 47, 49, 50, 63-64, 66, 74, 76, 168, 243
Nauvoo Expositor: 30
Nauvoo Legion: 30, 35
Nauvoo Temple: 31, 67, 68, 72
Nebeker, John: 97
The Needles: 225
Nephites: 115
New Mexico: 45, 54
Newman, Elijah: 130, 226, 233; bio, 341
Nickerson, Levi: 315-317
night guard: 119, 122, 290; organized, 114, 127
Niobrara River: 53, 104, 105, 111
Nishnabotna River: 64, 91, 94-97; West Fork, 97
Nixon, Stephen: 30
Nodaway River: 92
North Fork of the Platte: 22, 161, 189, 291, 297
North Platte, Nebraska: 153
Norton, John Wesley: 122, 130, 255, 356; bio, 341
Nowlin, Jabez T: 276

Oakley, James: 219, 255
Observation Bluff: 164
Oceanside, California: 344
odometer: 140, 153-54, 174, 322
Old Sow: *see* cannon
Omaha Indians: 60, 103, 106-08, 120, 125
Omaha, Nebraska: 34

INDEX

One Hundred and Two River: 92
Oregon: 22, 40, 41, 43, 45-47, 50, 112
Oregon Buttes: 202
Oregon Trail: 21, 48, 105, 116, 141, 161, 176, 208, 280
Oregon-California Trails Association: 198
Orient, Iowa: 64
Ottawa River: 93
Otter Creek: 105
Owen, Seeley: 122, 128, 130, 190, 249, 259; bio, 342
Ox company of returning pioneers, 258, 267-68, 307, 309, 312, departs Salt Lake, 260; breaks covenant, 314

Pace, James: 58
Pacific Springs: 203, 205
Pack, John: 123, 130, 132, 142, 146, 165, 172, 193, 228, 233-34, 259; bio, 342
Page, John E: 41
Papillion Creek: 118, 121
Papin, Pierre D: 146, 177, 304
Park, William A: 277, 303, 312, 362, 364
Parker, "Peepstone": 71
Parker, Henry Miller: 75, 78, 86, 96, 342
Parting of the Ways: 208, 280
Paw Paw Grove: 93
Pawnee Mission: 53, 128-29, 312; described, 129
Pawnee Town: 122, 129, 317-18; described, 131
Pawnee Indians: 53, 114, 122, 124, 129, 134, 145, 178, 311, 314; trade with, 126
Peck, Ezekiel: 75
Peck, Hezekiah: 89, 93; bio, 342
Peirce, Eli Harvey: 130, 191, 276, 361; bio, 342
Perce, Alonzo: 75
Perkins, David: 255
Perkins, William: 321
Perpetual Emigration Fund: 35, 37
Perry, Stephen Chadwick: 83, 86-87; bio, 342
Pettegrew, David: 56
Pied Riche (Pottawattamie): 99
Pierson, Ebenezer: bio, 342
Pierson, Harmon D: bio, 342
Pierson, Judson A: 277, 288, 362, 364; bio, 342
pioneer company: lack of draft animals, 18; composition, 112; women and children in, 112, 181; departs, 112; scientific equipment, 113; military organization, 123; laws written, 124; blazes new road, 22, 133, 135-36, 148, 223, 227; builds rafts, 129, 131, 191, 214, 216; entertainment, 138; sights buffalo, 142; meets Jim Bridger, 205; meets battalion advance party, 218; rebaptized, 248-253; irrigates, 234, 237-38, 244, 252
Pioneer Hollow: 223
Pioneer Memorial Museum: 25, 351
Pioneer Park: 247
plants: aloes, 134; artemisia, 187-88, 197, 200, 202-03, 208, 213, 220, 222-24, 229; buffalo grass, 105, 126-27, 139, 291, 299-300, 303-304, 311, 315; chamomile, 193; cherries, 270, 272; currants, 230, 278; flax, 187, 212, 220, 222; gooseberries, 199, 201-02, 208, 222, 228, 230, 262, 271-72; greasewood, 199-200; haws, 270; hollyhocks, 270; hops, 228, 272; mint, 197, 200, 222; mushrooms, 178, 189; mustard, 178, 188-89; onions, 188, 195, 201, 202, 223; peppermint, 184; pig weed, 178; prickly pear, 136, 139, 155, 162, 169, 172, 210, 219, 271, 294, 296-300; raspberries, 262; rushes, 136, 208, 231, 241, 311, 315; saffron, 271; sage, 198, 271, 273, 275, 282, 284, 296; service berries, 260, 270; southern wood, 162; strawberries, 201-02; sweet sicily, 184; thistles, 185, 195, 197, 199, 220, 299; wandering milk weed, 233; watercresses, 136; wild currants, 161; wild roses, 170; wild sage, 155, 193; wild wheat, 228, 231; yarrow, 184; *see also* crops, flowers
Platte River: 59, 105, 113, 116, 118, 121, 123, 299, 315; described, 126; *see also* North Fork of the Platte
Platte River Road: 111
Pogue, John: 192
Poison Spring Creek: 197
Poison Springs: 285
Polk, James Knox: 46, 49, 54-55, 60-61, 243, 340
polygamy: 29, 31, 195, 243, 285
Pomeroy, Francis Martin: 122, 130, 196; bio, 342
Ponca Indians: 53, 108
Pony Express: 175
Poor Camp: 16, 33, 51, 64, 65, 331, 336, 345; route, 66
popcorn: 98, 317
Porter's Rock: 292

Pottawattamies: 60, 64
Potter, Gardner: 315; bio, 342
Powder River: 297
Powell, David: 122, 130, 226, 276; bio, 342
Prairie Creek: 316
Prairie Slough: 134
Pratt's Pass: 229, 232
Pratt, Orson: diary, 20; in Washington, 41: in England; 45; *passim*, 49, 51, 105-06, 109; and 1847 trek, 113, 117-21, 123, 129-30, 140, 142, 151, 158, 160, 164, 179, 183, 191, 197, 199, 203, 216-17, 219, 223, 225; and odometer, 140; observations, 120, 153, 158, 164, 168, 177, 221, 254-55, 361; leads advance party, 226; 230-32; dedicates Salt Lake Valley, 233; in Salt Lake, 238-39, 241-42, 246-50, 252, 256-58, 261, 264; runs baseline, 250; with returning pioneers, 276, 278-79, 287, 290-91, 295, 299, 307, 314; on Mormon Time, 316; on forming First Presidency 320; *passim*, 328, 332, 341, 344-46, 356, 362-63; bio, 342-43
Pratt, Parley P: 31, 45, 48, 52, 113, 117, 120; leads 2nd division, 267, 273, meets returning pioneers, 279; Young rebukes; 267-68, 279; bio 342
Prayer Circle Bluffs: 171
Pressley, William H: 75, 83, 92
Prospect Hill: 197, 285
Pueblo, Colorado: 52, 57-58, 173, 176, 337
Pulpit Rock: 272
Pulsipher, Zera: 321

Raccoon Fork: 89
Rappleye, Tunis: 130, 179, 190, 237, 258, 259, 267; leads ox company, 257; bio, 343
rattlesnakes: *see* reptiles
Rattlesnake Caves: 261
Rattlesnake Creek: 305, 314
Rawhide Creek: 172, 175, 297
Red Buttes: 196
Red Fork: 210, 227, 272; *see also* Echo Canyon
Red Valley: 186
Redden, Return Jackson: 130, 132, 144, 147, 226, 259, 313-314; bio, 343
Register Cliff: 181-82
reptiles: bull snake, 165; garter snakes, 161; green racer, 154; mud turtles, 134, 155, 310; rattlesnakes, 64, 135, 158, 163-64, 168, 172, 188, 193, 232, 306; water snake, 157

returning pioneers: 267-318; depart Salt Lake, 269; feasted by 2nd division, 281; at Fort Laramie, 292-295; horses fail, 309
Revenue Cutter: 131, 151, 157-58, 160, 170, 178, 191, 193
Rich, Charles Colson: 152, 165, 179, 217-18, 229-30, 247, 280, 340; mail to, 157, 184; bio, 343
Richard, John Baptiste: 175, 300-01, 304
Richards, Franklin D: bio, 343
Richards, Levi: 102, 105; bio, 343
Richards, Willard: and Bullock, 13, 24, 28, 30-31, 64, 68, 81, 87, 99, 101, 102-05; and church records, 108; and 1847 trek, 42, 113, 117-19, 120, 122-25, 129-30, 142, 144-45, 148, 151-52, 155, 157-58, 160, 162, 163, 168, 171-72, 176, 178-80, 182-84, 189, 193, 196-98, 201, 216-22, 225-26, 228-29, 231, 233; in Salt Lake, 238-39, 241-42, 247-50, 253-56, 258, 260-62, 264-65; leaves messages, 149, 151, 152; smokes peace pipe, 166, 289; finds fossil, 162; clears road, 185, 201, 273; doctors Bullock, 172, 191, 228; posts guide board, 208; addresses pioneers, 246; wagon breaks, 270; with returning pioneers, 269, 271, 273, 279-80, 287-88, 290-93, 295, 297, 300, 302, 304, 306-07, 314-15, 330, 335-36, 343, 351, 356, 362-63; ejects Bullock from wagon, 310; on ox team company, 318; death, 37; bio, 343
Richardson's Point: 83
Richardson, Thomas: 256, 258
Richmond, Benjamin: 265, 276, 290, 316, 363
Rigdon, Sidney: 44
Rio Grande River: 57, 59, 140
Riter, Levi Evans: 108; bio, 343
Roberts, B. H: 15, 37, 49, 112, 115, 141, 185
Roberts, Benjamin: 219, 259
Robinson, John L: 68, 75, 83, 87, 95, 96, 108
Rock Creek: 202
rock rolling: 228
Rockwell, Orrin Porter: passes Poor Camp, 92-93; with 1847 trek, 125, 130, 134, 172, 217, 226-27, 277, 356; hunts, 132, 142-43, 147, 152, 197, 240; to meet 2nd division, 248; bio, 343–44
Rockwood, Albert P: with 1847 trex, 117, 121-22, 130, 153, 155-56, 159, 166, 170-71, 176, 179-80, 185, 189, 195, 202, 237,

248, 257, 260, 263, 274, 276, 285, 294-95, 362-63; as colonel, 123, 183, 258, 297; journal, 128; sick, 227-28; bio, 344
Rodgers, W. H: 104
Rolfe, Benjamin William: 130, 141, 259; bio, 344
Rolfe, Samuel: 108, 344
Rooker, Joseph: 122, 130, 303, 363,-64; bio, 344
Roundy, Shadrach: 123, 130, 176, 226, 233, 237, 258-60, 267; leads ox company, 257; bio, 344
Rouvoir, James: 186
Rowe, Caratat Conderset: 277, 363, 364
Rowe, William: 277, 303, 361-62, 364
Rushton, Edwin: 68
Rushton, Fanny: 101
Rushton, Isabella Alice: 102
Rushton, John: 74, 77, 85, 96, 102; bio, 344
Rushton, Margaret: 102
Rushton, Richard: 25; bio, 344
Russell, Daniel: 102, 126
Rust, W. William: 262, 264, 277, 362, 364

Sage Creek: 283
saleratus: 198, 200, 213, 284
San Francisco: 45, 183
Sanborn, Jesse: 97
Sand Hill Ruts: 154
Sanderson, George: 56-57
Sanderson, Henry W: 258
Sandstone Springs: 93
Santa Fé: 40, 57-58, 106, 179, 187
Sarjent, Abel M: 277, 362
Sarpy, Peter A: 52-53, 106, 126, 186
Savery, Samuel: 83, 88, 95-97, 101; sells wife, 85; bio, 344
Scholes, George: 86, 96, 122, 128, 130, 259, 345
Scofield, Joseph Smith: 130, 193, 274, 276, 357; bio, 345
Scott's Spring: 103
Scott, John: 102
Scott, Levi: 202
Scotts Bluff: 141, 169, 299, 300
Scottsbluff, Nebraska: 139
Sessions, Patty: 18, 359
Sevier Lake: 213
Shabne (Pottawatamie chief): 92
Shaw, John S: 313

Shefmolan (Pawnee chief): 115
Shell Creek: 126, 318
Shepherdson, Mary: 274
Sherman, Ephraim M: 75
Sherwood, Henry G: 43, 104, 130, 166, 230, 241; surveys city, 247, 255; bio, 345
Shipley, Joseph: 258
Shirtleff, Vinson: 282
Shumway, Andrew Purley: 130, 277; bio, 345
Shumway, Charles: 50, 124, 130, 172, 233, 252, 270, 277; bio, 345
Shupe, Andrew Jackson: 219, 240, 247, 259; bio, 345
Sioux Indians: *see* Lakotas
Smith, Andrew Jackson: 57
Smith, Emma: 42
Smith, George A: told to fire Bullock, 37; at Winter Quarters, 104, 106; and 1847 trek, 42, 118-21, 125, 130, 148, 182, 188, 191, 193, 198-99, 201, 203, 215-17, 219, 225-34, 238, 241-42, 247, 250, 252, 256-58, 261-62, 264-65, 275-76, 279, 290, 307; accident, 128; scouts road, 188-89, 278; clears road, 231; hunts, 287; preaches, 121, 132, 164, 239, 280; sick, 216-17; *passim*, 356, 362-63; bio, 345
Smith, Hyrum: 28, 31, 38, 42, 175, 203; martyrdom, 30; 42; bio, 345;
Smith, Jedediah Strong: 202, 235
Smith, Uncle John: 103-04, 122, 146, 252, 279, 282, 304, 345
Smith, Joseph F: 37
Smith, Joseph, III: 42
Smith, Joseph, Jr: founds LDS church, 39; bodyguards, 65, 326, 341, 343-44; martyrdom, 16, 30, 41, 175, 203, 341, 346; Indian prophecies, 115; petitions Congress, 41; succession problems, 16, 44; presidential campaign, 29, 40; prophesies, 73; and animals, 132; passim, 15, 28-29, 37, 40, 192, 243, 295, 330, 333, 335, 338-39, 347; bio, 345
Smith, Joseph, Sr: bio, 345
Smith, Mary Fielding: 73, 81; bio, 345
Smith, Nancy Adelid: death reported, 125
Smith, Richard D: 255
Smith, Samuel H: 42
Smith, Samuel Trunkey: 65, 96, 98; bio, 346
Smith, Sylvester: 149
Smith, William: 42, 47

Smithson, William C: 244
Smoot, Abraham Owen: 280, 331, 352; bio, 346
Smoot, William Cockran Adkinson: 122, 130, 150, 227; bio, 346
Snake Indians: 289
Snake River: 204
Snow, Erastus Fairbanks: 52, and 1847 trek, 122, 130, 140, 149, 164, 172, 221, 228-30, 231, 252, 274, 277, 332, 363; rebuked, 148, 149; preaches, 280; bio, 346
Soap Creek: 84-86
Soda Hollow: 223
Soda Lakes: 284
South Pass: 175, 268, 269, 305; pioneers cross, 203; returning pioneers cross, 281
Spencer, Daniel: 40, 126, 267, 278-79, 333-34; bio, 346
Sprague, James M: 65, 91
Sprague, Samuel: 105
Spring Creek: 157, 299, 306
Spurr, Peter: 75
Squires, William: 253
Staines, William Carter: 279; bio, 346
Steamboat Rock: 198
Steele, Catherine: 253
Steele, John: 253
Steele, Young Elizabeth: born, 253
Stegner, Wallace: 22, 39
Stephens-Murphy-Townsend party: 22, 116
Stevens, George: 140
Stevens, Roswell: 130, 132, 135, 151, 179, 239, 259; catches fawn, 157; bio, 346
Stewart, Benjamin Franklin: 124, 130, 132, 196, 277, 363, 364; damns orders, 293; bio, 346
Stewart, James Wesley: 130, 226, 259, 276; bio, 346-47
Stillman, Clark: 250, 258
Stillman, Dexter: 276, 309, 362, 363; bio, 347
Stockton, Robert Field: 58, 295-96; meets returning pioneers, 300
Stoddard, Amos: 97
Stout, Hosea: 55, 269, 314, 335, 352; leads relief, 269, 315; bio, 347
Stowe Creek: 223
Strang, James: 43
Strawberry Creek: 201
Stringham, Briant: 96, 131; bio, 347
Sublette Cutoff: 208, 280
Sublette, William L: 175, 198

Sugar Creek: 63, 77, 78
Sugar Loaf Peak: 249
Sulphur Spring: 224
Summe, Gilbard: 122, 130, 226; bio, 347
Sun Ranch: 199
Sutherland, Nebraska: 154
Sutter's Fort: 58-59
Sutter, John: 46
Swallows Cave: 225, 272; *see also* Cache Cave
Sweetwater Canyon: 201
Sweetwater Mountains: 197, 200, 284-85
Sweetwater River: 174, 198-204, 268, 281-82, 284

Table Rocks: 202
Taft, Seth: 124, 130, 176, 226, 233; plows first furrow, 234; bio, 347
Tanner, Miron: 258
Tanner, Thomas: 122, 128, 130, 248, 256, 265, 274, 276, 356, 362-63; bio, 347
Tar Spring: 224; *see also* Brigham Young Oil Well
Taylor, Allen: 94
Taylor, John: 45, 98; leads 2nd division, 113, 120, 124, 268, 273, 281, 327, 331; and Benbows, 280; and Widow Thompson, 282; bio, 347
Taylor, Norman: 130, 226, 258, 357, 362; bio, 347
Temple Block: 255
Terrill, Joel J: 219, 247, 276, 294, 362
Terrill, William: 277
Texas: 41, 44
Therlkill, George W: 176, 181, 226, 255, 257; bio, 347-48
Therlkill, Harriet Ann: born, 257
Therlkill, James William: 181
Therlkill, Matilda Jane Crow: 181, 255, 357; daughter born, 257
Therlkill, Milton Howard: 181; drowns, 255; funeral, 256
Thomas, Hayward: 277
Thomas, Robert T: 130, 158, 226, 276; bio, 347
Thompson, Mercy: 73
Thompson, Widow: 282
Thomson Fork: 90
Thornton, Horace: 122, 128, 130, 185, 225-26, 259; bio, 347
Thorpe, Marcus Ball: 130, 144, 226, 261, 276; bio, 348
Thorrington, Horace: *see* Thornton, Horace

Tippets, John Harvey: 59, 122, 128, 130, 145, 151, 178, 179; bio, 348
Tongue River: 105
Tooele Valley: 236, 249
Travis, Tommy: 70
Treaty of Guadalupe Hidalgo: 235
trees: ash, 160, 185, 187-88, 312; aspen, 201, 230-31, 270; Balm of Gilead, 270; balsam, 241, 262, 270; birch, 231, 270; box elder, 188, 288; cedar, 152, 158, 160, 162-64, 180, 191, 199, 211, 222-24, 272, 275, 285; choke cherry, 180, 185, 188; cottonwood, 119, 121, 123-25, 136, 180, 182-83, 187-89, 193, 210, 213-14, 224-25, 228, 230, 233, 271, 286, 294, 297, 308, 311, 316-18; fir, 231, 242, 262, 270-71, 291; maple, 231, 270; mountain cherry, 160; oak, 210, 231; Palm Tree, 117; petrified, 209; pine, 158, 160, 162, 180, 184, 191, 199, 210, 224, 240, 262; poplar, 210, 222, 231, 241, 270; slippery elm, 119; spruce, 262, 291; sugar maple, 270; willow, 99, 119, 133, 142, 153, 183, 188, 202, 208, 210, 213, 220, 222, 225, 228-33, 256, 270-73, 279, 282, 308, 313
trout: 170, 221, 229
Tubbs, Amos: 65, 93, 94
Tubbs, William: 248, 261
Tucker, William: 185-86
Twelve Apostles: 16-18, 30, 42, 44, 48, 49, 52, 65, 91, 111, 113, 120; members in Pioneer Camp, 119; in Salt Lake, 267; meet battalion, 244; send letters to California, 252
Twin Peaks: 249, 262, 264, 271, 273
Tyler, John: 46

Utah Lake: 210, 211, 238, 245, 248, 250, 256; Bridger describes, 213
Utah Valley: 36, 236
Utah War: 36
Utes: 213, 245-46; trade with pioneers, 240; killed, 250; visit pioneers, 255

Valley of Dry Bones: 154
Van Burklow, Luther: 78, 82, 84-85, 96
Van Wert, Iowa: 66
Vance, John: 108
Vance, William Perkins: 122, 130; bio, 348
Vancouver Island: 45
Vasquez, Louis: 210
Vermillion River: 43

Wagonhound Creek: 186
wagons: 50-51
Walker, Henson: 130, 233; bio, 348
Walker, Joseph R: 304
Walker, William: 219
Wallace, George Benjamin: 280; bio, 348
Wanship, Utah: 37
Wardle, Fanny: 70, 71
Wardle, George: 66-70, 72, 74, 79-80, 84-87, 96, 130, 216-17, 258; bio, 348
Wardsworth, William Shin: 122, 130, 201, 277; bio, 348
Warm Spring: 239, 244, 245, 256, 262
Warm Spring, Wyoming: 182, 292
Wasatch Mountains: 235
Wash te cha (Lakota chief): 166-68; meets returning pioneers, 289
Wassell, Ann: 103
Wassell, Mary: 103
Wassell, Richard: 103
Watt, George D: 28, 123-24
Weber Canyon: 229
Weber River: 205, 228-29, 232, 233, 239, 262, 271
Weiler, Jacob: 130, 185, 356; bio, 348
Welden Fork: 88
Wells, Captain: 210, 224, 256; visits pioneers, 262
Wells, Daniel H: 35, bio, 348
West Cottonwood Creek: 188
Wheeler, E. T: 81, 83
Wheeler, John: 122, 130, 255; bio, 348
Wheeler, Sister: 79, 96
Wheeler, William: 80
Whipple, Edson: 122, 130, 132, 304; bio, 348-49
White Oak Springs: 88
Whitebreast Creek: 66, 88
Whitehead, Benjamin: 74, 84-86, 92; bio, 349
Whitehead, James: 67: bio, 349
Whitetail Creek: 305
Whitney, Helen Mar: 349
Whitney, Horace Kimball: 128, 130, 185, 277, 363; bio, 349
Whitney, Newel K: 119-22; with relief party, 269; bio, 349
Whitney, Orson Kimball: 130, 165, 277, 362-63; bio, 349
Whittaker, Moses: 75
Wight, Lyman: 44
Wild Cat Grove: 87

Wild Cat Range: 165
wildlife: antelopes, 135-36, 140, 142, 144-49, 155-58, 168-70, 182, 184-85, 187-91, 194, 197, 202, 225-26, 254, 275, 283, 298-300; badgers, 254, 303; bats, 304; bears, 197, 223, 272; beavers, 170; bighorn sheep, 190, 240, 254; black bears, 191; chameleons, 134; deer, 152, 172, 184-85, 187, 188, 197, 200, 254, 288, 308; elk, 254, 305-06; frogs, 162, 287-88, 308; grizzly bears, 18, 287, 297; hares, 150, 163, 254; in journals, 20; mountain sheep, 262, 283; prairie dogs, 143-44, 187, 303, 311-14; skunks, 268, 298-300; squirrels, 117, 272; wild horses, 152; wolves, 20, 95, 131-32, 143-44, 147-48, 152, 159, 161, 168-69, 175, 254, 265, 286, 300, 302, 304, 307, 311-12; *see also* buffaloes
Williams, Almon Mack: 130, 235, 259; bio, 349
Williams, Thomas Stephen: 58, 205, 219, 221, 249, 253, 265; bio, 349
Williams, William: 75
Willis, William Wesley: 58, 237, 250, 252-53, 256, 260, 267
Willow Island: 148
Willow Springs, Utah: 270
Willow Springs, Wyoming: 197, 285
Wilsey, Washington: 75
Wilson, George: 262, 264, 274, 277, 362, 364
Wilson, Jonathan: 75, 85
Wilson, Robert: 313
Wind River Mountains: 200, 202
Winter Quarters: 16, 23, 34, 53, 59, 108, 112-13, 116-18, 120; deaths at, 17; distance from, 121, 128, 152, 159, 233; letters to, 146, 179; mill at, 101-02, 107-08, 280; relief from, 313
Wixom, Solomon: 86
Wolf Creek: 159
Wood Creek: 136
Wood River: 315
Woodrie, James: 186
Woodruff, Wilford: 19, 21, 22, 51, 106, 108; defends Bullock, 37; and 1847 trek, 113, 117-19, 122-23, 129-30, 141, 151, 160, 165, 171, 183, 186-89, 197-99, 201, 203, 217-19, 222, 225-27, 229; hunts, 118, 132, 135, 283, 287, 302, 313; sick, 222; describes Salt Lake, 235; in Salt Lake, 237-39, 241, 247, 252-53, 256-58, 261-62, 264-65; and returning pioneers, 267, 270-71, 275-76, 278-80, 286, 289, 295, 306-07, 309, 312, 315; supports Young, 319; *passim*, 331, 345, 356, 362-63; bio, 349
Woodward, George: 130, 217, 218; bio, 349
Woodworth, Lucien: 44
Woodworth, Lysander: 253
Woolsey, Thomas: 59, 122, 128, 129-30, 146, 151, 158, 178, 179, 277, 301, 310, 312-14, 347, 362-63; buffalo hunt captain, 132; bio, 349
The Word and Will of the Lord: 17, 111, 222, 226, 267
Word of Wisdom: 23
Wordsworth, William; *see* Wardsworth, William
Worsley, John: 75
Wreston, Isaac Newton: 277, 303, 362-63
Wreston, John P: 277, 362-63

Yellow Creek: 225
Yellowstone: 45, 105
Yellowstone River: 104
Yorkshire, ship: 27
Young, Abigail Howe: 349
Young, Brigham: rise to power, 16, 30, 42, 44, 319-321; *passim*, 15, 22, 33, 36, 43-44, 48-52, 101, 104, 108; papers, 23; rhetoric, 23; fires Bullock, 37; hopes for independence, 47, 55, 244; and U.S. government, 48, 50, 179, 244; and Mormon Battalion, 54-55, 57-60, 106, 108, 174, 179, 236, 243, 245, 248; writes Polk, 59-61; evacuates Nauvoo, 63; sends Poor Camp relief, 65; promise to Bullock, 99; as slave owner, 112, 334; sustained as president, 113; organizes 1847 emigration, 17, 119-22, 124, 267; leads 1847 trek, 18, 45, 111, 113, 117, 118, 123-24, 126, 129-31, 134-37, 140, 144-49, 151-52, 157-60, 163, 168, 171-72, 174, 176, 178-80, 182-83, 186, 191, 193, 198-01, 203, 205, 216-19, 221-22, 224, 226-27, 233-36; and Indians, 103, 105, 107, 115, 127, 269, 280; scouts road, 128, 135, 143, 154, 157, 187, 188, 197, 213, 217-18, 278, 310, 317; hunts, 135, 150, 161, 283, 287, 303; instructs pioneers, 132, 144, 145, 148, 164, 257; and animals, 133, 147, 148, 180; clears road, 127, 223, 273; rebukes pioneers, 141, 159, 171, 293; gives names, 158, 239, 257, 263; establishes Mormon Ferry, 174, 194, 196; builds rafts,

194, 214; on polygamy, 195, 243, 249; compliments Bullock, 197; meets Moses Harris, 208; meets Bridger, 206-07, 209, 213; health, 215-16, 225, 228-29, 246, 270, 309, 310; arrives in Salt Lake, 237; in Salt Lake, 238-41, 247, 252-53, 255, 258, 260-65; visits Great Salt Lake, 239; on city planning, 242, 256; selects temple lot, 241; on schools, 242; damns Polk, 243; orders Bullock to rest, 248; discourages hunting, 254; organizes returning pioneers, 274; leads returning pioneers, 267-73, 279, 284-85, 290-92, 294, 295-300, 302-04, 307-08, 313-14; rebukes P. P. Pratt, 267, 268, 279; smokes peace pipe, 289; warns Lakotas, 301; discusses foreign policy, 307; distributes spirits, 315, 317; praises pioneers, 269; issues General Epistle, 320; organizes 1848 emigration, 321; *passim*, 333-38, 340-41, 343, 345-49, 355-57, 362-63; bio, 350

Young, Clarissa Decker: 112, 130, 202; bio, 350

Young, Harriet Page Wheeler: 112, 130, 199, 237; tries saleratus, 198; bio, 331, 350

Young, Henry Isaac: 66, 70, bio, 350

Young, John: 117; bio, 349

Young, Joseph: 102, 120, 317; bio, 349

Young, Joseph Angell: 36; bio, 350

Young, Joseph Watson: 273; bio, 350

Young, Lorenzo Dow: 112, 121, 130, 157, 174, 191, 198-99, 217, 228, 264-65, 356; bio, 350

Young, Lorenzo Zobieski: 112, 130; bio, 349

Young, Phinehas H: 40, 124, 130, 132, 153, 157, 179, 191, 218; bio, 349

Zemmer, Ann: 75

Zion: 18, 21, 45, 112

Zion's Camp: 326, 328, 330-31, 333, 336, 338; and Twelve Apostles, 156